Chambers

BACK-WORDS
for Crosswords

Compiled by
J. C. P. Schwarz

© 1986 W & R Chambers Ltd
43-45 Annandale Street, Edinburgh EH7 4AZ

Reprinted 1987, 1988, 1989, 1991, 1992

British Library Cataloguing in Publication Data

A catalogue record for this book is available from the
British Library.

ISBN 0-550-19012-0

Cover design by Art Dept, Edinburgh.
Printed in Great Britain by Clay Ltd, St Ives plc

Preface

Crossword puzzle solvers often find themselves in the position of knowing the ending, but not the beginning, of certain words on the grid. In such instances conventional dictionaries—and even crossword dictionaries—are of no help, since they are always arranged according to the beginning letters of the words. But Chambers have set the computer to work on their famous Dictionary to produce BACK-WORDS FOR CROSSWORDS.

BACK-WORDS FOR CROSSWORDS is a huge list of about 120,000 words arranged by length and by alphabetical order *from the end of each word*. This means that, for example, all 5-letter words *ending* in 'A' are grouped together and precede all 5-letter words *ending* in 'B'. Also, words ending in 'BA' precede words ending in 'CA'; words ending in 'SER' come before those with 'TER' endings; and so on. At the end of each word-length section you will, of course, find all the words ending in 'Z'.

If you are faced with a clue for which you know only the ending, you can quickly find the full solution by consulting BACK-WORDS FOR CROSSWORDS. For example, consider the clue:

> It often keeps a union together (8)

If you know from the grid that the solution ends in 'I-E', simply look up the 8-letter section of the book; a rapid scan of the columns of words ending in 'E' will lead you to the solution ADHESIVE.

Alternatively:

> Mum cheers a broken pipe (10)

Given the ending 'A-M' look up the 10-letter words and locate those ending in 'M' (the headings at the top of each page will guide you).

Then scan the column of third-last letters until the letter 'A', and the solution MEERSCHAUM appears.

The scope of BACK-WORDS FOR CROSSWORDS can be further extended by taking into account possible word endings. It is usually clear from crossword clues whether their solutions end in '(E)S', 'ING' or '(E)D'. In these cases you should disregard the expected ending and look up the 'basic' word in the text. For example:

> Attacked from the wrong side, alas (8)

Knowing that the solution ends 'A-L-D' and that the word is probably in the past tense you should ignore the '-D' and look up 'A-L' in the 6-letter section. The discovery of ASSAIL will show you that the solution is ASSAILED.

A similar case would be:

> Making Bill better just before afternoon? (8)

where the letters 'D--G' are known. Disregarding the expected 'ING' ending, turn to 'D' in the 5-letter words to find AMEND, meaning both 'make better' and 'just before afternoon' (A.M. end). The solution is therefore AMENDING. A few minutes' practice with this ingenious and unusual book will greatly increase your solving power.

For crossword solvers *and* compilers, Chambers BACK-WORDS FOR CROSSWORDS is the most useful publication since its companion volumes WORDS and ANAGRAMS. BACK-WORDS FOR CROSSWORDS closes the frustrating gap between the end of the crossword and the tip of the tongue!

A	raja	gena	acta	gamb	marc	bled
baba	soja	vena	beta	iamb	merc	fled
caba	puja	kina	geta	jamb	torc	gled
Saba	haka	mina	keta	lamb	aesc	pled
abba	kaka	piña	seta	kemb	disc	sled
peba	weka	vina	zeta	wemb	fisc	sned
boba	dika	ulna	dita	limb	fusc	coed
arba	pika	anna	pita	zimb	douc	hoed
buba	sika	bona	vita	bomb	D	roed
juba	tika	dona	anta	comb	ecad	toed
tuba	ekka	Doña	iota	tomb	scad	sped
paca	ilka	mona	jota	womb	bead	ared
raca	EOKA	zona	lota	dumb	dead	bred
mica	fa-la	etna	rota	numb	head	used
pica	gala	buna	Ruta	blob	lead	hued
Inca	la-la	puna	paua	glob	mead	rued
coca	nala	tuna	skua	slob	read	sued
Orca	tala	myna	Java	knob	tead	awed
yuca	pela	whoa	kava	snob	yead	owed
Dada	tela	anoa	lava	boob	egad	dyed
Edda	vela	proa	deva	doob	igad	eyed
Veda	gila	stoa	leva	stob	chad	Wafd
sida	hila	capa	diva	swob	shad	gaid
coda	pila	papa	riva	barb	clad	kaid
soda	zila	tapa	Siva	garb	glad	laid
idea	olla	Nipa	viva	herb	goad	maid
odea	amla	pipa	Hova	kerb	load	paid
rhea	cola	dopa	nova	Serb	road	raid
shea	kola	pupa	urva	verb	toad	said
Thea	sola	zupa	pawa	sorb	woad	acid
flea	tola	mara	shwa	curb	brad	deid
ilea	vola	para	mowa	daub	prad	weid
Olea	aula	Pará	taxa	chub	trad	chid
plea	gula	tara	Bixa	blub	duad	whid
zoea	hula	vara	coxa	club	quad	ski'd
area	Cama	sera	moxa	flub	swad	skid
urea	Kama	Vera	maya	slub	dyad	olid
uvea	lama	lira	hiya	knub	wadd	slid
alfa	mama	Mira	soya	snub	redd	amid
sofa	Rama	okra	B	drub	rudd	loid
tufa	Yama	bora	scab	grub	sudd	void
gaga	bema	Dora	blab	stub	gaed	arid
naga	Xema	fora	flab	C	abed	grid
raga	lima	kora	slab	Waac	iced	irid
saga	rima	mora	snab	abac	deed	guid
vega	sima	sora	doab	spec	feed	muid
biga	alma	orra	Arab	laic	heed	quid
alga	emma	aura	crab	saic	meed	avid
toga	boma	dura	drab	odic	need	bald
yoga	coma	jura	frab	chic	reed	wald
juga	loma	sura	grab	zoic	seed	yald
yuga	noma	eyra	stab	epic	teed	geld
ha-ha	roma	Lyra	swab	spic	weed	held
taha	soma	vasa	Beeb	eric	yeed	meld
agha	duma	mesa	dieb	uric	aged	seld
epha	huma	visa	bleb	otic	she'd	veld
Naia	puma	Rosa	pleb	talc	shed	weld
obia	cyma	Xosa	sneb	banc	died	yeld
glia	kana	Ursa	Abib	zinc	gied	eild
ilia	lana	Musa	glib	sync	hied	gild
inia	mana	rusa	snib	choc	lied	kild
aria	nana	data	crib	bloc	pied	mild
huia	rana	rata	drib	croc	tied	sild
Naja	tana	ta-ta	bulb	atoc	vied	vild

4 -ILD

wild	mood	alae	Mede	rage	syke	lame
bold	pood	blae	rede	sage	tyke	lamé
cold	rood	slae	yede	wage	bale	name
fold	wood	spae	aide	edge	dale	same
gold	apod	brae	bide	tige	eale	tame
hold	brod	frae	hide	doge	gale	wame
sold	prod	twae	nide	urge	hale	acme
told	trod	babe	ride	euge	kale	deme
wold	quod	abbé	side	huge	male	feme
yold	bard	Hebe	tide	luge	pale	heme
auld	card	gibe	vide	ache	rale	leme
band	Dard	jibe	wide	eche	sale	semé
fand	eard	kibe	unde	he-he	tale	teme
hand	fard	vibe	bode	ethe	vale	dime
land	hard	albe	code	kaie	wale	lime
pand	lard	unbe	lode	plié	yale	mime
rand	nard	jobe	mode	Brie	able	rime
sand	pard	lobe	node	stie	idle	time
wand	sard	robe	rode	bake	dele	alme
bend	ward	to-be	yode	cake	hele	come
fend	yard	cube	urdé	fake	Pele	dome
hend	herd	jube	dude	hake	vele	home
lend	yerd	rube	gude	jake	ogle	mome
mend	bird	tube	nude	lake	bile	nome
pend	gird	gybe	rude	make	file	pome
rend	yird	dace	tyde	rake	mile	Rome
send	cord	face	idée	sake	pile	some
tend	ford	lace	agee	take	rile	tome
vend	lord	mace	ogee	wake	sile	fume
wend	sord	pace	ghee	leke	tile	cyme
Zend	word	race	thee	peke	vile	lyme
bind	burd	tace	whee	reke	wile	zyme
find	curd	ecce	ajee	bike	bole	bane
hind	Kurd	bice	akee	dike	cole	cane
kind	surd	dice	alee	fike	dole	Dane
lind	turd	lice	blee	hike	gole	fane
mind	fyrd	mice	flee	kike	hole	gane
rind	baud	nice	glee	like	jole	jane
sind	daud	pice	slee	mike	mole	lane
tind	gaud	rice	smee	Nike	pole	mane
wind	haud	sice	knee	pike	role	pane
bond	laud	tice	épée	sike	sole	sane
cond	maud	vice	bree	tike	tole	tane
fond	yaud	ance	cree	ylke	vole	vane
kond	'zbud	once	dree	coke	orle	wane
pond	scud	unce	free	joke	isle	acne
yond	feud	duce	gree	moke	dule	bene
bund	khud	luce	pree	poke	gule	dene
fund	thud	puce	tree	roke	hule	gene
rund	foud	syce	swee	soke	mule	mene
tund	loud	bade	twee	toke	pule	nene
rynd	you'd	cade	café	woke	rule	pene
synd	spud	fade	safe	yoke	tule	tene
tynd	crud	gade	fife	duke	yule	aïné
wynd	stud	hade	life	juke	axle	bine
feod	bawd	jade	nife	luke	fyle	dine
shod	dawd	kade	rife	nuke	hyle	eine
alod	gawd	lade	wife	puke	kyle	fine
clod	lewd	made	orfe	yuke	came	kine
plod	dowd	rade	ryfe	byke	dame	line
snod	gowd	vade	cage	dyke	fame	mine
food	ivy'd	wade	gage	fyke	game	nine
good	E	bede	mage	hyke	hame	pine
hood	thae	cede	page	ryke	kame	rine

sine	care	ease	kite	vive	jeff	G
tine	dare	lase	lite	wive	teff	peag
vine	fare	mase	mite	cove	biff	shag
wine	gare	rase	rite	dove	jiff	clag
bone	hare	vase	site	hove	miff	flag
cone	lare	wase	tite	Jove	niff	slag
done	mare	mese	vite	love	riff	knag
gone	nare	sese	wite	move	tiff	snag
hone	pare	bise	yite	rove	coff	brag
lone	rare	mise	ante	wove	doff	crag
none	tare	pisé	cote	gyve	goff	drag
pone	vare	rise	dote	ryve	koff	stag
rone	ware	vise	hote	wawe	toff	quag
sone	yare	visé	lote	howe	buff	swag
tone	acre	wise	mote	lowe	cuff	skeg
zone	bere	else	note	yowe	duff	cleg
erne	cere	cose	pote	Saxe	fuff	fleg
esne	dere	dose	rote	abye	guff	gleg
dune	fere	hose	tote	scye	huff	hagg
June	here	lose	vote	Skye	luff	magg
lune	lere	nose	cute	stye	muff	ragg
rune	mere	oose	jute	daze	puff	tegg
tune	père	pose	lute	faze	ruff	yegg
dyne	sere	posé	mute	gaze	tuff	bigg
eyne	were	rose	byte	haze	kaif	rigg
kyne	we're	rosé	cyte	laze	naïf	hogg
pyne	ogre	tose	gyte	maze	waif	thig
syne	ciré	apse	kyte	naze	neif	whig
tyne	dire	arse	lyte	raze	reif	snig
oboe	fire	Erse	tyte	adze	seif	brig
ygoe	hire	esse	wyte	meze	coif	frig
shoe	lire	fuse	ague	pize	cuif	grig
aloe	mire	muse	blue	size	calf	prig
floe	sire	ruse	clue	coze	half	trig
sloe	tire	rusé	flue	doze	delf	swig
evoe	wire	lyse	glue	moze	pelf	twig
cape	bore	bate	slue	ooze	self	bang
gape	core	cate	moue	toze	golf	cang
jape	fore	date	roué	fuze	wolf	dang
nape	gore	fate	spue	F	gulf	fang
pape	lore	gate	crue	haaf	bumf	gang
rape	more	hate	grue	Waaf	humf	hang
tape	pore	late	true	deaf	coof	kang
kipe	rore	mate	cave	leaf	goof	lang
pipe	sore	maté	gave	goaf	hoof	pang
ripe	tore	pate	have	loaf	loof	rang
sipe	wore	pâté	lave	Graf	poof	sang
wipe	yore	rate	nave	beef	roof	tang
olpe	cure	sate	pave	reef	woof	T'ang
cope	curé	tate	rave	chef	prof	vang
dope	dure	wate	save	fief	zarf	wang
hope	lure	yate	wave	lief	kerf	yang
lope	mure	bete	leve	nief	serf	leng
mope	pure	bête	névé	clef	corf	meng
nope	sure	fête	we've	tref	surf	bing
pope	owre	jeté	yeve	baff	turf	ding
rope	byre	mete	cive	caff	zurf	ging
tope	eyre	nete	dive	daff	houf	hing
dupe	gyre	rete	five	faff	pouf	king
hype	lyre	tête	give	gaff	dowf	ling
rype	pyre	bite	hive	haff	gowf	ming
sype	tyre	cite	jive	raff	howf	ping
type	base	dite	live	waff	sowf	ring
bare	case	gite	rive	yaff	wowf	sing

4 -ING

ting	sech	posh	yogi	J	muck	tink
wing	dich	tosh	Tshi	hadj	puck	wink
zing	lich	bush	haji	hajj	ruck	conk
dong	rich	cush	kaki	benj	suck	gonk
gong	sich	dush	Paki	K	tuck	honk
hong	tich	gush	raki	beak	yuck	konk
long	inch	hush	saki	leak	keek	monk
mong	coch	lush	tiki	peak	leek	bunk
nong	loch	mush	Loki	reak	meek	dunk
pong	roch	push	dali	teak	peek	funk
rong	arch	rush	kali	weak	reek	gunk
song	etch	tush	mali	dhak	seek	hunk
tong	itch	bath	Pali	flak	week	junk
bung	much	eath	vali	soak	trek	punk
dung	ouch	hath	wali	arak	faik	sunk
fung	such	lath	deli	nabk	haik	amok
hung	pegh	math	ugli	back	laik	book
lung	high	oath	pili	hack	maik	cook
rung	nigh	path	wili	jack	naik	dook
sung	sigh	rath	Holi	lack	paik	gook
scog	yogh	tath	soli	mack	raik	hook
agog	eugh	beth	kami	pack	reik	jook
shog	pugh	kith	rami	rack	chik	kook
biog	lakh	lith	semi	sack	hoik	look
clog	Sikh	pith	rani	tack	spik	nook
flog	ankh	sith	beni	yack	balk	pook
slog	rukh	with	peni	zack	calk	rook
smog	sukh	both	mini	beck	talk	sook
snog	tanh	coth	yoni	deck	walk	took
brog	sinh	doth	Zuni	feck	welk	atok
frog	phoh	Goth	mooi	geck	yelk	bark
grog	booh	loth	euoi	heck	bilk	cark
prog	pooh	moth	kepi	keck	milk	dark
trog	umph	Esth	pipi	neck	silk	hark
darg	soph	ruth	tipi	reck	folk	jark
marg	ouph	myth	impi	peck	polk	lark
berg	bash	pruh	topi	dick	yolk	mark
burg	cash	I	Tupi	hick	bulk	nark
scug	dash	chai	dari	kick	hulk	park
chug	fash	Thai	sari	lick	oulk	sark
thug	gash	Babi	meri	mick	pulk	wark
skug	hash	rabi	peri	nick	sulk	berk
glug	lash	lobi	Shri	pick	bank	jerk
plug	mash	unci	kiri	rick	dank	merk
slug	pash	foci	siri	sick	fank	serk
smug	rash	asci	sori	tick	hank	yerk
snug	sash	cadi	tori	wick	lank	birk
drug	tash	gadi	nisi	bock	rank	dirk
trug	wash	kadi	kati	cock	sank	firk
boyg	mesh	qadi	sati	dock	tank	kirk
H	nesh	wadi	zati	hock	wank	lirk
yeah	bish	cedi	yeti	jock	yank	mirk
shah	dish	midi	titi	lock	penk	yirk
blah	fish	nidi	anti	mock	bink	cork
amah	hish	modi	not-I	nock	dink	fork
opah	kish	nodi	Asti	pock	fink	pork
ayah	pish	glei	etui	rock	gink	work
bach	wish	vlei	divi	sock	jink	york
each	bosh	hi-fi	kiwi	wock	kink	burk
nach	cosh	Sofi	maxi	buck	link	lurk
rach	gosh	Sufi	taxi	duck	mink	murk
tach	josh	Magi	dixi	fuck	pink	Turk
hech	losh	ragi	Nazi	huck	rink	bask
pech	nosh	vagi		luck	sink	

cask	sial	noil	dull	mewl	vehm	gaum
hask	vial	roil	full	bowl	kaim	scum
mask	anal	soil	gull	cowl	maim	geum
task	coal	toil	hull	dowl	saim	neum
desk	foal	aril	lull	fowl	shim	chum
yesk	goal	vril	mull	gowl	whim	pium
bisk	opal	muil	null	howl	skim	Sium
disk	oral	null	pull	jowl	glim	alum
fisk	Ural	axil	wull	nowl	plim	glum
risk	dual	ball	gaol	sowl	slim	plum
bosk	aval	call	obol	yowl	brim	slum
busk	oval	fall	idol	idyl	grim	roum
cusk	twal	gall	viol	odyl	prim	soum
dusk	gyal	hall	cool	amyl	trim	arum
husk	myal	mall	dool	moyl	Urim	Brum
lusk	ryal	pall	fool	aryl	quim	drum
musk	bael	tall	gool	hwyl	swim	grum
rusk	Gael	wall	mool	M	balm	stum
tusk	tael	bell	pool	ma'am	calm	ovum
bauk	feel	cell	tool	naam	halm	swum
cauk	heel	dell	wool	scam	malm	hawm
wauk	jeel	fell	carl	Adam	palm	sowm
neuk	keel	he'll	earl	Edam	helm	azym
yeuk	peel	hell	farl	beam	holm	N
bouk	reel	jell	harl	leam	culm	naan
gouk	seel	kell	jarl	ream	mumm	scan
jouk	teel	mell	marl	team	whom	bean
pouk	weel	pell	herl	ogam	boom	dean
souk	bhel	sell	merl	cham	coom	gean
touk	riel	tell	birl	sham	doom	jean
youk	wiel	vell	cirl	wham	loom	lean
cawk	goel	we'll	dirl	clam	room	mean
dawk	Noël	well	girl	flam	soom	pean
gawk	duel	yell	nirl	glam	toom	rean
hawk	fuel	bill	pirl	slam	zoom	sean
lawk	axel	cill	tirl	imam	from	Tean
mawk	dahl	dill	virl	foam	prom	wean
pawk	kohl	fill	eorl	loam	atom	yean
gowk	buhl	gill	burl	roam	barm	khan
howk	bail	hill	curl	Spam ®	farm	shan
L	Dáil	jill	furl	cram	harm	than
Baal	fail	kill	gurl	dram	marm	Dian
taal	hail	lill	hurl	gram	warm	Xian
odal	jail	mill	murl	pram	berm	clan
udal	kail	nill	nurl	tram	derm	élan
deal	mail	pill	purl	dwam	ferm	flan
feal	nail	rill	rotl	swam	germ	plan
geal	pail	sill	caul	exam	herm	G-man
heal	rail	till	Gaul	lyam	perm	anan
leal	sail	vill	haul	haem	term	eoan
meal	tail	will	maul	deem	firm	koan
neal	vail	yill	paul	neem	corm	loan
peal	wail	boll	saul	seem	dorm	moan
real	ceil	coll	waul	teem	form	roan
seal	deil	doll	shul	weem	gorm	span
teal	seil	joll	elul	ahem	norm	Aran
veal	teil	loll	foul	them	worm	bran
weal	veil	moll	noul	riem	turm	cran
zeal	weil	noll	roul	clem	Würm	gran
egal	anil	poll	soul	ylem	gism	duan
chal	boil	roll	bawl	poem	jism	guan
dhal	coil	toll	pawl	item	caum	tuan
dial	foil	bull	wawl	stem		yuan
rial	moil	cull	yawl	fehm		swan

4 -YAN

cyan	skin	tarn	urao	halo	koto	golp
azan	blin	warn	Igbo	kilo	loto	holp
ta'en	coin	yarn	ambo	lilo	otto	gulp
Eden	foin	dern	umbo	milo	auto	pulp
been	join	fern	gobo	silo	Pavo	camp
deen	loin	hern	hobo	kolo	rivo	damp
keen	roin	kern	zobo	polo	vivo	gamp
peen	spin	pern	bubo	solo	arvo	lamp
reen	grin	tern	sybo	demo	kayo	ramp
seen	trin	airn	paco	memo	yo-yo	samp
teen	quin	firn	taco	ammo	ouzo	tamp
ween	ruin	girn	fico	homo	P	vamp
agen	twin	kirn	mico	jomo	heap	hemp
then	kiln	pirn	unco	sumo	leap	kemp
when	vuln	born	coco	leno	neap	temp
bien	damn	corn	joco	fino	reap	gimp
gien	limn	horn	loco	kino	chap	jimp
lien	hymn	lorn	toco	lino	whap	limp
mien	cann	morn	arco	mino	clap	pimp
sien	jann	Norn	dado	vino	flap	simp
glen	Finn	porn	fado	wino	plap	wimp
amen	ginn	sorn	eddo	mono	slap	comp
omen	jinn	torn	re-do	no-no	knap	pomp
doen	linn	worn	dido	Juno	snap	romp
J-pen	conn	burn	Fido	shoo	soap	bump
open	sunn	curn	lido	broo	crap	dump
bren	kaon	durn	undo	Kroo	drap	gump
wren	ebon	gurn	dodo	proo	frap	hump
eten	icon	ourn	to-do	capo	trap	jump
sten	aeon	turn	judo	gapó	wrap	lump
even	neon	hisn	ludo	pepo	atap	mump
oven	peon	bos'n	skeo	expo	stap	pump
oxen	agon	faun	oleo	hypo	swap	rump
syen	phon	gaun	info	typo	deep	sump
sign	thon	maun	bufo	faro	jeep	tump
föhn	lion	raun	dago	haro	keep	gymp
john	pion	shun	kago	taro	neep	tymp
cain	Zion	boun	sago	hero	peep	chop
fain	ikon	loun	bego	zero	seep	shop
gain	anon	noun	sego	afro	weep	whop
hain	boon	toun	figo	thro	skep	clop
Jain	coon	spun	gogo	Biro®	prep	flop
kain	goon	stun	logo	giro	step	plop
lain	loon	eevn	upgo	tiro	quep	slop
main	moon	bawn	Argo	inro	chip	knop
nain	noon	dawn	ergo	Moro	ship	coop
pain	poon	fawn	echo	duro	whip	co-op
rain	roon	lawn	coho	euro	skip	goop
sain	soon	pawn	Moho	pyro	blip	hoop
vain	toon	rawn	so-ho	tyro	clip	loop
wain	zoon	sawn	toho	odso	flip	moop
Odin	upon	yawn	yo-ho	peso	slip	noop
bein	iron	hewn	agio	miso	snip	poop
mein	tron	sewn	skio	also	drip	roop
pein	Eton	down	Clio	so-so	grip	soop
rein	muon	gown	olio	huso	trip	yoop
vein	axon	lown	Unio	jato	quip	crop
zein	exon	mown	brio	Nato	calp	drop
agin	Lyon	nown	trio	veto	palp	prop
chin	barn	pown	gajo	bito	salp	atop
shin	darn	sown	mako	alto	help	stop
thin	earn	town	boko	into	kelp	quop
whin	harn	O	moko	onto	yelp	swop
akin	larn	ciao	toko	unto	kilp	Lapp

yapp	knar	pair	S	Eros	onus	ybet
repp	snar	sair	baas	caps	nous	beet
kipp	boar	vair	ceas	reps	sous	feet
ripp	hoar	heir	bias	seps	opus	leet
barp	roar	keir	Lias	oops	urus	meet
carp	soar	leir	alas	Mars	taws	weet
harp	voar	weir	Xmas	hers	yaws	shet
warp	spar	shir	anas	vers	mews	whet
dorp	arar	thir	upas	ours	news	diet
burp	asar	whir	bras	bass	dows	piet
gasp	tsar	amir	utas	lass	Keys	blet
hasp	star	emir	'twas	mass	emys	poet
jasp	duar	smir	eyas	pass	T	spet
rasp	guar	coir	nyas	sass	scat	aret
wasp	czar	stir	nabs	tass	beat	fret
hesp	tzar	muir	vibs	cess	feat	tret
lisp	laer	puir	odds	fess	geat	stet
risp	Acer	odor	mods	jess	heat	duet
wisp	icer	khor	suds	less	leat	suet
cusp	beer	Thor	Ides	mess	meat	evet
caup	deer	boor	lees	ness	neat	pyet
gaup	feer	door	she's	sess	peat	baft
jaup	jeer	goor	does	diss	seat	daft
yaup	leer	loor	foes	hiss	teat	haft
scup	meer	moor	noes	kiss	chat	raft
coup	ne'er	poor	lues	miss	ghat	waft
doup	peer	carr	Aves	piss	khat	deft
loup	seer	parr	axes	Riss	shat	heft
moup	teer	yarr	exes	siss	that	left
noup	veer	Herr	eyes	boss	what	reft
roup	eger	serr	oyes	coss	fiat	weft
soup	bier	birr	mags	doss	skat	gift
gawp	kier	girr	fegs	foss	blat	lift
yawp	lier	tirr	digs	Goss	clat	rift
cowp	pier	dorr	dais	hoss	flat	sift
dowp	tier	torr	pais	joss	plat	tift
sowp	sker	burr	ibis	koss	slat	coft
R	omer	curr	feis	loss	gnat	loft
haar	oner	furr	reis	löss	boat	soft
maar	Boer	nurr	egis	moss	coat	toft
T-bar	doer	purr	this	poss	doat	tuft
scar	goer	baur	fris	soss	goat	yuft
Adar	hoer	gaur	gris	toss	moat	baht
bear	brer	waur	iris	buss	spat	echt
dear	user	scur	kris	cuss	brat	bait
fear	huer	blur	Isis	fuss	drat	gait
gear	puer	slur	utis	huss	grat	ha'it
hear	aver	smur	iwis	muss	prat	rait
lear	ever	knur	ywis	puss	buat	tait
near	over	dour	axis	Russ	quat	wait
pear	ewer	four	hols	suss	swat	obit
rear	ower	hour	tems	bats	twat	adit
sear	oxer	jour	alms	oats	kyat	edit
tear	dyer	lour	coms	rats	pyat	geit
wear	oyer	pour	kans	wats	debt	chit
year	tahr	sour	sans	cits	fact	shit
afar	lehr	tour	gens	wots	pact	whit
agar	tehr	your	lens	nuts	tact	skit
char	mohr	spur	sens	tuts	sect	alit
thar	fair	bawr	oons	Zeus	dict	flit
liar	gair	mawr	pons	rhus	Pict	glit
ajar	hair	bowr	naos	thus	duct	slit
alar	lair	skyr	loos	plus	haet	emit
gnar	Nair		epos	anus	abet	omit

4 -MIT

smit	fent	eyot	yest	slut	tatu	know
knit	gent	pyot	zest	smut	aitu	snow
unit	hent	ryot	cist	knut	tutu	arow
doit	kent	rapt	fist	bout	V	brow
moit	lent	kept	gist	dout	Slav	crow
spit	ment	sept	hist	gout	deev	drow
brit	pent	wept	kist	hout	chiv	frow
crit	rent	hipt	list	shiv	shiv	grow
frit	sent	ript	mist	nout	spiv	prow
grit	tent	tipt	sist	pout	derv	trow
writ	vent	Copt	wist	rout	perv	stow
cuit	went	cart	onst	tout	Mirv	avow
luit	ain't	dart	cost	brut	W	X
quit	bint	fart	dost	dawt	scaw	Ajax
suit	dint	gart	host	tawt	chaw	flax
twit	hint	hart	lost	newt	shaw	coax
exit	lint	kart	most	lowt	thaw	hoax
Balt	mint	mart	post	nowt	skaw	Crax
dalt	oint	part	tost	rowt	claw	ibex
halt	pint	tart	wost	towt	flaw	flex
malt	tint	wart	erst	next	slaw	ilex
salt	vint	cert	bust	sext	gnaw	ulex
belt	win't	pert	dust	text	spaw	apex
celt	don't	vert	fust	mixt	braw	prex
felt	font	wert	gust	bayt	craw	faix
gelt	oont	airt	just	U	draw	flix
kelt	ront	dirt	lust	beau	staw	calx
melt	won't	girt	must	unau	chew	falx
pelt	wont	bort	oust	frau	phew	lanx
telt	yont	dort	rust	prau	shew	Manx
welt	aunt	fort	cyst	babu	thew	jinx
yelt	bunt	mort	xyst	tabu	whew	minx
gilt	cunt	port	batt	zebu	view	Yunx
hilt	dunt	rort	matt	ombu	skew	iynx
jilt	hunt	sort	tatt	zobu	alew	jynx
kilt	lunt	tort	watt	Urdu	blew	lynx
lilt	punt	wort	fett	kudu	clew	flux
milt	runt	curt	Lett	lieu	flew	roux
silt	scot	hurt	nett	emeu	slew	crux
tilt	phot	yurt	sett	Rahu	smew	onyx
wilt	shot	bast	yett	Jehu	anew	Pnyx
bolt	riot	cast	bitt	juju	enew	oryx
colt	blot	east	ditt	kuku	knew	Styx
dolt	clot	fast	fitt	balu	spew	Y
holt	plot	gast	mitt	tolu	arew	D-day
jolt	slot	hast	ritt	lulu	brew	V-day
polt	knot	last	bott	pulu	crew	chay
tolt	snot	mast	cott	Zulu	drew	shay
volt	boot	oast	nott	rimu	grew	okay
cult	coot	past	pott	genu	trew	alay
bant	foot	rast	butt	menu	stew	blay
cant	hoot	vast	mutt	Ainu	scow	clay
can't	loot	wast	putt	non-U	meow	flay
dant	moot	best	haut	chou	chow	play
gant	poot	gest	saut	thou	dhow	slay
kant	root	hest	taut	clou	show	apay
lant	soot	jest	vaut	bapu	whow	spay
pant	toot	lest	abut	tapu	alow	bray
rant	woot	nest	scut	Ogpu	blow	dray
vant	spot	pest	chut	ecru	clow	fray
want	grot	rest	phut	Peru	flow	gray
bent	trot	test	shut	guru	glow	pray
cent	stot	vest	Blut	masu	slow	tray
dent	swot	west	glut	Jesu	enow	X-ray

stay	bley	Esky '	ismy	espy	oosy	gazy
quay	fley	yuky	fumy	I-spy	posy	hazy
away	gley	paly	cany	nary	rosy	jazy
M-way	sley	waly	many	oary	upsy	lazy
sway	joey	ably	wany	vary	busy	mazy
tway	drey	idly	zany	wary	maty	vizy
baby	grey	rely	deny	scry	city	cozy
gaby	prey	ugly	reny	adry	mity	dozy
inby	trey	lily	miny	aery	pity	fozy
goby	stey	oily	piny	eery	doty	oozy
go-by	quey	wily	tiny	hery	arty	Z
toby	defy	ally	viny	very	duty	Geëz
upby	affy	illy	winy	airy	cavy	chez
orby	cagy	inly	bony	miry	Davy	trez
ruby	edgy	only	cony	wiry	navy	oyez
lacy	eggy	holy	mony	skry	wavy	phiz
pacy	bogy	moly	pony	dory	bevy	whiz
racy	dogy	poly	tony	gory	levy	friz
ricy	fogy	duly	puny	lory	envy	quiz
fady	orgy	guly	tuny	pory	movy	swiz
lady	hugy	July	awny	rory	yawy	Günz
wady	achy	puly	gyny	Tory	dewy	lutz
eddy	ashy	ruly	ahoy	spry	nowy	Druz
tedy	caky	owly	pioy	'Arry	towy	jazz
tidy	laky	gamy	cloy	bury	waxy	razz
oldy	oaky	demy	ploy	fury	sexy	lezz
body	taky	limy	troy	jury	dixy	fizz
tody	icky	rimy	buoy	awry	mixy	gizz
urdy	fiky	elmy	pipy	eyry	nixy	hizz
judy	inky	Emmy	copy	easy	pixy	pozz
obey	joky	domy	dopy	jasy	coxy	buzz
they	poky	homy	mopy	cosy	doxy	fuzz
whey	roky	army	ropy	nosy	foxy	tuzz

A	chica	sorda	sol-fa	dacha	redia	sepia
Kaaba	plica	Gouda	loofa	kacha	oidia	rupia
araba	spica	vivda	yarfa	pacha	podia	maria
Sheba	erica	Picea	chufa	Mocha	Mafia	ceria
gamba	Binca ®	aldea	omega	nucha	tafia	moria
mamba	Vinca	Ardea	dagga	bigha	vigia	noria
samba	Phoca	bohea	saiga	aloha	logia	atria
rumba	Parca	galea	taiga	hoo-ha	orgia	stria
aroba	Perca	palea	belga	alpha	sakia	curia
yerba	circa	pilea	mulga	sopha	Melia	ossia
kasba	Musca	tinea	kanga	hypha	Tilia	entia
sauba	Eruca	apnea	panga	Typha	dolia	ostia
scuba	labda	usnea	tanga	pasha	folia	hutia
abaca	Vedda	zooea	renga	musha	dulia	hodja
bacca	kheda	ocrea	linga	labia	lamia	ouija
yacca	vifda	Butea	conga	tibia	zamia	ganja
Decca ®	cnida	hevea	donga	cobia	bania	zanja
Mecca	panda	fovea	longa	erbia	mania	khoja
ticca	fonda	trefa	tonga	nubia	tenia	Rioja
bocca	zonda	Jaffa	wonga	Rubia	amnia	pooja
yucca	Munda	buffa	darga	facia	conia	thuja
caeca	garda	luffa	virga	aecia	gonia	poaka
theca	zerda	halfa	Tsuga	media	bunia	pucka

vodka	sigma	varna	tetra	vitta	squib	Asdic
cheka	dogma	Lerna	ultra	cotta	stilb	pudic
laika	anima	Norna	sutra	gotta	weamb	theic
pakka	prima	fauna	extra	gutta	chimb	oleic
yakka	halma	sauna	laura	lytta	climb	Cufic
pukka	talma	abuna	Anura	scuta	A-bomb	Kufic
polka	pelma	downa	doura	sputa	H-bomb	Sufic
pulka	gamma	cocoa	Goura	adyta	V-bomb	magic
dumka	mamma	genoa	lavra	rhyta	rhomb	logic
tanka	gemma	scapa	mowra	vacua	clomb	yogic
punka	lemma	stipa	tayra	mahua	coomb	orgic
hooka	limma	calpa	omasa	brava	cromb	ethic
parka	comma	kalpa	presa	guava	rhumb	malic
nerka	momma	Salpa	paisa	sheva	thumb	salic
burka	gumma	talpa	balsa	Saiva	plumb	melic
scala	summa	pampa	sansa	Shiva	crumb	relic
koala	haoma	scopa	Mensa	halva	cabob	telic
Itala	aroma	L-dopa	Xhosa	malva	kabob	colic
tabla	groma	kappa	roosa	selva	nabob	Eolic
qibla	stoma	tappa	sarsa	silva	kebob	folic
chela	myoma	koppa	bursa	volva	Jacob	aulic
stela	karma	poppa	massa	vulva	demob	hylic
kwela	derma	cuppa	sessa	sylva	carob	xylic
sigla	herma	vespa	fossa	larva	throb	gamic
agila	Norma	stupa	Hausa	murva	coarb	demic
voilà	rusma	burqa	reata	mahwa	acerb	ogmic
calla	douma	chara	riata	schwa	inorb	ohmic
nalla	etyma	tiara	recta	fetwa	blurb	mimic
palla	thana	labra	dicta	abaya	slurb	comic
walla	Diana	sabra	theta	chaya	courb	nomic
cella	liana	zabra	pietà	khaya	zebub	Romic
fella	anana	zebra	softa	shaya	scrub	osmic
villa	asana	libra	Sakta	playa	shrub	humic
holla	guana	umbra	Malta	Oriya	C	zymic
molla	bwana	cobra	delta	bunya	bobac	manic
bulla	scena	lubra	pelta	Surya	ileac	panic
nulla	veena	sacra	volta	Thuya	oshac	genic
Idola	arena	picra	manta	plaza	iliac	dinic
shola	crena	Indra	pinta	colza	eniac	Sinic
viola	frena	Sudra	junta	hamza	Isiac	conic
moola	urena	hydra	biota	senza	lilac	ionic
stola	Avena	opera	diota	sarza	sumac	sonic
repla	hyena	infra	flota	Mirza	linac	tonic
tesla	Jaina	naira	quota	matza	serac	Punic
gusla	china	taira	lepta	motza	Anzac	runic
alula	spina	Moira	septa	Oryza	rebec	tunic
inula	quina	bajra	carta	tazza	xebec	cynic
uvula	Lemna	hejra	jarta	pizza	zebec	Troic
phyla	canna	hijra	yarta	huzza	cumec	stoic
kaama	manna	kokra	aorta	B	varec	azoic
Agama	nanna	agora	porta	kabab	cosec	topic
shama	tanna	flora	kurta	kebab	cusec	aspic
llama	henna	psora	basta	jelab	Aztec	typic
drama	penna	lepra	pasta	scrab	vraic	baric
grama	senna	copra	Rasta	squab	rabic	daric
padma	pinna	sopra	festa	nawab	cubic	seric
edema	winna	serra	testa	Chubb	pubic	xeric
Shema	Donna	terra	vesta	slubb	mucic	Afric
thema	gonna	morra	vista	cubeb	Eddic	Ugric
ulema	Sunna	sorra	costa	ardeb	medic	Doric
enema	Shona	durra	hosta	Deneb	Vedic	loric
trema	Anona	hurra	batta	sahib	Indic	roric
magma	krona	murra	pitta	ad-lib	iodic	toric
regma	trona	surra	Sitta	Carib	sodic	auric

lyric	embed	lined	hewed	rapid	shand	yeard
basic	imbed	tined	sewed	sapid	viand	chard
mesic	unbed	boned	unwed	vapid	aland	shard
music	lobed	toned	bowed	lepid	bland	liard
vatic	orbed	zoned	cowed	tepid	eland	board
ictic	tubed	urned	dowed	lipid	gland	hoard
metic	faced	runed	mowed	cupid	brand	guard
antic	laced	tuned	nowed	marid	grand	award
optic	paced	awned	sowed	acrid	stand	sward
artic	jaded	tyned	vowed	jerid	scend	izard
attic	laded	shoed	taxed	thrid	teend	sherd
civic	aided	aloed	sexed	virid	shend	caird
toxic	bided	cooed	vexed	unrid	fiend	laird
franc	sided	wooed	fixed	rorid	piend	raird
tronc	ended	biped	mixed	strid	blend	reird
adunc	ogee'd	piped	foxed	lurid	amend	weird
caboc	bleed	moped	payed	Hasid	emend	third
Médoc	gleed	roped	rayed	betid	an-end	abord
taroc	kneed	upped	keyed	fetid	spend	chord
siroc	speed	dared	joyed	nitid	up-end	fiord
estoc	breed	eared	styed	putid	trend	fjord
havoc	creed	oared	dazed	bluid	stend	loord
D	freed	acred	razed	fluid	by-end	sword
decad	greed	ydred	sized	squid	teind	faurd
cycad	steed	shred	Enzed	Druid	ahind	bourd
bedad	tweed	fired	dozed	pavid	blind	gourd
ahead	unfed	hired	plaid	livid	poind	paysd
plead	caged	tired	slaid	vivid	grind	scaud
knead	raged	wired	apaid	sayid	ycond	blaud
snead	edged	unred	braid	scald	blond	fraud
aread	toged	cored	staid	heald	frond	pseud
bread	shied	spred	rabid	weald	laund	bemud
dread	skied	erred	tabid	afald	maund	thou'd
oread	plied	tyred	rebid	skald	bound	aloud
tread	spied	based	unbid	spald	found	cloud
stead	cried	rased	lucid	stal'd	hound	proud
begad	dried	hosed	mucid	neeld	lound	yrivd
toga'd	fried	nosed	madid	bield	mound	crowd
jehad	pried	rosed	re-did	field	pound	apayd
jihad	tried	mused	undid	piel'd	round	spayd
naiad	stied	dated	bifid	wield	sound	quayd
eliad	ivied	fated	rigid	yield	wound	they'd
Iliad	baked	gated	algid	speld	lownd	alkyd
triad	naked	lated	aphid	gyeld	sownd	sloyd
salad	waked	pated	unkid	child	chynd	E
yclad	piked	rated	calid	trild	pagod	tubae
bemad	unked	sated	valid	build	ungod	zoeae
nomad	poked	meted	gelid	guild	ephod	bigae
gonad	ycled	moted	unlid	tell'd	halo'd	algae
monad	filed	noted	solid	acold	silo'd	nugae
A-road	tiled	muted	timid	scold	allod	telae
broad	unled	outed	humid	ahold	synod	volae
sepad	upled	agued	tumid	woold	agood	rimae
eupad	famed	glued	canid	world	blood	venae
farad	named	slued	geoid	cauld	flood	ulnae
ydrad	wamed	paved	sloid	hauld	snood	zonae
dorad	rimed	saved	zooid	tauld	brood	gynae
sprad	timed	waved	aroid	yauld	stood	stoae
strad	domed	lived	avoid	could	bipod	pupae
octad	armed	rived	ovoid	mould	sprod	scrae
squad	maned	coved	axoid	nould	unsod	thrae
hexad	paned	moved	hyoid	would	fa'ard	strae
dryad	vaned	jawed	myoid	fremd	beard	aurae
aredd	waned	sawed	pyoid	scand	heard	setae

5 -TAE

antae	bonce	erode	phage	targe	eerie	atoke
novae	nonce	exode	plage	cerge	oorie	stoke
sybbe	ponce	borde	image	merge	rorie	evoke
glebe	sonce	horde	apage	serge	curie	awoke
grebe	bunce	blude	Osage	verge	ourie	burke
bribe	dunce	elude	usage	dirge	owrie	fluke
tribe	ounce	coudé	étage	virge	ayrie	pouke
all-be	punce	crude	stage	forge	eyrie	gryke
jambe	farce	prude	swage	gorge	Kyrie	scale
bombe	perce	étude	badge	gurge	visie	veale
bombé	terce	exude	cadge	purge	tatie	shale
combe	force	gryde	fadge	surge	retie	whale
pombe	sauce	Babee	gadge	gauge	untie	spale
adobe	educe	albee	madge	bouge	uptie	stale
Niobe	deuce	abcee	hedge	gouge	cutie	avale
globe	douce	emcee	kedge	rouge	Eytie	dwale
probe	pruce	lycée	ledge	vouge	cavie	swale
barbe	truce	sycee	sedge	cache	revie	cable
garbe	teade	undée	wedge	nache	dovie	fable
gerbe	shade	urdee	fidge	rache	movie	gable
daube	blade	tehee	kidge	tache	tawie	hable
taube	glade	rakee	midge	fiche	dowie	sable
U-tube	slade	ackee	ridge	miche	zowie	table
howbe	spade	belee	bodge	niche	dixie	bible
maybe	grade	mêlée	dodge	boche	nixie	amble
peace	irade	aglee	Hodge	ruche	pixie	coble
glacé	trade	ramee	lodge	owche	ulyie	moble
place	stade	semée	podge	Tyche	ulzie	noble
apace	evade	ranee	wodge	raphe	tozie	roble
space	glede	donee	budge	ouphe	gadje	ruble
brace	arede	cooee	fudge	bathe	bunje	macle
grace	brede	tepee	judge	eathe	lapje	ancle
trace	suede	elpee	nudge	lathe	kopje	uncle
recce	swede	topee	pudge	rathe	gauje	socle
peece	abide	rupee	liege	Lethe	shake	cycle
niece	chide	saree	siege	hithe	flake	ladle
piece	elide	scree	grège	kithe	slake	padle
grece	glide	agree	legge	lithe	snake	addle
saice	slide	three	ligge	sithe	poake	sidle
de-ice	amide	boree	pogge	tithe	spake	bodle
Alice	imide	doree	beige	withe	brake	yodle
slice	snide	soree	bilge	hythe	crake	abele
amice	bride	spree	bulge	kythe	drake	neele
voice	gride	purée	mange	lythe	stake	anele
spice	pride	besee	range	sythe	quake	stele
grice	tride	upsee	henge	oldie	awake	rifle
price	aside	fusee	menge	régie	wacke	eagle
trice	guide	tutee	venge	bogie	alike	pagle
juice	oxide	levee	binge	cogie	glike	angle
twice	tilde	cuvée	dinge	dogie	ylike	ingle
dolce	vilde	ngwee	hinge	logie	spike	bogle
dance	solde	etwee	singe	vogie	grike	fogle
hance	lande	payee	tinge	fugie	trike	bugle
lance	ronde	razee	winge	belie	ranke	fugle
nance	sonde	fuzee	congé	folie	zinke	maile
pance	tynde	neafe	longe	kylie	choke	edile
rance	abode	chafe	gunge	ramie	bloke	agile
fence	geode	gaffe	lunge	semie	smoke	chile
hence	chode	buffe	agoge	pumie	snoke	while
pence	diode	ruffe	éloge	genie	spoke	smile
mince	anode	tuffe	barge	penie	broke	anile
since	apode	'slife	large	Minié	proke	voile
wince	epode	knife	parge	Ernie	troke	spile
yince	spode	adage	sarge	aerie	wroke	esile

stile	reame	agene	borne	leare	barré	halse
utile	seame	phene	morne	chare	narre	salse
guile	shame	akene	morné	phare	warre	valse
axile	blame	skene	mesne	share	serre	bulse
exile	flame	amene	visne	whare	kurre	dulse
ankle	brame	ctene	abune	blare	murre	pulse
inkle	crame	eigne	jeune	Clare	metre	temse
dalle	frame	ligne	prune	flare	petre	Hanse
belle	grame	seine	bowne	glare	litre	manse
selle	ysame	chine	lowne	snare	mitre	cense
fille	theme	rhine	rayne	spare	nitre	dense
mille	fleme	shine	sayne	crare	titre	mense
rille	mneme	thine	royne	stare	antre	sense
tulle	breme	whine	syboe	aware	outré	tense
wanle	creme	aline	mahoe	sware	alure	rinse
dhole	steme	cline	cohoe	cabré	emure	sonse
f-hole	queme	amine	evhoe	sabre	enure	chose
thole	exeme	Koine	pekoe	fibre	inure	those
whole	fehme	opine	kyloe	ombre	loure	whose
soole	vehme	spine	canoe	umbre	you're	close
drôle	chime	brine	throe	nacre	usure	boose
prole	clime	crine	kayoe	lucre	sture	goose
stole	slime	trine	scape	sucre	azure	loose
caple	anime	urine	agape	cadre	livre	moose
maple	crime	quine	chape	padre	howre	noose
ample	grime	avine	shape	yfere	skyre	roose
apple	prime	ovine	crape	shere	styre	arose
duple	stime	dwine	drape	there	abase	brose
farle	damme	swine	grape	where	cease	erose
marle	kamme	twine	trape	fiere	lease	prose
parle	gimme	exine	étape	arere	mease	lapse
merle	homme	panne	clepe	stere	pease	copse
birle	lumme	benne	crêpe	'twere	tease	carse
easle	biome	penne	clipe	eagre	chase	farse
aisle	gnome	renne	slipe	aygre	phase	parse
lisle	crome	tenné	snipe	ochre	ukase	herse
gusle	drome	bonne	gripe	vairé	blasé	perse
title	forme	conne	tripe	afire	erase	terse
istle	horme	sonne	stipe	shire	prase	verse
ettle	disme	tonne	swipe	moire	caese	birse
ixtle	neume	T-bone	golpe	moiré	obese	corse
Thule	flume	scone	Tempe	spire	geese	dorse
boule	glume	agone	scope	stire	neese	gorse
foulé	plume	ohone	elope	quire	phese	horse
joule	spume	phone	slope	swire	these	morse
noule	brume	rhone	grope	twire	grese	Norse
poule	grume	shone	trope	genre	prese	torse
spule	rowme	alone	stope	ybore	maise	worse
brûlé	chyme	clone	myope	score	raise	burse
mvule	rhyme	no-one	nappe	adore	peise	curse
ovule	thyme	crone	jaspé	afore	seise	nurse
dowle	styme	drone	taupe	chore	weise	purse
sowle	azyme	grone	coupe	shore	anise	basse
bayle	meane	krone	coupé	whore	hoise	massé
hayle	thane	prone	loupe	blore	noise	passé
kayle	liane	trone	poupe	smore	poise	rasse
rayle	plane	atone	drupe	snore	toise	sasse
odyle	slane	stone	stupe	spore	arise	tasse
chyle	inane	ozone	clype	crore	crise	fesse
phyle	spane	gerne	flype	frore	grise	gesse
soyle	crane	kerne	slype	prore	prise	Jesse
style	stane	Lerne	grype	store	guise	nisse
guyle	scene	terne	scare	swore	avise	fosse
aizle	teene	borné	feare	barre	false	posse

5 -SSE

musse	unite	vague	slive	maize	pluff	stang
cause	spite	segue	knive	peize	snuff	swang
hause	trite	gigue	drive	seize	houff	twang
pause	urite	cogue	stive	weize	gruff	kyang
abuse	write	rogue	calve	brize	stuff	kreng
scuse	quite	togue	halve	frize	howff	ba'ing
meuse	suite	vogue	salve	grize	sowff	icing
reuse	evite	argue	valve	prize	calif	being
chuse	twite	orgue	delve	avize	kalif	aging
sluse	volte	fugue	helve	wanze	quoif	thing
amuse	zante	salue	solve	zanze	serif	cling
bouse	rente	value	volve	winze	metif	fling
douse	conte	tenue	wolve	bonze	motif	sling
house	monte	venue	above	cloze	shelf	doing
louse	ronte	pique	shove	gloze	skelf	going
mouse	shote	roque	clove	booze	Guelf	bring
rouse	clote	toque	glove	croze	Wolof	wring
souse	flote	tuque	slove	froze	aloof	sting
touse	emote	sprue	amove	furze	kloof	ruing
cruse	smote	ensue	emove	gauze	spoof	suing
druse	soote	issue	hoove	touze	groof	a-wing
hawse	wrote	bevue	poove	Druze	M-roof	owing
tawse	quote	revue	drove	towze	proof	swing
bowse	azote	deave	grove	avyze	scarf	dying
dowse	carte	heave	prove	tazze	wharf	eying
lowse	forte	leave	stove	F	dwarf	hying
towse	Porte	reave	carve	sheaf	swarf	lying
peyse	torte	weave	varve	kenaf	swerf	tying
poyse	baste	agave	nerve	daraf	scurf	vying
pryse	caste	chave	serve	chief	grouf	thong
guyse	haste	shave	verve	thief	G	flong
abate	paste	clave	curve	brief	de-bag	among
reate	taste	slave	Fauve	grief	unbag	emong
agate	waste	knave	mauve	F-clef	oflag	boong
skate	geste	loave	you've	G-clef	gulag	prong
alate	teste	brave	cruve	scaff	scrag	wrong
blate	piste	crave	crewe	chaff	sprag	stong
elate	coste	grave	Yahwe	flaff	strag	clung
plate	matte	stave	alowe	draff	Uzbeg	flung
slate	patte	suave	knowe	graff	hyleg	slung
amate	patté	awave	Debye	staff	unpeg	young
enate	fitte	naeve	inbye	quaff	glogg	wrung
roate	botte	deeve	upbye	nyaff	craig	stung
spate	motte	keeve	bedye	whiff	staig	swung
crate	butte	reeve	ox-eye	skiff	re-jig	embog
grate	fytte	kieve	pioye	cliff	rejig	incog
irate	sauté	lieve	barye	gliff	renig	pi-dog
orate	vaute	nieve	herye	sniff	sprig	befog
prate	acute	sieve	leaze	spiff	strig	Magog
urate	scute	cleve	peaze	griff	bewig	cohog
wrate	chute	breve	teaze	stiff	obang	lolog
state	elute	greve	agaze	quiff	bhang	scoog
ovate	flute	preve	blaze	scoff	whang	scrog
weete	route	Yahve	glaze	feoff	kiang	sprog
thete	brute	naive	amaze	skoff	liang	bourg
arête	vawte	waive	toaze	cloff	alang	debug
wefte	skyte	neive	braze	in-off	clang	undug
shite	flyte	reive	craze	on-off	klang	almug
white	quyte	ogive	graze	go-off	slang	scoug
skite	imbue	chive	buaze	wauff	spang	shrug
blite	endue	shive	feeze	scuff	krang	sprug
élite	indue	skive	heeze	chuff	orang	H
flite	undue	alive	neeze	bluff	subah
smite	queue	olive	baize	fluff	prang	obeah

ephah	linch	leuch	plash	grith	dhobi	tholi
Shiah	pinch	teuch	slash	swith	abaci	gusli
rajah	winch	couch	smash	filth	cocci	styli
bekah	conch	mouch	gnash	tilth	succi	agami
galah	bunch	pouch	snash	illth	amici	e-la-mi
belah	dunch	touch	brash	tenth	sulci	swami
selah	hunch	vouch	crash	ninth	farci	elemi
Allah	lunch	psych	trash.	month	fasci	salmi
omlah	munch	bandh	stash	Thoth	Musci	Suomi
solah	punch	almeh	quash	cloth	khadi	fermi
almah	runch	caneh	awash	sloth	Mahdi	Adeni
donah	lynch	kaneh	swash	Y-moth	soldi	acini
Jonah	synch	maneh	flesh	booth	Hindi	blini
mynah	hooch	doseh	plesh	sooth	fundi	benni
marah	mooch	laigh	fresh	tooth	cardi	jinni
gerah	pooch	heigh	taish	broth	pardi	Sunni
omrah	epoch	neigh	whish	froth	scudi	garni
Torah	broch	weigh	slish	troth	Yezdi	envoi
arrah	larch	ahigh	apish	wroth	pilei	scapi
surah	march	thigh	arish	quoth	aurei	okapi
Pesah	parch	anigh	Irish	azoth	nisei	palpi
lotah	perch	brogh	cuish	depth	issei	sampi
rayah	birch	burgh	swish	earth	Naafi	tempi
beach	porch	faugh	welsh	garth	buffi	cippi
leach	torch	haugh	mulsh	berth	sci-fi	Iraqi
peach	curch	kaugh	dunsh	birth	thagi	acari
reach	lurch	laugh	flosh	firth	tragi	imari
teach	Pasch	saugh	slosh	girth	fungi	urari
Vlach	batch	waugh	hoosh	mirth	lungi	indri
coach	catch	heugh	woosh	forth	corgi	ard-ri
loach	hatch	leugh	sposh	north	Lurgi	uteri
poach	latch	teugh	harsh	worth	spahi	pagri
roach	match	bough	marsh	furth	shchi	aggri
brach	natch	cough	wersh	musth	lichi	bajri
orach	patch	dough	shush	couth	elchi	kukri
beech	ratch	hough	blush	fouth	qui-hi	Maori
keech	watch	lough	flush	mouth	Sophi	karri
leech	fetch	rough	plush	routh	tophi	cirri
reech	ketch	sough	slush	south	rishi	Tisri
Czech	letch	tough	snush	youth	imshi	kauri
Reich	retch	hewgh	brush	truth	sushi	houri
chich	vetch	sirih	crush	fowth	lathi	quasi
which	aitch	Haikh	frush	rowth	radii	Parsi
stich	bitch	graph	death	sowth	modii	tarsi
quich	ditch	staph	heath	crwth	genii	Amati
belch	fitch	aleph	neath	sixth	torii	coati
welch	hitch	Ralph	snath	uh-huh	hadji	cacti
filch	pitch	delph	loath	I	hajji	recti
hilch	titch	sylph	wrath	Bahai	shoji	Eyeti
milch	witch	oomph	tuath	Sakai	khaki	mufti
pilch	botch	bumph	swath	stoai	ozeki	Sakti
zilch	hotch	humph	width	perai	palki	Fanti
culch	notch	sumph	teeth	serai	parki	tanti
gulch	potch	lymph	uneth	terai	Turki	dhoti
mulch	rotch	nymph	doeth	pirai	Neski	parti
ganch	butch	morph	fifth	Masai	urali	fasti
hanch	cutch	glyph	faith	assai	obeli	katti
lanch	dutch	myrrh	haith	rabbi	ceili	putti
ranch	hutch	abash	laith	alibi	chili	tutti
bench	kutch	leash	saith	oribi	dilli	aguti
tench	mutch	shash	meith	iambi	villi	ennui
wench	lauch	blash	smith	nimbi	paoli	appui
cinch	sauch	clash	crith	zimbi	oboli	maqui
finch	heuch	flash	frith	zombi	choli	bravi

5 -EVI

naevi	slick	whilk	D-mark	zygal	sural	refel
ghazi	snick	baulk	snark	nahal	gyral	bagel
bwazi	hoick	caulk	spark	ethal	pyral	Rigel
darzi	yoick	waulk	stark	phial	basal	angel
K	spick	skulk	quark	glial	nasal	mohel
bobak	brick	chank	clerk	spial	vasal	chiel
Kodak ®	crick	shank	chirk	prial	mesal	shiel
bleak	erick	thank	shirk	trial	sisal	spiel
sneak	prick	blank	smirk	urial	datal	ariel
apeak	trick	clank	stirk	axial	fatal	oriel
speak	wrick	flank	quirk	pokal	natal	Sikel
break	stick	plank	stork	halal	ictal	yokel
creak	quick	spank	awork	salal	octal	allel
freak	acock	brank	abask	molal	fetal	camel
wreak	chock	crank	flask	hamal	metal	samel
steak	shock	drank	whisk	ramal	petal	gemel
tweak	block	frank	flisk	tamal	cital	panel
kaiak	clock	prank	glisk	femal	dital	lapel
umiak	flock	stank	brisk	hemal	vital	repel
kulak	smock	swank	frisk	comal	dotal	impel
Pomak	knock	twank	kiosk	domal	notal	cupel
cloak	brock	chink	torsk	romal	rotal	expel
croak	crock	think	taluk	rumal	total	merel
gopak	frock	skink	drouk	banal	artal	borel
strak	trock	blink	snowk	canal	equal	forel
Musak ®	stock	clink	L	fanal	usual	lorel
uptak	chuck	plink	graal	genal	naval	morel
kayak	shuck	slink	kraal	penal	nival	sorel
Muzak	cluck	spink	cabal	renal	rival	easel
aback	pluck	brink	Sabal	venal	arval	mesel
chack	amuck	drink	bubal	final	orval	eisel
shack	snuck	prink	tubal	vinal	coxal	losel
thack	cruck	stink	decal	annal	noxal	ousel
whack	truck	swink	fecal	monal	gayal	ratel
alack	nebek	twink	tical	tonal	riyal	betel
black	Uzbek	clonk	focal	zonal	loyal	botel
clack	cheek	plonk	local	urnal	royal	hotel
plack	theek	cronk	vocal	shoal	spyal	motel
slack	cleek	stonk	ducal	skoal	gazal	artel
smack	gleek	quonk	dedal	papal	Babel	cruel
knack	sleek	chunk	medal	sepal	label	gruel
snack	apeek	skunk	pedal	pipal	debel	cavel
brack	creek	blunk	nidal	copal	jebel	gavel
crack	Greek	clunk	tidal	nopal	nebel	javel
frack	steek	flunk	modal	appal	rebel	navel
track	a-week	plunk	nodal	pupal	gibel	ravel
wrack	Dalek	slunk	podal	typal	libel	bevel
stack	snoek	spunk	ideal	feral	umbel	devel
quack	topek	drunk	sheal	seral	Sicel	kevel
swack	tupek	trunk	wheal	viral	excel	level
check	terek	stunk	zoeal	coral	bedel	nevel
cleck	glaik	chook	areal	goral	kidel	revel
fleck	smaik	shook	ureal	horal	jodel	rivel
sneck	traik	snook	steal	loral	model	hovel
V-neck	sheik	spook	uveal	moral	yodel	novel
speck	mujik	brook	sweal	poral	sheel	jewel
treck	tupik	crook	offal	roral	wheel	newel
wreck	Nasik	drook	vagal	soral	kneel	sewel
haick	batik	stook	legal	aural	speel	tewel
saick	chalk	kapok	regal	dural	creel	bowel
chick	stalk	yapok	algal	fural	steel	dowel
thick	whelk	tarok	fugal	jural	aweel	Nowel
click	spelk	chark	jugal	mural	sweel	rowel
flick	thilk	shark	pygal	rural	tweel	towel

vowel	spell	snarl	hakam	carom	jorum	no-man
Texel	stell	chirl	Islam	besom	strum	roman
pixel	quell	thirl	cloam	bosom	durum	toman
gazel	dwell	whirl	pro-am	buxom	adsum	woman
hazel	swell	skirl	haram	rearm	datum	urman
bezel	chill	swirl	abram	charm	notum	atman
sizel	shill	twirl	scram	alarm	novum	human
zizel	thill	ceorl	ihram	smarm	shawm	Ruman
ouzel	skill	whorl	joram	enarm	N	sloan
puzel	spill	churl	nizam	inarm	Alban	groan
scail	brill	knurl	modem	unarm	amban	japan
skail	drill	miaul	adeem	swarm	koban	sapan
flail	frill	spaul	breem	therm	urban	zupan
snail	grill	babul	steem	inerm	Cuban	varan
brail	krill	picul	exeem	sperm	Tacan	scran
drail	trill	woful	begem	chirm	pecan	skran
frail	still	awful	golem	enorm	Sican	Koran
grail	quill	mogul	xylem	storm	Oscan	loran
T-rail	swill	schul	proem	chasm	redan	Qoran
trail	'twill	pikul	harem	miasm	sedan	toran
quail	twill	yokul	totem	plasm	Sudan	buran
avail	knoll	manul	pashm	spasm	paean	furan
sybil	droll	annul	thaim	odism	ocean	Qurân
steil	proll	afoul	claim	deism	skean	tyran
Rigil	troll	ghoul	fraim	seism	clean	basan
sigil	atoll	proul	bedim	zoism	glean	kisan
vigil	quoll	capul	hakim	apism	spean	Nisan
argil	scull	pipul	sclim	prism	stean	ratan
pugil	ahull	ampul	sklim	tuism	quean	Satan
nihil	skull	jarul	panim	abysm	lagan	titan
vakil	you'll	shawl	denim	glaum	pagan	witan
Tamil	trull	spawl	minim	imaum	began	Javan
armil	stull	brawl	harim	dwaum	vegan	pavan
aumil	idyll	crawl	abrim	sebum	ligan	divan
aboil	ghyll	drawl	scrim	album	wigan	Sivan
spoil	cibol	trawl	purim	locum	zigan	elvan
broil	Cobol	wrawl	aswim	ledum	ingan	jawan
droil	nicol	scowl	maxim	sedum	hogan	dewan
pupil	indol	thowl	goyim	odeum	logan	diwan
meril	she'ol	growl	realm	rheum	argan	ajwan
peril	segol	prowl	shalm	ileum	organ	cowan
zoril	rigol	swayl	smalm	oleum	Teian	gowan
April	Algol	sibyl	psalm	sagum	Chian	powan
basil	argol	ethyl	qualm	begum	Elian	rowan
fusil	thiol	alkyl	dwalm	degum	Ilian	Texan
intil	jokol	allyl	whelm	algum	apian	Mayan
until	xylol	xylyl	skelm	ungum	Arian	geyan
cavil	shool	vinyl	haulm	jugum	Asian	Aryan
devil	snool	beryl	stulm	ho-hum	avian	heben
civil	spool	cetyl	flamm	odium	bajan	laden
anvil	brool	butyl	Sodom	ilium	yojan	widen
scall	drool	M	idiom	opium	pekan	olden
be-all	stool	praam	axiom	oakum	uhlan	loden
shall	carol	madam	celom	hokum	solan	Woden
small	parol	undam	genom	kokum	kulan	sheen
do-all	enrol	abeam	venom	velum	yulan	wheen
spall	furol	I-beam	choom	hilum	caman	green
stall	eusol	fleam	bloom	pilum	daman	preen
myall	lysol	gleam	gloom	solum	ad-man	treen
shell	metol	bream	sloom	larum	he-man	steen
she'll	extol	cream	spoom	scrum	leman	queen
smell	pearl	dream	broom	serum	reman	'tween
knell	gnarl	steam	groom	thrum	amman	hogen
snell	knarl	ogham	vroom	forum	unman	ashen

5 -IEN

alien	dozen	quoin	inion	gluon	queyn	imago
baken	lozen	unpin	onion	unwon	proyn	grego
oaken	thegn	orpin	union	caxon	0	doggo
taken	deign	lupin	Orion	Saxon	cacao	amigo
waken	feign	sarin	avion	taxon	chiao	fango
liken	reign	abrin	eikon	rayon	yobbo	mango
soken	align	serin	salon	sayon	bilbo	tango
token	coign	agrin	talon	try-on	jambo	bingo
woken	V-sign	burin	felon	gazon	mambo	dingo
silen	foehn	purin	melon	dearn	sambo	jingo
solen	again	basin	colon	learn	zambo	lingo
samen	chain	sasin	Solon	yearn	kembo	bongo
yamen	blain	resin	nylon	sharn	kimbo	congo
semen	plain	elsin	pylon	starn	limbo	pongo
limen	slain	eosin	demon	awarn	timbó	mungo
elmen	amain	rosin	lemon	stern	combo	cargo
women	spain	lysin	Timon	quern	gombo	largo
lumen	brain	Latin	timon	bairn	bumbo	sargo
numen	drain	matin	ammon	cairn	gumbo	Virgo
rumen	grain	satin	canon	acorn	jumbo	borgo
hymen	train	sit-in	cañon	scorn	rumbo	forgo
linen	stain	untin	fanon	adorn	dsobo	sorgo
tapen	swain	potin	tenon	shorn	Garbo	misgo
ripen	twain	ettin	xenon	thorn	sorbo	outgo
unpen	cabin	cutin	ninon	doorn	turbo	tea-ho
aspen	sabin	cut-in	piñon	frorn	chaco	macho
Karen	robin	put-in	run-on	sworn	Draco	litho
siren	rubin	rutin	shoon	churn	guaco	Sotho
syren	ricin	Bruin	spoon	inurn	bacco	ngaio
risen	orcin	bavin	croon	bourn	secco	radio
hosen	mucin	pavin	swoon	mourn	cocco	addio
owsen	Ladin	ravin	capon	yourn	zocco	audio
eaten	eldin	savin	yapon	spurn	banco	folio
laten	sdein	levin	jupon	U-turn	zinco	polio
oaten	lie-in	covin	yupon	azurn	bunco	danio
paten	tie-in	sewin	baron	tabun	junco	curio
often	skein	powin	heron	begun	Turco	patio
hoten	olein	mix-in	seron	cajun	casco	ratio
moten	grein	toxin	giron	Injun	cisco	banjo
haven	stein	auxin	boron	stoun	disco	shako
paven	elfin	buy-in	moron	swoun	spado	decko
raven	Fagin	swoln	apron	rerun	credo	gecko
seven	begin	djinn	gyron	uprun	uredo	jocko
yeven	algin	stonn	bason	bosun	iaido	bucko
given	yogin	bacon	mason	jotun	dildo	dekko
liven	lakin	Maçon	meson	flawn	soldo	sanko
riven	takin	racon	bison	gnawn	kendo	pinko
coven	Pekin	ancon	vison	spawn	rondo	bunko
hoven	likin	radon	boson	drawn	tondo	smoko
woven	all-in	end-on	arson	prawn	good-o	cyclo
erven	colin	codon	urson	shewn	fordo	Anglo
sewen	kylin	paeon	hyson	adown	sordo	hallo
yewen	gamin	odeon	baton	shown	misdo	cello
rowen	tamin	pheon	acton	blown	outdo	hello
waxen	admin	pleon	béton	clown	scudo	jello
mixen	ulmin	Freon ®	jeton	flown	video	hillo
vixen	cumin	Dagon	seton	known	rodeo	hollo
boxen	renin	wagon	niton	brown	cameo	hullo
woxen	venin	tigon	piton	crown	Romeo	paolo
doyen	kinin	argon	futon	drown	roneo	ovolo
dizen	linin	ergon	muton	frown	vireo	matlo
mizen	run-in	zygon	put-on	grown	paseo	stylo
wizen	eloin	scion	cyton	stown	buffo	schmo
cozen	groin	anion	Fluon ®	sdayn	cuffo	

primo	torso	steep	swoop	smear	weber	agger
Salmo	basso	sweep	strop	anear	fiber	egger
pulmo	lasso	priep	estop	spear	giber	liger
commo	gesso	salep	psyop	arear	jiber	Niger
zhomo	fatso	julep	scarp	drear	liber	tiger
dsomo	howso	stoep	sharp	swear	amber	anger
duomo	say-so	strep	twerp	sofar	ember	Roger
gismo	Erato	graip	chirp	begar	umber	soger
gizmo	recto	redip	stirp	regar	sober	urger
beano	add-to	tulip	twirp	segar	suber	auger
piano	aweto	oxlip	thorp	eggar	tuber	Luger
llano	all-to	genip	slurp	cigar	facer	ocher
guano	molto	scrip	usurp	sugar	macer	usher
segno	canto	unrip	clasp	lahar	pacer	ether
Taino	manto	atrip	grasp	briar	racer	other
chino	panto	strip	crisp	friar	dicer	shier
rhino	cento	equip	knosp	makar	ricer	skier
ken-no	lento	unzip	scaup	eskar	ulcer	flier
dunno	pinto	scalp	whaup	malar	oncer	plier
corno	conto	whelp	tie-up	talar	wader	brier
porno	junto	skelp	all-up	velar	adder	crier
baboo	punto	ayelp	pin-up	filar	udder	drier
taboo	photo	sculp	ton-up	hilar	Seder	frier
wahoo	typto	poulp	run-up	molar	aider	prier
yahoo	yarto	scamp	sun-up	polar	cider	trier
baloo	basto	champ	scoup	solar	eider	osier
igloo	mesto	clamp	croup	volar	rider	twier
hoo-oo	visto	cramp	group	gular	sider	baker
napoo	gusto	tramp	stoup	damar	alder	daker
Karoo	set-to	stamp	two-up	cimar	elder	faker
gazoo	ditto	swamp	tip-up	simar	under	laker
kazoo	lotto	chimp	mop-up	jumar	order	maker
igapo	motto	skimp	pop-up	cymar	cyder	naker
quipo	potto	blimp	top-up	symar	cheer	oaker
tempo	cutto	flimp	sirup	dinar	sheer	raker
compo	putto	crimp	syrup	minar	fleer	saker
gippo	Pluto	primp	get-up	ulnar	ameer	taker
hippo	how-to	guimp	let-up	sonar	emeer	waker
zoppo	bravo	chomp	set-up	lunar	one-er	icker
gyppo	salvo	tromp	fit-up	hepar	emeer	ocker
micro	Provo	stomp	titup	tasar	sneer	diker
mucro	servo	chump	put-up	kesar	speer	hiker
pedro	diazo	thump	mix-up	Tatar	breer	liker
hydro	piezo	clump	lay-up	petar	freer	piker
fuero	matzo	flump	fry-up	sitar	steer	anker
Negro	mezzo	plump	scowp	altar	queer	inker
aggro	P	slump	polyp	antar	sweer	joker
Genro	recap	crump	R	attar	tweer	poker
Munro	uncap	frump	debar	ottar	wafer	roker
repro	aheap	trump	embar	feuar	defer	asker
appro	cheap	stump	imbar	douar	refer	esker
morro	sneap	bebop	unbar	Invar ®	offer	puker
zorro	jalap	galop	lobar	dowar	fifer	syker
burro	hanap	salop	tubar	jowar	lifer	baler
metro	scrap	orlop	vicar	sowar	infer	haler
retro	strap	scoop	in-car	Nayar	gofer	waler
intro	U-trap	whoop	Oscar	boyar	eager	idler
gadso	attap	cloop	radar	Iyyar	jäger	ogler
godso	cheep	sloop	cedar	bazar	lager	filer
aviso	sheep	snoop	abear	lazar	pager	miler
whoso	bleep	apoop	leear	sizar	rager	piler
dipso	cleep	droop	shear	spaer	wager	siler
verso	sleep	troop	blear	caber	yager	tiler
corso	creep	stoop	clear	Saber	leger	soler

5 -LER

puler	miser	sawer	arbor	gebur	plies	Eblis
ruler	riser	tawer	décor	occur	spies	Iblis
owler	loser	hewer	mucor	recur	Aries	Felis
tyler	noser	sewer	nidor	incur	cries	nelis
namer	poser	bower	pudor	regur	fries	allis
tamer	muser	cower	sudor	augur	pries	camis
Khmer	cater	dower	Tudor	mohur	tries	kamis
dimer	dater	lower	nagor	demur	sties	tamis
mimer	eater	mower	rigor	femur	exies	semis
rimer	hater	power	vigor	lemur	fakes	Canis
timer	later	rower	abhor	scour	jakes	Manis
emmer	mater	sower	ichor	odour	cokes	lenis
comer	pater	tower	ephor	clour	tales	penis
homer	rater	taxer	prior	flour	vales	finis
vomer	tater	waxer	trior	amour	arles	ornis
ormer	water	vexer	major	stour	gules	lapis
diner	deter	fixer	milor	satyr	james	tapis
finer	meter	mixer	rumor	S	limes	Paris
liner	peter	sixer	tumor	cabas	Times	Doris
miner	after	boxer	manor	Midas	fomes	loris
viner	biter	gayer	Señor	judas	manes	épris
inner	titer	layer	tenor	rudas	lenes	arris
boner	alter	payer	minor	Naias	penes	orris
goner	enter	sayer	donor	alias	Nones	Xyris
loner	inter	shyer	floor	Trias	shoes	basis
moner	doter	skyer	smoor	balas	dares	oasis
tuner	noter	flyer	spoor	palas	nares	apsis
awner	voter	slyer	stoor	bolas	Ceres	arsis
owner	aster	foyer	sapor	atlas	Xeres	lysis
shoer	ester	toyer	vapor	camas	mores	métis
wooer	otter	dryer	sopor	monas	bases	Vitis
twoer	utter	fryer	maror	psoas	gases	cutis
caper	luter	pryer	error	naras	oases	louis
gaper	outer	tryer	furor	teras	arses	mavis
paper	oxter	buyer	juror	liras	asses	pavis
raper	gluer	twyer	visor	Doras	buses	levis
taper	haver	gazer	actor	arras	cates	lewis
leper	laver	hazer	fetor	lavas	nates	taxis
neper	paver	mazer	motor	texas	eaves	pyxis
piper	raver	sizer	rotor	plebs	haves	kecks
riper	saver	dozer	sutor	combs	oaves	socks
viper	taver	chair	tutor	clubs	Dives	ducks
wiper	waver	flair	fluor	specs	fives	fenks
coper	bever	glair	cruor	circs	hives	finks
doper	fever	stair	livor	needs	lives	yonks
roper	lever	quair	taxor	winds	vives	hunks
toper	never	nadir	mayor	fonds	wives	zooks
upper	sever	mudir	razor	hards	elves	works
asper	diver	their	vizor	hurds	luxes	Yorks
duper	fiver	speir	charr	blaes	styes	lawks
super	giver	sweir	gnarr	claes	fezes	vails
hyper	hiver	Kafir	starr	tabes	beefs	noils
ryper	liver	kefir	chirr	Ribes	dregs	mools
parer	river	jagir	shirr	vibes	maggs	marls
airer	siver	fakir	whirr	pubes	tongs	mouls
firer	viver	choir	skirr	feces	jougs	hiems
hirer	elver	tapir	smirr	voces	maths	dooms
wirer	cover	aesir	mhorr	luces	meths	means
borer	dover	astir	churr	Hades	labis	glans
corer	hover	nazir	flurr	sedes	pubis	krans
porer	lover	wazir	knurr	grees	cedis	avens
curer	mover	vezir	scaur	wages	Sufis	evens
laser	rover	vizir	whaur	abies	aegis	mains
maser	syver	tabor	glaur	flies	aphis	reins

banns	gloss	humus	begat	fleet	izzet	fecit
jinns	cross	Janus	unhat	gleet	abaft	licit
harns	dross	manus	Uniat	sleet	chaft	on-dit
nouns	gross	genus	éclat	freet	shaft	audit
chaos	gauss	venus	splat	greet	craft	freit
mebos	truss	minus	Banat	sweet	draft	befit
ambos	abyss	sinus	qanat	tweet	graft	refit
dados	swats	Alnus	annat	beget	kraft	unfit
dodos	grits	bonus	beget	unget	theft	legit
kudos	quits	tonus	Donat	quiet	aleft	digit
speos	swits	thous	E-boat	upjet	cleft	unlit
Logos	gilts	pious	Q-boat	unket	shift	split
ethos	pants	smous	U-boat	palet	whift	admit
adios	gents	mopus	shoat	salet	clift	demit
sekos	Scots	lupus	bloat	valet	glift	remit
halos	boots	Larus	float	ablet	snift	limit
telos	foots	sarus	gloat	relet	drift	immit
demos	toots	varus	Croat	aglet	grift	vomit
nomos	terts	Abrus	groat	filet	swift	droit
topos	dorts	virus	troat	gilet	delft	stoit
saros	batts	Morus	stoat	inlet	thoft	quoit
tiros	tatts	sorus	bepat	unlet	aloft	nepit
altos	Cebus	torus	carat	volet	croft	pipit
lotos	rebus	Eurus	karat	islet	scuft	merit
heaps	gibus	gyrus	scrat	culet	yacht	afrit
chaps	embus	Pyrus	morat	owlet	fecht	amrit
shaps	lobus	Jesus	sprat	emmet	hecht	sprit
Elaps	Rubus	jesus	curat	comet	Pecht	absit
craps	Picus	nisus	jurat	armet	wecht	besit
chips	incus	risus	surat	fumet	dicht	resit
snips	oncus	Ursus	fouat	manet	licht	visit
timps	uncus	Fusus	squat	benet	richt	posit
mumps	focus	ictus	vivat	genet	docht	rosit
Scops	hocus	fetus	lovat	tenet	oucht	musit
elops	locus	lotus	bowat	Donet	Peght	petit
slops	arcus	Notus	doubt	nonet	bight	sluit
props	ascus	Equus	react	tapet	dight	Inuit
myops	fucus	favus	diact	caret	eight	squit
corps	mucus	Taxus	enact	beret	fight	bruit
turps	Gadus	nexus	coact	egret	hight	fruit
fiars	nidus	Anzus	epact	mpret	kight	g-suit
yours	modus	braws	bract	arrêt	light	davit
class	nodus	thews	fract	beset	might	pewit
glass	ileus	trews	tract	reset	night	tewit
amass	Fagus	adays	exact	inset	pight	inwit
brass	magus	X-rays	eject	onset	right	unwit
crass	vagus	aways	elect	unset	sight	rozit
frass	negus	Kotys	erect	roset	tight	welkt
grass	bogus	T	edict	upset	wight	dealt
trass	argus	rabat	evict	asset	aught	shalt
kvass	ankus	Sebat	mulct	muset	ought	smalt
chess	onkus	rybat	tinct	octet	plait	spalt
bless	talus	ducat	educt	motet	krait	exalt
loess	hilus	sceat	eruct	fouet	trait	P-Celt
cress	pilus	cheat	veldt	cruet	await	Q-Celt
dress	bolus	wheat	Tibet	revet	habit	P-Kelt
press	solus	bleat	zibet	civet	debit	Q-Kelt
tress	camus	cleat	facet	rivet	ambit	smelt
guess	ramus	pleat	lacet	covet	oobit	knelt
whiss	wamus	speat	tacet	duvet	Tobit	spelt
bliss	Mimus	great	cadet	bewet	orbit	dwelt
amiss	Ulmus	treat	bidet	unwet	cubit	swelt
Swiss	comus	sweat	godet	bowet	oubit	doilt
floss	Momus	exeat	sheet	rozet	tacit	spilt
			skeet			

atilt	joint	capot	exert	blist	arnut	**W**
stilt	noint	depot	chirt	foist	about	macaw
built	point	repot	shirt	hoist	scout	pshaw
guilt	print	impot	skirt	joist	chout	pi-jaw
quilt	stint	tarot	flirt	moist	shout	pilaw
twilt	quint	besot	snirt	roist	clout	in-law
U-bolt	suint	assot	spirt	zoist	flout	unlaw
smolt	biont	divot	quirt	frist	glout	bylaw
ymolt	front	pivot	abort	grist	smout	papaw
dault	ayont	guyot	short	trist	knout	scraw
fault	burnt	adapt	whort	wrist	snout	thraw
gault	'tisn't	leapt	amort	buist	spout	straw
hault	daunt	inapt	snort	muist	crout	squaw
sault	gaunt	unapt	poort	quist	grout	pawaw
vault	haunt	coapt	aport	ovist	trout	bedew
adult	jaunt	wrapt	sport	twist	stout	askew
boult	naunt	yrapt	blurt	exist	caput	emmew
moult	saunt	swapt	court	canst	kaput	immew
poult	taunt	adept	yourt	ghost	input	enmew
exult	vaunt	slept	spurt	boost	strut	unmew
scant	shunt	inept	sturt	roost	mazut	renew
idant	blunt	crept	beast	crost	smowt	sinew
leant	count	stept	feast	frost	'twixt	vinew
meant	fount	swept	least	ytost	**U**	screw
chant	mount	whipt	reast	karst	Medau	shrew
shan't	brunt	clipt	yeast	warst	pilau	threw
giant	grunt	slipt	ghast	verst	boyau	strew
hiant	prunt	dempt	blast	first	noyau	unsew
riant	stunt	kempt	boast	horst	jambu	navew
plant	meynt	nempt	coast	worst	urubu	miaow
slant	jabot	tempt	hoast	burst	nandu	elbow
drant	sabot	compt	roast	curst	Hindu	embow
grant	abbot	adopt	toast	durst	perdu	up-bow
orant	robot	co-opt	brast	hurst	adieu	ox-bow
trant	ox-bot	epopt	wrast	wurst	snafu	sybow
quant	picot	swopt	avast	adust	waefu'	widow
avant	escot	poupt	hadst	inust	samfu	endow
scent	cagot	erupt	didst	joust	prahu	theow
agent	fagot	Egypt	midst	moust	fichu	nohow
shent	magot	crypt	kydst	roust	buchu	ewhow
sient	begot	scart	reest	crust	sadhu	ablow
blent	bigot	T-cart	egest	frust	bucku	below
glent	gigot	heart	chest	trust	haiku	aglow
olent	jigot	peart	blest	mayst	hokku	pilow
ament	ingot	chart	doest	sayst	poilu	allow
anent	ungot	liart	crest	royst	voulu	scrow
spent	argot	skart	drest	tryst	cornu	serow
brent	ergot	smart	prest	scatt	sajou	shrow
prent	idiot	boart	wrest	arett	bijou	throw
urent	ariot	apart	guest	duett	tatou	arrow
yrent	helot	spart	quest	flitt	bayou	strow
usen't	Nilot	start	ewest	shott	quipu	tatow
stent	pilot	quart	angst	beaut	coypu	kotow
event	allot	tuart	saist	ghaut	uhuru	vrouw
faint	gemot	swart	waist	claut	lassu	**X**
paint	scoot	lyart	Idist	kraut	bussu	addax
saint	afoot	chert	odist	début	Bantu	malax
taint	'sfoot	piert	deist	rebut	vertu	relax
feint	shoot	alert	geist	incut	virtu	limax
meint	cloot	inert	heist	uncut	Kuo-yü	panax
ahint	sloot	apert	neist	Yakut	kudzu	borax
skint	smoot	avert	reist	galut	kanzu	hyrax
flint	snoot	evert	agist	gamut	**V**	untax
glint	wroot	overt	whist	donut	ollav	vibex

index	deray	zincy	moody	motey	ruggy	ducky
codex	foray	farcy	woody	cutey	vuggy	lucky
podex	moray	mercy	bardy	bluey	bilgy	mucky
telex	spray	gaucy	cardy	fluey	bulgy	yucky
silex	array	saucy	hardy	gluey	mangy	reeky
culex	stray	gawcy	lardy	savey	rangy	spiky
Pulex	resay	beady	mardy	wavey	tangy	yukky
remex	unsay	heady	pardy	covey	dingy	balky
cimex	assay	leady	tardy	lovey	lingy	milky
Rumex	essay	ready	vardy	yawey	mingy	silky
annex	Douay	shady	perdy	skyey	wingy	yolky
Ampex ®	alway	glady	wordy	leafy	zingy	bulky
carex	noway	toady	curdy	beefy	bungy	hulky
sorex	asway	baddy	gaudy	arefy	dungy	sulky
Lurex	byway	caddy	crudy	baffy	gungy	dumky
murex	Araby	daddy	study	daffy	elogy	hanky
Pyrex ®	cabby	faddy	bawdy	taffy	stogy	lanky
unsex	gabby	paddy	dowdy	jiffy	porgy	manky
latex	tabby	waddy	howdy	miffy	surgy	dinky
vitex	yabby	neddy	rowdy	niffy	azygy	kinky
radix	debby	reddy	abbey	toffy	techy	pinky
affix	webby	teddy	lacey	fuffy	tichy	sinky
infix	Bibby	biddy	pacey	huffy	Vichy	zinky
unfix	ribby	giddy	dicey	puffy	itchy	conky
calix	bobby	kiddy	ricey	edify	duchy	honky
salix	cobby	middy	cagey	deify	Sophy	wonky
helix	dobby	tiddy	bogey	reify	hashy	funky
bolix	hobby	widdy	fogey	unify	mashy	hunky
cylix	lobby	doddy	skiey	gulfy	washy	junky
kylix	mobby	noddy	dikey	comfy	meshy	choky
admix	nobby	poddy	jokey	goofy	dishy	smoky
immix	bubby	soddy	dykey	roofy	fishy	booky
varix	cubby	toddy	agley	woofy	imshy	cooky
embox	fubby	buddy	kiley	surfy	toshy	hooky
redox	hubby	cuddy	alley	turfy	bushy	kooky
phlox	nubby	muddy	coley	stagy	cushy	nooky
Xerox ®	tubby	puddy	holey	cadgy	gushy	rooky
beaux	gleby	ruddy	poley	hedgy	hushy	barky
Glaux	rugby	deedy	muley	kedgy	lushy	darky
Gueux	Dolby ®	needy	kyley	ledgy	mushy	larky
choux	comby	reedy	samey	sedgy	pushy	narky
Sioux	womby	seedy	limey	ridgy	rushy	parky
calyx	jumby	weedy	homey	dodgy	lathy	sarky
Y	globy	predy	waney	podgy	pithy	jerky
embay	booby	laldy	reney	pudgy	withy	perky
decay	looby	goldy	veney	elegy	bothy	mirky
today	warby	bandy	piney	baggy	mothy	corky
Tokay	derby	candy	winey	jaggy	bunjy	forky
Malay	herby	dandy	coney	naggy	leaky	porky
palay	o'erby	handy	honey	raggy	peaky	murky
belay	forby	kandy	money	leggy	shaky	pesky
delay	busby	pandy	poney	peggy	flaky	pisky
relay	outby	randy	toney	biggy	snaky	risky
allay	dauby	sandy	cooey	ciggy	braky	ensky
inlay	lay-by	bendy	gooey	piggy	quaky	bosky
unlay	fly-by	fendy	hooey	boggy	tacky	dusky
splay	spacy	rindy	dopey	doggy	wacky	husky
uplay	oracy	windy	jasey	foggy	dicky	musky
renay	baccy	gundy	absey	moggy	micky	tusky
repay	spicy	oundy	sesey	soggy	picky	fluky
unpay	pricy	a'body	mosey	buggy	wicky	gawky
appay	juicy	X-body	nosey	fuggy	cocky	pawky
scray	fancy	boody	upsey	muggy	pocky	scaly
beray	nancy	goody	matey	puggy	rocky	mealy

5 -ALY

vealy	manly	mammy	sunny	nappy	fairy	copsy
shaly	wanly	rammy	tunny	pappy	hairy	mopsy
coaly	fonly	Sammy	ebony	sappy	lairy	popsy
swaly	cooly	tammy	peony	zappy	vairy	gypsy
nobly	gooly	gemmy	agony	peppy	spiry	birsy
badly	hooly	jemmy	phony	dippy	awmry	gorsy
madly	mooly	jimmy	piony	gippy	Cymry	horsy
sadly	haply	mommy	loony	hippy	henry	pursy
oddly	reply	pommy	moony	lippy	flory	gassy
redly	amply	tommy	crony	nippy	glory	massy
godly	imply	dummy	drony	pippy	moory	sassy
jeely	apply	gummy	irony	tippy	frory	messy
seely	duply	lummy	atony	yippy	story	cissy
onely	early	mummy	stony	zippy	ivory	missy
daily	marly	rummy	carny	hoppy	carry	sissy
gaily	parly	tummy	ferny	moppy	harry	bossy
haily	ferly	yummy	corny	poppy	marry	lossy
saily	girly	anomy	horny	soppy	parry	mossy
veily	mirly	coomy	curny	duppy	tarry	tossy
shily	nirly	doomy	lawny	guppy	berry	fussy
slily	burly	roomy	Sawny	puppy	ferry	hussy
doily	curly	atomy	tawny	gyppy	Gerry	mussy
roily	gurly	barmy	yawny	harpy	herry	pussy
soily	hurly	dormy	downy	purpy	jerry	patsy
drily	murly	gormy	powny	gaspy	merry	gutsy
bally	surly	wormy	towny	paspy	perry	bousy
dally	fatly	gaumy	accoy	raspy	serry	lousy
gally	patly	plumy	decoy	waspy	terry	mousy
pally	fitly	spumy	peeoy	wispy	firry	tousy
rally	hotly	thymy	enjoy	roupy	lorry	crusy
sally	aptly	leany	alloy	soupy	sorry	drusy
tally	truly	meany	annoy	scary	worry	gawsy
wally	rawly	teeny	sepoy	deary	burry	newsy
belly	newly	weeny	stroy	leary	curry	towsy
felly	lowly	rainy	duroy	teary	furry	meaty
jelly	laxly	meiny	savoy	weary	gurry	peaty
nelly	shyly	veiny	envoy	chary	hurry	platy
telly	slyly	shiny	heapy	diary	lurry	slaty
welly	coyly	whiny	soapy	alary	murry	goaty
billy	dryly	spiny	crapy	clary	retry	praty
dilly	wryly	briny	grapy	flary	nitry	piety
filly	beamy	twiny	seepy	glary	entry	goety
gilly	reamy	canny	weepy	snary	saury	suety
hilly	seamy	fanny	snipy	hoary	loury	hefty
silly	flamy	nanny	kelpy	roary	usury	lefty
willy	foamy	fenny	gilpy	otary	azury	fifty
colly	loamy	henny	pulpy	ovary	Jewry	mifty
dolly	enemy	jenny	campy	ambry	cowry	nifty
folly	pigmy	penny	dampy	decry	dowry	lofty
golly	pygmy	wenny	hempy	faery	fubsy	softy
holly	blimy	finny	jimpy	beery	pudsy	tufty
jolly	slimy	hinny	bumpy	leery	sudsy	laity
lolly	grimy	linny	dumpy	peery	poesy	deity
molly	primy	ninny	humpy	veery	daisy	seity
polly	atimy	pinny	jumpy	aiery	noisy	whity
bully	stimy	tinny	lumpy	fiery	grisy	amity
cully	balmy	bonny	tumpy	emery	palsy	unity
dully	calmy	nonny	slopy	apery	pansy	malty
fully	palmy	sonny	goopy	query	tansy	salty
gully	filmy	bunny	loopy	every	sonsy	walty
hully	gammy	dunny	roopy	aggry	goosy	kelty
sully	hammy	funny	atopy	angry	prosy	kilty
dimly	jammy	gunny	gappy	ochry	gipsy	silty
rumly	lammy	runny	happy	dairy	tipsy	jolty

canty	party	fusty	dotty	chivy	stewy	fizzy
janty	tarty	lusty	motty	skivy	showy	tizzy
manty	warty	musty	potty	privy	blowy	pozzy
wanty	dirty	rusty	totty	stivy	snowy	buzzy
benty	dorty	batty	butty	senvy	frowy	fuzzy
genty	forty	catty	cutty	poovy	flaxy	huzzy
tenty	porty	fatty	gutty	carvy	braxy	muzzy
linty	rorty	natty	jutty	nervy	ataxy	Z
minty	purty	patty	nutty	curvy	prexy	topaz
tinty	hasty	ratty	putty	navvy	epoxy	kranz
jonty	masty	tatty	rutty	savvy	proxy	blitz
ponty	nasty	betty	tutty	bevvy	druxy	glitz
aunty	pasty	jetty	fluty	bivvy	glazy	spitz
bunty	tasty	netty	gouty	civvy	crazy	waltz
punty	vasty	petty	sixty	divvy	boozy	miltz
runty	resty	bitty	roguy	deawy	woozy	Nantz
zloty	testy	ditty	appuy	thawy	furzy	wootz
booty	yesty	kitty	heavy	flawy	ritzy	hertz
footy	zesty	Mitty	leavy	chewy	gauzy	pzazz
rooty	fisty	nitty	peavy	thewy	jazzy	whizz
sooty	misty	titty	gravy	viewy	lezzy	frizz
empty	busty	witty	chevy	spewy	dizzy	abuzz
umpty	dusty					

A	cicada	air-sea	murrha	aralia	aporia
indaba	bahada	nausea	geisha	amelia	latria
amoeba	bajada	protea	aphtha	dahlia	yttria
zareba	gelada	terefa	maltha	pallia	nutria
zereba	armada	Malaga	quotha	skolia	Sauria
gowf-ba'	cañada	bodega	bertha	antlia	anuria
sahiba	panada	telega	Aglaia	abulia	pyuria
zariba	espada	senega	Tupaia	thulia	tarsia
zeriba	posada	quagga	phobia	mia-mia	cassia
tsamba	lambda	striga	acacia	anemia	russia
rhumba	stadda	Auriga	Riccia	premia	clusia
dagoba	Reseda	brolga	atocia	uremia	Raetia
jojoba	la-di-da	khanga	fascia	pyemia	Scotia
arroba	agenda	Svarga	stadia	kalmia	tertia
aucuba	pagoda	Swarga	acedia	holmia	trivia
Yoruba	remuda	Swerga	Isodia	mummia	salvia
cloaca	garuda	beluga	semeia	crania	sylvia
alpaca	Elodea	cha-cha	pereia	Urania	ataxia
maraca	azalea	kwacha	Maffia	taenia	alexia
Seneca	quelea	chicha	raffia	zinnia	anoxia
cubica	cosmea	concha	loggia	bunnia	razzia
Judica	Aranea	epocha	alogia	Adonia	khodja
silica	guinea	lorcha	lochia	hernia	kanaka
vomica	cornea	cutcha	ischia	utopia	karaka
arnica	apnoea	kutcha	Raphia	myopia	jataka
Punica	Clupea	onycha	sophia	sharia	Pitaka
Carica	cow-pea	Buddha	lithia	hydria	eureka
lorica	ochrea	pakeha	Pythia	Egeria	troika
Myrica	spirea	pulkha	tankia	sheria	quokka
vesica	chorea	burkha	funkia	pteria	chukka
urtica	Ostrea	Gurkha	realia	scoria	judoka
motuca	sub-sea	sulpha	Thalia	choria	chapka
mutuca	mid-sea	yarpha	alalia	gloria	czapka

friska	panama	modena	pitara	sonata	papaya
manuka	retama	lagena	cembra	terata	piraya
cabala	squama	Athena	exedra	errata	kufiya
kabala	chacma	galena	sundra	strata	macoya
cicala	oedema	murena	tundra	batata	garrya
argala	schema	catena	Hedera	ejecta	Vaisya
kamala	cinema	novena	sclera	puncta	Peziza
impala	kinema	Mishna	camera	chaeta	stanza
inyala	eczema	Lucina	womera	zabeta	nyanza
Thecla	smegma	medina	genera	valeta	mezuza
kamela	bregma	vagina	monera	veleta	coryza
sheila	enigma	regina	Vipera	pineta	piazza
cafila	stigma	angina	patera	tapeta	B
kafila	zeugma	tahina	entera	peseta	baobab
Dalila	Brahma	salina	Onagra	boshta	serdab
kamila	asthma	lamina	Mithra	coaita	prefab
manila	jemima	lumina	epeira	orbita	confab
Aquila	minima	numina	hegira	capita	lablab
paella	conima	rumina	hejira	copita	scarab
scilla	ultima	carina	buckra	Nerita	mihrab
axilla	intima	farina	kia-ora	amrita	Cantab
abolla	optima	marina	Pecora	Shakta	neb-neb
arolla	maxima	patina	ancora	Shelta	cobweb
Scylla	stemma	retina	fedora	planta	pen-nib
eidola	zygoma	pruina	angora	quanta	midrib
areola	glioma	alumna	femora	amenta	excamb
Angola	xyloma	thanna	remora	omenta	enjamb
cupola	lipoma	goanna	Señora	quinta	aplomb
Pyrola	Abroma	sienna	korora	pelota	stromb
payola	chroma	duenna	aurora	sapota	entomb
hoop-la	stroma	maunna	Masora	charta	untomb
vizsla	myxoma	hebona	sierra	Sparta	enwomb
kgotla	dharma	Ancona	shirra	khurta	benumb
tabula	Phasma	aikona	dhurra	egesta	corymb
nebula	miasma	Pomona	Dectra	fiesta	ski-bob
fibula	plasma	Annona	mantra	siesta	earbob
facula	alisma	corona	Tantra	cuesta	sea-cob
macula	trauma	dharna	contra	Avesta	kincob
fecula	lucuma	whatna	footra	arista	hobjob
radula	pneuma	lacuna	sistra	crista	odd-job
cedula	struma	vicuña	rostra	crusta	hobnob
infula	mazuma	induna	lustra	frusta	haboob
regula	cabana	Varuna	foutra	chatta	athrob
tegula	jacana	koruna	elytra	anatta	decarb
ligula	arcana	balboa	Podura	cicuta	bicarb
ungula	befana	jerboa	pleura	valuta	comarb
pilula	nagana	halloa	Anoura	agouta	superb
ranula	yojana	holloa	gopura	Laputa	adverb
zonula	Bimana	quinoa	cesura	baryta	reverb
lunula	vimana	leipoa	datura	lingua	absorb
papula	banana	epizoa	satyra	cornua	adsorb
tipula	mañana	Carapa	Ganesa	Griqua	desorb
copula	zenana	Tulipa	shiksa	statua	resorb
ferula	Paraná	Atropa	ahimsa	noctua	suburb
morula	piraña	grappa	mucosa	mantua	bedaub
Torula	torana	sherpa	Lycosa	ottava	hubbub
masula	Purana	vihara	mimosa	geneva	cherub
insula	gitana	samara	serosa	Shaiva	C
rosula	iguana	tamara	glossa	saliva	tombac
Betula	Havana	Gemara	foussa	moorva	ipecac
situla	Tswana	kumara	medusa	pesewa	windac
rotula	fraena	curara	empusa	peshwa	zodiac
Luzula	hyaena	satara	albata	redowa	celiac
palama	ozaena	petara	balata	kabaya	heliac

oomiac	mythic	zoonic	Keltic	unread	air-bed
maniac	Pythic	ironic	cultic	spread	surbed
Syriac	Turkic	atonic	mantic	sol-fa'd	hotbed
Micmac	sialic	muonic	lentic	Pleiad	box-bed
caimac	Uralic	azonic	pontic	illiad	day-bed
tarmac	italic	hypnic	Scotic	eyliad	placed
Cognac	oxalic	echoic	photic	myriad	spaced
finnac	emblic	heroic	rhotic	Lusiad	graced
poonac	public	Eozoic	biotic	unclad	voiced
calpac	cyclic	adipic	erotic	unglad	spiced
ric-rac	Gaelic	biopic	exotic	ballad	priced
ovisac	exilic	tropic	myotic	Seanad	calced
ink-sac	Gallic	atopic	azotic	maenad	fenced
air-sac	Aeolic	myopic	haptic	ogdoad	minced
tic-tac	cholic	hippic	peptic	reload	zinced
tietac	frolic	etypic	septic	unload	forced
caduac	garlic	agaric	Coptic	abroad	deuced
fennec	Adamic	fabric	aortic	inroad	beaded
zarnec	agamic	cobric	Iastic	byroad	headed
tanrec	ogamic	lubric	mastic	lampad	leaded
tenrec	chemic	rubric	nastic	tiara'd	shaded
parsec	anemic	picric	gestic	forrad	bladed
Alcaic	mnemic	hydric	cistic	tetrad	loaded
Eddaic	eremic	cleric	fistic	new-sad	woaded
sodaic	uremic	steric	fustic	fantad	traded
Judaic	fehmic	oniric	rustic	pentad	gadded
Romaic	vehmic	spiric	cystic	heptad	padded
mosaic	filmic	Cymric	mystic	vista'd	wadded
Altaic	holmic	choric	Lettic	spayad	bedded
Arabic	anomic	psoric	nautic	huzza'd	tedded
iambic	gnomic	capric	toluic	ideaed	wedded
tombic	bromic	cupric	Slavic	togaed	kidded
phobic	dromic	ferric	pelvic	visaed	lidded
niobic	atomic	iatric	ataxic	seabed	ridded
terbic	Suomic	matric	alexic	dabbed	codded
calcic	dermic	metric	anoxic	nabbed	dodded
dyadic	formic	citric	rhizic	tabbed	godded
acidic	cosmic	nitric	bumalc	nebbed	nodded
iridic	etymic	vitric	tomboc	webbed	podded
Wendic	neanic	yttric	manioc	dibbed	budded
mundic	Iranic	tauric	escroc	fibbed	reeded
syndic	uranic	phasic	sciroc	jibbed	seeded
geodic	cyanic	Persic	nostoc	nibbed	weeded
rhodic	picnic	physic	fustoc	ribbed	sleded
anodic	pycnic	phatic	panisc	bobbed	abided
epodic	scenic	lactic	bonduc	jobbed	chided
exodic	Edenic	tactic	mucluc	lobbed	slided
bardic	phenic	hectic	D	mobbed	voided
Dardic	irenic	pectic	tebbad	robbed	gelded
herdic	ethnic	arctic	forbad	sobbed	gilded
Nordic	clinic	acetic	alidad	cubbed	banded
phaeic	quinic	thetic	doodad	dubbed	handed
maleic	pyknic	emetic	aoudad	rubbed	landed
deific	gymnic	anetic	behead	subbed	sanded
unific	hymnic	noetic	unhead	pig-bed	bended
tragic	tannic	poetic	oxhead	bulbed	sended
Belgic	Finnic	zoetic	tele-ad	limbed	tended
agogic	Hunnic	cretic	unlead	nimbed	wended
sophic	iconic	uretic	uplead	combed	minded
Orphic	Adonic	luetic	remead	numbed	rinded
pathic	agonic	critic	ennead	tan-bed	tinded
lithic	phonic	iritic	adread	sunbed	winded
Gothic	bionic	Baltic	reread	globed	bonded
Sothic	clonic	Celtic	thread	barbed	funded

6 -DED

hooded	tanged	spiked	aisled	conned	besped
wooded	menged	yolked	misled	donned	unsped
eroded	dinged	ranked	titled	dunned	cusped
barded	hinged	tanked	souled	punned	couped
parded	minged	pinked	cowled	sunned	feared
warded	ringed	zinked	howled	pioned	geared
girded	singed	zonked	jowled	mooned	seared
corded	winged	choked	teamed	stoned	chared
worded	lunged	smoked	shamed	darned	fibred
exceed	gorged	hooked	blamed	corned	inbred
indeed	niched	marked	flamed	horned	unbred
unfeed	inched	narked	deemed	morned	sacred
screed	arched	corked	premed	burned	meered
jereed	washed	forked	maimed	turned	haired
agreed	dished	worked	calmed	downed	paired
viséed	unshed	masked	palmed	gowned	spired
leafed	bushed	busked	helmed	locoed	all-red
puffed	hushed	husked	dammed	echoed	manred
ruffed	pushed	musked	jammed	haloed	barred
hoofed	tithed	tusked	rammed	siloed	garred
roofed	mothed	hawked	gemmed	Samoed	jarred
woofed	rubied	scaled	hemmed	intoed	marred
turfed	eddied	sealed	dimmed	leaped	tarred
poufed	bodied	opaled	nimmed	neaped	warred
staged	defied	fabled	rimmed	shaped	furred
sedged	affied	gabled	bummed	draped	hatred
wedged	belied	tabled	gummed	aliped	metred
ridged	relied	mobled	hummed	uniped	outred
bagged	lilied	macled	mummed	helped	wax-red
fagged	allied	addled	summed	humped	abased
gagged	denied	heeled	doomed	jumped	phased
hagged	renied	keeled	roomed	pumped	biased
jagged	honied	peeled	warmed	looped	erased
lagged	monied	angled	formed	pooped	seised
nagged	copied	failed	wormed	capped	hoised
ragged	espied	mailed	plumed	happed	poised
sagged	varied	nailed	rhymed	lapped	irised
tagged	scried	sailed	leaned	mapped	halsed
wagged	buried	tailed	omened	napped	pulsed
begged	busied	veiled	hained	rapped	sensed
legged	pitied	boiled	pained	sapped	closed
pegged	untied	doiled	veined	tapped	lapsed
digged	dutied	foiled	shined	lepped	hersed
figged	levied	soiled	spined	repped	versed
jigged	taxied	toiled	ruined	dipped	cursed
pigged	beaked	guiled	twined	hipped	gassed
rigged	peaked	ankled	vulned	lipped	passed
wigged	soaked	balled	damned	nipped	jessed
cogged	awaked	palled	hymned	pipped	pissed
dogged	backed	walled	canned	ripped	bossed
fogged	racked	celled	fanned	sipped	fossed
hogged	tacked	gelled	manned	tipped	tossed
jogged	vacked	billed	tanned	copped	cussed
logged	decked	hilled	vanned	hopped	amused
sogged	necked	milled	wanned	lopped	unused
bugged	recked	nilled	genned	mopped	soused
hugged	picked	bolled	kenned	popped	abated
jugged	ticked	polled	penned	sopped	heated
lugged	wicked	rolled	dinned	topped	seated
rugged	cocked	mulled	finned	cupped	teated
tugged	pocked	stoled	ginned	pupped	alated
banged	fucked	marled	pinned	supped	plated
fanged	sucked	nirled	sinned	gypped	slated
hanged		curled	tinned	warped	moated

grated	butted	inlaid	laroid	afawld	secund
stated	gutted	unlaid	toroid	riband	jocund
debted	hutted	repaid	cytoid	ligand	refund
wafted	jutted	unpaid	devoid	argand	osmund
gifted	nutted	appaid	toxoid	unhand	abound
tufted	putted	abraid	trepid	uphand	ybound
gaited	rutted	afraid	limpid	inland	around
raited	queued	spraid	torpid	Poland	ground
united	salued	resaid	hispid	Roland	stound
doited	valued	unsaid	cuspid	soland	swound
quited	ensued	navaid	stupid	upland	gerund
suited	heaved	forbid	acarid	island	obtund
exited	leaved	morbid	sparid	oxland	retund
malted	weaved	turbid	Hebrid	demand	rotund
salted	shaved	outbid	hybrid	remand	stownd
belted	graved	diacid	pierid	woman'd	swownd
melted	staved	placid	florid	repand	peacod
kilted	peeved	coccid	cyprid	expand	sea-god
tilted	reeved	rancid	horrid	farand	sungod
wanted	slived	viscid	torrid	tarand	war-god
tented	stived	roscid	putrid	errand	unshod
vented	salve'd	muscid	Chasid	strand	method
wonted	valved	raucid	capsid	unbend	period
bunted	gloved	candid	Hassid	accend	nid-nod
runted	proved	fordid	foetid	ascend	Pernod®
pioted	carved	sordid	mantid	addend	unhood
booted	varved	misdid	cystid	defend	'sblood
footed	nerved	remeid	liquid	offend	pea-pod
rooted	curved	Aeneid	gravid	fag-end	unipod
parted	revved	nereid	fulvid	lag-end	tripod
warted	clawed	trifid	fervid	tag-end	uropod
casted	flawed	sexfid	corvid	legend	isopod
masted	gnawed	frigid	sayyid	dog-end	exopod
tasted	unawed	fulgid	ribald	yshend	tie-rod
vested	stawed	pongid	aefald	friend	ramrod
cisted	thewed	turgid	herald	token'd	Nimrod
listed	skewed	orchid	steeld	on-lend	betrod
busted	flewed	all-hid	beheld	depend	retrod
rusted	slewed	masjid	upheld	impend	untrod
batted	stewed	Ozalid®	afield	append	fantod
fatted	showed	eyelid	chield	expend	motto'd
hatted	blowed	callid	shield	to-rend	ivy-tod
matted	flowed	pallid	hareld	upsend	tabard
patted	unowed	stolid	begild	obtend	sweard
ratted	crowed	pot-lid	engild	intend	cafard
betted	avowed	agamid	ungild	attend	regard
letted	jinxed	desmid	uphild	but-end	Asgard
netted	flayed	Leonid	kobold	extend	Utgard
petted	prayed	cuboid	bifold	wax-end	Briard
retted	stayed	fucoid	enfold	rebind	enlard
vetted	swayed	mucoid	infold	unbind	canard
wetted	bedyed	gadoid	unfold	upbind	aboard
bitted	undyed	algoid	behold	behind	nasard
ditted	gleyed	haloid	uphold	unkind	wisard
fitted	uneyed	keloid	jymold	remind	petard
pitted	ox-eyed	peloid	resold	rewind	retard
witted	cloyed	xyloid	unsold	enwind	dotard
cotted	agazed	cymoid	retold	inwind	vaward
dotted	crazed	zymoid	untold	unwind	reward
jotted	prized	ganoid	extold	upwind	inward
lotted	boozed	conoid	new-old	second	onward
potted	fezzed	zonoid	day-old	almond	coward
rotted	fizzed	lipoid	spauld	beyond	toward
sotted	relaid	hypoid	should	fecund	upward

6 -ARD

usward	scalae	plaice	decade	bum-bee	goatee
Bayard	stelae	bodice	arcade	bawbee	debtee
hazard	pallae	office	bejade	voidee	tee-tee
mazard	cellae	malice	salade	Culdee	Fantee
lizard	uvulae	delice	unlade	vendee	jantee
rizard	Palmae	cilice	remade	coffee	puntee
vizard	mammae	allice	unmade	toffee	bootee
wizard	gemmae	police	nomade	dragée	jestee
izzard	gnomae	splice	pomade	gidgee	mestee
braird	hermae	pumice	parade	gee-gee	testee
ox-bird	pennae	Venice	abrade	raggee	bustee
begird	pinnae	choice	tirade	congee	mustee
engird	faunae	thrice	pesade	pongee	pattée
ungird	agapae	entice	invade	bungee	settee
accord	scopae	notice	noyade	apogee	puttee
record	florae	sluice	accede	bargee	suttee
uncord	serrae	advice	recede	burgee	corvée
afford	terrae	device	secede	spahee	drawee
Oxford	bursae	novice	incede	lichee	peewee
milord	vittae	séance	remede	elchee	wee-wee
unlord	guttae	chance	impede	lychee	carafe
reword	euouae	fiancé	braide	teehee	strafe
in-word	silvae	elance	decide	lathee	unsafe
byword	evovae	glance	excide	lethee	priefe
absurd	larvae	prance	bedide	towhee	piaffe
invis'd	let-a-be	trance	iodide	gidjee	griffe
ribaud	need-be	usance	oreide	conjee	pouffe
uphaud	ephebe	stance	halide	bunjee	strife
belaud	phoebe	nuance	relide	hackee	ambage
maraud	ribibe	egence	bolide	palkee	cubage
red-bud	imbibe	thence	oroide	Yankee	tubage
big-bud	caribe	whence	lipide	parkee	encage
rum-bud	scribe	spence	deride	bailee	incage
disbud	clambe	prince	boride	mallee	uncage
Talmud	flambé	quince	arride	sallee	bocage
remoud	scrobe	evince	stride	coulée	socage
shroud	aerobe	sconce	beside	mammee	hidage
stroud	enrobe	jaunce	reside	jinnee	mid-age
bestud	unrobe	launce	inside	donnée	dégage
redwud	strobe	vaunce	onside	pawnee	engage
salewd	jujube	bounce	no-side	townee	engagé
shrewd	preace	jounce	upside	teepee	achage
appayd	deface	pounce	betide	wampee	triage
Ormazd	reface	rounce	divide	epopee	galage
Ormuzd	efface	veloce	blende	rappee	pelage
E	enface	scarce	amende	yippee	milage
thecae	palace	searce	blonde	coupee	silage
plicae	belace	fierce	Fronde	toupee	ullage
phocae	anlace	pierce	decode	decree	anlage
Parcae	enlace	tierce	encode	enfree	volage
muscae	inlace	alerce	triode	unfree	damage
cnidae	unlace	amerce	dynode	degree	homage
Suidae	solace	coerce	strode	soirée	romage
sundae	pomace	amorce	cytode	bajree	fumage
paleae	menace	source	gourde	choree	manage
zooeae	tenace	abduce	delude	sirree	ménage
ocreae	enrace	adduce	allude	retree	linage
foveae	rosace	deduce	illude	ti-tree	alnage
reggae	vivace	reduce	denude	entrée	nonage
hyphae	fleece	seduce	unrude	bo-tree	lynage
tibiae	greece	induce	bedyde	Parsee	pipage
rediae	apiece	spruce	Seabee	lessee	garage
teniae	griece	aubade	dog-bee	missee	oarage
striae	sea-ice	facade	jambee	coatee	parage

mirage	blunge	jumbie	rookie	cabrie	mozzie
enrage	plunge	corbie	darkie	faerie	nocake
enragé	emunge	specie	birkie	féerie	ashake
borage	lounge	gaucie	hawkie	Leerie	aslake
forage	spunge	roadie	mealie	peerie	remake
sorage	stooge	baddie	goalie	kierie	unmake
murage	charge	caddie	jeelie	awmrie	upmake
visage	sparge	haddie	keelie	toorie	unrake
dosage	cierge	laddie	bailie	corrie	strake
eatage	emerge	waddie	wellie	durrie	ywrake
metage	George	cuddie	billie	écurie	betake
dotage	storge	duddie	gillie	pourie	retake
potage	reurge	bridie	collie	cowrie	intake
outage	spurge	laldie	mollie	Lowrie	uptake
gavage	refuge	candie	humlie	laesie	belike
lavage	deluge	randie	coolie	falsie	unlike
pavage	takahe	boodie	doolie	donsie	scrike
ravage	apache	woodie	girlie	sonsie	shrike
savage	orache	pardie	nirlie	dassie	strike
rivage	obeche	perdie	outlie	lassie	alsike
lovage	cleché	birdie	saulie	tassie	ananke
sewage	flèche	burdie	trémie	jessie	decoke
cowage	crèche	bludie	stimie	cossie	in-joke
towage	seiche	howdie	lammie	mossie	mopoke
voyage	cliché	gadgie	commie	possie	stroke
fledge	quiche	wedgie	anomie	Aussie	ywroke
gledge	manche	bodgie	dormie	mousie	revoke
pledge	cloche	budgie	stymie	crusie	invoke
sledge	broché	biggie	beanie	grysie	unyoke
unedge	croche	ciggie	meanie	pratie	sparke
dredge	troche	piggie	meinie	Eyetie	rebuke
bridge	bosche	coggie	quinie	daftie	peruke
fridge	tusche	loggie	minnie	leftie	embale
stodge	eatche	luggie	pinnie	softie	locale
bludge	fitché	gilgie	tinnie	hogtie	steale
sludge	potche	tangie	bonnie	keltie	rafale
smudge	rotche	bungie	loonie	kiltie	regale
snudge	gauche	lungie	Moonie	tentie	mygale
drudge	bouche	boogie	sarnie	lintie	inhale
grudge	couché	stogie	girnie	pontie	exhale
trudge	douche	porgie	pirnie	auntie	tamale
allege	louche	bougie	Hornie	cup-tie	female
manège	touché	Archie	byrnie	sortie	finale
renege	psyche	mashie	Downie ®	histie	empale
barege	scathe	bothie	pownie	postie	impale
agrégé	snathe	bunjie	townie	tystie	morale
greige	loathe	sickie	nix-nie	tattie	resale
oblige	spathe	buckie	sea-pie	bittie	pot-ale
dirige	swathe	luckie	mud-pie	hottie	liable
saulge	seethe	reekie	deepie	tottie	viable
emulge	saithe	kie-kie	weepie	puttie	enable
voulge	blithe	talkie	magpie	dautie	unable
change	writhe	selkie	kelpie	toutie	doable
flange	clothe	silkie	lappie	dawtie	arable
grange	soothe	hankie	lippie	tawtie	usable
orange	berthe	yankie	doppie	shavie	stable
peenge	scythe	pinkie	koppie	clavie	suable
avenge	cabbie	honkie	gyppie	skivie	dyable
whinge	yabbie	junkie	purpie	garvie	babble
cringe	kebbie	sunkie	taupie	outvie	dabble
fringe	dobbie	bookie	tawpie	bonxie	gabble
swinge	mobbie	cookie	dearie	lunyie	jabble
twinge	lambie	kookie	hearie	heezie	rabble
sponge	zombie	nookie	roarie	vizzie	wabble

6 -BLE

pebble	heddle	muffle	vagile	parole	turtle
dibble	meddle	ruffle	awhile	furole	myrtle
kibble	peddle	trifle	simile	resole	castle
nibble	reddle	stifle	penile	insole	nestle
bobble	diddle	purfle	senile	citole	pestle
cobble	fiddle	beagle	virile	staple	mistle
gobble	kiddle	teagle	resile	triple	jostle
hobble	middle	daggle	visile	cample	bustle
mobble	piddle	gaggle	ensile	sample	hustle
nobble	riddle	haggle	fusile	kemple	justle
wobble	tiddle	raggle	untile	semple	rustle
bubble	boddle	waggle	motile	temple	battle
nubble	coddle	giggle	futile	dimple	cattle
rubble	hoddle	higgle	rutile	pimple	pattle
feeble	noddle	jiggle	sutile	simple	rattle
treble	toddle	niggle	revile	wimple	tattle
faible	buddle	wiggle	grakle	dumple	wattle
edible	cuddle	boggle	cackle	rumple	fettle
thible	fuddle	coggle	hackle	people	kettle
foible	guddle	goggle	mackle	dapple	mettle
crible	huddle	joggle	tackle	fipple	nettle
gamble	muddle	toggle	deckle	nipple	pettle
hamble	puddle	woggle	heckle	ripple	settle
ramble	ruddle	guggle	keckle	sipple	kittle
wamble	needle	juggle	fickle	tipple	little
remble	daidle	paigle	mickle	copple	tittle
semble	paidle	taigle	pickle	hopple	vittle
dimble	bridle	bangle	rickle	popple	bottle
fimble	candle	dangle	sickle	topple	dottle
nimble	dandle	fangle	tickle	supple	mottle
wimble	handle	jangle	cockle	hirple	pottle
bumble	wandle	mangle	buckle	purple	buttle
fumble	dindle	tangle	huckle	couple	cuttle
humble	kindle	wangle	muckle	souple	guttle
jumble	windle	bingle	ruckle	measle	suttle
mumble	fondle	dingle	suckle	fo'c'sle	epaule
rumble	bundle	gingle	fankle	enisle	nebule
tumble	rundle	jingle	rankle	inisle	nebulé
garble	boodle	kingle	wankle	warsle	lobule
marble	doodle	lingle	kinkle	birsle	tubule
warble	noodle	mingle	tinkle	hirsle	macule
jirble	poodle	pingle	winkle	nursle	locule
burble	girdle	single	runkle	hassle	vocule
bauble	curdle	tingle	darkle	fissle	oscule
double	hurdle	bungle	muskle	tussle	nucule
rouble	caudle	jungle	vielle	mousle	module
bawble	dawdle	google	ruelle	nousle	nodule
oracle	kabele	dargle	faille	tousle	ligule
icicle	kebele	gargle	grille	subtle	pilule
chicle	Cybele	burgle	tuille	beetle	venule
nuncle	unhele	gurgle	boulle	leetle	zonule
circle	allele	availe	bummle	cantle	lunule
mascle	sapele	habile	branle	hantle	papule
muscle	baffle	labile	dinnle	mantle	ampule
raucle	raffle	debile	ecbole	gentle	cupule
boucle	waffle	mobile	sobole	pintle	ferule
beadle	yaffle	nubile	indole	wintle	unrule
cradle	piffle	facile	areole	footle	curule
daddle	riffle	ancile	creole	rootle	titule
faddle	siffle	docile	oriole	tootle	mutule
paddle	coffle	aedile	cajole	dartle	prawle
raddle	poffle	sedile	Ankole	kirtle	wraxle
saddle	cuffle	audile	pinole	wortle	Kabyle
waddle	duffle	defile	dipole	hurtle	argyle

smoyle	chrome	Sabine	ravine	cuttoe	sclere
cotyle	ugsome	rubine	savine	ukiyo-e	ampere
teazle	awsome	picine	divine	sea-ape	misère
foozle	kiss-me	orcine	alvine	uncape	revere
touzle	mousmé	oscine	bovine	escape	severe
dazzle	heaume	Aldine	thyine	dog-ape	tuyère
razzle	legume	Andine	brenne	awhape	twyere
bezzle	inhume	ondine	frenne	canapé	Caffre
fizzle	exhume	undine	unbone	zarape	zaffre
mizzle	relume	iodine	re-done	scrape	gaufre
pizzle	illume	theine	undone	serape	meagre
sizzle	volume	define	begone	recipe	maigre
nozzle	resume	refine	orgone	illipe	chigre
sozzle	résumé	affine	bygone	unripe	émigré
fuzzle	assume	unfine	ochone	stripe	malgre
guzzle	enzyme	engine	azione	équipe	maugre
muzzle	urbane	ingine	Belone	poulpe	euchre
nuzzle	decane	wahine	kinone	guimpe	enfire
puzzle	arcane	ashine	ionone	trompe	admire
wuzzle	steane	saline	depone	uncope	bemire
became	ethane	valine	repone	aslope	venire
madame	alkane	feline	impone	stoope	empire
vidame	silane	reline	perone	unpope	umpire
defame	by-lane	on-line	throne	unrope	aspire
infame	immane	unline	ketone	pyrope	expire
ashame	humane	moline	ditone	metope	desire
salame	nonane	spline	intone	frappé	satire
aflame	borane	up-line	botone	steppe	retire
bename	forane	byline	pavone	grippe	entire
rename	furane	famine	anyone	thorpe	intire
agname	tisane	gamine	bizone	croupe	attire
to-name	insane	tamine	enzone	troupe	squire
by-name	octane	ermine	evzone	polype	rewire
sesame	cetane	lumine	scerne	ectype	unwire
entame	butane	canine	lierne	re-type	rebore
untame	pavane	ranine	eterne	unbare	encore
squame	hexane	conine	frorne	decare	before
raceme	Nicene	rapine	bourne	breare	tofore
scheme	picene	repine	spurne	steare	engore
sememe	Eocene	alpine	puisne	infare	bog-ore
toneme	indene	orpine	flaune	ulnare	ashore
carème	sagene	lupine	lagune	empare	galore
bireme	achene	supine	cohune	curare	splore
stigme	sphene	larine	triune	astare	ignore
décime	Athene	marine	jejune	square	furore
régime	ethene	narine	immune	beware	sempre
unlime	Selene	scrine	untune	unware	chypre
betime	silene	ferine	attune	Ghebre	scarre
intime	xylene	nerine	trayne	Guebre	sperre
optime	serene	shrine	hydyne	timbre	beurré
by-time	threne	Strine	groyne	sombre	goitre
gramme	sirene	murine	scryne	fiacre	centre
stemme	pyrene	purine	desyne	dièdre	ventre
become	Essene	sasine	haùyne	tendre	montre
ancome	retene	cosine	covyne	quaere	dartre
income	butene	arsine	dildoe	pheere	bistre
oncome	advene	ursine	chigoe	effere	lustre
upcome	hexene	rusine	unshoe	infere	rustre
radome	coigne	lysine	felloe	adhere	feutre
at-home	soigné	ratine	diploe	inhere	foutre
zymome	Progne	intine	schmoe	cohere	recure
genome	daphne	mutine	hoopoe	sphere	secure
droome	sdaine	extine	uphroe	a'where	obdure
merome	graine	equine	tiptoe	galère	endure

6 -URE

ordure	fraise	oppose	intuse	binate	hamite
figure	praise	expose	cayuse	innate	samite
ligure	incise	exposé	blowse	donate	acmite
abjure	excise	virose	browse	zonate	Semite
objure	Medise	morose	drowse	ornate	somite
adjure	iodise	porose	arayse	lunate	humite
injure	valise	uprose	debate	pupate	zymite
velure	walise	gyrose	rebate	hypate	Danite
allure	camise	setose	sebate	karate	venite
colure	tamise	favose	libate	aerate	ignite
demure	demise	Nivôse	lobate	berate	finite
immure	remise	hexose	jubate	cerate	pinite
armure	agnise	elapse	tubate	derate	tonite
manure	ionise	corpse	vacate	pirate	dunite
tenure	froise	hearse	Hecate	borate	gunite
avoure	cerise	coarse	micate	lorate	munite
repure	agrise	hoarse	uncate	uprate	sopite
impure	dorise	sparse	locate	aurate	barite
parure	uprise	a-per-se	mucate	curate	karite
rasure	cotise	sperse	pedate	gyrate	cerite
cesure	aguise	averse	sedate	lyrate	nerite
ensure	bruise	scorse	undate	ansate	norite
insure	cruise	ahorse	iodate	ensate	sprite
unsure	pavise	bourse	update	notate	pyrite
assure	advise	course	sudate	rotate	re-site
mature	devise	thyrse	ideate	estate	visite
nature	revise	chasse	oleate	mutate	ratite
future	unwise	chassé	create	nutate	petite
puture	nowise	wrasse	legate	eluate	levite
suture	grilse	ghesse	negate	fluate	invite
fixure	avulse	laisse	ligate	equate	svelte
razure	evulse	plissé	algate	savate	pointe
oeuvre	transe	cuisse	ingate	bovate	quinte
louvre	flense	crosse	dogate	fixate	picoté
stowre	jaunse	mousse	togate	luxate	zygote
they're	ribose	tsetse	ergate	stacte	behote
debase	lobose	clause	jugate	facete	Nilote
embase	jocose	accuse	rugate	Docete	tylote
imbase	aldose	recuse	oxgate	effete	demote
encase	nodose	incuse	Uniate	vegete	remote
incase	rugose	excuse	opiate	delete	denote
uncase	zygose	defuse	aviate	gamete	capote
please	otiose	refuse	malate	bemete	aptote
unease	arkose	effuse	palate	terete	devote
crease	eclose	infuse	ablate	Sûreté	peyote
grease	filose	ill-use	oblate	twaite	coyote
prease	pilose	bemuse	sclate	rebite	écarté
zymase	xylose	scouse	belate	albite	quarte
kinase	hamose	chouse	delate	dacite	chaste
lipase	ramose	blouse	relate	accite	snaste
phrase	vamose	flouse	velate	recite	triste
cytase	rimose	smouse	dilate	incite	arbute
cheese	comose	spouse	sklate	excite	émeute
pheese	osmose	arouse	T-plate	indite	refute
breese	dumose	crouse	hamate	podite	argute
creese	cymose	grouse	ramate	augite	salute
greese	lanose	trouse	inmate	ophite	dilute
kreese	venose	empuse	comate	Shiite	solute
camese	choose	ceruse	osmate	arkite	volute
chaise	broose	peruse	Banate	halite	minute
liaise	depose	disuse	lanate	pelite	croûte
blaise	repose	misuse	adnate	iolite	depute
araise	impose	obtuse	senate	oolite	repute
braise	appose	retuse	agnate	polite	impute

nasute	virtue	wharve	hop-off	talweg	edging
astute	battue	starve	far-off	sea-egg	urging
oocyte	encave	swarve	shroff	Liebig	luging
fescue	incave	enerve	let-off	fisgig	aching
rescue	sheave	swerve	set-off	fizgig	a'thing
miscue	theave	they've	cut-off	jigjig	skiing
subdue	cleave	ungyve	put-off	sea-pig	baking
vendue	sleave	mug-ewe	lay-off	lea-rig	caking
fondue	greave	ice-axe	pay-off	oil-rig	making
perdue	behave	annexe	rebuff	runrig	raking
feague	impave	maxixe	bepuff	bobwig	taking
league	thrave	aye-aye	scruff	tie-wig	waking
Teague	octave	scraye	khalif	bagwig	liking
blague	Zouave	bye-bye	kharif	bigwig	viking
plague	sleeve	leg-bye	sherif	earwig	unking
brigue	preeve	forbye	massif	gobang	poking
cangue	steeve	outbye	hussif	kobang	yoking
gangue	thieve	lay-bye	in-calf	padang	paling
langue	grieve	lac-dye	behalf	upgang	ogling
dengue	prieve	azodye	unself	oxgang	ailing
tongue	stieve	redeye	itself	unhang	filing
brogue	enlevé	pop-eye	myself	uphang	tiling
drogue	glaive	qui-hye	engulf	lalang	ulling
morgue	endive	tailye	ingulf	parang	holing
unglue	regive	spulye	hereof	serang	poling
évolué	Argive	keksye	behoof	thrang	toling
avenue	unhive	ennuyé	unroof	sprang	puling
claque	belive	bedaze	returf	musang	ruling
plaque	relive	upgaze	unturf	baaing	gaming
opaque	unlive	ablaze	shaduf	lobing	naming
Jacque	solive	pheeze	G	robing	taming
sacque	scrive	wheeze	tea-bag	tubing	liming
cheque	derive	sneeze	ice-bag	facing	timing
caique	shrive	breeze	rag-bag	lacing	coming
haique	thrive	freeze	sag-bag	racing	homing
saique	arrive	frieze	ink-bag	dicing	caning
clique	strive	blaize	gas-bag	arcing	waning
unique	visive	braize	ratbag	fading	fining
calque	essive	agrize	kit-bag	lading	lining
pulque	musive	assize	nurhag	wading	mining
manqué	dative	aguize	stalag	aiding	inning
cinque	native	stanze	malmag	biding	boning
cloqué	sative	quinze	pad-nag	hiding	woning
barque	active	bronze	tonnag	niding	zoning
marque	motive	snooze	bodrag	riding	urning
jerque	votive	defuze	updrag	siding	tuning
cirque	cruive	scruze	toe-rag	elding	awning
torque	revive	blowze	tagrag	ending	agoing
basque	unwive	agryze	rag-tag	onding	cooing
casque	fixive	F	sontag	boding	wooing
masque	shelve	undeaf	wigwag	roding	gaping
bisque	twelve	belief	zigzag	seeing	raping
risque	evolve	relief	atabeg	teeing	piping
risqué	alcove	sclaff	muskeg	ageing	wiping
mosque	behove	pilaff	redleg	hieing	coping
embrue	belove	straff	mid-leg	pieing	doping
imbrue	unlove	tariff	peg-leg	rueing	roping
accrue	remove	squiff	dog-leg	dyeing	upping
untrue	enmove	mid-off	pin-leg	eyeing	typing
persue	groove	one-off	proleg	pyeing	caring
pursue	shrove	ill-off	bow-leg	effing	daring
tissue	throve	run-off	nutmeg	offing	earing
statue	strove	rip-off	hatpeg	paging	paring
vertue	inwove	tip-off	Tuareg	raging	raring

6 -ING

airing	fixing	pygarg	k'thibh	diarch	tusseh
firing	boxing	kilerg	bodach	anarch	Jahveh
hiring	foxing	simorg	bleach	enarch	Yahveh
tiring	haying	coburg	pleach	inarch	Yahweh
wiring	laying	simurg	areach	eparch	creagh
enring	maying	bedbug	breach	starch	quaigh
boring	paying	humbug	creach	exarch	abeigh
goring	saying	dor-bug	preach	smirch	skeigh
loring	flying	sow-bug	queach	scorch	sleigh
spring	plying	may-bug	eriach	church	a-weigh
erring	toying	jug-jug	sumach	taisch	besigh
string	spying	unplug	broach	kirsch	sealgh
during	crying	H	Pesach	borsch	kiaugh
tyring	drying	jibbah	detach	Bursch	sheugh
basing	frying	gubbah	attach	kitsch	wheugh
casing	prying	jubbah	fleech	putsch	cleugh
besing	trying	casbah	sleech	Flysch	pleugh
rising	buying	kasbah	smeech	scatch	chough
losing	hazing	Agadah	speech	thatch	shough
nosing	sizing	keddah	breech	clatch	though
posing	dozing	numdah	Molech	smatch	clough
busing	bogong	doodah	varech	snatch	plough
musing	bugong	purdah	cosech	cratch	slough
bating	dugong	houdah	quaich	fratch	enough
eating	kalong	howdah	dreich	quatch	brough
gating	oblong	loofah	unlich	awatch	trough
rating	belong	beegah	Munich	thetch	sheikh
acting	oolong	kufiah	droich	sketch	ollamh
biting	so-long	rupiah	enrich	fletch	good-oh
anting	oulong	pariah	strich	spetch	matzoh
doting	sarong	poojah	fetich	wretch	paraph
luting	throng	punkah	sealch	quetch	seraph
outing	strong	hookah	quelch	kvetch	teraph
bluing	awrong	bablah	blanch	flitch	joseph
caving	bebung	keblah	flanch	glitch	caliph
having	bedung	kiblah	planch	knitch	ceriph
paving	unhung	nallah	branch	snitch	seriph
raving	sprung	pallah	cranch	stitch	Guelph
saving	strung	wallah	stanch	quitch	grumph
waving	besung	fellah	blench	switch	encash
diving	unsung	zillah	clench	twitch	bedash
giving	sea-dog	mollah	elench	cultch	fogash
living	red-dog	Gullah	flench	scotch	rehash
coving	pie-dog	mullah	drench	blotch	calash
loving	pye-dog	nullah	french	hootch	unlash
moving	fog-dog	koolah	trench	crotch	splash
roving	pug-dog	moolah	wrench	nautch	camash
cawing	bandog	Beulah	stench	scutch	gamash
jawing	sun-dog	thanah	quench	clutch	thrash
lawing	lapdog	beenah	hainch	smutch	potash
rawing	hopdog	numnah	chinch	crutch	squash
sawing	wardog	tannah	clinch	grutch	siwash
tawing	sea-fog	oompah	gaunch	sheuch	secesh
hewing	sea-hog	hijrah	haunch	cleuch	sneesh
sewing	quahog	Thorah	launch	pleuch	creesh
lowing	jig-jog	jarrah	paunch	Baluch	emmesh
mowing	dialog	sirrah	raunch	eunuch	immesh
sowing	unclog	gurrah	clunch	slouch	enmesh
towing	loglog	hurrah	brunch	smouch	afresh
aswing	putlog	tussah	crunch	crouch	thresh
taxing	eggnog	halvah	moloch	grouch	nebish
waxing	nig-nog	gunyah	smooch	avouch	eadish
hexing	tautog	hamzah	brooch	kirbeh	jadish
vexing	phizog	matzah	search	sakieh	radish

eddish	goyish	fourth	nielli	wapiti	undock
oddish	toyish	sleuth	chilli	miriti	Mohock
oldish	dryish	galuth	arilli	buriti	paiock
modish	debosh	scouth	neroli	Shakti	pajock
dudish	kibosh	drouth	muesli	dhooti	o'clock
rudish	kybosh	stouth	lobuli	bhisti	enlock
oafish	galosh	scowth	loculi	gomuti	inlock
offish	golosh	growth	moduli	agouti	unlock
Fifish	splosh	I	ramuli	cestui	uplock
elfish	whoosh	gardai	cumuli	J	bemock
lakish	swoosh	gilgai	tumuli	swaraj	yapock
rakish	ambush	nilgai	annuli	K	barock
fikish	upgush	kowhai	calami	tombak	mocuck
palish	ablush	haikai	salami	screak	beduck
relish	floush	kaikai	gurami	streak	canuck
polish	thrush	Adonai	tatami	squeak	Kanuck
mulish	inrush	simpai	Brahmi	pachak	struck
owlish	onrush	Moirai	mishmi	oomiak	untuck
famish	sprush	bonsai	decani	Ostiak	atabek
lamish	uprush	banzai	dewani	sanjak	lebbek
Romish	'sdeath	Wahabi	uncini	she-oak	unmeek
banish	sheath	ephebi	tahini	bogoak	streek
Danish	smeath	ourebi	bikini	kalpak	shriek
vanish	aneath	rhombi	gemini	anarak	straik
finish	sneath	colobi	Alpini	anorak	dik-dik
minish	uneath	incubi	alumni	Slovak	zendik
tonish	breath	flocci	djinni	Ostyak	muzhik
punish	wreath	miladi	tholoi	reback	moujik
papish	wroath	solidi	dromoi	hijack	suslik
impish	bypath	Yezidi	Dipnoi	ack-ack	schtik
mopish	strath	nuclei	octroi	Polack	embank
popish	Tebeth	glutei	renvoi	repack	shrank
uppish	smeeth	Alhagi	borzoi	unpack	enrank
barish	moneth	judogi	scampi	carack	enlink
garish	length	chichi	illupi	eirack	unlink
harish	eighth	shtchi	polypi	sprack	shrink
marish	highth	litchi	safari	arrack	debunk
parish	scaith	eltchi	nagari	strack	Podunk
perish	skaith	sandhi	askari	Y-track	begunk
ogrish	graith	Naskhi	tamari	awrack	bohunk
morish	wraith	Neskhi	kumari	untack	shrunk
arrish	staith	trophi	curari	attack	reebok
latish	hadith	scyphi	ourari	thwack	jambok
fetish	eolith	bukshi	souari	nebeck	bosbok
dotish	zenith	munshi	jawari	rebeck	unhook
aguish	Lapith	canthi	jowari	zebeck	uplook
bluish	inwith	wakiki	sundri	bedeck	betook
gluish	health	titoki	humeri	undeck	retook
squish	wealth	Russki	soneri	ripeck	debark
lavish	spilth	kabuki	gri-gri	copeck	embark
ravish	coolth	saluki	Tishri	kopeck	imbark
elvish	warmth	argali	Cabiri	rypeck	unbark
dovish	acanth	alkali	satori	medick	demark
dawish	Granth	ourali	gharri	tchick	remark
rawish	plinth	Divali	sbirri	panick	impark
Jewish	T-cloth	Dewali	pituri	unpick	uncork
newish	smooth	Diwali	chowri	aspick	rework
unwish	zeroth	seseli	papyri	tisick	inwork
cowish	scarth	puteli	cytisi	shtick	unwork
shyish	dearth	jungli	thyrsi	inwick	bywork
skyish	hearth	phalli	tsotsi	pranck	damask
slyish	skarth	shalli	manati	stanck	immask
boyish	sparth	thalli	jupati	uncock	unmask
coyish	swarth	ocelli	tapeti	mocock	out-ask

panisk	anneal	ostial	neural	sexual	scamel
Morisk	cuneal	gavial	plural	coeval	enamel
imbosk	zooeal	jovial	crural	ogival	pommel
unhusk	repeal	Novial	omasal	valval	hummel
padauk	appeal	jackal	mensal	vulval	kümmel
nebbuk	cereal	atokal	tarsal	larval	pummel
dybbuk	unreal	fallal	varsal	nerval	harmel
haiduk	boreal	hallal	versal	serval	oxymel
Seljuk	enseal	sallal	dorsal	avowal	weanel
mukluk	unseal	wadmal	morsal	cotwal	crenel
padouk	roseal	haemal	bursal	kotwal	spinel
mohawk	osteal	hiemal	cursal	biaxal	simnel
squawk	luteal	mahmal	vassal	ghazal	cannel
L	puteal	animal	missal	benzal	fannel
atabal	squeal	primal	dossal	dirndl	wannel
tribal	reveal	hammal	tussal	Azrael	fennel
gimbal	foveal	mammal	byssal	isabel	kennel
timbal	unweal	gimmal	causal	djebel	vennel
jumbal	plagal	gymmal	pausal	barbel	ginnel
cymbal	mangal	dermal	meatal	corbel	funnel
tymbal	gingal	formal	statal	cancel	gunnel
global	jingal	normal	rectal	rancel	runnel
herbal	fungal	dismal	rictal	pencel	tunnel
verbal	tergal	brumal	acetal	marcel	lionel
coccal	frugal	lienal	foetal	parcel	darnel
buccal	nuchal	regnal	hyetal	tarcel	kernel
caecal	hyphal	signal	obital	tercel	girnel
faecal	lethal	rhinal	chital	goidel	cornel
thecal	withal	spinal	unital	Mindel	chapel
laical	labial	crinal	coital	rondel	stipel
apical	tibial	trinal	spital	fardel	compel
epical	facial	urinal	avital	sardel	propel
sulcal	racial	hymnal	santal	bordel	rappel
tincal	fecial	pennal	cental	aludel	carpel
cercal	uncial	phonal	dental	sea-eel	curpel
furcal	social	clonal	mental	reheel	dispel
pascal	radial	zoonal	rental	awheel	gospel
rascal	medial	atonal	fontal	vakeel	drupel
mescal	podial	azonal	pontal	unreel	umbrel
fiscal	Belial	carnal	crotal	streel	barrel
faucal	filial	tarnal	septal	unseel	carrel
coucal	simial	ternal	hartal	atweel	parrel
daedal	tomial	vernal	aortal	keffel	ferrel
credal	denial	faunal	mortal	duffel	verrel
ooidal	genial	nounal	portal	ridgel	borrel
bridal	menial	in-foal	curtal	cudgel	sorrel
iridal	penial	palpal	festal	beigel	worrel
sandal	venial	pen-pal	vestal	mangel	burrel
vandal	xenial	carpal	distal	lingel	petrel
sendal	finial	vorpal	vistal	zingel	laurel
tindal	monial	bharal	instal	nochel	saurel
feodal	espial	umbral	costal	orchel	teasel
anodal	garial	sacral	postal	muchel	weasel
enodal	narial	bedral	scutal	Gadhel	diesel
apodal	parial	spiral	brutal	isohel	chisel
pardal	aerial	aboral	vidual	burhel	tolsel
caudal	ferial	choral	ungual	bushel	damsel
feudal	serial	floral	manual	bethel	hansel
ordeal	oorial	amoral	annual	samiel	ransel
unheal	atrial	parral	casual	Daniel	pensel
unleal	burial	worral	visual	seckel	tinsel
rameal	mesial	retral	actual	teckel	gunsel
lineal	fetial	mitral	ritual	nickel	woosel
pineal	retial	astral	mutual	shekel	tarsel

hirsel	serail	emball	school	fitful	fogram
dorsel	mesail	no-ball	jarool	potful	ashram
morsel	assail	becall	retool	artful	Bairam
torsel	detail	recall	escrol	lawful	marram
eassel	retail	end-all	sterol	boxful	murram
tassel	entail	befall	musrol	joyful	balsam
vessel	oxtail	infall	patrol	befoul	jetsam
missel	squail	onfall	petrol	defoul	tam-tam
dossel	unvail	to-fall	podsol	cagoul	bantam
mussel	bewail	thrall	cresol	kagoul	wigwam
pussel	jezail	you-all	amatol	ensoul	diadem
russel	mezail	squall	pistol	insoul	anadem
housel	bulbil	devall	wittol	peepul	ibidem
haysel	gerbil	enwall	toluol	trisul	randem
boatel	jerbil	inwall	frivol	consul	tandem
mantel	uracil	bedell	podzol	kittul	addeem
dentel	pencil	befell	benzol	acrawl	redeem
lintel	unveil	merell	imparl	scrawl	hareem
flotel	fulfil	sorell	aswirl	sprawl	beseem
cartel	ridgil	resell	schorl	sprawl	inseem
martel	archil	eisell	becurl	sea-owl	beteem
pastel	orchil	retell	uncurl	uncowl	esteem
wastel	vermil	newell	upcurl	behowl	dodgem
listel	reboil	unwell	unfurl	methyl	sachem
hostel	emboil	Nowell	upfurl	diamyl	dirhem
battel	upboil	upwell	uphurl	uranyl	anthem
cautel	accoil	lozell	shtetl	phenyl	mayhem
refuel	recoil	refill	bemaul	propyl	emblem
sequel	uncoil	infill	monaul	tetryl	Moslem
gravel	upcoil	upfill	saxaul	nitryl	phloem
travel	til-oil	uphill	bulbul	dactyl	semsem
A-level	bemoil	shrill	jambul	baetyl	montem
O-level	nim-oil	thrill	tubful	acetyl	restem
Y-level	ben-oil	up-till	aidful	protyl	system
thivel	assoil	squill	waeful	trotyl	apozem
snivel	betoil	unwill	woeful	benzyl	phlegm
drivel	entoil	rigoll	ireful	M	drachm
swivel	nut-oil	scroll	useful	Balaam	megohm
shovel	fibril	enroll	dueful	salaam	rhythm
grovel	umbril	unroll	rueful	goddam	misaim
carvel	deasil	uproll	eyeful	quidam	Elohim
marvel	chesil	stroll	bagful	beldam	pashim
varvel	tahsil	they'll	jugful	scream	Baalim
vervel	pensil	Argyll	mugful	stream	prelim
devvel	tonsil	engaol	wilful	enseam	Muslim
knawel	eassil	chibol	armful	inseam	painim
shewel	dossil	gambol	canful	unseam	paynim
crewel	fossil	symbol	manful	unteam	megrim
thowel	subtil	glycol	panful	lingam	betrim
trowel	dentil	cineol	penful	pelham	retrim
meazel	lentil	mongol	dinful	fulham	untrim
teazel	ventil	googol	sinful	derham	passim
ghazel	pontil	seghol	tinful	dirham	victim
drazel	pastil	frijol	urnful	Durham	partim
ranzel	distil	tol-lol	lapful	log-jam	embalm
donzel	pistil	wadmol	sapful	jimjam	becalm
puzzel	instil	formol	pepful	bedlam	encalm
embail	postil	thymol	cupful	fullam	napalm
aumail	coutil	phenol	barful	hammam	schelm
tenail	weevil	quinol	earful	befoam	unhelm
agnail	pulvil	uncool	jarful	stroam	nincom
unnail	brazil	befool	hatful	Vibram ®	non-com
derail	frazil	unfool	vatful	engram	sitcom
rerail	benzil	kagool	netful	ingram	apedom

6 -DOM

seldom	Shiism	Lolium	sputum	Fabian	cabman
fandom	holism	tomium	adytum	Sabian	subman
mandom	hylism	osmium	vacuum	Zabian	socman
random	Ramism	xenium	mutuum	ascian	badman
condom	nomism	minium	yum-yum	radian	madman
wisdom	Humism	omnium	scrawm	median	odd-man
fathom	nanism	ionium	anonym	Indian	red-man
slalom	bonism	Sapium	eponym	Lydian	dodman
coelom	eonism	sepium	exonym	Magian	hodman
whilom	Ionism	barium	N	kalian	rodman
waboom	monism	cerium	Theban	Salian	iceman
addoom	Maoism	Nerium	tulban	Delian	pieman
abloom	Taoism	corium	corban	bilian	one-man
simoom	egoism	atrium	turban	Eolian	foeman
byroom	papism	curium	siccan	Julian	apeman
pompom	merism	ostium	ash-can	Samian	bagman
vagrom	verism	bivium	oilcan	simian	ragman
pogrom	chrism	nickum	vulcan	Humian	leg-man
hansom	Dorism	dinkum	cancan	banian	gigman
ransom	porism	bunkum	tin-can	Janian	pig-man
lissom	purism	beflum	Tuscan	Fenian	fogman
jetsom	lyrism	vallum	toucan	Aonian	log-man
diatom	autism	vellum	maidan	Ionian	caiman
tom-tom	mutism	Idolum	soldan	Zuñian	obi-man
fantom	truism	peplum	randan	Popian	oil-man
custom	favism	replum	Dardan	Tupian	dolman
bottom	civism	phylum	Jordan	Marian	gemman
air-arm	laxism	amylum	lurdan	Parian	fenman
disarm	sexism	asylum	houdan	Ugrian	penman
aswarm	Nazism	hummum	Soudan	Sirian	pin-man
thairm	caecum	amomum	Idaean	Dorian	tinman
affirm	talcum	khanum	Sabean	durian	con-man
infirm	nincum	plenum	Andean	Syrian	gunman
unfirm	viscum	frenum	Judean	Tyrian	yeoman
squirm	dumdum	magnum	Augean	mesian	topman
deform	dirdum	lignum	uplean	Ossian	cupman
reform	durdum	hypnum	ramean	Latian	barman
biform	lyceum	wampum	bemean	titian	carman
enform	Phleum	alarum	demean	Jovian	harman
inform	pileum	asarum	Nemean	enzian	warman
unform	museum	labrum	Humean	finjan	german
by-form	red-gum	sacrum	Etnean	Trojan	merman
orgasm	Targum	ingrum	Berean	garjan	airman
chiasm	tergum	quorum	nosean	reckan	firman
telesm	humhum	marrum	sea-fan	achkan	norman
Babism	zythum	antrum	chagan	barkan	Burman
cubism	labium	omasum	moggan	chalan	gasman
racism	erbium	pensum	origan	Hielan'	desman
sadism	aecium	sensum	wangan	raglan	yes-man
Medism	radium	gypsum	fingan	leglan	disman
Vedism	medium	dorsum	longan	ballan	busman
iodism	tedium	possum	Scogan	hallan	batman
dudism	oidium	outsum	slogan	lallan	hetman
nudism	indium	factum	brogan	villan	met-man
obeism	podium	rectum	durgan	gollan	hit-man
ageism	sodium	dictum	kurgan	pollan	pitman
theism	kalium	Gnetum	machan	fullan	amtman
Sofism	Valium ®	multum	lochan	replan	pot-man
Sufism	helium	tum-tum	afghan	norlan'	outman
Magism	cilium	centum	arghan	murlan	tutman
yogism	Lilium	mentum	orphan	koulan	Rouman
schism	Allium	quotum	Pathan	seaman	lawman
Ophism	dolium	septum	Sathan	shaman	bow-man
obiism	folium	scutum	bothan	ataman	cowman

cayman	piecen	biogen	gemmen	bitten	fusain
layman	deaden	exogen	yeomen	kitten	obtain
skyman	leaden	myogen	germen	litten	detain
fly-man	loaden	largen	Ostmen	mitten	retain
toyman	madden	morgen	acumen	pitten	attain
finnan	sadden	oxygen	crumen	gotten	atwain
bemoan	ledden	pea-hen	kronen	rotten	dizain
Minoan	redden	lichen	stonen	lutten	arabin
trapan	bidden	richen	sea-pen	putten	rabbin
bedpan	hidden	Kuchen	shapen	tauten	bobbin
ice-pan	midden	eughen	deepen	gluten	dobbin
trepan	ridden	ewghen	pigpen	heaven	dubbin
ash-pan	god-den	sephen	hog-pen	leaven	ash-bin
taipan	hodden	hyphen	holpen	shaven	globin
Evipan®	sodden	washen	dampen	craven	niacin
jampan	hudden	Goshen	hempen	graven	farcin
sampan	pudden	rushen	lumpen	cheven	viscin
tympan	sudden	fat-hen	hen-pen	eleven	leucin
sanpan	reeden	lathen	reopen	uneven	glycin
sappan	hagden	sithen	happen	steven	lead-in
tarpan	maiden	eothen	lippen	sweven	gradin
inspan	hoiden	sazhen	luppen	sliven	hand-in
shoran	gilden	weaken	parpen	driven	orcein
garran	milden	shaken	loupen	cloven	fade-in
serran	bolden	soaken	gowpen	sloven	take-in
Terran	golden	kraken	dzeren	hooven	herein
sovran	holden	awaken	froren	proven	serein
ptisan	gulden	libken	barren	carven	Verein
Xhosan	gylden	sicken	warren	verven	unrein
messan	linden	ticken	Herren	flaxen	casein
gossan	wooden	wicken	arisen	weazen	ossein
tutsan	farden	docken	Bunsen	glazen	lutein
platan	garden	lucken	chosen	brazen	cave-in
Cretan	harden	sucken	coosen	frozen	live-in
caftan	warden	meeken	loosen	fizzen	Gräfin
kaftan	herden	milken	gipsen	gizzen	olefin
pultan	burden	silken	sarsen	mizzen	biffin
sultan	hurden	sunken	worsen	indign	tiffin
fan-tan	lurden	sloken	lessen	malign	boffin
suntan	louden	spoken	Nissen	benign	coffin
syntan	hoyden	broken	tossen	eloign	cuffin
captan	dudeen	wroken	causen	proign	muffin
partan	baleen	awoken	beaten	obsign	puffin
tartan	spleen	barken	neaten	design	ruffin
rattan	alpeen	darken	whaten	resign	bowfin
rottan	careen	harken	platen	ensign	pidgin
moutan	screen	birken	pecten	assign	laggin
sextan	skreen	murken	weeten	repugn	biggin
Paduan	boreen	misken	soften	impugn	piggin
taguan	moreen	dusken	erg-ten	oppugn	hoggin
Siouan	tureen	leglen	whiten	expugn	noggin
Papuan	beseen	fallen	luiten	wabain	origin
silvan	unseen	bollen	kanten	eucain	margin
sylvan	lateen	pollen	lenten	sodain	virgin
Hesvan	sateen	sullen	looten	ordain	plug-in
ajowan	poteen	stolen	marten	regain	Cochin
dioxan	voteen	flamen	fasten	ungain	urchin
Libyan	atween	stamen	hasten	demain	wash-in
banyan	deafen	examen	listen	remain	elshin
Minyan	halfen	foemen	batten	almain	arshin
Troyan	turfen	tegmen	fatten	domain	within
Tarzan	laggen	daimen	latten	papain	suck-in
gozzan	liggen	dolmen	patten	sprain	tuck-in
graben	pangen	culmen	ratten	strain	bodkin

dodkin	enjoin	beacon	turion	saloon	chaton
calkin	cojoin	deacon	nasion	simoon	craton
malkin	esloin	flacon	lesion	maroon	breton
walk-in	ganoin	chicon	vision	ceroon	chiton
welkin	heroin	ulicon	fusion	heroon	Briton
simkin	essoin	falcon	cation	seroon	triton
bumkin	tie-pin	non-con	kation	alsoon	nekton
rumkin	step-in	garçon	nation	ratoon	melton
nankin	chopin	zircon	ration	aswoon	Wilton
look-in	pippin	gascon	action	gazoon	pulton
napkin	coppin	mascon	ultion	Aizoon	canton
pipkin	hatpin	head-on	lotion	Eozoon	danton
parkin	key-pin	hagdon	motion	weapon	panton
jerkin	fibrin	guidon	notion	crepon	santon
merkin	aldrin	randon	potion	slip-on	wanton
perkin	pterin	tendon	option	tampon	ponton
firkin	fiorin	sindon	ustion	pompon	photon
girkin	florin	Diodon	donjon	tompon	spot-on
kirkin'	citrin	lardon	beckon	Nippon	croton
morkin	tocsin	pardon	reckon	Rippon	proton
work-in	raisin	cordon	ulikon	tarpon	lepton
gaskin	seisin	side-on	walk-on	yaupon	barton
siskin	kamsin	pigeon	etalon	coupon	carton
joskin	coosin	wigeon	myelon	Charon	parton
buskin	myosin	come-on	muflon	macron	burton
catkin	pepsin	hereon	tiglon	micron	seston
mawkin	versin	have-on	gallon	hadron	teston
dualin	cousin	gryfon	vellon	Oberon	piston
goblin	isatin	flagon	billon	mikron	boston
codlin	pectin	dragon	roll-on	thoron	ratton
myelin	emetin	waggon	pull-on	napron	jetton
leglin	cretin	epigon	Idolon	garron	cotton
riglin	chitin	trigon	stolon	perron	button
fall-in	dentin	long-on	diplon	latron	mutton
pull-in	muntin	trogon	merlon	matron	deuton
dunlin	biotin	isogon	Ceylon	natron	Teuton
kaolin	martin	jargon	daemon	patron	pluton
violin	Austin	gorgon	mnemon	citron	bouton
caplin	shut-in	Trygon	salmon	neuron	newton
poplin	beduin	archon	gammon	geason	Caxton
marlin	saguin	brehon	mammon	peason	sexton
berlin	beguin	siphon	'simmon	reason	phyton
merlin	sequin	euphon	common	season	rhyton
murlin	flavin	syphon	summon	odds-on	elevon
purlin	chevin	Typhon	gnomon	godson	flow-on
maslin	alevin	python	dromon	unison	diaxon
muslin	kelvin	gabion	sermon	foison	klaxon
ratlin	mauvin	Albion	Mormon	poison	crayon
inulin	outwin	legion	musmon	grison	canyon
moulin	alexin	region	towmon	orison	ronyon
haemin	dioxin	logion	etymon	prison	baryon
cummin	stay-in	talion	xoanon	kelson	scazon
harmin	Pinyin	camion	pycnon	nelson	blazon
germin	seizin	fanion	guenon	telson	amazon
vermin	wedeln	wanion	Memnon	damson	tenzon
uranin	solemn	minion	cannon	ramson	cedarn
guanin	column	pinion	pennon	Samson	decern
cyanin	autumn	amnion	phonon	tenson	secern
lignin	jötunn	gonion	baboon	ven'son	lucern
tannin	gibbon	bunion	cacoon	parson	aldern
rennin	ribbon	dupion	racoon	person	undern
sagoin	bonbon	virion	cocoon	lesson	modern
adjoin	carbon	morion	tycoon	bisson	casern
rejoin	Lisbon	durion	lagoon	jetson	altern

intern	unsown	poncho	bamboo	lean-to	dog-hep
astern	intown	gaucho	booboo	Shinto	duikep
extern	uptown	psycho	nandoo	pronto	schlep
cavern	poleyn	gung-ho	Hindoo	crypto	catnep
tavern	O	sorgho	hoodoo	quarto	sitrep
wivern	manoao	yo-ho-ho	koodoo	presto	instep
govern	lavabo	nympho	voodoo	aristo	unstep
wyvern	gazebo	Sappho	nardoo	giusto	dog-hip
luzern	crambo	morpho	vaudoo	anatto	reship
shairn	akimbo	chi-rho	samfoo	ghetto	inship
reborn	macaco	camsho	burgoo	duetto	unship
inborn	turaco	Clotho	boo-hoo	blotto	inclip
unborn	stucco	nuncio	yoo-hoo	grotto	fillip
suborn	medico	tercio	forhoo	gomuto	oxslip
dehorn	angico	fascio	tu-whoo	tenuto	turnip
cohorn	calico	studio	cuckoo	scruto	catnip
untorn	matico	adagio	halloo	Basuto	gossip
uptorn	blanco	gorgio	gooroo	incavo	bunyip
attorn	bronco	Gallio	Karroo	octavo	magilp
inworn	rococo	daimio	sissoo	one-two	megilp
unworn	fiasco	bagnio	gentoo	billy-o	repulp
tea-urn	fresco	vibrio	too-too	arroyo	decamp
auburn	mikado	barrio	tattoo	embryo	encamp
Tyburn	fumado	physio	shivoo	schizo	stramp
Saturn	dorado	baguio	zoozoo	stanzo	revamp
return	albedo	whacko	kakapo	corozo	scrimp
unturn	speedo	gingko	shippo	P	shrimp
upturn	make-do	stalko	troppo	sea-cap	skrimp
sea-bun	Toledo	finsko	ignaro	mob-cap	scrump
tundun	comedo	robalo	gabbro	hub-cap	skrump
tangun	teredo	pedalo	gombro	madcap	gazump
wangun	tuxedo	enhalo	Velcro®	red-cap	bishop
pen-gun	libido	catalo	cicero	ice-cap	Ethiop
shogun	aikido	pueblo	cheero	toecap	dallop
pop-gun	dosi-do	pomelo	bolero	ink-cap	gallop
air-gun	overdo	pumelo	Herero	ear-cap	wallop
pot-gun	hair-do	tupelo	torero	upheap	collop
outgun	weirdo	niello	sbirro	upleap	dollop
six-gun	escudo	duello	bistro	threap	gollop
tuchun	pseudo	trillo	arioso	air-gap	lollop
gurjun	stereo	apollo	zeloso	mishap	Dunlop
thin'un	Galago	zufolo	whatso	mayhap	inhoop
Mahoun	virago	gigolo	rabato	earlap	unhoop
unspun	vorago	palolo	rebato	oar-lap	saloop
ice-run	non-ego	rotolo	rubato	burlap	scroop
ski-run	sapego	modulo	legato	cat-lap	astoop
hen-run	forego	dynamo	fugato	dewlap	bedrop
outrun	indigo	paramo	pomato	kidnap	unprop
pultun	caligo	Eskimo	tomato	catnap	hyssop
pantun	Loligo	ultimo	potato	affrap	redtop
impawn	ginkgo	chromo	Alecto	riprap	peg-top
supawn	quango	lucumo	puncto	satrap	tiptop
thrawn	gringo	melano	hereto	entrap	unstop
unhewn	stingo	solano	righto	attrap	outtop
strewn	drongo	gitano	Pakhto	rewrap	escarp
unsewn	eryngo	albino	Pashto	enwrap	extirp
godown	stop-go	Ladino	Pushto	inwrap	unhasp
go-down	overgo	domino	subito	unwrap	teacup
ungown	albugo	Alpino	solito	gas-tap	hiccup
unmown	colugo	merino	vomito	upkeep	eggcup
renown	lanugo	zorino	manito	asleep	gilcup
thrown	re-echo	casino	bonito	bo-peep	huddup
strown	rancho	kimono	Rialto	threep	used-up
disown	sancho	yah-boo	smalto	beweep	paid-up

hold-up	outbar	tuskar	tulwar	deader	vender
send-up	towbar	chukar	psywar	header	binder
wind-up	siccar	scalar	magyar	leader	cinder
hard-up	tricar	medlar	rizzar	reader	finder
race-up	calcar	pedlar	sphaer	loader	hinder
fade-up	owl-car	stelar	dabber	trader	minder
make-up	trocar	ashlar	gabber	gadder	pinder
take-up	air-car	vallar	jabber	ladder	tinder
pile-up	circar	cellar	nabber	madder	winder
line-up	sircar	tellar	yabber	padder	bonder
rave-up	lascar	pillar	bibber	sadder	conder
bang-up	kit-car	villar	dibber	bedder	ponder
hang-up	box-car	collar	fibber	pedder	wonder
high-up	Veadar	dollar	gibber	redder	yonder
lash-up	chadar	gollar	jibber	tedder	dunder
wash-up	bandar	sollar	libber	bidder	sunder
nosh-up	pandar	poplar	cobber	didder	shoder
back-up	deodar	guslar	dobber	hidder	carder
kick-up	sirdar	ocular	jobber	kidder	larder
pick-up	bordar	ovular	robber	dodder	warder
cock-up	sea-ear	uvular	lubber	fodder	girder
lock-up	unbear	stylar	rubber	nodder	border
mock-up	upbear	palmar	tubber	dudder	furder
fuck-up	endear	Colmar	Gheber	judder	murder
link-up	undear	fulmar	Gueber	rudder	lauder
hook-up	ungear	dammar	briber	sudder	sawder
mark-up	dog-ear	summar	camber	feeder	powder
tail-up	rehear	bismar	jamber	needer	affeer
call-up	asmear	planar	tamber	reeder	meneer
roll-up	linear	chenar	member	seeder	veneer
pull-up	appear	thenar	limber	weeder	fineer
foul-up	uprear	chinar	timber	lieder	career
warm-up	arrear	spinar	bomber	raider	laveer
sannup	pasear	uproar	comber	chider	howe'er
burn-up	ensear	bow-oar	cumber	glider	chafer
turn-up	to-tear	bezoar	lumber	slider	loafer
recoup	uptear	unspar	number	moider	reefer
stroup	shofar	keasar	goober	voider	liefer
slap-up	alegar	quasar	barber	spider	prefer
step-up	saggar	caesar	Berber	guider	gaffer
slip-up	beggar	pulsar	dauber	gelder	Kaffer
cherup	seggar	bursar	placer	welder	zaffer
larrup	nuggar	hassar	spacer	gilder	differ
mess-up	Bulgar	hussar	bracer	wilder	niffer
toss-up	vulgar	avatar	tracer	folder	coffer
catsup	hangar	nectar	soccer	holder	doffer
beat-up	sangar	guitar	piecer	polder	goffer
pent-up	sungar	cantar	de-icer	solder	buffer
bust-up	cougar	kantar	slicer	dander	duffer
dust-up	eschar	qintar	voicer	gander	puffer
tittup	Nuphar	tartar	spicer	hander	suffer
blow-up	Jashar	mortar	juicer	lander	heifer
R	Cathar	gas-tar	twicer	pander	pilfer
bazaar	foliar	bestar	cancer	sander	golfer
bulbar	antiar	instar	dancer	wander	wolfer
sambar	caviar	co-star	lancer	zander	confer
mimbar	evejar	sittar	fencer	bender	roofer
lumbar	jamjar	cottar	mincer	fender	woofer
minbar	hanjar	soutar	pincer	gender	surfer
isobar	gas-jar	low-tar	wincer	lender	titfer
Herbar	nickar	jaguar	grocer	mender	gaufer
durbar	shikar	valvar	mercer	render	gowfer
disbar	kunkar	vulvar	forcer	sender	laager
bus-bar	sirkar	pulwar	saucer	tender	onager

usager	hunger	tother	seeker	thaler	antler
stager	droger	wuther	daiker	whaler	ostler
badger	merger	defier	yakker	fabler	butler
cadger	verger	relier	balker	ambler	cutler
hedger	virger	inlier	calker	cycler	outler
kedger	forger	cimier	talker	yodler	sutler
ledger	burger	denier	walker	feeler	hauler
lidger	purger	tinier	bilker	heeler	bawler
bodger	gauger	punier	milker	keeler	bowler
codger	sauger	rapier	bulker	peeler	fowler
dodger	lecher	copier	banker	reeler	howler
lodger	micher	varier	canker	rifler	jowler
sodger	nicher	verier	hanker	eggler	guyler
budger	tocher	étrier	janker	angler	beamer
jaeger	archer	visier	ranker	bugler	reamer
lieger	etcher	cosier	tanker	ashler	seamer
sieger	higher	hosier	wanker	bailer	teamer
dagger	cipher	rosier	yanker	jailer	shamer
gagger	gopher	métier	sinker	mailer	roamer
jagger	cypher	pitier	tinker	nailer	framer
lagger	basher	squier	winker	railer	seemer
nagger	dasher	envier	conker	sailer	roemer
sagger	Jasher	vizier	yonker	wailer	chimer
tagger	lasher	wizier	bunker	smiler	epimer
yagger	masher	cozier	Dunker	boiler	primer
legger	rasher	beaker	hunker	moiler	trimer
bigger	washer	leaker	junker	toiler	palmer
digger	fisher	shaker	Tunker	guiler	dammer
jigger	wisher	soaker	choker	caller	gammer
ligger	cosher	Quaker	smoker	waller	hammer
nigger	josher	dacker	cooker	feller	lammer
rigger	kosher	lacker	hooker	heller	mammer
cogger	tosher	packer	looker	seller	rammer
dogger	gusher	racker	broker	teller	yammer
fogger	husher	tacker	proker	filler	dimmer
hogger	lusher	yacker	stoker	killer	gimmer
jogger	musher	decker	barker	miller	kimmer
logger	pusher	pecker	larker	siller	limmer
bugger	rusher	bicker	marker	tiller	nimmer
lugger	bather	dicker	parker	willer	simmer
mugger	father	kicker	jerker	holler	zimmer
rugger	gather	licker	corker	loller	bummer
tugger	lather	nicker	forker	poller	cummer
leiger	rather	picker	porker	roller	hummer
bulger	aether	ricker	worker	soller	mummer
banger	nether	sicker	yorker	toller	rummer
danger	pether	ticker	lurker	buller	summer
ganger	tether	wicker	masker	culler	boomer
hanger	wether	cocker	tasker	fuller	roomer
manger	cither	docker	risker	guller	isomer
ranger	dither	hocker	bosker	muller	farmer
lenger	either	locker	busker	puller	warmer
venger	hither	mocker	husker	gaoler	termer
dinger	lither	rocker	tusker	choler	dormer
finger	mither	socker	cauker	violer	former
ginger	tither	bucker	cawker	cooler	wormer
linger	wither	ducker	hawker	proler	stumer
pinger	zither	fucker	howker	birler	rhymer
ringer	anther	mucker	duyker	burler	deaner
singer	bother	pucker	scaler	curler	planer
winger	fother	sucker	dealer	hurler	keener
conger	mother	tucker	healer	purler	opener
longer	pother	yucker	mealer	tatler	signer
monger	rother	keeker	sealer	titler	gainer

6 -NER

seiner	sniper	rasper	tusser	jolter	foster
shiner	griper	Hesper	motser	tolter	poster
whiner	swiper	vesper	causer	culter	roster
coiner	helper	lisper	Mauser	canter	zoster
joiner	yelper	pauper	pauser	panter	Auster
ruiner	pulper	Keuper	abuser	ranter	buster
twiner	camper	couper	amuser	wanter	duster
limner	damper	souper	douser	center	luster
banner	hamper	yawper	mouser	renter	muster
canner	pamper	scarer	rouser	tenter	ouster
fanner	ramper	bearer	touser	venter	oyster
lanner	tamper	hearer	hawser	linter	xyster
manner	vamper	nearer	bowser	minter	batter
tanner	kemper	rearer	dowser	sinter	fatter
vanner	semper	tearer	towser	tinter	hatter
henner	temper	wearer	wowser	winter	latter
kenner	simper	sharer	geyser	aunter	matter
penner	romper	snarer	acater	bunter	natter
tenner	bumper	roarer	beater	gunter	patter
dinner	dumper	sparer	heater	hunter	ratter
finner	jumper	starer	skater	punter	tatter
ginner	lumper	jeerer	elater	scoter	yatter
pinner	mumper	Führer	plater	rioter	better
sinner	pumper	scorer	slater	footer	fetter
tinner	Rumper	adorer	boater	hooter	getter
winner	eloper	shorer	doater	looter	letter
conner	cooper	snorer	crater	mooter	petter
cunner	hooper	storer	frater	Pooter	setter
gunner	looper	pourer	grater	rooter	tetter
punner	groper	tourer	prater	tooter	bitter
runner	proper	usurer	saeter	quoter	fitter
wunner	capper	leaser	teeter	nipter	hitter
pioner	dapper	teaser	dieter	barter	jitter
mooner	lapper	chaser	ureter	carter	litter
ironer	mapper	flaser	rafter	darter	pitter
kroner	napper	eraser	wafter	garter	ritter
atoner	rapper	kaiser	lifter	parter	sitter
stoner	sapper	raiser	sifter	dorter	titter
pyoner	tapper	poiser	lofter	porter	witter
darner	wapper	guiser	tufter	rorter	cotter
earner	yapper	falser	baiter	sorter	hotter
garner	pepper	halser	gaiter	hurter	jotter
warner	dipper	censer	waiter	caster	potter
corner	kipper	rinser	reiter	easter	rotter
horner	nipper	closer	smiter	faster	totter
sorner	ripper	cooser	uniter	laster	butter
burner	sipper	groser	goiter	master	cutter
turner	tipper	proser	loiter	paster	gutter
dauner	zipper	parser	writer	raster	mutter
pruner	bopper	verser	cuiter	taster	nutter
dawner	copper	dorser	falter	waster	putter
fawner	dopper	worser	halter	fester	rutter
pawner	hopper	curser	palter	jester	cauter
downer	lopper	nurser	salter	pester	neuter
undoer	mopper	purser	felter	rester	fluter
echoer	popper	passer	kelter	tester	couter
leaper	topper	lesser	pelter	wester	douter
reaper	cupper	kisser	welter	yester	fouter
shaper	supper	dosser	filter	bister	mouter
diaper	carper	josser	kilter	lister	pouter
draper	harper	rosser	milter	mister	router
keeper	warper	tosser	tilter	sister	souter
peeper	gasper	cusser	bolter	ulster	touter
weeper	jasper	fusser	colter	coster	fewter

pewter	stewer	diapir	lictor	cratur	Hyades
powter	shower	mahsir	victor	Kultur	irides
sowter	blower	santir	doctor	santur	Rhodes
baxter	flower	bestir	rhetor	zephyr	sordes
dexter	glower	faquir	foetor	martyr	emydes
arguer	knower	elixir	faitor	S	kamees
valuer	grower	succor	editor	anabas	dinges
issuer	stower	rancor	suitor	fracas	laches
beaver	answer	chador	cantor	Dorcas	riches
heaver	coaxer	weldor	lentor	windas	fishes
reaver	hoaxer	vendor	mentor	Boreas	sithes
weaver	E-layer	condor	captor	oil-gas	rabies
shaver	flayer	sordor	raptor	biogas	facies
claver	player	meteor	sartor	air-gas	ladies
slaver	slayer	fragor	castor	outgas	undies
craver	crayer	fulgor	pastor	unbias	bodies
graver	prayer	turgor	Nestor	golias	bogies
quaver	stayer	anchor	bettor	capias	orgies
peever	swayer	Senhor	fautor	Pallas	nelies
weever	obeyer	author	elutor	killas	allies
Q-fever	scryer	senior	liquor	pholas	sanies
liever	skryer	junior	octuor	dowlas	monies
clever	spryer	pavior	salvor	magmas	caries
soever	lawyer	chikor	flexor	Lammas	series
taiver	sawyer	chukor	plexor	ananas	movies
waiver	bowyer	jailor	mahzor	whenas	faikes
reiver	blazer	sailor	rizzor	lampas	stokes
shiver	glazer	tailor	squirr	pampas	umbles
skiver	grazer	pallor	sambur	charas	oodles
oliver	geezer	enamor	concur	madras	whiles
sliver	seizer	cremor	fadeur	degras	caules
driver	prizer	tremor	fureur	narras	boules
stiver	panzer	termor	poseur	tarras	Jeames
quiver	bonzer	signor	auteur	serras	Hermes
calver	boozer	mainor	voyeur	terras	kermes
halver	fizzer	kronor	furfur	dipsas	Termes
salver	rizzer	indoor	langur	portas	vermes
delver	rozzer	unmoor	kunkur	vestas	magnes
silver	buzzer	huzoor	murmur	canvas	hoboes
solver	nuzzer	torpor	giaour	abdabs	dadoes
wolver	sea-air	stupor	labour	crumbs	eddoes
culver	mid-air	terror	tabour	ethics	dodoes
pulver	affair	mirror	arbour	conics	dagoes
shover	unfair	horror	ardour	sonics	ingoes
clover	unhair	censor	rigour	optics	echoes
glover	mohair	sensor	vigour	civics	haloes
plover	éclair	tensor	valour	naiads	heroes
hoover	repair	tonsor	velour	aphids	tiroes
up-over	impair	cursor	colour	amends	tyroes
drover	Altair	lessor	dolour	zounds	vetoes
prover	hot-air	fossor	armour	gourds	trapes
trover	gambir	abator	humour	Thebes	stapes
stover	mandir	viator	rumour	faeces	cripes
carver	effeir	orator	tumour	ibices	stipes
nerver	co-heir	stator	honour	ilices	swipes
server	sea-fir	ovator	vapour	apices	Vulpes
louver	Kaffir	debtor	detour	grices	herpes
thawer	jaghir	factor	retour	calces	Glires
gnawer	menhir	hector	notour	falces	Sèvres
drawer	kephir	lector	favour	lances	vivres
viewer	corkir	rector	savour	fasces	phases
skewer	korkir	sector	devour	Pisces	crases
spewer	memoir	vector	dyvour	fauces	theses
brewer	devoir	fictor	Mensur	cruces	dieses

preses	rachis	otitis	Hypnos	speiss	Tungus
crises	orchis	mantis	tripos	bekiss	sargus
irises	raphis	fortis	pharos	unkiss	tophus
krises	turkis	syrtis	Hyksos	demiss	typhus
lenses	oxalis	pastis	lassos	remiss	mythus
menses	Majlis	testis	cantos	kumiss	radius
gooses	Mejlis	Anguis	centos	emboss	medius
lisses	cullis	unguis	nostos	imboss	modius
misses	caulis	tenuis	custos	endoss	regius
louses	epulis	maquis	xystos	kaross	genius
souses	Themis	clavis	set-tos	across	Sirius
mewses	salmis	travis	dittos	T-cross	ruckus
acates	commis	clevis	bravos	betoss	cyclus
whites	exomis	trevis	biceps	schuss	obelus
gentes	dermis	pelvis	Cynips	Greats	callus
pontes	kermis	parvis	thrips	groats	gallus
Boötes	vermis	brewis	clumps	assets	Rallus
quotes	tennis	praxis	glumps	drafts	Tellus
certes	Adonis	rhexis	ellops	lights	villus
Cortes	patois	orexis	Merops	nights	obolus
sortes	putois	deixis	stirps	tights	tholus
syrtes	kalpis	ptyxis	polyps	crants	peplus
testes	jaspis	specks	shears	faints	opulus
ungues	Charis	knicks	jabers	feints	stylus
tenues	debris	hoicks	cheers	Cloots	shamus
leaves	nebris	yoicks	sheers	sports	lacmus
claves	hubris	shucks	pliers	chiaus	animus
loaves	hybris	breeks	afters	Erebus	primus
graves	indris	branks	revers	iambus	wammus
staves	Iberis	chinks	divers	Limbus	hummus
beeves	Pieris	blinks	vivers	nimbus	cormus
knives	Pteris	snooks	cizers	air-bus	litmus
calves	Osiris	vitals	theirs	morbus	thymus
halves	cypris	cruels	adoors	abacus	Uranus
delves	cerris	'snails	Messrs	coccus	Olenus
pelves	derris	cecils	she-ass	succus	acinus
selves	morris	miasms	megass	Cnicus	Somnus
wolves	phasis	dedans	vakass	sulcus	clonus
hooves	crasis	Volans	camass	mancus	Cornus
looves	stasis	lemans	admass	juncus	mucous
corves	thesis	Octans	repass	crocus	iodous
turves	diesis	sowans	bypass	cercus	nodous
thewes	emesis	sowens	harass	circus	rufous
ibexes	tmesis	ablins	morass	discus	rugous
ilexes	noesis	matins	strass	viscus	odious
apexes	uresis	pylons	potass	cuscus	pilous
calxes	cyesis	ovibos	cavass	ruscus	famous
lynxes	crisis	saccos	kavass	caucus	hamous
cruxes	miosis	rondos	abbess	gradus	ramous
blazes	ulosis	cameos	access	fundus	limous
fezzes	enosis	imagos	recess	exodus	rimous
proofs	gnosis	bathos	excess	Turdus	timous
troggs	urosis	pathos	unless	uraeus	comous
delphs	ptosis	pithos	caress	adieus	osmous
cloths	myosis	mythos	egress	pileus	dumous
Arabis	sepsis	curios	ogress	coleus	fumous
Anubis	cassis	sakkos	stress	soleus	humous
glacis	missis	tholos	duress	Cereus	awmous
précis	tussis	peplos	obsess	aureus	cymous
caddis	abatis	dromos	assess	tragus	venous
vendis	gratis	cosmos	citess	valgus	vinous
Elaeis	Isatis	kosmos	Jewess	vulgus	serous
haggis	ulitis	llanos	vowess	dingus	virous
hachis	iritis	Kronos	gneiss	fungus	porous

aurous	in-laws	afloat	reluct	pocket	gullet
gyrous	always	throat	rabbet	rocket	mullet
favous	noways	bespat	gibbet	socket	pullet
joyous	lay-bys	pit-pat	gobbet	bucket	camlet
noyous	bogeys	cowpat	rubbet	sucket	hamlet
scapus	alleys	sea-rat	thibet	tucket	samlet
palpus	Tethys	Bharat	gambet	banket	gimlet
campus	Geomys	pig-rat	barbet	junket	armlet
wampus	Erinys	hog-rat	sorbet	sunket	runlet
rumpus	labrys	barrat	surbet	dooket	piolet
pappus	zlotys	carrat	placet	market	violet
cippus	T	comsat	dulcet	basket	duplet
hippus	sea-bat	diktat	lancet	casket	varlet
carpus	sabbat	rat-tat	avocet	gasket	gurlet
corpus	Shebat	loquat	tercet	lasket	haslet
gaupus	combat	asquat	faucet	wisket	taslet
gawpus	wombat	cravat	doucet	bosket	goslet
mawpus	numbat	tan-vat	syndet	busket	cutlet
acarus	fox-bat	raiyat	verdet	musket	nutlet
Scarus	sea-cat	subact	unmeet	chalet	outlet
Labrus	gib-cat	redact	afreet	eyalet	amulet
uterus	tib-cat	olfact	street	gablet	howlet
walrus	bobcat	unfact	haffet	tablet	raylet
Acorus	mud-cat	triact	buffet	giblet	stylet
chorus	ramcat	monact	tuffet	goblet	helmet
cyprus	tom-cat	impact	perfet	sublet	pelmet
cirrus	hep-cat	caract	gadget	omelet	mammet
citrus	tip-cat	intact	fidget	eyelet	mommet
Laurus	mercat	outact	midget	reflet	gromet
Taurus	forçat	hexact	nidget	eaglet	cermet
miurus	muscat	defect	widget	haglet	kismet
rhesus	fat-cat	refect	budget	leglet	maumet
census	Kitcat	affect	hogget	reglet	mawmet
tarsus	upbeat	effect	nugget	aiglet	fewmet
versus	defeat	infect	garget	giglet	elanet
cursus	orgeat	abject	parget	piglet	planet
passus	reheat	object	target	goglet	chenet
missus	repeat	deject	forget	buglet	magnet
byssus	hereat	reject	gorget	smilet	signet
meatus	threat	inject	cachet	toilet	cygnet
hiatus	reseat	select	sachet	stilet	spinet
flatus	unseat	humect	rochet	anklet	gannet
status	outeat	aspect	Tophet	auklet	bennet
cactus	caveat	expect	'Arriet	ballet	dennet
rectus	loggat	direct	curiet	callet	gennet
rictus	forgat	arrect	soviet	gallet	jennet
foetus	nougat	resect	ram-jet	mallet	kennet
coitus	orchat	bisect	fan-jet	pallet	rennet
saltus	red-hat	insect	gas-jet	sallet	sennet
cultus	lum-hat	exsect	outjet	tallet	linnet
cantus	sunhat	obtect	backet	wallet	pinnet
Myrtus	top-hat	detect	jacket	pellet	sinnet
cestus	cushat	addict	nacket	vellet	bonnet
cistus	pot-hat	indict	packet	billet	sonnet
costus	lariat	delict	racket	fillet	punnet
xystus	khalat	relict	tacket	gillet	runnet
Cottus	khilat	depict	becket	jillet	lionet
Plutus	ballat	strict	picket	millet	cronet
Brutus	tallat	peinct	ticket	oillet	dip-net
lituus	sea-mat	decoct	wicket	rillet	carnet
naevus	summat	abduct	cocket	willet	garnet
Milvus	format	adduct	docket	collet	cornet
corvus	Bannat	deduct	locket	bullet	hornet
plexus	donnat	induct	nocket	cullet	burnet

6 -NET

gurnet	grivet	elicit	tirrit	galant	dement
basnet	privet	re-edit	forrit	zelant	piment
posnet	trivet	credit	worrit	volant	foment
brunet	velvet	bandit	bed-sit	aslant	loment
tow-net	vervet	pandit	prosit	tenant	moment
drapet	corvet	pundit	outsit	sonant	ponent
limpet	curvet	verdit	lowsit	tonant	repent
lappet	chewet	albeit	doitit	dopant	unpent
tappet	upwaft	sobeit	tomtit	vorant	arpent
sippet	infeft	deceit	dittit	arrant	parent
tippet	bereft	haffit	tautit	errant	ybrent
moppet	begift	soffit	reduit	durant	gerent
poppet	uplift	comfit	schuit	jurant	virent
puppet	adrift	confit	Innuit	gyrant	unrent
carpet	shrift	profit	acquit	tyrant	to-rent
forpet	thrift	misfit	requit	pesant	sprent
toupet	strift	outfit	spruit	natant	absent
claret	unsoft	baggit	Jesuit	octant	resent
labret	fricht	Giggit	unsuit	dotant	wisent
tabret	waucht	mishit	intuit	optant	unsent
secret	height	outhit	godwit	mutant	assent
affret	keight	tewhit	peewit	nutant	latent
regret	weight	pookit	nitwit	extant	patent
floret	alight	poukit	outwit	eluant	detent
amoret	blight	hawkit	pinxit	truant	intent
barret	flight	twilit	cobalt	savant	untent
garret	plight	sunlit	stealt	levant	potent
berret	slight	nirlit	basalt	bezant	ostent
ferret	anight	gas-lit	desalt	pezant	attent
terret	knight	submit	unbelt	byzant	extent
torret	ypight	flemit	infelt	inbent	fluent
turret	aright	fremit	unfelt	unbent	advent
tea-set	bright	dammit	bepelt	jacent	invent
subset	fright	semmit	ungilt	accent	plaint
wadset	wright	commit	spoilt	decent	quaint
offset	quight	summit	uptilt	recent	splint
eel-set	twight	hermit	unbolt	nocent	anoint
sunset	caught	permit	uncolt	ascent	aroint
closet	haught	unknit	lavolt	lucent	forint
groset	naught	upknit	abvolt	cadent	sprint
avoset	raught	sennit	revolt	sedent	squint
verset	taught	pirnit	occult	bident	afront
corset	waught	dacoit	incult	eident	unwont
basset	bought	dakoit	indult	rident	learnt
tasset	dought	adroit	tumult	indent	chaunt
misset	fought	eye-pit	penult	rodent	flaunt
cosset	mought	ash-pit	result	ardent	draunt
posset	nought	pulpit	insult	pudent	avaunt
gusset	sought	armpit	dreamt	regent	exeunt
russet	klepht	sumpit	libant	cogent	amount
outset	whisht	tan-pit	vacant	argent	scrunt
cruset	karait	roopit	decant	urgent	strunt
saw-set	strait	tappit	recant	scient	aroynt
dowset	rabbit	keppit	secant	client	talbot
septet	rubbit	forpit	pedant	orient	burbot
sestet	tidbit	bespit	aidant	unkent	turbot
fustet	gag-bit	rat-pit	creant	talent	tricot
sextet	gambit	loupit	infant	yblent	doocot
minuet	hen-bit	roupit	naiant	relent	mascot
piquet	two-bit	sawpit	pliant	silent	filfot
coquet	turbit	cabrit	criant	dolent	fylfot
roquet	titbit	spirit	bejant	splent	faggot
brevet	woubit	esprit	sejant	lament	maggot
olivet	placit	territ	askant	cement	spigot

ill-got	script	recast	cueist	bedust	way-out
lingot	sculpt	dicast	legist	degust	try-out
forgot	exempt	upcast	schist	august	buy-out
red-hot	prompt	breast	oikist	adjust	mazout
unshot	abrupt	nefast	malist	unjust	offput
upshot	irrupt	aghast	enlist	thrust	Rajput
galiot	Aegypt	dikast	holist	browst	output
Samiot	uncart	oblast	hylist	frowst	put-put
heriot	go-cart	yplast	Ramist	encyst	astrut
loriot	endart	dynast	demist	sceatt	tut-tut
Nesiot	indart	repast	timist	domett	atwixt
Sukkot	'sheart	by-past	Humist	octett	konfyt
zealot	go-kart	saidst	tanist	motett	schuyt
shalot	comart	amidst	bonist	unbitt	U
job-lot	jumart	incest	Ionist	dewitt	landau
ocelot	tooart	eldest	monist	assott	cadeau
diglot	depart	oldest	Maoist	kaputt	bureau
giglot	impart	modest	Taoist	ablaut	réseau
ballot	assart	freest	oboist	umlaut	bateau
tallot	astart	queest	Idoist	Arnaut	gâteau
by-plot	tewart	infest	egoist	nobbut	coteau
carlot	thwart	regest	quoist	hagbut	nilgau
harlot	Tibert	digest	papist	woobut	pillau
firlot	albert	ingest	rapist	offcut	ynambu
commot	sweert	behest	tapist	anicut	aperçu
marmot	expert	shiest	typist	mid-gut	teledu
motmot	desert	driest	Marist	catgut	subfeu
unknot	insert	priest	verist	rotgut	milieu
cannot	assert	molest	Christ	log-hut	Kisleu
donnot	exsert	unnest	aorist	unshut	pangfu'
why-not	astert	honest	uprist	outjut	Telugu
unboot	tavert	funest	aurist	englut	Manchu
refoot	obvert	unrest	jurist	killut	saddhu
cahoot	advert	forest	purist	besmut	samshu
galoot	revert	uprest	lyrist	peanut	gomoku
enroot	divert	arrest	desist	cobnut	ormolu
unroot	invert	latest	resist	pig-nut	tamanu
uproot	covert	obtest	insist	oak-nut	ingénu
tea-pot	sweirt	detest	assist	walnut	détenu
inkpot	begirt	eftest	artist	oil-nut	Vishnu
jampot	engirt	attest	lutist	ben-nut	roucou
compot	ungirt	devest	unwist	econut	amadou
tinpot	T-shirt	revest	laxist	ragout	voudou
bespot	squirt	divest	sexist	rig-out	congou
despot	escort	invest	whilst	bug-out	cachou
hotpot	effort	lowest	haulst	dugout	acajou
bowpot	dehort	gayest	Nernst	mahout	wou-wou
sexpot	cohort	mayest	accost	schout	gay-you
agorot	exhort	sayest	oncost	all-out	gru-gru
sap-rot	deport	shyest	unlost	dim-out	jabiru
carrot	report	slyest	volost	cop-out	Pakhtu
garrot	import	'mongst	almost	aspout	Pashtu
parrot	apport	Babist	inmost	far-out	Pushtu
wet-rot	asport	vibist	upmost	sprout	abattu
dry-rot	export	cubist	utmost	strout	Basutu
enrapt	besort	racist	repost	get-out	muu-muu
accept	resort	oecist	impost	let-out	kikuyu
recept	assort	sadist	sperst	set-out	V
incept	detort	Vedist	hairst	fit-out	moshav
except	retort	codist	thirst	not-out	Kislev
unkept	extort	modist	waurst	cut-out	W
yclept	cavort	nudist	aburst	devout	guffaw
bewept	unhurt	ageist	robust	lay-out	gewgaw
unwept	yaourt	theist	locust	pay-out	heehaw

bashaw	fellow	imbrex	Friday	scabby	shindy
cashaw	mellow	astrex	all-day	shabby	maundy
unthaw	yellow	unisex	man-day	flabby	woundy
haw-haw	billow	dentex	Monday	slabby	embody
sea-law	pillow	vertex	Sunday	crabby	imbody
mob-law	willow	cortex	law-day	drabby	nobody
bye-law	follow	vortex	six-day	plebby	melody
byrlaw	hollow	frutex	box-day	slobby	monody
outlaw	go-slow	convex	lay-day	knobby	bloody
sea-maw	matlow	spadix	mayday	snobby	broody
begnaw	haymow	prefix	pay-day	chubby	dipody
pawpaw	erenow	suffix	heyday	slubby	parody
redraw	acknow	confix	perfay	knubby	corody
undraw	minnow	bollix	margay	snubby	swardy
updraw	winnow	prolix	morgay	grubby	gourdy
pad-saw	escrow	commix	pochay	stubby	sturdy
seesaw	upgrow	chenix	linhay	hereby	cloudy
jigsaw	barrow	fornix	sashay	trilby	spacey
log-saw	farrow	matrix	deejay	thumby	pricey
rip-saw	harrow	tutrix	mellay	brumby	wincey
pit-saw	marrow	tettix	replay	crumby	stagey
bow-saw	narrow	cervix	by-play	near-by	mangey
powwaw	tarrow	caranx	parlay	overby	dingey
subdew	yarrow	sphinx	o'erlay	owerby	stogey
mildew	borrow	meninx	mislay	abbacy	lackey
sun-dew	morrow	syrinx	outlay	legacy	dickey
may-dew	sorrow	larynx	waylay	lunacy	mickey
curfew	burrow	red-box	dismay	papacy	tickey
eschew	furrow	icebox	mornay	piracy	hockey
nephew	leasow	peg-box	sea-pay	curacy	jockey
cashew	bestow	egg-box	prepay	speccy	bed-key
review	unstow	tar-box	upbray	fleecy	off-key
unclew	kowtow	hatbox	defray	esnecy	ash-key
curlew	bowwow	outbox	affray	policy	crikey
sea-mew	powwow	jawbox	fin-ray	sluicy	donkey
Hebrew	wow-wow	haybox	sunray	chancy	monkey
redrew		pay-box	unpray	riancy	chokey
upgrew	X	sea-fox	warray	agency	hookey
fog-bow	bombax	kid-fox	forray	egency	darkey
pole-ax	dogfox	hurray	bouncy	horkey
sunbow	Ceefax ®	carfox	murray	rouncy	turkey
dew-bow	carfax	outfox	betray	idiocy	hawkey
sea-cow	banjax	trek-ox	in-tray	Arcady	low-key
dun-cow	smilax	musk-ox	astray	steady	medley
ant-cow	climax	lummox	estray	malady	podley
meadow	larnax	magnox	bewray	milady	bailey
shadow	thorax	cowpox	forsay	swaddy	galley
window	storax	Volvox	missay	smiddy	valley
row-dow	styrax	boyaux	nay-say	shoddy	willey
forhow	pre-tax	adieux	upstay	cloddy	volley
anyhow	syntax	reflux	dittay	spuddy	gulley
upblow	surtax	afflux	seaway	cruddy	mulley
by-blow	earwax	efflux	subway	speedy	pulley
reflow	paxwax	influx	midway	greedy	gooley
inflow	Bembex	hallux	leeway	remedy	hooley
upflow	caudex	Pollux	one-way	comedy	barley
callow	orifex	bijoux	runway	untidy	parley
fallow	forfex	Bombyx	two-way	bluidy	hurley
gallow	deflex	coccyx	airway	bieldy	wurley
hallow	reflex		Norway	wieldy	motley
mallow	pollex	Y	upsway	mouldy	bawley
sallow	scolex	hobday	key-way	shandy	yowley
tallow	diplex	midday	skyway	brandy	doyley
wallow	implex	off-day	anyway	trendy	blimey
bellow	duplex	Tagday			

kidney	spiffy	thingy	earthy	nimbly	merely
meiney	spoffy	clingy	forthy	dumbly	sorely
phoney	scuffy	stingy	worthy	humbly	purely
pioney	chuffy	spongy	couthy	jumbly	surely
gooney	fluffy	oology	mouthy	marbly	basely
barney	pluffy	eulogy	youthy	doubly	wisely
carney	snuffy	clergy	truthy	chicly	lately
sarney	stuffy	energy	forwhy	deadly	titely
curney	rubify	syzygy	bleaky	gladly	astely
jitney	pacify	beachy	sneaky	fiddly	mutely
sawney	ladify	leachy	creaky	tiddly	lively
powney	nidify	peachy	freaky	cuddly	vively
phooey	codify	coachy	croaky	puddly	lovely
swipey	modify	poachy	whacky	needly	deafly
gilpey	salify	reechy	knacky	laidly	bob-fly
pompey	uglify	conchy	checky	aridly	gadfly
scarey	vilify	bunchy	specky	avidly	hop-fly
ochrey	ramify	catchy	thicky	baldly	barfly
storey	humify	patchy	bricky	mildly	dor-fly
osprey	sanify	tetchy	cricky	vildly	purfly
warrey	lenify	vetchy	tricky	boldly	wet-fly
verrey	minify	bitchy	sticky	coldly	botfly
murrey	omnify	fitchy	talcky	kindly	outfly
surrey	munify	hitchy	zincky	fondly	saw-fly
pudsey	typify	pitchy	stocky	clodly	day-fly
milsey	verify	botchy	plucky	goodly	mayfly
tolsey	Torify	pouchy	cheeky	hardly	dry-fly
linsey	aurify	touchy	sleeky	lordly	waggly
tinsey	purify	dinghy	creeky	loudly	giggly
winsey	gasify	laughy	chalky	lewdly	niggly
goosey	ossify	doughy	stalky	cicely	wiggly
jersey	ratify	roughy	whelky	nicely	coggly
kersey	notify	tumphy	blanky	widely	goggly
causey	vivify	trophy	branky	nudely	trigly
mousey	Nazify	furphy	cranky	rudely	gangly
whitey	shelfy	murphy	pranky	wheely	jangly
maguey	scurfy	blashy	swanky	skeely	tangly
voguey	argufy	flashy	chinky	freely	jingly
peavey	ladyfy	plashy	slinky	steely	kingly
slavey	Toryfy	brashy	chunky	safely	singly
convey	fledgy	trashy	spunky	rifely	tingly
jarvey	stodgy	swashy	spooky	wifely	longly
kurvey	sludgy	fleshy	smirky	sagely	jungly
purvey	smudgy	swishy	quirky	hugely	googly
survey	shaggy	bolshy	mid-sky	likely	smugly
savvey	claggy	gun-shy	whisky	palely	snugly
clayey	flaggy	sloshy	flisky	vilely	richly
wheyey	slaggy	sposhy	brisky	solely	archly
tolzey	knaggy	marshy	frisky	gamely	muchly
boozey	snaggy	flushy	drosky	lamely	highly
sheafy	craggy	plushy	Russky	namely	nighly
tabefy	quaggy	slushy	shoaly	samely	gashly
rubefy	dreggy	brushy	drably	tamely	rashly
madefy	twiggy	deathy	stably	timely	poshly
calefy	cloggy	heathy	babbly	comely	lushly
humefy	smoggy	loathy	pebbly	homely	eathly
tumefy	froggy	apathy	wobbly	sanely	snaily
tepefy	groggy	wrathy	bubbly	finely	racily
rarefy	bluggy	swathy	nubbly	lonely	tidily
chaffy	stuggy	smithy	rubbly	troely	bodily
draffy	effigy	stithy	feebly	ripely	cagily
whiffy	otalgy	filthy	trebly	barely	uglily
cliffy	slangy	toothy	glibly	rarely	oilily
sniffy	twangy	frothy	wambly	yarely	wilily

holily	trimly	saltly	prismy	cowboy	bleary
family	calmly	gently	rheumy	lowboy	smeary
homily	warmly	partly	Albany	day-boy	speary
punily	termly	tartly	Almany	verdoy	dreary
ropily	firmly	pertly	Romany	popjoy	aweary
warily	glumly	portly	tetany	accloy	vagary
eerily	drumly	curtly	litany	Y-alloy	fegary
verily	grumly	fastly	botany	deploy	angary
airily	leanly	lastly	gowany	employ	sugary
wirily	meanly	vastly	sheeny	shamoy	apiary
gorily	keenly	wistly	greeny	Tannoy ®	friary
easily	openly	costly	sweeny	teapoy	aviary
cosily	evenly	mostly	tweeny	pomroy	salary
rosily	fainly	kittly	oogeny	Norroy	telary
busily	gainly	nextly	brainy	lenvoy	Hilary
dewily	mainly	nebuly	grainy	renvoy	volary
hazily	vainly	unduly	geminy	convoy	canary
lazily	thinly	raguly	jiminy	sheepy	panary
mazily	lionly	unruly	hominy	sleepy	denary
oozily	dernly	brawly	rosiny	creepy	senary
weakly	townly	crawly	satiny	steepy	binary
hackly	emboly	viewly	mutiny	sweepy	donary
feckly	unholy	slowly	squiny	stripy	nonary
rickly	dhooly	growly	shanny	crampy	zonary
sickly	grooly	greyly	branny	swampy	lunary
tickly	deeply	spryly	cranny	skimpy	horary
meekly	triply	mizzly	granny	crimpy	rosary
weekly	damply	sozzly	tranny	clumpy	datary
lankly	dimply	occamy	swanny	glumpy	petary
rankly	jimply	gleamy	blenny	plumpy	notary
tinkly	pimply	creamy	johnny	slumpy	rotary
darkly	simply	dreamy	shinny	crumpy	votary
parkly	comply	steamy	whinny	frumpy	vivary
duskly	two-ply	infamy	skinny	grumpy	covary
really	ripply	bigamy	spinny	stumpy	unwary
re-ally	popply	digamy	gobony	jalopy	aumbry
egally	supply	oogamy	incony	canopy	war-cry
whally	purply	belamy	paeony	droopy	descry
orally	dearly	goramy	aphony	ectopy	outcry
dually	nearly	bulimy	oniony	chappy	sundry
ovally	pearly	smalmy	briony	snappy	bawdry
shelly	rearly	qualmy	felony	drappy	tawdry
skelly	yearly	shammy	colony	trappy	ambery
smelly	gnarly	clammy	polony	preppy	umbery
snelly	snarly	Grammy	gemony	chippy	jadery
railly	anerly	chemmy	lemony	whippy	cidery
chilly	overly	shimmy	simony	slippy	rudery
whilly	fairly	whimmy	spoony	snippy	cheery
skilly	swirly	swimmy	barony	drippy	sneery
frilly	twirly	scummy	betony	grippy	steery
stilly	poorly	chummy	saxony	choppy	wafery
evilly	knurly	plummy	bryony	shoppy	eggery
twilly	hourly	slummy	sharny	floppy	tigery
wholly	sourly	crummy	thorny	sloppy	ochery
coolly	measly	sodomy	pigsny	croppy	sphery
woolly	grisly	ignomy	puisny	chirpy	ashery
brolly	featly	bloomy	brawny	crispy	briery
drolly	neatly	gloomy	browny	occupy	osiery
trolly	flatly	sloomy	sea-boy	croupy	bakery
foully	subtly	broomy	tomboy	groupy	rakery
seemly	meetly	bosomy	carboy	syrupy	fikery
slimly	daftly	smarmy	busboy	titupy	dukery
grimly	deftly	stormy	pot-boy	vicary	celery
primly	softly	chasmy	bow-boy	sudary	oilery

tilery	skerry	kecksy	shifty	dainty	smutty
volery	whirry	cocksy	clifty	fainty	beauty
owlery	smirry	folksy	snifty	painty	snouty
almery	scurry	booksy	drifty	shinty	spouty
venery	skurry	whimsy	eighty	flinty	grouty
finery	flurry	flimsy	mighty	stinty	trouty
pinery	slurry	slimsy	nighty	coonty	deputy
vinery	smurry	clumsy	orbity	jaunty	plaguy
winery	spurry	teensy	cecity	bounty	chequy
ornery	fratry	quinsy	oddity	county	exequy
napery	poetry	argosy	nudity	mounty	cliquy
papery	paltry	gelosy	freity	snooty	shelvy
empery	peltry	monosy	aseity	humpty	groovy
popery	sultry	choosy	polity	hearty	scurvy
ropery	gantry	floosy	dimity	clarty	chivvy
dupery	pantry	apepsy	enmity	smarty	skivvy
orrery	centry	biopsy	comity	swarty	spivvy
misery	gentry	dropsy	sanity	uberty	strawy
rosery	sentry	hearsy	vanity	cherty	sinewy
eatery	vintry	classy	lenity	shirty	screwy
watery	wintry	glassy	egoity	thirty	arrowy
nitery	riotry	brassy	bepity	shorty	galaxy
artery	pastry	grassy	uppity	snorty	eutaxy
wavery	wastry	cressy	parity	sporty	sleazy
revery	vestry	tressy	rarity	reasty	queazy
severy	hostry	prissy	ferity	yeasty	wheezy
livery	scaury	flossy	verity	reesty	sleezy
rivery	glaury	glossy	purity	chesty	sneezy
tawery	rebury	drossy	entity	pigsty	breezy
bowery	anbury	tootsy	acuity	feisty	franzy
lowery	unbury	curtsy	equity	wristy	frenzy
towery	decury	embusy	fruity	twisty	bronzy
belfry	fleury	unbusy	cavity	ghosty	floozy
hungry	augury	blowsy	levity	frosty	glitzy
glairy	injury	drowsy	novity	gousty	blowzy
unmiry	penury	frowsy	laxity	crusty	frowzy
expiry	floury	treaty	fixity	trusty	snazzy
theory	stoury	sweaty	fealty	scatty	frizzy
priory	dysury	floaty	lealty	chatty	Z
pelory	luxury	nicety	realty	fretty	suivez
memory	chowry	sheety	shelty	pretty	ersatz
armory	avowry	gleety	owelty	suetty	kibitz
motory	uneasy	sleety	stilty	chitty	krantz
savory	creasy	freety	guilty	gritty	chintz
scarry	greasy	sweety	faulty	Scotty	blintz
charry	queasy	safety	vaulty	blotty	quartz
gharry	phrasy	gaiety	scanty	clotty	Tammuz
sparry	extasy	ubiety	chanty	plotty	bazazz
starry	woodsy	moiety	shanty	knotty	pazazz
quarry	cheesy	ninety	teenty	snotty	bezazz
cherry	griesy	surety	plenty	spotty	bizazz
sherry	gamesy	rosety	twenty	grotty	pizazz
wherry	heresy	crafty			

A					
wallaba	takahea	Ophidia	ammonia	alluvia	vanilla
jellaba	trachea	conidia	boronia	apraxia	papilla
mastaba	Cyathea	gonidia	acapnia	pyrexia	barilla
zareeba	hop-flea	aspidia	petunia	eutexia	gorilla
copaiba	rat-flea	basidia	Digynia	hypoxia	maxilla
marimba	cochlea	pyxidia	polynia	Deutzia	vexilla
calumba	valonea	exordia	sequoia	ostraka	corolla
Columba	dyspnea	douleia	Olympia	mousaka	medulla
córdoba	ipomoea	ratafia	Xylopia	heureka	ampulla
araroba	cinerea	aphagia	sinopia	romaika	tombola
succuba	Chelsea	Panagia	atropia	paprika	barbola
paxiuba	deep-sea	patagia	ectopia	rusalka	mandola
catawba	oversea	otalgia	malaria	yamulka	gondola
ostraca	galatea	myalgia	talaria	ziganka	rubeola
polacca	ommatea	eulogia	velaria	palooka	mineola
Rebecca	herb-tea	refugia	Filaria	bazooka	aureola
zimocca	sage-tea	chéchia	Fumaria	gazooka	roseola
felucca	beeftea	onychia	ulnaria	mazurka	foveola
Jamaica	meat-tea	silphia	conaria	britska	pergola
replica	khalifa	morphia	puparia	zakuska	Modiola
Formica	alfalfa	penthia	dataria	kibitka	hemiola
erotica	Buphaga	Latakia	aquaria	britzka	variola
exotica	bottega	clarkia	vivaria	cabbala	Pianola ®
tapioca	hidalga	vedalia	fimbria	Kabbala	Salsola
carioca	galanga	regalia	apteria	falbala	octapla
Minorca	bubinga	Vinalia	asteria	scybala	hexapla
tedesca	seringa	rosalia	sangria	Zincala	exempla
sambuca	Moringa	novalia	mudiria	mandala	specula
farruca	myringa	lobelia	deliria	trehala	spicula
verruca	syringa	mycelia	ciboria	Sinhala	Avicula
Lactuca	cotinga	aphelia	peloria	harmala	falcula
Haggada	parerga	cimelia	emporia	Marsala	vincula
Kannada	meshuga	aurelia	decuria	candela	furcula
alameda	Solpuga	scaglia	Lemuria	Urodela	vascula
Rigveda	verruga	ganglia	Etruria	Cedrela	lingula
candida	langaha	sedilia	dysuria	Mustela	primula
Acarida	bruhaha	Palilia	argyria	vihuela	formula
Matilda	Halacha	monilia	aphasia	sequela	plumula
veranda	kachcha	ruellia	aplasia	acushla	planula
viranda	kuchcha	scholia	Aspasia	caffila	paenula
notanda	panocha	aboulia	xerasia	tequila	cannula
mutanda	sraddha	anaemia	freesia	coralla	pinnula
addenda	Goorkha	uraemia	algesia	cavalla	scapula
videnda	bourkha	pyaemia	silesia	labella	scopula
pudenda	piranha	bulimia	nemesia	sabella	serpula
delenda	pupunha	skimmia	amnesia	rubella	zebrula
osmunda	agrapha	encomia	atresia	sacella	trisula
rotunda	Corypha	anosmia	fuchsia	micella	fossula
Isopoda	tamasha	Logania	banksia	padella	spatula
monarda	ricksha	Titania	apepsia	nigella	fistula
Circaea	Maratha	tutania	quassia	lamella	valvula
Neogaea	paratha	Zizania	indusia	canella	propyla
althaea	naphtha	Eugenia	domatia	zanella	pteryla
Limnaea	acantha	Sirenia	Alsatia	Capella	bergama
Lymnaea	galabia	robinia	Rhaetia	parella	cariama
Dionaea	exurbia	lacinia	godetia	corella	ashrama
spiraea	malacia	actinia	militia	rosella	diorama
galabea	braccia	equinia	comitia	patella	grandma
panacea	breccia	begonia	notitia	novella	seriema
rosacea	Dioecia	oogonia	amentia	cedilla	emblema
Cetacea	zooecia	mahonia	opuntia	codilla	erotema
Helodea	soredia	aphonia	inertia	mamilla	empyema
hypogea	aecidia	valonia	minutia	armilla	kerygma
	ascidia	Polonia	synovia	manilla	drachma

Kallima	Acarina	tempera	fermata	romneya	musk-sac
stasima	ocarina	drosera	Odonata	Sankhya	dart-sac
digamma	tsarina	Bursera	cantata	Vaishya	bivouac
ack-emma	czarina	tessera	dejecta	jambiya	autovac
dilemma	Vitrina	tuatera	Insecta	polynya	Thebaic
maremma	retsina	Diptera	taffeta	chalaza	archaic
sarcoma	platina	Zostera	athleta	guereza	Aramaic
leucoma	cantina	podagra	secreta	mestiza	Hebraic
isodoma	sestina	Tanagra	excreta	organza	prosaic
osteoma	flutina	urethra	placita	bonanza	deltaic
angioma	rhytina	hetaira	amanita	cadenza	voltaic
myeloma	rabanna	mandira	partita	alcorza	ephebic
diploma	caranna	madeira	pituita	B	amoebic
adenoma	hosanna	pareira	lavolta	pedicab	alembic
fibroma	savanna	pereira	Vedanta	minicab	rhombic
pleroma	Gehenna	mandora	infanta	taxicab	plumbic
neuroma	antenna	pandora	Maranta	wide-gab	aerobic
Tritoma	Madonna	rhodora	magenta	nashgab	strobic
scotoma	Bellona	Senhora	polenta	inqilab	acerbic
adharma	cremona	amphora	ramenta	Pan-Arab	sebacic
chiasma	madroña	Signora	lomenta	Mozarab	boracic
schisma	persona	corpora	momenta	pea-crab	silicic
melisma	canzona	Massora	pronota	dog-crab	triadic
mahatma	taverna	zamarra	Lacerta	ewe-lamb	nomadic
curcuma	carauna	Viverra	canasta	mug-lamb	vanadic
satsuma	Calluna	begorra	catasta	reclimb	gonadic
ecthyma	curaçoa	Camorra	podesta	upclimb	monadic
anonyma	keitloa	saburra	ingesta	dislimb	faradic
ikebana	toheroa	goburra	celesta	coxcomb	octadic
bandana	parazoa	ondatra	balista	coulomb	Sotadic
beffana	metazoa	sumatra	genista	succumb	hexadic
Zingana	endozoa	plectra	locusta	bethumb	gonidic
pargana	Mesozoa	spectra	regatta	unplumb	juridic
omniana	ectozoa	shastra	mulatta	corn-cob	Hasidic
forlana	entozoa	Flustra	annatta	hob-a-nob	fluidic
furlana	Bryozoa	pandura	arietta	hip-knob	druidic
campana	Polyzoa	Ophiura	biretta	rhubarb	scaldic
tympana	grandpa	tempura	stretta	pot-herb	skaldic
guaraná	catalpa	Purpura	mozetta	proverb	Scandic
sultana	voluspa	Macrura	sagitta	perturb	ergodic
lantana	baccara	caesura	ricotta	disturb	melodic
ventana	cascara	vettura	battuta	whoobub	monodic
tartana	mascara	bravura	decidua	lion-cub	synodic
curtana	Zingara	palmyra	residua	rub-a-dub	parodic
nirvana	cithara	madrasa	piragua	mini-sub	paludic
echidna	kithara	oropesa	quechua	mash-tub	malefic
Lycaena	chikara	impresa	Quichua	wash-tub	benefic
Zygaena	woorara	shicksa	morrhua	bathtub	venefic
Sciaena	tuatara	margosa	punalua	bran-tub	traffic
muraena	tantara	curiosa	subaqua	meat-tub	sebific
verbena	algebra	amorosa	siliqua	whey-tub	pacific
duodena	terebra	potassa	madoqua	C	omnific
Euglena	ephedra	vanessa	baclava	cardiac	mirific
noumena	exhedra	toccata	mud-lava	elegiac	ossific
lasagna	Megaera	biodata	cassava	coeliac	vivific
Bologna	hetaera	Radiata	dvandva	Cluniac	Guelfic
Krishna	gerbera	Ciliata	copaiva	theriac	pelagic
buccina	viscera	themata	khediva	scoriac	ellagic
piscina	caldera	enemata	hellova	muntjac	myalgic
glucina	riviera	magmata	pavlova	seed-lac	energic
stamina	cholera	regmata	Minerva	shellac	georgic
tegmina	chimera	lemmata	helluva	almanac	Noachic
tormina	woomera	gummata	peishwa	champac	Bacchic
alumina	gunnera	stomata	atalaya	yolk-sac	Czechic

7 -HIC

stichic	Romanic	Amharic	practic	kenotic	pig-lead
psychic	Koranic	velaric	atactic	prootic	implead
edaphic	Puranic	Tataric	smectic	nepotic	mislead
graphic	satanic	cambric	orectic	parotic	lip-read
Delphic	tetanic	quadric	deictic	xerotic	aspread
nymphic	titanic	baldric	Rhaetic	mitotic	misread
trophic	botanic	baudric	tabetic	entotic	betread
Sapphic	eugenic	suberic	Docetic	aptotic	retread
morphic	sphenic	spheric	ascetic	sceptic	untread
glyphic	sthenic	etheric	pedetic	skeptic	bestead
myrrhic	Galenic	dimeric	eidetic	aseptic	instead
pyrrhic	selenic	Homeric	aphetic	glyptic	onstead
gnathic	splenic	numeric	gametic	cryptic	lymphad
spathic	phrenic	generic	mimetic	tryptic	Dunciad
ichthic	eirenic	piperic	cometic	styptic	eyeliad
xanthic	sirenic	icteric	genetic	quartic	chiliad
benthic	arsenic	enteric	kinetic	clastic	gwiniad
vocalic	technic	nephric	tonetic	elastic	gwyniad
podalic	Lychnic	Cabiric	aloetic	plastic	sun-clad
acyclic	Mishnic	oneiric	anoetic	spastic	skyclad
angelic	alginic	empiric	paretic	drastic	cupola'd
aphelic	aclinic	satiric	heretic	Avestic	pyjama'd
Tamilic	actinic	theoric	pyretic	deistic	horn-mad
phallic	stannic	caloric	zetetic	ekistic	offload
thallic	bubonic	peloric	auxetic	eristic	disload
idyllic	laconic	chloric	augitic	gnostic	pay-load
ecbolic	obconic	pyloric	ophitic	caustic	sea-road
embolic	meconic	Armoric	Shiitic	glottic	anyroad
bucolic	hedonic	fluoric	pelitic	barytic	notepad
Tamulic	paeonic	Tantric	oolitic	agravic	helipad
acrylic	aphonic	centric	politic	motivic	footpad
oghamic	anionic	gastric	Hamitic	pyrexic	megarad
Islamic	psionic	Austric	Semitic	hypoxic	kamerad
dynamic	avionic	dysuric	somitic	manihoc	gorsedd
ceramic	colonic	satyric	neritic	mandioc	bedridd
keramic	xylonic	butyric	soritic	futhorc	sol-faed
potamic	demonic	dibasic	pyritic	subfusc	hennaed
anaemic	nimonic	aphasic	levitic	mollusc	tiaraed
uraemic	canonic	Friesic	P-Celtic	D	vistaed
pyaemic	Japonic	amnesic	Q-Celtic	grandad	huzzaed
racemic	Aaronic	Liassic	P-Keltic	unidea'd	lie-abed
endemic	Neronic	classic	Q-Keltic	go-ahead	sofa-bed
polemic	chronic	Glossic	frantic	sub-head	scabbed
tonemic	moronic	prussic	quantic	red-head	blabbed
totemic	Byronic	Eleatic	identic	godhead	slabbed
bathmic	masonic	creatic	quintic	egghead	crabbed
celomic	mesonic	sciatic	odontic	bighead	grabbed
chromic	opsonic	triatic	deontic	dog-head	stabbed
entomic	metonic	Asiatic	biontic	log-head	swabbed
ptarmic	Saxonic	volatic	chaotic	lum-head	cribbed
thermic	caproic	nematic	robotic	pinhead	knobbed
spermic	epizoic	sematic	sybotic	saphead	swobbed
chasmic	benzoic	somatic	mycotic	hop-head	chubbed
miasmic	Neozoic	ismatic	zygotic	cuphead	clubbed
plasmic	priapic	fanatic	aphotic	warhead	slubbed
spasmic	jalapic	venatic	abiotic	cathead	snubbed
seismic	Sarapic	agnatic	idiotic	fat-head	drubbed
enzymic	Serapic	lunatic	meiotic	pithead	grubbed
sudanic	Olympic	hepatic	Nilotic	hothead	stubbed
oceanic	Canopic	piratic	dulotic	pot-head	road-bed
veganic	ectopic	erratic	demotic	rawhead	reed-bed
organic	metopic	astatic	osmotic	bowhead	seedbed
Asianic	entopic	extatic	zymotic	tow-head	sand-bed
melanic	stearic	aquatic	henotic	tea-lead	bone-bed

sick-bed	crowded	swagged	collied	shanked	trilled
bark-bed	succeed	shogged	dollied	beinked	quilled
coal-bed	proceed	clogged	bullied	blinked	twilled
nail-bed	misdeed	flogged	cullied	swinked	woolled
climbed	pigfeed	frogged	gullied	trunked	templed
thumbed	ink-feed	plugged	sullied	crooked	dimpled
down-bed	in-kneed	snugged	replied	unyoked	pimpled
bilobed	bespeed	drugged	implied	unasked	dappled
camp-bed	sea-reed	flanged	applied	stealed	pearled
peat-bed	inbreed	fringed	mummied	pebbled	gnarled
tent-bed	decreed	wringed	pennied	marbled	snarled
dirt-bed	bur-reed	stinged	poppied	circled	star-led
test-bed	red-seed	thonged	unspied	mascled	whorled
lazy-bed	hag-seed	pronged	wearied	muscled	knurled
po-faced	aniseed	unurged	decried	raddled	measled
unraced	oil-seed	beached	undried	tiddled	bobsled
fleeced	til-seed	reached	queried	fuddled	kirtled
grieced	allseed	clichéd	gloried	huddled	castled
tranced	linseed	finched	storied	bridled	wattled
pounced	mawseed	pinched	ivoried	handled	mettled
pierced	hayseed	bunched	carried	rundled	settled
reduced	goateed	parched	harried	girdled	bottled
arcaded	seaweed	perched	married	wheeled	dottled
pleaded	cudweed	matched	parried	kneeled	mottled
breaded	oreweed	patched	tarried	steeled	noduled
steaded	hag-weed	pitched	berried	meseled	raguled
unfaded	ragweed	notched	ferried	nose-led	unruled
unjaded	pigweed	pouched	serried	maffled	pixy-led
gladded	hog-weed	touched	worried	muffled	wrizled
sledded	pop-weed	weighed	curried	ruffled	sozzled
clodded	oarweed	abashed	hurried	stifled	dreamed
plodded	tarweed	slashed	retried	purfled	steamed
snodded	burweed	fleshed	untried	goggled	unfamed
prodded	matweed	sloshed	daisied	joggled	ashamed
scudded	outweed	flushed	palsied	bangled	benamed
studded	cow-weed	brushed	pansied	fangled	agnamed
speeded	mayweed	crushed	emptied	tangled	unnamed
plaided	cliffed	cowshed	dirtied	wing-led	untamed
unaided	self-fed	loathed	puttied	enfiled	racemed
braided	chuffed	spathed	appuied	unfiled	unaimed
decided	stuffed	seethed	navvied	unoiled	unlimed
sleided	high-fed	clothed	bevvied	spoiled	unrimed
betided	well-fed	toothed	unbaked	uppiled	shammed
fielded	full-fed	mouthed	wreaked	untiled	clammed
childed	corn-fed	scythed	yslaked	tackled	slammed
woolded	rump-fed	tabbied	unraked	deckled	crammed
worlded	scarfed	fancied	unwaked	pickled	stemmed
branded	dwarfed	farcied	whacked	sickled	skimmed
blended	overfed	toadied	cracked	cockled	slimmed
blinded	mast-fed	muddied	tracked	scalled	brimmed
brinded	snow-fed	ruddied	stacked	dialled	primmed
fronded	engaged	bandied	flecked	vialled	trimmed
bounded	nonaged	candied	V-necked	stalled	scummed
rounded	unpaged	studied	sticked	shelled	drummed
demoded	enraged	edified	zincked	spelled	stummed
blooded	visaged	deified	shocked	stelled	venomed
flooded	fledged	unified	blocked	duelled	bosomed
snooded	alleged	lethied	brocked	fuelled	charmed
bearded	shagged	dallied	frocked	dwelled	alarmed
sharded	flagged	rallied	plucked	swelled	enarmed
guarded	snagged	sallied	cleeked	chilled	unarmed
swarded	bragged	tallied	trekked	skilled	chasmed
deluded	cragged	bellied	stalked	spilled	rheumed
clouded	dragged	jellied	whelked	grilled	unfumed

7 -MED

volumed	semiped	osiered	exposed	scented	snouted
assumed	striped	tile-red	emersed	fainted	reputed
bitumed	unwiped	tapered	spersed	painted	rescued
gowaned	cramped	rose-red	biassed	sainted	subdued
aliened	unhoped	watered	classed	tainted	unfeued
wakened	scooped	fevered	blessed	jointed	langued
havened	stooped	livered	dressed	pointed	tongued
wizened	chapped	rivered	tressed	stinted	torqued
feigned	clapped	covered	crossed	fronted	basqued
chained	flapped	lovered	trussed	haunted	statued
brained	slapped	powered	accused	vaunted	sheaved
grained	knapped	towered	focused	counted	cleaved
trained	snapped	layered	hocused	mounted	sleaved
stained	trapped	unaired	fucused	prunted	behaved
refined	wrapped	staired	ill-used	stunted	unpaved
affined	swapped	unfired	blowsed	bigoted	unsaved
unlined	stepped	unhired	unbated	unnoted	sleeved
ermined	chipped	bemired	undated	devoted	glaived
groined	shipped	expired	nodated	pivoted	shrived
rosined	whipped	retired	sweated	adapted	thrived
patined	skipped	untired	togated	adopted	unwived
ravined	clipped	begored	opiated	hearted	beloved
scanned	slipped	ungored	belated	averted	unloved
planned	snipped	floored	related	skirted	removed
spanned	dripped	visored	velated	blasted	unmoved
thinned	gripped	vizored	dilated	toasted	starved
skinned	tripped	scarred	unmated	chested	ungyved
grinned	shopped	charred	zonated	crested	strawed
twinned	plopped	gnarred	lunated	waisted	sinewed
shunned	slopped	knarred	bloated	twisted	vinewed
stunned	cropped	sparred	aurated	frosted	screwed
taloned	dropped	starred	lyrated	oersted	strewed
swooned	propped	averred	ansated	worsted	unsewed
throned	stopped	overred	unsated	bursted	embowed
untoned	swopped	shirred	doubted	chatted	unbowed
unzoned	scarped	whirred	unacted	flatted	endowed
learned	usurped	stirred	fracted	platted	allowed
sterned	cedared	blurred	erected	slatted	strowed
acorned	sheared	slurred	mulcted	dratted	untaxed
thorned	bleared	spurred	fructed	abetted	unsexed
corsned	uneared	goitred	faceted	whetted	invexed
untuned	speared	cantred	sheeted	bletted	unvexed
brawned	sugared	centred	greeted	fretted	unfixed
unowned	briared	bistred	unmeted	stetted	unmixed
crowned	unpared	rustred	riveted	flitted	decayed
drowned	para-red	uncured	coveted	emitted	delayed
kimboed	squared	figured	shafted	omitted	relayed
tangoed	mad-bred	odoured	shifted	knitted	renayed
pinnoed	ill-bred	unsured	clifted	spitted	sprayed
tabooed	outbred	assured	lighted	fritted	strayed
unwooed	low-bred	natured	nighted	quitted	essayed
lassoed	sky-bred	sutured	sighted	twitted	unwayed
web-toed	kindred	louvred	plaited	shotted	sad-eyed
hen-toed	wondred	ruby-red	excited	blotted	pie-eyed
fin-toed	hundred	debased	limited	clotted	one-eyed
tiptoed	ambered	embased	vomited	plotted	doe-eyed
mottoed	umbered	pleased	posited	knotted	pig-eyed
T-shaped	ulcered	arrased	fruited	spotted	bug-eyed
U-shaped	uddered	cheesed	exalted	trotted	alleyed
V-shaped	ridered	incised	swelted	abutted	owl-eyed
ycleped	sweered	agrised	stilted	glutted	pin-eyed
lobiped	offered	advised	quilted	smutted	honeyed
taliped	sphered	reposed	vaulted	voluted	moneyed
soliped	briered	unposed	slanted	clouted	two-eyed

pop-eyed	Geminid	cissoid	mistold	town-end	orotund
cat-eyed	hominid	byssoid	aefauld	stipend	ichabod
dry-eyed	globoid	arctoid	remould	compend	stucco'd
Samoyed	phacoid	deltoid	unmould	rump-end	rock-cod
annoyed	placoid	dentoid	ribband	propend	musk-cod
appuyed	coccoid	lentoid	salband	wappend	peascod
bedazed	cricoid	mastoid	armband	parpend	fish-god
unfazed	ericoid	cestoid	proband	perpend	demigod
ungazed	helcoid	histoid	disband	dispend	moon-god
bemazed	zincoid	cystoid	husband	suspend	goat-god
friezed	sarcoid	mattoid	hatband	uptrend	wet-shod
unsized	percoid	cottoid	hayband	godsend	dry-shod
bronzed	discoid	naevoid	deodand	missend	sea-food
blowzed	muscoid	obovoid	brigand	subtend	all-good
whizzed	Veddoid	rhizoid	red-hand	pretend	cubhood
frizzed	osteoid	insipid	offhand	contend	godhood
quizzed	fungoid	Pelopid	two-hand	protend	apehood
Thebaid	xiphoid	subarid	bow-hand	portend	elfhood
deaf-aid	typhoid	ascarid	cowhand	distend	hoghood
mislaid	lithoid	sciarid	midland	butt-end	manhood
new-laid	anthoid	scabrid	Iceland	minuend	nunhood
sea-maid	tenioid	epacrid	Hieland	provend	cathood
barmaid	sialoid	Homerid	elfland	miswend	boyhood
mermaid	hyaloid	asterid	bogland	hopbind	oxblood
prepaid	tabloid	diagrid	golland	abscind	upstood
low-paid	cycloid	epeirid	holland	rescind	redwood
embraid	oceloid	bestrid	fenland	exscind	dye-wood
upbraid	cheloid	satyrid	garland	mankind	dagwood
air-raid	myeloid	Abbasid	norland	unblind	dogwood
missaid	colloid	Chassid	wetland	Amerind	logwood
unstaid	haploid	hydatid	cotland	regrind	oak-wood
overbid	diploid	carotid	outland	sea-wind	cam-wood
subacid	amyloid	parotid	lawland	outwind	sap-wood
triacid	styloid	plastid	gowland	turbond	barwood
monacid	agamoid	languid	lowland	abscond	fir-wood
antacid	sigmoid	pinguid	command	plafond	boxwood
oxy-acid	pygmoid	noctuid	summand	diamond	plywood
flaccid	ethmoid	impavid	gormand	dromond	decapod
culicid	desmoid	piebald	operand	towmond	hexapod
katydid	adenoid	pyebald	farrand	despond	copepod
cepheid	glenoid	twafald	astrand	respond	musk-pod
araneid	ctenoid	riggald	sea-sand	dew-pond	lycopod
clupeid	crinoid	emerald	weasand	bausond	pleopod
Perseid	hypnoid	Tynwald	tar-sand	iracund	tylopod
proteid	vespoid	infield	upstand	rebound	octopod
triffid	acaroid	wergild	provand	embound	polypod
octofid	sparoid	unchild	ellwand	unbound	dasypod
energid	labroid	rebuild	weazand	upbound	dambrod
sylphid	zebroid	unbuild	prebend	redound	vine-rod
syrphid	fibroid	upbuild	descend	refound	king-rod
non-skid	ambroid	ice-cold	dead-end	unfound	nail-rod
pyralid	android	key-cold	road-end	Mahound	hot-trod
squalid	hydroid	onefold	fore-end	impound	ycleap'd
invalid	theroid	twifold	self-end	expound	gabbard
skid-lid	aneroid	penfold	forfend	aground	libbard
annelid	steroid	tenfold	prehend	enround	lubbard
cichlid	negroid	pinfold	back-end	unround	bombard
unsolid	tigroid	twofold	weekend	resound	lombard
pyramid	ochroid	sixfold	book-end	unsound	sea-card
Fatimid	spiroid	twyfold	tail-end	astound	placard
phasmid	choroid	mangold	forlend	unwound	brocard
plasmid	astroid	toe-hold	reamend	upwound	discard
tabanid	sauroid	cuckold	commend	lispund	doddard
oceanid	thyroid	Reynold	open-end	contund	affear'd

7 -ARD

unheard	skyward	Araneae	fat-face	creance	alidade
Midgard	halyard	strigae	outface	enhance	prefade
haggard	lanyard	nymphae	anelace	askance	brigade
laggard	tanyard	aphthae	bullace	balance	fougade
saggard	innyard	antliae	replace	valance	Pleiade
niggard	hop-yard	taeniae	emplace	romance	cockade
boggard	mazzard	scoriae	unplace	penance	scalade
belgard	dizzard	spuriae	byplace	finance	ballade
pochard	gizzard	exuviae	grimace	sonance	roulade
orchard	buzzard	Grallae	pinnace	durance	chamade
die-hard	halberd	axillae	furnace	surance	man-made
beghard	pig-herd	areolae	dispace	advance	mismade
goliard	cowherd	tabulae	outpace	joyance	new-made
laniard	sea-bird	nebulae	rebrace	noyance	grenade
poniard	ice-bird	faculae	embrace	licence	tornade
pockard	poe-bird	maculae	unbrace	cadence	charade
tankard	egg-bird	radulae	aggrace	defence	degrade
tailard	fig-bird	infulae	engrace	offence	regrade
mallard	oil-bird	regulae	barrace	ox-fence	aggrade
bollard	awlbird	tegulae	terrace	regence	upgrade
collard	dun-bird	ungulae	retrace	cogence	comrade
lollard	sun-bird	papulae	untrace	urgence	corrade
pollard	wosbird	situlae	outrace	faience	estrade
dullard	catbird	cotylae	ambs-ace	science	torsade
foulard	ant-bird	palamae	ames-ace	valence	passade
poulard	cowbird	squamae	choc-ice	silence	crusade
donnard	may-bird	intimae	caddice	ha'pence	boutade
gurnard	poy-bird	thermae	suffice	absence	pervade
reynard	concord	strumae	edifice	essence	couvade
inboard	rip-cord	catenae	orifice	latence	precede
unhoard	discord	vaginae	pack-ice	potence	epicede
uphoard	net-cord	Felinae	chalice	potencé	concede
jeopard	dichord	laminae	anglice	fayence	arreede
leopard	sea-lord	retinae	Gallice	asconce	regrede
guisard	warlord	alumnae	dormice	patonce	carbide
Hansard	May-lord	coronae	titmice	chaunce	deicide
mansard	bug-word	lacunae	cornice	flounce	suicide
leotard	o'erword	exedrae	rejoice	enounce	ovicide
bastard	misword	paterae	devoice	frounce	ecocide
dastard	nayword	pleurae	invoice	trounce	biocide
costard	applaud	serosae	unvoice	inherce	discide
bustard	defraud	medusae	tappice	emperce	confide
custard	rose-bud	chaetae	coppice	od-force	raphide
mustard	leafbud	Docetae	bespice	deforce	rawhide
enguard	marybud	Ratitae	hospice	afforce	cowhide
unguard	becloud	crustae	auspice	efforce	nuclide
seaward	encloud	aufgabe	avarice	enforce	collide
bedward	uncloud	would-be	oporice	inforce	bromide
godward	mim-mou'd	ascribe	caprice	divorce	uranide
leeward	E	escribe	morrice	quiesce	cyanide
steward	amoebae	englobe	matrice	tumesce	hydride
off-ward	cloacae	inglobe	nourice	dehisce	hag-ride
hogward	loricae	trilobe	statice	traduce	tan-ride
awkward	vesicae	microbe	pentice	subduce	nitride
vanward	Cebidae	saprobe	Scotice	conduce	astride
sunward	Gadidae	disrobe	D-notice	produce	outride
froward	Felidae	ice-cube	mortice	prepuce	joy-ride
airward	Canidae	j'adoube	justice	lettuce	seaside
forward	Ranidae	myotube	lattice	tribade	subside
norward	Laridae	sea-dace	crevice	forbade	bedside
outward	Muridae	vendace	service	succade	preside
hayward	Equidae	preface	snow-ice	falcade	offside
nayward	araceae	proface	vacance	brocade	topside
wayward	Irideae	surface	aidance	cascade	outside

wayside	vouchee	giraffe	sullage	rootage	anagoge
ebb-tide	Quashee	unruffe	haulage	cartage	apagoge
peptide	bukshee	od's-life	primage	portage	epagoge
riptide	banshee	low-life	rummage	lastage	isagoge
provide	prithee	sea-wife	plumage	wastage	scrooge
dioxide	prythee	midwife	thanage	restage	enlarge
epoxide	thankee	alewife	apanage	hostage	Fabergé
seconde	jubilee	hen-wife	cranage	postage	auberge
aliunde	galilee	huswife	teenage	upstage	demerge
forbode	mishmee	Tartufe	amenage	wattage	remerge
zincode	mousmee	cabbage	lignage	cottage	immerge
sarcode	alienee	garbage	wainage	pottage	asperge
cladode	soignée	herbage	coinage	scutage	deterge
cathode	trainee	ribcage	spinage	ajutage	diverge
kathode	ordinee	soccage	pannage	escuage	spairge
implode	nominee	brocage	tannage	viduage	regorge
explode	Shawnee	discage	tonnage	assuage	engorge
alamode	escapee	boscage	dunnage	scavage	splurge
commode	calipee	trucage	gunnage	salvage	scourge
outmode	whoopee	guidage	tunnage	selvage	expurge
spinode	frappée	faldage	peonage	brewage	resurge
corrode	referee	bandage	carnage	flowage	upsurge
tetrode	ice-free	vendage	cornage	stowage	scrouge
episode	tax-free	windage	seepage	drayage	relâche
pentode	puggree	bondage	rampage	quayage	panache
cestode	congree	pondage	compage	buoyage	earache
custode	machree	sondage	propage	disedge	attaché
vaivode	retiree	fardage	kippage	outedge	gouache
waivode	bourrée	yardage	umbrage	saw-edge	caliche
voivode	tea-tree	cordage	peerage	abridge	moriche
woiwode	pad-tree	wordage	pierage	swindge	fetiche
occlude	fig-tree	mileage	average	splodge	potiche
seclude	oak-tree	lineage	over-age	adjudge	tranche
include	oil-tree	acreage	lairage	rejudge	quinche
exclude	hop-tree	leafage	moorage	besiege	brioche
prelude	fir-tree	serfage	storage	assiege	galoche
collude	nut-tree	lee-gage	barrage	college	caroche
obtrude	yew-tree	baggage	vitrage	protégé	soroche
detrude	cow-tree	foggage	outrage	cortège	basoche
intrude	wax-tree	luggage	courage	negligé	ecorché
extrude	box-tree	burgage	presage	ventige	babuche
Wahabee	foresee	cowhage	prisage	vestige	capuche
hive-bee	devisee	foliage	corsage	indulge	nuraghe
Frisbee	look-see	arriage	massage	effulge	strophe
fiancée	oversee	leakage	passage	divulge	coryphe
Yezidee	hicatee	soakage	message	Falange	embathe
Zezidee	legatee	package	sausage	mélange	imbathe
Chaldee	manatee	sackage	abusage	derange	sheathe
killdee	draftee	dockage	plusage	enrange	breathe
grandee	visitee	lockage	paysage	arrange	wreathe
spondee	grantee	mockage	waftage	strange	staithe
feoffee	jauntee	tankage	weftage	wheenge	smoothe
alms-fee	picotee	linkage	voltage	revenge	sparthe
pledgee	devotee	sinkage	vantage	lozenge	sperthe
thuggee	bhistee	brokage	wantage	accinge	freebie
obligee	trustee	corkage	centage	unhinge	stiddie
perigee	spattee	keelage	tentage	impinge	accidie
whangee	dilutee	tallage	ventage	springe	weirdie
refugee	amputee	pillage	mintage	syringe	geordie
coachee	evacuee	tillage	vintage	allonge	crowdie
leechee	marquee	village	montage	chaunge	scaffie
trochee	fedayee	collage	pontage	expunge	gaudgie
fitchée	enchafe	tollage	flotage	camboge	swaggie
couchee	agraffe	fullage	footage	gamboge	teachie

macchie	dhurrie	odd-like	volable	audible	wheedle
conchie	smytrie	godlike	rulable	legible	tweedle
rotchie	scourie	rodlike	namable	delible	spindle
roughie	scowrie	manlike	tamable	risible	brindle
toughie	cruisie	sunlike	tenable	visible	trindle
Quashie	booksie	warlike	finable	fusible	dwindle
bolshie	primsie	dislike	tunable	patible	swindle
couthie	floosie	mislike	capable	scamble	roundle
routhie	brassie	cat-like	papable	shamble	trundle
nartjie	tootsie	sea-pike	ropable	bramble	croodle
quickie	sweetie	rampike	dupable	tremble	strodle
chuckie	shoe-tie	garpike	parable	thimble	urodele
dovekie	nightie	gas-coke	hirable	whomble	ukelele
Chinkie	necktie	hardoke	mirable	scumble	ukulele
spunkie	realtie	abrooke	errable	crumble	pommele
chookie	sheltie	bespoke	curable	drumble	parafle
pliskie	chantie	unspoke	durable	grumble	snaffle
wheelie	coontie	upspoke	disable	stumble	whiffle
troelie	jauntie	cowpoke	losable	ignoble	skiffle
forelie	mountie	unbroke	batable	ennoble	sniffle
Ramilie	Clootie	convoke	datable	unnoble	scuffle
baillie	smartie	provoke	eatable	soluble	shuffle
taillie	shortie	disyoke	hatable	voluble	snuffle
ghillie	beastie	misyoke	ratable	trouble	soufflé
troolie	hirstie	may-duke	retable	debâcle	souffle
stoolie	toustie	netsuke	citable	treacle	truffle
Charlie	Scottie	Vandyke	notable	manacle	finagle
overlie	plottie	lamb-ale	potable	cenacle	draggle
steamie	tuilyie	timbale	astable	miracle	sniggle
Brummie	spulyie	percale	mutable	coracle	wriggle
remanié	brulyie	rescale	equable	cubicle	smuggle
insanie	tailzie	unscale	savable	radicle	snuggle
dominie	tuilzie	daedale	livable	pedicle	spangle
grannie	spulzie	rundale	lovable	vehicle	brangle
trannie	brulzie	mace-ale	movable	silicle	trangle
johnnie	prenzie	gregale	dowable	panicle	wrangle
inconie	floozie	unshale	taxable	sanicle	twangle
polonie	prezzie	radiale	fixable	funicle	shingle
starnie	naartje	sea-kale	payable	tunicle	cringle
pigsnie	tea-cake	propale	sayable	utricle	tringle
niks-nie	hoe-cake	chorale	flyable	auricle	atingle
brownie	oil-cake	four-ale	buyable	vesicle	swingle
queynie	pancake	scytale	sizable	ossicle	shoogle
cap-à-pie	carcake	setuale	scabble	reticle	bauchle
scrapie	oatcake	gunwale	shabble	article	stabile
creepie	lac-lake	holy-ale	snabble	cuticle	gracile
pork-pie	mismake	pacable	brabble	binocle	profile
riempie	bespake	vocable	drabble	pinocle	misfile
plumpie	upspake	fadable	grabble	monocle	fragile
bran-pie	to-brake	ridable	prabble	opuscle	nargile
chappie	forsake	seeable	cribble	recycle	umwhile
drappie	offtake	sueable	dribble	bicycle	sea-mile
clippie	partake	dyeable	fribble	calycle	estoile
charpie	pertake	affable	gribble	treadle	compile
meat-pie	mistake	effable	pribble	staddle	febrile
dirt-pie	outtake	skiable	tribble	swaddle	sterile
groupie	reawake	pliable	stibble	twaddle	puerile
fedarie	prancke	amiable	quibble	treddle	nitrile
foudrie	paiocke	friable	knobble	griddle	pensile
niterie	pajocke	triable	knubble	quiddle	sensile
coterie	sea-like	makable	grubble	twiddle	tensile
reverie	unalike	takable	stubble	scuddle	sessile
prairie	riblike	likable	deleble	cruddle	fissile
calorie	siclike	salable	ribible	studdle	missile

subtile	condole	stipple	ferrule	big-time	profane
tactile	cineole	swipple	misrule	all-time	origane
sectile	aureole	dropple	capsule	centime	tsigane
fictile	alveole	stopple	spatule	two-time	Zingane
coctile	foveole	decuple	noctule	septime	abthane
ductile	mud-hole	scruple	pustule	wartime	methane
pantile	eye-hole	octuple	valvule	airtime	sea-lane
gentile	doghole	whaisle	nervule	pastime	lee-lane
pontile	ash-hole	bransle	guayule	mistime	biplane
reptile	armhole	noursle	entayle	rut-time	emplane
fertile	manhole	pightle	condyle	daytime	air-lane
cortile	pinhole	betitle	scroyle	laytime	hog-mane
tortile	top-hole	entitle	protyle	May-time	germane
hostile	ear-hole	scantle	restyle	anytime	propane
sextile	airhole	brantle	distyle	off-come	parpane
textile	cat-hole	gruntle	enstyle	welcome	platane
beguile	rat-hole	startle	eustyle	non-come	Beltane
servile	bothole	whirtle	systyle	o'ercome	pentane
flexile	pothole	snirtle	wheezle	outcome	montane
shackle	jawhole	spirtle	whaizle	newcome	heptane
crackle	foxhole	chortle	snoozle	dishome	tartane
grackle	keyhole	spurtle	frazzle	coelome	soutane
quackle	spy-hole	trestle	drizzle	caulome	dogvane
speckle	foliole	wrestle	frizzle	hadrome	dioxane
freckle	cariole	thistle	grizzle	plerome	epicene
brickle	dariole	whistle	swizzle	twasome	Miocene
prickle	variole	epistle	snuzzle	waesome	obscene
trickle	petiole	bristle	ducdame	beesome	epigene
stickle	ostiole	gristle	beldame	woesome	pangene
grockle	frijole	apostle	ill-fame	awesome	Neogene
chuckle	schoole	brattle	disfame	noisome	Ruthene
knuckle	tadpole	prattle	endgame	irksome	hygiene
bruckle	ale-pole	twattle	war-game	fulsome	scalene
truckle	hop-pole	whittle	May-game	winsome	stelene
crankle	maypole	skittle	beshame	urosome	Trilene ®
prankle	safrole	knittle	réclame	twosome	Hellene
crinkle	console	spittle	inflame	lissome	amylene
wrinkle	rissole	brittle	pen-name	gaysome	propene
twinkle	outsole	cuittle	sirname	noysome	terpene
crunkle	scatole	shottle	surname	toysome	Cairene
sparkle	skatole	crottle	misname	epitome	terrene
bubukle	pistole	scuttle	outname	leptome	styrene
gabelle	systole	shuttle	macramé	rhizome	pentene
nacelle	vacuole	skuttle	reframe	gisarme	toluene
micelle	benzole	globule	enframe	perfume	prevene
pucelle	wheeple	barbule	paracme	deplume	convene
jumelle	steeple	saccule	academe	emplume	Slovene
parelle	maniple	spicule	beteeme	unplume	benzene
Moselle	whample	bascule	phoneme	subsume	Cocagne
roselle	trample	tragule	spireme	presume	lasagne
écuelle	example	virgule	trireme	consume	sdeigne
novelle	stemple	cellule	supreme	costume	insigne
gazelle	whimple	gemmule	extreme	dogbane	epergne
rozelle	crimple	plumule	triseme	bugbane	cocaine
Braille	crumple	granule	eroteme	henbane	eucaine
codille	frumple	spinule	sublime	mirbane	sodaine
treille	scapple	pinnule	millime	myrbane	delaine
manille	knapple	cagoule	gas-lime	cowbane	demaine
zorille	grapple	kagoule	begrime	flybane	Almaine
mouillé	stapple	ampoule	reprime	chicane	moraine
whemmle	aripple	stipule	tea-time	lindane	sixaine
whommle	cripple	zebrule	bedtime	mundane	stibine
whummle	gripple	caerule	old-time	lurdane	combine
bricole	tripple	sporule	ragtime	demeane	hopbine

7 -INE

carbine	crimine	bez-tine	Diasone	outrope	fen-fire
turbine	primine	beguine	dapsone	towrope	pin-fire
hyacine	fulmine	anguine	cassone	guy-rope	bonfire
vaccine	bromine	genuine	acetone	isotope	gunfire
calcine	carmine	flavine	tritone	échappé	gas-fire
phocine	harmine	olivine	isotone	schappe	misfire
percine	jasmine	milvine	duotone	genappe	jaghire
hircine	desmine	sylvine	two-tone	Euterpe	outhire
porcine	thymine	provine	peptone	subtype	pismire
fascine	guanine	hop-vine	histone	tintype	armoire
piscine	cyanine	cervine	yu-stone	ecotype	rampire
leucine	adenine	nervine	oxytone	zootype	sampire
doucine	erg-nine	corvine	flavone	isotype	vampire
brucine	asinine	Iguvine	subzone	isobare	respire
glycine	quinine	entwine	trizone	baccare	inspire
gradine	pennine	intwine	canzone	outdare	suspire
uredine	leonine	untwine	lucarne	eelfare	saltire
nandine	heroine	lauwine	acharné	welfare	acquire
nundine	alepine	rhizine	lucerne	fanfare	require
pardine	vulpine	fanzine	caserne	warfare	enquire
sardine	chopine	benzine	alterne	misfare	inquire
sordine	propine	tyranne	interne	bus-fare	esquire
turdine	forpine	cayenne	externe	wayfare	haywire
codeine	vespine	doyenne	to-torne	Zingare	forbore
olefine	nut-pine	beginne	to-worne	sea-hare	rescore
confine	acarine	façonné	demesne	deciare	moidore
imagine	otarine	rib-bone	posaune	caviare	bandore
machine	pébrine	jambone	tribune	backare	pandore
errhine	zebrine	hip-bone	dejeune	declare	windore
beshine	eccrine	ear-bone	disjune	ensnare	inshore
arshine	cedrine	jawbone	commune	insnare	onshore
coniine	uterine	rawbone	Neptune	prepare	asthore
Rankine	tigrine	mud-cone	fortune	compare	bewhore
sea-line	chorine	fir-cone	distune	hectare	fahlore
opaline	caprine	condone	mistune	laetare	deplore
praline	cyprine	fordone	demayne	tartare	implore
hyaline	terrine	misdone	anodyne	upstare	explore
decline	murrine	someone	esloyne	T-square	Signore
recline	latrine	half-one	essoyne	sea-ware	iron-ore
incline	Petrine	doggone	sinsyne	unaware	oospore
dyeline	citrine	epigone	arch-foe	tinware	bedsore
off-line	vitrine	forgone	backhoe	macabre	eyesore
logline	taurine	misgone	gumshoe	calibre	tussore
aniline	neurine	outgone	tap-shoe	Félibre	restore
ralline	dourine	waygone	ice-floe	chambré	simarre
hem-line	azurine	diphone	forsloe	polacre	bizarre
kaoline	cuisine	beshone	euphroe	conacre	theatre
choline	pepsine	hemione	peep-toe	chancre	plectre
isoline	versine	abalone	crow-toe	chondre	spectre
two-line	byssine	chalone	inscape	sphaere	philtre
top-line	isatine	cyclone	half-ape	sincere	sceptre
carline	dietine	pallone	reshape	nowhere	dioptre
marline	emetine	violone	unshape	rivière	piastre
berline	pantine	anemone	igarapé	chimere	epicure
purline	dentine	hormone	red-tape	commère	procure
set-line	tontine	quinone	ycleepe	uromere	obscure
outline	tartine	hypnone	estrepe	isomere	dry-cure
cauline	destine	alsoone	cob-pipe	compere	perdure
Pauline	sestine	componé	bagpipe	umbrere	verdure
bowline	Sistine	propone	dip-pipe	austere	bordure
towline	sittine	dispone	gas-pipe	Gruyère	outdure
bay-line	bottine	ladrone	syncope	maulgre	hachure
skyline	routine	padrone	apocope	affaire	conjure
examine	bay-tine	neurone	wanhope	sea-fire	perjure

failure	discase	iconise	enclose	endorse	juncate
soilure	nutcase	adonise	inclose	indorse	evocate
recoure	oxidase	agonise	unclose	unhorse	furcate
guipure	decease	lionise	upclose	remorse	educate
purpure	release	ironise	villose	imburse	gradate
coupure	appease	ozonise	thylose	accurse	predate
measure	disease	echoise	marmose	uncurse	oxidate
seasure	misease	heroise	plumose	excurse	mandate
erasure	enchase	despise	grumose	scourse	deodate
leisure	inchase	rearise	hog-nose	unpurse	cordate
brisure	inphase	diarise	pug-nose	preasse	misdate
censure	euclase	sunrise	spinose	bagasse	outdate
tonsure	inulase	reprise	crinose	megasse	caudate
closure	amylase	emprise	mannose	filasse	exudate
morsure	diapase	apprise	pannose	Molasse	dogeate
fissure	sucrase	low-rise	carnose	vinasse	galeate
abature	anatase	pectise	caboose	impasse	maleate
feature	lactase	poetise	unloose	tirasse	pileate
stature	maltase	unitise	vamoose	idlesse	lineate
facture	diocese	pentise	shmoose	finesse	cuneate
lecture	Auslese	egotise	papoose	duresse	ocreate
picture	siamese	riotise	adipose	pelisse	aureate
wafture	Burmese	azotise	compose	hérissé	roseate
voiture	Sienese	baptise	propose	métisse	foveate
culture	Chinese	peptise	pappose	because	sea-gate
multure	Genoese	mortise	suppose	vareuse	frigate
pulture	imprese	cottise	purpose	diseuse	vulgate
vulture	Maltese	previse	dispose	poseuse	virgate
denture	fadaise	parvise	tea-rose	diffuse	outgate
venture	Judaise	endwise	labrose	suffuse	saw-gate
monture	malaise	sunwise	fibrose	confuse	Newgate
cloture	upraise	mapwise	umbrose	profuse	rechate
capture	arabise	anywise	necrose	perfuse	lithate
rapture	soubise	repulse	sucrose	enthuse	labiate
rupture	Grecise	impulse	acerose	recluse	sociate
torture	precise	appulse	operose	rehouse	radiate
nurture	laicise	expulse	dog-rose	in-house	mediate
pasture	concise	insulse	beprose	unhouse	ciliate
gesture	iridise	cleanse	leprose	jalouse	filiate
vesture	oxidise	expanse	cirrose	delouse	foliate
posture	anodise	recense	lactose	zamouse	osmiate
couture	atheise	license	pectose	espouse	teniate
texture	elegise	incense	acetose	carouse	miniate
fixture	mythise	defense	maltose	uprouse	expiate
mixture	dockise	offense	pentose	overuse	variate
gravure	realise	immense	ventose	contuse	ebriate
nervure	coalise	expense	Ventôse	pertuse	seriate
flexure	obelise	unsense	sinuose	dialyse	striate
plexure	utilise	intense	delapse	analyse	muriate
dasyure	gallise	extense	relapse	limbate	satiate
seizure	idolise	gibbose	illapse	globate	vitiate
out-owre	stylise	globose	synapse	probate	ostiate
empayre	chamise	herbose	traipse	barbate	obviate
diabase	chemise	verbose	eclipse	sorbate	deviate
isobase	premise	succose	ellipse	surbate	oxalate
air-base	itemise	talcose	glimpse	placate	sublate
surbase	promise	dulcose	demerse	baccate	chelate
egg-case	atomise	viscose	immerse	saccate	prelate
uricase	surmise	muscose	asperse	thecate	deflate
pen-case	cyanise	glucose	obverse	plicate	reflate
pincase	kyanise	glycose	adverse	emicate	inflate
cap-case	trenise	foliose	reverse	spicate	epilate
carcase	cognise	ebriose	diverse	falcate	gallate
percase	ebonise	reclose	inverse	sulcate	fellate

collate	caprate	accrete	axinite	unquote	autocue
bullate	narrate	secrete	Samnite	outvote	residue
violate	ferrate	excrete	mannite	synapte	overdue
prolate	serrate	naïveté	Sonnite	Astarte	treague
isolate	cirrate	Bahaite	Sunnite	impaste	renague
implate	disrate	Karaite	ebonite	celeste	renegue
oculate	misrate	Sivaite	aconite	modiste	fatigue
adulate	retrate	thwaite	zoonite	batiste	embogue
ululate	citrate	Moabite	kernite	artiste	eclogue
emulate	nitrate	niobite	bornite	riposte	exergue
ovulate	titrate	calcite	reunite	auguste	devalue
stylate	epurate	dulcite	alunite	rabatte	revalue
imamate	irisate	zincite	Rappite	vedette	upvalue
cremate	pulsate	leucite	despite	vidette	sea-blue
sigmate	lactate	brucite	respite	mofette	ice-blue
climate	dictate	Luddite	nacrite	ariette	sky-blue
animate	nictate	lyddite	picrite	aviette	bee-glue
primate	acetate	cordite	eucrite	palette	ingénue
palmate	agitate	erudite	bedrite	ailette	détenue
mammate	imitate	jadeite	thorite	fumette	revenue
gemmate	evitate	Janeite	diorite	genette	detinue
bromate	saltate	turfite	cuprite	dinette	retinue
formate	peltate	tergite	ferrite	minette	macaque
mismate	cantate	zorgite	nitrite	nonette	grecque
plumate	dentate	Cushite	attrite	cunette	cacique
khanate	septate	lithite	azurite	lunette	Salique
emanate	portate	göthite	rewrite	pipette	oblique
cyanate	curtate	bee-kite	unwrite	lorette	relique
phenate	hastate	box-kite	zoisite	burette	silique
crenate	gestate	Baalite	felsite	curette	comique
magnate	restate	Coalite®	Hussite	rosette	repique
cognate	testate	uralite	apatite	musette	perique
spinate	instate	hyalite	tektite	octette	antique
crinate	unstate	Peelite	biotite	bluette	cazique
urinate	costate	spilite	partite	fouetté	bezique
quinate	upstate	mellite	Hittite	navette	baroque
ruinate	vittate	tillite	pittite	cuvette	brusque
tannate	guttate	zeolite	requite	layette	congrue
pennate	scutate	zoolite	pituite	gazette	wall-rue
pinnate	vacuate	hoplite	attuite	cocotte	reissue
connate	arcuate	perlite	Saivite	calotte	habitué
neonate	valuate	thulite	sylvite	culotte	concave
phonate	sinuate	stylite	Servite	garotte	upheave
pronate	liquate	Adamite	bauxite	gavotte	bereave
ternate	actuate	Shemite	zeuxite	tribute	threave
palpate	situate	eremite	vicomte	execute	unreave
scopate	clavate	gummite	andante	elocute	inweave
cuspate	elevate	marmite	infante	confute	unweave
exarate	private	termite	volante	pollute	forgave
librate	valvate	azymite	pesante	evolute	misgave
vibrate	solvate	granite	détente	fat-lute	enclave
picrate	vulvate	uranite	entente	commute	exclave
cedrate	obovate	cyanite	slàinte	permute	beslave
hydrate	larvate	kyanite	hay-bote	veloute	enslave
operate	nervate	pycnite	epidote	compute	beknave
iterate	curvate	Owenite	Samiote	dispute	embrave
regrate	suffete	syenite	promote	embrute	engrave
aggrate	exegete	lignite	unsmote	imbrute	deprave
migrate	machete	gahnite	connote	versute	sea-wave
ingrate	athlete	ichnite	keynote	hirsute	airwave
emirate	deplete	Cainite	unsoote	statute	screeve
evirate	replete	kainite	compote	oophyte	unreeve
odorate	implete	crinite	rewrote	acolyte	achieve
prorate	compete	erinite	myosote		believe

relieve	outmove	midriff	golf-bag	banteng	sliding
scrieve	behoove	sheriff	work-bag	dabbing	voiding
shrieve	reprove	caitiff	musk-bag	nabbing	guiding
khedive	improve	pontiff	mail-bag	webbing	balding
tardive	approve	mastiff	toolbag	dibbing	gelding
deceive	innerve	hand-off	bean-bag	fibbing	welding
receive	unnerve	send-off	tear-bag	jibbing	eilding
forgive	observe	face-off	post-bag	ribbing	gilding
misgive	deserve	enfeoff	grow-bag	bobbing	hilding
outgive	reserve	rake-off	Rigsdag	jobbing	wilding
archive	recurve	take-off	Riksdag	mobbing	folding
beehive	incurve	come-off	fish-fag	robbing	holding
unalive	overawe	long-off	moss-hag	sobbing	banding
mislive	servewe	push-off	peat-hag	cubbing	landing
outlive	survewe	kick-off	time-lag	dubbing	sanding
connive	cracowe	sell-off	grey-lag	rubbing	bending
redrive	leasowe	well-off	tutenag	subbing	lending
on-drive	pole-axe	spin-off	outbrag	tubbing	mending
deprive	pickaxe	turn-off	nose-rag	numbing	pending
suasive	poll-axe	turnoff	dish-rag	daubing	sending
evasive	curtaxe	sawn-off	Landtag	spacing	binding
pensive	good-bye	jump-off	chinwag	bracing	finding
tensive	gang-bye	stop-off	filabeg	tracing	winding
plosive	overdye	left-off	filibeg	slicing	bonding
erosive	dead-eye	lift-off	fanteeg	voicing	funding
corsive	goldeye	cast-off	hindleg	dancing	farding
torsive	blue-eye	show-off	foreleg	fencing	warding
cursive	fisheye	play-off	gateleg	mincing	birding
massive	cockeye	sea-calf	long-leg	wincing	girding
passive	sockeye	law-calf	milk-leg	zincing	cording
fissive	buck-eye	cow-calf	cork-leg	farcing	lording
missive	pink-eye	box-calf	bootleg	beading	wording
jussive	wall-eye	out-half	shoe-peg	heading	feuding
tussive	mill-eye	fly-half	tent-peg	leading	inbeing
abusive	moon-eye	oneself	vent-peg	reading	unbeing
elusive	overeye	himself	thalweg	yeading	fleeing
amusive	cat's-eye	herself	wind-egg	shading	freeing
elative	shut-eye	ourself	nest-egg	loading	lugeing
amative	bumbaze	thyself	shindig	roading	shoeing
stative	spreaze	sea-wolf	goat-fig	trading	blueing
factive	emblaze	rye-wolf	fishgig	gadding	leafing
fictive	mizmaze	warwolf	mail-gig	madding	loafing
caitive	spreeze	werwolf	fizzgig	padding	reefing
unitive	squeeze	thereof	jigajig	wadding	daffing
emotive	trapeze	whereof	pfennig	bedding	gaffing
captive	reseize	Gasthof	long-pig	redding	tiffing
tortive	man-size	shadoof	headrig	tedding	puffing
furtive	capsize	ale-hoof	corn-rig	wedding	golfing
festive	outsize	witloof	periwig	bidding	wolfing
restive	tan-ooze	sun-roof	buzz-wig	kidding	roofing
costive	blintze	reproof	shebang	ridding	surfing
survive	F	hip-roof	lumbang	codding	turfing
midwive	tea-leaf	approof	probang	nodding	staging
fluxive	fig-leaf	bedwarf	sladang	podding	hedging
bivalve	disleaf	saw-kerf	yardang	sodding	wedging
absolve	flyleaf	G	o'ergang	budding	ridging
resolve	cobloaf	flea-bag	sirgang	pudding	lodging
devolve	shereef	grab-bag	endlang	feeding	bagging
revolve	debrief	handbag	siamang	reeding	fagging
involve	cantref	sandbag	trepang	seeding	gagging
sea-dove	engraff	wind-bag	linsang	weeding	jagging
unglove	restaff	game-bag	sea-tang	abiding	lagging
premove	distaff	wine-bag	mustang	chiding	ragging
commove	bailiff	nosebag	ginseng	gliding	sagging

tagging	sea-king	cabling	fooling	rouming	echoing
wagging	shaking	fabling	tooling	souming	heaping
begging	unaking	tabling	sapling	leaning	leaping
legging	soaking	sibling	fopling	meaning	shaping
pegging	quaking	ambling	darling	loaning	keeping
digging	awaking	gadling	harling	opening	weeping
figging	backing	madling	Karling	evening	T'ai-p'ing
jigging	hacking	hidling	marling	haining	sniping
pigging	lacking	kidling	warling	seining	griping
rigging	packing	codling	herling	veining	helping
wigging	racking	godling	merling	shining	yelping
cogging	sacking	feeling	birling	whining	lamping
dogging	tacking	heeling	hirling	coining	tamping
hogging	vacking	keeling	morling	joining	vamping
jogging	decking	peeling	curling	ruining	kemping
logging	necking	reeling	hurling	twining	limping
nogging	pecking	rifling	purling	damning	pimping
sogging	licking	pigling	unsling	limning	jumping
bugging	picking	rigling	gosling	hymning	lumping
hugging	ticking	angling	catling	canning	sloping
jugging	docking	failing	fatling	fanning	looping
lugging	mocking	mailing	kitling	manning	stoping
mugging	rocking	nailing	titling	panning	capping
pugging	arcking	railing	witling	tanning	happing
rugging	bucking	sailing	cutling	vanning	lapping
tugging	ducking	tailing	wauling	kenning	mapping
bulging	fucking	wailing	devling	penning	napping
banging	sucking	ceiling	bawling	dinning	rapping
ganging	reeking	veiling	wawling	ginning	sapping
hanging	balking	smiling	bowling	pinning	tapping
panging	talking	boiling	cowling	sinning	dipping
hinging	walking	foiling	fowling	tinning	hipping
ringing	milking	soiling	howling	winning	lipping
singing	erl-king	toiling	yowling	conning	nipping
tinging	hulking	spiling	beaming	donning	pipping
longing	ranking	oakling	reaming	cunning	ripping
lunging	tanking	inkling	teaming	dunning	sipping
forging	yanking	balling	flaming	funning	tipping
purging	pinking	calling	foaming	gunning	dopping
surging	sinking	falling	framing	punning	hopping
gauging	winking	galling	seeming	running	lopping
miching	zinking	halling	teeming	sunning	mopping
etching	smoking	lalling	Fleming	tunning	popping
ruching	booking	palling	maiming	pioning	sopping
sighing	looking	walling	briming	looning	topping
bashing	carking	gelling	priming	nooning	cupping
dashing	marking	telling	damming	ironing	pupping
lashing	sarking	welling	jamming	darning	supping
mashing	jerking	yelling	lamming	earning	carping
washing	kirking	billing	ramming	warning	warping
meshing	corking	dilling	gemming	horning	gasping
dishing	Dorking	filling	hemming	morning	rasping
fishing	working	killing	lemming	sorning	lisping
wishing	lurking	milling	dimming	burning	bearing
gushing	tasking	tilling	rimming	turning	hearing
pushing	busking	willing	gumming	pruning	searing
lathing	husking	colling	humming	dawning	tearing
nithing	hawking	polling	mumming	fawning	wearing
tithing	scaling	rolling	summing	yawning	charing
Althing	dealing	tolling	booming	undoing	sharing
in-thing	healing	culling	dooming	ingoing	flaring
nothing	sealing	nulling	farming	ongoing	glaring
by-thing	whaling	eanling	warming	upgoing	snaring
peaking	swaling	tanling	forming	bygoing	roaring

soaring	skating	rusting	stewing	war-song	almirah
sparing	plating	batting	showing	art-song	menorah
staring	slating	fatting	flowing	paktong	Masorah
inbring	boating	hatting	glowing	biltong	waratah
upbring	coating	matting	slowing	morwong	cheetah
sacring	doating	patting	knowing	geebung	pooftah
jeering	grating	ratting	growing	cow-dung	pouftah
leering	prating	tatting	stowing	upflung	shittah
veering	meeting	betting	lapwing	unslung	halavah
fairing	weeting	getting	inswing	unwrung	Jehovah
pairing	wafting	letting	upswing	peat-bog	mitzvah
scoring	sifting	netting	outwing	wild-dog	kajawah
shoring	tufting	petting	waxwing	bird-dog	kufiyah
snoring	Lagting	retting	flaying	firedog	genizah
mooring	baiting	setting	fraying	wolf-dog	mezuzah
c-spring	raiting	vetting	praying	hangdog	impeach
barring	waiting	wetting	staying	bulldog	appeach
earring	whiting	fitting	swaying	flip-dog	unteach
jarring	uniting	hitting	rubying	cantdog	toshach
marring	writing	pitting	eddying	megafog	pellach
tarring	quiting	sitting	tidying	road-hog	dorlach
warring	suiting	witting	undying	sand-hog	stomach
herring	halting	dotting	bodying	wart-hog	spinach
firring	malting	jotting	defying	jigajog	cannach
furring	salting	lotting	affying	Tagalog	abroach
purring	belting	potting	belying	catelog	currach
gas-ring	felting	rotting	relying	semilog	screech
G-string	melting	sotting	allying	antilog	beseech
louring	pelting	totting	inlying	backlog	scriech
pouring	tilting	wotting	uplying	hack-log	skriech
souring	bolting	gutting	denying	homolog	toisech
touring	banting	hutting	renying	moorlog	scraich
usuring	canting	jutting	cloying	crannog	nebbich
key-ring	panting	nutting	copying	iceberg	screich
ceasing	wanting	putting	espying	Hamburg	schlich
leasing	tenting	rutting	varying	Homburg	zarnich
teasing	venting	fluting	scrying	quahaug	estrich
biasing	tinting	pouting	burying	gold-bug	ostrich
raising	bunting	routing	busying	firebug	mastich
sensing	hunting	flyting	pitying	rose-bug	distich
rinsing	munting	queuing	untying	pill-bug	squelch
closing	rioting	roguing	levying	hornbug	scranch
prosing	footing	ensuing	revying	ladybug	two-inch
parsing	mooting	heaving	envying	toby-jug	squinch
versing	rooting	leaving	taxying	earplug	craunch
horsing	darting	weaving	glazing	sea-slug	staunch
cursing	karting	shaving	amazing	H	scrunch
gassing	parting	craving	grazing	djibbah	torgoch
passing	sorting	graving	seizing	Pooh-Bah	sea-loch
hissing	basting	skiving	glozing	sahibah	yelloch
missing	casting	driving	boozing	khotbah	raploch
sossing	easting	salving	fizzing	khutbah	pibroch
tossing	fasting	wolving	buzzing	chuddah	endarch
bussing	lasting	proving	pakfong	terefah	triarch
pausing	tasting	stoving	mah-jong	stengah	nomarch
amusing	wasting	carving	up-along	Messiah	monarch
bousing	jesting	serving	endlong	zaptiah	toparch
housing	resting	curving	agelong	Halakah	xerarch
mousing	testing	revving	erelong	Dalilah	mesarch
rousing	vesting	sea-wing	prolong	Delilah	navarch
sousing	westing	thawing	furlong	Mishnah	hexarch
tousing	listing	drawing	daylong	thannah	unperch
beating	misting	viewing	kampong	alannah	goyisch
seating	posting	brewing	pop-song	pitarah	quetsch

7 -SCH

bortsch	eyelash	mud-fish	fullish	boarish	bulrush
ambatch	taplash	ice-fish	gullish	guarish	outrush
upcatch	outlash	raffish	abolish	cherish	Sabbath
bycatch	goulash	toffish	coolish	tigrish	mud-bath
unlatch	quamash	huffish	foolish	fairish	eye-bath
splatch	badmash	hagfish	carlish	whorish	oil-bath
rematch	budmash	pig-fish	girlish	boorish	sun-bath
scratch	gabnash	dogfish	Gaulish	moorish	isobath
stretch	hoop-ash	hog-fish	stylish	poorish	hip-bath
unhitch	Midrash	selfish	beamish	currish	air-bath
scritch	gytrash	wolfish	Rhemish	nourish	beneath
shritch	eye-wash	pinfish	blemish	sourish	unneath
squitch	bagwash	dun-fish	Flemish	falsish	Goliath
bewitch	pigwash	sun-fish	filmish	missish	sea-path
unwitch	hogwash	pupfish	rammish	goatish	warpath
cowitch	Pugwash	garfish	dimmish	Pictish	towpath
splotch	car-wash	oar-fish	rummish	ooftish	breadth
thrutch	dry-wash	serfish	gnomish	softish	turpeth
debauch	enflesh	catfish	Suomish	whitish	listeth
scrauch	unflesh	net-fish	alumish	British	wotteth
debouch	refresh	saw-fish	planish	saltish	twelfth
retouch	nebbish	jewfish	Spanish	coltish	alength
cleruch	bobbish	cowfish	evanish	doltish	youngth
nonsuch	hobbish	haggish	Rhenish	Kentish	unfaith
diptych	mobbish	waggish	plenish	runtish	turbith
ceilidh	cubbish	biggish	roinish	tartish	trilith
khotbeh	rubbish	jiggish	brinish	fastish	tallith
zabtieh	tubbish	piggish	swinish	cattish	neolith
zaptieh	Sorbish	riggish	mannish	fattish	zoolith
sakiyeh	furbish	doggish	wannish	rattish	urolith
spreagh	tea-dish	hoggish	fennish	pettish	otolith
curragh	baddish	muggish	wennish	meltith	
skriegh	caddish	puggish	Finnish	wettish	outwith
scraigh	faddish	longish	donnish	hottish	stealth
screigh	Kaddish	largish	tonnish	sottish	greenth
skreigh	Qaddish	highish	dunnish	ruttish	seventh
inveigh	saddish	hashish	Hunnish	loutish	dozenth
reweigh	reddish	snakish	nunnish	brutish	jacinth
sky-high	Yiddish	peckish	moonish	beauish	Corinth
ard-righ	piedish	sickish	dronish	anguish	absinth
simurgh	Swedish	buckish	garnish	roguish	Sabaoth
scraugh	maidish	puckish	tarnish	voguish	Succoth
through	baldish	dankish	varnish	slavish	Sukkoth
enrough	wildish	pinkish	kernish	knavish	bee-moth
unrough	coldish	monkish	Cornish	peevish	pug-moth
borough	goldish	bookish	hornish	wolvish	owl-moth
Pharaoh	Wendish	rookish	burnish	dervish	mammoth
right-oh	tun-dish	darkish	furnish	slowish	wax-moth
billy-oh	goodish	larkish	townish	snowish	insooth
digraph	hardish	parkish	roynish	clayish	betroth
epitaph	wordish	Yorkish	dampish	babyish	matzoth
acaleph	Kurdish	murkish	gampish	ladyish	in-depth
triumph	loudish	Turkish	vampish	wheyish	inearth
galumph	prudish	duskish	wampish	greyish	unearth
dimorph	niceish	luskish	rompish	fogyish	rebirth
diglyph	fineish	hawkish	dumpish	'Arryish	ungirth
catarrh	ogreish	mawkish	lumpish	Romansh	hap'orth
earbash	moreish	publish	mumpish	baboosh	unworth
kurbash	doveish	English	Lappish	ale-bush	azimuth
wood-ash	sea-fish	hellish	hippish	rag-bush	bismuth
burdash	lubfish	rellish	foppish	tarbush	uncouth
unleash	tubfish	dollish	waspish	ivy-bush	bemouth
bone-ash	redfish	bullish	bearish	outgush	untruth
dobhash	codfish	dullish	wearish	unflush	'strewth

acolyth	tsunami	K	rollick	rullock	pin-tuck
sun-myth	macrami	offpeak	cowlick	hemlock	bestuck
I	gourami	bespeak	gimmick	Wenlock	unstuck
assagai	Lakshmi	respeak	mimmick	gun-lock	mid-week
assegai	jamdani	unspeak	pannick	hoolock	man-week
ghilgai	Zingani	upspeak	Kennick	hip-lock	rooinek
didakai	anziani	inbreak	minnick	carlock	olykoek
remblai	jampani	to-break	dornick	earlock	souslik
quillai	timpani	upbreak	ice-pick	oar-lock	dvornik
samurai	Guaraní	muntjak	rampick	warlock	beatnik
Panjabi	guarani	tokamak	earpick	air-lock	sputnik
Punjabi	soprani	yashmak	nit-pick	fetlock	outtalk
syllabi	biryani	live-oak	derrick	putlock	cat-walk
bilimbi	sordini	cork-oak	patrick	rowlock	outwalk
thrombi	crimini	uncloak	hayrick	laylock	jaywalk
succubi	termini	holm-oak	seasick	Shylock	ewe-milk
menisci	amorini	champak	dogsick	schmock	oil-silk
effendi	martini	nunatak	car-sick	gammock	jap-silk
étourdi	pulvini	dieback	airsick	hammock	sea-folk
dinky-di	Karenni	hogback	fossick	mammock	menfolk
glutaei	rabboni	finback	pot-sick	hommock	kinfolk
caducei	Marconi	setback	bedtick	bummock	merfolk
didakei	epigoni	wetback	dog-tick	hummock	Norfolk
sarangi	padroni	cutback	schtick	mummock	cot-folk
gnocchi	canzoni	outback	bestick	bannock	sea-bank
kamichi	pronaoi	layback	unstick	jannock	fog-bank
elenchi	rhomboi	oomiack	lustick	finnock	pot-bank
rhonchi	didicoi	manjack	outwick	minnock	cab-rank
bronchi	stichoi	skyjack	kebbock	pinnock	disrank
Baluchi	pindari	pellack	meacock	winnock	outrank
nuraghi	sundari	pollack	peacock	dunnock	gas-tank
Marathi	Zingari	cromack	sea-cock	bedrock	ratfink
bacchii	shikari	finnack	bibcock	defrock	bethink
nauplii	Campari	mudpack	gorcock	unfrock	methink
basenji	saouari	icepack	petcock	tarrock	rethink
mono-ski	alizari	prepack	bawcock	sourock	unthink
zakuski	colibri	calpack	dawcock	cassock	prejink
astatki	chondri	six-pack	haycock	hassock	perjink
Zincali	kacheri	barrack	shy-cock	lassock	dislink
Bengali	Lyomeri	carrack	daddock	tussock	sea-pink
serkali	Cabeiri	hatrack	haddock	castock	ice-rink
hallali	saimiri	amtrack	paddock	restock	chewink
woorali	venturi	ransack	piddock	unstock	eye-wink
wourali	pachisi	hopsack	puddock	custock	undrunk
Israeli	reversi	Cossack	ruddock	hattock	sjambok
sondeli	uva-ursi	subtack	candock	mattock	stembok
Ismaili	molossi	tietack	windock	bittock	blesbok
gingili	Senussi	tin-tack	hordock	buttock	gemsbok
Swahili	chapati	unstack	burdock	futtock	grysbok
jinjili	chupati	Purbeck	wet-dock	puttock	blaubok
nautili	Bharati	sun-deck	dry-dock	garvock	bloubok
vitelli	dakoiti	recheck	unblock	kebbuck	angekok
bacilli	emeriti	uncheck	padlock	roebuck	red-book
lapilli	wistiti	redneck	wedlock	jumbuck	rag-book
bouilli	oustiti	ewe-neck	daglock	hawbuck	log-book
Osmanli	Chianti	wryneck	schlock	saw-buck	boobook
alveoli	démenti	rye-peck	pellock	sea-duck	law-book
ravioli	alfaquí	henpeck	hillock	heyduck	day-book
tripoli	charqui	conteck	killock	ill-luck	flybook
sacculi	Pahlavi	maffick	sillock	misluck	sea-cook
calculi	Pehlevi	Gothick	pollock	pot-luck	precook
stimuli	neo-Nazi	fly-kick	rollock	schmuck	man-cook
origami	Jacuzzi ®	niblick	bullock	Calmuck	olycook
thalami		killick	mullock	Kalmuck	bandook

bundook	dorhawk	oatmeal	trivial	puberal	clausal
mud-hook	goshawk	nut-meal	eluvial	bederal	accusal
eyehook	bashlyk	balneal	fluvial	federal	excusal
pothook	L	corneal	pluvial	hederal	refusal
nut-hook	wadmaal	clypeal	exuvial	sideral	spousal
wet-look	nagmaal	glareal	abaxial	ruderal	arousal
outlook	kursaal	Floréal	adaxial	spheral	perusal
schnook	scribal	surreal	biaxial	scleral	palatal
chinook	Isiacal	deiseal	coaxial	cameral	edictal
forsook	cloacal	tar-seal	epaxial	gomeral	proctal
partook	caracal	fur-seal	brinjal	humeral	vegetal
mistook	cubical	lacteal	decimal	numeral	gametal
tan-bark	radical	gluteal	minimal	general	tapetal
disbark	medical	pluteal	optimal	mineral	orbital
futhark	nodical	illegal	maximal	funeral	cubital
meal-ark	magical	peregal	thermal	lateral	recital
sea-lark	logical	epochal	miasmal	literal	digital
mudlark	ethical	trochal	seismal	enteral	comital
titlark	helical	paschal	abysmal	apteral	somital
skylark	mimical	burghal	decanal	several	genital
seamark	comical	nymphal	bimanal	enthral	capital
cup-mark	domical	marshal	tetanal	admiral	marital
earmark	finical	gnathal	lumenal	retiral	unvital
daymark	conical	narwhal	hymenal	sudoral	quantal
waymark	cynical	stibial	adrenal	preoral	edental
carpark	stoical	cambial	arsenal	chloral	amental
dispark	topical	glacial	juvenal	femoral	omental
bulwark	typical	spacial	vicinal	nemoral	trental
hauberk	lyrical	special	ordinal	immoral	quintal
berserk	vesical	asocial	paginal	unmoral	frontal
Dunkirk	musical	fascial	vaginal	humoral	pivotal
pit-mirk	optical	faucial	reginal	caporal	cryptal
hayfork	lexical	crucial	anginal	sororal	coastal
futhork	toxical	trucial	feminal	auroral	borstal
ribwork	truncal	predial	seminal	mayoral	crustal
bedwork	bifocal	iridial	liminal	central	crystal
die-work	unvocal	mondial	nominal	ventral	quittal
dye-work	decadal	sundial	luminal	castral	glottal
ragwork	creedal	alodial	shrinal	oestral	abuttal
legwork	bemedal	cordial	matinal	vestral	refutal
all-work	bipedal	syzgial	actinal	mistral	gradual
lapwork	amygdal	rachial	retinal	rostral	subdual
network	geoidal	lochial	equinal	austral	lingual
artwork	ovoidal	ischial	umbonal	lustral	cornual
outwork	apsidal	pallial	digonal	neutral	unequal
tutwork	co-tidal	gremial	ammonal	dextral	coequal
waxwork	fluidal	cranial	coronal	elytral	rorqual
day-work	scandal	somnial	bitonal	pleural	accrual
gas-mask	poundal	hernial	bizonal	figural	censual
dismask	synodal	gharial	eternal	augural	mensual
pay-desk	chordal	diarial	sternal	hypural	sensual
key-desk	acaudal	decrial	diurnal	natural	pursual
sun-disk	paludal	pairial	journal	sutural	unusual
odalisk	conceal	uxorial	lacunal	satyral	factual
obelisk	unideal	cerrial	sea-coal	phrasal	tactual
sea-risk	irideal	patrial	gas-coal	uprisal	victual
lentisk	misdeal	retrial	pit-coal	devisal	obitual
subfusk	epigeal	spatial	day-coal	revisal	virtual
mollusk	congeal	initial	Oedipal	sponsal	textual
putchuk	apogeal	nuptial	frampal	deposal	asexual
chabouk	oscheal	martial	ectypal	reposal	octaval
chibouk	allheal	partial	membral	exposal	salival
Volapük	nucleal	tertial	diedral	glossal	co-rival
sea-hawk	disleal	bestial	liberal	abyssal	arrival

datival	colonel	trysail	scissil	tassell	bandrol
revival	grapnel	bobtail	apostil	outsell	control
removal	charnel	tag-tail	jonquil	nousell	parasol
renewal	scalpel	wagtail	Pasquil	Kartell	girasol
bathyal	stempel	pigtail	bedevil	mistell	aerosol
unroyal	graupel	fantail	fox-evil	outtell	girosol
quetzal	apparel	pintail	uncivil	knevell	Capitol
Ishmael	cambrel	curtail	chervil	spa-well	Bristol
Jezebel	gambrel	rat-tail	oddball	indwell	bepearl
decibel	timbrel	fox-tail	cue-ball	inkwell	impearl
limacel	wimbrel	travail	eyeball	oil-well	ensnarl
radicel	tumbrel	prevail	pinball	gas-well	unsnarl
pedicel	mandrel	codicil	proball	upswell	busgirl
chancel	haverel	domicil	patball	outwell	cowgirl
spancel	doggrel	stencil	netball	maxwell	day-girl
lioncel	gangrel	council	miscall	twibill	upwhirl
tiercel	langrel	Bobadil	catcall	saw-bill	Nahuatl
citadel	mongrel	dysodil	hold-all	wax-bill	axolotl
infidel	quarrel	corbeil	cure-all	pay-bill	outhaul
roundel	poitrel	vermeil	save-all	way-bill	box-haul
remodel	wastrel	conseil	ice-fall	wrybill	saksaul
strudel	kestrel	monofil	misfall	ice-hill	caracul
sand-eel	costrel	strigil	pitfall	ant-hill	deedful
tar-heel	custrel	lyophil	outfall	pug-mill	heedful
enwheel	dottrel	dika-oil	jawfall	oil-mill	needful
cowheel	handsel	crab-oil	dew-fall	saw-mill	handful
log-reel	nainsel'	gumboil	oak-gall	pennill	mindful
hair-eel	counsel	garboil	gingall	athrill	foodful
manteel	damosel	parboil	cupgall	moor-ill	tubeful
genteel	chessel	seed-oil	nut-gall	bestill	bodeful
unsteel	tressel	wood-oil	lack-all	distill	gleeful
falafel	scissel	bone-oil	heal-all	instill	lifeful
felafel	floatel	rape-oil	overall	drevill	rageful
evangel	pointel	trefoil	hersall	ill-will	wakeful
tinchel	Prestel®	milfoil	install	rag-doll	pokeful
hatchel	chattel	tinfoil	sea-wall	wax-doll	baleful
satchel	prequel	jetfoil	cob-wall	wadmoll	taleful
notchel	caravel	sexfoil	gadwall	redpoll	wileful
futchel	unravel	long-oil	know-all	escroll	doleful
burrhel	shrivel	tung-oil	setwall	bed-roll	wameful
brothel	bejewel	fish-oil	witwall	rye-roll	baneful
farthel	embowel	rock-oil	out-wall	log-roll	tuneful
Zadkiel	stanyel	coal-oil	fog-bell	pay-roll	pipeful
spaniel	damozel	tall-oil	bar-bell	topfull	hopeful
staniel	pretzel	wool-oil	air-bell	dewfull	careful
ba'spiel	jeofail	palm-oil	cowbell	seagull	dareful
snorkel	abigail	turmoil	low-bell	leg-pull	direful
caramel	all-hail	poon-oil	egg-cell	caracol	dureful
trammel	air-mail	despoil	air-cell	gasahol	easeful
stammel	hobnail	embroil	wet-cell	alcohol	museful
trommel	toe-nail	hair-oil	sex-cell	gasohol	fateful
stummel	trenail	deasoil	dry-cell	myrrhol	hateful
calomel	pedrail	subsoil	misfell	menthol	gazeful
oenomel	engrail	top-soil	enshell	vitriol	mazeful
caromel	air-rail	nombril	inshell	ethanol	loofful
columel	vitrail	tumbril	unshell	xylenol	songful
empanel	entrail	mandril	fannell	Guignol	sighful
impanel	lugsail	tendril	respell	orcinol	bashful
unpanel	topsail	gomeril	unspell	retinol	gashful
spignel	vassail	imperil	carrell	jambool	dishful
channel	wassail	scurril	borrell	damfool	fishful
flannel	vessail	testril	lorrell	tomfool	wishful
stannel	outsail	nostril	burrell	rag-wool	pushful
chunnel	skysail	utensil	woosell	fusarol	pithful

ruthful	fern-owl	legitim	upswarm	tachism	Pittism
pitiful	dismayl	shittim	exoderm	tychism	babuism
dutiful	spondyl	oil-palm	sea-term	Sikhism	Slavism
sackful	cacodyl	dum-palm	mid-term	sophism	atavism
lockful	kakodyl	wax-palm	preterm	Orphism	Saivism
tankful	diethyl	wych-elm	non-term	mythism	Fauvism
bookful	prothyl	dishelm	misterm	Babiism	Marxism
sarkful	benzoyl	rock-elm	confirm	Sufiism	bruxism
workful	dibutyl	rhabdom	zoeform	Naziism	ladyism
riskful	M	freedom	preform	Baalism	bogyism
zealful	macadam	dukedom	difform	realism	fogyism
vialful	milldam	popedom	aciform	dualism	zanyism
pailful	grandam	boredom	deiform	myalism	copyism
wailful	quondam	serfdom	uniform	Zoilism	Toryism
skilful	holydam	kingdom	triform	idolism	hummaum
toilful	tie-beam	halidom	aviform	wholism	plumbum
soulful	eye-beam	dolldom	oviform	Carlism	modicum
teemful	sun-beam	earldom	conform	odylism	Panicum
brimful	amalgam	filmdom	perform	chemism	offscum
palmful	whangam	hobodom	disform	animism	popadum
doomful	trangam	tsardom	misform	Thomism	smeddum
roomful	polygam	stardom	bestorm	atomism	solidum
harmful	brecham	czardom	sea-worm	cosmism	notaeum
moanful	beef-ham	heirdom	webworm	pianism	Hordeum
gainful	gingham	babudom	lobworm	onanism	vitreum
painful	mashlam	Slavdom	ice-worm	uranism	sorghum
skinful	Surinam	fogydom	ragworm	Owenism	stibium
dernful	grannam	envenom	lugworm	Jainism	cambium
hornful	sea-foam	jib-boom	eelworm	donnism	niobium
skepful	findram	predoom	cutworm	peonism	terbium
shipful	wolfram	rebloom	maw-worm	lionism	calcium
helpful	diagram	embloom	dew-worm	Zionism	stadium
shopful	anagram	begloom	sarcasm	hoboism	taedium
cropful	epigram	engloom	Syriasm	echoism	uredium
fearful	trigram	sea-room	fantasm	heroism	iridium
tearful	pangram	tea-room	Sabaism	Titoism	rhodium
tactful	tangram	bedroom	Dadaism	tropism	alodium
fretful	grogram	legroom	Judaism	utopism	spodium
tentful	program	gunroom	Bahaism	charism	erodium
plotful	isogram	taproom	Zolaism	tsarism	plagium
hurtful	myogram	bar-room	Lamaism	czarism	elogium
mastful	lockram	boxroom	Mosaism	diorism	ischium
jestful	buckram	diadrom	Sivaism	amorism	lithium
pestful	mantram	chrisom	Arabism	entrism	pythium
restful	gopuram	transom	Hobbism	heurism	Krilium®
zestful	flotsam	embosom	cambism	tourism	ballium
fistful	ramstam	imbosom	phobism	sensism	gallium
listful	misdeem	unbosom	etacism	Parsism	pallium
mistful	misseem	blossom	itacism	Persism	thulium
wistful	epithem	subatom	Grecism	statism	cadmium
gustful	requiem	Euratom	epicism	tactism	premium
lustful	problem	phantom	fascism	pietism	holmium
playful	phellem	symptom	faddism	cretism	fermium
trayful	theorem	yard-arm	Luddism	leftism	alumium
preyful	microhm	free-arm	Mahdism	elitism	cranium
deasiul	acclaim	tone-arm	maidism	elitism	uranium
karakul	declaim	fire-arm	phaeism	cultism	rhenium
bradawl	reclaim	forearm	fideism	Comtism	hafnium
asprawl	exclaim	fee-farm	atheism	Kantism	muonium
red-cowl	mashlim	becharm	asteism	Scotism	oxonium
wood-owl	Thummim	encharm	Couéism	egotism	zoarium
pea-fowl	interim	uncharm	selfism	photism	orarium
sea-fowl	Isegrim	rein-arm	imagism	erotism	Librium®
lich-owl	pilgrim	overarm	leggism	baptism	thorium

natrium	synonym	costean	Iranian	headman	bellman
yttrium	toponym	sarafan	Uranian	roadman	billman
caesium	paronym	yatagan	Owenian	landman	pollman
Elysium	acronym	Mohegan	Johnian	sandman	tollman
tritium	metonym	wanigan	Lemnian	bondman	Pullman
protium	antonym	clachan	aeonian	goodman	woolman
trivium	autonym	tulchan	Etonian	hoodman	dawn-man
eluvium	N	brochan	Oxonian	woodman	gownman
trankum	Caliban	barchan	salpian	yardman	locoman
trinkum	soroban	ataghan	utopian	herdman	kroo-man
hoodlum	exurban	barkhan	acarian	spaeman	Ottoman
mashlum	Yoruban	darshan	Icarian	faceman	unwoman
skellum	baracan	urethan	diarian	lace-man	chapman
chillum	Senecan	Achaian	orarian	gude-man	shipman
egg-plum	indican	Cataian	ovarian	gleeman	shopman
hog-plum	Mohican	Arabian	Umbrian	freeman	star-man
pabulum	pelican	Tsabian	Locrian	wakeman	overman
seculum	pemican	ouabian	Iberian	pikeman	door-man
osculum	African	Hobbian	Pierian	sokeman	moorman
minimum	Vatican	Grobian	cyprian	isleman	mobsman
optimum	Mexican	Serbian	Nitrian	lineman	gadsman
maximum	coon-can	Sorbian	saurian	fireman	oddsman
arcanum	stew-can	lesbian	etesian	wire-man	rodsman
ladanum	Ramadan	Grecian	Capsian	foreman	magsman
organum	graddan	Apician	Jersian	byreman	alms-man
solanum	yakhdan	Arician	Persian	baseman	kinsman
fraenum	oppidan	Roscian	hessian	caseman	tapsman
sternum	souldan	crucian	Rissian	hoseman	topsman
jejunum	Sabaean	Acadian	Russian	gateman	oarsman
pantoum	Nicaean	iridian	crusian	trueman	passman
labarum	Judaean	pridian	Drusian	caveman	batsman
fulcrum	Achaean	suidian	Elysian	surfman	artsman
humdrum	Sinaean	Ovidian	Raetian	turfman	newsman
eardrum	sea-bean	Rhodian	Noetian	drag-man	daysman
war-drum	bogbean	Wardian	Comtian	swagman	meat-man
Lythrum	Niobean	Gordian	Kantian	yeggman	peatman
decorum	lyncean	Hygeian	gentian	hangman	boatman
tantrum	Circean	Peneian	Laotian	ringman	raftman
centrum	Joycean	saffian	Scotian	songman	maltman
rastrum	subdean	ruffian	Grotian	frogman	mint-man
oestrum	Pandean	Wolfian	Martian	Brahman	footman
sistrum	Vendean	Belgian	tertian	highman	mootman
nostrum	Mazdean	Jungian	fustian	bushman	portman
rostrum	epigean	Vosgian	Shavian	heliman	postman
lustrum	apogean	Ogygian	Flavian	Ahriman	dustman
elytrum	Vosgean	Stygian	Sylvian	taximan	text-man
grassum	Orphean	Paphian	Servian	jackman	decuman
opossum	lethean	orthian	Latvian	packman	inhuman
alyssum	unclean	Pythian	Marxian	sick-man	unhuman
pomatum	spelean	Lockian	Zeuxian	lockman	hanuman
erratum	Zoilean	idalian	Günzian	milkman	showman
stratum	Cadmean	thalian	Harijan	silk-man	snowman
sanctum	pigmean	Uralian	oolakan	linkman	Manxman
punctum	pygmean	Italian	oulakan	junkman	drayman
pinetum	Linnean	Anglian	Catalan	bookman	bogy-man
tapetum	lernean	Azilian	gamelan	jarkman	juryman
quantum	Aetnean	hallian	challan	markman	jazzman
amentum	pampean	Tullian	Trullan	workman	dipnoan
omentum	Zairean	aeolian	ortolan	Turkman	epizoan
scrotum	taurean	Paulian	Gosplan	meal-man	catapan
frustum	azurean	Permian	courlan	coalman	dead-pan
triduum	Hulsean	vermian	Ameslan	keelman	skidpan
trionym	Dantean	Wormian	sagaman	mailman	hard-pan
homonym	protean	Würmian	clubman	railman	knee-pan

firepan	has-been	chicken	smarten	certain	finikin
iron-pan	crubeen	thicken	shorten	pertain	minikin
harn-pan	good-e'en	slicken	chasten	curtain	cutikin
moor-pan	arsheen	bricken	guesten	abstain	barmkin
outspan	potheen	quicken	glisten	bestain	simpkin
salt-pan	buckeen	slocken	moisten	distain	bumpkin
dust-pan	nankeen	drucken	bursten	sustain	lumpkin
stewpan	colleen	sleeken	whatten	vervain	pumpkin
Saharan	terreen	drunken	flatten	corn-bin	gherkin
foreran	kamseen	ywroken	spitten	Jacobin	redskin
cateran	fifteen	betoken	written	dust-bin	kid-skin
Lateran	canteen	hearken	twitten	turacin	doe-skin
veteran	umpteen	starken	shotten	salicin	pigskin
Alcoran	posteen	brisken	grutten	tunicin	dogskin
Alkoran	ratteen	woollen	stouten	sericin	hog-skin
also-ran	sixteen	swollen	odd-even	gliadin	griskin
sierran	unqueen	sudamen	enliven	baladin	oilskin
overran	misween	velamen	shriven	paladin	kip-skin
sporran	between	foramen	thriven	mueddin	catskin
Fortran	stiffen	duramen	enriven	acridin	sow-skin
dextran	mutagen	putamen	unriven	speldin	doitkin
artisan	smidgen	dead-men	striven	in-and-in	ladykin
medusan	trudgen	freemen	inwoven	stand-in	ptyalin
Tibetan	twiggen	foremen	unwoven	hirudin	quiblin
shaitan	lucigen	highmen	strawen	trade-in	quodlin
capitan	mucigen	regimen	bedizen	hordein	maudlin
puritan	antigen	molimen	denizen	nuclein	Gobelin
quintan	endogen	hillmen	citizen	villein	ermelin
Spartan	halogen	abdomen	bronzen	mullein	capelin
quartan	xylogen	agnomen	impregn	phone-in	javelin
Avestan	humogen	shipmen	deraign	therein	ravelin
capstan	zymogen	footmen	arraign	wherein	hafflin
Laputan	acrogen	albumen	condign	write-in	mafflin
triduan	kerogen	cacumen	foreign	protein	halflin
Mantuan	pyrogen	cerumen	realign	drive-in	Mechlin
caravan	cryogen	bitumen	consign	xerafin	mashlin
Genevan	röntgen	jurymen	sky-sign	griffin	phallin
Heshvan	loxygen	flannen	Mas-John	beaufin	gremlin
mail-van	beechen	cheapen	Mes-John	smidgin	kremlin
corn-van	larchen	steepen	disdain	sloe-gin	drumlin
Chesvan	Märchen	bull-pen	bargain	Scoggin	etiolin
cob-swan	birchen	plumpen	enchain	lying-in	lanolin
Malayan	kitchen	shippen	unchain	spongin	cipolin
Catayan	witchen	sharpen	villain	teach-in	complin
mista'en	leuchen	play-pen	explain	kinchin	pearlin
Saracen	leughen	greisen	murlain	weigh-in	eastlin
unladen	roughen	samisen	unslain	tanghin	westlin
broaden	toughen	unrisen	germain	delphin	rattlin
gladden	cain-hen	uprisen	gas-main	dolphin	littlin
abidden	moorhen	coarsen	refrain	dauphin	lupulin
chidden	freshen	hoarsen	engrain	xanthin	torulin
slidden	harshen	glassen	ingrain	break-in	insulin
good-den	heathen	Meissen	darrain	ramakin	patulin
trodden	writhen	wheaten	terrain	canakin	prawlin
asudden	earthen	uneaten	murrain	manakin	thiamin
studden	burthen	greaten	detrain	lambkin	vitamin
Wealden	wrythen	sweeten	retrain	brodkin	Brahmin
standen	anywhen	quieten	vitrain	lordkin	adermin
bounden	greyhen	unoften	entrain	bawdkin	plasmin
stooden	betaken	lighten	up-train	ramekin	albumin
Dresden	retaken	righten	uptrain	wolfkin	legumin
sarsden	untaken	tighten	huitain	bodikin	melanin
shebeen	blacken	moulten	contain	canikin	meconin
gombeen	bracken	hearten	captain	manikin	saponin

opsonin	Pasquin	Pandion	abusion	raccoon	neutron
subjoin	Angevin	semeion	elusion	puccoon	elytron
conjoin	chauvin	pereion	elation	bridoon	fleuron
disjoin	bedawin	E-region	enation	cardoon	pleuron
misjoin	Baldwin	fashion	oration	lardoon	chevron
sirloin	throw-in	cushion	station	buffoon	treason
purloin	relaxin	fushion	ovation	dragoon	good-son
surloin	hoatzin	sea-lion	faction	jargoon	wheeson
fibroin	muezzin	obelion	paction	typhoon	name-son
ligroin	goddamn	hallion	taction	balloon	pi-meson
benzoin	condemn	hellion	lection	galloon	mu-meson
jalapin	contemn	billion	rection	Walloon	waveson
nine-pin	dislimn	gillion	section	midnoon	liaison
fivepin	birlinn	million	diction	lampoon	malison
king-pin	bourbon	pillion	fiction	pompoon	benison
inchpin	limaçon	zillion	miction	harpoon	venison
push-pin	Comecon	bullion	unction	gadroon	cloison
hook-pin	rubicon	cullion	coction	godroon	parison
sculpin	Vidicon ®	mullion	auction	patroon	warison
skulpin	silicon	rullion	ruction	monsoon	keelson
galopin	sericon	skolion	suction	gorsoon	stemson
atropin	lexicon	ant-lion	edition	bassoon	crimson
hairpin	soupçon	exomion	unition	gossoon	chanson
leg-spin	celadon	fermion	coition	platoon	sponson
crispin	Abaddon	franion	tuition	pultoon	stepson
topspin	gladdon	opinion	cantion	pontoon	caisson
tent-pin	yealdon	wannion	mention	cartoon	frisson
stearin	abandon	munnion	emotion	festoon	Stetson
tamarin	mylodon	runnion	caption	testoon	blouson
cumarin	Monodon	ternion	emption	madzoon	sabaton
heparin	guerdon	reunion	portion	epizoon	megaton
Patarin	bourdon	grunion	bastion	matzoon	phaeton
navarin	Corydon	campion	caution	crampon	exciton
savarin	peraeon	lampion	elution	metopon	Honiton
atabrin	Actaeon	rampion	mixtion	shippon	positon
atebrin	pidgeon	tampion	flexion	croupon	kirkton
suberin	widgeon	pompion	fluxion	sit-upon	Stilton
poperin	dudgeon	tompion	knock-on	megaron	fronton
roper-in	gudgeon	pumpion	enfelon	omicron	daunton
chagrin	dungeon	clarion	echelon	caldron	crypton
glairin	burgeon	orarion	mamelon	puldron	krypton
aspirin	murgeon	alerion	mouflon	dendron	ribston
taborin	surgeon	pterion	epsilon	tendron	neuston
dextrin	nucleon	chorion	upsilon	caudron	fletton
aneurin	galleon	carrion	ypsilon	enderon	foot-ton
cerasin	thereon	morrion	Aquilon	Acheron	glutton
ceresin	whereon	erasion	shallon	aileron	croûton
emulsin	chiffon	suasion	moellon	moneron	baryton
khamsin	griffon	evasion	paillon	hyperon	hard-won
erepsin	decagon	elision	quillon	enteron	well-won
trypsin	nonagon	mansion	eidolon	saffron	triaxon
poussin	paragon	pension	salamon	nephron	monaxon
gelatin	octagon	tension	telamon	pea-iron	spray-on
keratin	hexagon	plosion	kirimon	sad-iron	halcyon
wood-tin	perigon	erosion	norimon	andiron	Procyon
built-in	fourgon	mersion	musimon	endiron	tachyon
carotin	polygon	tersion	Solomon	leg-iron	hallyon
elastin	ulichon	version	kikumon	pig-iron	embryon
mess-tin	torchon	torsion	organon	bog-iron	carry-on
volutin	sorehon	passion	hebenon	bar-iron	borazon
penguin	gryphon	cession	chignon	environ	horizon
pinguin	Brython	session	lorgnon	tow-iron	tridarn
bedouin	Erewhon	fission	actinon	box-iron	unlearn
sagouin	symbion	mission	chronon	isotron	forwarn

concern	vulturn	guanaco	heigh-ho	Gestapo	fagotto
discern	outturn	huanaco	navarho	plenipo	arnotto
ice-fern	turndun	touraco	tally-ho	up-tempo	risotto
oak-fern	hand-gun	tobacco	braccio	Zingaro	Kotytto
salfern	wind-gun	squacco	senecio	saguaro	cornuto
cithern	unbegun	barocco	papilio	piffero	centavo
zithern	time-gun	sirocco	rosolio	budgero	relievo
stonern	punt-gun	morocco	scorpio	non-hero	rilievo
lampern	shotgun	Tampico	etaerio	arriero	eightvo
lectern	blowgun	barrico	cheerio	zanjero	zemstvo
saltern	thick'un	patrico	histrio	primero	mestizo
lantern	pronoun	persico	azulejo	llanero	scherzo
eastern	hard-run	cantico	finnsko	pampero	P
pastern	forerun	portico	cembalo	padrero	knee-cap
testern	milk-run	mistico	cymbalo	pedrero	bluecap
western	overrun	Tabasco ®	Zincalo	patrero	huff-cap
yestern	Whitsun	tedesco	beefalo	brasero	half-cap
cistern	vingt-un	Moresco	buffalo	montero	flat-cap
postern	mash-tun	Morisco	bummalo	vaquero	root-cap
pattern	sun-dawn	gambado	cattalo	subzero	snowcap
bittern	suppawn	avocado	tangelo	allegro	ash-heap
cittern	indrawn	soldado	pompelo	zamarro	outleap
gittern	updrawn	mockado	morello	electro	stop-gap
silvern	unshewn	scalado	zorillo	maestro	mud-flap
sea-born	rubdown	tornado	criollo	so-and-so	eye-flap
misborn	lie-down	downa-do	diabolo	whereso	earflap
newborn	hoedown	passado	tombolo	chamiso	fly-flap
low-born	hagdown	crusado	piccolo	proviso	shiplap
skyborn	run-down	pintado	zoccolo	giocoso	overlap
rye-corn	sundown	bravado	zuffolo	mafioso	road-map
unicorn	let-down	privado	tremolo	furioso	star-map
tricorn	set-down	torpedo	nathemo	oloroso	genipap
pilcorn	sitdown	bushido	supremo	amoroso	caltrap
popcorn	put-down	calando	proximo	calypso	mantrap
coehorn	low-down	virando	verismo	reverso	suntrap
leghorn	sea-gown	morendo	Meccano ®	marcato	dip-trap
bighorn	tea-gown	secondo	chicano	sfumato	air-trap
foghorn	rug-gown	underdo	secondo	vibrato	gas-trap
Kuh-horn	disgown	testudo	volcano	agitato	unstrap
inkhorn	unshown	howdy-do	oregano	forzato	rat-trap
alphorn	unblown	lumbago	Zingano	stand-to	fox-trap
dishorn	upblown	Chicago	timpano	Orvieto	fly-trap
unshorn	new-mown	long-ago	pompano	magneto	wine-sap
althorn	beknown	viliago	tympano	thereto	wiretap
saxhorn	unknown	smarago	soprano	whereto	heel-tap
forlorn	embrown	farrago	Marrano	Peshito	lip-deep
May-morn	imbrown	sapsago	paisano	hornito	outpeep
sea-worn	decrown	serpigo	ripieno	Negrito	day-peep
woeworn	uncrown	porrigo	bambino	coquito	ensteep
war-worn	ingrown	prurigo	gradino	Appalto	ensweep
forworn	ungrown	lentigo	rondino	sciolto	upsweep
unsworn	upgrown	tentigo	tondino	ailanto	outweep
outworn	dogtown	vertigo	sordino	coranto	bee-skep
wayworn	Miltown	hidalgo	pianino	memento	parsnep
sunburn	cottown	embargo	volpino	pimento	demirep
outburn	darrayn	botargo	amorino	steep-to	onestep
mowburn	homelyn	albergo	cassino	esparto	two-step
cothurn	O	undergo	madroño	impasto	misstep
adjourn	curaçao	ferrugo	inferno	mulatto	outstep
rejourn	peekabo	hollaho	bugaboo	annatto	rose-hip
sojourn	placebo	malicho	manchoo	nonetto	sibship
sea-turn	nelumbo	Jericho	samshoo	stretto	midship
nocturn	theorbo	broncho	shampoo	cavetto	end-ship
ill-turn	viliaco	smoke-ho	Pushtoo	ridotto	godship

ludship	outcrop	stuck-up	sun-bear	pilular	knobber
dogship	eye-drop	snarl-up	forbear	hamular	swobber
log-ship	gumdrop	clean-up	ant-bear	ramular	blubber
kinship	eardrop	grown-up	low-gear	simular	slubber
donship	wardrop	regroup	mishear	tumular	snubber
sonship	air-drop	ingroup	unclear	annular	grubber
gunship	dew-drop	pea-soup	nuclear	zonular	imbiber
nunship	pit-prop	steep-up	besmear	lunular	caliber
warship	caltrop	bull-pup	compear	papular	scriber
hership	milk-sop	cover-up	crop-ear	copular	chamber
airship	sour-sop	chirrup	upspear	popular	clamber
worship	treetop	stirrup	redsear	cupular	climber
foxship	foretop	knees-up	dog's-ear	morular	Scomber
tie-clip	roof-top	balls-up	cat's-ear	insular	scumber
toeclip	high-top	press-up	Jew's-ear	titular	clumber
seedlip	worktop	hunt's-up	unswear	vitular	plumber
hare-lip	hilltop	built-up	outwear	astylar	slumber
egg-flip	roll-top	start-up	mid-year	jacamar	f-number
leg-slip	maintop	burst-up	man-year	picamar	October
non-slip	whip-top	R	insofar	patamar	coluber
cowslip	overtop	sea-haar	overfar	grammar	defacer
pay-slip	non-stop	megabar	vinegar	ordinar	filacer
parsnip	airstop	choc-bar	realgar	laminar	fleecer
non-drip	bus-stop	sand-bar	koftgar	seminar	officer
tide-rip	pit-stop	type-bar	shophar	lacunar	enticer
cantrip	schlepp	fire-bar	handjar	pair-oar	chancer
ego-trip	epicarp	five-bar	bell-jar	outroar	prancer
unstrip	syncarp	drag-bar	lashkar	four-oar	spencer
drip-tip	exocarp	milk-bar	tutelar	outsoar	bouncer
re-equip	discerp	roll-bar	burglar	ice-spar	piercer
insculp	enclasp	toll-bar	bifilar	felspar	adducer
arc-lamp	inclasp	bilobar	similar	wood-tar	reducer
fog-lamp	unclasp	kilobar	basilar	mukhtar	seducer
sun-lamp	Arimasp	bass-bar	ocellar	semitar	inducer
gas-lamp	engrasp	footbar	stellar	simitar	pleader
enstamp	cage-cup	draw-bar	axillar	fenitar	kneader
bethump	kingcup	crow-bar	escolar	rock-tar	dreader
pig-jump	giltcup	handcar	areolar	mooktar	treader
outjump	speed-up	sidecar	scholar	coal-tar	invader
mud-lump	clued-up	forecar	bipolar	plantar	bladder
oak-lump	mixed-up	minicar	dipolar	sea-star	shedder
air-pump	build-up	tank-car	cupolar	Dogstar	shidder
no-trump	stand-up	mail-car	templar	Telstar	whidder
mugwump	round-up	rail-car	fabular	all-star	glidder
bellhop	shake-up	tram-car	pabular	daystar	slidder
tea-shop	frame-up	gyrocar	nebular	couguar	plodder
pie-shop	flare-up	autocar	fibular	bolivar	scudder
rum-shop	close-up	twiscar	lobular	samovar	shudder
ginshop	write-up	subadar	tubular	Gaekwar	acceder
kip-shop	paste-up	jamadar	facular	Gaikwar	seceder
cop-shop	carve-up	jemadar	macular	man-o'-war	bleeder
pop-shop	booze-up	tanadar	secular	post-war	speeder
pot-shop	punch-up	chobdar	jocular	pheazar	breeder
toyshop	catchup	chaddar	locular	janizar	decider
escalop	patch-up	khaddar	vocular	blabber	broider
develop	ketchup	Cheddar	oscular	clabber	derider
envelop	smash-up	chuddar	radular	slabber	insider
scallop	brush-up	subedar	modular	drabber	divider
shallop	sneak-up	jemidar	nodular	grabber	scalder
scollop	break-up	amildar	regular	stabber	chalder
trollop	check-up	sea-bear	tegular	swabber	fielder
rollmop	snick-up	cudbear	ligular	dribber	wielder
hen-coop	stickup	she-bear	angular	clobber	yielder
outroop	knock-up	bugbear	jugular	slobber	skelder

7 -DER

spelder	all-seer	armiger	slasher	collier	flecker
builder	whate'er	changer	smasher	dollier	wrecker
guilder	aquafer	clanger	swasher	Grolier	shicker
scolder	chiefer	avenger	flesher	replier	whicker
smolder	chaffer	whinger	fresher	earlier	clicker
woolder	piaffer	slinger	Irisher	fitlier	flicker
boulder	flaffer	bringer	swisher	outlier	slicker
foulder	staffer	cringer	welsher	haulier	smicker
moulder	quaffer	wringer	blusher	premier	knicker
bowlder	whiffer	stinger	flusher	larmier	snicker
meander	sniffer	swinger	brusher	pannier	pricker
slander	scoffer	sponger	crusher	vernier	tricker
brander	feoffer	wronger	feather	drapier	sticker
stander	proffer	blunger	heather	pompier	chocker
blender	bluffer	plunger	leather	rippier	shocker
slender	snuffer	lounger	weather	decrier	blocker
amender	stuffer	charger	blather	sucrier	clocker
spender	lucifer	sparger	slather	barrier	knocker
blinder	conifer	peacher	loather	carrier	shucker
flinder	porifer	reacher	seether	farrier	plucker
joinder	rotifer	teacher	thether	harrier	trucker
poinder	aquifer	coacher	whether	marrier	sleeker
grinder	chamfer	poacher	blether	tarrier	moniker
thonder	granfer	belcher	neither	perrier	striker
daunder	spoofer	welcher	thither	terrier	trekker
launder	Engager	filcher	whither	sorrier	chukker
maunder	homager	pilcher	blither	worrier	stalker
chunder	manager	rancher	slither	currier	caulker
thunder	tanager	bencher	swither	furrier	skulker
blunder	alnager	wencher	panther	courier	thanker
plunder	forager	pincher	smother	brasier	flanker
bounder	ravager	luncher	another	crosier	spanker
founder	dowager	muncher	soother	tarsier	swanker
lounder	voyager	puncher	brother	dossier	thinker
pounder	spadger	moocher	farther	saltier	skinker
rounder	pledger	marcher	norther	rentier	blinker
sounder	sledger	percher	further	emptier	clinker
wounder	dredger	torcher	murther	cottier	klinker
asunder	leidger	lurcher	mauther	puttier	slinker
decoder	stodger	catcher	mouther	heavier	drinker
brooder	bludger	hatcher	pouther	clavier	stinker
boarder	smudger	matcher	souther	klavier	plonker
hoarder	drudger	patcher	mawther	brevier	stonker
reorder	trudger	watcher	scyther	glazier	blunker
unorder	reneger	ditcher	gambier	brazier	plunker
sworder	integer	hitcher	jambier	grazier	younker
bourder	stagger	pitcher	glacier	crozier	snooker
deluder	swagger	botcher	fancier	sneaker	stooker
scowder	skegger	potcher	saucier	speaker	stroker
chowder	chigger	wotcher	readier	breaker	sharker
crowder	thigger	butcher	kiddier	wreaker	shirker
roe-deer	snigger	gutcher	ruddier	upmaker	whisker
pig-deer	frigger	blucher	soldier	croaker	frisker
hog-deer	prigger	moucher	studier	rosaker	rebuker
encheer	trigger	toucher	edifier	retaker	stealer
upcheer	swigger	voucher	deifier	whacker	inhaler
mynheer	twigger	weigher	unifier	clacker	drabler
pickeer	clogger	drogher	cashier	flacker	stabler
whene'er	slogger	burgher	luthier	slacker	babbler
pioneer	plugger	laugher	rockier	smacker	dabbler
compeer	slugger	cougher	atelier	knacker	gabbler
outpeer	drugger	rougher	dallier	cracker	rabbler
where'er	veliger	telpher	rallier	tracker	wabbler
mahseer	lamiger	flasher	hellier	checker	dibbler

nibbler	dangler	tattler	mariner	flapper	admirer
cobbler	jangler	fettler	loriner	slapper	desirer
gobbler	mangler	settler	resiner	knapper	taborer
hobbler	tangler	bottler	Latiner	snapper	ignorer
nobbler	wangler	prouler	diviner	trapper	floorer
wobbler	jingler	brawler	scanner	wrapper	spoorer
gambler	mingler	crawler	planner	swapper	sparrer
rambler	pingler	drawler	spanner	stepper	stirrer
fumbler	tingler	trawler	thinner	chipper	spurrer
jumbler	bungler	growler	skinner	shipper	securer
mumbler	trailer	prowler	spinner	whipper	endurer
rumbler	defiler	foozler	scunner	skipper	augurer
tumbler	spoiler	dazzler	chunner	clipper	abjurer
garbler	broiler	sizzler	stunner	flipper	injurer
marbler	reviler	muzzler	wagoner	slipper	manurer
warbler	cackler	puzzler	almoner	snipper	scourer
doubler	hackler	creamer	tenoner	fripper	insurer
circler	tackler	dreamer	crooner	gripper	assurer
paddler	heckler	steamer	coroner	tripper	debaser
saddler	pickler	metamer	intoner	chopper	pleaser
meddler	tickler	schemer	bywoner	shopper	greaser
peddler	buckler	claimer	learner	whopper	phraser
diddler	suckler	lorimer	scorner	cropper	praiser
fiddler	Szekler	shammer	mourner	dropper	bruiser
piddler	tinkler	slammer	spurner	stopper	cruiser
riddler	odaller	crammer	Pilsner	swopper	adviser
tiddler	udaller	stammer	centner	scupper	deviser
toddler	dialler	skimmer	vintner	crupper	reviser
fuddler	sheller	glimmer	partner	scarper	chooser
muddler	smeller	slimmer	spawner	sharper	deposer
puddler	speller	brimmer	crowner	chirper	imposer
needler	dueller	crimmer	drowner	scorper	apposer
bridler	fueller	krimmer	misdoer	usurper	opposer
handler	queller	trimmer	outgoer	clasper	exposer
ländler	dweller	swimmer	escaper	grasper	scorser
kindler	sweller	brommer	hanaper	whisper	courser
fondler	thiller	prommer	repaper	crisper	grasser
doodler	spiller	scummer	unpaper	prosper	dresser
girdler	stiller	skummer	scraper	scauper	presser
hurdler	swiller	slummer	cheeper	grouper	guesser
scudler	proller	brummer	bleeper	trouper	cuisser
skudler	troller	drummer	sleeper	shearer	glosser
dawdler	sculler	ionomer	creeper	clearer	trusser
wheeler	cruller	monomer	steeper	swearer	accuser
kneeler	cajoler	bloomer	sweeper	squarer	end-user
speeler	spooler	charmer	juniper	orderer	refuser
spieler	stapler	swarmer	scalper	cheerer	infuser
baffler	sampler	exhumer	scamper	fleerer	non-user
raffler	simpler	polymer	clamper	sneerer	smouser
piffler	rippler	cleaner	tramper	steerer	arouser
riffler	tippler	gleaner	stamper	offerer	grouser
muffler	coupler	pardner	swamper	wagerer	peruser
ruffler	pearler	widener	whimper	adherer	misuser
trifler	snarler	bigener	crimper	coherer	debater
stifler	whirler	ingener	thumper	venerer	rebater
beagler	twirler	wakener	plumper	caperer	cheater
haggler	pantler	cozener	stumper	taperer	theater
giggler	turtler	drainer	no-hoper	caterer	greater
higgler	hostler	grainer	scooper	waterer	treater
niggler	bustler	trainer	whooper	enterer	sweater
wiggler	hustler	stainer	snooper	utterer	relater
boggler	rustler	refiner	trooper	waverer	dilater
goggler	battler	enginer	stooper	reverer	bloater
juggler	rattler	repiner	clapper	Fuehrer	floater

unwater	re-enter	bolster	clutter	empower	decolor
doubter	eventer	holster	flutter	thrower	settlor
exacter	painter	hamster	sputter	strower	athanor
specter	reinter	minster	stutter	indexer	alienor
erecter	jointer	conster	refuter	delayer	jib-door
skeeter	pointer	monster	saluter	allayer	pandoor
tweeter	printer	punster	diluter	inlayer	outdoor
quieter	stinter	booster	scouter	forayer	emperor
lameter	twinter	rooster	shouter	sprayer	Windsor
dimeter	haunter	tapster	plouter	strayer	incisor
ammeter	saunter	yapster	spouter	assayer	advisor
osseter	taunter	hepster	trouter	essayer	devisor
riveter	vaunter	hipster	imputer	métayer	revisor
shafter	chunter	tipster	plowter	moneyer	divisor
drafter	shunter	burster	Pinxter	enjoyer	unvisor
grafter	counter	bluster	rescuer	caloyer	emulsor
shifter	mounter	cluster	subduer	filazer	sponsor
snifter	grunter	fluster	leaguer	sneezer	plessor
drifter	scooter	rouster	lacquer	freezer	scissor
grifter	shooter	truster	chequer	assizer	creator
swifter	acroter	shyster	conquer	snoozer	legator
poofter	pivoter	clyster	jerquer	Switzer	aviator
crofter	adapter	royster	masquer	waltzer	ablator
poufter	chapter	tryster	pursuer	seltzer	delator
yachter	tempter	scatter	cadaver	whizzer	relator
fighter	compter	chatter	cleaver	quizzer	dilator
lighter	sumpter	shatter	palaver	rag-fair	senator
righter	diopter	blatter	Papaver	funfair	venator
sighter	charter	clatter	griever	forfair	donator
boshter	starter	flatter	minever	furfair	aerator
plaiter	quarter	platter	whoever	Mayfair	curator
arbiter	skirter	slatter	forever	machair	rotator
orbiter	snorter	smatter	assever	open-air	equator
reciter	sporter	spatter	however	two-pair	levator
inciter	feaster	swatter	whyever	despair	laxator
exciter	shaster	abetter	ashiver	corsair	abactor
inditer	blaster	whetter	caliver	Kashmir	reactor
lamiter	plaster	chitter	deliver	Mjölnir	X-factor
femiter	boaster	skitter	reliver	boudoir	enactor
limiter	coaster	clitter	miniver	pochoir	tractor
igniter	roaster	flitter	shriver	racloir	exactor
stoiter	toaster	glitter	thriver	couloir	ejector
quoiter	dabster	slitter	upriver	pissoir	elector
Jupiter	wabster	omitter	striver	sautoir	erector
inviter	webster	knitter	vetiver	Elzevir	evictor
re-alter	fibster	spitter	reviver	duumvir	proctor
Psalter	lobster	critter	recover	mormaor	eductor
shelter	mobster	fritter	uncover	picador	praetor
skelter	oldster	quitter	all-over	mirador	traitor
smelter	rodster	twitter	remover	matador	excitor
spelter	wrester	blotter	popover	humidor	auditor
swelter	quester	clotter	estover	stridor	janitor
philter	dyester	plotter	out-over	feoffor	genitor
stilter	gagster	slotter	flyover	pledgor	monitor
quilter	maister	knotter	swerver	obligor	paritor
gaulter	waister	snotter	flivver	isochor	heritor
vaulter	heister	spotter	renewer	chikhor	visitor
boulter	leister	trotter	screwer	markhor	Realtor ®
coulter	agister	stotter	strewer	camphor	chantor
poulter	blister	swotter	embower	biophor	grantor
chanter	glister	abutter	imbower	Signior	stentor
planter	foister	scutter	recower	warrior	adaptor
granter	roister	reutter	widower	squalor	questor
tranter	twister	shutter	endower	similor	agistor

abettor	rakshas	apsides	mangoes	seraphs	scepsis
quittor	Xiphias	upsides	dingoes	wreaths	skepsis
dilutor	Ananias	pyxides	cargoes	milreis	asepsis
ally-tor	Messias	incudes	schmoes	rhachis	tripsis
languor	verglas	données	Negroes	arachis	krypsis
septuor	pajamas	ambages	lassoes	rhaphis	stypsis
sextuor	pyjamas	remiges	mottoes	Graphis	chassis
revivor	miasmas	Striges	bravoes	bubalis	classis
machzor	Satanas	emonges	salvoes	alkalis	whatsis
schnorr	vaginas	marches	talipes	Pyralis	ecdysis
centaur	coronas	clothes	stripes	Nasalis	ileitis
clotbur	Mithras	scabies	stirpes	Chablis	uveitis
Bahadur	caritas	darbies	polypes	challis	colitis
farceur	abraxas	species	Antares	trellis	parotis
douceur	habdabs	kiddies	unwares	parulis	abattis
primeur	ski-bobs	candies	Rasores	lychnis	glottis
flâneur	od's-bobs	hurdies	lustres	coronis	marquis
signeur	cherubs	piggies	lemures	Vaudois	vis-à-vis
proneur	agogics	turkies	oeuvres	chamois	synaxis
danseur	irenics	tallies	aliases	travois	hijinks
masseur	phonics	billies	atlases	Sarapis	odzooks
amateur	bionics	willies	praeses	Serapis	casuals
hauteur	sferics	gullies	geneses	sinopis	marrels
liqueur	vitrics	goolies	pubises	ascaris	battels
sulphur	physics	wurlies	tyloses	cidaris	crewels
Réaumur	statics	pennies	fourses	Polaris	cruells
tambour	tactics	funnies	rebuses	epacris	consols
harbour	photics	pionies	focuses	sherris	bagfuls
succour	haptics	Moonies	fucuses	myiasis	jugfuls
rancour	peptics	otaries	ictuses	ectasis	mugfuls
candour	nautics	berries	algates	entasis	panfuls
pandour	Pleiads	falsies	ergates	ascesis	tinfuls
haveour	Lusiads	fifties	Achates	pedesis	cupfuls
two-four	calends	panties	penates	algesis	jarfuls
fulgour	kalends	sonties	annates	aphesis	hatfuls
mid-hour	emerods	empties	mycetes	askesis	potfuls
man-hour	innards	forties	tagetes	telesis	boxfuls
haviour	inwards	sixties	isoetes	nemesis	meseems
paviour	onwards	stovies	ascites	mimesis	Dodgems
saviour	towards	civvies	limites	genesis	prelims
parlour	upwards	Musales	fomites	kinesis	lyceums
clamour	limaces	yibbles	sorites	synesis	asylums
glamour	hyraces	humbles	pyrites	anoesis	orleans
enamour	vibices	numbles	xerotes	paresis	Juglans
mainour	radices	soboles	litotes	auxesis	Lallans
outpour	indices	sapples	barytes	mycosis	atamans
acatour	codices	measles	sheaves	sycosis	hetmans
faitour	salices	papules	greaves	zygosis	caymans
santour	helices	cotyles	thieves	abiosis	cadrans
contour	Filices	betimes	shelves	meiosis	sextans
dortour	culices	tzimmes	scarves	dulosis	sithens
flavour	cylices	Romanes	wharves	tylosis	dickens
fervour	cimices	Oscines	ingowes	limosis	siemens
Hotspur	carices	no-fines	indexes	osmosis	Fastens
vacatur	varices	Malines	murexes	zymosis	elevens
Fraktur	murices	joannes	helixes	kenosis	crivens
crittur	latices	ambones	calyxes	monosis	remains
S	calyces	umbones	Erinyes	xerosis	gubbins
klipdas	oreades	ancones	quizzes	virosis	juggins
csárdás	naiades	bygones	sea-legs	porosis	muggins
czardas	dryades	triones	ant-eggs	sorosis	Jenkins
whereas	Alcides	tyrones	tidings	pyrosis	gaskins
coal-gas	aphides	bilboes	innings	ketosis	aiblins
tear-gas	besides	spadoes	aurochs	mitosis	hidlins

oodlins	compass	gutless	repress	floccus	minimus
Collins	surpass	lawless	empress	Dyticus	trismus
tenpins	hey-pass	sexless	impress	Quercus	Tabanus
mattins	zebrass	rayless	appress	Oniscus	Balanus
epigons	cuirass	wayless	oppress	Glaucus	Calanus
commons	matrass	keyless	express	rhabdus	Varanus
summons	canvass	joyless	cypress	solidus	tetanus
buttons	success	kermess	actress	archeus	Totanus
pronaos	precess	kirmess	tutress	Cepheus	silenus
rhombos	process	badness	usuress	Orpheus	Ricinus
stuccos	abscess	madness	possess	nucleus	uncinus
parados	goddess	sadness	poetess	malleus	echinus
dos-à-dos	herdess	oddness	portess	clypeus	Rhamnus
reredos	confess	redness	hostess	choreus	alumnus
rear-dos	profess	oldness	prowess	Perseus	Avernus
stichos	doggess	waeness	absciss	proteus	Sturnus
ponchos	largess	oneness	vendiss	gluteus	gibbous
benthos	burgess	bigness	submiss	pluteus	glebous
porthos	duchess	iciness	premiss	urachus	bulbous
adagios	Turkess	shiness	air-miss	Bacchus	limbous
thermos	braless	illness	dismiss	jacchus	globous
temenos	ebbless	dulness	koumiss	trochus	herbous
threnos	ribless	fulness	treviss	Syrphus	opacous
albinos	unbless	dimness	bugloss	scyphus	succous
merinos	jobless	wanness	schloss	cyathus	talcous
stamnos	cubless	lioness	sea-moss	canthus	zincous
apropos	sacless	twoness	bog-moss	Roscius	sarcous
Atropos	aidless	farness	cup-moss	gladius	viscous
orthros	lidless	harness	recross	sardius	fuscous
embryos	endless	fatness	uncross	Gordius	raucous
perhaps	godless	patness	engross	ziffius	rhodous
schnaps	rodless	setness	matross	Ziphius	apodous
triceps	budless	wetness	degauss	Celsius	piceous
forceps	ageless	fitness	succuss	Tarsius	hideous
ethiops	tieless	witness	concuss	Bubalus	hugeous
cyclops	useless	hotness	percuss	angelus	atheous
Mormops	hueless	aptness	discuss	Mytilus	rameous
lace-ups	aweless	outness	untruss	phallus	timeous
sanders	eyeless	rawness	caddyss	thallus	igneous
taggers	legless	fewness	rickets	ocellus	cereous
Highers	wigless	newness	giblets	arillus	caseous
withers	fogless	lowness	starets	embolus	gaseous
jankers	aimless	laxness	bandits	Carolus	osseous
bonkers	rimless	gayness	blewits	nonplus	piteous
conkers	armless	shyness	G-agents	surplus	duteous
hunkers	sumless	slyness	V-agents	lobulus	luteous
Kommers	finless	coyness	bureaus	loculus	aqueous
jeepers	kinless	dryness	Kurhaus	modulus	niveous
bitters	sinless	wryness	Bauhaus	regulus	fungous
jitters	sonless	ancress	Carabus	famulus	azygous
clivers	sunless	address	ephebus	hamulus	typhous
halvers	awnless	redress	Phoebus	ramulus	dubious
indoors	hapless	undress	fidibus	limulus	rubious
velours	napless	peeress	helibus	mimulus	vicious
sea-bass	sapless	Negress	minibus	cumulus	badious
carcass	lipless	regress	omnibus	tumulus	tedious
corcass	pipless	aggress	railbus	annulus	bilious
wild-ass	topless	digress	rhombus	torulus	nimious
jackass	earless	tigress	jacobus	Corylus	simious
declass	oarless	ingress	colobus	calamus	osmious
cutlass	airless	heiress	aerobus	isthmus	impious
eggmass	hatless	Mooress	autobus	dedimus	copious
biomass	witless	adpress	post-bus	vidimus	carious
sea-pass	artless	depress	incubus	bulimus	various

serious	routous	chlamys	bum-boat	reflect	plashet
corious	vacuous	lamboys	gunboat	inflect	freshet
curious	nocuous	T	pap-boat	neglect	blushet
furious	viduous	dingbat	catboat	collect	epithet
obvious	arduous	bullbat	kit-boat	tranect	misdiet
devious	tenuous	hurl-bat	rowboat	connect	palmiet
bivious	sinuous	acrobat	flyboat	respect	inquiet
envious	fatuous	placcat	pea-coat	inspect	unquiet
invious	fulvous	wild-cat	redcoat	suspect	jump-jet
anxious	nervous	polecat	top-coat	re-erect	prop-jet
noxious	Priapus	bush-cat	car-coat	carrect	flacket
atokous	Oedipus	musk-cat	surcoat	correct	placket
jealous	euripus	hell-cat	box-coat	porrect	bracket
zealous	grampus	palm-cat	wildoat	trisect	stacket
callous	Olympus	whipcat	pitapat	dissect	thicket
villous	Canopus	bear-cat	talipat	protect	clicket
parlous	Xenopus	meercat	kail-pat	predict	smicket
perlous	pyropus	salt-cat	nacarat	verdict	cricket
emulous	octopus	copy-cat	apparat	afflict	pricket
agamous	Scirpus	sea-beat	quadrat	inflict	brocket
gummous	polypus	offbeat	land-rat	astrict	crocket
plumous	Dasypus	sun-beat	molerat	convict	glaiket
spumous	humerus	drybeat	pack-rat	extinct	blanket
brumous	Cyperus	recheat	musk-rat	defunct	trinket
grumous	icterus	escheat	majorat	adjunct	bycoket
chymous	pelorus	red-heat	rat-a-tat	injunct	flasket
onymous	pylorus	preheat	habitat	expunct	whisket
azymous	churrus	moth-eat	latitat	concoct	brisket
uranous	oestrus	pigmeat	cumquat	percoct	frisket
heinous	Sciurus	pap-meat	kumquat	infarct	medalet
veinous	Silurus	thereat	wine-vat	viaduct	royalet
ominous	Xenurus	whereat	mash-vat	subduct	driblet
spinous	Zonurus	overeat	redoubt	oviduct	triblet
urinous	papyrus	floreat	abreact	conduct	herblet
ruinous	pegasus	retreat	re-enact	product	doublet
burnous	thiasus	entreat	compact	drabbet	circlet
pulpous	bonasus	estreat	overact	sherbet	bendlet
pompous	petasus	extreat	refract	salicet	rundlet
pappous	Croesus	disseat	infract	pouncet	lobelet
fibrous	cytisus	box-seat	carract	sea-beet	lakelet
umbrous	thyrsus	key-seat	detract	decreet	pikelet
nacrous	conatus	wine-fat	retract	regreet	osselet
hydrous	stratus	woolfat	tetract	unsweet	notelet
uberous	tractus	salt-fat	attract	whiffet	wavelet
acerous	Sanctus	tile-hat	extract	deep-fet	covelet
onerous	linctus	plug-hat	pentact	beaufet	dovelet
ochrous	quietus	high-hat	contact	pledget	leaflet
odorous	Boletus	pith-hat	inexact	unbeget	jinglet
amorous	impetus	silk-hat	play-act	drugget	kinglet
leprous	cubitus	chip-hat	polyact	overget	ringlet
cuprous	halitus	shariat	pandect	brachet	singlet
ferrous	caestus	sheriat	prefect	guichet	winglet
cirrous	arbutus	meerkat	A-effect	manchet	froglet
petrous	carduus	mud-flat	confect	linchet	archlet
citrous	gallows	runflat	perfect	lynchet	devilet
nitrous	bellows	cork-mat	traject	crochet	hacklet
anurous	dogdays	automat	subject	merchet	necklet
usurous	man-days	doormat	conject	hatchet	booklet
featous	endways	quinnat	project	latchet	swallet
acetous	anyways	sea-boat	disject	ratchet	skillet
lentous	donkeys	mud-boat	dialect	watchet	quillet
riotous	gulleys	ice-boat	re-elect	fitchet	chamlet
azotous	gooleys	pigboat	prelect	nymphet	hornlet
portous	ichthys	tug-boat	deflect	prophet	cacolet

7 -LET

triolet	snippet	sleight	king-hit	akvavit	coolant
chaplet	trippet	freight	song-hit	half-wit	replant
triplet	cabaret	behight	overhit	want-wit	implant
templet	tabaret	delight	stickit	unpinkt	explant
droplet	minaret	relight	brockit	asphalt	ululant
ripplet	lazaret	enlight	,cleekit	sea-salt	adamant
couplet	sakeret	yplight	sleekit	dry-salt	clamant
scarlet	leveret	benight	steekit	oxy-salt	calmant
starlet	riveret	tonight	glaikit	gestalt	dormant
deerlet	sea-fret	empight	traikit	ice-belt	formant
sterlet	coffret	shright	toolkit	dog-belt	emanant
harslet	pomfret	alright	drookit	oil-belt	regnant
corslet	taboret	unright	droukit	hip-belt	urinant
flatlet	arboret	spright	moonlit	flybelt	remnant
cantlet	wherret	upright	starlit	indwelt	pennant
gantlet	whirret	insight	readmit	unspilt	vernant
mantlet	skirret	unsight	delimit	in-built	reboant
fontlet	whitret	uptight	Thermit ®	unbuilt	rampant
rootlet	ioduret	claught	manumit	eyebolt	amarant
martlet	fleuret	flaught	invenit	elf-bolt	vibrant
partlet	dead-set	draught	subunit	hagbolt	hydrant
tartlet	headset	fraught	exploit	ragbolt	operant
fortlet	handset	abought	introit	dogbolt	iterant
epaulet	hard-set	thought	flea-pit	tap-bolt	vagrant
annulet	boneset	brought	sand-pit	default	regrant
zonulet	high-set	drought	cockpit	assault	migrant
rivulet	backset	wrought	pockpit	envault	spirant
playlet	well-set	wheesht	coal-pit	sun-cult	odorant
ceramet	seam-set	parfait	shilpit	singult	farrant
grommet	twin-set	unplait	marl-pit	consult	warrant
plummet	moonset	extrait	crampit	bergylt	currant
grummet	overset	megabit	corn-pit	peccant	entrant
gourmet	brasset	inhabit	tear-pit	alicant	intrant
calumet	Knesset	cohabit	cesspit	emicant	courant
alkanet	cresset	frabbit	salt-pit	descant	peasant
remanet	quintet	rarebit	clay-pit	discant	versant
hose-net	quartet	ringbit	inherit	oxidant	passant
drag-net	languet	frogbit	demerit	pendant	jessant
fish-net	droguet	adhibit	Prakrit	fondant	rousant
cabinet	racquet	inhibit	culprit	wood-ant	blatant
tabinet	picquet	cohibit	revisit	gardant	statant
basinet	docquet	exhibit	transit	verdant	imitant
satinet	rocquet	hawkbit	deposit	mordant	saltant
quannet	briquet	kilobit	reposit	pageant	montant
spinnet	banquet	traybit	whatsit	sejeant	flotant
jaconet	croquet	treybit	baby-sit	unmeant	reptant
baronet	parquet	deficit	cole-tit	elegant	gestant
coronet	bouquet	illicit	bush-tit	enchant	distant
Euronet	minivet	solicit	coal-tit	etchant	instant
bayonet	unrivet	quiddit	wren-tit	radiant	sextant
clapnet	vilayet	snoddit	oven-tit	median	piquant
keepnet	isohyet	subedit	circuit	defiant	issuant
drop-net	redraft	chindit	biscuit	valiant	provant
overnet	indraft	plaudit	conduit	reliant	servant
hair-net	engraft	excudit	mesquit	variant	buoyant
sarsnet	ski-lift	howbeit	recruit	resiant	lambent
draw-net	airlift	conceit	floruit	deviant	cumbent
crownet	hayloft	forfeit	nonsuit	duck-ant	sorbent
parapet	borscht	surfeit	sunsuit	sealant	bowbent
crampet	thatcht	benefit	pursuit	zealant	concent
crumpet	claucht	ague-fit	missuit	Hielant	nascent
trumpet	bedight	thiggit	catsuit	ballant	descent
whippet	undight	ringgit	lawsuit	callant	credent
skippet	aheight	hard-hit	aquavit	gallant	trident

evident	manrent	monocot	galipot	dispart	sitfast
candent	horrent	peridot	talipot	bit-part	orgiast
pendent	torrent	hard-got	jackpot	outpart	arblast
erodent	current	unbegot	kail-pot	restart	ballast
mordent	pew-rent	saligot	eye-spot	upstart	outlast
prudent	present	Manihot	sunspot	blewart	oak-mast
student	consent	full-hot	tar-spot	athwart	topmast
reagent	dissent	one-shot	piss-pot	rizzart	durmast
co-agent	missent	eye-shot	tosspot	halbert	dismast
exigent	content	elf-shot	fuss-pot	filbert	gymnast
fulgent	portent	mugshot	pint-pot	gilbert	accoast
tangent	distent	gunshot	stewpot	lambert	upcoast
ringent	unguent	hip-shot	blue-rot	concert	hop-oast
pungent	diluent	ear-shot	hoof-rot	grosert	upbrast
margent	sequent	hotshot	pierrot	dessert	peltast
surgent	attuent	pot-shot	dogtrot	subvert	fantast
turgent	prevent	outshot	jog-trot	taivert	maddest
forhent	solvent	bowshot	tom-trot	culvert	reddest
unshent	convent	Italiot	footrot	convert	middest
ambient	fervent	galliot	fox-trot	pervert	saidest
ancient	forwent	chariot	paletot	pay-dirt	gabfest
audient	miswent	Cypriot	viretot	sea-girt	liefest
salient	outwent	patriot	aliquot	comfort	confest
lenient	bepaint	Zantiot	talayot	alamort	biggest
sapient	depaint	Cheviot	usucapt	seaport	suggest
patient	repaint	bibelot	readapt	comport	lengest
totient	impaint	camelot	periapt	gunport	congest
unblent	unpaint	matelot	dewlapt	rapport	longest
mid-Lent	spraint	triglot	precept	support	bargest
asklent	straint	melilot	concept	carport	disgest
tallent	besaint	copilot	percept	airport	highest
pollent	unsaint	reallot	discept	purport	rathest
violent	attaint	shallot	unswept	besport	tiniest
forlent	varmint	maillot	upswept	disport	puniest
opulent	catmint	subplot	receipt	outport	veriest
oddment	abjoint	complot	unwhipt	row-port	outjest
clement	adjoint	marplot	unclipt	consort	unblest
element	injoint	filemot	pre-empt	contort	willest
ragment	unjoint	halimot	unkempt	bistort	fullest
segment	repoint	have-not	benempt	distort	earnest
figment	appoint	top-knot	dirempt	blawort	disnest
pigment	reprint	whatnot	attempt	ribwort	anapest
augment	imprint	gumboot	accompt	madwort	tempest
raiment	enprint	top-boot	readopt	mudwort	nearest
aliment	asquint	web-foot	bedropt	ragwort	Everest
ailment	isodont	ice-foot	excerpt	figwort	leg-rest
comment	isokont	ten-foot	prerupt	bugwort	imprest
garment	diplont	two-foot	corrupt	mugwort	contest
sarment	dinmont	hotfoot	disrupt	felwort	protest
varment	towmont	outfoot	decrypt	saw-wort	fattest
ferment	affront	jaw-foot	gabbart	yoghurt	wottest
torment	unburnt	six-foot	dogcart	accourt	acquest
fitment	romaunt	dry-foot	tip-cart	lambast	bequest
butment	manhunt	upshoot	tax-cart	bombast	request
hutment	fox-hunt	Rajpoot	Jeddart	die-cast	inquest
payment	account	red-root	unheart	precast	lievest
wayment	recount	cheroot	Jethart	miscast	harvest
eminent	demount	taproot	folk-art	metcast	Midwest
fornent	remount	disroot	unsmart	outcast	prowest
parpent	unmount	outroot	foumart	abreast	nor'-west
perpent	dovecot	firepot	donnart	nor'-east	spryest
serpent	haricot	glue-pot	rampart	tubfast	alongst
unspent	apricot	dash-pot	compart	bedfast	amongst
stupent	plumcot	wash-pot	two-part	sunfast	emongst

Dadaist	agonist	copyist	hind-gut	bandeau	fretsaw
Judaist	Zionist	against	foregut	rondeau	buzz-saw
Bahaist	ironist	alecost	shea-nut	tableau	choctaw
Lamaist	cornist	low-cost	crab-nut	rouleau	ring-taw
dumaist	hornist	teleost	pili-nut	trumeau	whittaw
Arabist	faunist	sepiost	lock-nut	moineau	ally-taw
Hobbist	judoist	periost	gall-nut	tonneau	flamfew
cambist	echoist	midmost	horn-nut	chapeau	fitchew
gambist	uphoist	endmost	coconut	château	morphew
iambist	poloist	topmost	Arnaout	plateau	sea-view
phobist	soloist	farmost	comb-out	manteau	preview
herbist	hyloist	harmost	lead-out	Watteau	purview
epicist	Titoist	aftmost	read-out	nylghau	surview
fascist	tropist	outmost	fold-out	fabliau	fire-new
faddist	utopist	unroost	handout	cattabu	insinew
Mahdist	mappist	bedpost	fade-out	cardecu	unsinew
exodist	Rappist	compost	hideout	camaieu	span-new
feudist	harpist	dispost	take-out	purlieu	bran-new
atheist	diarist	outpost	time-out	basbleu	air-crew
Couéist	piarist	way-post	line-out	double-u	unscrew
selfist	tsarist	defrost	hangout	laithfu'	beshrew
dry-fist	czarist	sea-tost	hip-gout	catechu	bestrew
imagist	sacrist	provost	wash-out	bunraku	oversew
elegist	querist	athirst	unshout	seppuku	longbow
oligist	chorist	inburst	without	parvenu	rainbow
elogist	florist	upburst	lockout	inconnu	moon-bow
tachist	amorist	accurst	tuck-out	marabou	downbow
Elohist	ivorist	mightst	walk-out	caribou	milk-cow
sophist	metrist	infaust	lookout	sapajou	killcow
mythist	entrist	inhaust	work-out	tinamou	mudscow
Lockist	attrist	exhaust	fall-out	manitou	ladycow
chekist	Maurist	combust	sell-out	bebeeru	re-endow
Yorkist	tourist	sea-dust	roll-out	babassu	hoosgow
realist	subsist	rag-dust	full-out	ju-jitsu	salchow
dialist	sensist	pin-dust	pull-out	chanoyu	somehow
unalist	consist	sawdust	spinout	V	ice-show
dualist	persist	disgust	worn-out	Pan-Slav	leg-show
biblist	statist	encrust	burn-out	Chislev	know-how
cyclist	dietist	incrust	turn-out	W	flyblow
anglist	pietist	entrust	spun-out	jackdaw	outflow
Zoilist	leftist	untrust	eelpout	trishaw	sunglow
cellist	elitist	otocyst	drop-out	cumshaw	high-low
idolist	cultist	analyst	bespout	lock-jaw	shallow
violist	Comtist	Corbett	asprout	foot-jaw	swallow
Carlist	Dantist	rackett	passout	club-law	forslow
oculist	Kantist	cornett	cab-tout	dew-claw	fly-slow
law-list	dentist	Debrett	surtout	land-law	whitlow
pay-list	Scotist	wadsett	shut-out	danelaw	good-now
stylist	egotist	septett	blow-out	case-law	misknow
chemist	protist	sestett	cajuput	corn-law	eyebrow
Rhemist	baptist	sextett	occiput	poor-law	pit-brow
animist	flutist	babbitt	shot-put	bourlaw	low-brow
palmist	vacuist	boycott	cajuput	fist-law	sea-crow
summist	fuguist	kellaut	skew-put	pickmaw	pilcrow
Thomist	casuist	halibut	subtext	forepaw	jim-crow
atomist	Yahvist	holibut	pretext	cat's-paw	gorcrow
cosmist	Fauvist	hackbut	context	misdraw	windrow
plumist	Yahwist	sackbut	mar-text	band-saw	outgrow
rhymist	entwist	woodcut	betwixt	handsaw	upthrow
pianist	intwist	rose-cut	U	foresaw	sparrow
plenist	untwist	annicut	jambeau	backsaw	oversow
Owenist	re-exist	linocut	corbeau	hack-saw	disavow
hymnist	co-exist	trap-cut	ponceau	buck-saw	X
ebonist	Marxist	haircut	morceau	whip-saw	panchax

anthrax	bateaux	gainsay	mediacy	whiskey	jellify
land-tax	coteaux	hearsay	prelacy	passkey	jollify
poll-tax	vitraux	outstay	fallacy	fiddley	mollify
overtax	jambeux	die-away	primacy	tiddley	nullify
wood-wax	milieux	welaway	testacy	trolley	amplify
seal-wax	Benelux	runaway	eustacy	Charley	mummify
beeswax	conflux	caraway	privacy	paisley	chymify
narthex	vaudoux	faraway	secrecy	parsley	magnify
triplex	apteryx	lyra-way	vacancy	hackney	dignify
simplex	bostryx	getaway	infancy	cockney	lignify
complex	Y	cutaway	pliancy	chimney	signify
apoplex	rose-bay	layaway	tenancy	spinney	damnify
perplex	sick-bay	flyaway	sonancy	baloney	reunify
reannex	ilkaday	headway	truancy	boloney	pulpify
Siporex	faraday	roadway	decency	spooney	scarify
Scandix	good-day	raceway	recency	stepney	clarify
antefix	name-day	sideway	lucency	blarney	nigrify
postfix	someday	tide-way	cadency	journey	scorify
choenix	foreday	freeway	ardency	tourney	glorify
Phoenix	love-day	someway	pudency	pigsney	caprify
oratrix	half-day	ropeway	regency	chutney	terrify
rectrix	flag-day	wire-way	cogency	stripey	horrify
tectrix	wash-day	gateway	urgency	palfrey	petrify
victrix	fish-day	halfway	oriency	comfrey	nitrify
tortrix	holiday	ringway	valency	orphrey	vitrify
phalanx	Hock-day	each-way	latency	lamprey	thurify
salpinx	weekday	lichway	patency	spurrey	falsify
pharynx	work-day	archway	potency	backsey	salsify
seedbox	term-day	highway	fluency	woolsey	tipsify
band-box	noonday	fish-way	vivency	whimsey	versify
sand-box	Asmoday	pathway	remercy	malmsey	Russify
dice-box	leap-day	packway	idiotcy	choosey	beatify
side-box	ne'erday	walkway	tribady	odyssey	gratify
juke-box	fair-day	folkway	thready	curtsey	rectify
axle-box	Tuesday	parkway	already	chantey	acetify
firebox	rent-day	railway	unready	plaguey	pontify
live-box	fast-day	hallway	byrlady	lacquey	Scotify
puff-box	rest-day	tramway	May-lady	cliquey	certify
tuck-box	post-day	ship-way	squaddy	sprayey	fortify
work-box	play-day	slipway	shreddy	salsafy	mortify
coal-box	nosegay	fairway	unheedy	torpefy	testify
mail-box	twankay	doorway	tragedy	stupefy	justify
call-box	rokelay	spur-way	raggedy	torrefy	mystify
hell-box	virelay	footway	perfidy	putrefy	brutify
pill-box	forelay	cartway	subsidy	liquefy	Slavify
toolbox	Morglay	thruway	unhandy	squiffy	satisfy
coin-box	rocklay	play-way	sebundy	scruffy	cabbagy
soapbox	gunplay	rag-baby	naebody	plebify	splodgy
gearbox	display	cry-baby	man-body	specify	scraggy
poor-box	misplay	hushaby	anybody	calcify	spriggy
spit-box	net-play	wallaby	Methody	dulcify	scroggy
salt-box	outplay	lullaby	hymnody	zincify	prodigy
post-box	overlay	Barnaby	tripody	farcify	lozengy
show-box	dead-pay	sassaby	corrody	mercify	springy
snow-box	half-pay	squabby	prosody	crucify	stringy
play-box	backpay	scrubby	custody	re-edify	anagogy
jury-box	overpay	shrubby	unhardy	acidify	analogy
princox	respray	stand-by	shroudy	dandify	trilogy
paradox	outpray	by-and-by	disobey	mundify	ecology
flummox	tea-tray	thereby	crickey	undeify	geology
equinox	ash-tray	whereby	pipe-key	fishify	neology
draft-ox	portray	swing-by	swankey	zinkify	ufology
bureaux	out-tray	lewdsby	turnkey	qualify	biology
réseaux	foresay	rudesby	flunkey	anglify	noology

apology	skreaky	vividly	snow-fly	rockily	dustily
orology	streaky	childly	grayfly	luckily	lustily
urology	squeaky	worldly	ladyfly	spikily	rustily
otology	colicky	blandly	spangly	milkily	nattily
myology	panicky	grandly	shingly	silkily	tattily
dyslogy	finicky	blindly	dyingly	bulkily	pettily
telergy	unlucky	spindly	lyingly	sulkily	wittily
allergy	droshky	roundly	vyingly	smokily	heavily
synergy	malarky	soundly	wrongly	perkily	weevily
theurgy	autarky	ungodly	youngly	murkily	privily
splurgy	squawky	weirdly	roughly	peskily	showily
zymurgy	anomaly	thirdly	toughly	riskily	snowily
liturgy	apetaly	buirdly	nymphly	duskily	crazily
preachy	affably	proudly	fleshly	huskily	boozily
queachy	pliably	doucely	freshly	muskily	woozily
sleechy	amiably	gradely	apishly	pawkily	jazzily
queechy	salably	snidely	harshly	sea-lily	dizzily
droichy	tunably	crudely	deathly	godlily	fuzzily
branchy	durably	largely	loathly	pig-lily	muzzily
Frenchy	ratably	lithely	fifthly	sillily	bleakly
stenchy	notably	stalely	tenthly	jollily	slackly
paunchy	mutably	agilely	ninthly	surlily	crackly
raunchy	equably	primely	monthly	lowlily	freckly
crunchy	movably	pronely	soothly	day-lily	thickly
diarchy	taxably	shapely	earthly	may-lily	slickly
anarchy	dribbly	sparely	youthly	beamily	smickly
eparchy	knobbly	falsely	sixthly	slimily	prickly
starchy	knubbly	tensely	nobbily	grimily	trickly
duarchy	stubbly	closely	loobily	rummily	quickly
exarchy	audibly	loosely	spicily	roomily	sleekly
dyarchy	legibly	tersely	saucily	cannily	blankly
churchy	visibly	grysely	headily	bonnily	frankly
kitschy	brambly	irately	readily	funnily	crinkly
snatchy	crumbly	stately	shadily	sunnily	wrinkly
fratchy	grumbly	whitely	giddily	stonily	starkly
sketchy	stumbly	tritely	muddily	soapily	clerkly
switchy	ignobly	acutely	ruddily	jumpily	briskly
twitchy	volubly	vaguely	deedily	lumpily	locally
Scotchy	treacly	bravely	needily	happily	vocally
blotchy	dreadly	gravely	seedily	soppily	ducally
acouchy	broadly	suavely	dandily	wearily	modally
slouchy	twaddly	naïvely	handily	charily	ideally
grouchy	twiddly	sand-fly	windily	hoarily	legally
sloughy	fadedly	chiefly	moodily	fierily	regally
froughy	jadedly	briefly	hardily	angrily	fugally
atrophy	nakedly	firefly	tardily	fairily	axially
splashy	notedly	stiffly	wordily	merrily	banally
squashy	vexedly	bluffly	gaudily	sorrily	penally
creeshy	fixedly	gruffly	bawdily	noisily	venally
squishy	mixedly	dung-fly	dowdily	prosily	finally
cockshy	dazedly	tail-fly	rowdily	tipsily	papally
work-shy	staidly	gall-fly	huffily	messily	morally
sheathy	rabidly	cornfly	puffily	tossily	aurally
breathy	lucidly	aloofly	goofily	fussily	jurally
wreathy	rigidly	lamp-fly	stagily	lousily	rurally
sagathy	validly	dropfly	baggily	loftily	gyrally
empathy	gelidly	overfly	foggily	saltily	nasally
lengthy	solidly	meat-fly	soggily	sootily	mesally
healthy	timidly	boat-fly	nargily	dirtily	disally
wealthy	humidly	beet-fly	mushily	hastily	fatally
timothy	tumidly	frit-fly	pithily	nastily	metally
swarthy	rapidly	test-fly	shakily	tastily	vitally
drouthy	vapidly	goutfly	snakily	testily	totally
somewhy	luridly	blowfly	cockily	mistily	equally

squally	nightly	scotomy	bell-boy	mammary	gaudery
usually	rightly	zootomy	gownboy	nummary	prudery
cavally	sightly	perfumy	kroo-boy	summary	powdery
loyally	tightly	alchymy	ship-boy	granary	puffery
royally	wightly	tiffany	shop-boy	scenary	pilfery
injelly	tacitly	tzigany	newsboy	plenary	imagery
cruelly	licitly	villany	footboy	signary	stagery
vowelly	unfitly	Tammany	hautboy	trinary	dodgery
hazelly	scantly	Rommany	draw-boy	urinary	faggery
frailly	giantly	company	playboy	quinary	jaggery
shrilly	slantly	tympany	didicoy	hymnary	raggery
thrilly	faintly	rhatany	killjoy	ternary	waggery
civilly	saintly	dittany	overjoy	zedoary	figgery
wofully	jointly	larceny	saveloy	library	niggery
awfully	gauntly	spleeny	charpoy	petrary	piggery
aphylly	bluntly	geogeny	viceroy	bursary	wiggery
cleanly	inaptly	biogeny	pomeroy	pessary	doggery
unmanly	unaptly	zoogeny	destroy	peatary	hoggery
womanly	ineptly	orogeny	nun-buoy	nectary	toggery
humanly	heartly	progeny	gas-buoy	sectary	buggery
greenly	peartly	isogeny	therapy	dietary	puggery
queenly	smartly	neoteny	satrapy	unitary	gingery
vixenly	startly	kitteny	cacoepy	dentary	congery
plainly	alertly	vermiiny	gossipy	Tartary	mongery
dearnly	inertly	destiny	scrimpy	January	forgery
sternly	overtly	calumny	scrumpy	ossuary	surgery
bairnly	shortly	uncanny	miscopy	actuary	lechery
trifoly	courtly	scranny	entropy	estuary	archery
duopoly	beastly	tyranny	eutropy	olivary	fashery
cheaply	ghastly	dewanny	isotopy	Calvary	fishery
steeply	thistly	ha'penny	unhappy	slumbry	coshery
plumply	moistly	squinny	scrappy	mimicry	tushery
panoply	bristly	gyronny	strappy	bone-dry	lathery
reapply	gristly	unfunny	jaloppy	guildry	mothery
sharply	ghostly	unsunny	stroppy	shandry	pothery
overply	firstly	ribbony	hiccupy	diandry	hosiery
crisply	stoutly	balcony	concupy	spin-dry	hackery
clearly	masculy	London	tittupy	kiln-dry	pickery
friarly	untruly	geogony	Barbary	laundry	mockery
soberly	scrawly	zoogony	herbary	foundry	rockery
elderly	sprawly	euphony	turbary	drip-dry	puckery
orderly	drizzly	Anthony	peccary	blow-dry	cankery
cheerly	frizzly	haemony	piscary	fibbery	monkery
sheerly	grizzly	alimony	feodary	bobbery	cookery
queerly	streamy	harmony	feudary	jobbery	jookery
eagerly	trigamy	compony	alveary	robbery	rookery
tigerly	pangamy	pit-pony	unweary	fubbery	brokery
angerly	syngamy	tantony	beggary	rubbery	joukery
miserly	zoogamy	syntony	Hungary	bribery	sealery
utterly	apogamy	bottony	unchary	daubery	whalery
loverly	isogamy	cottony	biliary	tracery	nailery
crassly	exogamy	buttony	ciliary	spicery	boilery
crossly	balsamy	muttony	miliary	duncery	gallery
grossly	jessamy	scrawny	laniary	grocery	Sillery
piously	academy	epigyny	topiary	mercery	gullery
greatly	alchemy	attaboy	retiary	sorcery	foolery
exactly	phlegmy	sand-boy	ostiary	laddery	butlery
erectly	scrummy	herdboy	pedlary	doddery	cutlery
fleetly	thrummy	wide-boy	vallary	duddery	sutlery
sweetly	economy	page-boy	bullary	weedery	gemmery
quietly	zoonomy	highboy	obolary	spidery	mummery
swiftly	isonomy	linkboy	gramary	bindery	farmery
lichtly	visnomy	call-boy	primary	cindery	wormery
lightly	anatomy	tallboy	palmary	tindery	plumery

deanery	quavery	sweltry	nimiety	dignity	thretty
scenery	shivery	choltry	omniety	trinity	rosetty
joinery	silvery	poultry	impiety	dacoity	ambitty
swinery	clovery	chantry	variety	charity	unwitty
cannery	plovery	giantry	ebriety	clarity	off-duty
tannery	poovery	re-entry	satiety	spirity	feu-duty
hennery	servery	gauntry	anxiety	obesity	planxty
ginnery	brewery	country	rackety	falsity	overbuy
gunnery	showery	bigotry	tackety	density	fall-guy
nunnery	flowery	helotry	rickety	tensity	obsequy
fernery	chiefry	sceptry	furmety	varsity	obloquy
turnery	deep-fry	avoutry	ferrety	vastity	replevy
drapery	stir-fry	tilbury	russety	vacuity	tantivy
grapery	ahungry	mercury	naïvety	viduity	Muscovy
tripery	Irishry	conjury	velvety	tenuity	anchovy
coopery	enquiry	perjury	thrifty	annuity	mildewy
zoopery	inquiry	planury	weighty	fatuity	meadowy
mappery	cavalry	coloury	blighty	gravity	shadowy
peppery	rivalry	armoury	flighty	pravity	sallowy
coppery	camelry	vapoury	haughty	suavity	tallowy
foppery	revelry	savoury	naughty	brevity	mellowy
jaspery	jewelry	dyvoury	paughty	privity	yellowy
Moorery	devilry	century	doughty	curvity	billowy
goosery	felonry	martyry	foughty	penalty	pillowy
nursery	demonry	fantasy	rabbity	loyalty	willowy
mousery	almonry	ecstasy	probity	royalty	marrowy
peatery	canonry	eustasy	edacity	cruelty	furrowy
fratery	heronry	geodesy	opacity	novelty	ataraxy
sintery	masonry	cramesy	siccity	frailty	epitaxy
wintery	succory	clerisy	unicity	faculty	zootaxy
esotery	chicory	tricksy	paucity	aplenty	cachexy
mastery	gregory	unsonsy	acidity	untenty	anorexy
wastery	euphory	tea-cosy	aridity	seventy	hydroxy
mistery	hickory	egg-cosy	avidity	flaunty	asphyxy
mystery	pillory	leprosy	surdity	scrunty	squeezy
battery	signory	easy-osy	crudity	maggoty	chintzy
cattery	suasory	eupepsy	paneity	enomoty	quartzy
mattery	sensory	autopsy	omneity	carroty	Z
nattery	cursory	ambassy	aureity	parroty	showbiz
rattery	elusory	embassy	gaseity	liberty	schmelz
tattery	amatory	ampassy	reality	puberty	tendenz
rettery	oratory	morassy	egality	poverty	kolkhoz
jittery	factory	teentsy	duality	unhasty	fahlerz
littery	rectory	circusy	quality	dynasty	staretz
lottery	victory	prelaty	ability	modesty	kibbutz
pottery	olitory	throaty	agility	bheesty	thammuz
tottery	castory	encraty	anility	majesty	bazzazz
buttery	history	insecty	utility	amnesty	pazzazz
cautery	sleepry	streety	exility	honesty	bezzazz
roguery	remarry	taffety	jollity	Christy	bizzazz
beavery	unmarry	fidgety	nullity	thirsty	pizzazz
slavery	sowarry	nuggety	furmity	frowsty	gin-fizz
knavery	equerry	dubiety	inanity	squatty	humbuzz
bravery	phratry	society	amenity		

A	chick-pea	physalia	herbaria	Marattia
djellaba	sweetpea	dentalia	cercaria	zoocytia
piassaba	heartpea	battalia	cnidaria	alleluia
zambomba	glory-pea	Spigelia	Fragaria	effluvia
algaroba	undersea	parhelia	Scalaria	impluvia
bona-roba	brick-tea	anthelia	adularia	ataraxia
carnauba	Nemertea	bromelia	Arenaria	cachexia
macahuba	caper-tea	dysmelia	troparia	dyslexia
simaruba	rutabaga	stapelia	sacraria	anorexia
theriaca	Zoophaga	Caecilia	terraria	apyrexia
jararaca	meshugga	Marsilia	dentaria	panmixia
oiticica	geropiga	Reptilia	montaria	asphyxia
angelica	quadriga	camellia	septaria	trapezia
basilica	churinga	beryllia	wistaria	Vellozia
maiolica	caatinga	hemiolia	manubria	quillaja
majolica	araponga	magnolia	synedria	maharaja
japonica	arapunga	Scopolia	Diandria	takamaka
veronica	Saratoga	adynamia	hetaeria	jararaka
brassica	sastruga	toxaemia	progeria	moussaka
sciatica	zastruga	academia	Eutheria	babushka
Hepatica	kaliyuga	pandemia	krameria	svastika
barranca	brouhaha	ischemia	gesneria	swastika
mandioca	biscacha	anthemia	bacteria	yarmulka
anasarca	viscacha	paroemia	criteria	schapska
Mollusca	bizcacha	hydremia	wisteria	britzska
Samaveda	vizcacha	astigmia	hysteria	amygdala
Araneida	cachucha	zoonomia	Hatteria	polygala
Annelida	shraddha	Funtumia	pizzeria	Kalevala
Griselda	acalepha	raphania	hetairia	zarzuela
reddenda	Golgotha	egomania	triforia	strobila
credenda	sapucaia	encaenia	euphoria	Valhalla
hacienda	quillaia	gardenia	Signoria	Walhalla
anaconda	gallabia	asthenia	victoria	glabella
Golconda	Amphibia	insignia	Suctoria	isabella
Decapoda	coenobia	vaccinia	zoiatria	cribella
Hexapoda	rhizobia	Puccinia	gematria	Roccella
Copepoda	ytterbia	Garcinia	ischuria	marcella
Tylopoda	suburbia	Virginia	chyluria	predella
Octopoda	conurbia	pollinia	planuria	flagella
Nematoda	Monoecia	Salvinia	polyuria	shigella
Bethesda	alopecia	gloxinia	dichasia	orchella
hypogaea	estancia	insomnia	gymnasia	Tremella
Notogaea	semuncia	Polymnia	Laurasia	glumella
Nymphaea	epicedia	zirconia	fantasia	Brunella
Furcraea	cymbidia	sinfonia	malvasia	prunella
Mithraea	coccidia	Gorgonia	Rhodesia	ombrella
gastraea	sporidia	euphonia	ecclesia	umbrella
Schizaea	presidia	Chelonia	magnesia	terrella
gallabea	sympodia	vallonia	akinesia	vulsella
Campodea	buddleia	Bignonia	symposia	tessella
synaphea	epopoeia	tritonia	ambrosia	clitella
diarrhea	Panhagia	miltonia	eupepsia	scutella
barathea	vestigia	Slavonia	autopsia	rachilla
sand-flea	hypalgia	Saturnia	intarsia	orchilla
snow-flea	coxalgia	Trigynia	parousia	mammilla
trochlea	apologia	paranoia	Dionysia	fibrilla
Marsilea	pterygia	metanoia	Sarmatia	guerilla
Castanea	synechia	hemiopia	hospitia	spirilla
prytanea	petechia	diplopia	apositia	sensilla
Dulcinea	branchia	Cecropia	syssitia	mantilla
zoogloea	bronchia	subtopia	Rodentia	flotilla
paranoea	agraphia	scotopia	dementia	tortilla
dyspnoea	radialia	photopia	strontia	Anguilla
earth-pea	Mammalia	dystopia	hamartia	tequilla

coquilla	chloasma	Porifera	Atalanta	hecatomb
parabola	cathisma	Rotifera	placenta	plumb-bob
metabola	charisma	ephemera	sarmenta	goosegob
Denebola	Rhytisma	habanera	adespota	rent-a-mob
Coca-Cola®	platysma	antisera	non-quota	swell-mob
Arvicola	gymkhana	isoptera	Fascista	doorknob
Saxicola	dulciana	pellagra	ballista	nose-herb
minneola	shamiana	chiragra	Protista	reabsorb
fasciola	fistiana	anaphora	subcosta	well-curb
massoola	katakana	plethora	starosta	sillabub
tetrapla	Ramayana	lecanora	Mahratta	syllabub
mandorla	tridacna	diaspora	faldetta	golf-club
cunabula	Dracaena	semantra	vendetta	over-club
nubecula	Phocaena	dicentra	zuchetta	sea-shrub
lodicula	subpoena	calyptra	fughetta	subshrub
silicula	campagna	kalyptra	burletta	rum-shrub
Canicula	zampogna	palestra	operetta	souse-tub
auricula	trichina	fenestra	terzetta	leach-tub
vesicula	kinakina	claustra	mozzetta	swill-tub
navicula	semolina	dielytra	Peshitta	dolly-tub
opercula	Carolina	Xanthura	Zoophyta	C
opuscula	sudamina	Anoplura	tamandua	bacchiac
subucula	velamina	tamboura	periagua	dochmiac
scrofula	foramina	velatura	continua	demoniac
Spergula	putamina	Porphyra	menstrua	simoniac
hula-hula	pashmina	rakshasa	Saxicava	ammoniac
squamula	Filipina	marchesa	lava-lava	celeriac
vaginula	Atherina	Responsa	piassava	aphasiac
retinula	glossina	Scabiosa	Mahadeva	Genesiac
gastrula	sonatina	gloriosa	Kamadeva	amnesiac
clausula	cavatina	mariposa	septleva	stick-lac
capitula	Neritina	virtuosa	Casanova	shell-lac
blastula	bandanna	abscissa	conferva	Armagnac
Symphyla	platanna	vibrissa	antefixa	sandarac
Cinerama®	Podogona	mantissa	Himalaya	tric-trac
panorama	Cinchona	tsaritsa	calisaya	cul-de-sac
parabema	Ochotona	stoccata	xenophya	tac-au-tac
myxedema	cromorna	Tunicata	galabiya	hypothec
anathema	avifauna	Chordata	credenza	forinsec
epithema	tsarevna	viewdata	czaritza	Chaldaic
erythema	czarevna	Craniata	B	spondaic
sclerema	water-boa	Ungulata	lemon-dab	trochaic
diastema	holla-hoa	Annulata	smear-dab	Cyrenaic
blastema	dyschroa	matamata	land-crab	Mishnaic
stalagma	Anthozoa	Squamata	king-crab	mesaraic
syntagma	Heliozoa	schemata	black-neb	Mithraic
sterigma	Hydrozoa	bregmata	mem-sahib	un-mosaic
arapaima	Sporozoa	stigmata	quill-nib	stanzaic
engramma	protozoa	ultimata	cross-rib	syllabic
trilemma	chinampa	stemmata	short-rib	cannabic
semicoma	capybara	gliomata	choliamb	Columbic
glaucoma	caracara	lipomata	choriamb	microbic
trachoma	toxocara	stromata	forelimb	ascorbic
lymphoma	chinkara	automata	time-bomb	cherubic
xanthoma	sayonara	myxomata	fire-bomb	thoracic
melanoma	sasarara	miasmata	dive-bomb	enneadic
atheroma	demerara	traumata	nail-bomb	Haggadic
scleroma	gurdwara	serenata	aerobomb	palladic
Pyrosoma	vertebra	resinata	catacomb	Helladic
steatoma	Alhambra	Edentata	side-comb	maenadic
teratoma	penumbra	analecta	rose-comb	tornadic
mycetoma	cathedra	saliceta	back-comb	sporadic
odontoma	chimaera	arboreta	wool-comb	tetradic
pro-forma	tapadera	Señorita	flax-comb	pentadic

molybdic	Vandalic	zoonomic	daemonic	choleric
premedic	pachalic	isonomic	pulmonic	chimeric
conoidic	cephalic	trisomic	gnomonic	epimeric
Chasidic	kephalic	diatomic	harmonic	trimeric
Hassidic	omphalic	anatomic	sermonic	isomeric
heraldic	phthalic	epitomic	hormonic	turmeric
sarcodic	rhopalic	zootomic	geoponic	mesmeric
cathodic	tantalic	endermic	vibronic	bacteric
methodic	republic	orgasmic	hadronic	ureteric
periodic	dicyclic	marasmic	subsonic	neoteric
episodic	encyclic	Targumic	parsonic	esoteric
prosodic	eucyclic	volcanic	diatonic	exoteric
Talmudic	Goidelic	vulcanic	platonic	hysteric
apogaeic	Gadhelic	rhodanic	subtonic	podagric
dyspneic	parhelic	manganic	tectonic	spagiric
morbific	nickelic	mechanic	epitonic	diapiric
specific	dysmelic	Ossianic	Miltonic	vampiric
calcific	Pentelic	shamanic	syntonic	meteoric
prolific	gentilic	Germanic	protonic	enchoric
magnific	medallic	tympanic	isotonic	amphoric
somnific	metallic	Hispanic	Teutonic	euphoric
cornific	orsellic	sultanic	plutonic	rhetoric
febrific	Cyrillic	galvanic	Newtonic	historic
terrific	Lucullic	biogenic	Slavonic	theatric
horrific	diabolic	Diogenic	saturnic	electric
petrific	anabolic	zoogenic	anechoic	dimetric
pulsific	symbolic	erogenic	epiploic	dioptric
beatific	carbolic	orogenic	paranoic	mercuric
lactific	Mongolic	myogenic	gabbroic	telluric
pontific	catholic	pyogenic	unheroic	hippuric
mortific	hemiolic	dysgenic	dichroic	purpuric
salvific	phenolic	hyphenic	metazoic	spagyric
choragic	epipolic	asthenic	endozoic	diabasic
choregic	petrolic	ruthenic	holozoic	tribasic
gambogic	systolic	hygienic	Cenozoic	gymnasic
anagogic	methylic	Hellenic	Mesozoic	geodesic
apagogic	phenylic	ecumenic	ectozoic	phthisic
epagogic	propylic	neotenic	entozoic	forensic
isagogic	caprylic	morainic	polyzoic	epinosic
dialogic	dactylic	rabbinic	satrapic	Triassic
analogic	epigamic	succinic	syncopic	Jurassic
epilogic	pangamic	pollinic	Ethiopic	potassic
ecologic	syngamic	encrinic	hemiopic	gneissic
geologic	isogamic	platinic	cyclopic	banausic
neologic	exogamic	tyrannic	hydropic	Tungusic
urologic	thalamic	carbonic	ectropic	pop-music
telergic	cinnamic	draconic	eutropic	anabatic
allergic	adynamic	aniconic	scotopic	sabbatic
synergic	dioramic	zirconic	photopic	cuneatic
theurgic	balsamic	glyconic	isotopic	phreatic
liturgic	toxaemic	sardonic	Calippic	emphatic
Pelasgic	academic	trigonic	zootypic	muriatic
Halachic	epidemic	geogonic	isobaric	prelatic
diarchic	pandemic	isogonic	barbaric	villatic
anarchic	alchemic	Tychonic	Pindaric	dramatic
seraphic	ischemic	siphonic	Bulgaric	haematic
agraphic	phonemic	euphonic	margaric	rhematic
strophic	trisemic	typhonic	coumaric	thematic
empathic	systemic	chthonic	tartaric	poematic
eolithic	sphygmic	pythonic	cerebric	trematic
ornithic	rhythmic	Panionic	dyhydric	magmatic
anorthic	coelomic	nepionic	glyceric	sigmatic
autarkic	economic	chalonic	spageric	dogmatic
daedalic	bionomic	cyclonic	sopheric	climatic

primatic	pyelitic	synoptic	pike-head	side-road
dalmatic	spilitic	entoptic	bonehead	ring-road
pelmatic	mellitic	autoptic	forehead	highroad
aromatic	zeolitic	dicastic	sorehead	railroad
stomatic	zoolitic	orgastic	stag-head	tram-road
Sarmatic	poplitic	chiastic	long-head	cart-road
dermatic	perlitic	gelastic	bulkhead	dirt-road
umbratic	Adamitic	aplastic	forkhead	post-road
Socratic	eremitic	monastic	nail-head	crashpad
hieratic	palmitic	dynastic	railhead	Upanisad
operatic	granitic	asbestic	well-head	tightwad
protatic	uranitic	majestic	billhead	superadd
ecstatic	syenitic	eclestic	bullhead	cupolaed
eustatic	lignitic	telestic	drumhead	pyjamaed
silvatic	aconitic	domestic	skinhead	slug-a-bed
sylvatic	zoonitic	agrestic	pump-head	piss-a-bed
caryatic	eccritic	tungstic	hoarhead	vartabed
didactic	eucritic	sadistic	pier-head	unwebbed
galactic	dioritic	theistic	overhead	unribbed
synectic	ferritic	Sufistic	hogshead	demobbed
eutectic	neuritic	logistic	flathead	throbbed
elenctic	pruritic	holistic	softhead	undubbed
Nearctic	felsitic	nomistic	gilt-head	scrubbed
diabetic	myositic	monistic	bolt-head	unrubbed
syndetic	rectitic	Taoistic	jolthead	childbed
geodetic	Jesuitic	egoistic	mort-head	bride-bed
exegetic	bauxitic	papistic	masthead	death-bed
Japhetic	cobaltic	meristic	misplead	flock-bed
bathetic	basaltic	veristic	fair-lead	plank-bed
pathetic	pedantic	poristic	tea-bread	uncombed
enthetic	Vedantic	juristic	bee-bread	untombed
sovietic	gigantic	puristic	rye-bread	benumbed
athletic	Atlantic	myristic	sow-bread	divan-bed
balletic	semantic	artistic	waybread	wagon-bed
amuletic	romantic	autistic	misdread	unilobed
phyletic	xerantic	truistic	foreread	trilobed
hermetic	gerontic	agnostic	unthread	unbarbed
cosmetic	narcotic	acrostic	well-read	osier-bed
planetic	epidotic	acoustic	deep-read	water-bed
frenetic	lordotic	maieutic	bespread	river-bed
magnetic	kyphotic	toreutic	dispread	hover-bed
limnetic	orthotic	dialytic	star-read	chair-bed
phonetic	semiotic	analytic	overread	absorbed
unpoetic	amniotic	slivovic	bedstead	disorbed
herpetic	periotic	ataraxic	jeremiad	uncurbed
anoretic	psilotic	dyslexic	Olympiad	press-bed
heuretic	epulotic	anorexic	vine-clad	sad-faced
diuretic	cyanotic	orichalc	turf-clad	red-faced
enuretic	hypnotic	quidnunc	mail-clad	pig-faced
apyretic	enzootic	perisarc	iron-clad	dog-faced
apatetic	despotic	endosarc	overclad	pug-faced
dietetic	fibrotic	ectosarc	hebdomad	ill-faced
erotetic	necrotic	D	hey-go-mad	two-faced
Helvetic	dicrotic	granddad	moody-mad	surfaced
klephtic	hidrotic	veranda'd	freeload	fat-faced
Sinaitic	neurotic	pale-dead	case-load	unplaced
leucitic	amitotic	half-dead	peak-load	embraced
rachitic	quixotic	club-head	pack-load	unbraced
orchitic	synaptic	dead-head	deck-load	ungraced
mephitic	eupeptic	feed-head	workload	terraced
Cushitic	ecliptic	acid-head	ship-load	untraced
Kushitic	elliptic	bald-head	overload	chaliced
uralitic	holoptic	hindhead	boat-load	corniced
enclitic	panoptic	hardhead	cartload	unvoiced

unpriced	godspeed	lozenged	verified	embarked
balanced	subbreed	unhinged	purified	unbarked
valanced	outbreed	unringed	ossified	remarked
advanced	miscreed	stringed	ratified	unmarked
cadenced	free-reed	untinged	notified	unworked
defenced	birdseed	unwinged	ladyfied	unmasked
unfenced	cole-seed	thronged	trophied	vandyked
scienced	gapeseed	enlarged	sicklied	unscaled
silenced	rape-seed	unforged	unallied	unhealed
unforced	beniseed	engorged	complied	unsealed
brocaded	worm-seed	ungorged	supplied	unfabled
unshaded	moonseed	unpurged	mutinied	disabled
unloaded	fern-seed	ungauged	crannied	cribbled
degraded	hemp-seed	unrouged	whinnied	stubbled
ungraded	lintseed	detached	canopied	troubled
untraded	flax-seed	attached	unespied	pedicled
unbedded	bindweed	breeched	occupied	paniced
shredded	pondweed	flanched	awearied	auricled
unwedded	pokeweed	planched	salaried	articled
unlidded	fireweed	branched	unvaried	calyced
unbudded	blueweed	caboched	descried	brindled
undeeded	gulfweed	enarched	sun-dried	unpeeled
unheeded	itchweed	starched	liveried	unaneled
unneeded	neckweed	scorched	belfried	teaseled
unseeded	rockweed	thatched	prairied	truffled
unweeded	duckweed	wretched	quarried	unrifled
one-sided	milk-weed	stitched	flurried	smuggled
two-sided	hawkweed	blotched	unburied	spangled
lop-sided	loco-weed	crotched	dropsied	shingled
unguided	knapweed	crutched	tape-tied	writhled
provided	goatweed	sloughed	unpitied	unhailed
ungilded	knotweed	uncashed	cavitied	unmailed
unfolded	wartweed	undashed	unenvied	unsailed
unbanded	goutweed	unsashed	frenzied	detailed
stranded	flix-weed	unwashed	sun-baked	bewailed
unbended	earth-fed	woodshed	streaked	unveiled
defended	midwifed	unfished	unshaked	unsoiled
friended	stall-fed	polished	unslaked	pantiled
intended	spoon-fed	finished	unbacked	weeviled
untended	unroofed	perished	unhacked	speckled
extended	underfed	tool-shed	unpacked	freckled
unminded	herbaged	caboshed	unracked	wrinkled
unfunded	foliaged	unbathed	undecked	caballed
grounded	packaged	sheathed	unrecked	uncalled
exploded	full-aged	breathed	invecked	so-called
dismoded	plumaged	wreathed	unlicked	medalled
outmoded	apanaged	unpathed	mimicked	pedalled
unhooded	teen-aged	steadied	panicked	ungalled
unwooded	cottaged	remedied	tunicked	phialled
retarded	unhedged	brandied	unpicked	appalled
unwarded	two-edged	embodied	undocked	metalled
vizarded	saw-edged	unbodied	unlocked	petalled
begirded	enridged	parodied	uplocked	totalled
ungirded	scragged	sturdied	havocked	equalled
unlorded	spragged	undefied	unsucked	rivalled
unworded	unrigged	tumefied	untucked	unwalled
secluded	sprigged	rarefied	unmilked	labelled
included	bewigged	ladified	unbanked	debelled
excluded	unwigged	codified	unlinked	rebelled
shrouded	shrugged	modified	unpinked	libelled
flambéed	effulged	salified	unbooked	excelled
alms-deed	unhanged	vilified	uncooked	modelled
drip-feed	unpanged	ramified	unlooked	refelled
overfeed	deranged	typified	sheep-ked	unfelled

orielled	mistimed	cayenned	ungeared	flowered
panelled	becalmed	unpinned	dog-eared	unhaired
lapelled	unhelmed	untinned	lop-eared	unpaired
repelled	unfilmed	unsunned	upreared	oil-fired
impelled	undammed	rawboned	unshared	all-fired
cupelled	bedimmed	doggoned	declared	gas-fired
expelled	undimmed	gabioned	collared	inspired
ravelled	ungummed	legioned	dollared	dog-tired
bevelled	thrummed	visioned	prepared	acquired
levelled	strummed	pennoned	unspared	required
revelled	unsummed	weaponed	infra-red	brick-red
rivelled	undoomed	unironed	ultrared	unadored
jewelled	customed	reasoned	nectared	mirrored
newelled	bottomed	seasoned	home-bred	liquored
bowelled	unharmed	unatoned	pure-bred	debarred
rowelled	unwarmed	cantoned	true-bred	embarred
towelled	deformed	unearned	half-bred	unbarred
vowelled	reformed	unwarned	high-bred	unmarred
unfilled	informed	caverned	calibred	untarred
unmilled	unformed	unburned	hell-bred	deferred
perilled	unwormed	unturned	well-bred	referred
untilled	perfumed	upturned	blood-red	inferred
cavilled	beplumed	unpruned	membered	deterred
devilled	costumed	fortuned	timbered	interred
unwilled	unrhymed	ungowned	cumbered	abhorred
unpolled	turbaned	renowned	laddered	occurred
carolled	unweaned	uncoyned	doddered	recurred
scrolled	unyeaned	stuccoed	wildered	incurred
enrolled	hog-maned	frescoed	wandered	unfurred
extolled	unmoaned	nielloed	wondered	demurred
unculled	tartaned	tattooed	sundered	sceptred
undulled	hardened	yoke-toed	bordered	sun-cured
annulled	unweened	unreaped	powdered	verdured
unpulled	lichened	unshaped	affeered	perjured
aureoled	stamened	unsoaped	unpeered	uninured
petioled	unopened	undraped	coffered	laboured
schooled	pattened	milleped	buffered	arboured
steepled	mittened	cheliped	jiggered	coloured
crumpled	weazened	filliped	fingered	armoured
stippled	resigned	milliped	withered	humoured
uncurled	unsigned	palmiped	wickered	honoured
untitled	unpained	plumiped	suckered	vapoured
gruntled	strained	pinniped	cankered	unsoured
startled	unsained	fissiped	bunkered	favoured
bristled	combined	multiped	antlered	savoured
engouled	turbined	anguiped	bannered	measured
besouled	unreined	unhelped	mannered	leisured
unsouled	confined	undamped	cornered	tonsured
stipuled	margined	scrimped	tempered	fissured
uncowled	buskined	scrapped	raftered	featured
grizzled	reclined	strapped	centered	statured
unseamed	inclined	unsapped	wintered	cultured
unshamed	muslined	untapped	ulstered	raptured
unblamed	vermined	undipped	nattered	vestured
inflamed	uncoined	unripped	tattered	textured
unframed	spavined	stripped	bettered	surbased
diademed	undamned	equipped	lettered	deceased
meseemed	columned	unlopped	littered	unleased
esteemed	unfanned	stropped	tottered	diseased
systemed	unmanned	estopped	beavered	enchased
rhythmed	japanned	unwarped	quivered	unbiased
unmaimed	untanned	hiccuped	calvered	unraised
sublimed	unkenned	endeared	clovered	upraised
ill-timed	unpenned	unfeared	louvered	opalised

premised	striated	closeted	unposted	winnowed
agonised	muriated	corseted	encysted	borrowed
unpoised	unelated	cosseted	unhatted	sorrowed
unhalsed	afflated	breveted	squatted	unavowed
licensed	inflated	velveted	unnetted	newly-wed
unsensed	oculated	curveted	rosetted	deflexed
unclosed	animated	infefted	revetted	reflexed
cyanosed	palmated	ungifted	rivetted	inflexed
stenosed	mismated	uplifted	bewetted	convexed
pug-nosed	crenated	unsifted	unwetted	hobdayed
composed	crinated	alighted	gazetted	defrayed
supposed	pinnated	blighted	unbitted	affrayed
purposed	throated	flighted	befitted	unstayed
disposed	not-pated	plighted	unfitted	unswayed
relapsed	umbrated	unbaited	splitted	wool-dyed
demersed	spirated	inedited	admitted	deep-dyed
immersed	serrated	unedited	remitted	unobeyed
reversed	irisated	pulpited	immitted	bird-eyed
unversed	agitated	spirited	allotted	wide-eyed
suversed	hastated	requited	garotted	pale-eyed
addorsed	unstated	unsuited	unrotted	mole-eyed
endorsed	costated	intuited	besotted	sloe-eyed
accursed	guttated	unsalted	assotted	fire-eyed
harassed	sinuated	unbelted	rebutted	dove-eyed
recessed	situated	unmelted	strutted	weak-eyed
stressed	clavated	uptilted	polluted	cockeyed
unkissed	elevated	unbolted	cornuted	pink-eyed
unmissed	larvated	revolted	sprouted	hawk-eyed
embossed	curvated	occulted	unimbued	wall-eyed
enmossed	indebted	unwanted	fatigued	volleyed
embussed	affected	indented	unargued	dull-eyed
hocussed	dejected	oriented	rose-hued	full-eyed
uncaused	selected	talented	unvalued	open-eyed
nimbused	expected	lamented	revenued	moon-eyed
diffused	obtected	demented	bereaved	storeyed
confused	invected	untented	unshaved	sour-eyed
unamused	addicted	unvented	enslaved	boss-eyed
unhoused	rabbeted	undinted	engraved	causeyed
chorused	lanceted	unwonted	depraved	lynx-eyed
pertused	streeted	unhunted	shrieved	grey-eyed
unabated	fidgeted	balloted	received	many-eyed
combated	budgeted	unfooted	low-lived	dewy-eyed
globated	pargeted	unrooted	deprived	employed
barbated	targeted	parroted	midwived	unglazed
surbated	jacketed	prompted	resolved	unseized
plicated	racketed	thwarted	unsolved	unprized
spicated	picketed	inserted	ungloved	man-sized
falcated	docketed	exserted	unproved	outsized
sulcated	pocketed	reverted	unnerved	medicaid
furcated	socketed	inverted	deserved	deep-laid
outdated	junketed	unsorted	reserved	overlaid
caudated	marketed	assorted	recurved	handmaid
unheated	toileted	retorted	incurved	bondmaid
galeated	palleted	intorted	upcurved	milkmaid
pileated	billeted	breasted	unthawed	cookmaid
lineated	filleted	impasted	unflawed	unrepaid
repeated	helmeted	untasted	unchewed	post-paid
unseated	signeted	unwasted	unviewed	duty-paid
alveated	bonneted	enfested	windowed	unafraid
ill-fated	lappeted	forested	unblowed	foresaid
radiated	carpeted	untested	wallowed	gainsaid
ciliated	garreted	attested	billowed	first-aid
foliated	ferreted	unlisted	pillowed	underbid
ebriated	turreted	assisted	willowed	unforbid

unturbid	ypsiloid	eupatrid	neck-band	yardwand
wood-acid	mytiloid	ophiurid	fahlband	metewand
thio-acid	phalloid	caryatid	rain-band	reascend
monoacid	thalloid	obliquid	hair-band	dividend
tetracid	phelloid	illiquid	moor-band	gable-end
polyacid	phylloid	skewbald	platband	nerve-end
scolecid	triploid	danegeld	dead-hand	reoffend
dytiscid	liguloid	horngeld	free-hand	scrag-end
Seleucid	cotyloid	hand-held	forehand	befriend
pellucid	sesamoid	withheld	longhand	unfriend
bombycid	prismoid	midfield	nigh-hand	forelend
uncandid	humanoid	ice-field	backhand	resplend
splendid	paranoid	oil-field	deck-hand	vilipend
underdid	tetanoid	urnfield	mill-hand	forspend
limnaeid	sphenoid	airfield	farm-hand	misspend
tracheid	galenoid	gas-field	rein-hand	reverend
sclereid	solenoid	outfield	join-hand	rope's-end
multifid	Armenoid	hayfield	whip-hand	wallsend
non-rigid	pyrenoid	enshield	near-hand	repetend
sphingid	echinoid	bushveld	overhand	co-extend
synergid	hominoid	backveld	hour-hand	woodbind
tailskid	actinoid	spot-weld	left-hand	bellbind
whizz-kid	coronoid	weregild	text-hand	prescind
Heraclid	sturnoid	godchild	slobland	overkind
coverlid	polypoid	elf-child	headland	sun-blind
serranid	Polaroid	twichild	wild-land	purblind
Sassanid	gabbroid	man-child	woodland	tamarind
zygaenid	cancroid	merchild	yardland	dead-wind
sciaenid	dendroid	overbold	homeland	landwind
arachnid	amberoid	sour-cold	foreland	woodwind
salmonid	spheroid	outscold	oil-gland	side-wind
amoeboid	scleroid	snow-cold	gangland	forewind
rhomboid	asteroid	clay-cold	highland	withwind
pinacoid	nephroid	world-old	lackland	downwind
coracoid	tapiroid	ninefold	dockland	overwind
hyracoid	centroid	gatefold	folkland	vagabond
autacoid	sciuroid	fivefold	bookland	backbond
helicoid	siluroid	scaffold	parkland	bail-bond
soricoid	lemuroid	manifold	filmland	Eurobond
scincoid	pityroid	billfold	mainland	pair-bond
calycoid	emulsoid	overfold	cornland	overfond
rhabdoid	thyrsoid	fourfold	downland	keeshond
lambdoid	medusoid	marigold	townland	ash-blond
doridoid	sinusoid	handhold	overland	Garamond
clupeoid	hydatoid	freehold	moorland	fishpond
thyreoid	ergatoid	lifehold	mossland	duck-pond
spongoid	nematoid	withhold	shetland	millpond
trichoid	ceratoid	overhold	Scotland	stewpond
conchoid	keratoid	foothold	portland	reed-rond
trochoid	teratoid	roothold	eastland	pudibund
psychoid	athetoid	copyhold	Lettland	moribund
scaphoid	odontoid	frampold	gourmand	furibund
cardioid	blastoid	oversold	ordinand	infecund
taenioid	volutoid	foretold	re-expand	verecund
chorioid	omohyoid	Cotswold	reed-rand	rubicund
tarsioid	geomyoid	old-world	cider-and	wage-fund
histioid	botryoid	saraband	iron-sand	reinfund
pinakoid	schizoid	headband	thousand	ice-bound
alkaloid	pezizoid	reed-band	cab-stand	egg-bound
homaloid	intrepid	side-band	ash-stand	fogbound
sepaloid	bicuspid	nose-band	inkstand	pot-bound
petaloid	dihybrid	waveband	hatstand	outbound
cameloid	subacrid	reef-band	outstand	mawbound
cichloid	hesperid	backband	graduand	dumfound

confound	coltwood	way-board	nowt-herd	Vespidae
profound	bentwood	keyboard	reed-bird	Scaridae
new-found	myriapod	camisard	rice-bird	Sparidae
sea-hound	tetrapod	brassard	cagebird	Labridae
elkhound	amphipod	mud-guard	game-bird	Pieridae
foxhound	orthopod	leg-guard	fire-bird	Corvidae
compound	myriopod	vanguard	wire-bird	Theaceae
ten-pound	theropod	hatguard	lyre-bird	Oleaceae
propound	pteropod	rat-guard	bluebird	Fagaceae
lispound	sauropod	outguard	lovebird	Limaceae
unground	rhizopod	jacquard	puff-bird	Ulmaceae
all-round	smørbrød	thraward	surf-bird	Moraceae
surround	out-Herod	landward	hangbird	Rosaceae
ostracod	lease-rod	hindward	king-bird	Musaceae
pease-cod	dowel-rod	windward	songbird	Vitaceae
water-god	stair-rod	woodward	cockbird	Rutaceae
river-god	down-trod	sideward	rock-bird	Taxaceae
belly-god	trout-rod	homeward	jail-bird	Bixaceae
slipshod	impasto'd	Romeward	call-bird	tracheae
babyfood	scabbard	rereward	bell-bird	induciae
maidhood	guimbard	foreward	gaol-bird	laciniae
wifehood	food-card	hiveward	oven-bird	actiniae
pagehood	face-card	backward	rain-bird	Picariae
idlehood	race-card	parkward	whipbird	facetiae
popehood	time-card	kirkward	snow-bird	minutiae
wivehood	railcard	hellward	ladybird	induviae
selfhood	wool-card	woolward	sash-cord	sequelae
serfhood	brancard	Zionward	rheocord	lamellae
kinghood	coat-card	downward	whipcord	patellae
monkhood	postcard	untoward	Hereford	novellae
dollhood	show-card	bearward	trichord	mamillae
girlhood	standard	rearward	urochord	papillae
pump-hood	well-far'd	leftward	landlord	maxillae
misshood	savegard	eastward	overlord	medullae
babyhood	staggard	westward	headword	ampullae
ladyhood	sluggard	vineyard	foreword	formulae
ill-blood	pilchard	boneyard	owreword	plumulae
shampoo'd	galliard	meteyard	backword	planulae
holy-rood	halliard	backyard	loan-word	cannulae
lima-wood	billiard	rickyard	overword	serpulae
crab-wood	milliard	dockyard	password	fistulae
dead-wood	Spaniard	junk-yard	cuss-word	pterylae
wild-wood	whiniard	kirkyard	ill-faurd	drachmae
hardwood	blinkard	kailyard	taste-bud	piscinae
cord-wood	stinkard	sail-yard	fruit-bud	Corvinae
lime-wood	drunkard	willyard	farcy-bud	antennae
pine-wood	stunkard	farmyard	enshroud	tenebrae
firewood	baselard	mainyard	unshroud	exhedrae
rosewood	gaillard	whinyard	top-proud	tesserae
beef-wood	overlard	barnyard	misproud	urethrae
Wedgwood	seaboard	Savoyard	star-pav'd	amphorae
kingwood	tea-board	shipyard	E	Saururae
rock-wood	lee-board	door-yard	succubae	Labiatae
milkwood	off-board	tilt-yard	verrucae	locustae
corkwood	pegboard	show-yard	Coccidae	describe
wormwood	logboard	navy-yard	Phocidae	inscribe
ovenwood	damboard	unvizard	Percidae	diatribe
poon-wood	lap-board	blizzard	Muscidae	subtribe
ironwood	mopboard	land-herd	Tineidae	buncombe
coco-wood	cupboard	swanherd	Gobiidae	lyophobe
pulpwood	garboard	shepherd	Rallidae	seed-lobe
basswood	larboard	potsherd	Agamidae	conglobe
softwood	outboard	neat-herd	Aranidae	gas-globe
giltwood	pax-board	goatherd	Talpidae	wardrobe

8 -OBE

anaerobe	booklice	tadvance	sun-shade	ringside
bathrobe	shell-ice	abeyance	blockade	backside
bathcube	semplice	buoyance	stockade	hillside
boob-tube	complice	nascence	escalade	Ironside
fire-tube	surplice	credence	saw-blade	burnside
worm-tube	egg-slice	evidence	defilade	flip-side
test-tube	woodmice	tendence	enfilade	diopside
draw-tube	reremice	prudence	oeillade	nearside
thridace	rearmice	exigence	grillade	overside
deuce-ace	overnice	pungence	accolade	quayside
dispeace	outvoice	mergence	overlade	yuletide
club-face	allspice	sithence	handmade	half-tide
hardface	water-ice	nowhence	home-made	hock-tide
side-face	licorice	ambience	self-made	meal-tide
pale-face	cut-price	audience	well-made	eventide
type-face	gentrice	salience	serenade	noontide
half-face	practice	lenience	marinade	neaptide
boniface	drift-ice	sapience	lemonade	misguide
coal-face	poultice	patience	escapade	redivide
full-face	prentice	violence	croupade	suboxide
moon-face	solstice	opulence	disgrade	trioxide
postface	brattice	clemence	speisade	monoxide
whey-face	brettice	commence	palisade	peroxide
gold-lace	Scottice	eminence	camisade	forebode
bone-lace	log-juice	tenpence	glissade	Postcode
shoe-lace	verjuice	twopence	persuade	arillode
Lovelace	unsluice	fippence	dissuade	phyllode
necklace	riddance	tuppence	antecede	displode
displace	toe-dance	dispence	Ganymede	threnode
misplace	egg-dance	sixpence	stampede	palinode
bootlace	abidance	clarence	pax-brede	antinode
populace	voidance	florence	Samoyede	megapode
stay-lace	guidance	presence	regicide	antipode
reed-mace	tendance	pretence	algicide	monopode
carapace	tap-dance	sentence	aphicide	wind-rode
halfpace	war-dance	sequence	filicide	centrode
airspace	outdance	intrince	silicide	bestrode
footpace	elegance	convince	homicide	rhapsode
vambrace	bechance	province	viricide	nematode
headrace	ambiance	ensconce	vaticide	preclude
landrace	radiance	insconce	feticide	conclude
tide-race	defiance	denounce	viticide	postlude
bongrace	affiance	renounce	coincide	semi-nude
disgrace	valiance	announce	genocide	subtrude
sack-race	reliance	symploce	nucleide	protrude
tail-race	alliance	effierce	rhaphide	transude
millrace	variance	enfierce	sulphide	hebetude
flat-race	resiance	empierce	sylphide	quietude
boatrace	deviance	commerce	sodamide	habitude
foot-race	parlance	sesterce	selenide	solitude
sea-piece	ordnance	renforce	arsenide	finitude
cod-piece	crepance	perforce	actinide	latitude
one-piece	iterance	resource	polypide	altitude
toe-piece	entrance	coalesce	chloride	aptitude
eye-piece	outrance	evanesce	fluoride	attitude
two-piece	nuisance	compesce	override	aldehyde
earpiece	exitance	liquesce	bestride	Punjabee
say-piece	portance	cognosce	Abbaside	scarabee
jaundice	sortance	estacade	kerb-side	Caribbee
malefice	pastance	aquacade	curbside	queen-bee
benefice	distance	autocade	roadside	honey-bee
artifice	instance	frescade	wind-side	divorcee
woodlice	pittance	renegade	fireside	Sadducee
bird-lice	issuance	eyeshade	foreside	frank-fee

penny-fee	jack-tree	wharfage	squirage	refringe
squeegee	sack-tree	re-engage	tutorage	infringe
protégée	milk-tree	mortgage	wood-sage	astringe
negligee	cork-tree	weighage	envisage	prolonge
squiligee	meal-tree	roughage	dressage	disponge
Faringee	wall-tree	verbiage	plussage	enraunge
Portugee	palm-tree	carriage	ill-usage	straunge
chee-chee	plum-tree	marriage	spousage	implunge
Manichee	rain-tree	ferriage	disusage	scrounge
coryphee	gauntree	breakage	misusage	dispunge
moonshee	bountree	trackage	floatage	paragoge
Cherokee	coco-tree	wreckage	driftage	horologe
hard-a-lee	soap-tree	blockage	maritage	scarmoge
shiralee	pear-tree	truckage	heritage	row-barge
expellee	bourtree	pucelage	fruitage	recharge
jampanee	upas-tree	fuselage	vaultage	encharge
assignee	boottree	tutelage	chantage	uncharge
detainee	releasee	mucilage	plantage	litharge
examinee	promisee	spoilage	frontage	sea-marge
overknee	Pharisee	ensilage	vauntage	submerge
disponee	licensee	diallage	cabotage	re-emerge
internee	endorsee	smallage	sabotage	commerge
pindaree	sightsee	enallage	agiotage	absterge
puggaree	hiccatee	stallage	helotage	converge
sangaree	neckatee	spillage	pilotage	disgorge
dungaree	indictee	grillage	shortage	demiurge
shikaree	frailtee	stillage	substage	lee-gauge
bummaree	absentee	thirlage	off-stage	oil-gauge
rapparee	patentee	endamage	frottage	rampauge
shivaree	ballotee	chummage	adjutage	apophyge
conferee	repartee	appanage	language	headache
kedgeree	deportee	alienage	truquage	rondache
budgeree	arrestee	cozenage	messuage	face-ache
folk-free	remittee	drainage	cleavage	bone-ache
toll-free	tirrivee	grainage	strewage	backache
overfree	employee	vicinage	tasswage	mustache
rent-free	auto-da-fé	badinage	malaxage	soutache
scot-free	fail-safe	wagonage	métayage	corniche
shot-free	meat-safe	baronage	fire-edge	pastiche
cost-free	mort-safe	sternage	fore-edge	postiche
post-free	repriefe	equipage	ice-ledge	cynanche
duty-free	Tartuffe	full-page	impledge	revanche
filagree	wildlife	stumpage	selvedge	menarche
disagree	pond-life	wrappage	Oxbridge	tedesche
greegree	home-life	slippage	porridge	babouche
pedigree	half-life	stoppage	estridge	pabouche
filigree	self-life	overpage	pulsidge	débouché
jamboree	long-life	footpage	dislodge	barouche
sowarree	penknife	groupage	prejudge	farouche
shea-tree	wakerife	vicarage	forjudge	acalephe
crab-tree	waukrife	clearage	misjudge	nebbishe
rood-tree	goodwife	altarage	begrudge	sunbathe
dule-tree	spaewife	under-age	scrowdge	spreathe
axle-tree	fishwife	steerage	urostege	enswathe
lime-tree	cribbage	acierage	meshugge	inswathe
pine-tree	birdcage	amperage	prestige	unswathe
shoe-tree	carucage	waterage	promulge	spreethe
sloetree	T-bandage	beverage	exchange	nepenthe
pipe-tree	blindage	leverage	phalange	absinthe
rose-tree	frondage	coverage	citrange	reclothe
date-tree	poundage	sewerage	estrange	enclothe
roof-tree	guardage	suffrage	fontange	unclothe
tung-tree	cloudage	langrage	scavenge	Medjidie
pith-tree	staffage	umpirage	befringe	organdie

dinky-die	overtake	telltale	bankable	mootable
scroggie	ale-stake	tell-tale	smokable	quotable
killogie	seaquake	woodwale	workable	portable
swelchie	likewake	probable	scalable	sortable
grumphie	lykewake	curbable	healable	tastable
smoothie	latewake	clubable	bailable	testable
Ramillie	lichwake	placable	mailable	bistable
underlie	push-bike	peccable	sailable	instable
bonhomie	fail-dike	amicable	fellable	unstable
visnomie	klondike	educable	sellable	gustable
forhooie	crablike	readable	tellable	arguable
squab-pie	lamblike	gradable	tillable	valuable
shred-pie	seed-like	evadable	rollable	liquable
mince-pie	lifelike	beddable	tollable	issuable
umble-pie	wife-like	biddable	gullable	salvable
apple-pie	homelike	voidable	syllable	solvable
magot-pie	pipelike	guidable	violable	provable
foedarie	wise-like	weldable	isolable	drawable
Tartarie	roselike	fundable	blamable	viewable
lingerie	wavelike	fordable	filmable	knowable
flânerie	hivelike	laudable	loanable	avowable
causerie	dovelike	rideable	amenable	playable
métairie	leaf-like	makeable	openable	seizable
Valkyrie	self-like	takeable	gainable	prizable
Walkyrie	roof-like	likeable	opinable	bedabble
malvesie	kinglike	saleable	ruinable	scrabble
plurisie	song-like	nameable	damnable	squabble
dricksie	suchlike	tameable	tannable	scribble
jalousie	rush-like	tuneable	winnable	enfeeble
intertie	pithlike	ropeable	runnable	dry-bible
bheestie	milklike	hireable	shapable	fencible
Christie	parklike	hateable	palpable	vincible
dress-tie	swanlike	rateable	culpable	runcible
cross-tie	lion-like	liveable	bearable	forcible
tirrivie	starlike	loveable	wearable	miscible
spuilzie	what-like	moveable	inarable	educible
bruilzie	snowlike	sizeable	sparable	crucible
Sobranje	ladylike	diggable	operable	inedible
hardbake	half-pike	huggable	adorable	credible
clambake	turnpike	hangable	storable	mandible
seedcake	yarmulke	singable	exorable	vendible
rape-cake	fog-smoke	warhable	leasable	eludible
ague-cake	meal-poke	washable	erasable	eligible
loaf-cake	slowpoke	fishable	raisable	exigible
beefcake	pembroke	oathable	rinsable	tangible
fishcake	upstroke	tithable	lapsable	fallible
rock-cake	equivoke	sociable	passable	gullible
plum-cake	archduke	reliable	reusable	terrible
corn-cake	Mameluke	deniable	amusable	horrible
salt-cake	ring-dyke	expiable	unusable	thurible
rout-cake	klondyke	variable	abatable	feasible
off-shake	musicale	satiable	beatable	suasible
soda-lake	bud-scale	pitiable	tea-table	evasible
salt-lake	Airedale	vitiable	statable	sensible
Merimake	amygdale	dutiable	bed-table	tensible
sea-snake	bride-ale	leviable	liftable	rinsible
hub-brake	white-ale	enviable	imitable	passible
rim-brake	overhale	inviable	writable	possible
air-brake	oil-shale	unviable	suitable	partible
mandrake	fin-whale	shakable	evitable	flexible
muck-rake	small-ale	kickable	pantable	preamble
overrake	maid-pale	mockable	rentable	scramble
namesake	generale	talkable	pintable	atremble
keepsake	folk-tale	walkable	loo-table	resemble

ensemble	paraffle	sardelle	capriole	floscule
assemble	gefuffle	Rochelle	carriole	opuscule
assemblé	kefuffle	kyrielle	sand-mole	calycule
emmarble	bemuffle	quenelle	iron-mole	schedule
ox-warble	unmuffle	prunelle	Seminole	amygdule
redouble	unruffle	mamselle	clodpole	glandule
undouble	pea-rifle	dentelle	flagpole	squamule
chasuble	pantofle	rocaille	antipole	pack-mule
binnacle	sea-eagle	canaille	beanpole	flammule
pinnacle	inveagle	tenaille	tent-pole	vaginule
barnacle	espiègle	gerbille	punt-pole	spherule
spiracle	bedaggle	spadille	escarole	overrule
pentacle	scriggle	tredille	fumarole	footrule
tentacle	squiggle	orseille	fusarole	spansule
obstacle	struggle	reveille	girasole	punctule
bittacle	enveigle	chenille	camisole	intitule
fascicle	inveigle	bastille	cork-sole	plantule
pendicle	triangle	pastille	plimsole	frustule
caudicle	sprangle	coutille	turnsole	live-axle
pellicle	strangle	aiguille	diastole	ventayle
follicle	entangle	cheville	asystole	dysodyle
caulicle	untangle	pulville	manciple	staphyle
pannicle	immingle	parabole	disciple	prothyle
vernicle	springle	hypobole	multiple	gargoyle
cornicle	keybugle	caracole	ensample	gurgoyle
curricle	pinochle	borecole	repeople	diastyle
versicle	shauchle	tubicole	empeople	substyle
canticle	trauchle	nucleole	unpeople	epistyle
denticle	forhaile	sand-hole	mad-apple	prostyle
lenticle	ventaile	wood-hole	egg-apple	urostyle
monticle	immobile	kneehole	oak-apple	pyroxyle
particle	strobile	dane-hole	thrapple	bedazzle
testicle	imbecile	dene-hole	may-apple	undazzle
clavicle	domicile	nine-hole	thropple	embezzle
peduncle	indocile	borehole	empurple	unmuzzle
homuncle	dysodile	arsehole	impurple	good-dame
caruncle	serafile	bung-hole	subduple	gude-dame
furuncle	nail-file	sink-hole	uncouple	stepdame
tubercle	narghile	funkhole	centuple	holydame
encircle	symphile	coal-hole	septuple	card-game
unicycle	zoophile	nail-hole	sextuple	love-game
epicycle	lyophile	hell-hole	unsubtle	deck-game
tricycle	umquhile	well-hole	subtitle	ball-game
hen-padle	erewhile	worm-hole	mistitle	wall-game
encradle	nine-mile	kiln-hole	immantle	skin-game
straddle	camomile	peep-hole	unmantle	code-name
unsaddle	juvenile	weephole	ungentle	forename
co-meddle	wood-pile	lamphole	thristle	nickname
unriddle	eolipile	loophole	throstle	overname
striddle	scurrile	peat-hole	embattle	hog-frame
stroddle	scissile	bolthole	scrattle	airframe
befuddle	emissile	vent-hole	sprattle	saw-frame
bemuddle	volatile	shot-hole	squattle	grapheme
bone-idle	saxatile	knot-hole	resettle	morpheme
unbridle	tractile	porthole	unsettle	millième
rehandle	erectile	post-hole	belittle	teleseme
rekindle	quintile	dust-hole	throttle	glosseme
enkindle	quartile	blowhole	floccule	excuse-me
unbundle	sprackle	hidy-hole	molecule	polyseme
caboodle	untackle	fasciole	radicule	analcime
canoodle	strickle	gladiole	ridicule	isochime
engirdle	unbuckle	ovariole	lodicule	soda-lime
somedele	sprinkle	cabriole	silicule	bird-lime
triskele	strinkle	gloriole	reticule	seed-time

8 -IME

goodtime	foursome	gangrene	isocline	iron-mine
lifetime	playsome	neoprene	deadline	salt-mine
sometime	polysome	isoprene	headline	relumine
foretime	cloysome	arrasene	lead-line	illumine
calf-time	rheotome	kerosene	load-line	enlumine
half-time	gendarme	carotene	hand-line	solanine
ring-time	tachisme	pyroxene	land-line	long-nine
maritime	étatisme	Cocaigne	hardline	oscinine
meal-time	reillume	thebaine	zibeline	arginine
realtime	displume	procaine	lobeline	feminine
full-time	transume	poulaine	side-line	pavonine
term-time	reassume	Alemaine	tree-line	sturnine
meantime	eye-rhyme	ptomaine	life-line	jack-pine
downtime	rat-rhyme	germaine	cameline	huon-pine
xenotime	isocryme	migraine	capeline	atropine
overtime	coenzyme	darraine	tapeline	resupine
part-time	lysozyme	stovaine	pipeline	polypine
post-time	flea-bane	carabine	wire-line	stearine
Flextime ®	inurbane	woodbine	base-line	curarine
playtime	dog'sbane	bearbine	date-line	Patarine
consommé	ratsbane	Eugubine	coteline	mazarine
owrecome	dumb-cane	limacine	dragline	exocrine
down-come	silicane	déraciné	Catiline	algerine
overcome	barchane	telecine	aquiline	atherine
semi-dome	stephane	medicine	neckline	pelerine
stereome	camphane	salicine	balkline	vomerine
trichome	urethane	culicine	thalline	piperine
zoothome	seaplane	soricine	goal-line	viperine
rest-home	triplane	hyoscine	suilline	anserine
phyllome	volplane	calycine	apolline	icterine
menopome	warplane	baladine	tram-line	riverine
seadrome	airplane	sanidine	slimline	enshrine
syndrome	jetplane	acridine	mainline	inshrine
prodrome	tow-plane	pyridine	down-line	aegirine
airdrome	purslane	amandine	lanoline	chlorine
fleasome	inhumane	sourdine	Caroline	leporine
gladsome	membrane	paludine	gasoline	fluorine
handsome	jib-crane	caffeine	compline	doctrine
gleesome	triptane	mauveine	tump-line	lustrine
lifesome	camstane	gate-fine	loop-line	dextrine
jokesome	dry-stane	overfine	hairline	figurine
dolesome	paravane	baregine	gantline	sciurine
gamesome	terebene	strigine	contline	lemurine
lonesome	stilbene	zecchine	buntline	xenurine
tiresome	Pliocene	elaphine	trotline	daturine
gruesome	Holocene	trephine	girtline	andesine
lovesome	indigene	sylphine	rattline	ceresine
twigsome	hypogene	morphine	baculine	fuchsine
longsome	virogene	dauphine	induline	cytisine
tedisome	gasogene	murrhine	reguline	kerosine
darksome	gazogene	myrrhine	figuline	tyrosine
mirksome	phosgene	sunshine	lupuline	cytosine
worksome	polygene	outshine	Ursuline	glassine
murksome	camphene	Banthine ®	vituline	Theatine
healsome	Tyrrhene	ianthine	snowline	creatine
duelsome	xanthene	xanthine	sycamine	kreatine
toilsome	disthene	tarwhine	thiamine	legatine
roomsome	gasolene	sylviine	calamine	palatine
ribosome	ethylene	bubaline	melamine	gelatine
liposome	Terylene ®	alkaline	dopamine	astatine
merosome	butylene	sepaline	coramine	diactine
pyrosome	hexylene	petaline	gold-mine	nicotine
autosome	Gadarene	club-line	land-mine	serotine
fearsome	Nazarene	syncline	coal-mine	pristine

matutine	overtone	skyscape	kalotype	backfire
brow-tine	pea-stone	misshape	holotype	hell-fire
trey-tine	ribstone	sea-grape	homotype	drumfire
sanguine	rubstone	fox-grape	genotype	camp-fire
basquine	mudstone	name-tape	Linotype ®	overfire
undivine	ice-stone	inch-tape	monotype	spit-fire
pipe-wine	roestone	night-ape	serotype	port-fire
palm-wine	axe-stone	stay-tape	autotype	camphire
sea-swine	ragstone	sea-snipe	medicare	samphire
port-wine	inkstone	feed-pipe	easy-care	sapphire
magazine	felstone	reed-pipe	solidare	redshire
topazine	oilstone	sand-pipe	redshare	Ayrshire
armozine	camstone	windpipe	milliare	quagmire
éolienne	gemstone	hosepipe	centiare	wagmoire
julienne	tinstone	liripipe	outglare	grimoire
Sorbonne	gunstone	seal-pipe	play-mare	conspire
chaconne	sunstone	tail-pipe	ore-stare	perspire
dragonné	capstone	soil-pipe	outstare	goodsire
raisonné	lapstone	cornpipe	hardware	gudesire
cretonne	top-stone	hornpipe	liveware	transire
boutonné	potstone	downpipe	firmware	head-tire
edgebone	rot-stone	vent-pipe	ovenware	ship-tire
barebone	keystone	blowpipe	ironware	overtire
ringbone	dry-stone	clay-pipe	slipware	verquire
fish-bone	barytone	rope-ripe	flatware	gold-wire
wishbone	naloxone	rathripe	software	live-wire
backbone	everyone	drop-ripe	wiseacre	trip-wire
neck-bone	time-zone	overripe	cornacre	albacore
trombone	tin-terne	pericope	massacre	hardcore
shin-bone	Sauterne	episcope	mediocre	albicore
rump-bone	seaborne	iriscope	bayadère	halicore
wind-cone	airborne	bioscope	while-ere	corocore
pine-cone	forborne	otoscope	torchère	hog-score
nose-cone	tricorne	stanhope	co-inhere	ten-score
silicone	slogorne	Calliope	ensphere	two-score
half-done	cremorne	escalope	insphere	sixscore
overdone	cromorne	antelope	unsphere	soft-core
wobegone	nocturne	envelope	oosphere	matadore
foregone	sand-dune	Antilope	isothere	ochidore
perigone	demi-lune	ski-slope	anywhere	pinafore
diaphone	semilune	dip-slope	première	zoochore
triphone	perilune	gantlope	meunière	isochore
sulphone	fine-tune	antipope	umbriere	biophore
geophone	folk-tune	dead-rope	portière	seashore
earphone	picayune	headrope	metamere	offshore
pay-phone	acknowne	wire-rope	dungmere	word-lore
zabaione	Cockayne	bush-rope	cashmere	folklore
let-alone	megadyne	back-rope	abampere	booklore
high-lone	endodyne	tail-rope	beau-pere	sycamore
argemone	homodyne	bell-rope	Miserere	sagamore
rotenone	aerodyne	zoetrope	confrère	sycomore
one-to-one	gyrodyne	raft-rope	eglatere	evermore
corn-pone	autodyne	bolt-rope	verquere	claymore
postpone	night-foe	tent-rope	trouvère	diaspore
cicerone	tuckahoe	foot-rope	canaigre	epispore
dethrone	prong-hoe	zootrope	Frimaire	zoospore
enthrone	sand-shoe	Aganippe	Brumaire	exospore
unthrone	slip-shoe	Xantippe	dead-fire	footsore
aleurone	overshoe	Zantippe	need-fire	omnivore
half-tone	soft-shoe	Zentippe	wildfire	overwore
semitone	snow-shoe	antitype	bale-fire	forswore
baritone	log-canoe	moon-type	home-fire	parterre
mean-tone	seedy-toe	logotype	sure-fire	mismetre
monotone	seascape	calotype	hangfire	bien-être

recentre	bookcase	localise	porpoise	elsewise
incentre	slip-case	vocalise	portoise	ringwise
cadastre	gear-case	nodalise	tortoise	longwise
aplustre	door-case	idealise	macarise	archwise
accoutre	suit-case	legalise	velarise	suchwise
mind-cure	showcase	alkalise	polarise	teamwise
sinecure	surcease	canalise	solarise	stepwise
insecure	sublease	penalise	curarise	dropwise
pedicure	nuclease	finalise	notarise	overwise
manicure	decrease	annalise	soberise	pairwise
corn-cure	increase	papalise	suberise	thuswise
rest-cure	degrease	moralise	maderise	flatwise
roundure	protease	ruralise	etherise	tentwise
coiffure	purchase	nasalise	dimerise	convulse
refigure	anaphase	vitalise	emperise	condense
brochure	prophase	totalise	high-rise	prepense
ciselure	catalase	equalise	satirise	propense
encolure	idocrase	rivalise	moonrise	dispense
scrimure	rephrase	royalise	theorise	suspense
disinure	dioptase	ptyalise	aphorise	nonsense
tournure	diastase	novelise	valorise	subtense
pleasure	preceese	vowelise	memorise	protense
treasure	cargeese	Tebilise	vaporise	response
incisure	marchese	mobilise	sororise	floccose
cocksure	Tyrolese	similise	motorise	varicose
reinsure	paramese	civilise	tutorise	frondose
cynosure	Sudanese	fabulise	comprise	overdose
reposure	Japanese	nebulise	surprise	paludose
exposure	Javanese	regulise	misprise	strigose
reassure	Pekinese	infamise	treatise	fire-hose
pressure	Balinese	Islamise	hepatise	spathose
tressure	Siennese	racemise	practise	boothose
scissure	Viennese	polemise	aphetise	pluviose
cubature	Congoese	minimise	athetise	parclose
creature	Canarese	optimise	monetise	disclose
ligature	Kanarese	maximise	appetise	sabulose
filature	Genevese	sodomise	covetise	maculose
colature	Genovese	urbanise	albitise	undulose
immature	po'chaise	paganise	digitise	nodulose
armature	archaise	organise	Semitise	rugulose
denature	Hebraise	Arianise	sanitise	ramulose
fixature	bepraise	Romanise	pyritise	cumulose
enacture	unpraise	womanise	quantise	annulose
fracture	appraise	humanise	ergotise	papulose
cincture	Graecise	tetanise	amortise	torulose
lincture	solecise	botanise	chastise	levulose
tincture	logicise	Aryanise	deputise	ankylose
juncture	ethicise	feminise	Hinduise	squamose
puncture	sinicise	resinise	disguise	racemose
geniture	Ionicise	Latinise	euphuise	exosmose
painture	Atticise	cutinise	marquise	strumose
tainture	exercise	divinise	to-bruise	bluenose
jointure	exorcise	ebionise	readvise	diagnose
aperture	nomadise	unionise	televise	farinose
overture	faradise	colonise	rerevise	pruinose
moisture	paradise	polonise	lyra-wise	star-nose
annexure	rigidise	demonise	crabwise	dog's-nose
database	fluidise	Timonise	comb-wise	lacunose
leaf-base	brandise	canonise	bendwise	mongoose
pupa-case	melodise	caponise	sidewise	mungoose
card-case	disseise	Saxonise	edgewise	bargoose
pipe-case	eulogise	eternise	likewise	cargoose
note-case	energise	immunise	palewise	waygoose
wing-case	focalise	jumboise	somewise	pappoose

reimpose	richesse	delibate	runagate	mutilate
cribrose	duchesse	dealbate	divagate	ocellate
windrose	noblesse	plumbate	tide-gate	stellate
suberose	vainesse	bilobate	delegate	arillate
tuberose	porpesse	hylobate	relegate	areolate
sclerose	impresse	acerbate	somegate	segolate
shoe-rose	bretesse	incubate	abnegate	etiolate
literose	portesse	titubate	renegate	immolate
rock-rose	abscisse	intubate	lichgate	desolate
musk-rose	saucisse	aguacate	lychgate	insolate
primrose	coulisse	braccate	obligate	bed-plate
soporose	lacrosse	defecate	alligate	vamplate
moss-rose	repoussé	radicate	remigate	template
dextrose	petuntse	abdicate	fumigate	tin-plate
comatose	concause	dedicate	irrigate	omoplate
keratose	applause	medicate	strigate	key-plate
stratose	diapause	indicate	fatigate	dry-plate
fructose	disabuse	delicate	litigate	log-slate
virtuose	farceuse	silicate	mitigate	tabulate
flexuose	berceuse	pumicate	navigate	ambulate
woodwose	vendeuse	tunicate	levigate	lobulate
botryose	danseuse	loricate	lock-gate	subulate
collapse	masseuse	apricate	tail-gate	tubulate
prolapse	time-fuse	muricate	hell-gate	jaculate
incorpse	reinfuse	suricate	tollgate	maculate
rehearse	tea-house	vesicate	evulgate	peculate
enhearse	madhouse	urticate	elongate	loculate
inhearse	ice-house	aduncate	abrogate	osculate
unhearse	bee-house	truncate	derogate	radulate
submerse	ale-house	relocate	arrogate	undulate
disperse	dye-house	allocate	leachate	modulate
traverse	dog-house	advocate	conchate	regulate
subverse	log-house	invocate	self-hate	ligulate
universe	bughouse	carucate	sulphate	ungulate
renverse	mug-house	vanadate	xanthate	jugulate
converse	hen-house	foredate	glaciate	hamulate
perverse	ginhouse	antedate	emaciate	simulate
sea-horse	tap-house	validate	speciate	cumulate
one-horse	air-house	solidate	fasciate	annulate
pilhorse	dishouse	lapidate	cruciate	lunulate
two-horse	cathouse	back-date	gladiate	vapulate
war-horse	cot-house	emendate	eradiate	copulate
dishorse	hothouse	inundate	palliate	populate
bathorse	pothouse	up-to-date	talliate	cupulate
saw-horse	nut-house	chordate	spoliate	insulate
premorse	outhouse	postdate	antliate	rosulate
retrorse	cowhouse	acaudate	formiate	ethylate
antrorse	try-house	ecaudate	taeniate	palamate
introrse	jealouse	denudate	patriate	squamate
extrorse	dog-louse	trabeate	initiate	racemate
disburse	sea-mouse	calceate	tritiate	yoke-mate
precurse	dormouse	croceate	breviate	casemate
wet-nurse	titmouse	nucleate	perviate	decimate
dry-nurse	burnouse	malleate	exuviate	ultimate
recourse	underuse	aculeate	ice-skate	intimate
sea-purse	reperuse	permeate	escalate	optimate
egg-purse	abstruse	clypeate	regelate	estimate
dispurse	paralyse	recreate	sufflate	book-mate
cutpurse	catalyse	increate	conflate	work-mate
fougasse	atmolyse	uncreate	sibilate	team-mate
déclassé	pyrolyse	ochreate	jubilate	room-mate
lampasse	autolyse	laureate	depilate	chromate
crevasse	makebate	nauseate	oppilate	automate
largesse	celibate	indagate	pupilate	shipmate

helpmate	acierate	cristate	sulphite	kalinite
messmate	tolerate	constate	Memphite	melinite
flatmate	numerate	ecostate	gnathite	ciminite
inhumate	generate	apostate	perthite	Leninite
exhumate	venerate	prostate	bob-white	retinite
playmate	asperate	misstate	off-white	stannite
impanate	superate	crustate	non-white	Ebionite
titanate	literate	amputate	Shafiite	meionite
alienate	enterate	evacuate	hell-kite	mylonite
selenate	emigrate	graduate	brookite	Xylonite ®
arsenate	aspirate	evaluate	sodalite	zylonite
catenate	levirate	adequate	tonalite	limonite
stagnate	vizirate	torquate	fayalite	ammonite
uncinate	bank-rate	excavate	sea-blite	saponite
ordinate	decorate	tidivate	Bakelite ®	Maronite
paginate	priorate	salivate	noselite	arsonite
saginate	pejorate	derivate	melilite	essonite
vaginate	chlorate	activate	troilite	saxonite
alginate	perorate	titivate	phyllite	sternite
echinate	sororate	motivate	cimolite	disunite
laminate	stuprate	subovate	impolite	autunite
geminate	aberrate	renovate	unpolite	crocoite
seminate	overrate	innovate	aerolite	sinopite
dominate	poor-rate	acervate	mesolite	polypite
nominate	filtrate	enervate	pisolite	sybarite
ruminate	cultrate	malaxate	datolite	liparite
supinate	contrate	entr'acte	rhyolite	Nazarite
carinate	tartrate	inficete	cryolite	dendrite
marinate	castrate	aesthete	pearlite	amberite
resinate	rostrate	obsolete	baculite	Abderite
rosinate	lustrate	complete	lazulite	siderite
Latinate	inaurate	paranete	calamite	ankerite
stannate	accurate	concrete	Islamite	sclerite
umbonate	obdurate	discrete	dynamite	dolerite
meconate	indurate	Masorete	catamite	laterite
coronate	figurate	mansuete	Ottamite	nephrite
resonate	depurate	verligte	wood-mite	tephrite
assonate	maturate	uintaite	itch-mite	aegirite
detonate	saturate	Shivaite	psammite	Nazirite
intonate	obturate	flea-bite	Sodomite	Taborite
inornate	butyrate	Wahabite	dolomite	chlorite
lacunate	tractate	backbite	chromite	tenorite
inchoate	spectate	stilbite	epsomite	minorite
caproate	punctate	plumbite	Ottomite	fluorite
benzoate	eructate	ayenbite	thermite	epitrite
baldpate	hebetate	Jacobite	urbanite	contrite
clodpate	vegetate	cenobite	aphanite	roburite
crispate	dubitate	overbite	melanite	lazurite
occupate	oscitate	boracite	basanite	miswrite
vicarate	meditate	sericite	titanite	iodyrite
stearate	digitate	analcite	elvanite	argyrite
separate	cogitate	expedite	stibnite	parasite
glabrate	militate	viridite	queenite	gibbsite
cribrate	volitate	Araldite ®	sagenite	bomb-site
execrate	sanitate	plaudite	galenite	andesite
fulcrate	capitate	cleveite	selenite	fuchsite
quadrate	irritate	phengite	ilmenite	lewisite
liberate	hesitate	eclogite	Ibsenite	Burnsite
suberate	levitate	eklogite	arsenite	apposite
lacerate	edentate	trichite	euxenite	opposite
macerate	denotate	trochite	re-ignite	jarosite
ulcerate	annotate	onychite	prehnite	campsite
federate	aseptate	graphite	definite	Glassite
moderate	aristate	psephite	infinite	Jebusite

cerusite	pianiste	curlicue	engrieve	unactive
steatite	ébeniste	purlicue	reprieve	coactive
hematite	drabette	shore-due	retrieve	practive
hepatite	barbette	portague	Congreve	tractive
zaratite	dancette	intrigue	evincive	ejective
mimetite	dancetté	fantigue	coercive	elective
appetite	suedette	portigue	crescive	erective
smaltite	pochette	harangue	nose-dive	vegetive
picotite	jockette	meringue	fish-dive	quietive
mesquite	diskette	ox-tongue	conceive	deletive
Shaivite	omelette	pishogue	perceive	additive
eutaxite	toilette	dialogue	overgive	auditive
beauxite	roulette	analogue	proclive	fugitive
Darbyite	palmette	aeglogue	overlive	volitive
Puseyite	pianette	epilogue	off-drive	vomitive
Vichyite	vignette	collogue	jet-drive	genitive
monazite	reinette	apologue	outdrive	lenitive
bronzite	spinette	prologue	contrive	monitive
wurtzite	brunette	isologue	abrasive	punitive
diamanté	umbrette	duologue	invasive	positive
courante	aigrette	prorogue	adhesive	totitive
diapente	barrette	redargue	cohesive	fruitive
sirvente	anisette	disvalue	decisive	by-motive
enceinte	noisette	outvalue	incisive	adaptive
affronté	grisette	half-blue	derisive	adoptive
fire-bote	cassette	navy-blue	divisive	co-optive
dovecote	fossette	rice-glue	emulsive	eruptive
bellcote	amusette	fish-glue	aversive	exertive
salt-cote	septette	continue	inessive	abortive
anecdote	sestette	inconnue	emissive	sportive
lepidote	sextette	odalique	omissive	egestive
peridote	baguette	appliqué	plausive	solutive
antidote	maquette	vehmique	excusive	eye-salve
Italiote	coquette	clinique	effusive	lipsalve
Cypriote	moquette	physique	infusive	univalve
Zantiote	roquette	pratique	delusive	trivalve
matelote	corvette	critique	allusive	dissolve
zopilote	fauvette	lustique	illusive	convolve
ward-mote	garrotte	mystique	locative	ring-dove
halimote	subacute	boutique	vocative	rock-dove
locomote	peracute	pétanque	sedative	true-love
headnote	resalute	filioque	ideative	calf-love
wood-note	archlute	breloque	creative	self-love
side-note	absolute	colloque	negative	kid-glove
half-note	resolute	remarqué	ablative	foxglove
wolf-note	obvolute	Moresque	relative	lack-love
bank-note	revolute	embusqué	dilative	lady-love
call-note	involute	perruque	sanative	engroove
footnote	malamute	goat's-rue	innative	ingroove
creasote	malemute	construe	unnative	mangrove
kreasote	deaf-mute	unvirtue	conative	disprove
creosote	semi-mute	bone-cave	donative	gas-stove
kreosote	megabyte	disleave	curative	dry-stove
triptote	presbyte	way-leave	vitative	wirewove
misquote	kamacyte	conclave	rotative	subserve
card-vote	gonocyte	outbrave	optative	preserve
lambaste	trachyte	margrave	mutative	conserve
outcaste	epiphyte	burgrave	putative	disserve
cinéaste	geophyte	palstave	laxative	slate-axe
unchaste	neophyte	tide-wave	taxative	white-eye
distaste	zoophyte	long-wave	fixative	bindi-eye
forwaste	barbecue	hair-wave	reactive	pearl-eye
tanaiste	cardecue	hog-reeve	enactive	tiger-eye
tachiste	pirlicue	aggrieve	inactive	aftereye

bird's-eye	handcuff	shear-leg	gladding	maraging
bull's-eye	plum-duff	short-leg	shedding	sledging
Sobranye	footmuff	scaly-leg	sledding	bridging
gramarye	puff-puff	moss-hagg	clodding	grudging
star-gaze	dandruff	peat-hagg	plodding	trudging
kamikaze	woodruff	goose-egg	prodding	flagging
defreeze	overruff	pasch-egg	scudding	bragging
refreeze	calc-tuff	shell-egg	studding	dragging
enfreeze	sob-stuff	mah-jongg	receding	thigging
unfreeze	dyestuff	stravaig	bleeding	frigging
anticize	sanserif	caprifig	speeding	prigging
disseize	aperitif	hedgepig	breeding	shogging
racemize	tree-calf	tithe-pig	wingding	flogging
macarize	half-calf	penny-pig	plaiding	chugging
disprize	bull-calf	polliwig	braiding	plugging
misprize	mooncalf	lime-twig	dividing	snugging
outprize	yourself	pollywig	scalding	drugging
gold-size	aardwolf	gang-bang	fielding	obliging
life-size	werewolf	jingbang	yielding	clanging
king-size	demi-wolf	slap-bang	spelding	slanging
oversize	bull-hoof	seladang	childing	twanging
bulldoze	curb-roof	quandang	building	avenging
schmooze	wood-roof	overgang	scolding	flinging
quatorze	span-roof	overhang	woolding	bringing
petuntze	sunproof	kaoliang	moulding	cringing
F	war-proof	upsprang	standing	wringing
tone-deaf	disproof	parasang	blending	stinging
seed-leaf	ratproof	zugzwang	unending	swinging
gold-leaf	pentroof	sol-faing	spending	plunging
lace-leaf	langlauf	huzzaing	blinding	lounging
vine-leaf	G	blabbing	poinding	emerging
nose-leaf	shake-bag	grabbing	grinding	leaching
rose-leaf	brief-bag	stabbing	bounding	reaching
overleaf	earth-bag	swabbing	founding	teaching
four-leaf	cloak-bag	cribbing	rounding	unaching
half-loaf	green-bag	swobbing	sounding	coaching
milk-loaf	water-bag	clubbing	wounding	poaching
hung-beef	scent-bag	slubbing	unboding	filching
neck-beef	money-bag	snubbing	flooding	ranching
bull-beef	Jiffybag	drubbing	boarding	pinching
corn-beef	doggy-bag	grubbing	thirding	bunching
kerchief	lucky-bag	stubbing	clouding	perching
mischief	dilly-bag	scribing	ill-being	Fasching
unbelief	emery-bag	blimbing	not-being	batching
sea-brief	ditty-bag	climbing	unseeing	catching
fee-grief	lallygag	plumbing	singeing	hatching
giff-gaff	lollygag	menacing	lungeing	matching
niffnaff	night-hag	enticing	canoeing	patching
riff-raff	sand-flag	glancing	queueing	fetching
misgraff	fire-flag	prancing	briefing	pitching
bed-staff	sick-flag	vauncing	chaffing	witching
palstaff	corn-flag	bouncing	whiffing	botching
tipstaff	mail-drag	piercing	gliffing	notching
tau-staff	shake-rag	reducing	sniffing	butching
sea-cliff	stone-rag	seducing	spiffing	couching
dandriff	ballyrag	arcading	scoffing	touching
stand-off	bullyrag	sheading	snuffing	weighing
trade-off	price-tag	pleading	stuffing	laughing
write-off	scalawag	treading	proofing	coughing
brush-off	philabeg	steading	scarfing	clashing
check-off	philibeg	unfading	wharfing	flashing
blast-off	fillibeg	salading	engaging	plashing
badly-off	white-leg	unlading	managing	slashing
bully-off	blackleg	cladding	garaging	smashing

crashing	pranking	handling	suckling	footling
swashing	swanking	sandling	tinkling	mortling
swishing	thinking	kindling	darkling	turtling
blushing	skinking	fondling	porkling	eastling
flushing	blinking	bundling	dialling	nestling
brushing	clinking	bardling	stalling	jostling
crushing	drinking	lordling	shelling	hustling
scathing	stinking	hurdling	smelling	rustling
loathing	plonking	sideling	spelling	rattling
naething	trunking	sheeling	duelling	tattling
seething	drooking	wheeling	fuelling	wattling
teething	stroking	steeling	dwelling	fettling
Lagthing	sharking	cageling	swelling	settling
writhing	overking	atheling	chilling	littling
non-thing	whisking	shieling	shilling	mottling
clothing	frisking	dukeling	skilling	shawling
soothing	drouking	popeling	spilling	brawling
farthing	shealing	hireling	drilling	crawling
northing	stealing	tireling	frilling	trawling
southing	swealing	wiseling	grilling	scowling
anything	shoaling	baffling	trilling	growling
sneaking	stabling	maffling	stilling	prowling
speaking	babbling	piffling	quilling	wraxling
breaking	dabbling	ruffling	swilling	grayling
unmaking	gabbling	trifling	drolling	swayling
upmaking	rabbling	stifling	trolling	foozling
croaking	wabbling	halfling	sculling	dazzling
retaking	pebbling	wolfling	weanling	mizzling
whacking	nibbling	purfling	yeanling	sizzling
blacking	cobbling	outfling	twinling	puzzling
smacking	hobbling	beagling	townling	gleaming
cracking	wobbling	ridgling	tripling	dreaming
tracking	saibling	gaggling	sampling	steaming
stacking	lambling	giggling	simpling	defaming
clecking	rambling	higgling	dumpling	ashaming
wrecking	wambling	niggling	rippling	gloaming
clicking	humbling	goggling	coupling	scheming
slicking	mumbling	joggling	dearling	qualming
bricking	rumbling	juggling	pearling	shamming
pricking	tumbling	dangling	yearling	clamming
tricking	snobling	gangling	snarling	slamming
sticking	garbling	jangling	sparling	cramming
zincking	marbling	tangling	starling	stemming
shocking	warbling	wangling	sperling	skimming
blocking	burbling	jingling	sterling	slimming
smocking	baubling	kingling	whirling	brimming
knocking	doubling	mingling	skirling	primming
frocking	circling	pingling	knurling	trimming
stocking	muscling	singling	spurling	swimming
shucking	cradling	bungling	Riesling	scumming
trucking	paddling	frogling	brisling	slumming
vice-king	waddling	quailing	quisling	drumming
sleeking	meddling	availing	gin-sling	stumming
foreking	peddling	sheiling	nursling	becoming
striking	fiddling	deviling	housling	incoming
trekking	middling	reviling	flatling	oncoming
stalking	piddling	weakling	gnatling	blooming
caulking	riddling	tackling	goatling	glooming
skulking	toddling	keckling	bratling	spooming
bean-king	fuddling	reckling	beetling	charming
thanking	puddling	tickling	softling	alarming
clanking	reedling	rockling	whitling	swarming
planking	seedling	buckling	bantling	storming
spanking	daidling	duckling	mantling	assuming

cleaning	thumping	catering	pressing	mounting
gleaning	clumping	watering	guessing	grunting
steaning	scooping	entering	amissing	fagoting
groaning	whooping	uttering	swissing	shooting
greening	stooping	wavering	crossing	pivoting
steening	clapping	covering	trussing	tempting
queening	flapping	sewering	focusing	starting
wakening	slapping	lowering	hocusing	shirting
ravening	knapping	towering	browsing	skirting
feigning	snapping	layering	bleating	flirting
plaining	trapping	rush-ring	treating	snorting
graining	wrapping	semi-ring	sweating	sporting
training	swapping	aspiring	bloating	Storting
staining	stepping	expiring	floating	blurting
swaining	chipping	retiring	derating	courting
steining	shipping	untiring	unsating	feasting
refining	whipping	attiring	doubting	blasting
groining	skipping	junk-ring	enacting	boasting
repining	clipping	seal-ring	exacting	coasting
scanning	flipping	bull-ring	sheeting	roasting
planning	slipping	flooring	fleeting	toasting
spanning	snipping	tutoring	greeting	questing
pfenning	dripping	upspring	sweeting	hoisting
thinning	gripping	scarring	quieting	roisting
skinning	tripping	charring	valeting	twisting
spinning	chopping	sparring	riveting	frosting
grinning	shopping	starring	coveting	trusting
twinning	whopping	unerring	shafting	roysting
shunning	plopping	averring	grafting	chatting
stunning	slopping	shirring	shifting	flatting
crooning	cropping	whirring	crofting	platting
swooning	dropping	stirring	yachting	abetting
intoning	propping	blurring	fighting	whetting
learning	stopping	slurring	lighting	fretting
yearning	swopping	spurring	righting	stetting
scorning	scarping	centring	plaiting	flitting
churning	sharping	restring	exciting	slitting
mourning	chirping	unstring	limiting	emitting
spurning	usurping	lustring	vomiting	omitting
spawning	clasping	enduring	visiting	knitting
clowning	grasping	adjuring	positing	spitting
browning	grouping	alluring	fruiting	fritting
crowning	uncaring	manuring	inviting	quitting
drowning	shearing	scouring	smelting	twitting
frowning	clearing	naturing	stilting	shotting
der-doing	drearing	banxring	quilting	blotting
fordoing	swearing	pixy-ring	vaulting	clotting
misdoing	sugaring	debasing	boulting	plotting
sea-going	squaring	pleasing	moulting	knotting
forgoing	headring	phrasing	planting	spotting
outgoing	yeldring	greesing	slanting	trotting
way-going	yoldring	praising	awanting	swotting
tabooing	sobering	uprising	scenting	abutting
lassoing	nidering	bruising	eventing	shutting
sneaping	ordering	advising	fainting	glutting
scraping	fleering	sponsing	painting	scouting
sleeping	sneering	imposing	pointing	shouting
creeping	steering	opposing	printing	grouting
sweeping	offering	coursing	stinting	trouting
striping	legering	biassing	haunting	reputing
skelping	ushering	grassing	jaunting	rescuing
scamping	papering	blessing	taunting	briguing
stamping	tapering	dressing	vaunting	tonguing
skimping	nose-ring	gressing	shunting	jerquing

pursuing	applying	unsprung	peishwah	besmirch
cleaving	outlying	upsprung	jambiyah	unchurch
steeving	mummying	unstrung	sea-beach	Romansch
thieving	decrying	shantung	ash-leach	Rumansch
ungiving	querying	house-dog	impleach	Rumonsch
unliving	dairying	coachdog	unpreach	seecatch
shriving	glorying	watch-dog	outreach	unthatch
thriving	storying	ditch-dog	toiseach	nuthatch
striving	carrying	shock-dog	misteach	potlatch
reviving	harrying	sheepdog	caillach	mismatch
shelving	marrying	underdog	kreplach	outmatch
beloving	parrying	water-dog	drammach	despatch
unloving	tarrying	night-dog	coranach	dispatch
unmoving	berrying	penny-dog	coronach	dog-watch
starving	ferrying	puppy-dog	sea-loach	outwatch
swerving	worrying	pettifog	encroach	eldritch
hind-wing	currying	goosegog	reproach	carritch
lace-wing	hurrying	hedgehog	approach	parritch
renewing	retrying	whole-hog	tribrach	unstitch
screwing	emptying	earth-hog	ceterach	top-notch
forewing	dirtying	shear-hog	sea-orach	declutch
strewing	puttying	river-hog	clarsach	unclutch
bluewing	fly-tying	jickajog	reattach	besmutch
corkwing	appuying	shot-clog	dog-leech	insomuch
gull-wing	navvying	waterlog	cow-leech	overmuch
throwing	dizzying	footslog	penneech	inasmuch
strowing	wheezing	brick-nog	by-speech	cartouch
overwing	sneezing	tree-frog	unbreech	disvouch
beeswing	freezing	bullfrog	cromlech	nonesuch
batswing	bronzing	leap-frog	tristich	triptych
outswing	waltzing	golliwog	sandwich	dahabieh
left-wing	whizzing	polliwog	alebench	galabieh
relaxing	quizzing	gollywog	disbench	mudirieh
indexing	ding-dong	pollywog	unclench	nargileh
delaying	quandong	osnaburg	bedrench	kaffiyeh
allaying	packfong	faubourg	indrench	keffiyeh
inlaying	souchong	scuppaug	retrench	kuffiyeh
renaying	headlong	water-bug	entrench	danelagh
repaying	sidelong	mealy-bug	nine-inch	outweigh
straying	lifelong	bunny-hug	hawfinch	knee-high
assaying	livelong	fire-plug	rum-punch	type-high
essaying	span-long	vent-plug	camshoch	jack-high
tabbying	yearlong	love-drug	mashloch	bank-high
lobbying	overlong	steam-tug	agalloch	well-nigh
fancying	hourlong	H	gralloch	Hamburgh
toadying	flatlong	coolabah	skelloch	hiccough
muddying	ping-pong	Haggadah	rere-arch	although
ruddying	love-song	lah-di-dah	research	furlough
bandying	singsong	verandah	oligarch	turlough
studying	folk-song	galabeah	Syriarch	thorough
honeying	swan-song	khalifah	taxiarch	pooh-pooh
edifying	evensong	Halachah	phylarch	diagraph
deifying	coon-song	padishah	outmarch	epigraph
unifying	boat-song	galabiah	ethnarch	trigraph
dallying	part-song	Jeremiah	hipparch	syngraph
rallying	quantong	Kabbalah	rear-arch	odograph
sallying	jelutong	blah-blah	hierarch	biograph
tallying	tile-hung	masoolah	overarch	apograph
bellying	well-hung	Shekinah	tetrarch	myograph
bullying	overhung	savannah	pentarch	bar-graph
cullying	aqualung	chutzpah	heptarch	airgraph
sullying	Nibelung	Massorah	unstarch	cenotaph
replying	far-flung	begorrah	polyarch	gallumph
implying	low-slung	madrasah	sea-perch	harrumph

8 -MPH

sea-nymph	pipe-fish	briskish	sweetish	ensheath
theosoph	rosefish	stablish	lightish	bequeath
biomorph	bluefish	feeblish	tightish	opsimath
zoomorph	draffish	babelish	stiltish	polymath
isomorph	stiffish	yokelish	faintish	book-oath
diaglyph	wolf-fish	camelish	saintish	race-path
anaglyph	spoffish	novelish	bluntish	side-path
triglyph	surf-fish	tinglish	idiotish	telepath
manna-ash	gruffish	frailish	startish	allopath
calabash	kingfish	Aprilish	flirtish	footpath
squabash	lung-fish	devilish	shortish	myriadth
kourbash	frogfish	ticklish	flattish	fiftieth
slap-dash	weakfish	smallish	brattish	umptieth
Malagash	rock-fish	swellish	skittish	fortieth
outflash	milkfish	drollish	Scottish	sixtieth
backlash	monk-fish	demolish	sluttish	isopleth
whiplash	dealfish	unpolish	stoutish	Masoreth
pearl-ash	coalfish	purplish	languish	strength
stramash	sail-fish	churlish	cliquish	misfaith
mishmash	wallfish	ghoulish	vanquish	monteith
bran-mash	foul-fish	qualmish	enravish	megalith
calipash	scomfish	slimmish	thievish	regolith
rose-rash	scumfish	skirmish	shrewish	xenolith
overrash	drumfish	paganish	well-wish	monolith
musquash	moon-fish	Romanish	nohowish	acrolith
limewash	lumpfish	womanish	essayish	aerolith
wish-wash	scarfish	greenish	boobyish	god-smith
backwash	boarfish	vixenish	toadyish	tinsmith
buck-wash	starfish	plainish	dandyish	gunsmith
rain-wash	dwarfish	brainish	sandyish	poortith
overwash	overfish	swainish	dowdyish	hamewith
pig's-wash	flatfish	diminish	rowdyish	herewith
hasheesh	goat-fish	clannish	puppyish	unhealth
hen-flesh	baitfish	thinnish	sorryish	perianth
disflesh	crawfish	admonish	fiftyish	amaranth
drabbish	crayfish	astonish	fortyish	hydranth
snobbish	grey-fish	clownish	tarboosh	eleventh
clubbish	Whiggish	brownish	shadbush	hyacinth
snubbish	priggish	jingoish	sloebush	helminth
broadish	sluggish	sheepish	rose-bush	Visigoth
cloddish	slangish	steepish	hempbush	tea-cloth
side-dish	youngish	scampish	salt-bush	pad-cloth
solidish	roughish	blimpish	flax-bush	oilcloth
childish	toughish	glumpish	hush-hush	wax-cloth
tolldish	sylphish	plumpish	outflush	box-cloth
blandish	sumphish	frumpish	tarboush	behemoth
brandish	nymphish	snappish	bellpush	hawk-moth
standish	freshish	quippish	pear-push	corn-moth
fiendish	sneakish	sharpish	tar-brush	puss-moth
roundish	freakish	vagarish	air-brush	goat-moth
unmodish	blackish	squarish	hatbrush	dart-moth
clapdish	knackish	tovarish	club-rush	tolbooth
soap-dish	brackish	queerish	fox-brush	unsmooth
alms-dish	thickish	tigerish	toad-rush	forsooth
proudish	trickish	pokerish	gold-rush	eye-tooth
tuna-fish	blockish	viperish	wood-rush	gag-tooth
toad-fish	stockish	emperish	downrush	egg-tooth
seed-fish	Greekish	waterish	sand-bath	dogtooth
goldfish	Frankish	feverish	birdbath	jaw-tooth
band-fish	prankish	liverish	stop-bath	saw-tooth
land-fish	spookish	flourish	foot-bath	sea-froth
file-fish	sparkish	Friesish	dust-bath	shofroth
tilefish	clerkish	coarsish	sitz-bath	mitzvoth
line-fish	quirkish	crossish	sea-heath	mezuzoth

fox-earth	ciceroni	hardback	main-deck	bale-dock
misbirth	cothurni	Zwieback	boat-deck	bail-dock
far-forth	diddicoi	come-back	penneeck	slip-dock
penn'orth	cunjevoi	bareback	roll-neck	putchock
wanworth	koftgari	fire-back	swan-neck	wig-block
outworth	canthari	blueback	deer-neck	bum-clock
selcouth	hari-kari	half-back	kenspeck	deadlock
badmouth	daiquari	kickback	Benedick	gridlock
vermouth	ryotwari	pickback	pea-chick	sidelock
Plymouth	beriberi	talk-back	dabchick	tide-lock
regrowth	kachahri	hark-back	dobchick	fire-lock
ingrowth	hara-kiri	tailback	dipchick	forelock
upgrowth	duumviri	fall-back	grub-kick	gavelock
I	tandoori	pull-back	side-kick	havelock
shanghai	Dioscuri	turnback	goal-kick	lovelock
drachmai	sannyasi	humpback	drop-kick	picklock
hetairai	virtuosi	hog's-back	calf-lick	stenlock
kohlrabi	narcissi	moss-back	deer-lick	charlock
capricci	Senoussi	softback	salt-lick	drammock
pasticci	antenati	fastback	bootlick	slummock
maravedi	post-nati	clawback	hand-pick	crummock
cicisbei	Gujarati	drawback	redbrick	drummock
Ganoidei	Gujerati	skew-back	air-brick	phinnock
Holostei	literati	slowback	baldrick	yeldrock
solfeggi	castrati	playback	baudrick	laverock
bostangi	perfecti	sway-back	limerick	disfrock
mariachi	acoemeti	hardhack	maverick	folkrock
diadochi	graffiti	highjack	pin-prick	shamrock
tedeschi	ouistiti	flapjack	dog-trick	trap-rock
Feringhi	Trimurti	slapjack	paitrick	wind-sock
Gurmukhi	Fascisti	whipjack	homesick	tick-tock
bimbashi	chapatti	skipjack	lovesick	sea-stock
Swadeshi	chupatti	boot-jack	soul-sick	die-stock
perradii	concetti	lazy-jack	iron-sick	penstock
komitaji	confetti	jet-black	cropsick	linstock
sukiyaki	libretti	good-lack	wood-tick	non-stock
piroshki	amoretti	forslack	politick	gunstock
pirozhki	banditti	crummack	tick-tick	palebuck
hydroski	dividivi	wolf-pack	sea-stick	blue-buck
water-ski	streltzi	backpack	ski-stick	bush-buck
après-ski	K	wool-pack	malstick	stembuck
bouzouki	kaka-beak	tamarack	canstick	surf-duck
strobili	half-beak	shabrack	gunstick	musk-duck
teocalli	hornbeak	gimcrack	mapstick	shelduck
cancelli	grosbeak	jimcrack	dip-stick	muckluck
morbilli	forepeak	sun-crack	lipstick	chipmuck
pulvilli	forspeak	pipe-rack	mopstick	unstruck
broccoli	misspeak	roof-rack	cat-stick	peat-reek
nucleoli	outspeak	rick-rack	pot-stick	Whitweek
gladioli	newspeak	overrack	joy-stick	Brezonek
flocculi	tea-break	coatrack	herdwick	pashalik
utriculi	tie-break	one-track	woodcock	nastalik
durukuli	off-break	sea-wrack	sage-cock	refusnik
pastrami	leg-break	eelwrack	game-cock	town-talk
prodromi	parbreak	rucksack	half-cock	overtalk
ginglymi	outbreak	woolsack	abricock	eyestalk
maharani	daybreak	knapsack	apricock	baby-talk
biriyani	ecofreak	gripsack	ballcock	sidewalk
scaldini	bestreak	hardtack	full-cock	cakewalk
zucchini	Russniak	tick-tack	princock	likewalk
fedelini	holly-oak	haystack	turncock	rope-walk
soffioni	feed-back	bethwack	stop-cock	fire-walk
taglioni	laid-back	foredeck	moorcock	ring-walk
macaroni	holdback	well-deck	shaddock	milk-walk

dog-whelk	playbook	firework	tragical	gyroidal
rice-milk	copybook	wirework	alogical	cuspidal
skim-milk	rock-cook	case-work	surgical	pudendal
kirn-milk	fire-hook	fluework	sophical	cathodal
near-silk	fish-hook	ringwork	mythical	dianodal
workfolk	billhook	mesh-work	biblical	tripodal
hillfolk	clip-hook	backwork	cyclical	episodal
alms-folk	trip-hook	hack-work	pollical	unfeudal
kinsfolk	boat-hook	rackwork	Adamical	epigaeal
overbulk	canthook	rock-work	chemical	glutaeal
databank	boot-hook	linkwork	inimical	dead-deal
sand-bank	overlook	bookwork	dromical	somedeal
peat-bank	nainsook	taskwork	atomical	perigeal
left-bank	Ragnarök	desk-work	cosmical	hypogeal
clay-bank	lacebark	mill-work	chymical	tracheal
red-shank	shag-bark	woolwork	scenical	self-heal
outflank	ring-bark	team-work	irenical	deisheal
fore-rank	re-embark	formwork	ethnical	limbmeal
rear-rank	ironbark	ironwork	clinical	wood-meal
overrank	soap-bark	hornwork	ironical	bone-meal
forthink	saw-shark	soap-work	heroical	inchmeal
misthink	fox-shark	slopwork	tropical	fish-meal
outthink	sand-lark	overwork	atypical	hymeneal
iceblink	wood-lark	hair-work	etypical	unlineal
sun-blink	rock-lark	fretwork	lubrical	perineal
bobolink	headmark	koftwork	rubrical	peroneal
snap-link	landmark	salt-work	clerical	dyspneal
rose-pink	tidemark	tent-work	iatrical	sidereal
outdrink	telemark	knotwork	metrical	ethereal
hoodwink	fire-mark	footwork	physical	venereal
cheewink	kite-mark	partwork	statical	cinereal
forswink	hoof-mark	bodywork	tactical	funereal
salt-junk	pockmark	wine-cask	hectical	Sangreal
chipmunk	bookmark	hip-flask	thetical	arboreal
sow-drunk	hallmark	antimask	emetical	empyreal
forswunk	rillmark	overtask	poetical	monk-seal
bontebok	swan-mark	humoresk	critical	harp-seal
boschbok	monomark	trochisk	tritical	hair-seal
steenbok	mint-mark	egg-whisk	erotical	bracteal
angekkok	footmark	basilisk	vertical	warragal
road-book	postmark	tamarisk	cortical	astragal
handbook	deer-park	fire-risk	vortical	prodigal
herd-book	aardvark	asterisk	fistical	madrigal
wordbook	knee-jerk	satyrisk	rustical	warrigal
stud-book	mud-clerk	cornhusk	mystical	galangal
casebook	rock-cork	zomboruk	nautical	springal
notebook	dung-fork	tomahawk	cervical	laryngal
songbook	more-pork	mopehawk	epifocal	conjugal
lung-book	cribwork	sore-hawk	trifocal	monachal
cash-book	dead-work	fish-hawk	univocal	rhonchal
bank-book	headwork	duck-hawk	Lupercal	diarchal
cook-book	cold-work	spar-hawk	novercal	anarchal
workbook	handwork	newshawk	knapscal	zenithal
billbook	woodwork	L	oviducal	bilabial
hornbook	studwork	Sangraal	beheadal	bifacial
chapbook	life-work	cannibal	tripedal	especial
year-book	cagework	zodiacal	deicidal	judicial
overbook	wage-work	heliacal	suicidal	official
mass-book	salework	maniacal	biocidal	unsocial
pass-book	pilework	dithecal	cuboidal	fiducial
gift-book	time-work	Judaical	fucoidal	gonadial
jestbook	homework	farcical	keloidal	praedial
textbook	pipework	syndical	conoidal	remedial
text-book	ropework	deifical	toroidal	soredial

ring-dial	inertial	neuronal	sceptral	Emmental
pygidial	exequial	seasonal	plastral	parental
conidial	lixivial	unisonal	binaural	pronotal
gonidial	synovial	personal	monaural	uprootal
peridial	induvial	cantonal	epidural	subtotal
basidial	diluvial	subzonal	furfural	teetotal
prandial	alluvial	trizonal	fulgural	pubertal
allodial	uniaxial	hibernal	tellural	immortal
exordial	triaxial	infernal	macrural	pedestal
patagial	monaxial	supernal	caesural	agrestal
remigial	pyrexial	maternal	mensural	forestal
brachial	rhythmal	paternal	pictural	sagittal
mycelial	lacrimal	internal	cultural	remittal
unfilial	septimal	external	nurtural	rebuttal
familial	proximal	tribunal	pastural	decidual
supplial	informal	shogunal	gestural	residual
endemial	unformal	communal	vestural	dividual
proemial	abnormal	wood-coal	postural	exergual
binomial	Landsmål	dice-coal	guttural	biannual
monomial	chrismal	charcoal	textural	subequal
acromial	lacrymal	drop-goal	flexural	punctual
domanial	tympanal	benthoal	subbasal	habitual
ungenial	duodenal	entozoal	prenasal	eventual
achenial	noumenal	satrapal	chamisal	bisexual
splenial	crumenal	syncopal	surmisal	unsexual
hymenial	domainal	wood-opal	despisal	upheaval
biennial	morainal	fire-opal	reprisal	medieval
oogonial	turbinal	semi-opal	proposal	shrieval
colonial	vaccinal	funebral	supposal	primeval
baronial	nundinal	cerebral	disposal	khedival
troopial	cardinal	dihedral	petrosal	receival
troupial	imaginal	chondral	triapsal	gingival
vicarial	original	visceral	demersal	archival
malarial	marginal	falderal	reversal	carnival
filarial	virginal	ponderal	envassal	deprival
conarial	declinal	zooperal	colossal	outrival
riparial	staminal	vesperal	occlusal	aestival
puparial	criminal	tesseral	espousal	festival
notarial	germinal	ureteral	carousal	survival
etherial	terminal	dipteral	climatal	reproval
imperial	torminal	podagral	primatal	approval
biserial	encrinal	integral	stomatal	interval
material	Quirinal	urethral	prenatal	reviewal
soterial	pectinal	clithral	neonatal	bestowal
arterial	inguinal	acquiral	societal	suffixal
prairial	columnal	cup-coral	parietal	defrayal
vizirial	autumnal	balmoral	varietal	betrayal
memorial	antennal	non-moral	skeletal	conveyal
armorial	diaconal	temporal	non-metal	surveyal
manorial	diagonal	corporal	gunmetal	disloyal
sororial	trigonal	pectoral	prometal	surroyal
rasorial	isogonal	rectoral	pot-metal	spur-ryal
motorial	siphonal	sectoral	decretal	capsizal
sutorial	regional	doctoral	barbital	cascabel
tutorial	visional	clitoral	eremital	barbicel
spur-rial	national	pastoral	compital	lenticel
mistrial	rational	littoral	hospital	penoncel
reburial	motional	deferral	detrital	muscadel
manurial	notional	referral	requital	asphodel
tenurial	optional	saburral	curvital	new-model
indusial	hormonal	demurral	octantal	snake-eel
abbatial	matronal	theatral	bidental	paste-eel
palatial	patronal	spectral	cliental	forefeel
agential	tetronal	arbitral	oriental	wire-heel

cork-heel	Emmanuel	alguacil	pithball	bonibell
webwheel	Immanuel	verticil	moth-ball	hawkbell
bobwheel	rondavel	daffodil	musk-ball	soul-bell
ragwheel	disgavel	overveil	coalball	shop-bell
cog-wheel	dishevel	multifil	heel-ball	hairbell
cam-wheel	sea-level	oenophil	bail-ball	doorbell
pin-wheel	wye-level	Sinophil	wool-ball	mass-bell
flywheel	top-level	colza-oil	corn-ball	mortbell
joy-wheel	day-level	pulza-oil	soap-ball	fuel-cell
hose-reel	disbowel	overboil	trap-ball	germ-cell
newsreel	tea-towel	soft-boil	hair-ball	pikadell
wheat-eel	bergmehl	snake-oil	four-ball	rowndell
aasvogel	iron-mail	spike-oil	fuss-ball	woolfell
stanchel	stub-nail	shale-oil	meat-ball	rakehell
switchel	treenail	whale-oil	softball	seashell
threshel	shoe-nail	stone-oil	football	eggshell
shlemiel	hangnail	olive-oil	dust-ball	ark-shell
bonspiel	doornail	parafoil	blowball	top-shell
matériel	sea-snail	gold-foil	snowball	ear-shell
pannikel	slop-pail	aerofoil	fuzz-ball	gas-shell
parallel	headrail	sept-foil	birdcall	nutshell
sewellel	handrail	beech-oil	roll-call	pell-mell
béchamel	landrail	shark-oil	toll-call	misspell
strammel	live-rail	fusel-oil	overcall	nainsell
schimmel	taffrail	sperm-oil	spendall	oversell
bepommel	Sangrail	train-oil	dead-fall	soft-sell
strummel	rack-rail	rosin-oil	landfall	bestsell
Philomel	monorail	carap-oil	windfall	foretell
hydromel	motorail	strap-oil	free-fall	outdwell
fontanel	sliprail	niger-oil	leaf-fall	tube-well
sentinel	cant-rail	free-soil	bergfall	farewell
cracknel	contrail	grass-oil	backfall	live-well
spicknel	wind-sail	sweet-oil	rock-fall	gromwell
impannel	foresail	joint-oil	evenfall	pump-well
unpannel	gaff-sail	overtoil	rainfall	outswell
scrannel	full-sail	short-oil	downfall	draw-well
unkennel	mainsail	poppy-oil	trap-fall	kaka-bill
mangonel	moonsail	spandril	overfall	handbill
petronel	stunsail	cheveril	pratfall	time-bill
shrapnel	oversail	coistril	footfall	shoe-bill
enkernel	staysail	coystril	snowfall	duckbill
ritornel	dovetail	Ygdrasil	wind-gall	bank-bill
sapropel	bang-tail	mofussil	vine-gall	hornbill
estoppel	ring-tail	redistil	overgall	boatbill
langspel	long-tail	fauteuil	spur-gall	show-bill
whimbrel	hightail	tranquil	catch-all	crow-bill
spandrel	fish-tail	sea-devil	moot-hall	play-bill
tafferel	cocktail	she-devil	pall-mall	landfill
doggerel	duck-tail	wood-evil	femerall	backfill
hoggerel	silktail	alguazil	coverall	overfill
mackerel	sark-tail	hand-ball	bethrall	sand-hill
pickerel	fork-tail	handball	enthrall	mole-hill
cockerel	mill-tail	race-ball	borstall	mote-hill
dotterel	aventail	time-ball	lay-stall	dung-hill
cheverel	horntail	fire-ball	dead-wall	downhill
squirrel	whip-tail	baseball	ring-wall	wanthill
chaptrel	hair-tail	puffball	longwall	foothill
coistrel	cat's-tail	golf-ball	hickwall	moot-hill
minstrel	rat's-tail	goofball	cetywall	overkill
coystrel	boattail	korfball	carry-all	back-lill
thrissel	gilt-tail	highball	dumb-bell	hand-mill
carousel	ruby-tail	wash-ball	handbell	windmill
brocatel	pony-tail	fishball	harebell	tidemill
muscatel	paravail	push-ball	bluebell	cane-mill

bone-mill	glycerol	wrongful	unartful	panislam
tuck-mill	folderol	watchful	startful	rehoboam
walk-mill	banderol	pouchful	sportful	jeroboam
wauk-mill	bannerol	laughful	feastful	diazepam
wool-mill	disenrol	blushful	ghastful	decagram
corn-mill	furfurol	deathful	boastful	skiagram
pulpmill	entresol	loathful	chestful	paragram
malt-mill	cortisol	wrathful	tristful	hexagram
post-mill	sorbitol	faithful	trustful	telegram
flax-mill	dulcitol	slothful	troutful	decigram
clay-mill	mannitol	soothful	god-awful	marigram
minipill	inositol	toothful	unlawful	lexigram
mandrill	clay-marl	trothful	bellyful	ideogram
testrill	landgirl	mirthful	unjoyful	logogram
clap-sill	work-girl	worthful	disannul	ergogram
door-sill	call-girl	mouthful	oversoul	echogram
pot-still	mill-girl	youthful	pub-crawl	kilogram
goodwill	shop-girl	truthful	bescrawl	hologram
free-will	newsgirl	fanciful	rose-bowl	nomogram
self-will	showgirl	merciful	wash-bowl	tomogram
poorwill	playgirl	weariful	slop-bowl	nanogram
pigswill	leaf-curl	freakful	dust-bowl	monogram
clodpoll	kiss-curl	wreakful	eagle-owl	lipogram
clotpoll	spit-curl	wrackful	wild-fowl	barogram
inscroll	nudicaul	wreckful	garefowl	aerogram
bead-roll	club-haul	stickful	gairfowl	brockram
land-roll	long-haul	thankful	moorfowl	marjoram
leaf-roll	keelhaul	prankful	churn-owl	Moharram
bankroll	down-haul	trunkful	night-owl	Muharram
rent-roll	overhaul	friskful	cacomixl	water-ram
plimsoll	dreadful	spoilful	triethyl	nicky-tam
semibull	speedful	unwilful	dimethyl	water-yam
pang-full	fraudful	shellful	mersalyl	unbeseem
cram-full	peaceful	spellful	diphenyl	overteem
brim-full	graceful	dreamful	carbonyl	exanthem
overfull	voiceful	gloomful	carbaryl	periblem
skua-gull	forceful	charmful	glyceryl	Muharrem
monohull	spadeful	stormful	metopryl	pipe-stem
numskull	tradeful	groanful	didactyl	meristem
dead-pull	prideful	plainful	epicotyl	apothegm
push-pull	vengeful	basinful	carboxyl	paradigm
bellpull	surgeful	wagonful	hydroxyl	didrachm
prophyll	tableful	spoonful	nitroxyl	non-claim
protocol	ladleful	dearnful	M	proclaim
catechol	smileful	scornful	caimacam	disclaim
naphthol	guileful	mournful	mokaddam	cherubim
geraniol	shameful	scoopful	muqaddam	isocheim
lyra-viol	blameful	udderful	schiedam	Niflheim
Comsomol	crimeful	cheerful	hollidam	Blenheim
Komsomol	noiseful	powerful	rood-beam	seraphim
methanol	menseful	glassful	hardbeam	teraphim
over-cool	senseful	pressful	moonbeam	xeraphim
jack-fool	purseful	blissful	hornbeam	Nethinim
cesspool	pauseful	doubtful	sea-bream	snap-brim
sesspool	unuseful	lightful	ice-cream	sopherim
sash-tool	houseful	mightful	daydream	Isengrim
tint-tool	plateful	rightful	on-stream	mahzorim
wood-wool	grateful	fruitful	upstream	alastrim
pine-wool	spiteful	faultful	phenogam	pichurim
slag-wool	tasteful	scentful	brougham	cullysim
skin-wool	wasteful	eventful	whim-wham	verbatim
cony-wool	nieveful	vauntful	sealyham	gradatim
Interpol	griefful	fountful	kaimakam	seriatim
gossypol	shelf-ful	snootful	flim-flam	moshavim

overswim	pump-room	ensiform	Graecism	novelism
wine-palm	mess-room	fusiform	solecism	Stahlism
date-palm	newsroom	natiform	dioecism	pugilism
doom-palm	rest-room	retiform	ethicism	nihilism
doum-palm	showroom	stem-form	hylicism	familism
coco-palm	playroom	reinform	Sinicism	troilism
sago-palm	here-from	iodoform	cynicism	virilism
hemp-palm	caschrom	slipform	stoicism	devilism
witch-elm	angstrom	platform	Doricism	phallism
telefilm	disbosom	Januform	lyricism	psellism
intercom	gram-atom	sea-storm	Atticism	Gaullism
villadom	christom	sand-worm	exorcism	embolism
pappadom	accustom	lindworm	merycism	sciolism
duncedom	round-arm	wood-worm	nomadism	simplism
liegedom	sword-arm	tube-worm	monadism	populism
thanedom	white-arm	pile-worm	faradism	botulism
whoredom	stud-farm	gapeworm	Braidism	Occamism
chiefdom	home-farm	tapeworm	solidism	Islamism
leechdom	fish-farm	fireworm	Hasidism	dynamism
birthdom	small-arm	wire-worm	druidism	racemism
Greekdom	arm-in-arm	case-worm	Stundism	endemism
sheikdom	underarm	flag-worm	paludism	totemism
clerkdom	lukewarm	ringworm	Mazdeism	bathmism
thraldom	milk-warm	inch-worm	Babeeism	minimism
babeldom	periderm	muck-worm	caffeism	intimism
rebeldom	endoderm	silkworm	ditheism	optimism
unseldom	hypoderm	bookworm	pacifism	seismism
noveldom	mesoderm	hook-worm	drudgism	acosmism
devildom	ectoderm	meal-worm	Whiggism	paganism
swelldom	entoderm	pill-worm	priggism	veganism
queendom	isotherm	boll-worm	thuggism	organism
Saxondom	episperm	cornworm	dirigism	Arianism
queerdom	zoosperm	hornworm	Orangism	melanism
unwisdom	half-term	ship-worm	swingism	Romanism
saintdom	long-term	whipworm	obeahism	humanism
puppydom	taghairm	hair-worm	psychism	satanism
fairydom	reaffirm	flat-worm	Buddhism	Titanism
gypsydom	long-firm	maltworm	psephism	Wodenism
cardamom	lavaform	glow-worm	sapphism	eugenism
outvenom	waveform	slow-worm	Irishism	alienism
head-boom	cubiform	plateasm	Baathism	tokenism
spekboom	nubiform	isochasm	erethism	Galenism
tail-boom	tubiform	chiliasm	zombiism	Ibsenism
mainboom	unciform	neoplasm	Mahdiism	Essenism
foredoom	paliform	bioplasm	Parsiism	albinism
may-bloom	filiform	exoplasm	cabalism	Molinism
hand-loom	piliform	pleonasm	localism	feminism
heirloom	coliform	phantasm	vocalism	Leninism
clubroom	janiform	Mazdaism	modalism	alpinism
headroom	maniform	sol-faism	idealism	Marinism
ward-room	raniform	archaism	legalism	Latinism
sale-room	reniform	Aramaism	regalism	actinism
anteroom	omniform	ultraism	trialism	laconism
washroom	coniform	prosaism	finalism	hedonism
mushroom	napiform	voltaism	papalism	ebionism
bathroom	variform	Shivaism	moralism	unionism
backroom	aeriform	Wahabism	ruralism	polonism
cookroom	auriform	strabism	fatalism	demonism
dark-room	muriform	snobbism	petalism	Timonism
workroom	lyriform	clubbism	vitalism	Byronism
sail-room	pyriform	scribism	navalism	Saxonism
ball-room	gasiform	plumbism	royalism	Brownism
well-room	vasiform	betacism	ptyalism	jingoism
toolroom	pisiform	iotacism	babelism	negroism

escapism	paroxysm	encomium	speculum	Jamaican
priapism	guaiacum	chromium	spiculum	barbican
sinapism	capsicum	phormium	vinculum	publican
atropism	viaticum	didymium	inoculum	Anglican
metopism	Triticum	geranium	vasculum	Gallican
macarism	canticum	titanium	pendulum	hoolican
solarism	poppadum	ingenium	coagulum	pemmican
tigerism	mocuddum	achenium	cingulum	American
etherism	notandum	selenium	Erysimum	jerrican
dimerism	mutandum	splenium	isodomum	Scotican
eumerism	addendum	hymenium	olibanum	Etruscan
asterism	videndum	illinium	galbanum	billy-can
fakirism	pudendum	actinium	labdanum	jerrycan
rigorism	tenendum	meconium	laudanum	acaridan
algorism	corundum	syconium	origanum	harridan
aphorism	puppodum	oogonium	tympanum	kalamdan
pelorism	hypogeum	polonium	duodenum	qalamdan
tutorism	linoleum	ammonium	Sphagnum	isopodan
Tantrism	perineum	coronium	Buccinum	Circaean
centrism	Serapeum	opsonium	succinum	Mandaean
aneurism	mezereum	europium	glucinum	epigaean
naturism	coliseum	sudarium	aluminum	Neogaean
futurism	ommateum	velarium	platinum	Archaean
somatism	kauri-gum	solarium	laburnum	Hyblaean
donatism	sugar-gum	samarium	viburnum	spelaean
teratism	zooecium	ranarium	alburnum	Aramaean
Docetism	lutecium	conarium	Apocynum	pygmaean
quietism	silicium	puparium	cerebrum	Linnaean
Ophitism	francium	rosarium	delubrum	lernaean
Semitism	Caladium	ossarium	side-drum	Tyrtaean
Shaktism	vanadium	aquarium	mire-drum	Phoebean
giantism	soredium	vivarium	variorum	buckbean
saintism	rubidium	imperium	scalprum	Jacobean
sybotism	aecidium	apterium	veratrum	panacean
ergotism	oncidium	delirium	electrum	cetacean
idiotism	ascidium	ciborium	plectrum	Medicean
helotism	pygidium	emporium	spectrum	mid-ocean
acrotism	conidium	motorium	humstrum	caducean
chartism	gonidium	masurium	abomasum	Sotadean
Hinduism	aspidium	indusium	striatum	vice-dean
euphuism	peridium	solatium	testatum	Chaldean
cliquism	basidium	domatium	placitum	Shandean
altruism	pyxidium	cymatium	aconitum	perigean
untruism	scandium	lutetium	pulpitum	hypogean
sensuism	allodium	lixivium	rum-ti-tum	nymphean
Shaivism	Taxodium	diluvium	Adiantum	morphean
incivism	exordium	alluvium	ramentum	dry-clean
nativism	patagium	Leucojum	lomentum	Galilean
activism	eryngium	scybalum	momentum	Chellean
hobbyism	eulogium	rock-alum	tomentum	Carolean
boobyism	refugium	paspalum	Psilotum	Tyrolean
toadyism	graphium	Santalum	pronotum	cerulean
Paddyism	silphium	tantalum	factotum	foremean
dandyism	cyathium	crotalum	teetotum	hymenean
dowdyism	xanthium	corallum	residuum	Pyrenean
rowdyism	ordalium	labellum	tautonym	eburnean
bogeyism	nobelium	sacellum	polyonym	Pareoean
Puseyism	mycelium	schellum	N	Typhoean
bullyism	thallium	vexillum	berghaan	Priapean
puppyism	bdellium	date-plum	Columban	Oedipean
fairyism	trillium	musk-plum	suburban	European
gypsyism	scholium	exemplum	conurban	trappean
partyism	nebulium	cocoplum	barracan	Briarean
aneurysm	peculium	saeculum	trash-can	Cesarean

Nazarean	ordalian	riparian	urodelan	Turcoman
venerean	regalian	agrarian	rubellan	dragoman
aurorean	Hegelian	rosarian	Lucullan	Turkoman
empyrean	Sahelian	Tatarian	jambolan	sea-woman
Pegasean	aphelian	Rotarian	portolan	madwoman
Odyssean	Sikelian	nutarian	rataplan	ragwoman
cotquean	aurelian	aquarian	foreplan	pig-woman
turbofan	Stahlian	Cambrian	open-plan	obi-woman
neopagan	Sicilian	Teucrian	Indiaman	penwoman
taboggan	Tamilian	Abderian	hielaman	airwoman
toboggan	Aprilian	Algerian	Chinaman	batwoman
cardigan	Basilian	valerian	Rastaman	day-woman
hooligan	civilian	Sumerian	freedman	dey-woman
larrigan	idyllian	Naperian	plaidman	toywoman
Ramadhan	creolian	Cabirian	swordman	scrap-man
yataghan	Siculian	placeman	placeman	shearman
sneeshan	Bohemian	Bactrian	spaceman	spearman
Langshan	isthmian	Sartrian	sauceman	alderman
Jonathan	Albanian	Austrian	spademan	underman
Cathaian	Sicanian	Silurian	brideman	superman
Ghanaian	Oceanian	lemurian	three-man	waterman
Polabian	Zelanian	Etrurian	liegeman	peter-man
Eusebian	Romanian	Illyrian	bargeman	riverman
Jacobian	Rumanian	Assyrian	forgeman	chairman
magician	Turanian	Eurasian	whale-man	choirman
logician	Titanian	Ephesian	nobleman	motorman
musician	Athenian	Friesian	rifleman	beadsman
optician	Armenian	Salesian	fugleman	headsman
Bajocian	sirenian	Milesian	scene-man	leadsman
Volscian	Socinian	Jamesian	tripeman	goadsman
Accadian	Arminian	Artesian	shareman	roadsman
Arcadian	actinian	Parisian	shireman	seedsman
Orcadian	Baconian	Lewisian	shoreman	bandsman
Akkadian	Laconian	Wellsian	proseman	landsman
Canadian	Dodonian	Burnsian	verse-man	bondsman
comedian	Maeonian	gaussian	horseman	woodsman
ascidian	Polonian	Prussian	Norseman	herdsman
aphidian	Demonian	Venusian	houseman	bedesman
ophidian	Senonian	Pepysian	plateman	sidesman
meridian	Junonian	Ignatian	prize-man	tides-man
viridian	Maronian	Croatian	coachman	lodesman
obsidian	Neronian	Horatian	ranchman	dalesman
Scandian	Tironian	Alsatian	henchman	salesman
guardian	Huronian	Novatian	winchman	talesman
Claudian	Ausonian	Rhaetian	marchman	islesman
Freudian	Catonian	Venetian	watchman	linesman
plebeian	Ultonian	Lutetian	Dutchman	meresman
Harleian	Estonian	Swiftian	truchman	cragsman
Pompeian	Favonian	nicotian	freshman	dragsman
Tarpeian	pavonian	Boeotian	Irishman	swagsman
Graafian	Devonian	Egyptian	Welshman	gangsman
Wolffian	bezonian	Erastian	marshman	kings-man
Pelagian	Brownian	faustian	Northman	talisman
Georgian	digynian	Venutian	trackman	tacksman
Phrygian	Olympian	Laputian	stockman	locksman
Noachian	salopian	Moravian	truckman	banksman
bacchian	thespian	Batavian	brinkman	marksman
Delphian	picarian	Menevian	wheelman	wealsman
Memphian	apiarian	Racovian	gavelman	bailsman
xanthian	malarian	diluvian	stallman	Paul's-man
Parthian	Kolarian	Peruvian	quillman	helmsman
Scythian	aularian	Vesuvian	Musulman	doomsman
Hawaiian	ranarian	Hertzian	abram-man	clansman
dedalian	lunarian	piazzian	apron-man	Klansman

reinsman	rambutan	hydrogen	threaten	mountain
gownsman	sapi-utan	nitrogen	heighten	reattain
townsman	Quechuan	photogen	brighten	cinquain
rampsman	Quichuan	histogen	frighten	cordwain
oversman	punaluan	allergen	boughten	coxswain
door's-man	brake-van	roentgen	foughten	log-cabin
classman	Cheshvan	groschen	straiten	cannabin
glassman	cordovan	burschen	unfasten	thrombin
chessman	Biscayan	heath-hen	sebesten	sea-robin
pressman	Cathayan	water-hen	tungsten	cherubin
raftsman	Wesleyan	parishen	christen	clavecin
huntsman	Strepyan	wreathen	begotten	capsicin
puntsman	bartizan	lengthen	ungotten	oxytocin
Scotsman	partizan	smoothen	unrotten	resorcin
trewsman	cistvaen	somewhen	henequen	neomycin
night-man	kistvaen	dandy-hen	bereaven	muscadin
frontman	threaden	unshaken	unshaven	xyloidin
stuntman	menhaden	forsaken	engraven	Girondin
pivot-man	unbidden	partaken	good-even	xanthein
hoastman	unhidden	mistaken	God-given	acrolein
hoistman	unridden	outtaken	forgiven	fräulein
subhuman	stridden	reawaken	misgiven	cerulein
prehuman	unsodden	stricken	undriven	chow-mein
squawman	embolden	insucken	uncloven	gate-vein
widow-man	beholden	shrunken	unproven	paraffin
bandyman	ybounden	bespoken	unfrozen	toboggin
handyman	grounden	unspoken	campaign	aborigin
bogey-man	faburden	unbroken	darraign	jowing-in
bothyman	unburden	to-broken	misfeign	fellahin
sally-man	Aberdeen	bedarken	outreign	matachin
tallyman	spalpeen	Magdalen	unbenign	faulchin
Everyman	bescreen	befallen	disloign	chin-chin
dairyman	pea-green	unfallen	redesign	parochin
ferryman	sea-green	cyclamen	shop-sign	capuchin
merryman	shagreen	clinamen	reassign	seraphin
party-man	sengreen	gravamen	Autobahn	sneeshin
call-loan	sap-green	noblemen	demijohn	lecithin
parazoan	squireen	henchmen	poor-john	acanthin
metazoan	yestreen	Dutchmen	mass-john	byrlakin
ectozoan	seldseen	specimen	mess-john	dunnakin
polyzoan	foreseen	cognomen	marocain	brodekin
saucepan	well-seen	bed-linen	reordain	baudekin
brine-pan	overseen	velskoen	Sicelain	mousekin
marzipan	nineteen	unshapen	chaplain	mutchkin
brainpan	eighteen	music-pen	complain	spelikin
tragopan	poshteen	steel-pen	overlain	spilikin
lifespan	thirteen	quill-pen	purslain	cannikin
wingspan	fourteen	unholpen	pearmain	mannikin
jelly-pan	may-queen	wide-open	mortmain	pannikin
trimaran	overween	behappen	madbrain	larrikin
Lutheran	fedayeen	sheep-pen	mid-brain	cuitikin
dipteran	armozeen	unheppen	hot-brain	bootikin
furfuran	bedeafen	children	air-drain	cootikin
ophiuran	collagen	brethren	riverain	devilkin
diocesan	staragen	mensuren	suzerain	Algonkin
Parmesan	miscegen	reed-wren	quatrain	ciderkin
bartisan	aborigen	wood-wren	owl-train	damaskin
partisan	florigen	shamisen	restrain	lambskin
pentosan	cultigen	unarisen	distrain	wood-skin
tarlatan	glycogen	new-risen	way-train	moleskin
Orvietan	pathogen	unchosen	plantain	wine-skin
Olivetan	diplogen	unloosen	maintain	foreskin
sumpitan	cyanogen	enfrosen	quintain	calfskin
Augustan	androgen	unbeaten	fountain	wolf-skin

fishskin	looker-in	hurcheon	invasion	solation
buckskin	Palmerin	Pantheon	adhesion	himation
sealskin	phoner-in	cameleon	inhesion	limation
swan-skin	elaterin	napoleon	cohesion	adnation
turnskin	sitter-in	mezereon	decision	venation
bearskin	culverin	glucagon	recision	agnation
deerskin	veratrin	enneagon	incision	conation
goatskin	Mathurin	tarragon	excision	donation
pony-skin	tabourin	tetragon	illision	zonation
mescalin	purpurin	pentagon	derision	lunation
phthalin	moccasin	heptagon	irrision	pupation
harmalin	sarrasin	martagon	revision	aeration
formalin	mocassin	box-wagon	division	deration
santalin	damassin	analogon	envision	duration
gridelin	assassin	parergon	emulsion	gyration
zeppelin	Limousin	eulachon	avulsion	natation
glutelin	bog-Latin	oulachon	evulsion	citation
franklin	dog-Latin	cabochon	scansion	dotation
vitellin	neo-Latin	agraphon	sponsion	notation
fluellin	haematin	Strephon	eclosion	potation
vanillin	desyatin	antiphon	emersion	rotation
percolin	bulletin	colophon	aversion	mutation
mandolin	secretin	polyphon	eversion	nutation
luteolin	palmitin	marathon	pression	equation
pangolin	block-tin	Phaethon	scission	lavation
sassolin	lamantin	telethon	emission	novation
globulin	invertin	coercion	omission	taxation
aesculin	sheet-tin	Triodion	refusion	vexation
benjamin	Calixtin	melodion	affusion	fixation
prolamin	ramequin	religion	effusion	luxation
Moslemin	henequin	falchion	infusion	reaction
euonymin	maroquin	panchion	delusion	enaction
manganin	replevin	gumphion	allusion	inaction
safranin	teguexin	vocalion	illusion	coaction
lichenin	thyroxin	aphelion	bibation	fraction
santonin	zootoxin	ganglion	cibation	traction
syntonin	sarrazin	pavilion	libation	exaction
sainfoin	hoactzin	scallion	jobation	ejection
talapoin	limekiln	stallion	lobation	election
terrapin	malt-kiln	stellion	pacation	erection
thole-pin	unsolemn	skillion	vacation	C-section
scarf-pin	ostracon	orillion	location	evection
linchpin	isodicon	trillion	vocation	emiction
dowel-pin	orthicon	stillion	sedation	friction
underpin	irenicon	scullion	nidation	eviction
backspin	salpicon	epyllion	nodation	sanction
tail-spin	methadon	scholion	nudation	function
overspin	tacked-on	encomion	sudation	junction
driftpin	Poseidon	acromion	ideation	eduction
shirt-pin	myrmidon	thermion	creation	deletion
wrest-pin	guéridon	dominion	legation	ambition
wrist-pin	off-and-on	trunnion	negation	addition
bobby-pin	stegodon	sea-onion	ligation	sedition
mandarin	Rhinodon	non-union	rogation	audition
warfarin	mastodon	disunion	aviation	nolition
margarin	melodeon	champion	halation	volition
coumarin	smidgeon	scorpion	ablation	lenition
alizarin	bludgeon	etherion	oblation	ignition
speldrin	bourgeon	allerion	delation	monition
chondrin	sturgeon	Hyperion	gelation	munition
dobber-in	pancheon	histrion	relation	punition
glycerin	luncheon	decurion	dilation	position
gorgerin	nuncheon	occasion	illation	petition
licker-in	puncheon	abrasion	colation	fruition

scontion	octoroon	unseason	true-born	homespun
demotion	poltroon	diapason	live-born	fine-spun
remotion	ducatoon	grandson	self-born	long-spun
devotion	spontoon	gambeson	high-born	thin-spun
adaption	frontoon	whoreson	hell-born	fresh-run
gumption	spittoon	goings-on	well-born	sheep-run
adoption	parazoon	empoison	fool-born	underrun
co-option	metazoon	unpoison	mean-born	print-run
sorption	endozoon	imprison	twin-born	shrew-run
eruption	ectozoon	unprison	sea-acorn	cub-drawn
exertion	entozoon	garrison	seed-corn	air-drawn
abortion	polyzoon	warrison	ward-corn	rock-hewn
egestion	unweapon	jettison	mongcorn	bestrewn
question	hereupon	scoinson	mungcorn	hand-sewn
inustion	mascaron	sternson	naricorn	fade-down
locution	fanfaron	squarson	cavicorn	take-down
ablution	squadron	Anderson	amelcorn	comedown
dilution	dihedron	unperson	outscorn	backdown
solution	chaldron	cavesson	disadorn	kickdown
volution	cauldron	herisson	waldhorn	mark-down
oblivion	pauldron	lewisson	hand-horn	hull-down
diluvion	pouldron	advowson	shoehorn	even-down
alluvion	chawdron	ciclaton	staghorn	torn-down
annexion	erigeron	Sheraton	longhorn	turn-down
ostrakon	hanger-on	skeleton	slughorn	step-down
oerlikon	longeron	magneton	buckhorn	meltdown
gonfalon	walker-on	haqueton	bull-horn	shut-down
pantalon	looker-on	mirliton	crumhorn	show-down
matfelon	vigneron	graviton	krumhorn	blowdown
moufflon	chaperon	plankton	deer-horn	slow-down
biathlon	hapteron	rebutton	ram's-horn	stowdown
abutilon	setter-on	unbutton	lanthorn	stay-down
papillon	putter-on	follow-on	post-horn	bluegown
carillon	deuteron	feast-won	hawthorn	new-blown
cotillon	cheveron	tetraxon	lovelorn	fly-blown
bouillon	chaffron	polyaxon	lasslorn	nut-brown
propylon	southron	Apollyon	time-worn	discrown
cardamon	gridiron	eucaryon	careworn	outfrown
cinnamon	beak-iron	eukaryon	toil-worn	bestrown
sea-lemon	beck-iron	emblazon	well-worn	self-sown
episemon	bick-iron	outlearn	shopworn	thin-sown
phlegmon	boom-iron	forewarn	overworn	home-town
stasimon	wear-iron	rope-yarn	mansworn	kirktown
uncommon	flatiron	spun-yarn	forsworn	down-town
isodomon	cast-iron	tara-fern	footworn	post-town
gonfanon	oophoron	hard-fern	windburn	O
noumenon	oxymoron	tree-fern	overburn	scirocco
rigadoon	ice-apron	male-fern	taciturn	charneco
doubloon	negatron	lady-fern	downturn	politico
shalloon	skiatron	leathern	star-turn	barranco
epiploon	dynatron	northern	overturn	flamenco
half-moon	empatron	southern	near-gaun	locofoco
forenoon	betatron	quartern	omadhaun	alfresco
teaspoon	bevatron	slattern	cream-bun	mameluco
egg-spoon	electron	flittern	cross-bun	tucotuco
pap-spoon	plectron	forfairn	honeybun	tucutuco
macaroon	teletron	stubborn	mouse-dun	sticcado
picaroon	ignitron	dead-born	siege-gun	stoccado
octaroon	positron	wild-born	flash-gun	renegado
gambroon	mesotron	wood-born	radar-gun	escalado
spadroon	cryotron	bawd-born	elder-gun	escapado
quadroon	plastron	freeborn	spray-gun	malgrado
shagroon	klystron	home-born	tommy-gun	Sangrado
tenoroon	unreason	base-born	farm-toun	Eldorado

8 -ADO

palisado	bargello	espresso	handclap	lantskip
camisado	prunello	staccato	coal-flap	wool-clip
stampedo	umbrello	spiccato	flip-flap	underlip
how-d'ye-do	martello	sticcato	underlap	landslip
daring-do	spadillo	scordato	snip-snap	side-slip
mancando	caudillo	ostinato	soft-soap	long-slip
parlando	Negrillo	moderato	sand-trap	overslip
commando	tapacolo	literato	tank-trap	handgrip
saltando	tapaculo	castrato	fall-trap	hair-grip
lentando	twelvemo	sforzato	claptrap	overtrip
forzando	Fascismo	smorzato	star-trap	airstrip
reddendo	machismo	perfecto	gift-wrap	outstrip
perdendo	capitano	unsued-to	water-tap	pedipalp
innuendo	vargueño	graffito	knee-deep	self-help
well-to-do	scaldino	mosquito	skin-deep	lady-help
cicisbeo	zecchino	trecento	mug-sheep	wood-pulp
sigisbeo	palamino	seicento	overkeep	firedamp
plumbago	palomino	pimiento	dog-sleep	headlamp
suppeago	Filipino	assiento	outsleep	rear-lamp
villiago	peperino	hereunto	sand-peep	blowlamp
Ustilago	neutrino	concerto	peesweep	glowlamp
subimago	duettino	hitherto	side-step	Davy-lamp
galapago	ottavino	Mephisto	fire-step	pita-hemp
Plantago	kakemono	concetto	half-step	carl-hemp
super-ego	makimono	zuchetto	lockstep	sunn-hemp
vitiligo	contorno	stiletto	overstep	overjump
impetigo	peekaboo	varletto	doorstep	feed-pump
fandango	hubbuboo	palmetto	footstep	sand-pump
contango	toodle-oo	cornetto	sheep-dip	beer-pump
Mandingo	choo-choo	rispetto	lucky-dip	lift-pump
flamingo	ballyhoo	libretto	blue-chip	foot-pump
cacafogo	vindaloo	amoretto	rajaship	speed-cop
sentry-go	hallaloo	falsetto	headship	attercop
gazpacho	jordeloo	sestetto	land-ship	pork-chop
mallecho	Waterloo	terzetto	bardship	chop-chop
Monarcho	gardyloo	bozzetto	hardship	hedge-hop
whoa-ho-ho	kangaroo	Peshitto	wardship	seed-shop
libeccio	jackaroo	risoluto	lordship	shoe-shop
presidio	buckaroo	ritenuto	treeship	swagshop
preludio	wallaroo	continuo	mageship	grog-shop
villagio	gillaroo	terrazzo	dogeship	unbishop
coraggio	jillaroo	P	dukeship	tick-shop
arpeggio	wanderoo	goose-cap	popeship	tuck-shop
borachio	jackeroo	whitecap	fireship	junk-shop
finochio	groo-groo	death-cap	foreship	bookshop
Kuroshio	cockatoo	cloth-cap	serfship	cookshop
Struthio	guacharo	handicap	flagship	workshop
seraglio	tapadero	blackcap	Whigship	dram-shop
intaglio	ranchero	skull-cap	kingship	pawnshop
rosoglio	anti-hero	thrum-cap	longship	swap-shop
Noctilio	sombrero	crown-cap	deanship	slop-shop
pulvilio	paderero	ethercap	clanship	gift-shop
curculio	pederero	ettercap	tranship	lorry-hop
besognio	paterero	foolscap	twinship	clip-clop
Lothario	teru-tero	nightcap	township	clop-clop
scenario	cruzeiro	screw-cap	heroship	flip-flop
tenebrio	autogiro	dog-cheap	heirship	escallop
oratorio	corocoro	sand-heap	peatship	slipslop
intarsio	autogyro	dung-heap	poetship	dolly-mop
fellatio	gracioso	muck-heap	ladyship	hula-hoop
chechako	doloroso	overleap	demyship	war-whoop
makomako	maestoso	spark-gap	landskip	liripoop
finnesko	virtuoso	water-gap	townskip	lollipop
bordello	sargasso	baasskap	overskip	killcrop

overcrop	runner-up	overwear	consular	sea-adder
moss-crop	setter-up	forswear	capsular	shredder
root-crop	follow-up	outswear	spatular	Enzedder
paradrop	R	knitwear	fistular	conceder
name-drop	cinnabar	footwear	pustular	screeder
rose-drop	sound-bar	goodyear	valvular	confider
backdrop	millibar	half-year	nervular	outrider
raindrop	snack-bar	leap-year	condylar	joy-rider
pear-drop	unilobar	overyear	dactylar	offsider
tear-drop	microbar	agar-agar	pulvinar	consider
snowdrop	crossbar	resalgar	columnar	outsider
rosy-drop	draft-bar	unvulgar	Achernar	provider
calthrop	tommy-bar	nenuphar	sublunar	shielder
vine-prop	cable-car	gangliar	cislunar	bewilder
agitprop	cycle-car	familiar	wild-boar	unfolder
sweet-sop	horsecar	auxiliar	eight-oar	beholder
round-top	steam-car	peculiar	calcspar	inholder
table-top	turbocar	nightjar	feldspar	upholder
housetop	Caryocar	unifilar	komissar	empolder
blacktop	ricercar	tonsilar	selictar	impolder
reed-stop	hover-car	micellar	scimitar	unsolder
knee-stop	motor-car	nucellar	loadstar	shoulder
long-stop	leaf-scar	lamellar	sand-star	smoulder
helistop	killadar	patellar	lodestar	oleander
backstop	silladar	bacillar	bedeguar	malander
tram-stop	thanadar	mamillar	cultivar	bilander
screwtop	subahdar	papillar	tug-of-war	filander
mericarp	chokidar	medullar	man-of-war	inlander
pericarp	talukdar	alveolar	Guicowar	colander
endocarp	risaldar	modiolar	interwar	Polander
xylocarp	havildar	variolar	class-war	solander
monocarp	calendar	petiolar	kala-azar	uplander
mesocarp	kalendar	premolar	subsizar	islander
autocarp	zamindar	unipolar	ad-libber	bylander
autoharp	zemindar	subsolar	scrubber	demander
Jew's-harp	gospodar	vacuolar	Mulciber	pomander
moldwarp	hospodar	hexaplar	zingiber	expander
gold-wasp	taberdar	examplar	December	squander
sand-wasp	forebear	exemplar	remember	ascender
wood-wasp	cave-bear	globular	November	defender
gall-wasp	overbear	piacular	unlimber	offender
gemma-cup	mouse-ear	oracular	encumber	engender
death-cup	headgear	saccular	cucumber	calender
sneak-cup	high-gear	specular	renumber	expender
acorn-cup	neck-gear	acicular	absorber	entender
cider-cup	worm-gear	spicular	surfacer	intender
washed-up	spur-gear	calcular	replacer	untender
booked-up	footgear	circular	embracer	attender
balled-up	draw-gear	torcular	Quebecer	extender
warmed-up	overhear	furcular	opificer	lavender
jumped-up	all-clear	vascular	rejoicer	cylinder
hopped-up	cochlear	muscular	justicer	reminder
souped-up	musk-pear	pendular	balancer	seconder
tarted-up	reappear	lingular	romancer	refunder
hotted-up	eel-spear	singular	silencer	flounder
stived-up	hare's-ear	cellular	trouncer	grounder
pick-me-up	bear's-ear	nummular	divorcer	fly-under
steepe-up	wheat-ear	formular	traducer	exploder
freeze-up	wheatear	plumular	producer	do-gooder
owerloup	burnt-ear	planular	threader	regarder
subgroup	neckwear	granular	spreader	retarder
pop-group	workwear	scapular	unloader	rewarder
rice-soup	swimwear	stipular	forrader	emborder
higher-up		sporular	crusader	imborder

8 -DER

suborder	springer	scowther	mimicker	pedaller
accorder	stringer	steadier	monicker	moraller
recorder	stronger	greffier	unsicker	squaller
preorder	enhunger	pacifier	musicker	gabeller
disorder	expunger	codifier	shrieker	rebeller
misorder	geologer	modifier	misliker	libeller
marauder	enlarger	vilifier	embanker	modeller
colluder	asperger	typifier	shrinker	yodeller
obtruder	scourger	verifier	onlooker	repeller
intruder	scrouger	purifier	gas-poker	impeller
extruder	bleacher	gasifier	provoker	reteller
bepowder	preacher	ratifier	remarker	beveller
herb-beer	treacher	notifier	co-worker	leveller
rice-beer	broacher	vivifier	unmasker	reveller
near-beer	brancher	clothier	squawker	hoveller
root-beer	stancher	pedalier	annealer	jeweller
caboceer	drencher	espalier	repealer	schiller
mule-deer	trencher	gasalier	squealer	thriller
musk-deer	quencher	cavalier	revealer	caviller
killdeer	clincher	goodlier	drabbler	caroller
reindeer	flincher	gaselier	dribbler	enroller
cameleer	launcher	hotelier	fribbler	stroller
fusileer	searcher	motelier	stibbler	consoler
engineer	starcher	sanglier	quibbler	frampler
domineer	scorcher	fusilier	scambler	trampler
mutineer	thatcher	seemlier	trembler	trippler
timoneer	snatcher	gasolier	grumbler	stippler
life-peer	sketcher	complier	stumbler	scrupler
overpeer	fletcher	supplier	troubler	startler
mounseer	kvetcher	overlier	treadler	wrestler
overseer	snitcher	caponier	swaddler	whistler
muleteer	spitcher	occupier	twaddler	epistler
squiffer	stitcher	croupier	quiddler	prattler
chauffer	twitcher	quarrier	twiddler	twattler
crucifer	scutcher	scurrier	wheedler	scuttler
Chelifer	sloucher	spurrier	chandler	scrawler
mammifer	plougher	destrier	swindler	sprawler
Spirifer	decipher	roturier	teaseler	grizzler
thurifer	encipher	huissier	weaseler	screamer
transfer	uncipher	bénitier	hosteler	streamer
bondager	splasher	frontier	batteler	inflamer
schläger	thrasher	sabotier	whiffler	gossamer
pillager	squasher	quartier	sniffler	redeemer
villager	feldsher	courtier	scuffler	outremer
rummager	secesher	trustier	shuffler	extremer
teenager	thresher	streaker	snuffler	Bessemer
presager	polisher	squeaker	sniggler	mon-khmer
vintager	vanisher	cly-faker	wriggler	dulcimer
cottager	finisher	bedmaker	smuggler	old-timer
scavager	punisher	wig-maker	spangler	ragtimer
abridger	papisher	pin-maker	wrangler	egg-timer
besieger	perisher	gunmaker	shingler	two-timer
colleger	ravisher	topmaker	derailer	embalmer
ostreger	breather	law-maker	retailer	aglimmer
oak-egger	wreather	haymaker	entailer	thrummer
rejigger	a-weather	way-maker	squailer	welcomer
lammiger	regather	fly-maker	unveiler	newcomer
scutiger	upgather	partaker	profiler	misnomer
claviger	together	hijacker	compiler	ransomer
indulger	comether	unpacker	beguiler	customer
endanger	untether	attacker	stickler	tautomer
stranger	smoother	thwacker	twinkler	affirmer
revenger	scouther	ox-pecker	sparkler	deformer
malinger	shouther	vraicker	caballer	reformer

informer	gammoner	lumberer	perjurer	pomwater
perfumer	commoner	numberer	murmurer	tap-water
presumer	summoner	sorcerer	labourer	tar-water
consumer	sermoner	dodderer	armourer	gas-water
costumer	schooner	fodderer	rumourer	cut-water
chicaner	marooner	solderer	honourer	affecter
profaner	ratooner	wanderer	vapourer	effecter
bemoaner	disponer	renderer	favourer	rejecter
piecener	reasoner	tenderer	devourer	expecter
larcener	seasoner	hinderer	measurer	depicter
parcener	poisoner	ponderer	lecturer	pargeter
deadener	prisoner	wonderer	multurer	catheter
gardener	bijwoner	sunderer	venturer	racketer
hardener	blazoner	larderer	torturer	picketer
screener	taverner	verderer	nurturer	rocketer
congener	suborner	borderer	vesturer	marketer
weakener	by-corner	murderer	posturer	belleter
sickener	dehorner	veneerer	releaser	diameter
suckener	Zigeuner	sufferer	Judaiser	viameter
reopener	renowner	pilferer	oxidiser	trimeter
warrener	stuccoer	lingerer	realiser	oximeter
Pilsener	frescoer	cosherer	utiliser	ohmmeter
loosener	evil-doer	gatherer	idoliser	odometer
softener	well-doer	ditherer	promiser	udometer
whitener	overdoer	dummerer	atomiser	geometer
fastener	racegoer	pamperer	surmiser	gas-meter
hastener	foregoer	tamperer	ozoniser	luxmeter
listener	filmgoer	temperer	despiser	ferreter
fattener	play-goer	simperer	waywiser	masseter
convener	tattooer	pepperer	cleanser	physeter
maligner	end-paper	kipperer	licenser	uplifter
designer	rag-paper	loiterer	incenser	flichter
resigner	cap-paper	palterer	encloser	teuchter
impugner	tar-paper	banterer	incloser	blighter
oppugner	wax-paper	barterer	composer	plighter
ordainer	flypaper	pesterer	proposer	daughter
regainer	hag-taper	fosterer	supposer	laughter
strainer	douzeper	patterer	disposer	rabbiter
obtainer	calliper	letterer	relapser	circiter
detainer	bagpiper	titterer	reverser	verditer
retainer	pit-viper	potterer	endorser	profiter
cordiner	pen-wiper	totterer	harasser	chapiter
confiner	obtemper	mutterer	finesser	pulpiter
imaginer	untemper	mouterer	embosser	requiter
recliner	attemper	pewterer	diffuser	infilter
one-liner	shrimper	slaverer	profuser	revolter
eyeliner	galloper	quaverer	espouser	insulter
milliner	walloper	flowerer	carouser	decanter
top-liner	improper	answerer	dialyser	recanter
airliner	unproper	repairer	analyser	Levanter
jetliner	outroper	inspirer	bee-eater	indenter
examiner	didapper	requirer	reheater	scienter
terminer	strapper	enquirer	man-eater	fomenter
enjoiner	bepepper	inquirer	sin-eater	repenter
essoiner	stripper	implorer	repeater	resenter
tontiner	appearer	explorer	ant-eater	assenter
japanner	seafarer	hectorer	deflater	splinter
beginner	warfarer	restorer	idolater	sprinter
falconer	wayfarer	deferrer	zoolater	disinter
Londoner	declarer	abhorrer	regrater	squinter
pardoner	cellarer	demurrer	sea-water	chaunter
waggoner	preparer	procurer	red-water	flaunter
visioner	jabberer	obscurer	ice-water	enaunter
reckoner	cumberer	conjurer	eye-water	promoter

8 -TER

uprooter	doomster	absolver	long-hair	sash-door
parroter	spinster	resolver	back-hair	back-door
outvoter	imposter	revolver	deer-hair	hall-door
accepter	whipster	bedcover	overhair	open-door
prompter	quipster	air-cover	root-hair	main-door
departer	hampster	discover	plein-air	barndoor
imparter	dempster	handover	debonair	trap-door
thwarter	sempster	once-over	air-to-air	shop-door
deserter	thirster	take-over	unrepair	next-door
inserter	maltster	moreover	fish-weir	sea-floor
asserter	adjuster	rove-over	joint-fir	subfloor
inverter	baluster	hangover	tabashir	peat-moor
squirter	thruster	hung-over	souvenir	land-poor
dehorter	brewster	push-over	peignoir	conjuror
exhorter	frowster	walk-over	voussoir	nonjuror
reporter	splatter	work-over	abattoir	releasor
importer	squatter	pullover	grattoir	embrasor
exporter	enfetter	turnover	trottoir	promisor
resorter	unfetter	wrapover	decemvir	sun-visor
assorter	begetter	slip-over	triumvir	provisor
retorter	go-getter	stop-over	Dukhobor	licensor
oleaster	besetter	sea-rover	roncador	incensor
pilaster	resetter	reprover	toreador	extensor
canaster	onsetter	improver	Labrador	assessor
pinaster	upsetter	approver	provedor	occlusor
disaster	embitter	Passover	cuspidor	Mercator
goadster	imbitter	left-over	corridor	piscator
roadster	aglitter	observer	Messidor	educator
bandster	splitter	reviewer	providor	predator
lewdster	remitter	shadower	expandor	mandator
digester	sea-otter	beflower	splendor	radiator
molester	garotter	deflower	heliodor	mediator
gamester	rebutter	enflower	louis-d'or	expiator
semester	splutter	wallower	pledgeor	vitiator
mimester	strutter	bellower	therefor	deviator
bepester	tributer	follower	wherefor	chelator
forester	executer	winnower	unanchor	deflator
arrester	polluter	sea-power	up-anchor	inflator
attester	commuter	manpower	metaphor	epilator
dragster	computer	air-power	canephor	collator
bangster	disputer	outpower	phosphor	violator
gangster	reneguer	borrower	co-author	isolator
lingster	beslaver	sorrower	seignior	adulator
ringster	enslaver	bestower	inferior	emulator
gongster	engraver	reanswer	superior	cremator
songster	screever	gunlayer	ulterior	animator
plaister	believer	waylayer	anterior	urinator
slaister	reliever	tax-payer	interior	pronator
magister	buplever	defrayer	exterior	vibrator
register	whomever	betrayer	subprior	operator
demister	whenever	conveyer	bachelor	regrator
banister	wherever	employer	unicolor	migrator
canister	whosever	squeezer	tricolor	barrator
ganister	dissever	ebenezer	concolor	narrator
minister	whatever	apprizer	demeanor	pulsator
sinister	sandiver	kibitzer	convenor	sectator
cloister	dun-diver	howitzer	assignor	dictator
huckster	sky-diver	creutzer	pundonor	agitator
linkster	deceiver	kreutzer	dishonor	imitator
Pinkster	receiver	Landwehr	governor	testator
pollster	all-giver	lug-chair	side-door	valuator
seamster	law-giver	armchair	half-door	actuator
teamster	conniver	pew-chair		elevator
deemster	desilver	wire-hair		redactor

Rh-factor	signieur	graphics	larynges	Passeres
varactor	monsieur	dynamics	asperges	halteres
defector	ciseleur	polemics	coccyges	cursores
effector	bateleur	eugenics	breeches	Raptores
infector	jongleur	technics	cratches	emphases
objector	seigneur	hedonics	britches	diereses
rejector	écraseur	avionics	potashes	glacises
injector	chasseur	cryonics	uneathes	premises
selector	secateur	olympics	unnethes	narcoses
director	saboteur	spherics	effigies	thyloses
bisector	frotteur	kinesics	syzygies	zoonoses
detector	longueur	genetics	murphies	supposes
depictor	claqueur	kinetics	worthies	neuroses
abductor	truqueur	politics	chuckies	ellipses
adductor	trouveur	Semitics	alkalies	thripses
seductor	underfur	deontics	Ramilies	synopses
inductor	testamur	robotics	frillies	molasses
elicitor	remurmur	glyptics	woollies	chausses
traditor	belabour	plastics	pearlies	iambuses
creditor	malodour	ekistics	spinnies	nimbuses
proditor	clangour	adenoids	vagaries	funguses
cursitor	half-hour	badlands	sundries	Tunguses
servitor	lamp-hour	hollands	wherries	geniuses
accentor	watt-hour	air-bends	nineties	galluses
assentor	rye-flour	gold-ends	eighties	meatuses
patentor	decolour	beam-ends	nudities	hiatuses
promotor	encolour	dry-goods	canities	cactuses
gas-motor	paramour	seawards	verities	plexuses
recaptor	downpour	bedwards	exequies	galowses
acceptor	vavasour	godwards	larnakes	dialyses
receptor	stentour	offwards	Gnetales	analyses
inceptor	cockspur	sunwards	movables	Primates
exceptor	larkspur	frowards	shingles	diabetes
sculptor	partitur	airwards	naythles	Rhodites
assertor	loquitur	forwards	satelles	stipites
invertor	S	outwards	frijoles	Charites
quaestor	succubas	skywards	skittles	Quirites
ancestor	Bermudas	soap-suds	saccules	Atlantes
arrestor	pancreas	thoraces	mesdames	cerastes
attestor	overseas	scoleces	entremes	Argestes
investor	marsh-gas	spadices	oft-times	culottes
varistor	hidalgas	caudices	turbines	dock-dues
resistor	water-gas	pollices	uredines	all-fives
impostor	sewer-gas	imbrices	imagines	midwives
adjustor	verrugas	matrices	pectines	alewives
remittor	Asterias	altrices	johannes	caudexes
executor	bucellas	vertices	saw-bones	vortexes
alley-tor	drachmas	cortices	spadones	matrixes
disfavor	Sathanas	vortices	epigones	syrinxes
survivor	Maecenas	frutices	Geckones	larynxes
gillyvor	antennas	halluces	pulmones	nine-eyes
conveyor	copperas	Pleiades	saw-tones	four-eyes
kurveyor	corporas	pholades	calicoes	snow-eyes
purveyor	alcatras	dipsades	frescoes	earmuffs
surveyor	taffetas	rachides	dominoes	long-legs
allosaur	gravitas	raphides	Hereroes	ants'-eggs
dinosaur	tarantas	Pierides	tomatoes	jibbings
semitaur	sceattas	cyprides	potatoes	combings
Minotaur	never-was	Sarcodes	forcipes	sindings
clotebur	mestizas	hartbees	bagpipes	syndings
grandeur	aerobics	compages	Pan-pipes	diggings
frondeur	fluidics	sphinges	Tarsipes	hidlings
coiffeur	melodics	meninges	cyclopes	moslings
voyageur	psychics	syringes	unawares	coamings

gainings	narcosis	cathexis	omphalos	nit-grass
pyonings	acidosis	syntexis	lichanos	rotgrass
earnings	apodosis	endeixis	landdros	nut-grass
mornings	lordosis	panmixis	enhydros	cowgrass
harpings	homeosis	apomixis	dipteros	princess
rispings	kyphosis	elflocks	Negritos	Druidess
rinsings	heliosis	ballocks	asbestos	chiefess
hastings	cyclosis	bollocks	mestizos	clerkess
hustings	psilosis	bedsocks	anableps	idealess
leavings	ptilosis	waesucks	midships	rivaless
sea-lungs	kyllosis	menfolks	gig-lamps	limbless
Volsungs	thylosis	methinks	no-trumps	combless
long-togs	phimosis	gadzooks	Strigops	tombless
mezuzahs	gummosis	dye-works	Echinops	herbless
distichs	cyanosis	gas-works	sun-drops	verbless
cannabis	stenosis	all-risks	schnapps	curbless
wood-ibis	zoonosis	bifocals	lacunars	headless
lecythis	hypnosis	emendals	bejabers	leadless
miniskis	fibrosis	harigals	glanders	deedless
pardalis	necrosis	ringhals	snuffers	heedless
physalis	hidrosis	rinkhals	preggers	needless
syphilis	neurosis	genitals	butcher's	seedless
propolis	amitosis	hornfels	smithers	weedless
Dactylis	kurtosis	fattrels	crackers	maidless
imprimis	phytosis	Brussels	knickers	weldless
tyrannis	synapsis	entrails	starkers	goldless
Dinornis	thlipsis	fewtrils	sucklers	handless
notornis	ellipsis	tan-balls	bloomers	landless
Epyornis	synopsis	bristols	calipers	kindless
hautbois	reversis	handfuls	champers	mindless
Capparis	methysis	sackfuls	trossers	rindless
ex-libris	dialysis	cropfuls	trousers	windless
berberis	analysis	himseems	hipsters	fundless
Hesperis	emptysis	herseems	cleavers	foodless
grisgris	clematis	horn-rims	tweezers	hoodless
clitoris	carditis	sidearms	upstairs	woodless
cantoris	osteitis	doldrums	duumvirs	cordless
Hippuris	rachitis	darkmans	porthors	lordless
anabasis	orchitis	quadrans	outdoors	wordless
emphasis	mephitis	habitans	scissors	tubeless
teniasis	myelitis	has-beens	jodphurs	faceless
siriasis	pyelitis	agrémens	all-fours	fadeless
epitasis	uvulitis	crivvens	man-hours	redeless
protasis	adenitis	proggins	galleass	tideless
ecstasis	rhinitis	Gobelins	galliass	treeless
syndesis	samnitis	eastlins	subclass	lifeless
diegesis	ovaritis	stowlins	outclass	wifeless
exegesis	uteritis	ninepins	windlass	edgeless
Lachesis	metritis	fivepins	eyeglass	makeless
mathesis	neuritis	eftsoons	egg-glass	wakeless
anthesis	myositis	Baudrons	log-glass	ruleless
cosmesis	bursitis	environs	owl-glass	fameless
akinesis	rectitis	embryons	spyglass	nameless
dieresis	aortitis	kottabos	landmass	tameless
diuresis	mastitis	Barbados	overpass	timeless
enuresis	cystitis	intrados	trespass	homeless
centesis	sinuitis	extrados	sea-grass	maneless
erotesis	vulvitis	pintados	rib-grass	vaneless
empyesis	Atlantis	bravados	rye-grass	fineless
phthisis	haliotis	Calvados	dog-grass	boneless
enclisis	myosotis	epanodos	eelgrass	toneless
eccrisis	semi-axis	hidalgos	lopgrass	zoneless
chorisis	twin-axis	dolichos	matgrass	tuneless
xeransis	geotaxis	lekythos	oat-grass	shoeless

tapeless	toilless	mastless	bareness	maziness
pipeless	gall-less	restless	rareness	siziness
hopeless	wall-less	listless	hereness	doziness
careless	soulless	dustless	sereness	foziness
wareless	beamless	lustless	soreness	ooziness
fireless	seamless	rustless	pureness	weakness
tireless	foamless	thawless	sureness	sickness
wireless	seemless	clawless	baseness	meekness
coreless	teemless	flawless	wiseness	dankness
cureless	stemless	thewless	lateness	lankness
tyreless	brimless	viewless	muteness	rankness
baseless	helmless	thowless	blueness	pinkness
noseless	harmless	snowless	trueness	darkness
roseless	termless	browless	deafness	duskness
bateless	firmless	stayless	selfness	realness
dateless	formless	cloyless	dowfness	evilness
gateless	gormless	Titaness	trigness	tallness
hateless	gaumless	drabness	longness	fellness
mateless	planless	glibness	smugness	dullness
sateless	spanless	dumbness	snugness	fullness
witeless	signless	deadness	richness	nullness
noteless	gainless	gladness	archness	coolness
voteless	painless	seedness	muchness	foulness
clueless	rainless	agedness	suchness	slimness
waveless	reinless	piedness	highness	grimness
hiveless	chinless	voidness	nighness	primness
loveless	skinless	aridness	rashness	trimness
moveless	moonless	baldness	neshness	calmness
leafless	hornless	mildness	poshness	warmness
calfless	shunless	vildness	lushness	firmness
selfless	echoless	wildness	albiness	glumness
hoofless	chapless	boldness	raciness	grumness
roofless	soapless	coldness	tidiness	leanness
fangless	shipless	kindness	caginess	meanness
pangless	helpless	fondness	edginess	keenness
kingless	rumpless	goodness	inkiness	openness
ringless	stopless	hardness	ugliness	evenness
wingless	scarless	loudness	oiliness	fainness
songless	fearless	lewdness	wiliness	vainness
bashless	tearless	niceness	holiness	beinness
nathless	starless	wideness	liminess	thinness
pathless	peerless	nudeness	tininess	demoness
pithless	hairless	rudeness	boniness	canoness
ruthless	heirless	freeness	puniness	baroness
bodiless	stirless	safeness	ropiness	deepness
pitiless	spurless	rifeness	wariness	dampness
deviless	passless	sageness	eeriness	jimpness
sackless	meatless	hugeness	airiness	dearness
feckless	seatless	likeness	miriness	nearness
reckless	coatless	haleness	wiriness	searness
luckless	tactless	paleness	poriness	fairness
saikless	ductless	idleness	easiness	poorness
milkless	weetless	vileness	cosiness	dourness
bookless	saltless	soleness	nosiness	sourness
barkless	tintless	gameness	rosiness	thisness
workless	wontless	lameness	business	thusness
tuskless	plotless	sameness	waviness	neatness
zealless	knotless	tameness	dewiness	thatness
railless	bootless	saneness	waxiness	whatness
sailless	rootless	fineness	sexiness	flatness
tailless	sootless	doneness	coxiness	meetness
veilless	spotless	goneness	foxiness	daftness
skilless	wartless	loneness	haziness	deftness
soilless	hurtless	ripeness	laziness	softness

saltness	sourpuss	entellus	gypseous	bigamous
tartness	analects	bacillus	nauseous	digamous
pertness	have-nots	urceolus	feateous	oogamous
curtness	sea-boots	alveolus	lacteous	squamous
fastness	slyboots	modiolus	porteous	venomous
vastness	off-sorts	periplus	wrongous	astomous
justness	Fascists	overplus	pyrrhous	spermous
tautness	fish-guts	cost-plus	aphthous	enormous
nextness	Gasthaus	sacculus	xanthous	miasmous
slowness	syllabus	Cocculus	scabious	strumous
greyness	cottabus	calculus	edacious	didymous
cagyness	arquebus	surculus	spacious	melanous
spryness	thrombus	Aesculus	gracious	bimanous
busyness	strombus	stimulus	specious	titanous
vicaress	water-bus	volvulus	precious	selenous
votaress	hover-bus	mandamus	luscious	ravenous
sun-dress	motor-bus	thalamus	fiddious	geminous
top-dress	succubus	sphygmus	studious	luminous
wardress	amaracus	rhythmus	oragious	numinous
usheress	Dipsacus	mittimus	fashious	resinous
cateress	opinicus	chiasmus	eximious	mutinous
interess	Hibiscus	marasmus	scarious	covinous
congress	meniscus	tenesmus	ovarious	stannous
progress	Dytiscus	euonymus	scorious	aphonous
squiress	Sapindus	Pandanus	glorious	digynous
prioress	archaeus	Raphanus	uxorious	dipnoous
minoress	glutaeus	Serranus	yttrious	atropous
tutoress	caduceus	Platanus	spurious	acarpous
mayoress	Asmodeus	subgenus	usurious	croupous
oil-press	Morpheus	terminus	caesious	polypous
compress	peroneus	Quirinus	factious	biparous
suppress	Typhoeus	Cyprinus	stotious	scabrous
hot-press	choragus	pulvinus	captious	glabrous
oratress	choregus	Fraxinus	tortious	sombrous
lectress	Podargus	cicinnus	cautious	cumbrous
rectress	Monachus	hemionus	tenuious	wondrous
victress	elenchus	plumbous	previous	amberous
doctress	rhonchus	incubous	pervious	suberous
waitress	bronchus	anticous	pluvious	tuberous
editress	khuskhus	muticous	frabjous	ulcerous
suitress	Zalophus	aduncous	ditokous	ocherous
huntress	Zizyphus	couscous	kouskous	sclerous
fortress	scirrhus	glaucous	sepalous	temerous
portress	acanthus	caducous	petalous	dimerous
distress	dianthus	vanadous	sibilous	numerous
mistress	Zoanthus	paludous	nubilous	generous
instress	Lecythus	poaceous	perilous	viperous
fostress	bacchius	araceous	thallous	asperous
mattress	Orbilius	croceous	sciolous	apterous
buttress	nauplius	epigeous	fabulous	waverous
satyress	Merulius	gorgeous	pabulous	feverous
reassess	dochmius	gemmeous	sabulous	desirous
giantess	splenius	araneous	nebulous	arborous
saintess	Blennius	ligneous	bibulous	decorous
countess	Scorpius	carneous	tubulous	jocorous
marquess	denarius	corneous	sedulous	nidorous
isogloss	senarius	glareous	undulous	sudorous
lipgloss	Aquarius	nacreous	nodulous	rigorous
club-moss	tantalus	ochreous	orgulous	vigorous
tree-moss	Crotalus	cupreous	ramulous	ichorous
wall-moss	Scopelus	ferreous	papulous	valorous
peat-moss	nautilus	citreous	populous	chlorous
outcross	nucellus	vitreous	patulous	dolorous
tau-cross	vitellus	griseous	infamous	nemorous

timorous	amiantus	mostwhat	gallivat	discreet
humorous	Scolytus	remediat	rubaiyat	congreet
rumorous	crab-yaws	salariat	book-debt	by-street
tumorous	nowadays	cervelat	play-debt	peetweet
canorous	bobstays	table-mat	misdoubt	planchet
sonorous	sideways	diplomat	benefact	ricochet
saporous	edgeways	assignat	artefact	bratchet
vaporous	someways	alternat	artifact	crotchet
soporous	longways	externat	retroact	superhet
savorous	flatways	foldboat	cataract	antithet
goitrous	spinneys	lifeboat	underact	disquiet
dartrous	lampreys	surf-boat	interact	pulsejet
oestrous	Hydromys	longboat	diffract	turbo-jet
lustrous	T	hush-boat	subtract	pulsojet
dextrous	advocaat	cockboat	contract	super-jet
ordurous	brickbat	workboat	protract	water-jet
anourous	whirl-bat	keelboat	abstract	motor-jet
stratous	whorl-bat	mail-boat	distract	empacket
covetous	fruit-bat	sail-boat	transact	bloncket
halitous	hellicat	well-boat	praefect	impocket
pyritous	black-cat	flatboat	pre-elect	sprocket
exiguous	tiger-cat	faltboat	non-elect	unsocket
cernuous	soul-scat	tilt-boat	reselect	up-market
sensuous	tabby-cat	show-boat	idiolect	chevalet
featuous	toddy-cat	seed-coat	complect	dribblet
flatuous	pussy-cat	bluecoat	prospect	roundlet
unctuous	samizdat	buff-coat	suberect	cloudlet
vertuous	dead-beat	maxi-coat	redirect	herbelet
virtuous	wingbeat	sack-coat	indirect	bracelet
tortuous	drumbeat	tail-coat	vivisect	lancelet
fastuous	downbeat	raincoat	transect	tercelet
flexuous	overbeat	turncoat	maledict	bandelet
grievous	browbeat	overcoat	Benedict	spikelet
unjoyous	love-feat	dust-coat	derelict	flamelet
rhizopus	dead-heat	grey-coat	conflict	plumelet
Eohippus	overheat	pitty-pat	abstrict	drupelet
encarpus	dog-wheat	baccarat	restrict	murrelet
platypus	cow-wheat	firebrat	district	verselet
Tartarus	compleat	mobocrat	succinct	corselet
chondrus	box-pleat	theocrat	precinct	platelet
Cerberus	dead-meat	democrat	procinct	mantelet
Hesperus	bakemeat	monocrat	discinct	valvelet
susurrus	dog's-meat	autocrat	distinct	nervelet
diestrus	cat's-meat	scelerat	instinct	spanglet
Arcturus	overneat	wharf-rat	conjunct	pamphlet
Dasyurus	maltreat	water-rat	disjunct	tricklet
lathyrus	ill-treat	river-rat	bile-duct	brooklet
abomasus	mistreat	sewer-rat	aqueduct	sparklet
excursus	love-seat	ziggurat	gall-duct	capellet
bonassus	jump-seat	zikkurat	tear-duct	récollet
colossus	rout-seat	Intelsat	usufruct	greenlet
molossus	khilafat	despotat	obstruct	queenlet
afflatus	cocoa-fat	aegrotat	destruct	chainlet
inflatus	khalifat	appestat	instruct	crownlet
serratus	pressfat	antistat	alphabet	pistolet
Cricetus	puppy-fat	rheostat	zerumbet	sextolet
cathetus	opera-hat	barostat	scilicet	nonuplet
fremitus	wood-chat	aerostat	forefeet	octuplet
tinnitus	backchat	gyrostat	ice-sheet	underlet
crepitus	whinchat	pyrostat	pay-sheet	coverlet
emeritus	chitchat	cryostat	fly-sheet	crosslet
spiritus	crush-hat	paraquat	parakeet	bractlet
detritus	straw-hat	amadavat	lorikeet	swiftlet
pruritus	somewhat	avadavat	helpmeet	plantlet

8 -LET

frontlet	camshaft	arraught	sculpsit	mitigant
gauntlet	airshaft	straught	egg-fruit	arrogant
heartlet	lay-shaft	untaught	key-fruit	bacchant
courtlet	seacraft	unbought	bejesuit	penchant
wristlet	ice-craft	unfought	love-suit	merchant
troutlet	pencraft	do-nought	swimsuit	couchant
globulet	aircraft	besought	playsuit	elephant
Baphomet	zoograft	unsought	cognovit	oliphant
carcanet	misgraft	live-bait	blood-wit	olefiant
toucanet	self-left	toll-bait	underwit	unpliant
burganet	rich-left	portrait	misdealt	hauriant
pound-net	unbereft	distrait	rock-salt	proviant
sarcenet	manshift	dishabit	thio-salt	inhalant
stake-net	day-shift	wait-a-bit	lifebelt	exhalant
seine-net	dead-lift	stiff-bit	seat-belt	semblant
sarsenet	face-lift	prohibit	home-felt	sibilant
purse-net	forelift	post-obit	forefelt	jubilant
tabbinet	unthrift	auger-bit	deep-felt	vigilant
bobbinet	rood-loft	cucurbit	danegelt	rutilant
jirkinet	cockloft	implicit	full-pelt	pea-plant
toilinet	sail-loft	explicit	misspelt	tea-plant
muslinet	cornloft	accredit	unspoilt	ice-plant
moulinet	semi-soft	Ewigkeit	full-tilt	pie-plant
clarinet	ice-yacht	retrofit	air-built	egg-plant
bassinet	straicht	photo-fit	dead-bolt	ash-plant
martinet	straucht	two-digit	bird-bolt	supplant
trail-net	straight	pinch-hit	stud-bolt	air-plant
trawl-net	misdight	smash-hit	king-bolt	gas-plant
unbonnet	sea-fight	bullshit	ring-bolt	displant
balconet	tea-fight	breaskit	hackbolt	hat-plant
falconet	dog-fight	floodlit	stay-bolt	pot-plant
dragonet	bun-fight	wagon-lit	megavolt	cow-plant
burgonet	gunfight	resubmit	demi-volt	ambulant
siphonet	outfight	recommit	kilovolt	osculant
ballonet	arc-light	intromit	catapult	undulant
salmonet	red-light	intermit	undreamt	simulant
sermonet	in-flight	transmit	sauba-ant	insulant
canzonet	twilight	well-knit	excubant	petulant
sweep-net	owl-light	who-dun-it	titubant	claimant
scoop-net	fanlight	time-unit	corybant	untenant
drift-net	penlight	threapit	cosecant	co-tenant
arch-poet	sunlight	precepit	radicant	revenant
strumpet	gaslight	threepit	abdicant	covenant
cellaret	mislight	snake-pit	dedicant	stagnant
unsecret	wax-light	rifle-pit	indicant	pregnant
solleret	daylight	slime-pit	vesicant	poignant
banneret	skylight	brine-pit	urticant	plainant
lanneret	midnight	stone-pit	toxicant	ordinant
velveret	unknight	decrepit	abradant	vaginant
floweret	all-night	catch-pit	abundant	dominant
anchoret	sennight	chalkpit	inundant	luminant
electret	outnight	kalumpit	guardant	ruminant
whittret	bedright	toad-spit	sergeant	absonant
carburet	affright	frog-spit	serjeant	resonant
cyanuret	outright	turnspit	fainéant	assonant
tabouret	eyesight	Sanscrit	recreant	tulipant
thickset	dissight	disherit	segreant	flippant
quickset	outsight	preterit	nauseant	trippant
thornset	day-sight	dispirit	white-ant	occupant
marmoset	airtight	inspirit	slave-ant	quadrant
sharp-set	gas-tight	Sanskrit	bouffant	lacerant
underset	uncaught	bowsprit	obligant	tolerant
somerset	upcaught	pop-visit	fumigant	generant
paroquet	do-naught	oviposit	litigant	alterant

flagrant	decadent	agrément	rack-rent	mowburnt
fragrant	decedent	virement	seam-rent	headhunt
emigrant	accident	basement	corn-rent	drag-hunt
aspirant	occident	casement	besprent	stag-hunt
expirant	incident	easement	seat-rent	discount
roborant	strident	batement	quit-rent	miscount
colorant	resident	lavement	appetent	viscount
ignorant	scandent	pavement	penitent	sea-mount
sonorant	frondent	movement	renitent	surmount
aberrant	impudent	gazement	bell-tent	dismount
inerrant	subagent	mazement	impotent	sederunt
figurant	law-agent	fragment	existent	kail-runt
injurant	co-regent	lodgment	defluent	persicot
depurant	indigent	judgment	refluent	massicot
insurant	diligent	pediment	affluent	masticot
saturant	dirigent	sediment	effluent	Rome-scot
pheasant	emulgent	rudiment	influent	soul-scot
pleasant	plangent	regiment	frequent	wainscot
obeisant	emergent	liniment	eloquent	carrycot
naissant	forehent	miniment	non-event	polka-dot
puissant	overhent	muniment	bung-vent	microdot
recusant	nescient	sepiment	evolvent	misbegot
dilatant	inscient	orpiment	forewent	escargot
floatant	gradient	wariment	overwent	unforgot
reactant	obedient	diriment	oil-paint	blood-hot
hebetant	dormient	bailment	acquaint	white-hot
vegetant	aperient	immoment	gunflint	dead-shot
habitant	reorient	shipment	calamint	birdshot
incitant	hirrient	averment	vee-joint	free-shot
oscitant	nutrient	passment	conjoint	case-shot
excitant	haurient	abetment	hip-joint	drag-shot
militant	prurient	ointment	disjoint	wing-shot
volitant	esurient	sortment	pinpoint	cockshot
irritant	sentient	vestment	parpoint	buckshot
hesitant	quotient	abutment	mispoint	duck-shot
visitant	servient	document	outpoint	hailshot
latitant	bivalent	tegument	dewpoint	soul-shot
equitant	divalent	argument	dry-point	swan-shot
exultant	covalent	monument	half-pint	moonshot
mountant	forelent	cloyment	noverint	snapshot
questant	redolent	remanent	pre-print	chip-shot
constant	indolent	immanent	offprint	camp-shot
débutant	vinolent	imminent	comprint	drop-shot
adjutant	insolent	desinent	sun-print	overshot
evacuant	feculent	deponent	misprint	dust-shot
aliquant	esculent	imponent	aquatint	stradiot
pursuant	luculent	opponent	half-tint	Siceliot
paravant	muculent	exponent	monotint	Sikeliot
relevant	temulent	strepent	secodont	timariot
adjuvant	virulent	ill-spent	creodont	Fanariot
relaxant	purulent	far-spent	zygodont	cachalot
honey-ant	ligament	forspent	mylodont	eschalot
hell-bent	filament	misspent	homodont	hexaglot
adjacent	armament	apparent	monodont	monoglot
indecent	ornament	deferent	bunodont	polyglot
undecent	parament	referent	symbiont	cow-pilot
reticent	atrament	afferent	Piedmont	sky-pilot
innocent	needment	efferent	isobront	misallot
reascent	weldment	life-rent	sea-front	cacholot
acescent	bodement	adherent	ice-front	seed-plot
crescent	vehement	inherent	confront	water-lot
abducent	fakement	coherent	schizont	bergamot
adducent	tenement	haterent	unlearnt	philamot
relucent	cerement	reverent	sunburnt	philomot

martenot	sheep-rot	outsport	shouldst	melodist
Huguenot	liver-rot	raft-port	anapaest	monodist
rose-knot	heart-rot	re-export	immodest	parodist
love-knot	tommy-rot	sandwort	chiefest	Erdgeist
reef-knot	eucaryot	pilewort	slugfest	ditheist
wall-knot	eukaryot	cole-wort	manifest	canoeist
slip-knot	snow-capt	pipewort	talkfest	pacifist
root-knot	transept	lungwort	Almagest	puckfist
lace-boot	adscript	modiwort	indigest	druggist
half-boot	rescript	milkwort	emongest	oologist
jackboot	insculpt	wall-wort	alcahest	eulogist
snow-boot	contempt	wallwort	alkahest	psychist
bald-coot	consumpt	bellwort	sea-chest	Buddhist
club-foot	bankrupt	pillwort	tea-chest	sapphist
hind-foot	eucalypt	moonwort	barghest	Baathist
lobe-foot	dead-cart	hornwort	farthest	Mahdiist
tube-foot	hand-cart	soapwort	furthest	stockist
nine-foot	dung-cart	drop-wort	sauciest	corn-kist
barefoot	push-cart	starwort	readiest	cabalist
hare-foot	hock-cart	salt-wort	ruddiest	arbalist
forefoot	buckcart	wartwort	earliest	vocalist
foalfoot	mail-cart	goutwort	fitliest	modalist
four-foot	dust-cart	hen-court	unpriest	idealist
cat's-foot	sand-dart	law-court	sorriest	legalist
flat-foot	aerodart	yoghourt	heaviest	regalist
salt-foot	braggart	sand-cast	slimmest	trialist
poltfoot	sea-chart	telecast	hive-nest	finalist
slow-foot	bar-chart	molecast	love-nest	annalist
crowfoot	foulmart	typecast	hangnest	papalist
offshoot	Euromart	forecast	thinnest	moralist
elf-shoot	outsmart	worm-cast	unhonest	ruralist
outshoot	name-part	open-cast	fowl-pest	fatalist
folkmoot	forepart	downcast	headrest	vitalist
hall-moot	champart	overcast	interest	loyalist
hanepoot	overpart	newscast	utterest	royalist
muir-poot	four-part	sea-beast	bookrest	hand-list
clubroot	brassart	headfast	deforest	wine-list
rose-root	grossart	hold-fast	afforest	novelist
pinkroot	red-start	handfast	enforest	pugilist
alum-root	thrawart	cragfast	rearrest	nihilist
soap-root	stalwart	lockfast	footrest	Familist
prop-root	willyart	root-fast	outwrest	homilist
beetroot	Cuthbert	elegiast	high-test	civilist
chay-root	navicert	chiliast	mightest	sick-list
many-root	malapert	utopiast	soap-test	niellist
choy-root	inexpert	epiblast	conquest	duellist
hoot-toot	undesert	bioblast	reinvest	Gaullist
thumbpot	reinsert	zooblast	sol-faist	idyllist
cache-pot	reassert	myoblast	bargaist	re-enlist
entrepot	antevert	bioplast	archaist	sciolist
white-pot	ambivert	bootlast	Hebraist	simplist
hotchpot	wash-dirt	portlast	ultraist	subtlist
boughpot	red-shirt	foremast	prosaist	wait-list
flesh-pot	tee-shirt	half-mast	clubbist	fabulist
gallipot	outskirt	mainmast	solecist	populist
crackpot	hill-fort	overmast	ethicist	navy-list
stock-pot	Beaufort	jurymast	hylicist	Occamist
stink-pot	redshort	pleonast	hypocist	bigamist
water-pot	hot-short	sea-coast	exorcist	digamist
starspot	heliport	rib-roast	triadist	dynamist
heatspot	Coalport	pot-roast	solidist	ceramist
plant-pot	reimport	antepast	Hasidist	polemist
quart-pot	mar-sport	overpast	Stundist	totemist
honeypot	passport	contrast		minimist

intimist	Tantrist	seas-tost	layabout	fernshaw
optimist	centrist	renverst	sea-scout	hernshaw
maximist	contrist	sunburst	in-and-out	break-jaw
psalmist	figurist	airburst	shake-out	slack-jaw
alarmist	silurist	outburst	share-out	crackjaw
acosmist	naturist	gold-dust	thereout	stickjaw
volumist	futurist	bone-dust	whereout	under-jaw
arcanist	luxurist	coal-dust	white-out	lumpy-jaw
organist	somatist	star-dust	racahout	sword-law
Romanist	Donatist	overdust	tacahout	lynch-law
humanist	Docetist	malt-dust	watch-out	son-in-law
satanist	quietist	readjust	weigh-out	cole-slaw
botanist	rightist	piecrust	break-out	scout-law
lutanist	Semitist	upthrust	freak-out	mackinaw
eugenist	odontist	distrust	blackout	southpaw
alienist	demotist	mistrust	knockout	fine-draw
Galenist	nepotist	amethyst	muir-pout	wire-draw
lutenist	chartist	catalyst	moor-pout	withdraw
Molinist	duettist	mistryst	sea-trout	overdraw
feminist	flautist	megawatt	print-out	stone-raw
luminist	linguist	gigawatt	count-out	pea-straw
Leninist	euphuist	kilowatt	shoot-out	bedstraw
alpinist	altruist	forswatt	hout-tout	rye-straw
Marinist	sensuist	quintett	undevout	frame-saw
burinist	nativist	quartett	throw-out	chainsaw
Latinist	activist	retraitt	carry-out	tenon-saw
hedonist	Jehovist	forebitt	sinciput	crown-saw
unionist	had-I-wist	oceanaut	Lilliput	sweep-saw
colonist	pre-exist	aquanaut	wall-newt	alley-taw
demonist	essayist	argonaut	teletext	oldsquaw
simonist	hobbyist	aeronaut	half-text	williwaw
Timonist	lobbyist	surrebut	spintext	manna-dew
canonist	fornenst	sword-cut	U	field-dew
arsonist	yglaunst	table-cut	flambeau	honey-dew
Saxonist	free-cost	sabre-cut	aboideau	feverfew
Brownist	kink-host	wheel-cut	aboiteau	rough-hew
tangoist	disclost	clean-cut	Esquimau	clerihew
jingoist	self-lost	sharp-cut	hausfrau	foreshew
banjoist	headmost	clear-cut	feldgrau	side-view
centoist	amidmost	undercut	surucucu	teleview
escapist	hindmost	intercut	pirarucu	overview
Trappist	foremost	crosscut	pyengadu	transmew
groupist	highmost	shortcut	pot-au-feu	brand-new
apiarist	backmost	blind-gut	prie-dieu	fresh-new
aviarist	downmost	pinchgut	skene-dhu	split-new
solarist	deepmost	cockshut	skean-dhu	home-brew
lunarist	rearmost	areca-nut	sucurujú	airscrew
votarist	eastmost	cocoanut	cariacou	set-screw
aquarist	westmost	breadnut	carjacou	withdrew
Lazarist	geognost	doughnut	piou-piou	heronsew
etherist	hen-roost	earth-nut	carcajou	fish-stew
reverist	hand-post	betel-nut	kinkajou	sound-bow
satirist	side-post	hazelnut	kabeljou	stone-bow
arborist	gate-post	cream-nut	frou-frou	steelbow
theorist	ante-post	pecan-nut	pirrauru	crossbow
rigorist	kingpost	carap-nut	jiu-jitsu	milch-cow
aphorist	book-post	cedar-nut	tityre-tu	wirricow
calorist	goalpost	tiger-nut	V	worricow
armorist	signpost	cokernut	Jugoslav	water-cow
humorist	lamppost	chestnut	Yugoslav	worrycow
tenorist	rump-post	ivory-nut	W	beshadow
errorist	overpost	gadabout	Bradshaw	unshadow
motorist	doorpost	runabout	kickshaw	rowdedow
subtrist	footpost	marabout	rickshaw	disendow

rowdydow	intersex	châteaux	wash-away	theodicy
hoosegow	videotex	plateaux	soakaway	impolicy
chow-chow	biconvex	manteaux	rockaway	normalcy
heich-how	appendix	fabliaux	walk-away	peccancy
dumb-show	crucifix	microlux	wellaway	verdancy
roadshow	transfix	epicalyx	tearaway	mordancy
side-show	anthelix	sardonyx	carraway	elegancy
foreshow	intermix	Y	thataway	unchancy
talk-show	ready-mix	sweet-bay	castaway	radiancy
peep-show	mirepoix	lackaday	stowaway	valiancy
chat-show	Ulothrix	workaday	broadway	deviancy
silly-how	cicatrix	welladay	speedway	clamancy
bungalow	creatrix	pound-day	floodway	geomancy
overblow	aviatrix	birthday	three-way	zoomancy
rumbelow	curatrix	trial-day	ridgeway	myomancy
furbelow	tractrix	seven-day	cableway	dormancy
downflow	genetrix	day-to-day	cycleway	pernancy
overflow	janitrix	paper-day	horseway	rampancy
moss-flow	genitrix	Saturday	Fosseway	vibrancy
unhallow	heritrix	doomsday	causeway	vagrancy
disallow	phorminx	Thursday	driveway	imitancy
enwallow	quincunx	eight-day	coach-way	instancy
rebellow	music-box	court-day	hatchway	piquancy
upfollow	sound-box	feast-day	trackway	abeyancy
foreslow	voice-box	first-day	spillway	buoyancy
soft-slow	spice-box	gaudy-day	sternway	lambency
foreknow	sauce-box	worky-day	Galloway	nascency
don't-know	knife-box	everyday	clearway	pendency
corn-snow	stage-box	lancegay	waterway	tendency
highbrow	smoke-box	popinjay	riverway	reagency
overbrow	loose-box	pipeclay	stairway	co-agency
king-crow	snuffbox	fire-clay	motorway	exigency
cock-crow	coach-box	iron-clay	oversway	fulgency
overcrow	matchbox	handplay	crossway	tangency
hedgerow	patch-box	dice-play	drift-way	pungency
budgerow	watch-box	role-play	hoistway	vergency
overgrow	touch-box	foreplay	alleyway	saliency
elf-arrow	flush-box	foul-play	everyway	leniency
tomorrow	clack-box	palm-play	bush-baby	clemency
unburrow	wagon-box	overplay	kirn-baby	eminency
cross-row	water-box	underlay	corn-baby	currency
curassow	poor's-box	interlay	cobwebby	solvency
undertow	grass-box	Hogmanay	box-lobby	fervency
break-vow	press-box	underpay	hobnobby	ensigncy
X	scent-box	eagle-ray	rhubarby	gramercy
battle-ax	paint-box	sting-ray	passer-by	cornetcy
curtal-ax	money-box	iron-gray	sneaksby	unsteady
pita-flax	glorybox	death-ray	celibacy	landlady
toadflax	ditty-box	fly-spray	efficacy	charlady
parallax	orthodox	disarray	delicacy	tea-caddy
opopanax	black-fox	misarray	advocacy	tom-noddy
Scolopax	swine-pox	soothsay	delegacy	ill-deedy
blood-tax	smallpox	southsay	ultimacy	surquedy
supertax	sheep-pox	undersay	intimacy	haploidy
sales-tax	water-pox	forestay	pharmacy	diploidy
white-wax	jambeaux	long-stay	isocracy	unwieldy
grave-wax	ponceaux	mainstay	federacy	cuckoldy
earthwax	morceaux	overstay	numeracy	discandy
spinifex	bandeaux	Paraguay	literacy	burgundy
carnifex	rondeaux	fade-away	retiracy	wide-body
pontifex	Bordeaux	hideaway	accuracy	somebody
disannex	tableaux	take-away	obduracy	type-body
haruspex	rouleaux	hereaway	adequacy	fore-body
interrex	trumeaux	giveaway	prophecy	antibody

re-embody	repurify	typology	tussocky	sacredly
dog's-body	emulsify	aerology	hoky-poky	cursedly
busybody	classify	serology	kromesky	amusedly
sepalody	glassify	agrology	kolinsky	elatedly
petalody	Prussify	virology	undersky	statedly
phyllody	stratify	horology	probably	giftedly
psalmody	sanctify	ourology	placably	unitedly
threnody	fructify	misology	amicably	rootedly
palinody	stultify	dosology	readably	pettedly
unbloody	quantify	nosology	laudably	avowedly
octapody	identify	posology	saleably	amazedly
hexapody	flintify	batology	rateably	morbidly
polypody	moistify	cetology	moveably	turbidly
rhapsody	prettify	sitology	sociably	placidly
goliardy	Scottify	ontology	reliably	candidly
Lollardy	beautify	optology	deniably	sordidly
jeopardy	sanguify	autology	variably	frigidly
bastardy	revivify	cytology	pitiably	turgidly
dastardy	detoxify	sexology	enviably	pallidly
wanwordy	bronzify	doxology	violably	stolidly
uncloudy	quizzify	Mayology	blamably	limpidly
pandowdy	geophagy	bryology	amenably	torpidly
powsowdy	omophagy	lethargy	damnably	stupidly
mangabey	exophagy	chemurgy	palpably	floridly
latchkey	dysphagy	micrurgy	culpably	horridly
watch-key	strategy	hierurgy	bearably	putridly
check-key	zigzaggy	headachy	adorably	liquidly
malarkey	earwiggy	stomachy	passably	fervidly
shift-key	puddingy	naumachy	unusably	friendly
tipsy-key	pedagogy	screechy	suitably	unkindly
tomalley	demagogy	squelchy	quotably	secondly
garganey	paralogy	scrunchy	arguably	jocundly
rag-money	antilogy	thearchy	valuably	rotundly
commoney	cacology	triarchy	issuably	inwardly
pin-money	oncology	nomarchy	provably	onwardly
spy-money	tocology	dinarchy	scribbly	cowardly
Alderney	mycology	monarchy	forcibly	towardly
attorney	pedology	synarchy	credibly	upwardly
blue-grey	kidology	toparchy	vendibly	wizardly
iron-grey	podology	autarchy	eligibly	unlordly
ashy-grey	ideology	navarchy	tangibly	absurdly
guernsey	rheology	scratchy	fallibly	shrewdly
chop-suey	theology	stretchy	terribly	choicely
reconvey	oreology	splotchy	horribly	princely
resurvey	algology	cleruchy	feasibly	scarcely
pinguefy	ethology	eutrophy	sensibly	fiercely
unstuffy	axiology	pansophy	passibly	sprucely
silicify	tokology	rubbishy	possibly	unsafely
reaedify	pelology	bulrushy	flexibly	unwifely
rigidify	xylology	sympathy	assembly	savagely
solidify	demology	zoopathy	superbly	evangely
humidify	gemology	dyspathy	publicly	louchely
lapidify	homology	stealthy	heroicly	blithely
fluidify	nomology	synanthy	forcedly	unlikely
remodify	pomology	unworthy	deucedly	facilely
zinckify	atmology	keepsaky	jaggedly	futilely
alkalify	zymology	garlicky	raggedly	untimely
stellify	menology	gimmicky	doggedly	uncomely
simplify	oenology	picnicky	ruggedly	unhomely
resinify	penology	physicky	wingedly	urbanely
divinify	Sinology	peacocky	variedly	arcanely
saponify	vinology	hillocky	wickedly	immanely
esterify	monology	hummocky	markedly	humanely
gentrify	topology	hassocky	forkedly	insanely

serenely	straggly	sniffily	starrily	carnally
supinely	scriggly	stuffily	paltrily	fern-ally
divinely	squiggly	stodgily	sultrily	vernally
jejunely	gibingly	smudgily	uneasily	spirally
squarely	jibingly	shaggily	greasily	chorally
unwarely	ragingly	slangily	queasily	florally
sombrely	takingly	stingily	whimsily	retrally
severely	unkingly	spongily	flimsily	plurally
meagrely	jokingly	patchily	clumsily	dorsally
entirely	pulingly	tetchily	glassily	causally
squirely	cooingly	hitchily	brassily	rectally
securely	gapingly	touchily	glossily	mentally
demurely	hopingly	symphily	craftily	mortally
impurely	mopingly	flashily	shiftily	festally
maturely	daringly	trashily	mightily	distally
unwisely	erringly	wrathily	guiltily	brutally
jocosely	losingly	filthily	faultily	manually
rugosely	posingly	frothily	scantily	annually
morosely	musingly	worthily	daintily	casually
coarsely	ravingly	sneakily	flintily	visually
hoarsely	savingly	creakily	jauntily	actually
sparsely	lovingly	croakily	heartily	ritually
aversely	movingly	trickily	sportily	mutually
crousely	rovingly	stickily	frostily	sexually
obtusely	vexingly	stockily	crustily	trevally
pedately	pryingly	pluckily	trustily	red-belly
sedately	tryingly	cheekily	prettily	tunbelly
innately	strongly	crankily	snottily	gor-belly
ornately	plug-ugly	spookily	spottily	pot-belly
effetely	stanchly	friskily	smuttily	gingelly
politely	churchly	kindlily	plaguily	sea-jelly
finitely	kitschly	pond-lily	scurvily	kernelly
spritely	shauchly	tree-lily	sleazily	weaselly
remotely	modishly	homelily	wheezily	tinselly
chastely	rakishly	livelily	breezily	tasselly
argutely	mulishly	lovelily	bi-weekly	gravelly
minutely	tonishly	sicklily	tribally	snivelly
astutely	impishly	chillily	globally	subtilly
opaquely	mopishly	unholily	verbally	weevilly
uniquely	popishly	lent-lily	apically	sea-holly
steevely	uppishly	flax-lily	epically	loblolly
stievely	garishly	dreamily	rascally	ice-lolly
unlively	aguishly	steamily	feudally	wittolly
natively	lavishly	smalmily	lineally	woefully
actively	Jewishly	clammily	unreally	irefully
behovely	boyishly	gloomily	frugally	usefully
unlovely	coyishly	smarmily	labially	ruefully
snake-fly	toyishly	stormily	facially	wilfully
crane-fly	yongthly	spoonily	socially	manfully
stone-fly	eighthly	sleepily	radially	fitfully
horsefly	graithly	skimpily	medially	artfully
house-fly	smoothly	grumpily	filially	lawfully
white-fly	fourthly	stumpily	genially	joyfully
catchfly	shabbily	droopily	venially	beseemly
flesh-fly	bouncily	snappily	aerially	unseemly
froth-fly	steadily	floppily	serially	randomly
greenfly	shoddily	sloppily	mesially	infirmly
alder-fly	speedily	chirpily	jovially	seamanly
water-fly	greedily	smearily	animally	yeomanly
hover-fly	untidily	drearily	primally	leadenly
wheat-fly	woundily	unwarily	formally	hiddenly
night-fly	bloodily	tawdrily	normally	suddenly
fruit-fly	sturdily	cheerily	dismally	maidenly
scraggly	cloudily	hungrily	signally	goldenly

woodenly	unfairly	thingamy	eudemony	nucleary
brokenly	sailorly	endogamy	hegemony	balneary
sullenly	hectorly	allogamy	ceremony	dog-weary
lumpenly	doctorly	homogamy	palimony	war-weary
moltenly	pastorly	xenogamy	acrimony	forweary
rottenly	savourly	monogamy	agrimony	outweary
heavenly	diversly	porogamy	antimony	vinegary
cravenly	demissly	misogamy	scammony	petchary
unevenly	remissly	autogamy	saffrony	plagiary
slovenly	odiously	polygamy	chevrony	congiary
brazenly	famously	Bartlemy	catatony	milliary
malignly	timously	polysemy	homotony	vespiary
benignly	joyously	eurythmy	monotony	tertiary
ungainly	abjectly	gorblimy	gluttony	bestiary
virginly	directly	antinomy	perigyny	vestiary
cousinly	strictly	theonomy	monogyny	breviary
solemnly	unmeetly	aeronomy	hypogyny	tutelary
commonly	secretly	agronomy	misogyny	burglary
matronly	slightly	autonomy	polygyny	pupilary
wantonly	knightly	taxonomy	knife-boy	arillary
modernly	brightly	phisnomy	horse-boy	axillary
monopoly	straitly	blossomy	houseboy	phyllary
roly-poly	adroitly	polysomy	Whiteboy	calamary
three-ply	occultly	phantomy	dough-boy	rosemary
multiply	vacantly	lobotomy	blackboy	spermary
scrimply	pliantly	colotomy	cabin-boy	costmary
disapply	errantly	tenotomy	under-boy	vicenary
misapply	decently	autotomy	paper-boy	catenary
cross-ply	recently	land-army	choirboy	novenary
linearly	nocently	homonymy	nancy-boy	ordinary
beggarly	ardently	synonymy	billyboy	culinary
vulgarly	ungently	toponymy	bully-boy	laminary
ocularly	cogently	paronymy	canticoy	seminary
uvularly	urgently	metonymy	diddycoy	luminary
tartarly	silently	quiddany	dalmahoy	stannary
lubberly	momently	mahogany	kantikoy	coronary
lumberly	absently	Epiphany	overcloy	octonary
panderly	latently	endogeny	redeploy	lacunary
tenderly	intently	homogeny	corduroy	vivipary
badgerly	potently	nomogeny	paduasoy	polypary
gingerly	fluently	monogeny	life-buoy	federary
hungerly	quaintly	ectogeny	bell-buoy	numerary
fatherly	promptly	ontogeny	sonobuoy	cinerary
litherly	abruptly	autogeny	orthoepy	funerary
motherly	thwartly	cryogeny	enthalpy	siserary
quakerly	expertly	polygeny	episcopy	literary
sickerly	covertly	villainy	zooscopy	honorary
summerly	modestly	sunshiny	uroscopy	contrary
formerly	priestly	ignominy	trollopy	emissary
mannerly	honestly	scrutiny	anatropy	glossary
properly	Christly	port-winy	isotropy	legatary
dapperly	uncostly	tenpenny	schleppy	donatary
winterly	robustly	twopenny	mud-puppy	femetary
porterly	augustly	tuppenny	syncarpy	cometary
easterly	unjustly	sixpenny	geocarpy	monetary
masterly	devoutly	zebrinny	reoccupy	military
westerly	fellowly	seacunny	pea-soupy	solitary
sisterly	mellowly	telegony	chirrupy	limitary
latterly	hollowly	theogony	homotypy	sanitary
bitterly	narrowly	monogony	poticary	salutary
souterly	reflexly	merogony	solidary	February
cleverly	convexly	polygony	lapidary	statuary
silverly	prolixly	symphony	quandary	noctuary
lawyerly	sunbeamy	cushiony	boundary	obituary

mortuary	furriery	recovery	feretory	choultry
textuary	knackery	spivvery	auditory	pedantry
salivary	quackery	quizzery	vomitory	infantry
janizary	trickery	quagmiry	fumitory	tenantry
balladry	crockery	vassalry	vanitory	errantry
smoke-dry	spookery	chivalry	monitory	truantry
rough-dry	whiskery	chapelry	punitory	non-entry
ribaldry	diablery	tinselry	petitory	misentry
heraldry	cobblery	hostelry	sob-story	Coventry
smouldry	saddlery	missilry	locutory	chauntry
monandry	jugglery	paynimry	gossipry	zealotry
gynandry	snailery	yeomanry	miscarry	harlotry
misandry	raillery	wardenry	mismarry	parrotry
legendry	drollery	slovenry	peaberry	quixotry
calendry	scullery	brazenry	seaberry	synastry
cowardry	cajolery	cousinry	teaberry	ancestry
hazardry	samplery	ribbonry	ale-berry	tapestry
wizardry	growlery	deaconry	hagberry	forestry
ribaudry	creamery	falconry	dogberry	revestry
slabbery	dreamery	pigeonry	bilberry	registry
glibbery	shimmery	cannonry	mulberry	tanistry
slobbery	glimmery	weaponry	fen-berry	ministry
snobbery	flummery	blazonry	barberry	papistry
plumbery	bloomery	chiccory	Burberry	artistry
slumbery	polymery	allegory	nisberry	industry
Chancery	greenery	category	dew-berry	executry
bladdery	refinery	zoochory	cowberry	advoutry
gliddery	enginery	seignory	waxberry	centaury
sliddery	swannery	apospory	foxberry	sulphury
shuddery	spinnery	isospory	bayberry	bistoury
broidery	clownery	vavasory	podiatry	treasury
grindery	sleepery	decisory	geriatry	outlawry
thundery	trumpery	derisory	idolatry	panegyry
pseudery	slippery	irrisory	geolatry	porphyry
chiefery	frippery	advisory	zoolatry	Malagasy
chaffery	trippery	revisory	barratry	docimasy
spoofery	whispery	infusory	gadgetry	athanasy
savagery	lamasery	delusory	rocketry	euphrasy
drudgery	cheatery	illusory	basketry	phantasy
Whiggery	unwatery	libatory	musketry	apostasy
priggery	cemetery	sudatory	toiletry	isostasy
froggery	fruitery	aleatory	varletry	prophesy
groggery	psaltery	negatory	mammetry	trophesy
thuggery	sheltery	rogatory	symmetry	Japanesy
snuggery	smeltery	nugatory	odometry	courtesy
orangery	adultery	dilatory	geometry	upadaisy
hatchery	lientery	filatory	biometry	dog-daisy
patchery	vauntery	fumatory	noometry	cramoisy
bitchery	plastery	sanatory	zoometry	pleurisy
witchery	blistery	minatory	isometry	geognosy
botchery	blustery	donatory	maumetry	primrosy
butchery	clustery	moratory	mawmetry	epilepsy
cutchery	flustery	curatory	gannetry	dyspepsy
trashery	scattery	juratory	sonnetry	eclampsy
feathery	shattery	gyratory	puppetry	necropsy
heathery	flattery	natatory	coquetry	hydropsy
leathery	slattery	citatory	Babbitry	photopsy
slithery	glittery	potatory	rabbitry	undrossy
smithery	twittery	rotatory	banditry	circussy
smothery	snottery	mutatory	punditry	hen-hussy
frothery	sluttery	lavatory	summitry	overbusy
soldiery	sputtery	vexatory	pulpitry	jealousy
colliery	thievery	emictory	Jesuitry	entreaty
farriery	delivery	deletory	deviltry	unsafety

hatchety	validity	nubility	temerity	guaranty
sobriety	gelidity	facility	asperity	warranty
thickety	solidity	docility	alterity	curranty
blankety	timidity	vagility	severity	sovranty
subtlety	humidity	nihility	priority	suddenty
peripety	tumidity	humility	majority	fromenty
snippety	rapidity	senility	minority	furmenty
entirety	sapidity	virility	sonority	frumenty
toplofty	vapidity	motility	sorority	plenarty
almighty	tepidity	futility	security	tea-party
draughty	cupidity	civility	impurity	hen-party
droughty	acridity	sedulity	maturity	non-party
acerbity	viridity	calamity	futurity	property
dicacity	fluidity	intimity	jocosity	epinasty
audacity	lividity	enormity	mucosity	swine-sty
sagacity	vividity	urbanity	nodosity	travesty
fugacity	conceity	organity	rugosity	sacristy
salacity	velleity	immanity	otiosity	touristy
tenacity	perseity	humanity	pilosity	harmosty
minacity	multeity	insanity	gulosity	starosty
capacity	locality	satanity	dumosity	sawdusty
rapacity	vocality	serenity	fumosity	untrusty
feracity	modality	vicinity	venosity	dancetty
veracity	nodality	Ladinity	vinosity	ricketty
voracity	sodality	affinity	serosity	pommetty
furacity	ideality	infinity	morosity	unpretty
vivacity	legality	salinity	porosity	panic-buy
free-city	regality	felinity	sparsity	underbuy
pudicity	triality	feminity	obtusity	hay-de-guy
felicity	molality	caninity	sanctity	colloquy
solicity	femality	Latinity	scantity	musk-cavy
tonicity	banality	equinity	quantity	top-heavy
basicity	venality	divinity	identity	cum-savvy
toxicity	finality	eternity	chastity	rainbowy
aduncity	tonality	triunity	circuity	mixy-maxy
velocity	morality	jejunity	exiguity	apoplexy
ferocity	rurality	immunity	inequity	paradoxy
atrocity	nasality	impunity	iniquity	cacodoxy
scarcity	fatality	disunity	gratuity	trot-cozy
caducity	natality	self-pity	fortuity	Z
astucity	vitality	hilarity	nativity	razmataz
quiddity	totality	molarity	activity	pince-nez
heredity	equality	polarity	motivity	barometz
rabidity	rivality	imparity	unfixity	Seidlitz
lucidity	fidelity	alacrity	casualty	strelitz
rigidity	debility	queerity	subtilty	schmaltz
algidity	mobility	legerity	unguilty	kok-sagyz
calidity	nobility	celerity	unfaulty	

A	santonica	Arachnida	Myriapoda	barracuda
endamoeba	hieratica	Ophiurida	Amphipoda	Arctogaea
entamoeba	Myristica	asafetida	Chilopoda	propylaea
algarroba	slivovica	Bretwalda	Pteropoda	Crustacea
carnahuba	noctiluca	jacaranda	Sauropoda	Crinoidea
portulaca	enchilada	memoranda	Rhizopoda	Cystoidea
mandiocca	andromeda	referenda	Trematoda	hydrangea
harmonica	Yajurveda	Ostracoda	Urochorda	logorrhea

menorrhea	sponsalia	urticaria	golomynka	condyloma
gonorrhea	genitalia	araucaria	dharmsala	carcinoma
water-flea	Thargelia	Stellaria	Cicindela	Theobroma
Staphylea	triskelia	Tubularia	Philomela	hydrosoma
Hirudinea	neuroglia	Stigmaria	nemophila	haematoma
diarrhoea	mirabilia	spermaria	Shangri-la	Melastoma
otorrhoea	notabilia	Laminaria	talegalla	hypoderma
pyorrhoea	zoophilia	Saponaria	varicella	xeroderma
mesogloea	juvenilia	lacunaria	squamella	phantasma
string-pea	subsellia	cineraria	columella	empyreuma
pigeon-pea	sterculia	militaria	Chlorella	Americana
Dioscorea	Polygamia	sanitaria	panatella	poinciana
Phillyrea	Didynamia	Decandria	capitella	siciliana
Xylophaga	leucaemia	Triandria	haustella	nicotiana
ossifraga	cachaemia	calandria	sabadilla	jambolana
Saxifraga	ischaemia	Monandria	cebadilla	pozzolana
arracacha	leukaemia	Octandria	cevadilla	puzzolana
cha-cha-cha	cholaemia	Hexandria	sapodilla	marihuana
proseucha	spanaemia	rancheria	camarilla	marijuana
pentalpha	hydraemia	cafeteria	guerrilla	Lippizana
apocrypha	sapraemia	osmeteria	scintilla	Scorpaena
whillywha	tularemia	psalteria	zapotilla	cantilena
ecophobia	hypoxemia	acroteria	Ametabola	phenomena
neophobia	arhythmia	dysphoria	carambola	philopena
zoophobia	dysthymia	infusoria	hyperbola	malagueña
euphorbia	theomania	fumatoria	girandola	contadina
beccaccia	melomania	moratoria	scagliola	Sarcodina
zoothecia	oenomania	auditoria	acetabula	Commelina
apothecia	xenomania	haustoria	vibracula	Neopilina
paramecia	monomania	trattoria	spiracula	santolina
cryptadia	hypomania	zoolatria	tentacula	Balsamina
stichidia	typomania	Manchuria	trabecula	Gregarina
chromidia	pyromania	melanuria	vallecula	Casuarina
praesidia	opsomania	porphyria	corbicula	ballerina
ommatidia	Ruritania	Colocasia	Forficula	erythrina
compendia	Frankenia	dysphasia	febricula	Signorina
plasmodia	catamenia	dyscrasia	curricula	toccatina
parapodia	xenomenia	analgesia	matricula	quinquina
Richardia	urolagnia	parrhesia	clavicula	feiseanna
synapheia	strychnia	aesthesia	calendula	transenna
gorgoneia	peridinia	dysthesia	maxillula	Tarragona
Rauwolfia	neoteinia	Rafflesia	Campanula	fanfarona
Kniphofia	delphinia	artemisia	peninsula	cesarevna
omophagia	Britannia	dyspepsia	pennatula	whoa-ho-hoa
dysphagia	millennia	eclampsia	tarantula	Scyphozoa
aquilegia	septennia	hemiopsia	melodrama	Actinozoa
aqua-regia	dysphonia	micropsia	monodrama	Mycetozoa
neuralgia	eudemonia	photopsia	myriorama	grandpapa
tarsalgia	pneumonia	spermatia	cyclorama	Monotropa
nostalgia	Dicksonia	agalactia	cosmorama	dulcamara
sporangia	Adansonia	aubrietia	myxoedema	terramara
Sinningia	catatonia	peripetia	epirrhema	nullipara
paralogia	paulownia	Astrantia	exanthema	primipara
asynergia	Decagynia	Salientia	hyalonema	pluripara
naumachia	Hexagynia	sclerotia	treponema	multipara
batrachia	Monogynia	sestertia	protonema	sassarara
cleruchia	Octogynia	consortia	Nototrema	sussarara
Malpighia	Polygynia	colloquia	emphysema	tantarara
Didelphia	dyschroia	paralexia	didrachma	solfatara
forsythia	principia	stegomyia	terza-rima	tarantara
rudbeckia	hyperopia	bilharzia	penultima	sternebra
paralalia	cacotopia	Tripitaka	syphiloma	king-cobra
echolalia	amblyopia	britschka	papilloma	ambulacra
generalia	zelotypia	balalaika	granuloma	simulacra

octahedra	ribattuta	Pan-Arabic	stomachic	arhythmic
polyhedra	Bryophyta	Mozarabic	thearchic	antinomic
Cassandra	chihuahua	coxcombic	monarchic	ergonomic
clepsydra	Balaclava	lyophobic	autarchic	agronomic
chelicera	Vaishnava	anaerobic	epedaphic	autonomic
Oenothera	supernova	anthracic	epitaphic	taxonomic
box-camera	gallabiya	ischiadic	didelphic	syndromic
subgenera	Kshatriya	paramedic	eutrophic	prodromic
Hemiptera	cherimoya	logaoedic	pansophic	dichromic
Mecoptera	chirimoya	Samoyedic	dimorphic	subatomic
Homoptera	Fourcroya	pyramidic	isobathic	triatomic
Xenarthra	Pernettya	Chassidic	trilithic	monatomic
manticora	mycorhiza	Icelandic	Neolithic	epidermic
adiaphora	influenza	hydriodic	zoolithic	coseismic
canephora	B	aperiodic	oenanthic	pancosmic
herbivora	hansom-cab	psalmodic	synanthic	dysthymic
Carnivora	sheep-scab	spasmodic	Neo-Gothic	homonymic
triquetra	shore-crab	threnodic	acoluthic	synonymic
palaestra	devil-crab	octapodic	alicyclic	toponymic
orchestra	glass-crab	rhapsodic	epicyclic	acronymic
Thysanura	spider-web	Lombardic	tricyclic	metonymic
Xanthoura	taste-bulb	Sephardic	concyclic	inorganic
Xiphosura	flash-bulb	goliardic	isocyclic	epiphanic
jettatura	dithyramb	bezoardic	evangelic	Messianic
fioritura	smoke-bomb	Notogaeic	autotelic	Brahmanic
tessitura	depth-bomb	diarrheic	trochilic	melomanic
partitura	stink-bomb	zoogloeic	olephilic	hypomanic
Angostura	toothcomb	paranoeic	geophilic	puritanic
Brachyura	cockscomb	dyspnoeic	lyophilic	Saracenic
Spirogyra	honeycomb	felicific	pre-exilic	mutagenic
tirra-lyra	curry-comb	lapidific	parabolic	telegenic
Appaloosa	disentomb	sudorific	katabolic	lysigenic
dogaressa	altar-tomb	calorific	metabolic	antigenic
babirussa	jiggumbob	colorific	shambolic	oncogenic
ricercata	cherry-bob	dolorific	zinc-colic	endogenic
emboscata	honey-blob	honorific	alcoholic	zymogenic
Tracheata	hob-and-nob	vaporific	vitriolic	pyrogenic
alpargata	loll-shrob	soporific	diastolic	ectogenic
chipolata	Beelzebub	classific	epistolic	ontogenic
emblemata	goose-club	omophagic	apostolic	cryogenic
sarcomata	slate-club	dysphagic	hydraulic	polygenic
angiomata	underclub	diallagic	salicylic	oecumenic
Coelomata	yacht-club	strategic	pyroxylic	pyroxenic
adenomata	night-club	neuralgic	pre-adamic	strychnic
fibromata	C	nostalgic	endogamic	Jacobinic
scotomata	tacamahac	pedagogic	homogamic	neoteinic
melismata	paroemiac	demagogic	monogamic	proteinic
Pulmonata	egomaniac	paragogic	porogamic	triclinic
inamorata	insomniac	mycologic	autogamic	isoclinic
substrata	paranoiac	ideologic	polygamic	lupulinic
Notonecta	symposiac	rheologic	cineramic	Brahminic
Trilobita	Dionysiac	theologic	panoramic	diactinic
manzanita	pontianac	ethologic	cevitamic	nicotinic
incognita	bric-à-brac	zymologic	cachaemic	Alemannic
Senhorita	pollen-sac	monologic	ischaemic	Britannic
revalenta	embryo-sac	topologic	cholaemic	pharaonic
ervalenta	flûte-à-bec	agrologic	spanaemic	theogonic
aquatinta	smart-alec	horologic	sapraemic	cinchonic
Notodonta	Ptolemaic	ontologic	graphemic	sulphonic
Rhynchota	stenopaic	chop-logic	morphemic	symphonic
anaglypta	algebraic	lethargic	tularemic	dysphonic
autopista	choleraic	isenergic	epistemic	Pyrrhonic
paramatta	pharisaic	demiurgic	hypoxemic	gnathonic
satinetta	premosaic	chemurgic	nystagmic	benthonic

Brythonic	paregoric	grammatic	oogenetic	dracontic
eudemonic	isochoric	zygomatic	splenetic	archontic
hegemonic	anaphoric	idiomatic	phrenetic	rhapontic
antimonic	camphoric	axiomatic	threnetic	scazontic
Salomonic	zoophoric	celomatic	epainetic	silicotic
Solomonic	dysphoric	chromatic	dianoetic	peridotic
pneumonic	plethoric	stromatic	syncretic	dizygotic
uncanonic	euchloric	automatic	theoretic	psychotic
macaronic	folkloric	spermatic	Masoretic	morphotic
Ciceronic	zoosporic	miasmatic	equisetic	anabiotic
thrasonic	aleatoric	plasmatic	diapyetic	prebiotic
transonic	bishopric	spasmatic	Jacobitic	symbiotic
paratonic	geriatric	prismatic	sericitic	zoobiotic
stratonic	diametric	traumatic	trichitic	semeiotic
catatonic	symmetric	rheumatic	graphitic	scoliotic
semitonic	udometric	pneumatic	Memphitic	patriotic
homotonic	geometric	strumatic	erethitic	thermotic
monotonic	biometric	enzymatic	perthitic	exosmotic
hypotonic	zoometric	aplanatic	proclitic	melanotic
monaxonic	isometric	pancratic	typhlitic	stegnotic
embryonic	obstetric	isocratic	zymolitic	albinotic
trichroic	eccentric	quadratic	impolitic	epizootic
allantoic	excentric	nephratic	unpolitic	tricrotic
heliozoic	catoptric	diastatic	aerolitic	sclerotic
Caenozoic	digastric	anastatic	pisolitic	chlorotic
Cainozoic	colostric	epistatic	rhyolitic	amaurotic
Kainozoic	sulphuric	geostatic	pearlitic	symptotic
saprozoic	melanuric	apostatic	Islamitic	embryotic
protozoic	panegyric	prostatic	psammitic	analeptic
orthoepic	monobasic	isostatic	sodomitic	epileptic
zooscopic	polybasic	stalactic	dolomitic	sylleptic
anthropic	diastasic	climactic	sagenitic	proleptic
diatropic	analgesic	ataractic	selenitic	dyspeptic
subtropic	paradisic	syntactic	phrenitic	eclamptic
zoetropic	intrinsic	geotactic	ebionitic	syncoptic
geotropic	extrinsic	isotactic	mylonitic	sarcoptic
inotropic	virtuosic	cachectic	limonitic	orthoptic
isotropic	thalassic	cathectic	sternitic	hydroptic
philippic	klendusic	dialectic	sybaritic	cathartic
Callippic	folk-music	analectic	Nazaritic	bombastic
geocarpic	adiabatic	dyslectic	diacritic	sarcastic
antitypic	katabatic	anorectic	epicritic	orgiastic
holotypic	metabatic	dystectic	dendritic	inelastic
homotypic	aquabatic	apodictic	sideritic	emplastic
genotypic	acrobatic	endeictic	doleritic	onomastic
monotypic	Hanseatic	apomictic	nephritic	epinastic
polytypic	aliphatic	subarctic	tephritic	gymnastic
saccharic	sulphatic	Holarctic	arthritic	peirastic
theandric	lymphatic	Antarctic	Prakritic	fantastic
cylindric	apophatic	copacetic	chloritic	empaestic
trihydric	ischiatic	asyndetic	pleuritic	orchestic
metameric	mydriatic	cynegetic	parasitic	Dadaistic
monomeric	psoriatic	energetic	andesitic	Judaistic
poromeric	fluviatic	prophetic	Genesitic	lamaistic
polymeric	schematic	morphetic	Thersitic	Sivaistic
bigeneric	athematic	diathetic	Jebusitic	fascistic
trieteric	cinematic	apathetic	steatitic	atheistic
lienteric	kinematic	epithetic	eutaxitic	imagistic
isosteric	pragmatic	synthetic	asphaltic	Elohistic
cadaveric	bregmatic	prothetic	systaltic	sophistic
chiragric	enigmatic	aesthetic	geomantic	Sufiistic
upaithric	stigmatic	dysthetic	zoomantic	realistic
chivalric	zeugmatic	homiletic	myomantic	dualistic
allegoric	asthmatic	epaenetic	authentic	ballistic

wholistic	lowlihead	fire-robed	unavoided	greenweed
stylistic	lustihead	filter-bed	slab-sided	rosin-weed
animistic	blackhead	oyster-bed	iron-sided	lemon-weed
Thomistic	thickhead	flower-bed	many-sided	water-weed
atomistic	shock-head	full-orbed	misguided	riverweed
pianistic	blockhead	perturbed	undivided	dyer's-weed
onanistic	rowel-head	disturbed	unmoulded	drift-weed
agonistic	still-head	carpet-bed	mob-handed	smart-weed
faunistic	besom-head	crab-faced	redhanded	two-leafed
panoistic	crown-head	chub-faced	one-handed	unsnuffed
meroistic	negrohead	bald-faced	offhanded	unstuffed
tropistic	spearhead	bold-faced	ham-handed	unengaged
hubristic	water-head	good-faced	two-handed	undamaged
dioristic	river-head	undefaced	descended	unmanaged
floristic	stairhead	barefaced	unblended	appanaged
patristic	floorhead	uneffaced	unamended	languaged
heuristic	cross-head	half-faced	open-ended	unfledged
touristic	rivet-head	self-faced	suspended	unpledged
statistic	arrow-head	long-faced	pretended	gilt-edged
pietistic	jollyhead	smug-faced	unblinded	unbridged
Scotistic	hornyhead	dish-faced	man-minded	ill-judged
egotistic	poppy-head	full-faced	air-minded	ungrudged
protistic	blacklead	lean-faced	low-minded	zigzagged
casuistic	sheet-lead	thin-faced	diamonded	red-legged
atavistic	dika-bread	moon-faced	unbounded	one-legged
encaustic	loaf-bread	fair-faced	unfounded	dog-legged
methystic	corn-bread	boot-faced	unrounded	two-legged
scorbutic	clapbread	whey-faced	unsounded	bow-legged
paedeutic	diet-bread	gold-laced	astounded	nutmegged
paideutic	shewbread	unsolaced	unwounded	cat-rigged
halieutic	showbread	slow-paced	unblooded	unclogged
trachytic	proof-read	vambraced	unbearded	humbugged
epiphytic	bedspread	jaundiced	unguarded	unplugged
symphytic	outspread	beneficed	concluded	unchanged
geophytic	sight-read	unpoliced	undeluded	estranged
neophytic	roadstead	surpliced	unclouded	unavenged
zoophytic	homestead	unnoticed	uncrowded	ceilinged
paralytic	farmstead	verjuiced	title-deed	net-winged
catalytic	heapstead	high-viced	trust-deed	uncharged
pyrolytic	door-stead	discalced	force-feed	submerged
autolytic	Upanishad	affianced	stall-feed	unreached
Pan-Slavic	bromeliad	unpierced	spoon-feed	stomached
anticivic	asclepiad	unamerced	underfeed	beseeched
homotaxic	colubriad	unreduced	nose-bleed	up-perched
antitoxic	corn-salad	unseduced	weak-kneed	unhatched
cytotoxic	steel-clad	big-headed	good-speed	unmatched
char-à-banc	underclad	pigheaded	high-speed	bepatched
charabanc	subpoena'd	rug-headed	full-speed	unwatched
opodeldoc	truck-load	ill-headed	half-breed	stretched
coenosarc	wagon-load	two-headed	pedigreed	debauched
D	sail-broad	sapheaded	filigreed	untouched
volksraad	drove-road	mop-headed	grapeseed	unweighed
luckie-dad	coach-road	fat-headed	benne-seed	seemlihed
hermandad	trackroad	hotheaded	grapeseed	unabashed
stone-dead	trunk-road	not-headed	benni-seed	alewashed
brain-dead	crossroad	tow-headed	heartseed	bloodshed
scald-head	megafarad	undreaded	poppy-seed	unfleshed
Roundhead	undergrad	retreaded	snakeweed	tarnished
whale-head	hamadryad	besteaded	shore-weed	furnished
scare-head	sluggabed	disgodded	catchweed	cherished
White-head	settle-bed	uncrudded	chickweed	anguished
beachhead	spring-bed	unimpeded	slinkweed	yravished
youthhead	bethumbed	unbraided	brookweed	watershed
hardihead	unplumbed	undecided	jewel-weed	unbrushed

unscathed	kiln-dried	enkindled	shovelled	unassumed
unclothed	traceried	unkindled	grovelled	uncleaned
betrothed	galleried	uncurdled	marvelled	caravaned
unearthed	draperied	red-heeled	varvelled	unqueened
ungirthed	masonried	unbaffled	vervelled	unwakened
unscythed	pilloried	unruffled	trowelled	ill-omened
remercied	unmarried	toruffled	pencilled	unripened
disbodied	unworried	unstifled	fulfilled	chastened
unstudied	unhurried	triangled	gas-filled	bedizened
stupefied	fantasied	untangled	unskilled	unfeigned
torrefied	ecstasied	unmingled	unspilled	consigned
putrefied	unpalsied	hobnailed	undrilled	disdained
liquefied	jalousied	bobtailed	uptrilled	unchained
specified	qualitied	fantailed	distilled	unplained
dulcified	unemptied	pintailed	instilled	undrained
crucified	half-baked	fat-tailed	unstilled	engrained
acidified	unwreaked	travailed	weevilled	ingrained
dandified	bow-backed	domiciled	pulvilled	murrained
qualified	prepacked	undefiled	gambolled	untrained
Englified	jam-packed	trefoiled	symbolled	unstained
mollified	untracked	well-oiled	red-polled	sustained
nullified	unchecked	unspoiled	patrolled	surreined
amplified	ewe-necked	spreckled	petrolled	net-veined
mummified	low-necked	unsickled	pistolled	undefined
magnified	wry-necked	sandalled	worm-holed	unrefined
dignified	frolicked	jackalled	air-cooled	tree-lined
lignified	chemicked	gimmalled	gas-cooled	well-lined
signified	picnicked	signalled	rope-soled	conjoined
scarified	rampicked	overalled	unrumpled	chagrined
clarified	up-pricked	installed	unpeopled	unrosined
glorified	physicked	sea-walled	uncoupled	goddamned
terrified	unshocked	corbelled	embattled	condemned
horrified	fetlocked	marcelled	unsettled	contemned
petrified	hummocked	parcelled	scheduled	unscanned
nitrified	unfrocked	cudgelled	hard-ruled	unplanned
vitrified	cassocked	nickelled	bedazzled	ill-manned
falsified	unstocked	enamelled	undazzled	trepanned
versified	unplucked	pommelled	unmuzzled	inspanned
gratified	fen-sucked	pummelled	sunbeamed	suntanned
rectified	unthanked	crenelled	undreamed	unskinned
Scotified	unplanked	unknelled	well-famed	unshunned
certified	unfranked	kennelled	unashamed	abandoned
fortified	sex-linked	funnelled	code-named	cushioned
mortified	overinked	tunnelled	forenamed	mullioned
testified	red-looked	compelled	misdeemed	opinioned
justified	unrevoked	propelled	himseemed	passioned
mystified	twiforked	dispelled	unclaimed	portioned
brutified	two-forked	barrelled	well-aimed	bastioned
liquified	twyforked	laurelled	well-timed	gallooned
satisfied	unrebuked	teaselled	cat-hammed	gadrooned
atrophied	syllabled	chiselled	unskimmed	saffroned
misallied	unhumbled	hanselled	untrimmed	chevroned
unsullied	betumbled	tinselled	kingdomed	high-toned
panoplied	untumbled	tasselled	ungroomed	deep-toned
unapplied	ungarbled	mussselled	two-roomed	unlearned
Volkslied	pinnacled	housselled	uncharmed	concerned
Kunstlied	barnacled	lintelled	open-armed	unadorned
companied	tentacled	martelled	confirmed	sunburned
unpennied	fascicled	unfuelled	uniformed	unmourned
balconied	tubercled	unquelled	triformed	uncrowned
proud-pied	unsaddled	gravelled	twiformed	undrowned
passepied	scroddled	travelled	malformed	porticoed
unwearied	unbridled	snivelled	twyformed	embargoed
high-dried	unhandled	drivelled	unillumed	shampooed

impastoed	sheltered	practised	aculeated	subjected
fan-shaped	sweltered	disguised	uncreated	unelected
urn-shaped	unentered	debruised	floreated	deflected
misshaped	chartered	unbruised	untreated	reflected
unstriped	quartered	misavised	elongated	collected
unstamped	plastered	unadvised	hell-hated	connected
developed	bolstered	unrevised	emaciated	suspected
enveloped	holstered	dispensed	fasciated	dissected
scalloped	clustered	ankylosed	herniated	protected
dewlapped	scattered	snub-nosed	floriated	afflicted
kidnapped	shattered	hardnosed	storiated	crocheted
unwhipped	shuttered	leaf-nosed	unrelated	thicketed
unclipped	unuttered	hook-nosed	irrelated	ringleted
two-lipped	chequered	hawk-nosed	mutilated	chapleted
uncropped	unsevered	bull-nosed	rutilated	completed
bedropped	uncovered	star-nosed	pixilated	corsleted
unpropped	red-haired	soft-nosed	ocellated	coroneted
unstopped	ill-haired	unimposed	niellated	bayoneted
quadruped	coal-fired	unopposed	stellated	parapeted
shageared	sapphired	unexposed	arillated	trumpeted
long-eared	unadmired	sclerosed	areolated	banqueted
uncleared	unexpired	primrosed	cupolated	parqueted
misleared	undesired	unhearsed	lobulated	god-gifted
flap-eared	sick-tired	submersed	tubulated	twa-lofted
crop-eared	unattired	traversed	undulated	delighted
unsquared	pinafored	ill-versed	nodulated	unlighted
earth-bred	unfloored	renversed	tegulated	uplighted
underbred	untutored	unbiassed	angulated	benighted
interbred	unrazored	unclassed	simulated	unsighted
crossbred	unscarred	processed	cumulated	thoughted
ribaudred	preferred	confessed	annulated	unplaited
blubbered	conferred	professed	lunulated	fore-cited
calibered	concurred	unblessed	casemated	unincited
chambered	accoutred	addressed	uncinated	unexcited
bladdered	hard-cured	undressed	vaginated	conceited
meandered	unsecured	adpressed	echinated	surfeited
glandered	unfigured	depressed	laminated	benefited
brandered	uninjured	unpressed	patinated	illimited
unordered	unmanured	untressed	coronated	unlimited
uncheered	unscoured	possessed	baldpated	unmerited
upcheered	enamoured	unguessed	clodpated	unvisited
unoffered	contoured	prowessed	crispated	uninvited
proffered	uninsured	unglossed	lacerated	unexalted
chamfered	unassured	uncrossed	hederated	tip-tilted
staggered	tressured	engrossed	camerated	enchanted
ahungered	immatured	percussed	decorated	unplanted
co-sphered	unmatured	untrussed	zero-rated	warranted
unushered	cinctured	unaccused	cultrated	unscented
feathered	punctured	unfocused	castrated	tridented
weathered	undebased	unrebated	rostrated	segmented
smothered	iron-cased	radicated	saturated	pigmented
panniered	unpleased	dedicated	punctated	augmented
crosiered	unpraised	medicated	vegetated	garmented
knackered	feralised	tunicated	meditated	fermented
checkered	civilised	muricated	digitated	tormented
shickered	trellised	aduncated	crustated	contented
knickered	creolised	truncated	graduated	unpainted
whiskered	organised	unlocated	torquated	besainted
unpapered	unionised	long-dated	redoubted	untainted
creepered	velarised	overdated	undoubted	unjointed
slippered	polarised	trabeated	compacted	unpointed
trousered	pelorised	calceated	refracted	appointed
unwatered	surprised	nucleated	infracted	unprinted
unaltered	misprised	unpleated	retracted	unstinted

affronted	rue-leaved	underlaid	arachnoid	overbuild
undaunted	two-leaved	bridemaid	staminoid	stone-cold
unhaunted	cut-leaved	table-maid	cyprinoid	supercold
unblunted	ivy-leaved	nursemaid	platinoid	blindfold
uncounted	aggrieved	housemaid	cretinoid	threefold
unmounted	long-lived	lady's-maid	salmonoid	linen-fold
unpiloted	unshrived	dairymaid	polyzooid	sevenfold
top-booted	unmotived	underpaid	scombroid	sheepfold
web-footed	trivalved	sneak-raid	chancroid	interfold
fin-footed	unbeloved	aforesaid	chondroid	eightfold
two-footed	moon-loved	amino-acid	bacteroid	stokehold
oar-footed	unremoved	tortricid	hysteroid	leasehold
unadapted	self-moved	apartheid	sangfroid	household
untempted	disproved	quadrifid	meteoroid	threshold
unadopted	down-gyved	pedatifid	ophiuroid	twice-told
encrypted	unrenewed	septemfid	ellipsoid	auld-warld
uncharted	unsinewed	semi-rigid	gneissoid	play-world
two-parted	bestrewed	phalangid	haematoid	hood-mould
concerted	wire-sewed	monorchid	trematoid	leaf-mould
consorted	rainbowed	nymphalid	dermatoid	iron-mould
contorted	unendowed	chrysalid	thanatoid	broadband
distorted	unrelaxed	amaryllid	eutectoid	space-band
ballasted	unindexed	rock-solid	planetoid	dance-band
two-masted	oversexed	bipyramid	herpetoid	bugle-band
war-wasted	basifixed	scaraboid	granitoid	lease-band
congested	undecayed	gynaecoid	allantoid	blackband
ore-rested	undelayed	pithecoid	hypnotoid	train-band
contested	unallayed	scolecoid	scolytoid	crossband
ham-fisted	displayed	myrmecoid	mylohyoid	shirt-band
two-fisted	unassayed	corticoid	ichthyoid	waistband
dry-fisted	unessayed	meniscoid	trapezoid	wristband
untwisted	round-eyed	carangoid	tricuspid	belly-band
exhausted	eagle-eyed	pterygoid	cantharid	duplicand
disgusted	young-eyed	eunuchoid	trihybrid	trenchand
unfretted	thick-eyed	rhamphoid	ephemerid	roundhand
regretted	quick-eyed	scirrhoid	geometrid	third-hand
coquetted	stalk-eyed	ornithoid	priest-rid	sword-hand
brevetted	pearl-eyed	acanthoid	therapsid	stage-hand
curvetted	thrum-eyed	aspidioid	spermatid	aforehand
submitted	green-eyed	nauplioid	lithistid	small-hand
committed	hackneyed	scorpioid	semifluid	greenhand
permitted	onion-eyed	bungaloid	arch-druid	underhand
acquitted	unmoneyed	omphaloid	perfervid	right-hand
hen-witted	journeyed	syphiloid	isoniazid	shorthand
cat-witted	sharp-eyed	reptiloid	wind-shak'd	court-hand
fat-witted	blear-eyed	coralloid	Archibald	first-hand
nitwitted	clear-eyed	metalloid	springald	scrubland
outwitted	palfreyed	labelloid	seed-field	cloudland
unblotted	cross-eyed	lamelloid	goldfield	force-land
bespotted	argus-eyed	mongoloid	rice-field	sedgeland
unspotted	slant-eyed	varioloid	mine-field	Dixieland
garrotted	unalloyed	octaploid	long-field	tableland
besmutted	destroyed	hexaploid	coalfield	wasteland
unrefuted	good-sized	octoploid	open-field	milk-gland
unsaluted	life-sized	polyploid	cornfield	silk-gland
undiluted	king-sized	celluloid	snowfield	musk-gland
obvoluted	oversized	planuloid	gumshield	tear-gland
involuted	pint-sized	condyloid	boschveld	crash-land
unsubdued	unbrizzed	sphygmoid	dyer's-weld	marshland
unplagued	camanachd	serranoid	frithgild	northland
harangued	shanghai'd	zygaenoid	maid-child	southland
continued	twice-laid	sciaenoid	name-child	dreamland
remarqued	cable-laid	lichenoid	love-child	crown-land
unpursued	cream-laid	arytenoid	stepchild	swampland

engarland	break-wind	rough-shod	tiger-wood	billboard
sea-island	whirlwind	sharp-shod	brier-wood	mill-board
grassland	storm-wind	wholefood	aloeswood	bull-board
Lotus-land	interwind	angel-food	cocus-wood	signboard
drift-land	crosswind	spoon-food	sweetwood	clapboard
heartland	withywind	childhood	drift-wood	chipboard
pennyland	heart-bond	pixie-hood	fruitwood	shipboard
fairyland	mappemond	thanehood	heartwood	clip-board
reprimand	horse-pond	swinehood	Hollywood	slip-board
firebrand	wages-fund	falsehood	pseudopod	pulpboard
dust-brand	dachshund	statehood	peraeopod	shopboard
integrand	wind-bound	thinghood	scaphopod	starboard
semigrand	wordbound	flesh-hood	cirrhopod	overboard
doctorand	hide-bound	youthhood	pereiopod	cant-board
sea-strand	homebound	hardihood	phyllopod	footboard
quicksand	case-bound	gawkihood	heteropod	dart-board
shell-sand	calf-bound	lustihood	arthropod	maquisard
greensand	half-bound	angelhood	gastropod	face-guard
ampersand	hoof-bound	womanhood	chaetopod	safeguard
river-sand	rock-bound	queenhood	schizopod	lifeguard
bandstand	bark-bound	king's-hood	stadia-rod	axle-guard
handstand	soil-bound	monkshood	riding-rod	home-guard
ringstand	full-bound	adulthood	boning-rod	fireguard
wash-stand	rain-bound	gianthood	golden-rod	wire-guard
withstand	iron-bound	sainthood	piston-rod	roof-guard
rickstand	cropbound	beasthood	carpet-rod	rear-guard
bookstand	overbound	widowhood	lowrie-tod	snow-guard
cask-stand	root-bound	tabbyhood	Langobard	bodyguard
hallstand	westbound	needy-hood	Longobard	boulevard
overstand	snow-bound	puppyhood	three-card	fieldward
news-stand	brow-bound	fairyhood	score-card	shoreward
coatstand	duty-bound	life-blood	false-card	deathward
amperzand	dumbfound	gore-blood	punch-card	earthward
sheet-bend	well-found	pure-blood	microcard	northward
redescend	lime-hound	half-blood	trump-card	southward
transcend	lyme-hound	full-blood	court-card	sternward
candle-end	horehound	land-flood	lack-beard	afterward
single-end	gaze-hound	foul-brood	greybeard	nightward
deprehend	wolf-hound	withstood	disregard	rightward
reprehend	drag-hound	cocoa-wood	misregard	frontward
apprehend	staghound	zebra-wood	trenchard	coastward
dope-fiend	buckhound	bloodwood	stone-hard	mooseyard
drug-fiend	hellhound	lance-wood	interlard	graveyard
arch-fiend	lyam-hound	snakewood	spikenard	olive-yard
pen-friend	boarhound	eaglewood	communard	cloth-yard
boyfriend	hoarhound	copsewood	aquaboard	stackyard
lease-lend	deer-hound	whitewood	headboard	brickyard
recommend	newshound	zante-wood	cardboard	stockyard
forespend	grewhound	peach-wood	hardboard	steelyard
overspend	slow-hound	beech-wood	sideboard	scrap-yard
hinder-end	greyhound	matchwood	free-board	courtyard
finger-end	half-pound	touchwood	bakeboard	straw-yard
nurse-tend	ship-pound	brushwood	baseboard	biohazard
misintend	foot-pound	blackwood	half-board	haphazard
spellbind	half-round	prickwood	roof-board	swineherd
gavelkind	look-round	stink-wood	surf-board	goose-herd
womankind	turnround	sapan-wood	gangboard	weel-faird
humankind	wrapround	greenwood	dashboard	cocklaird
womenkind	whip-round	satinwood	wash-board	kirkyaird
sand-blind	year-round	carap-wood	buckboard	kailyaird
word-blind	overwound	tulip-wood	duck-board	scrub-bird
moon-blind	ororotund	cedarwood	sailboard	mound-bird
snow-blind	hodmandod	spear-wood	tail-board	blood-bird
Gradgrind	nature-god	underwood	wall-board	sedge-bird

snakebird	Zapodidae	Gramineae	free-space	fainéance
rifle-bird	Clupeidae	quadrigae	wall-space	recreance
plume-bird	Trochidae	letter-gae	aerospace	arrogance
flute-bird	Syrphidae	Solifugae	hair-space	off-chance
heath-bird	Tupaiidae	petechiae	rerebrace	mumchance
blackbird	Xiphiidae	branchiae	fore-brace	perchance
stink-bird	Ziphiidae	primitiae	mainbrace	mischance
skunk-bird	Arctiidae	reliquiae	vantbrace	snaphance
storm-bird	Sylviidae	strobilae	herb-grace	dalliance
satin-bird	Pyralidae	glabellae	torch-race	appliance
cedar-bird	Cichlidae	vulsellae	smock-race	tarriance
friarbird	Mytilidae	tessellae	wheel-race	imbalance
umber-bird	Oriolidae	fibrillae	leaf-trace	unbalance
water-bird	Tipulidae	nubeculae	relay-race	semblance
bower-bird	Phasmidae	lodiculae	headpiece	free-lance
wheat-bird	Tabanidae	vaginulae	timepiece	eye-glance
night-bird	Varanidae	retinulae	nose-piece	sibilance
stilt-bird	Iguanidae	clausulae	backpiece	jubilance
widow-bird	Hyaenidae	Dicotylae	neck-piece	vigilance
paddy-bird	Hominidae	trichinae	workpiece	demi-lance
honey-bird	Unionidae	Sylviinae	heel-piece	ambulance
dicky-bird	Belonidae	Totaninae	tailpiece	insulance
undergird	Sturnidae	Satyrinae	hair-piece	petulance
disaccord	Cynipidae	vertebrae	showpiece	sovenance
pop-record	Meropidae	Coniferae	cowardice	pregnance
match-cord	Ascaridae	ephemerae	prejudice	ordinance
decachord	Sciaridae	abscissae	suboffice	dominance
octachord	Homeridae	vibrissae	box-office	luminance
hexachord	Viperidae	aqua-vitae	pay-office	resonance
rheochord	Icteridae	placentae	sacrifice	assonance
monochord	Epeiridae	Isokontae	pontifice	occupance
notochord	Sciuridae	confervae	fortalice	clearance
liege-lord	Siluridae	astrolabe	sheep-lice	cumbrance
nonce-word	Zonuridae	subscribe	eye-splice	hindrance
rhyme-word	Satyridae	prescribe	fish-slice	tolerance
catchword	Lycosidae	conscribe	plant-lice	esperance
watchword	Neritidae	proscribe	stream-ice	utterance
swear-word	Noctuidae	xenophobe	shrew-mice	severance
afterword	Geomyidae	garderobe	precipice	flagrance
half-sword	Ericaceae	night-robe	anchor-ice	fragrance
backsword	Juncaceae	flashcube	liquorice	ignorance
crossword	Iridaceae	faith-cube	sale-price	aberrance
ghost-word	Typhaceae	sugar-cube	half-price	securance
weel-faur'd	Rubiaceae	hypercube	cicatrice	endurance
sour-gourd	Meliaceae	sieve-tube	armistice	manurance
cuckoo-bud	Liliaceae	make-peace	injustice	insurance
winter-bud	Tiliaceae	white-face	lime-juice	assurance
flower-bud	Violaceae	volte-face	love-juice	pleasance
blood-feud	Ebenaceae	cliff-face	in-service	obeisance
rain-cloud	Lemnaceae	poker-face	ex-service	puissance
overcloud	Anonaceae	interface	sand-dance	recusance
overproud	Cornaceae	about-face	impedance	reactance
press-stud	Aizoaceae	gin-palace	rope-dance	hesitance
shirt-stud	Characeae	blond-lace	stag-dance	exultance
overcrowd	Aceraceae	someplace	ring-dance	sportance
E	Lauraceae	fireplace	clogdance	elastance
Hepaticae	Cactaceae	high-place	avoidance	substance
Carabidae	Gnetaceae	workplace	folk-dance	omittance
Helicidae	Myrtaceae	farm-place	bull-dance	quittance
Culicidae	Cistaceae	show-place	abondance	pursuance
Pulicidae	Malvaceae	interlace	abundance	calavance
Cimicidae	Orchideae	tight-lace	step-dance	caravance
Soricidae	Florideae	point-lace	vengeance	readvance
Dorididae	Uredineae	sink-a-pace	permeance	grievance

relevance	frequence	antitrade	waterside	garnishee
arrivance	eloquence	overtrade	riverside	confirmee
allowance	pigsconce	embassade	night-side	maharanee
annoyance	pronounce	croustade	seamy-side	consignee
on-licence	land-force	retrocede	floodtide	Brahminee
reticence	life-force	intercede	multitide	menominee
innocence	workforce	millepede	river-tide	thick-knee
acescence	task-force	millipede	night-tide	knock-knee
decadence	re-enforce	palmipede	waveguide	boutonnée
accedence	reinforce	pinnipede	subdivide	abandonee
accidence	recalesce	cirripede	worldwide	trollopee
incidence	obsolesce	fissipede	statewide	stingaree
stridence	intumesce	multipede	basin-wide	chickaree
residence	luminesce	centipede	hydroxide	jigamaree
impudence	fluoresce	anguipede	tetroxide	recoveree
line-fence	reminisce	supersede	pentoxide	tithe-free
ring-fence	fish-sauce	Barmecide	protoxide	scart-free
rail-fence	jack-sauce	herbicide	allemande	heart-free
worm-fence	mint-sauce	verbicide	ash-blonde	fancy-free
deer-fence	reproduce	weedicide	demi-monde	bread-tree
indigence	introduce	fungicide	incommode	shade-tree
diligence	barricade	prolicide	staminode	smoke-tree
emulgence	cavalcade	germicide	internode	apple-tree
emergence	motorcade	vermicide	melampode	flame-tree
nescience	ambuscade	vulpicide	electrode	plane-tree
inscience	orangeade	acaricide	trematode	grapetree
obedience	cross-fade	uxoricide	Oudenarde	clove-tree
prurience	lampshade	parricide	disillude	gauze-tree
esurience	overshade	matricide	interlude	staff-tree
sentience	marmalade	patricide	giant-rude	swingtree
bivalence	tway-blade	foeticide	desuetude	peach-tree
redolence	moon-glade	menticide	assuetude	pitch-tree
indolence	everglade	pesticide	dulcitude	coral-tree
insolence	ebrillade	larvicide	longitude	pecan-tree
feculence	fusillade	ethnocide	amplitude	rowan-tree
temulence	remoulade	Antrycide	plenitude	covin-tree
virulence	judge-made	oxy-iodide	magnitude	thorntree
purulence	mouth-made	tracheide	lippitude	tulip-tree
vehemence	reformade	sclereide	torpitude	cigar-tree
remanence	ready-made	lysergide	turpitude	Judas-tree
immanence	esplanade	horsehide	negritude	grass-tree
imminence	promenade	phosphide	nigritude	crosstree
desinence	bastinade	oxy-halide	celsitude	fruit-tree
ninepence	colonnade	landslide	lassitude	macaw-tree
fivepence	carbonade	backslide	beatitude	bully-tree
halfpence	Gasconade	hair-slide	platitude	ivory-tree
fourpence	gabionade	carbamide	gratitude	fricassee
deference	cannonade	cyanamide	rectitude	déclassée
reference	tamponade	acetamide	certitude	sublessee
efference	carronade	polyamide	fortitude	addressee
inference	cassonade	anhydride	vastitude	dedicatee
adherence	cottonade	glyceride	servitude	cohabitee
inherence	estrapade	sand-pride	bumble-bee	consultee
coherence	gallopade	telluride	humble-bee	guarantee
reverence	mole-spade	five-a-side	Punjaubee	warrantee
unessence	turf-spade	broadside	chickadee	presentee
appetence	peat-spade	blind-side	dispondee	appointee
penitence	fanfarade	ingle-side	rye-coffee	affrontée
impotence	hit-parade	shore-side	mortgagee	dancettee
existence	gingerade	stateside	galiongee	muffettee
refluence	high-grade	alongside	ditrochee	committee
affluence	citigrade	glucoside	debauchee	Portuguee
effluence	downgrade	spear-side	Feringhee	détraquée
influence	free-trade	underside		autos-da-fé

vouchsafe	matronage	forejudge	humble-pie	undertake
réchauffé	patronage	spicilege	numble-pie	entertake
shelf-life	parsonage	sacrilege	lumber-pie	grub-stake
still-life	personage	sortilege	maggot-pie	soopstake
after-life	cartonage	privilege	cherry-pie	moonquake
short-life	title-page	misallege	bain-marie	wide-awake
reed-knife	scrippage	disoblige	federarie	kittiwake
case-knife	estoppage	Félibrige	menagerie	graywacke
jack-knife	interpage	Malebolge	gaucherie	greywacke
moon-knife	front-page	sea-change	diablerie	patchocke
cauld-rife	decoupage	sex-change	gaminerie	motor-bike
wasterife	arrearage	free-range	confrérie	march-dike
child-wife	cellarage	long-range	brasserie	hitch-hike
apple-wife	disparage	sea-orange	papeterie	look-alike
tripewife	pilferage	rearrange	sparterie	childlike
housewife	brokerage	challenge	Jacquerie	fiend-like
sousewife	butlerage	restringe	stouthrie	ungodlike
witch-wife	cooperage	sun-lounge	bolletrie	swordlike
appendage	waiterage	surcharge	bulletrie	snakelike
groundage	porterage	discharge	trashtrie	scalelike
bavardage	fosterage	mischarge	megacurie	nurselike
middle-age	flowerage	concierge	signeurie	thief-like
squireage	ossifrage	demi-gorge	Tod-lowrie	sylph-like
shroffage	saxifrage	overgorge	malvoisie	nymph-like
greengage	anchorage	sun-spurge	string-tie	deathlike
pre-engage	factorage	wind-gauge	assoilzie	truthlike
disengage	demurrage	ring-gauge	slack-bake	clerk-like
water-gage	arbitrage	rain-gauge	friedcake	rebel-like
repechage	encourage	calcifuge	pound-cake	snail-like
xylophage	entourage	vermifuge	spice-cake	shell-like
shrinkage	pasturage	febrifuge	bridecake	unmanlike
vassalage	ambassage	toothache	angel-cake	woman-like
barrelage	embassage	sea-orache	cream-cake	humanlike
cartilage	repassage	heartache	queen-cake	queen-like
fortilage	by-passage	moustache	spawn-cake	aspen-like
curtilage	streetage	bellyache	wafer-cake	bairnlike
hypallage	secretage	tête-bêche	layer-cake	unwarlike
treillage	knightage	parfleche	fruit-cake	lazar-like
pupillage	hermitage	Orobanche	shortcake	riverlike
school-age	dacoitage	avalanche	lardy-cake	glasslike
petrolage	hospitage	guilloche	tipsy-cake	plant-like
consulage	advantage	recherché	headshake	saintlike
self-image	clientage	bretasche	handshake	courtlike
archimage	parentage	proseuche	ring-shake	beastlike
scrimmage	escortage	cartouche	milk-shake	ghost-like
skrimmage	reportage	Roxburghe	sootflake	fairylike
scrummage	forestage	ensheathe	snowflake	handspike
orphanage	backstage	insheathe	merrymake	awestrike
villanage	downstage	unsheathe	sand-snake	air-strike
mismanage	curettage	embreathe	tree-snake	outstrike
careenage	galravage	inbreathe	ring-snake	artichoke
villenage	gilravage	enwreathe	rock-snake	peat-smoke
engrenage	knife-edge	inwreathe	whip-snake	sunstroke
recoinage	pearl-edge	unwreathe	hoop-snake	twostroke
voisinage	kentledge	rigwiddie	parabrake	keystroke
cousinage	kintledge	discandie	band-brake	unprovoke
beguinage	knowledge	rigwoodie	hand-brake	sail-fluke
empennage	razor-edge	pousowdie	cane-brake	march-dyke
siphonage	gall-midge	howtowdie	rock-brake	triticale
gabionage	Cambridge	shanachie	corn-brake	timescale
espionage	air-bridge	sennachie	corncrake	full-scale
gallonage	langridge	bum-baylie	fire-drake	Nithsdale
commonage	cartridge	bonhommie	sheldrake	standgale
tamponage	partridge	pictarnie	wapentake	galengale

galingale	touchable	alterable	habitable	irascible
sweet-gale	weighable	enterable	dubitable	adducible
church-ale	laughable	utterable	excitable	deducible
alum-shale	crushable	reverable	cogitable	reducible
rationale	mouthable	severable	limitable	inducible
pastorale	merciable	admirable	ignitable	inaudible
wholesale	unifiable	expirable	heritable	illegible
hospitale	talliable	desirable	veritable	dirigible
fairy-tale	unpliable	untirable	irritable	frangible
carrytale	appliable	memorable	visitable	indelible
intervale	unamiable	ignorable	equitable	intenible
clubbable	speakable	vaporable	work-table	exponible
scribable	breakable	motorable	plantable	cohesible
climbable	unmakable	razorable	grantable	derisible
impacable	unlikable	inerrable	paintable	divisible
abdicable	thinkable	filtrable	printable	invisible
medicable	drinkable	securable	turntable	sponsible
judicable	rebukable	incurable	countable	eversible
allocable	exhalable	uncurable	denotable	classible
revocable	unsalable	endurable	shootable	amissible
pleadable	semblable	figurable	unpotable	omissible
unfadable	available	insurable	adaptable	plausible
inaidable	habilable	assurable	temptable	infusible
unaidable	spellable	maturable	comptable	appetible
decidable	unnamable	saturable	pier-table	ignitible
avoidable	untamable	excisable	avertable	comptible
unridable	claimable	demisable	sportable	avertible
dividable	estimable	advisable	twistable	dissemble
wieldable	flammable	devisable	constable	rose-noble
yieldable	crammable	revisable	Dunstable	resoluble
mouldable	swimmable	unlosable	biostable	insoluble
amendable	resumable	deposable	refutable	immanacle
emendable	assumable	imposable	immutable	unmanacle
spendable	alienable	opposable	reputable	spectacle
woundable	disenable	classable	imputable	adminicle
guardable	intenable	amassable	scrutable	chronicle
deludable	untenable	guessable	skew-table	ventricle
peaceable	pregnable	accusable	rescuable	fernticle
traceable	drainable	excusable	subduable	X-particle
agreeable	trainable	refusable	inequable	carbuncle
unseeable	definable	debatable	unequable	siphuncle
imageable	laminable	uneatable	pursuable	dip-circle
vengeable	nominable	createable	cleavable	hut-circle
forgeable	learnable	treatable	unlivable	corpuscle
gaugeable	incunable	sofa-table	derivable	megacycle
shakeable	untunable	palatable	revivable	life-cycle
malleable	incapable	dilatable	evolvable	song-cycle
permeable	uncapable	floatable	unlovable	push-cycle
shapeable	escapable	unsatable	removable	pericycle
raiseable	graspable	get-at-able	immovable	kilocycle
ineffable	reparable	rotatable	unmovable	autocycle
delegable	separable	doubtable	renewable	cock-padle
relegable	execrable	unactable	allowable	skedaddle
irrigable	lacerable	tractable	repayable	dog-paddle
fatigable	deferable	sand-table	unpayable	hen-paddle
litigable	referable	card-table	unsayable	astraddle
mitigable	offerable	bird-table	assayable	pad-saddle
navigable	inferable	side-table	enjoyable	offsaddle
levigable	tolerable	tide-table	freezable	unswaddle
reachable	numerable	life-table	unsizable	condiddle
teachable	generable	vegetable	air-bubble	hen-paidle
catchable	venerable	timetable	evincible	crab-sidle
matchable	superable	covetable	indocible	manhandle
patchable	miserable	rightable	coercible	panhandle

9 -DLE

mishandle	vibratile	judas-hole	fascicule	enthymeme
sea-girdle	umbratile	Judas-hole	vermicule	monotreme
hip-girdle	pulsatile	rivet-hole	febricule	semanteme
hydrocele	versatile	sight-hole	graticule	white-lime
cystocele	portatile	blast-hole	poeticule	quicklime
banjulele	insectile	spout-hole	monticule	brooklime
clientèle	inductile	cubby-hole	homuncule	shell-lime
pantoffle	ridge-tile	hidey-hole	tubercule	pantomime
carfuffle	infantile	gully-hole	majuscule	peacetime
kerfuffle	drain-tile	glory-hole	minuscule	space-time
curfuffle	infertile	apsidiole	hierodule	spare-time
reshuffle	exsertile	arteriole	propagule	aforetime
pantoufle	turnstile	guacamole	umbellule	lunch-time
porbeagle	unbeguile	septimole	papillule	flexitime
bald-eagle	ranshakle	water-mole	petiolule	small-time
sore-eagle	unshackle	ridge-pole	gallinule	bairn-time
soar-eagle	bespeckle	lodgepole	pulvinule	undertime
gier-eagle	spraickle	bargepole	antennule	aftertime
bedraggle	tan-pickle	catchpole	megajoule	night-time
porwiggle	enranckle	rantipole	plumb-rule	short-time
misguggle	ear-cockle	turcopole	chondrule	first-time
fandangle	parbuckle	barcarole	slide-rule	oriflamme
wide-angle	unwrinkle	rigmarole	glomerule	programme
newfangle	mirabelle	banderole	chain-rule	prudhomme
semi-angle	rubicelle	title-role	night-rule	misbecome
bespangle	lioncelle	casserole	strongyle	forthcome
embrangle	organelle	cameo-rôle	aeolipyle	unwelcome
imbrangle	aquarelle	furfurole	micropyle	steam-dome
hour-angle	filoselle	lemon-sole	decastyle	macrodome
sea-tangle	bagatelle	piacevole	octastyle	astrodome
rectangle	rascaille	water-vole	hexastyle	metronome
pentangle	mitraille	principle	free-style	aquadrome
surcingle	grisaille	merpeople	peristyle	helidrome
commingle	corbeille	dispeople	areostyle	peridrome
kent-bugle	vermeille	crab-apple	pygostyle	velodrome
sprauchle	surveille	sorb-apple	monostyle	aerodrome
overhaile	quadrille	sage-apple	hypostyle	loxodrome
aventaile	tredrille	bakeapple	octostyle	zoechrome
cantabile	pointillé	pineapple	hairstyle	trichrome
prenubile	apostille	rose-apple	coat-style	urochrome
reconcile	amphibole	love-apple	polystyle	threesome
crocodile	rocambole	king-apple	ramfeezle	lithesome
serrefile	carambole	John-apple	bamboozle	wholesome
paper-file	hyperbole	star-apple	shemozzle	curvesome
iodophile	clerecole	quadruple	shimozzle	laughsome
halophile	calcicole	quintuple	schnozzle	loathsome
homophile	terricole	oil-beetle	Notre-Dame	toothsome
oenophile	clearcole	dor-beetle	hippodame	youthsome
xenophile	farandole	may-beetle	board-game	wearisome
Sinophile	girandole	half-title	blackgame	worrisome
somewhile	bracteole	gas-mantle	strap-game	tricksome
meanwhile	caprifole	dismantle	aftergame	pranksome
erstwhile	thumb-hole	outmantle	rakeshame	amplosome
facsimile	sound-hole	sea-turtle	brand-name	microsome
dissimile	stoke-hole	red-rattle	tradename	hydrosome
chamomile	mouse-hole	tea-kettle	stage-name	leptosome
campanile	hawsehole	sea-nettle	melodrame	timorsome
three-pile	bench-hole	dae-nettle	headframe	quietsome
aeolipile	touch-hole	day-nettle	cold-frame	eightsome
stockpile	shell-hole	sea-bottle	lace-frame	lightsome
screw-pile	dreamhole	ink-bottle	sash-frame	heartsome
unsterile	creep-hole	two-bottle	mainframe	leucotome
expansile	auger-hole	gas-bottle	telepheme	osteotome
extensile	water-hole	vestibule	blaspheme	lithotome

harmotome	acetylene	phosphine	party-line	wolverine
microtome	pentylene	catarhine	alabamine	pulverine
peristome	Philomene	monorhine	rhodamine	tanagrine
dirigisme	Melpomene	shoeshine	cardamine	peregrine
arrivisme	spodumene	moonshine	prolamine	victorine
disinhume	wolverene	starshine	monoamine	viverrine
transhume	reconvene	overshine	jessamine	veratrine
semiplume	supervene	acanthine	protamine	petaurine
filoplume	intervene	percaline	histamine	Mathurine
impostume	champagne	bengaline	glutamine	vulturine
monorhyme	Cockaigne	harmaline	re-examine	bombasine
apoenzyme	darraigne	crotaline	shale-mine	nigrosine
proenzyme	Novocaine	rhumb-line	gelsemine	haversine
spulebane	copataine	plumb-line	strip-mine	subursine
hause-bane	capotaine	pericline	undermine	limousine
wolfsbane	yohimbine	anticline	determine	sabbatine
sarbacane	recombine	monocline	extermine	nitratine
sword-cane	uncombine	breadline	curcumine	triactine
hurricane	columbine	Ghibeline	safranine	monactine
sugar-cane	succubine	guideline	mezzanine	aconitine
Cispadane	concubine	nepheline	echidnine	infantine
littleane	thylacine	nickeline	zygaenine	galantine
salangane	fettucine	whale-line	Johannine	eglantine
cymophane	muscadine	scare-line	falconine	Levantine
hedyphane	rhoeadine	shoreline	saturnine	Byzantine
halothane	grenadine	house-line	macedoine	argentine
bird-alane	Bernadine	musteline	stone-pine	valentine
burd-alane	contadine	touch-line	pitchpine	narcotine
rotaplane	pethidine	girthline	kauri-pine	libertine
aquaplane	thymidine	inquiline	subalpine	lacertine
land-plane	quinidine	trunk-line	Cisalpine	nemertine
peneplane	xyloidine	caballine	sugar-pine	asbestine
jack-plane	pieridine	coralline	reserpine	Celestine
mail-plane	histidine	metalline	albespine	forestine
sailplane	toluidine	zibelline	porcupine	intestine
tailplane	benzidine	capelline	screw-pine	Augustine
twin-plane	celandine	vitelline	gossypine	veloutine
monoplane	almandine	gorilline	calcarine	Calixtine
aeroplane	farandine	corolline	muscarine	ungenuine
gyroplane	secundine	trawl-line	mandarine	grapevine
marchpane	hirundine	Sibylline	gregarine	keelivine
filigrane	gabardine	datum-line	margarine	ovibovine
pentosane	gaberdine	bandoline	submarine	water-vine
iso-octane	haberdine	mandoline	rosmarine	keelyvine
hare-stane	interdine	crinoline	nectarine	Rhinewine
calmstane	madeleine	quinoline	estuarine	pack-twine
caumstane	vicereine	crepoline	alizarine	thyroxine
whunstane	sparteine	fibroline	balzarine	bombazine
hydrovane	predefine	benzoline	colubrine	hydrazine
chloracne	paraffine	underline	mepacrine	organzine
Oligocene	giraffine	leger-line	endocrine	landdamne
Pleiocene	unconfine	water-line	holocrine	persienne
damascene	superfine	interline	ectocrine	cloisonné
drop-scene	miscegine	night-line	volucrine	blade-bone
miscegene	aborigine	sight-line	ephedrine	spade-bone
photogene	pug-engine	front-line	Paludrine	ridge-bone
toxaphene	malengine	coastline	berberine	whalebone
phosphene	oil-engine	waistline	glycerine	spulebone
coryphene	air-engine	masculine	bebeerine	aitchbone
polythene	gas-engine	penduline	tangerine	thigh-bone
butadiene	protogine	traguline	ballerine	bellibone
magdalene	aubergine	primuline	passerine	cheek-bone
methylene	parochine	nummuline	butterine	shank-bone
propylene	seraphine	cordyline	polverine	pedal-bone

9 -ONE

speal-bone	limestone	importune	interlope	biosphere
whirl-bone	wine-stone	opportune	phalarope	noosphere
green-bone	hone-stone	disattune	guide-rope	exosphere
raven-bone	pipestone	albespyne	ridge-rope	somewhere
cramp-bone	cope-stone	Mnemosyne	slack-rope	elsewhere
storm-cone	merestone	brake-shoe	crack-rope	lavaliere
soda-scone	firestone	horseshoe	glass-rope	caponiere
drop-scone	bluestone	clout-shoe	emmetrope	brassière
methadone	flagstone	thrust-hoe	tight-rope	misoclere
sphendone	arch-stone	surf-canoe	hemitrope	cassimere
underdone	penistone	mistletoe	rheotrope	doucepere
woebegone	minkstone	hammer-toe	azeotrope	decastere
megaphone	hailstone	landscape	allotrope	decistere
Ansaphone ®	gall-stone	gas-escape	guest-rope	persevere
headphone	millstone	moonscape	straw-rope	sepulchre
telephone	marlstone	townscape	presbyope	luminaire
audiphone	brimstone	snowscape	lagniappe	numeraire
Tisiphone	calmstone	cityscape	Xanthippe	solitaire
idiophone	caumstone	waveshape	archetype	rapid-fire
allophone	alum-stone	shipshape	touch-type	cease-fire
xylophone	plum-stone	wild-grape	kallitype	watch-fire
homophone	caen-stone	broomrape	chemitype	brush-fire
aerophone	rain-stone	videotape	talbotype	death-fire
pyrophone	veinstone	Sellotape ®	heliotype	quick-fire
optophone	whinstone	mire-snipe	collotype	trial-fire
saxophone	moonstone	jack-snipe	cyanotype	shellfire
viewphone	ironstone	stand-pipe	phenotype	underfire
polyphone	cornstone	peace-pipe	stenotype	crossfire
menadione	hornstone	drone-pipe	phonotype	nightfire
bird-alone	turnstone	hawsepipe	ambrotype	coach-hire
Agapemone	soapstone	waste-pipe	ferrotype	Yorkshire
pheromone	step-stone	stove-pipe	phototype	pourboire
lithopone	drip-stone	pitchpipe	prototype	baignoire
interpone	pulpstone	quail-pipe	ricercare	écritoire
lazzarone	drop-stone	steam-pipe	aftercare	scrutoire
squadrone	hoar-stone	organ-pipe	dromedare	transpire
chaperone	star-stone	drain-pipe	inspheare	reinspire
isochrone	buhrstone	wincopipe	fieldfare	acrospire
disthrone	door-stone	water-pipe	autoflare	grandsire
cortisone	burrstone	blast-pipe	terramare	subentire
touch-tone	Jew's-stone	cassaripe	nightmare	disattire
barbitone	whetstone	ratheripe	unprepare	reacquire
Dulcitone	gritstone	under-ripe	overstare	piano-wire
eigentone	siltstone	rock-tripe	tee-square	microwire
orthotone	font-stone	pin-stripe	self-aware	chokebore
microtone	mort-stone	sideswipe	China-ware	hellebore
undertone	holystone	megascope	table-ware	small-bore
slabstone	chest-tone	somascope	stoneware	manticore
tombstone	schiavone	vitascope	whiteware	water-core
kerbstone	interzone	telescope	steel-ware	nine-score
curbstone	road-borne	engiscope	holloware	overscore
headstone	self-borne	koniscope	outerware	fourscore
loadstone	rail-borne	periscope	glassware	stevedore
toad-stone	sail-borne	auriscope	Delftware	provedore
goldstone	sloggorne	endoscope	wood-fibre	cuspidore
band-stone	sloghorne	hodoscope	simulacre	commodore
sandstone	slughorne	baroscope	involucre	therefore
bondstone	plenilune	horoscope	esclandre	wherefore
wood-stone	root-prune	poroscope	insincere	semaphore
lodestone	dance-tune	gyroscope	adipocere	canephore
freestone	psalm-tune	pyroscope	belvedere	gonophore
bakestone	befortune	mutoscope	interfere	gynophore
milestone	infortune	cryoscope	ecosphere	foreshore
tile-stone	unfortune	engyscope	geosphere	longshore

bandalore	chaussure	upper-case	epilogise	economise
pencil-ore	plicature	lower-case	syllogise	anatomise
plant-lore	defeature	staircase	geologise	epitomise
hackamore	foliature	mummy-case	neologise	customise
mattamore	miniature	lend-lease	apologise	volcanise
nathemore	striature	displease	prologise	vulcanise
Baltimore	tablature	misplease	catechise	rhodanise
sophomore	prelature	metaphase	franchise	sloganise
nevermore	premature	telophase	molochise	mechanise
massymore	climature	monophase	anarchise	Indianise
millepore	crenature	polyphase	empathise	Balkanise
madrepore	signature	periclase	globalise	Germanise
palampore	ill-nature	reductase	verbalise	star-anise
palempore	connature	synaptase	sulcalise	galvanise
extempore	serrature	invertase	vandalise	Trubenise ®
phonopore	dictature	wild-geese	feudalise	oxygenise
water-pore	nervature	ewe-cheese	unrealise	hyphenise
megaspore	curvature	nip-cheese	labialise	hellenise
ascospore	depicture	tip-cheese	socialise	recognise
endospore	stricture	Pekingese	radialise	cocainise
zygospore	decocture	Cingalese	genialise	luteinise
heart-sore	structure	Sinhalese	serialise	hyalinise
drug-store	comfiture	Congolese	animalise	kaolinise
bookstore	confiture	Carlylese	formalise	aluminise
herbivore	garniture	Soudanese	normalise	platinise
carnivore	furniture	manganese	signalise	solemnise
kidney-ore	fioriture	Bolognese	carnalise	tyrannise
decametre	nouriture	Londonese	vernalise	carbonise
decimetre	vestiture	Ceylonese	pluralise	preconise
kilometre	sepulture	Nipponese	tantalise	Londonise
nanometre	debenture	Cantonese	mortalise	dragonise
saltpetre	indenture	calabrese	brutalise	jargonise
decalitre	calenture	polonaise	annualise	gorgonise
decilitre	adventure	béarnaise	casualise	euphonise
kilolitre	recapture	dispraise	visualise	harmonise
jobcentre	enrapture	mispraise	actualise	sermonise
off-centre	scripture	écossaise	ritualise	matronise
epicentre	sculpture	syllabise	mutualise	patronise
concentre	prompture	ostracise	sexualise	personise
rencontre	departure	rhotacise	nickelise	Platonise
dislustre	coverture	synoecise	gospelise	wantonise
outlustre	depasture	imprecise	dieselise	peptonise
water-cure	repasture	unprecise	cartelise	Teutonise
procedure	insisture	gothicise	stabilise	Slavonise
engendure	imposture	mythicise	syphilise	hibernise
prefigure	exposture	italicise	sterilise	modernise
configure	retexture	publicise	fossilise	communise
disfigure	admixture	gaelicise	subtilise	equipoise
lay-figure	deflexure	anglicise	gentilise	overpoise
cannelure	inflexure	gallicise	fertilise	turquoise
chevelure	embrazure	metricise	metallise	barbarise
disimmure	manoeuvre	Persicise	powellise	Pindarise
intermure	melaphyre	poeticise	diabolise	vulgarise
belamoure	sea-satyre	Briticise	symbolise	gargarise
simon-pure	wheelbase	criticise	Mongolise	catharise
admeasure	leuco-base	rusticise	formulise	summarise
remeasure	music-case	subincise	capsulise	marmarise
embrasure	spore-case	hybridise	euphemise	scenarise
licensure	brief-case	subsidise	emblemise	tartarise
enclosure	watch-case	liquidise	systemise	Magyarise
inclosure	crankcase	deoxidise	rhythmise	rubberise
exclosure	jewel-case	methodise	sublimise	mercerise
composure	braincase	dialogise	victimise	tenderise
disposure	paper-case	analogise	randomise	isomerise

mesmerise	spokewise	juxtapose	veilleuse	rest-house
jasperise	tablewise	decompose	charmeuse	posthouse
pauperise	anglewise	recompose	chanteuse	brew-house
bacterise	slopewise	superpose	superfuse	playhouse
winterise	spirewise	interpose	interfuse	crab-louse
neoterise	fesse-wise	indispose	transfuse	woodlouse
Listerise	scarfwise	transpose	cornemuse	bird-louse
cauterise	clockwise	tenebrose	lobscouse	fish-louse
silverise	shoalwise	blush-rose	clubhouse	booklouse
pulverise	spoonwise	squarrose	bead-house	woodmouse
vampirise	altarwise	gneissose	dead-house	cole-mouse
deodorise	otherwise	edematose	roadhouse	reremouse
Sanforise	taperwise	galactose	coldhouse	coal-mouse
authorise	stairwise	cespitose	woodhouse	rearmouse
pillorise	crosswise	tomentose	yird-house	deer-mouse
glamorise	slantwise	schistose	bakehouse	hydrolyse
temporise	frontwise	siliquose	pine-house	breed-bate
terrorise	leastwise	quartzose	rope-house	columbate
factorise	coastwise	time-lapse	warehouse	trilobate
rhetorise	guestwise	neckverse	firehouse	tholobate
mainprise	screw-wise	reredorse	gate-house	stylobate
cicatrise	money-wise	rear-dorse	dove-house	reprobate
electrise	penny-wise	wood-horse	corf-house	approbate
carburise	road-sense	stud-horse	long-house	ascorbate
epicurise	thrombose	racehorse	wash-house	adsorbate
tellurise	corymbose	fore-horse	lush-house	desiccate
rapturise	bellicose	pack-horse	bathhouse	exsiccate
texturise	vorticose	cockhorse	deck-house	defaecate
martyrise	fruticose	workhorse	sick-house	deprecate
emphasise	verrucose	philhorse	lockhouse	imprecate
fantasise	pantihose	fill-horse	milk-house	eradicate
ecstasise	trunk-hose	mill-horse	cookhouse	predicate
Gallisise	grandiose	rearhorse	dark-house	vindicate
sabbatise	religiose	pair-horse	workhouse	syndicate
mediatise	spongiose	four-horse	coal-house	forficate
prelatise	minutiose	malt-horse	peel-house	vellicate
dramatise	foreclose	salt-horse	jailhouse	replicate
dogmatise	half-close	cart-horse	well-house	implicate
climatise	lamellose	post-horse	gill-house	applicate
aromatise	papillose	dray-horse	toll-house	duplicate
Socratise	foliolose	dextrorse	cool-house	explicate
privatise	calculose	reimburse	toolhouse	formicate
sovietise	surculose	sick-nurse	palmhouse	fornicate
palletise	cellulose	concourse	farmhouse	auspicate
pelletise	plumulose	discourse	townhouse	fabricate
magnetise	granulose	pick-purse	chop-house	imbricate
sonnetise	spinulose	palliasse	flophouse	lubricate
uralitise	fistulose	matelassé	rasp-house	rubricate
granitise	laevulose	paillasse	beer-house	cle cleericate
sensitise	anchylose	demitasse	poorhouse	affricate
pedantise	lacrimose	princesse	alms-house	metricate
narcotise	endosmose	humblesse	doss-house	intricate
hypnotise	lacrymose	hostlesse	joss-house	extricate
necrotise	lichenose	poetresse	neat-house	corticate
rebaptise	arabinose	reredosse	boathouse	masticate
unbaptise	raffinose	retroussé	malt-house	rusticate
expertise	calaboose	root-cause	penthouse	defalcate
advertise	wild-goose	subclause	moothouse	inculcate
misadvise	wase-goose	menopause	root-house	bisulcate
improvise	swan-goose	ionopause	cart-house	suffocate
supervise	snow-goose	self-abuse	porthouse	collocate
broadwise	grey-goose	arquebuse	masthouse	dislocate
wedgewise	wayzgoose	coiffeuse	oast-house	embrocate
snakewise	foot-loose	précieuse .	pesthouse	convocate

demarcate	bilabiate	urceolate	stipulate	fulminate
altercate	officiate	lineolate	scopulate	comminate
bifurcate	noviciate	faveolate	sporulate	abominate
expiscate	enunciate	alveolate	serrulate	germinate
obfuscate	associate	segholate	consulate	terminate
infuscate	reradiate	ciliolate	capsulate	verminate
coruscate	irradiate	foliolate	fossulate	acuminate
re-educate	remediate	hariolate	spatulate	aluminate
manducate	immediate	variolate	gratulate	inopinate
molybdate	sorediate	petiolate	postulate	pectinate
depredate	dimidiate	ostiolate	pustulate	obstinate
out-of-date	repudiate	inviolate	clavulate	destinate
elucidate	retaliate	phenolate	methylate	festinate
candidate	gangliate	consolate	caprylate	inquinate
rhipidate	affiliate	vacuolate	carbamate	pulvinate
cuspidate	humiliate	gold-plate	cyclamate	perennate
liquidate	emolliate	face-plate	glutamate	bipinnate
deoxidate	defoliate	sole-plate	stalemate	carbonate
fecundate	bifoliate	name-plate	incremate	diaconate
rotundate	exfoliate	baseplate	house-mate	siphonate
periodate	arseniate	half-plate	sublimate	pulmonate
retardate	laciniate	roof-plate	acclimate	tycoonate
obcordate	vicariate	fish-plate	collimate	mucronate
decaudate	bivariate	backplate	reanimate	personate
excaudate	inebriate	bookplate	inanimate	centonate
tracheate	fimbriate	dial-plate	exanimate	incarnate
anucleate	excoriate	coal-plate	proximate	hibernate
enucleate	elutriate	wall-plate	checkmate	alternate
cochleate	infuriate	soup-plate	coelomate	tribunate
delineate	luxuriate	door-plate	diplomate	coadunate
concreate	prussiate	hourplate	copes-mate	shogunate
procreate	indusiate	meat-plate	classmate	sublunate
miscreate	expatiate	footplate	despumate	fortunate
new-create	insatiate	draw-plate	rhodanate	mancipate
bracteate	unsatiate	mica-slate	manganate	dissipate
khalifate	novitiate	legislate	hetmanate	inculpate
propagate	negotiate	alum-slate	sultanate	exculpate
moss-agate	alleviate	translate	oxygenate	syncopate
floodgate	lixiviate	whet-slate	hyphenate	apocopate
lodge-gate	induviate	clay-slate	obsignate	extirpate
variegate	cephalate	ejaculate	designate	nuncupate
segregate	phthalate	speculate	rabbinate	parhypate
aggregate	tantalate	aciculate	bombinate	calcarate
waste-gate	correlate	apiculate	combinate	disparate
colligate	misrelate	spiculate	turbinate	celebrate
castigate	bombilate	calculate	vaccinate	cerebrate
instigate	ventilate	falculate	succinate	terebrate
fustigate	umbellate	inoculate	lancinate	calibrate
divulgate	locellate	circulate	runcinate	obumbrate
subrogate	lamellate	acidulate	circinate	adumbrate
prorogate	appellate	pendulate	fascinate	inumbrate
surrogate	patellate	coagulate	raffinate	lucubrate
Watergate	vacillate	lingulate	evaginate	obsecrate
water-gate	oscillate	virgulate	originate	desecrate
objurgate	sigillate	pullulate	marginate	third-rate
expurgate	mamillate	tremulate	machinate	dehydrate
subjugate	papillate	stimulate	declinate	verberate
conjugate	pupillate	formulate	reclinate	exuberate
corrugate	titillate	plumulate	pollinate	piece-rate
ivory-gate	decollate	granulate	staminate	cancerate
eparchate	cucullate	crenulate	examinate	viscerate
exarchate	medullate	spinulate	eliminate	ponderate
caliphate	chocolate	cannulate	criminate	vizierate
phosphate	percolate	pinnulate	culminate	scelerate

9 -ATE

glomerate	palmitate	trilobite	phonolite	bentonite
enumerate	crepitate	coenobite	scapolite	amazonite
pignerate	stipitate	underbite	fibrolite	monzonite
itinerate	palpitate	crossbite	microlite	mizzonite
vulnerate	mussitate	frostbite	saprolite	tribunite
exonerate	inusitate	chalybite	coprolite	bytownite
temperate	nictitate	omphacite	natrolite	hercynite
co-operate	gravitate	phenacite	sassolite	dichroite
cooperate	decantate	scolecite	pectolite	tephroite
desperate	bidentate	variscite	globulite	merozoite
pulse-rate	orientate	tetradite	cellulite	wood-spite
reiterate	dementate	extradite	nummulite	mugearite
masterate	potentate	recondite	granulite	margarite
deuterate	connotate	incondite	serpulite	goslarite
fire-grate	despotate	exopodite	tachylite	Himyarite
integrate	devastate	scorodite	bathylite	hypocrite
remigrate	intestate	inerudite	propylite	chondrite
immigrate	tungstate	pyreneite	Balaamite	anhydrite
denigrate	reinstate	Wyclifite	atacamite	enhydrite
death-rate	overstate	Irvingite	Gothamite	sphaerite
clathrate	degustate	dialogite	bedlamite	ozocerite
birth-rate	sagittate	uintahite	fogramite	witherite
elaborate	commutate	malachite	Thelemite	ozokerite
perforate	deciduate	phosphite	willemite	millerite
meliorate	devaluate	anorthite	diatomite	Hitlerite
deflorate	attenuate	zinc-white	sugar-mite	Wagnerite
pignorate	extenuate	milk-white	tridymite	wernerite
evaporate	insinuate	mark-white	prozymite	kieserite
corporate	antiquate	near-white	torbanite	geyserite
porporate	infatuate	lintwhite	vulcanite	elaterite
lectorate	reactuate	snow-white	manganite	preterite
rectorate	punctuate	lily-white	morganite	erythrite
doctorate	fluctuate	Wahabiite	polianite	Stagirite
pastorate	fructuate	phenakite	vivianite	meteorite
underrate	habituate	larvikite	ceylanite	anchorite
biserrate	eventuate	lardalite	sylvanite	feast-rite
water-rate	aggravate	socialite	Cobdenite	fulgurite
penetrate	re-elevate	marialite	hiddenite	tellurite
impetrate	khedivate	cheralite	wulfenite	Labourite
arbitrate	cultivate	theralite	zinkenite	favourite
denitrate	captivate	tantalite	austenite	hippurite
dioptrate	aestivate	Israelite	olivenite	typewrite
substrate	tittivate	scheelite	gelignite	overwrite
erostrate	binervate	nephelite	rabbinite	Stagyrite
prostrate	innervate	Carmelite	succinite	marcasite
first-rate	incurvate	ottrelite	coffinite	pargasite
flustrate	synoecete	corallite	gmelinite	anglesite
frustrate	logothete	rubellite	kaolinite	kermesite
carburate	nomothete	satellite	uraninite	magnesite
pandurate	sinoekete	wavellite	penninite	requisite
fulgurate	paraclete	covellite	vulpinite	exquisite
tellurate	dithelete	powellite	encrinite	epidosite
suppurate	décolleté	argillite	sylvinite	spilosite
micturate	locuplete	phacolite	belemnite	composite
triturate	zoogamete	laccolite	rhodonite	cerussite
insensate	isogamete	niccolite	Gibeonite	diphysite
intensate	Massorete	coccolite	Simeonite	goniatite
decussate	tête-à-tête	rhodolite	aragonite	haematite
pertusate	tinguaite	elaeolite	ceylonite	pegmatite
humectate	Rechabite	batholite	mammonite	Encratite
coarctate	Barnabite	sepiolite	Harmonite	enstatite
reluctate	snakebite	variolite	Mormonite	impactite
suscitate	columbite	tremolite	Mennonite	magnetite
flagitate		ichnolite	hessonite	granitite

cobaltite	epaulette	hylophyte	waldgrave	recursive
argentite	solenette	aerophyte	wildgrave	incursive
cementite	lorgnette	xerophyte	landgrave	excursive
carnotite	midinette	mesophyte	palsgrave	impassive
bipartite	serinette	ectophyte	suboctave	recessive
albertite	satinette	entophyte	rune-stave	excessive
proustite	jeannette	bryophyte	sound-wave	obsessive
muscovite	wagonette	eudialyte	pulse-wave	admissive
Muscovite	escopette	proselyte	brainwave	demissive
uvarovite	salopette	ampholyte	microwave	remissive
blood-wite	cigarette	hydrolyte	water-wave	diffusive
chabazite	soubrette	tachylyte	short-wave	perfusive
quartzite	usherette	colleague	parasceve	occlusive
bacchante	majorette	red-plague	sea-sleeve	reclusive
vigilante	Pierrette	gyrovague	land-reeve	seclusive
Rosinante	fleurette	distingué	wood-reeve	inclusive
Rozinante	amourette	outtongue	portreeve	exclusive
figurante	chevrette	pedagogue	unbelieve	prelusive
debutante	crossette	demagogue	champlevé	obtrusive
vivamente	poussette	synagogue	semibreve	intrusive
confronté	roussette	paragogue	yestereve	extrusive
hedge-bote	quintette	decalogue	embracive	contusive
house-bote	quartette	idealogue	subsecive	combative
theftbote	languette	trialogue	enhancive	probative
entrecôte	pirouette	catalogue	divorcive	siccative
sheep-cote	plaquette	ideologue	conducive	precative
redingote	briquette	theologue	crash-dive	fricative
holophote	etiquette	homologue	gerundive	evocative
papillote	banquette	Sinologue	power-dive	educative
stamp-note	croquette	monologue	undeceive	predative
undernote	statuette	land-value	spoil-five	laudative
chest-note	essayette	overvalue	forty-five	exudative
babacoote	storyette	news-value	revengive	purgative
asymptote	palafitte	steel-blue	superhive	sociative
monoptote	wyandotte	ortanique	dead-alive	radiative
predevote	charlotte	technique	wild-olive	mediative
eucaryote	retribute	véronique	self-drive	variative
eukaryote	attribute	demipique	overdrive	talkative
half-caste	prosecute	theorique	test-drive	inflative
overhaste	persecute	politique	assuasive	collative
post-haste	parachute	monocoque	pervasive	violative
pleonaste	waldflute	equivoque	precisive	prolative
hard-paste	nose-flute	bourasque	repulsive	isolative
puff-paste	dissolute	fantasque	impulsive	emulative
meat-paste	convolute	arabesque	expulsive	calmative
soft-paste	transmute	burlesque	revulsive	gemmative
foretaste	comminute	Junoesque	divulsive	summative
visagiste	autoroute	Dantesque	expansive	formative
dirigiste	disrepute	grotesque	ascensive	normative
simpliste	destitute	odalisque	defensive	emanative
arriviste	restitute	chibouque	offensive	urinative
langouste	institute	triptyque	expensive	vibrative
mangouste	leucocyte	meadow-rue	intensive	lucrative
estafette	phagocyte	side-issue	ostensive	operative
georgette	haemocyte	overissue	extensive	iterative
courgette	thymocyte	biconcave	implosive	narrative
couchette	fibrocyte	take-leave	explosive	pulsative
oubliette	macrocyte	sick-leave	purposive	causative
storiette	microcyte	folk-weave	corrosive	agitative
serviette	athrocyte	misbehave	aspersive	imitative
côtelette	endophyte	laticlave	detersive	writative
novelette	zygophyte	autoclave	inversive	tentative
paillette	halophyte	bond-slave	extorsive	quotative
tuillette	holophyte	Jack-slave	decursive	hortative

portative	retortive	misbelief	vanity-bag	unfolding
gestative	extortive	bas-relief	house-flag	beholding
gustative	digestive	outrelief	water-flag	upholding
privative	ingestive	tenor-clef	sweet-flag	demanding
curvative	arrestive	scaff-raff	pilot-flag	unbending
olfactive	resistive	handstaff	wallydrag	ascending
defective	executive	pikestaff	Reichstag	friending
affective	pollutive	flagstaff	scallawag	all-ending
effective	evolutive	jack-staff	scallywag	depending
infective	reflexive	packstaff	phillabeg	impending
objective	connexive	cowl-staff	phillibeg	unbinding
adjective	equivalve	whipstaff	beglerbeg	unwinding
selective	blowvalve	overstaff	sitzkrieg	abounding
humective	reinvolve	skew-whiff	square-leg	grounding
directive	patercove	plaintiff	jockteleg	ill-boding
detective	stock-dove	taking-off	spider-leg	regarding
invective	tug-of-love	setter-off	off-the-peg	rewarding
addictive	transmove	fisticuff	puzzle-peg	according
depictive	line-grove	ruff-a-duff	tuning-peg	recording
decoctive	cream-wove	cross-ruff	whore's-egg	shrouding
adductive	undeserve	feedstuff	whirligig	strouding
deductive	unreserve	food-stuff	guinea-pig	obtruding
reductive	archilowe	veinstuff	hairst-rig	well-being
seductive	double-axe	overstuff	whizz-bang	decreeing
inductive	battle-axe	leitmotif	chain-gang	all-seeing
forgetive	holing-axe	whale-calf	press-gang	far-seeing
depletive	cache-sexe	scrum-half	butty-gang	whingeing
expletive	tie-and-dye	bookshelf	cliffhang	swingeing
accretive	heddle-eye	underself	strap-hang	tiptoeing
decretive	swivel-eye	clock-golf	spur-whang	centreing
secretive	golden-eye	earthwolf	back-slang	tie-dyeing
excretive	saucer-eye	tiger-wolf	boom-slang	midwifing
lambitive	sheep's-eye	unheard-of	boomerang	packaging
traditive	tiger's-eye	wagon-roof	woomerang	vintaging
primitive	squint-eye	bombproof	ad-libbing	assuaging
dormitive	mother-lye	bead-proof	squibbing	besieging
cognitive	rybaudrye	page-proof	demobbing	de-bagging
aperitive	overglaze	fireproof	throbbing	spragging
nutritive	salt-glaze	ague-proof	scrubbing	sprigging
sensitive	overgraze	high-proof	bilimbing	strigging
factitive	sea-breeze	moth-proof	absorbing	effulging
partitive	hazardize	ball-proof	surfacing	revenging
intuitive	fortunize	foolproof	embracing	impinging
attuitive	overprize	rainproof	terracing	springing
incentive	queen-size	damp-proof	sufficing	stringing
resentive	wire-gauze	star-proof	rejoicing	diverging
assentive	F	overproof	unvoicing	bleaching
retentive	stone-deaf	shot-proof	romancing	preaching
intentive	broad-leaf	plot-proof	flouncing	fleeching
attentive	scale-leaf	dustproof	trouncing	breeching
adventive	table-leaf	rust-proof	traducing	flanching
inventive	title-leaf	under-roof	beheading	branching
plaintive	flame-leaf	G	spreading	stanching
promotive	loose-leaf	pounce-bag	unloading	wrenching
connotive	album-leaf	sponge-bag	degrading	quenching
acceptive	strip-leaf	saddle-bag	shredding	searching
deceptive	water-leaf	rattlebag	preceding	scorching
receptive	interleaf	muzzle-bag	exceeding	churching
inceptive	curry-leaf	string-bag	unheeding	thatching
exceptive	sugar-loaf	fardel-bag	screeding	fratching
irruptive	roast-beef	schoolbag	confiding	stitching
assertive	bully-beef	rennet-bag	cyaniding	switching
revertive	coral-reef	carpet-bag	nitriding	twitching
divertive	disbelief	monkey-bag	joy-riding	blotching

scutching	scumbling	metalling	twattling	inburning
slouching	thumbling	totalling	troutling	upburning
sleighing	grumbling	equalling	all-ruling	unturning
unsighing	troubling	squalling	scrawling	upturning
ploughing	treadling	rivalling	sprawling	lightning
splashing	twaddling	labelling	strayling	communing
thrashing	twiddling	debelling	screaming	undawning
sneeshing	wheedling	rebelling	streaming	frescoing
threshing	stridling	libelling	redeeming	well-doing
vanishing	worldling	excelling	beseeming	harm-doing
finishing	brandling	modelling	unseeming	race-going
punishing	spindling	refelling	subliming	foregoing
perishing	swindling	panelling	two-timing	down-going
ravishing	foundling	repelling	embalming	overgoing
unwishing	unfeeling	impelling	bedimming	play-going
upgushing	teaseling	cupelling	thrumming	easy-going
inrushing	nurseling	expelling	strumming	nielloing
sheathing	shaveling	gruelling	unharming	upheaping
breathing	chiefling	ravelling	disarming	filliping
something	whiffling	bevelling	presuming	bagpiping
do-nothing	shuffling	levelling	consuming	gossiping
smoothing	snuffling	revelling	chicaning	shrimping
Storthing	fledgling	jewelling	unmeaning	galloping
plaything	sniggling	bowelling	no-meaning	walloping
streaking	wriggling	rowelling	bemoaning	scrapping
squeaking	smuggling	towelling	deadening	strapping
cly-faking	spangling	upwelling	maddening	unripping
pin-making	brangling	infilling	puddening	stripping
topmaking	wrangling	upfilling	gardening	equipping
haymaking	twangling	schilling	screening	stropping
forsaking	shingling	perilling	deafening	estopping
partaking	swingling	shrilling	awakening	hiccuping
mistaking	youngling	thrilling	sickening	unbearing
unpacking	hatchling	cavilling	happening	endearing
thwacking	vetchling	devilling	lippening	unfearing
vraicking	fleshling	unwilling	softening	rehearing
mimicking	monthling	carolling	whitening	seafaring
panicking	earthling	enrolling	fastening	warfaring
finicking	unfailing	strolling	battening	misfaring
musicking	squailing	extolling	fattening	wayfaring
havocking	bewailing	annulling	rattening	ashlaring
shrieking	abseiling	potholing	leavening	unsparing
misliking	unveiling	schooling	designing	upstaring
unwinking	unsmiling	stripling	straining	thumb-ring
onlooking	untoiling	trampling	retaining	speldring
provoking	pantiling	crumpling	combining	guard-ring
embarking	crackling	crippling	confining	jabbering
underking	freckling	stippling	imagining	timbering
inworking	chickling	shearling	reclining	lumbering
unworking	prickling	niderling	inclining	niddering
unmasking	trickling	underling	examining	doddering
squawking	chuckling	steerling	adjoining	foddering
annealing	truckling	uncurling	japanning	wildering
appealing	Greekling	scantling	beginning	soldering
squealing	twinkling	plantling	jawboning	wandering
revealing	sparkling	saintling	pardoning	rendering
ting-a-ling	clerkling	heartling	visioning	tendering
drabbling	caballing	startling	reckoning	wondering
fribbling	emballing	courtling	gammoning	sundering
quibbling	medalling	wrestling	marooning	veneering
scambling	pedalling	whistling	reasoning	goffering
shambling	befalling	bristling	seasoning	suffering
brambling	phialling	firstling	lessoning	pilfering
trembling	appalling	brattling	governing	fingering

lingering	offspring	buffeting	unhatting	borrowing
mongering	outspring	fidgeting	squatting	sorrowing
ciphering	dayspring	budgeting	begetting	tuptowing
coshering	debarring	pargeting	go-getting	clearwing
gathering	embarring	racketing	besetting	underwing
withering	deferring	picketing	onsetting	liver-wing
mothering	referring	docketing	upsetting	downswing
wuthering	inferring	pocketing	revetting	right-wing
hankering	deterring	socketing	rivetting	defraying
tinkering	interring	bucketing	gazetting	missaying
ashlering	abhorring	Folketing	befitting	unstaying
hammering	occurring	junketing	refitting	steadying
yammering	recurring	marketing	unfitting	remedying
summering	incurring	billeting	splitting	embodying
diapering	demurring	filleting	admitting	parodying
tampering	bangsring	jenneting	remitting	surveying
tempering	gee-string	sonneting	immitting	tumefying
simpering	eye-string	carpeting	besitting	rarefying
coopering	maistring	ferreting	upsitting	codifying
peppering	hamstring	closeting	unwitting	modifying
coppering	bowstring	corseting	allotting	salifying
poppering	conjuring	cosseting	repotting	vilifying
raftering	non-juring	russeting	garotting	ramifying
waitering	murmuring	breveting	besotting	typifying
loitering	colouring	velveting	rebutting	verifying
faltering	vapouring	curveting	up-putting	purifying
weltering	inpouring	uplifting	strutting	ossifying
bantering	devouring	weighting	sprouting	ratifying
centering	measuring	blighting	fatiguing	notifying
mastering	venturing	profiting	engraving	down-lying
westering	torturing	ski-kiting	screeving	complying
sistering	fairy-ring	spiriting	believing	supplying
fostering	unceasing	unwriting	relieving	overlying
rostering	trapesing	unsuiting	sky-diving	mutinying
yattering	realising	desalting	forgiving	whinnying
bettering	promising	revolting	misgiving	canopying
gettering	surmising	occulting	outgiving	occupying
lettering	agonising	resulting	law-giving	unvarying
tittering	sunrising	insulting	surviving	descrying
pottering	cleansing	relenting	midwiving	quarrying
tottering	supposing	lamenting	revolving	flurrying
muttering	disposing	parenting	sea-roving	unpitying
slavering	relapsing	sprinting	reproving	unenvying
quavering	traipsing	squinting	improving	squeezing
shivering	reversing	flaunting	unnerving	apprizing
silvering	harassing	faggoting	observing	billabong
showering	finessing	balloting	deserving	underfong
flowering	caressing	uprooting	delta-wing	wobbegong
prize-ring	embussing	non-voting	sabre-wing	diphthong
scarf-ring	hocussing	excepting	goose-wing	currajong
troth-ring	sight-sing	prompting	whitewing	kurrajong
requiring	unamusing	departing	swing-wing	sing-along
inquiring	rehousing	thwarting	shadowing	cacholong
gemel-ring	chorusing	diverting	reflowing	nightlong
jingo-ring	combating	squirting	inflowing	binturong
authoring	sin-eating	reporting	wallowing	self-wrong
skijoring	repeating	unhasting	billowing	torch-song
sailoring	animating	unwasting	following	death-song
tailoring	operating	Landsting	unknowing	prick-song
exploring	regrating	unresting	winnowing	plainsong
mirroring	affecting	unsisting	ingrowing	undersong
factoring	expecting	Odelsting	upgrowing	currawong
cramp-ring	rabbeting	thrusting	harrowing	delundung
cee-spring	unweeting	rabatting	narrowing	underhung

hamstrung	decastich	Jew's-pitch	lagomorph	jellyfish
bowstrung	octastich	hem-stitch	allomorph	tunny-fish
wasp-stung	hexastich	dip-switch	homomorph	strongish
cat-and-dog	telestich	hop-scotch	xeromorph	bakhshish
police-dog	hemistich	cranreuch	mesomorph	backshish
poodle-dog	monostich	Hexateuch	ectomorph	buckshish
sleeve-dog	tsarevich	forasmuch	polymorph	smoothish
badger-dog	czarevich	musk-pouch	frithborh	Slovakish
dog-eat-dog	Greenwich	slop-pouch	ground-ash	unbookish
yellow-dog	anabranch	disavouch	interdash	establish
ground-hog	subbranch	polyptych	news-flash	fribblish
dannebrog	disbranch	gallabieh	cornbrash	republish
inselberg	free-bench	medresseh	gatecrash	disrelish
dramaturg	back-bench	dahabiyeh	cane-trash	un-English
shield-bug	nut-wrench	bobsleigh	succotash	gentilish
coffee-bug	flax-wench	foreweigh	whitewash	embellish
tumble-bug	pack-cinch	overweigh	toothwash	tol-lolish
doodlebug	goldfinch	ultra-high	mouthwash	startlish
jitterbug	pine-finch	waist-high	black-wash	squeamish
litter-bug	chaffinch	camsheugh	brainwash	Germanish
claret-jug	bullfinch	kink-cough	sheep-wash	maidenish
spark-plug	snow-finch	chincough	baksheesh	hoydenish
hearth-rug	outlaunch	sour-dough	nun's-flesh	spleenish
prayer-rug	hand-punch	rib-plough	squabbish	replenish
H	card-punch	cuddeehih	refurbish	kittenish
djellabah	rack-punch	tragelaph	snuff-dish	Londonish
gallabeah	milk-punch	skiagraph	clackdish	dragonish
dahabeeah	bell-punch	cymagraph	uplandish	premonish
gallabiah	monotroch	paragraph	cavendish	mammonish
alleluiah	roundarch	telegraph	scald-fish	sermonish
maharajah	chiliarch	marigraph	blindfish	baboonish
shillelah	matriarch	serigraph	hound-fish	parsonish
mashallah	patriarch	eidograph	round-fish	degarnish
inshallah	scholarch	hodograph	swordfish	refurnish
boxwallah	dead-march	ideograph	globe-fish	unfurnish
bismillah	polemarch	oleograph	spike-fish	viragoish
ayatollah	frogmarch	logograph	scale-fish	Tocharish
shamianah	slow-march	ergograph	swine-fish	Tokharish
Shechinah	trierarch	idiograph	stonefish	outparish
pergunnah	squirarch	allograph	snipe-fish	gibberish
madrassah	Aristarch	holograph	goose-fish	loaferish
barmizvah	pike-perch	xylograph	whitefish	niggerish
basmizvah	rock-perch	homograph	sting-fish	ratherish
batmizvah	overperch	nomograph	blackfish	Quakerish
dahabiyah	blowtorch	tomograph	stockfish	lickerish
galabiyah	dischurch	cymograph	trunkfish	copperish
sgian-dubh	backfisch	kymograph	coral-fish	bitterish
cailleach	Roumansch	monograph	angel-fish	cleverish
sea-breach	overcatch	barograph	unselfish	quiverish
headreach	cony-catch	aerograph	jewelfish	authorish
forereach	love-match	cerograph	snail-fish	liquorish
overreach	cockmatch	rotograph	April-fish	vapourish
taoiseach	overmatch	autograph	devil-fish	vulturish
foreteach	test-match	polygraph	shellfish	prelatish
cailliach	slow-match	logogriph	trawl-fish	strictish
Sassenach	sasquatch	perilymph	cramp-fish	slightish
mail-coach	doomwatch	endolymph	spearfish	un-British
slip-coach	stop-watch	paranymph	amber-fish	sallowish
slowcoach	overwatch	wood-nymph	razor-fish	tallowish
cockroach	bomb-ketch	autotroph	crossfish	yellowish
sandarach	milk-vetch	gymnosoph	sheat-fish	willowish
bacharach	last-ditch	paramorph	sweetfish	marrowish
Ausgleich	half-hitch	perimorph	pilot-fish	Mondayish
soothlich	overpitch	endomorph	Tartufish	monkeyish

9 -ISH

twentyish	pyracanth	goalmouth	wind-break	bootblack
thirtyish	chrysanth	home-truth	fire-break	foreslack
prettyish	fifteenth	half-truth	jail-break	well-smack
macintosh	umpteenth	misgrowth	gaol-break	pickapack
salt-marsh	sixteenth	outgrowth	snow-break	barmbrack
spice-bush	terebinth	**I**	redstreak	sand-crack
smoke-bush	labyrinth	lamaserai	lapstreak	wisecrack
scrog-bush	billionth	dziggetai	beefsteak	music-rack
thorn-bush	millionth	gonococci	pipsqueak	sword-rack
underbush	colocynth	garibaldi	krakowiak	plate-rack
caper-bush	Ostrogoth	jaborandi	pontianak	towel-rack
overflush	piña-cloth	latifondi	ground-oak	racetrack
four-flush	headcloth	coryphaei	poison-oak	side-track
sagebrush	gold-cloth	pronuclei	forest-oak	pipe-track
shoe-brush	face-cloth	Ricinulei	zamboorak	half-track
nail-brush	cere-cloth	Teleostei	yakety-yak	Minitrack ®
hair-brush	forecloth	Lotophagi	yakity-yak	backtrack
dust-brush	long-cloth	bahuvrihi	pickaback	toast-rack
spike-rush	wash-cloth	maharishi	huckaback	cart-track
ant-thrush	dish-cloth	Gujarathi	ridgeback	dirt-track
blood-bath	back-cloth	Gujerathi	whale-back	hornwrack
earth-bath	pack-cloth	octonarii	leaseback	haversack
water-bath	sackcloth	comitadji	horseback	thumb-tack
megadeath	neck-cloth	kathakali	write-back	peat-stack
philomath	sail-cloth	campanili	sling-back	pinchbeck
aftermath	barm-cloth	prothalli	swing-back	three-deck
Jagannath	loin-cloth	stornelli	hunchback	'tween-deck
flare-path	haircloth	fasciculi	hatchback	underdeck
homeopath	tent-cloth	homunculi	notchback	water-deck
osteopath	footcloth	ranunculi	touch-back	lower-deck
sociopath	mortcloth	patchouli	flash-back	raincheck
neuropath	tray-cloth	glomeruli	breakback	overcheck
feldspath	plume-moth	Pakistani	crookback	pass-check
hundredth	tiger-moth	fettucini	camelback	spot-check
foreteeth	grass-moth	contadini	shellback	snowfleck
ninetieth	wheat-moth	vetturini	greenback	goose-neck
eightieth	ghost-moth	lazzaroni	thornback	stiff-neck
twentieth	tollbooth	Pedipalpi	sweepback	rough-neck
thirtieth	foretooth	Zanzibari	paperback	breakneck
brandreth	wolf-tooth	zamindari	razor-back	shipwreck
Ashtoreth	wang-tooth	zemindari	fight-back	place-kick
cholelith	pick-tooth	Rastafari	fightback	skinflick
phacolith	bucktooth	kalamkari	swept-back	snowflick
laccolith	milk-tooth	Carbonari	swart-back	toothpick
coccolith	mill-tooth	pifferari	piggyback	gold-brick
batholith	dog's-tooth	impresari	fishyback	firebrick
sialolith	Ashtaroth	charivari	rusty-back	bath-brick
cyclolith	beef-broth	eleutheri	bushwhack	rope-trick
rhinolith	cook-broth	decemviri	bullwhack	overtrick
microlith	hell-broth	triumviri	lance-jack	brainsick
statolith	alembroth	pot-pourri	smoke-jack	heart-sick
cystolith	snow-broth	chaprassi	ankle-jack	fancy-sick
bathylith	shophroth	foederati	apple-jack	sheep-tick
goldsmith	bone-earth	sgraffiti	blackjack	crabstick
wordsmith	rare-earth	contralti	cheap-jack	knob-stick
jokesmith	cave-earth	bummaloti	river-jack	headstick
tunesmith	cole-garth	eucalypti	crossjack	goldstick
songsmith	fish-garth	spaghetti	pilot-jack	yardstick
jacksmith	sick-berth	scarpetti	bone-black	fire-stick
locksmith	live-birth	**K**	shoeblack	metestick
ironsmith	twin-birth	area-sneak	blue-black	buff-stick
therewith	stalworth	unbespeak	coal-black	flagstick
wherewith	loudmouth	forespeak	hell-black	gong-stick
forthwith	frogmouth	sand-break	lamp-black	nickstick

rickstick	eider-duck	overstink	framework	fatidical
mahlstick	decoy-duck	kiddywink	stonework	druidical
maulstick	woodchuck	honky-tonk	falsework	monodical
drumstick	fork-chuck	dandyfunk	housework	synodical
pogo-stick	corn-shuck	dead-drunk	out-of-work	parodical
slapstick	dumb-cluck	tree-trunk	coachwork	venefical
trap-stick	mallemuck	overstunk	patchwork	pacifical
gear-stick	awe-struck	springbok	swashwork	mirifical
joss-stick	sunstruck	guard-book	brushwork	illogical
seat-stick	half-cheek	guide-book	earthwork	unlogical
bailiwick	door-cheek	table-book	handiwork	psychical
Zernebock	house-leek	style-book	brickwork	graphical
steinbock	fenugreek	waste-book	clockwork	nymphical
pinchcock	open-steek	block-book	stockwork	unethical
heathcock	Ember-week	psalm-book	trunk-work	angelical
pillicock	hygrodeik	scrap-book	metal-work	umbilical
blackcock	refusenik	order-book	wheelwork	basilical
ouzel-cock	Raskolnik	class-book	steelwork	bucolical
storm-cock	chinovnik	press-book	shellwork	dynamical
water-cock	Bolshevik	story-book	chainwork	endemical
dandy-cock	Menshevik	plain-cook	plainwork	polemical
billycock	table-talk	undercook	drawn-work	thermical
poppycock	small-talk	clove-hook	crownwork	seismical
wood-shock	seed-stalk	flesh-hook	strap-work	organical
foreshock	yoke-stalk	spoon-hook	scamp-work	satanical
hollyhock	sales-talk	sheep-hook	stump-work	botanical
chubb-lock	leaf-stalk	grasshook	underwork	Galenical
roadblock	beanstalk	ingle-nook	poker-work	arsenical
woodblock	cornstalk	bully-rook	water-work	technical
back-block	cross-talk	undertook	interwork	dominical
jack-block	footstalk	spoil-bark	stair-work	laconical
joss-block	sweet-talk	shellbark	glasswork	obconical
tint-block	boardwalk	disembark	press-work	canonical
time-clock	sheepwalk	crown-bark	guesswork	Aaronical
hause-lock	crosswalk	cramp-bark	shift-work	chronical
matchlock	night-walk	scaly-bark	night-work	untypical
stock-lock	churn-milk	pitch-dark	frostwork	lumbrical
wheel-lock	nitro-silk	land-shark	fancywork	spherical
wagon-lock	womenfolk	loan-shark	handywork	etherical
scalp-lock	townsfolk	thumb-mark	water-cask	numerical
interlock	shear-hulk	floodmark	bergamask	generical
flintlock	sheer-hulk	trademark	death-mask	icterical
lady-smock	cantabank	plate-mark	bergomask	empirical
antiknock	weigh-bank	caste-mark	visor-mask	satirical
coat-frock	interbank	shelf-mark	plaid-neuk	centrical
coral-rock	river-bank	proof-mark	zumbooruk	satyrical
bobbysock	right-bank	bench-mark	eagle-hawk	whimsical
headstock	piggy-bank	touch-mark	stone-hawk	dropsical
feedstock	penny-bank	birthmark	night-hawk	classical
vine-stock	pick-thank	shoal-mark	mollymawk	unmusical
livestock	gangplank	watermark	L	sciatical
bank-stock	front-rank	press-mark	Landsmaal	ismatical
whip-stock	think-tank	cutty-sark	nachtmaal	fanatical
overstock	pen-and-ink	antiquark	preverbal	venatical
lintstock	forethink	steenkirk	dandiacal	agnatical
rootstock	snow-blink	burnt-cork	cardiacal	hepatical
prongbuck	interlink	slave-fork	elegiacal	piratical
blackbuck	index-link	pitchfork	theriacal	erratical
water-buck	clove-pink	fieldwork	Hebraical	practical
sheldduck	goldspink	piece-work	prosaical	ascetical
shielduck	gowdspink	spadework	monadical	mimetical
shellduck	alms-drink	parge-work	aphidical	genetical
raven-duck	diet-drink	scale-work	veridical	kinetical
scaup-duck	pre-shrink	table-work	juridical	heretical

ascitical	whole-meal	uncordial	textorial	regiminal
political	pease-meal	preludial	mercurial	abdominal
soritical	witch-meal	collegial	centurial	binominal
pyritical	wheat-meal	vestigial	dichasial	cacuminal
levitical	sweetmeal	uropygial	gymnasial	voluminal
quantical	calcaneal	pterygial	ecclesial	doctrinal
identical	cochineal	petechial	symposial	abactinal
idiotical	stamineal	branchial	ambrosial	diactinal
sceptical	pectineal	rhonchial	prelatial	matutinal
cryptical	dyspnoeal	bronchial	primatial	decagonal
styptical	sex-appeal	parochial	primitial	octagonal
deistical	nectareal	anarchial	cadential	hexagonal
eristical	marmoreal	vindemial	sciential	polygonal
gnostical	corporeal	paroemial	essential	versional
indexical	purpureal	trinomial	potential	torsional
frenzical	underseal	congenial	impartial	passional
quizzical	water-seal	vaccinial	unpartial	sessional
Provençal	popliteal	uredinial	celestial	stational
equivocal	foresteal	decennial	agrestial	factional
obeliscal	endosteal	vicennial	preputial	pactional
archducal	subniveal	triennial	syncytial	sectional
forbiddal	vice-regal	perennial	obsequial	fictional
back-pedal	phalangal	octennial	khedivial	tuitional
soft-pedal	pharyngal	novennial	convivial	emotional
regicidal	synagogal	sexennial	effluvial	emptional
homicidal	basifugal	marsupial	ingluvial	fluxional
feticidal	stomachal	bursarial	epitaxial	monsoonal
genocidal	distichal	nectarial	polyaxial	piperonal
pyramidal	monarchal	sectarial	trapezial	polytonal
phacoidal	seneschal	actuarial	erythemal	embryonal
discoidal	mareschal	estuarial	undecimal	polyzonal
fungoidal	marischal	funebrial	isochimal	hodiernal
xiphoidal	triumphal	manubrial	vicesimal	fraternal
typhoidal	catarrhal	synedrial	vigesimal	coeternal
lithoidal	sublethal	subaerial	prodromal	eviternal
cycloidal	Emmenthal	vizierial	liposomal	hesternal
cheloidal	betrothal	uniserial	autosomal	pre-vernal
colloidal	azimuthal	bacterial	epidermal	nocturnal
amyloidal	microbial	enchorial	exodermal	diuturnal
sigmoidal	adverbial	authorial	conformal	blind-coal
ethmoidal	connubial	signorial	subnormal	stone-coal
adenoidal	prefacial	censorial	coseismal	block-coal
glenoidal	trifacial	sensorial	baptismal	small-coal
crinoidal	edificial	tonsorial	trionymal	steam-coal
hypnoidal	orificial	cursorial	toponymal	paper-coal
negroidal	surficial	fossorial	isocrymal	antipapal
mastoidal	altricial	viatorial	lachrymal	municipal
rhizoidal	rusticial	amatorial	ring-canal	principal
prebendal	financial	oratorial	ship-canal	episcopal
antinodal	semuncial	factorial	bacchanal	antitypal
decapodal	precocial	rectorial	olecranal	homotypal
antipodal	dissocial	sectorial	fog-signal	palpebral
subcaudal	triradial	tectorial	cloacinal	vertebral
hypogaeal	perradial	vectorial	medicinal	penumbral
perinaeal	epicedial	pictorial	officinal	subsacral
beau-ideal	stapedial	doctorial	vaticinal	trihedral
interdeal	rachidial	auctorial	calycinal	cathedral
meningeal	sporidial	suctorial	libidinal	illiberal
syringeal	presidial	editorial	paludinal	poriferal
uncongeal	gerundial	cantorial	semifinal	rotiferal
laryngeal	sympodial	mentorial	synclinal	armigeral
coccygeal	episodial	tentorial	isoclinal	isotheral
diarrheal	prosodial	raptorial	sudaminal	bicameral
piecemeal	custodial	sartorial	foraminal	ephemeral

puerperal	bicipital	dash-wheel	clout-nail	light-ball
bilateral	ancipital	mill-wheel	screw-nail	screwball
biliteral	recruital	worm-wheel	guard-rail	bandy-ball
cleithral	sextantal	gear-wheel	guide-rail	bugle-call
antiviral	placental	star-wheel	plate-rail	trunk-call
duumviral	percental	four-wheel	towel-rail	quail-call
seed-coral	tridental	spur-wheel	water-rail	photocall
stercoral	submental	cartwheel	night-rail	party-call
seignoral	elemental	bilge-keel	smoke-sail	earthfall
exosporal	segmental	fish-creel	storm-sail	waterfall
electoral	tegmental	peat-creel	drift-sail	crossfall
chaparral	pigmental	conger-eel	spritsail	nightfall
diametral	alimental	cockateel	broadtail	shortfall
symmetral	Simmental	ungenteel	sword-tail	crown-gall
subastral	isodontal	cast-steel	horsetail	water-gall
cadastral	anecdotal	archangel	mouse-tail	glass-gall
Monastral	antidotal	astrophel	disentail	music-hall
ancestral	sclerotal	moygashel	tiger-tail	guildhall
semestral	subcostal	arc-en-ciel	mare's-tail	dance-hall
fenestral	committal	schlemiel	cart's-tail	Whitehall
magistral	acquittal	Domdaniel	shirt-tail	cloth-hall
sinistral	epiphytal	langspiel	forky-tail	ring-small
cloistral	bilingual	singspiel	widow-wail	governall
claustral	subungual	cockatiel	envermeil	headstall
plaustral	continual	mispickel	nonpareil	homestall
palustral	menstrual	schnorkel	Turcophil	forestall
subneural	effectual	entrammel	audiophil	backstall
inaugural	aspectual	personnel	anglophil	bookstall
creatural	revictual	uncharnel	gallophil	reinstall
unnatural	perpetual	pimpernel	ombrophil	whipstall
post-nasal	spiritual	sans-appel	negrophil	neat-stall
appraisal	accentual	reapparel	hygrophil	foot-stall
paradisal	commutual	unapparel	Russophil	stonewall
comprisal	unisexual	scoundrel	photophil	multi-wall
surprisal	pansexual	groundsel	Slavophil	brickwall
commensal	longaeval	ring-ousel	spark-coil	river-wall
squamosal	mediaeval	moschatel	level-coil	party-wall
rehearsal	primaeval	barbastel	almond-oil	death-bell
dispersal	rounceval	holy-cruel	multifoil	bonnibell
subversal	reprieval	spirituel	hydrofoil	alarm-bell
universal	retrieval	pay-gravel	eight-foil	larum-bell
disbursal	ablatival	outtravel	castor-oil	night-bell
succursal	relatival	dead-level	undersoil	guard-cell
subvassal	genitival	high-level	night-soil	stone-cell
dismissal	disproval	anti-novel	courbaril	nerve-cell
pertussal	disavowal	spur-rowel	Yggdrasil	death-cell
rearousal	antefixal	handtowel	Largactil ®	canal-cell
reperusal	paradoxal	dish-towel	sea-lentil	sperm-cell
antenatal	portrayal	semivowel	tormentil	photocell
perinatal	half-royal	wych-hazel	sand-devil	water-cell
post-natal	pair-royal	shlimazel	yoke-devil	ensorcell
dialectal	spur-royal	ring-ouzel	dare-devil	astrofell
oviductal	pre-cancel	schlemihl	demi-devil	dratchell
road-metal	pennoncel	drink-hail	dust-devil	bombshell
hard-metal	involucel	blackmail	nut-weevil	hardshell
type-metal	lark's-heel	trunk-mail	king's-evil	date-shell
leaf-metal	band-wheel	chain-mail	speed-ball	half-shell
bush-metal	hind-wheel	thumbnail	smoke-ball	wing-shell
semi-metal	side-wheel	spike-nail	beach-ball	tusk-shell
bell-metal	free-wheel	pond-snail	punch-ball	clam-shell
basipetal	idle-wheel	wing-snail	dough-ball	aeroshell
acropetal	fore-wheel	frost-nail	blackball	lamp-shell
isohyetal	nose-wheel		stink-ball	harp-shell
occipital	buff-wheel		stoolball	tear-shell

9 -ELL

star-shell	choke-full	praiseful	water-fowl	Brummagem
soft-shell	avizefull	reposeful	night-fowl	stratagem
bodyshell	chock-full	spriteful	shriek-owl	Jerusalem
pannikell	chuck-full	behoveful	jobernowl	title-poem
ritornell	multihull	throngful	trimethyl	prose-poem
play-spell	numbskull	speechful	polyvinyl	straw-stem
undersell	knapskull	unbashful	isopropyl	ecosystem
speedwell	snuff-mull	unwishful	tridactyl	chernozem
bridewell	cataphyll	breathful	syndactyl	diaphragm
stair-well	mesophyll	lengthful	hypocotyl	epiphragm
knee-swell	terpineol	healthful	M	logarithm
overswell	panthenol	unpitiful	commendam	algorithm
sword-bill	undercool	plentiful	coffer-dam	quit-claim
hedgebill	supercool	bountiful	scale-beam	Sephardim
watch-bill	water-cool	beautiful	whitebeam	Midrashim
acock-bill	court-fool	undutiful	quickbeam	have-at-him
spoonbill	preschool	barrelful	crossbeam	broad-brim
razor-bill	ski-school	shovelful	truss-beam	Sanhedrim
hawksbill	day-school	unskilful	foregleam	machzorim
crossbill	whirlpool	unharmful	full-cream	phantasim
crow's-bill	toadstool	spleenful	pipe-dream	literatim
money-bill	faldstool	gowpenful	midstream	kibbutzim
piccadill	camp-stool	designful	off-stream	peach-palm
spauld-ill	footstool	ungainful	jetstream	sugar-palm
aspergill	pixy-stool	unpainful	white-seam	macaw-palm
flirt-gill	steel-wool	unhelpful	monk's-seam	toddy-palm
treadmill	lamb's-wool	teacupful	bairn-team	ivory-palm
stone-mill	carvacrol	unfearful	phaenogam	Stahlhelm
snuff-mill	decontrol	saucerful	cryptogam	overwhelm
waulk-mill	house-carl	wonderful	mutton-ham	sound-film
stamp-mill	seed-pearl	hungerful	petersham	microfilm
sugar-mill	shell-marl	masterful	Malayalam	Houyhnhnm
paper-mill	goose-girl	wasterful	razor-clam	princedom
water-mill	paper-girl	matterful	tetragram	Yankeedom
light-mill	choir-girl	quiverful	pentagram	enfreedom
grist-mill	salesgirl	showerful	cablegram	savagedom
overspill	bunny-girl	prayerful	tephigram	Bumbledom
seed-drill	rhizocaul	colourful	calligram	beadledom
knee-drill	steam-haul	stressful	centigram	noodledom
fire-drill	backspaul	threatful	tachogram	puzzledom
pack-drill	caterwaul	streetful	nephogram	squiredom
rock-drill	unheedful	forgetful	sociogram	sheikhdom
drop-drill	unneedful	pocketful	radiogram	polypidom
cross-sill	remindful	bucketful	audiogram	rascaldom
check-till	unmindful	basketful	angiogram	thralldom
sea-squill	regardful	regretful	sialogram	cuckoldom
crow-quill	rewardful	plightful	pyelogram	sachemdom
come-o'-will	choiceful	frightful	anemogram	bishopdom
glycocoll	adviceful	deceitful	phonogram	beggardom
Hobbinoll	deviceful	spiritful	microgram	dufferdom
catchpoll	chanceful	resultful	hierogram	niggerdom
doddipoll	strifeful	resentful	deprogram	Quakerdom
dottipoll	grudgeful	plaintful	ferrogram	junkerdom
doddypoll	changeful	unhurtful	neurogram	kaiserdom
music-roll	avengeful	molestful	hectogram	masterdom
death-roll	chargeful	unrestful	pictogram	martyrdom
rock-'n'-roll	scatheful	thirstful	photogram	wagenboom
poor's-roll	rebukeful	sorrowful	cartogram	doorn-boom
comptroll	needleful	dismayful	histogram	zinc-bloom
court-roll	kettleful	proconsul	cheong-sam	broadloom
dandy-roll	bottleful	back-crawl	opobalsam	overgloom
sting-bull	untuneful	punch-bowl	misbeseem	power-loom
water-bull	unhopeful	scrub-fowl	disesteem	music-room
knapscull	uncareful	heath-fowl	misesteem	breadroom

boardroom	jelliform	earthworm	Orangeism	Powellism
guard-room	villiform	auger-worm	tritheism	diabolism
smoke-room	cauliform	churr-worm	pantheism	anabolism
storeroom	styliform	wheat-worm	egotheism	symbolism
house-room	mammiform	taint-worm	zootheism	mongolism
plate-room	mummiform	joint-worm	misoneism	epipolism
stateroom	vermiform	straw-worm	Monroeism	Carlylism
staffroom	cteniform	screw-worm	Tartufism	Ockhamism
shelfroom	aciniform	Landsturm	falangism	bedlamism
herd-groom	spiniform	Hesychasm	vikingism	euphemism
stud-groom	penniform	cataclasm	Irvingism	Moslemism
crush-room	corniform	cataplasm	syllogism	extremism
cloakroom	salpiform	metaplasm	panlogism	Muslimism
stack-room	fibriform	germ-plasm	neologism	pessimism
checkroom	cobriform	endoplasm	monergism	reformism
stock-room	floriform	idioplasm	synergism	volcanism
grill-room	capriform	alloplasm	monachism	vulcanism
still-room	cirriform	ectoplasm	catechism	Orleanism
greenroom	mitriform	cytoplasm	Munichism	mechanism
classroom	vitriform	sporidesm	fetichism	orphanism
press-room	tauriform	chaldaism	masochism	Fabianism
chartroom	versiform	Mithraism	anarchism	Sabianism
guest-room	bursiform	syllabism	churchism	Magianism
elbow-room	cactiform	labdacism	eunuchism	Fenianism
therefrom	tectiform	Syriacism	amorphism	Syrianism
wherefrom	multiform	ostracism	fetishism	shamanism
maelstrom	dentiform	rhotacism	Wahabiism	pelmanism
unchrisom	lentiform	monoecism	swarajism	Germanism
reblossom	septiform	synoecism	phenakism	Montanism
emblossom	restiform	mosaicism	cabbalism	galvanism
sea-bottom	cystiform	Gothicism	tribalism	Cobdenism
store-farm	scutiform	mythicism	verbalism	hoydenism
truck-farm	anguiform	italicism	rascalism	Origenism
trout-farm	unguiform	biblicism	mescalism	lichenism
dairy-farm	claviform	cyclicism	vandalism	hyphenism
strongarm	pelviform	gaelicism	feudalism	Hellenism
love-charm	vulviform	anglicism	unrealism	ecumenism
fire-alarm	larviform	gallicism	nephalism	Jansenism
queen's-arm	curviform	irenicism	labialism	cocainism
placoderm	plexiform	ethnicism	racialism	rabbinism
osteoderm	Cominform	physicism	socialism	Stalinism
pachyderm	Kominform	poeticism	serialism	diclinism
wheat-germ	misinform	Briticism	curialism	Paulinism
ectotherm	unconform	criticism	animalism	terminism
eurytherm	bromoform	triticism	formalism	vulpinism
perisperm	microform	Celticism	pennalism	Petrinism
endosperm	transform	Kelticism	atonalism	cretinism
zygosperm	dress-form	eroticism	carnalism	voltinism
short-term	cairngorm	exoticism	rhopalism	routinism
disaffirm	sand-storm	vorticism	amoralism	Calvinism
reconfirm	line-storm	mysticism	pluralism	Darwinism
cambiform	fire-storm	witticism	tantalism	Ribbonism
cymbiform	hail-storm	Sadducism	mentalism	draconism
bacciform	rainstorm	tribadism	crotalism	aniconism
sacciform	barnstorm	Poujadism	casualism	Gasconism
falciform	dust-storm	hybridism	ritualism	Londonism
lanciform	snowstorm	Chasidism	mutualism	dragonism
perciform	blindworm	Hassidism	sexualism	fusionism
pisciform	round-worm	Girondism	Mendelism	mammonism
cruciform	blood-worm	methodism	dithelism	Mormonism
eruciform	gourd-worm	do-goodism	Ismailism	Platonism
cordiform	flukeworm	Yankeeism	puerilism	Daltonism
cuneiform	angle-worm	Parseeism	gentilism	Miltonism
fungiform	fleshworm	sutteeism	servilism	Teutonism

Plutonism	solipsism	mausoleum	plutonium	snare-drum
modernism	sabbatism	calcaneum	Alcyonium	storm-drum
saturnism	defeatism	prytaneum	neptunium	conundrum
communism	prelatism	castoreum	encolpium	antiserum
panegoism	sigmatism	colosseum	ectropium	barathrum
albinoism	dogmatism	endosteum	entropium	pyrethrum
voodooism	animatism	fee-faw-fum	marsupium	indecorum
dichroism	thanatism	cowdie-gum	Gossypium	zygantrum
Averroism	Encratism	bubble-gum	herbarium	colostrum
Shintoism	sovietism	spirit-gum	caldarium	claustrum
hylozoism	magnetism	excambium	sacrarium	responsum
red-tapism	phonetism	nelumbium	terrarium	ultimatum
barbarism	klephtism	columbium	septarium	separatum
Pindarism	Babbitism	epilobium	manubrium	emplectum
welfarism	mephitism	coenobium	synedrium	vitecetum
vulgarism	Adamitism	rhizobium	pomoerium	salicetum
gargarism	eremitism	ytterbium	elaterium	quercetum
Catharism	spiritism	Hieracium	bacterium	combretum
Caesarism	Jesuitism	gynoecium	deuterium	arboretum
Magyarism	occultism	americium	triforium	diatretum
tenebrism	pedantism	palladium	Cichorium	equisetum
ex-librism	gigantism	epicedium	sensorium	quaesitum
hetaerism	tarantism	cymbidium	tentorium	asphaltum
ganderism	scientism	coccidium	anthurium	submentum
panderism	narcotism	pycnidium	tellurium	tegmentum
careerism	zealotism	rhipidium	collyrium	sarmentum
dufferism	hypnotism	Pteridium	dichasium	tormentum
niggerism	despotism	sporidium	gymnasium	prescutum
Lutherism	dicrotism	presidium	magnesium	Symphytum
shakerism	quixotism	diacodium	symposium	continuum
Quakerism	rebaptism	desmodium	potassium	menstruum
junkerism	Utraquism	sympodium	helvetium	pseudonym
Hitlerism	passivism	tripudium	hospitium	heteronym
isomerism	bashawism	contagium	strontium	cryptonym
mesmerism	Hebrewism	collegium	Cerastium	N
Wagnerism	Grundyism	fastigium	syncytium	basilican
mannerism	jockeyism	vestigium	zoocytium	spellican
pauperism	monkeyism	synangium	deliquium	Dominican
kaiserism	prettyism	uropygium	effluvium	Armorican
ranterism	neo-Nazism	pterygium	impluvium	molluscan
neoterism	Spinozism	magnalium	trapezium	antelucan
Pooterism	macrocosm	dentalium	flabellum	meropidan
esoterism	microcosm	berkelium	cribellum	qualamdan
Listerism	cataclysm	beryllium	flagellum	decapodan
cauterism	Taraxacum	trifolium	vulsellum	amoebaean
erythrism	vade-mecum	prooemium	clitellum	Chaldaean
hetairism	colchicum	Gelsemium	castellum	hypogaean
memoirism	Hypericum	neodymium	rostellum	Notogaean
vampirism	practicum	germanium	scutellum	Mycenaean
meteorism	Verbascum	drepanium	spirillum	Pyrenaean
Gongorism	avisandum	achaenium	sensillum	Dodonaean
authorism	avizandum	ruthenium	hordeolum	Nabataean
meliorism	reddendum	Asplenium	sugar-plum	Maccabean
apriorism	credendum	vaccinium	tenaculum	tonga-bean
tutiorism	hypogaeum	glucinium	reticulum	tonka-bean
terrorism	nymphaeum	uredinium	operculum	Caribbean
hectorism	Athenaeum	virginium	opusculum	broad-bean
historism	perinaeum	pollinium	capitulum	sword-bean
Camorrism	Mithraeum	aluminium	diachylum	sugar-bean
epicurism	gastraeum	decennium	subphylum	Chalybean
voyeurism	gynaeceum	zirconium	lanthanum	jellybean
labourism	propodeum	purdonium	sagapenum	Laodicean
vulturism	salt-rheum	euphonium	polygonum	Sadducean
lathyrism	petroleum	harmonium	Saccharum	Euclidean

jaspidean	periscian	prosimian	topiarian	Dinantian
acaridean	antiscian	Neocomian	Euskarian	Terentian
Hebridean	Traducian	neonomian	palmarian	Mozartian
floridean	Confucian	volcanian	planarian	lacertian
cystidean	Barbadian	vulcanian	librarian	nemertian
Manichean	circadian	Dardanian	Caesarian	Christian
Sisyphean	Palladian	Jordanian	sectarian	Proustian
Tantalean	steradian	Tasmanian	dietarian	Cracovian
Heraclean	Dalradian	Roumanian	Unitarian	Muscovian
Periclean	epicedian	Sassanian	septarian	Pavlovian
Damoclean	tragedian	Ruthenian	Tartarian	Harrovian
Achillean	rachidian	Slovenian	Ripuarian	Vitruvian
Lucullean	acaridian	Ukrainian	estuarian	semi-bajan
mausolean	Hebridian	Sardinian	dimyarian	myrobalan
Herculean	quotidian	Virginian	meandrian	castellan
Acheulean	Dravidian	Paulinian	cerberian	cameraman
caerulean	prosodian	Rosminian	Napierian	odd-jobman
Carlylean	custodian	Aretinian	Millerian	groundman
misdemean	Ricardian	Darwinian	Keplerian	policeman
calcanean	Edwardian	Serbonian	Cimmerian	sallee-man
Johannean	Oxfordian	draconian	Wagnerian	unfreeman
Meliboean	sherifian	Uriconian	Wernerian	Orangeman
cyclopean	Tartufian	Londonian	Turnerian	charge-man
cornopean	collegian	sardonian	Popperian	scytheman
Menippean	Galwegian	gorgonian	Hesperian	birlieman
Euterpean	Norwegian	Typhonian	bacterian	stable-man
Caesarean	Varangian	Bathonian	Hunterian	muscle-man
nectarean	gambogian	chthonian	Listerian	raddleman
Tartarean	neologian	Esthonian	Oliverian	reddleman
Cytherean	Pelasgian	chelonian	Isidorian	middleman
Solutrean	coccygian	Memnonian	Gregorian	ruddleman
Epicurean	Walachian	Brunonian	censorian	sickleman
gigantean	selachian	Daltonian	amatorian	gentleman
Atlantean	Eutychian	Waltonian	oratorian	cattleman
nemertean	Slovakian	Miltonian	Victorian	engine-man
Thyestean	epinikian	Huttonian	sartorian	venireman
subnivean	Algonkian	Plutonian	Nestorian	pleaseman
zoophagan	Seljukian	Newtonian	historian	phraseman
suffragan	Daedalian	Slavonian	Liguorian	exciseman
ptarmigan	mammalian	amazonian	Solutrian	minuteman
reed-organ	Tantalian	Hibernian	Arthurian	strongman
hand-organ	Castalian	Falernian	tellurian	churchman
pipe-organ	Mendelian	Saturnian	Caucasian	switchman
hoolachan	Mindelian	Mancunian	Afro-Asian	Scotchman
parischan	Spigelian	Neptunian	Laurasian	ploughman
spleuchan	carnelian	Hercynian	Hobbesian	signalman
astrakhan	cornelian	trigynian	Rhodesian	flugelman
acalephan	Zwinglian	Iroquoian	magnesian	bushel-man
leviathan	Ismailian	Ethiopian	Keynesian	kennel-man
amphibian	caecilian	cyclopian	Cartesian	ranzelman
Columbian	Vergilian	Fallopian	precisian	schoolman
macrobian	Virgilian	subtopian	ambrosian	patrolman
microbian	reptilian	dystopian	Molossian	Mussulman
Paulician	Castilian	barbarian	banausian	landamman
Phenician	Brazilian	herbarian	Tungusian	muffin-man
clinician	Corallian	verbarian	homousian	ribbon-man
epinician	Sabellian	cercarian	Malaysian	motion-man
rubrician	Orwellian	gregarian	Dionysian	clubwoman
patrician	gorillian	Bulgarian	Dalmatian	bond-woman
metrician	Lucullian	vulgarian	Sarmatian	freewoman
physician	Mongolian	Hungarian	Helvetian	tire-woman
tactician	Anatolian	Tocharian	Brechtian	forewoman
dietician	Acheulian	Tokharian	Nigritian	byrewoman
mortician	pandemian	semi-Arian	dietitian	fish-woman

work-woman	quarryman	vice-queen	jet-driven	cock-robin
shopwoman	wherryman	Hallowe'en	unshriven	litter-bin
charwoman	pantryman	in-between	disproven	indirubin
alms-woman	vestryman	go-between	garryowen	bilirubin
kinswoman	shantyman	phellogen	wood-waxen	capsaicin
oarswoman	heliozoan	oestrogen	endenizen	unlived-in
newswoman	hydrozoan	teratogen	half-dozen	properdin
post-woman	protozoan	dictyogen	champaign	phthalein
Manxwoman	frying-pan	guinea-hen	sovereign	check-rein
jurywoman	Aldebaran	cup-lichen	predesign	Zechstein
beggar-man	catamaran	mallee-hen	undersign	intervein
cellarman	poriferan	refreshen	misassign	tarboggin
timber-man	courtesan	tappit-hen	preordain	cotton-gin
lumberman	salvarsan	unburthen	turnagain	sea-margin
spider-man	charlatan	everywhen	side-chain	baldachin
doggerman	Mahometan	turkey-hen	drag-chain	sea-urchin
Pan-German	Samaritan	gymnasien	long-chain	endorphin
washerman	securitan	overtaken	back-chain	slammakin
fisherman	isokontan	requicken	lock-chain	princekin
hammerman	mercaptan	outspoken	open-chain	spellikin
corner-man	sacristan	foretoken	chilblain	spillikin
wasserman	mangostan	love-token	porcelain	heartikin
gutter-man	Bantustan	book-token	châtelain	grimalkin
repairman	Manhattan	misfallen	peneplain	kilderkin
ealdorman	harmattan	jaw-fallen	underlain	nipperkin
anchorman	orang-utan	new-fallen	self-slain	sooterkin
sailor-man	sapi-outan	gentlemen	baisemain	scarfskin
colourman	prison-van	ploughmen	water-main	thickskin
fieldsman	Himalayan	Mussulmen	hind-brain	slinkskin
roundsman	phycocyan	praenomen	fore-brain	sharkskin
synodsman	anthocyan	freewomen	lack-brain	onion-skin
guardsman	courtezan	forewomen	turf-drain	hyson-skin
thirdsman	Nickie-ben	jurywomen	well-drain	sheepskin
swordsman	overladen	energumen	blood-rain	clear-skin
ombudsman	outredden	marrow-men	chamfrain	cloacalin
tribesman	forbidden	lack-linen	sand-grain	amygdalin
spadesman	bedridden	veldskoen	rice-grain	Adrenalin ®
tradesman	hag-ridden	misshapen	filigrain	digitalin
bridesman	betrodden	overripen	overgrain	hobgoblin
brakes-man	retrodden	mishappen	grosgrain	metheglin
spokesman	untrodden	mislippen	road-train	francolin
sharesman	mermaiden	schlieren	pack-train	trampolin
shoresman	quarenden	sedge-wren	mail-train	tarpaulin
statesman	upbounden	jenny-wren	down-train	pyroxylin
deathsman	tea-garden	sea-beaten	aerotrain	ovalbumin
cracksman	hop-garden	sun-beaten	overtrain	duralumin
spoilsman	subwarden	moth-eaten	eyestrain	eumelanin
groomsman	way-warden	worm-eaten	constrain	hecogenin
plainsman	disburden	enlighten	outstrain	diosgenin
steersman	Willesden	benighten	boat-train	tanghinin
craftsman	carrageen	thoughten	chieftain	cytokinin
draftsman	palankeen	enhearten	uncertain	serotonin
yachtsman	damaskeen	fly-bitten	ascertain	saintfoin
eightsman	fasten-e'en	sex-kitten	appertain	surrejoin
pointsman	fillipeen	unsmitten	entertain	interjoin
sportsman	pistareen	rewritten	encurtain	chincapin
select-man	sage-green	unwritten	uncurtain	chinkapin
market-man	blue-green	ill-gotten	overstain	saddle-pin
quadruman	leaf-green	forgotten	overstain	tuning-pin
byrlaw-man	back-green	misgotten	cockswain	cotter-pin
fellow-man	evergreen	withouten	boatswain	wheel-spin
donkey-man	overgreen	mid-heaven	forecabin	breastpin
clergyman	velveteen	break-even	myoglobin	safety-pin
liveryman	seventeen	well-given	wake-robin	saccharin

Sanhedrin	endungeon	troparion	seclusion	epulation
luciferin	habergeon	Hipparion	inclusion	ovulation
whipper-in	sconcheon	synedrion	exclusion	cremation
Pellagrin	scuncheon	tricerion	prelusion	sigmation
pyrethrin	truncheon	criterion	collusion	animation
pituitrin	scutcheon	tellurion	prolusion	palmation
tambourin	pantaleon	centurion	obtrusion	gammation
lake-basin	chameleon	corrasion	detrusion	gemmation
wash-basin	endecagon	pervasion	intrusion	summation
rock-basin	dodecagon	precision	extrusion	formation
slop-basin	chiliagon	concision	contusion	planation
sannyasin	sea-dragon	collision	pertusion	emanation
oleo-resin	galdragon	prevision	probation	arenation
comings-in	pendragon	provision	jawbation	crenation
disseisin	bandwagon	repulsion	placation	cognation
rhodopsin	buck-wagon	impulsion	plication	urination
spadassin	tank-wagon	expulsion	emication	ruination
lack-Latin	Ctesiphon	revulsion	falcation	damnation
chromatin	trilithon	divulsion	sulcation	connation
prolactin	excambion	expansion	avocation	nunnation
needle-tin	Ostracion	accension	evocation	phonation
stream-tin	epinicion	recension	furcation	pronation
indigotin	suspicion	ascension	education	ozonation
unslept-in	gammadion	dimension	gradation	carnation
travertin	rhipidion	intension	predation	tarnation
progestin	stasidion	extension	oxidation	vernation
baragouin	diacodion	implosion	pandation	reboation
baldaquin	collodion	explosion	laudation	palpation
harlequin	accordion	prerosion	exudation	exaration
mannequin	trisagion	corrosion	lineation	libration
palanquin	contagion	delapsion	caseation	vibration
Algonquin	subregion	demersion	evagation	hydration
damasquin	faulchion	immersion	purgation	operation
bog-spavin	stanchion	aspersion	raciation	iteration
pyridoxin	refashion	detersion	radiation	migration
antitoxin	Malathion	obversion	mediation	spiration
mycotoxin	epinikion	reversion	filiation	adoration
autotoxin	battalion	diversion	foliation	proration
cytotoxin	dandelion	inversion	miniation	exoration
disseizin	parhelion	detorsion	expiation	narration
brick-kiln	anthelion	retorsion	variation	serration
Dobermann	mandilion	intorsion	seriation	latration
gas-carbon	vermilion	decursion	striation	nitration
chaw-bacon	postilion	recursion	satiation	titration
subdeacon	medallion	incursion	vitiation	neuration
stramaçon	tabellion	excursion	obviation	epuration
basilicon	rebellion	impassion	deviation	irisation
eirenicon	decillion	accession	sublation	pulsation
idioticon	modillion	decession	chelation	sensation
gerfalcon	nonillion	recession	prelation	cassation
jerfalcon	octillion	secession	deflation	cessation
gyrfalcon	cotillion	egression	reflation	causation
cotyledon	mandylion	obsession	afflation	jactation
pyramidon	anthemion	admission	inflation	lactation
clarendon	prooemion	demission	epilation	mactation
Rhineodon	companion	remission	lallation	dictation
Zeuglodon	tree-onion	immission	fellation	nictation
Iguanodon	phelonion	diffusion	collation	luctation
sphenodon	communion	suffusion	violation	ructation
chaetodon	usucapion	confusion	prolation	agitation
Glyptodon	encolpion	profusion	isolation	imitation
bombardon	ectropion	perfusion	adulation	evitation
reguerdon	entropion	occlusion	ululation	saltation
propodeon	orpharion	reclusion	emulation	siltation

dentation	depletion	incaution	resnatron	longicorn
mentation	repletion	execution	thyratron	Capricorn
tentation	impletion	elocution	magnetron	serricorn
flotation	accretion	pollution	semantron	clavicorn
quotation	secretion	evolution	cyclotron	broom-corn
reptation	excretion	deflexion	cosmotron	negro-corn
septation	tradition	reflexion	phytotron	wheat-corn
hortation	rendition	inflexion	encheason	sweet-corn
sortation	vendition	implexion	mid-season	bugle-horn
curtation	condition	connexion	offseason	pronghorn
gestation	perdition	prefixion	sand-mason	coach-horn
testation	erudition	defluxion	freemason	stinkhorn
gustation	largition	affluxion	livraison	krummhorn
guttation	coalition	effluxion	rat-poison	greenhorn
vacuation	abolition	influxion	caparison	alpenhorn
arcuation	dormition	misreckon	disprison	buck's-horn
valuation	inanition	arch-felon	encrimson	hartshorn
sinuation	evanition	pademelon	non-person	sloethorn
liquation	cognition	musk-melon	barperson	buckthorn
actuation	detrition	padymelon	layperson	short-horn
situation	attrition	decathlon	foster-son	water-worn
clavation	nutrition	tenaillon	saucisson	heartburn
elevation	dentition	semicolon	automaton	day-return
privation	quotition	diachylon	emplecton	handstun
salvation	partition	monoxylon	asyndeton	about-turn
solvation	sortition	cacodemon	epitheton	needle-gun
nervation	intuition	penstemon	doubleton	grease-gun
curvation	attuition	sea-salmon	singleton	minute-gun
subaction	indention	dog-salmon	simpleton	spring-gun
redaction	obtention	persimmon	hacqueton	swivel-gun
ice-action	detention	discommon	lamington	turret-gun
olfaction	retention	ichneumon	Orpington	Southroun
impaction	intention	olecranon	unbuilt-on	ciclatoun
defection	attention	Parthenon	witwanton	tip-and-run
refection	obvention	Cro-Magnon	badminton	hit-and-run
affection	invention	Agamemnon	melocoton	monkey-run
infection	premotion	colcannon	Pinkerton	vingt-et-un
abjection	commotion	barracoon	guncotton	cold-drawn
objection	promotion	Pantaloon	Semi-Saxon	hard-drawn
dejection	prenotion	honeymoon	procaryon	fine-drawn
rejection	recaption	afternoon	prokaryon	wiredrawn
injection	deception	soupspoon	stramazon	long-drawn
balection	reception	salt-spoon	tithe-barn	withdrawn
selection	inception	quintroon	plain-darn	deep-drawn
bolection	exception	frigatoon	unconcern	rough-hewn
direction	obreption	saskatoon	scale-fern	foreshewn
resection	ademption	musketoon	beech-fern	climb-down
bisection	coemption	Diplozoon	water-fern	up-and-down
insection	exemption	hydrozoon	holly-fern	shake-down
exsection	preoption	protozoon	sempitern	close-down
detection	abruption	thereupon	subaltern	write-down
advection	irruption	whereupon	Comintern	touch-down
addiction	desertion	submicron	Komintern	Southdown
indiction	insertion	trihedron	misgovern	breakdown
depiction	assertion	tierceron	stepbairn	crackdown
T-junction	exsertion	sticheron	twice-born	knock-down
inunction	co-portion	percheron	hedge-born	spelldown
decoction	apportion	Decameron	slave-born	steep-down
abduction	detortion	ephemeron	earthborn	clampdown
adduction	retortion	brand-iron	quick-born	eiderdown
deduction	intortion	scrap-iron	still-born	swansdown
reduction	extortion	cramp-iron	woman-born	swans-down
seduction	digestion	sheet-iron	first-born	right-down
induction	ingestion	sigmatron	bread-corn	count-down

screw-down	libecchio	telephoto	lairdship	chokedamp
throw-down	finocchio	wire-photo	spaceship	death-damp
stuff-gown	finnochio	antipasto	guideship	after-damp
undergown	embroglio	capotasto	judgeship	wood-stamp
nightgown	imbroglio	manifesto	uncleship	crack-hemp
shortgown	punctilio	hey-presto	thaneship	sisal-hemp
seldshown	spadillio	zucchetto	store-ship	bottle-imp
foreshown	pulvillio	larghetto	plate-ship	queue-jump
high-blown	portfolio	borghetto	rogueship	water-jump
full-blown	porphyrio	gruppetto	slave-ship	sugar-lump
overblown	gear-ratio	scarpetto	knaveship	force-pump
high-flown	cheechako	lazaretto	chiefship	bilge-pump
overflown	Euraquilo	vaporetto	subahship	chain-pump
unbeknown	stornello	neutretto	rajahship	water-pump
foreknown	albarello	quintetto	block-ship	overtrump
well-known	armadillo	quartetto	clerkship	Jew's-trump
half-crown	cigarillo	sostenuto	rivalship	tripe-shop
weed-grown	water-polo	chechaquo	bedelship	truck-shop
home-grown	guanazolo	four-by-two	devilship	print-shop
lung-grown	duodecimo	twenty-two	steamship	tallyshop
high-grown	altissimo	proembryo	queenship	dolly-shop
rush-grown	sixteenmo	gallinazo	clownship	tommy-shop
full-grown	major-domo	paparazzo	troop-ship	jerry-shop
overgrown	escribano	**P**	vicarship	hammerkop
moss-grown	hurricano	forage-cap	sizarship	redevelop
thick-sown	siciliano	fuddle-cap	eldership	belly-flop
Chinatown	dumb-piano	muffin-cap	ushership	heliscoop
O	boliviano	barret-cap	rulership	cock-a-hoop
algarrobo	portolano	good-cheap	ownership	nicompoop
beccafico	fish-guano	dirt-cheap	vizirship	stonecrop
magnifico	rock-guano	spoil-heap	priorship	share-crop
simpatico	contadino	shell-heap	majorship	catch-crop
catafalco	cipollino	scrap-heap	minorship	after-crop
calamanco	sopranino	after-clap	motor-ship	intercrop
Ayahuasco	solferino	saddle-lap	rotor-ship	wheat-crop
gauchesco	vetturino	glass-soap	tutorship	cough-drop
barricado	campesino	fish-scrap	mayorship	water-drop
ambuscado	andantino	mouse-trap	augurship	eavesdrop
zapateado	Argentino	death-trap	transship	wrist-drop
reformado	lanterloo	stink-trap	cadetship	punch-prop
bastinado	smasheroo	steel-trap	lightship	turboprop
carbonado	parleyvoo	smell-trap	giantship	underprop
strappado	pifferaro	steam-trap	saintship	turnip-top
desperado	cavaliero	drain-trap	countship	short-stop
enamorado	caballero	jockstrap	abbotship	sarcocarp
muscovado	bandolero	chinstrap	courtship	anthocarp
derring-do	campanero	booby-trap	about-ship	cremocarp
glissando	Politburo	quarry-sap	envoyship	sporocarp
sforzando	lagrimoso	waist-deep	horsewhip	cystocarp
smorzando	spiritoso	musk-sheep	coachwhip	rhizocarp
crescendo	pizzicato	underkeep	stock-whip	vibraharp
Quasimodo	obbligato	oversleep	paper-clip	mouth-harp
pearl-sago	inamorato	wink-a-peep	coverslip	card-sharp
come-and-go	talking-to	underpeep	short-slip	mouldwarp
cacafuego	sgraffito	cassareep	toodle-pip	hand-clasp
deck-cargo	sanbenito	peaseweep	land-scrip	galliwasp
chechacho	incognito	mint-julep	eavesdrip	coffee-cup
quebracho	paraquito	goose-step	kirbigrip	loving-cup
yo-heave-ho	contralto	route-step	kirby-grip	buttercup
capriccio	Esperanto	quickstep	round-trip	claret-cup
pasticcio	thereinto	tallow-dip	orange-tip	pillow-cup
solfeggio	whereinto	microchip	fingertip	trumped-up
pistachio	thereunto	chelaship	filter-tip	ballsed-up
mustachio	whereunto	guard-ship	paper-pulp	redding-up

washing-up	loaf-sugar	clausular	misguider	applauder
summing-up	milk-sugar	capitular	rose-elder	defrauder
topping-up	palm-sugar	blastular	sow-gelder	piepowder
totting-up	lump-sugar	substylar	infielder	egg-powder
cantaloup	colcothar	uniplanar	inkholder	gunpowder
task-group	justiciar	by-ordinar	penholder	table-beer
playgroup	conciliar	semi-lunar	innholder	balladeer
pease-soup	monkey-jar	stroke-oar	gas-holder	mouse-deer
pint-stoup	glabellar	pearl-spar	pew-holder	water-deer
knocker-up	cribellar	satin-spar	asmoulder	tabasheer
snapper-up	tessellar	fluorspar	bargander	canceleer
well-set-up	clitellar	registrar	bergander	bandoleer
wrought-up	rostellar	balthasar	two-hander	pistoleer
R	scutellar	commissar	coriander	buccaneer
lounge-bar	fibrillar	earth-star	Icelander	muffineer
double-bar	spirillar	superstar	Englander	routineer
saddle-bar	tonsillar	balthazar	philander	jargoneer
handlebar	pulvillar	hobjobber	mallander	sermoneer
saloon-bar	dog-collar	odd-jobber	Hollander	cannoneer
isallobar	rix-dollar	nutjobber	Finlander	pontoneer
window-bar	tubicolar	beslobber	Laplander	whatsoe'er
palace-car	lanceolar	sea-robber	Ausländer	backspeer
inside-car	nucleolar	beslubber	uitlander	sightseer
caddie-car	malleolar	describer	outlander	privateer
bubble-car	milk-molar	inscriber	lowlander	gadgeteer
tumble-car	homopolar	gris-amber	commander	targeteer
estate-car	lunisolar	non-member	germander	racketeer
racing-car	vocabular	dismember	compander	rocketeer
dining-car	bilobular	September	goosander	marketeer
saloon-car	floccular	discumber	bystander	musketeer
street-car	molecular	outnumber	dittander	sonneteer
berg-cedar	unsecular	wardrober	forwander	puppeteer
chowkidar	orbicular	perturber	descender	garreteer
ressaldar	radicular	disturber	muckender	profiteer
tahsildar	pedicular	disgracer	week-ender	pulpiteer
jaghirdar	vehicular	artificer	tail-ender	volunteer
white-bear	canicular	tap-dancer	mallender	oversteer
sloth-bear	funicular	geomancer	cullender	gazetteer
underbear	utricular	nuisancer	suspender	mortgager
teddy-bear	auricular	sentencer	quarender	non-usager
honey-bear	vesicular	denouncer	surrender	frontager
heart-dear	ossicular	renouncer	pretender	toe-ragger
bevel-gear	reticular	announcer	contender	outrigger
chain-gear	coticular	impleader	bartender	humbugger
night-gear	articular	misleader	Eastender	Zwanziger
trochlear	cuticular	end-reader	chavender	exchanger
wellanear	navicular	lip-reader	provender	pot-hanger
sublinear	avuncular	serenader	remainder	phalanger
trilinear	subocular	low-loader	attainder	sea-ranger
collinear	bilocular	persuader	tap-cinder	estranger
non-linear	binocular	dissuader	rejoinder	porrenger
outlinear	monocular	puff-adder	absconder	passenger
choke-pear	opercular	berg-adder	responder	messenger
disappear	floscular	succeeder	hereunder	scavenger
fish-spear	glandular	proceeder	upthunder	harbinger
boar-spear	irregular	cowfeeder	refounder	humdinger
underwear	slangular	hundreder	impounder	sea-ginger
overswear	acellular	upbraider	expounder	hog-ringer
nightwear	stellular	embroider	dissunder	derringer
light-year	retinular	sea-spider	foreboder	herringer
pottingar	manipular	free-rider	jeoparder	porringer
wood-sugar	unpopular	rank-rider	forwarder	pop-singer
cane-sugar	spherular	overrider	box-girder	pottinger
date-sugar	grossular	ringsider	mail-order	inswinger

prolonger	scarifier	barracker	fulfiller	consigner
warmonger	clarifier	ransacker	distiller	bargainer
wit-monger	scorifier	Quebecker	postiller	explainer
lawmonger	metrifier	two-decker	log-roller	engrainer
scrounger	falsifier	fig-pecker	lap-roller	container
cataloger	versifier	nutpecker	patroller	abstainer
theologer	gratifier	mafficker	leg-puller	sustainer
horologer	rectifier	picnicker	epistoler	karabiner
hamburger	certifier	rag-picker	bay-antler	mediciner
limburger	fortifier	hop-picker	bez-antler	headliner
impeacher	mortifier	fossicker	throttler	hardliner
stomacher	testifier	sapsucker	outhauler	mainliner
screecher	justifier	jaywalker	ridiculer	goldminer
beseecher	mystifier	oil-tanker	home-ruler	coal-miner
squelcher	satisfier	die-sinker	overruler	iron-miner
scratcher	seraskier	non-smoker	embezzler	illuminer
stretcher	mono-skier	gas-cooker	lion-tamer	purloiner
debaucher	chevalier	berserker	coco-de-mer	contemner
retoucher	cancelier	outworker	declaimer	trepanner
epitapher	bandelier	tutworker	reclaimer	ale-conner
triumpher	Cordelier	waxworker	pilgrimer	cab-runner
refresher	sommelier	scuddaler	half-timer	rum-runner
nebbisher	high-flier	scrabbler	full-timer	gunrunner
furbisher	bandolier	squabbler	autotimer	outrunner
Yiddisher	gondolier	scribbler	overtimer	dungeoner
sea-fisher	costumier	scrambler	part-timer	fashioner
cod-fisher	buccanier	resembler	midsummer	pensioner
rodfisher	centenier	assembler	home-comer	versioner
fly-fisher	cuisinier	pendicler	late-comer	missioner
publisher	cannonier	tricycler	taxonomer	stationer
English	pontonier	unriddler	unbosomer	portioner
planisher	chain-pier	straggler	elastomer	cautioner
garnisher	town-crier	struggler	confirmer	lampooner
tarnisher	spin-drier	inveigler	conformer	harpooner
varnisher	hair-drier	strangler	performer	pontooner
burnisher	voiturier	wassailer	co-polymer	postponer
furnisher	couturier	half-miler	Africaner	dethroner
nourisher	sottisier	pot-boiler	Afrikaner	discerner
Britisher	corsetier	despoiler	ergataner	easterner
ill-wisher	thriftier	subsoiler	caravaner	westerner
pen-pusher	compotier	pasquiler	shebeener	oil-burner
sea-bather	road-maker	sprinkler	fifteener	gas-burner
sunbather	robe-maker	signaller	sixteener	sojourner
godfather	pacemaker	rentaller	stiffener	copartner
all-father	homemaker	pot-waller	kitchener	landowner
forgather	shoemaker	dry-waller	toughener	sun-downer
thegither	rope-maker	cudgeller	freshener	low-downer
nowhither	casemaker	busheller	thickener	mine-owner
godmother	love-maker	enameller	quickener	coal-owner
financier	king-maker	hummeller	hearkener	mill-owner
brigadier	bookmaker	tunneller	cheapener	ship-owner
grenadier	toolmaker	propeller	eye-opener	part-owner
vivandier	rain-maker	gospeller	can-opener	torpedoer
custodier	horn-maker	teaseller	tin-opener	wrong-doer
stupefier	tent-maker	weaseller	pew-opener	underdoer
liquefier	bootmaker	hosteller	sharpener	shampooer
crucifier	stay-maker	traveller	sweetener	hand-paper
re-edifier	spinnaker	sniveller	tightener	sandpaper
qualifier	muck-raker	driveller	shortener	wood-paper
mollifier	moonraker	shoveller	chastener	lace-paper
nullifier	nunataker	groveller	enlivener	rice-paper
amplifier	caretaker	indweller	scrivener	notepaper
magnifier	outbacker	troweller	arraigner	bank-paper
signifier	skyjacker	penciller	foreigner	wallpaper

curl-paper	chatterer	appetiser	parameter	dynamiter
newspaper	clatterer	digitiser	octameter	exploiter
test-paper	flatterer	disguiser	hexameter	memoriter
ale-draper	smatterer	merganser	telemeter	law-writer
high-taper	fritterer	condenser	dose-meter	recruiter
beekeeper	twitterer	dispenser	wavemeter	waghalter
innkeeper	sputterer	responser	machmeter	drysalter
barkeeper	stutterer	rehearser	focimeter	enshelter
boxkeeper	avouterer	disperser	salimeter	inshelter
sandpiper	lacquerer	traverser	konimeter	defaulter
top-hamper	palaverer	canvasser	perimeter	assaulter
ill-temper	deliverer	witnesser	tasimeter	consulter
contemper	recoverer	addresser	dosimeter	enchanter
destemper	shotfirer	redresser	lysimeter	mishanter
distemper	conspirer	engrosser	altimeter	warranter
mistemper	wood-borer	untrusser	taximeter	instanter
no-trumper	rock-borer	paralyser	phonmeter	concenter
landloper	cork-borer	catalyser	oncometer	augmenter
developer	well-borer	crab-eater	pedometer	commenter
outrooper	corn-borer	egg-beater	hodometer	carpenter
kidnapper	scissorer	toad-eater	rheometer	presenter
schnapper	preferrer	fire-eater	areometer	dissenter
entrapper	conferrer	beefeater	ergometer	preventer
unstopper	schnorrer	frog-eater	eriometer	mid-winter
dispauper	precurrer	gas-heater	mekometer	misaunter
pea-souper	advoutrer	twoseater	milometer	bug-hunter
Varityper ®	mind-curer	meat-eater	Nilometer	mug-hunter
cupbearer	soul-curer	root-eater	bolometer	pot-hunter
calendrer	body-curer	clay-eater	xylometer	fox-hunter
slabberer	harbourer	monolater	osmometer	encounter
chamberer	succourer	pyrolater	atmometer	six-footer
slumberer	clamourer	desolater	zymometer	attempter
broiderer	outpourer	soda-water	manometer	corrupter
slanderer	pleasurer	dead-water	oenometer	disrupter
launderer	treasurer	head-water	monometer	restarter
maunderer	reinsurer	feed-water	tonometer	subverter
thunderer	reassurer	wild-water	barometer	converter
blunderer	increaser	rice-water	aerometer	perverter
plunderer	purchaser	tide-water	pyrometer	comforter
pickeerer	ink-eraser	limewater	gasometer	supporter
chafferer	archaiser	pome-water	potometer	out-porter
profferer	Hebraiser	fire-water	optometer	consorter
staggerer	appraiser	rose-water	auxometer	alabaster
swaggerer	exerciser	dish-water	cryometer	nor'-easter
sniggerer	exorciser	backwater	kryometer	arblaster
decoherer	localiser	rockwater	voltmeter	beplaster
smotherer	vocaliser	dill-water	slot-meter	emplaster
furtherer	idealiser	rain-water	wattmeter	job-master
murtherer	moraliser	pump-water	volumeter	beemaster
cashierer	vitaliser	Teeswater	flowmeter	cremaster
stammerer	totaliser	salt-water	herb-Peter	two-master
whimperer	equaliser	melt-water	trumpeter	surmaster
fripperer	noveliser	snow-water	banqueter	paymaster
whisperer	civiliser	polywater	hereafter	say-master
fruiterer	nebuliser	character	freighter	spymaster
shelterer	organiser	perfecter	benighter	spiraster
adulterer	romaniser	reflecter	flaughter	tea-taster
poulterer	womaniser	neglecter	slaughter	poetaster
saunterer	polariser	connecter	draughter	speedster
charterer	theoriser	respecter	exhibiter	fraudster
plasterer	aphoriser	sphincter	backbiter	Leicester
roisterer	vaporiser	concocter	forfeiter	worcester
roysterer	surpriser	cricketer	surfeiter	suggester
scatterer	practiser	trinketer	gauleiter	trimester

rhymester	gaol-fever	top-sawyer	televisor	resonator
protester	worm-fever	pit-sawyer	prehensor	detonator
requester	ship-fever	star-gazer	suspensor	intonator
sequester	camp-fever	calfdozer	responsor	separator
harvester	whichever	bulldozer	precursor	liberator
nor'-wester	retriever	schnauzer	valvassor	macerator
sou'-wester	gear-lever	headchair	successor	moderator
polyester	whosoever	cane-chair	processor	tolerator
youngster	howsoever	high-chair	confessor	numerator
sophister	free-diver	push-chair	professor	generator
Philister	skin-diver	deck-chair	sublessor	venerator
fillister	perceiver	camp-chair	addressor	cinerator
gannister	redeliver	easy-chair	aggressor	imperator
quirister	free-liver	horsehair	depressor	literator
chorister	hen-driver	goat's-hair	repressor	aspirator
barrister	pen-driver	three-pair	oppressor	decorator
sob-sister	contriver	disrepair	possessor	depurator
trickster	cat-silver	forestair	promissor	saturator
prankster	dish-cover	downstair	percussor	obturator
upholster	overcover	trap-stair	incubator	glossator
Axminster	dust-cover	joint-heir	defecator	dilatator
bemonster	up-and-over	backspeir	dedicator	tractator
defroster	voice-over	spruce-fir	indicator	spectator
exhauster	going-over	silver-fir	judicator	cunctator
throwster	wind-hover	antechoir	advocator	punctator
bescatter	spillover	aspersoir	emendator	irritator
hamfatter	Land-Rover ®	reservoir	escheator	hesitator
bespatter	crossover	septemvir	indagator	visitator
forgetter	preserver	centumvir	abnegator	annotator
sea-letter	conserver	Doukhobor	alligator	amputator
subletter	top-drawer	campeador	fumigator	scrutator
red-letter	whittawer	comprador	irrigator	evacuator
dog-letter	bee-flower	hundredor	mitigator	graduator
vignetter	safflower	Thermidor	navigator	excavator
wadsetter	sunflower	Fructidor	abrogator	rotavator
jet-setter	wax-flower	compandor	gladiator	activator
gas-fitter	mayflower	embraceor	spoliator	renovator
outfitter	swallower	confiteor	initiator	innovator
submitter	lawn-mower	called-for	escalator	rotovator
permitter	fire-power	unsued-for	inhalator	malaxator
bed-sitter	overpower	mortgagor	revelator	compactor
garrotter	rood-tower	sea-anchor	depilator	refractor
bog-butter	gate-tower	ice-anchor	mutilator	infractor
rum-butter	peel-tower	disanchor	immolator	detractor
nut-butter	bell-tower	posterior	desolator	retractor
vee-gutter	overtower	excelsior	tabulator	attractor
unshutter	shot-tower	fife-major	ambulator	extractor
off-putter	paradoxer	drum-major	jaculator	contactor
presbyter	mine-layer	état-major	peculator	play-actor
beleaguer	pipe-layer	antichlor	joculator	perfector
intriguer	germ-layer	councilor	modulator	projector
haranguer	displayer	sun-parlor	regulator	prelector
continuer	net-player	confirmor	simulator	deflector
exchequer	man-slayer	consignor	insulator	reflector
reconquer	ratepayer	Monsignor	decimator	collector
construer	portrayer	contemnor	estimator	connector
face-saver	gainsayer	stage-door	alienator	inspector
life-saver	journeyer	swing-door	laminator	prorector
flag-waver	tourneyer	shop-floor	dominator	corrector
hair-waver	high-flyer	malt-floor	nominator	trisector
whencever	destroyer	conqueror	ruminator	prosector
gold-fever	spin-dryer	recoveror	supinator	dip-sector
milk-fever	hair-dryer	misfeasor	divinator	dissector
jail-fever	sea-lawyer	disseisor	stannator	protector

convector	day-labour	symbolics	rectrices	torpedoes
predictor	neighbour	phonemics	tectrices	mirligoes
concoctor	unharbour	rhythmics	tortrices	embargoes
mad-doctor	pompadour	economics	praecoces	buffaloes
conductor	uncandour	bionomics	rhachides	lignaloes
inhabitor	splendour	mechanics	rhaphides	volcanoes
inhibitor	cul-de-four	dysgenics	pyramides	pettitoes
exhibitor	three-four	euthenics	oceanides	dogshores
capacitor	two-by-four	hygienics	Eumenides	Scansores
solicitor	treachour	ecumenics	Maeonides	syntheses
subeditor	lunch-hour	radionics	ascarides	Japaneses
admonitor	eight-hour	gnomonics	Ironsides	diaereses
apparitor	scurriour	harmonics	Aristides	Valdenses
inheritor	behaviour	geoponics	glottides	Waldenses
coheritor	pot-valour	tectonics	antipodes	elevenses
depositor	soya-flour	hysterics	octopodes	psychoses
repositor	wood-flour	theatrics	chlamydes	diagnoses
expositor	rice-flour	zoiatrics	phalanges	prognoses
consultor	rock-flour	dioptrics	pharynges	mongooses
subcantor	corn-flour	forensics	Boanerges	forcepses
guarantor	off-colour	dramatics	cacoethes	syllepses
warrantor	unicolour	didactics	nepenthes	prolepses
succentor	tricolour	eclectics	Ramillies	cyclopses
precentor	oil-colour	synectics	maniplies	abscisses
augmentor	discolour	geodetics	moniplies	omnibuses
commentor	miscolour	exegetics	manyplies	incubuses
tormentor	sky-colour	athletics	monyplies	octopuses
appointor	ill-humour	hermetics	guaranies	anacruses
dynamotor	dishumour	dianetics ®	congeries	linctuses
rail-motor	demeanour	magnetics	draperies	impetuses
locomotor	dishonour	phonetics	subseries	gallowses
aeromotor	caliatour	dietetics	mysteries	epiphyses
vasomotor	tregetour	semantics	oratories	apophyses
preceptor	endeavour	orthotics	varieties	Hylobates
susceptor	disfavour	semiotics	mollities	optimates
pre-emptor	prick-spur	entoptics	calvities	Eumycetes
excerptor	rowel-spur	logistics	novelties	Cordaites
disruptor	exequatur	acoustics	seventies	phengites
convertor	quaeritur	maieutics	obsequies	Baculites
protestor	S	toreutics	ingluvies	Aleurites
hygristor	En-Tout-Cas ®	caryatids	colluvies	ephialtes
thyristor	bottle-gas	Filicales	Sarcoptes
coadjutor	poison-gas	harigalds	Xyridales	Herpestes
tan-liquor	psychogas	highlands	Mucorales	agonistes
gas-liquor	asclepias	parklands	moveables	light-dues
pot-liquor	primitias	outbounds	fungibles	tipstaves
perfervor	parabolas	soft-goods	isosceles	ourselves
disseizor	plumdamas	backwoods	anopheles	antefixes
teleosaur	anathemas	billiards	strangles	long-sixes
stegosaur	Candlemas	landwards	nine-holes	phalanxes
deinosaur	Martinmas	windwards	sometimes	pharynxes
hadrosaur	Christmas	sidewards	teredines	crab's-eyes
pterosaur	Hallowmas	homewards	Ecardines	tipstaffs
Bucentaur	hippocras	Romewards	clew-lines	scaldings
cockle-bur	Dinoceras	hivewards	scarpines	fleshings
Excalibur	sassafras	backwards	side-bones	tea-things
butterbur	abscissas	parkwards	lazy-bones	riddlings
chauffeur	iconostas	hellwards	Telamones	darklings
voltigeur	cocoa-nibs	downwards	dib-stones	flatlings
souteneur	syllabics	leftwards	Sauternes	eastlings
shamateur	significs	eastwards	porticoes	scummings
raconteur	isagogics	westwards	Barbadoes	amornings
desulphur	liturgics	knee-cords	tornadoes	trappings
Valkyriur	bioethics	simplices	bravadoes	speerings

afterings	syneresis	rhachitis	small-arms	encompass
haverings	athetesis	trachitis	man-at-arms	underpass
speirings	diapyesis	conchitis	idle-worms	coal-brass
beastings	synizesis	onychitis	phantasms	vant-brass
beestings	silicosis	typhlitis	aquariums	gama-grass
biestings	homoeosis	strumitis	factotums	toad-grass
lazy-tongs	trichosis	balanitis	Afrikaans	reed-grass
fustilugs	psychosis	splenitis	dragomans	sand-grass
Franglais	gomphosis	phrenitis	perforans	hardgrass
Charolais	morphosis	vaginitis	impatiens	cord-grass
Planorbis	cirrhosis	laminitis	water-lens	rice-grass
proboscis	anabiosis	retinitis	seraphins	lyme-grass
promuscis	symbiosis	scleritis	thumbkins	tape-grass
Charybdis	scoliosis	enteritis	'sbodikins	wire-grass
Haloragis	alkalosis	arteritis	stownlins	bluegrass
bee-orchis	torulosis	nephritis	ganglions	silk-grass
man-orchis	ankylosis	arthritis	fire-irons	worm-grass
encanthis	exosmosis	gastritis	side-burns	star-grass
Corydalis	melanosis	pleuritis	impeticos	overgrass
chrysalis	diagnosis	glossitis	tournedos	hair-grass
Digitalis	stegnosis	sinusitis	innuendos	soft-grass
Hamamelis	geognosis	hepatitis	contangos	bent-grass
mirabilis	prognosis	ceratitis	flamingos	knotgrass
amaryllis	hypinosis	keratitis	promachos	debarrass
acropolis	resinosis	proctitis	akoluthos	embarrass
rosa-solis	polyposis	parotitis	Asclepios	tarantass
epidermis	madarosis	synovitis	theotokos	non-access
exodermis	siderosis	Buprestis	aryballos	unsuccess
macaronis	sclerosis	ovotestis	prunellos	reprocess
Deinornis	heterosis	pontlevis	Negrillos	vassaless
Aepyornis	nephrosis	pseudaxis	peribolos	vistaless
Québecois	arthrosis	orthoaxis	monoceros	thumbless
bourgeois	chlorosis	clinoaxis	periaktos	plumbless
allantois	fluorosis	macroaxis	concertos	throbless
anacharis	amaurosis	parataxis	crow-steps	shrubless
cantharis	steatosis	rheotaxis	amidships	dreadless
herb-Paris	keratosis	homotaxis	thick-lips	speedless
ephemeris	athetosis	hypotaxis	Stringops	shredless
verdigris	halitosis	aerotaxis	nyctalops	sapidless
mistigris	symptosis	epistaxis	sky-troops	wieldless
ambergris	proptosis	catalexis	goodyears	childless
parabasis	exostosis	endomixis	bleachers	blindless
katabasis	syllepsis	diazeuxis	douzepers	boundless
metabasis	prolepsis	epizeuxis	callipers	soundless
lithiasis	caryopsis	anaptyxis	strossers	woundless
taeniasis	catharsis	skeesicks	decemvirs	bloodless
acariasis	katharsis	boondocks	messieurs	beardless
mydriasis	pertussis	workfolks	secateurs	guardless
psoriasis	paracusis	kinsfolks	plus-fours	swordless
diastasis	anacrusis	golf-links	twalhours	cloudless
anastasis	synchysis	crop-marks	four-hours	tribeless
epistasis	diaphysis	ropeworks	whitebass	peaceless
diathesis	epiphysis	soapworks	white-hass	placeless
epithesis	symphysis	salt-works	high-class	spaceless
synthesis	apophysis	clericals	hand-glass	graceless
prothesis	paralysis	viaticals	sand-glass	traceless
aesthesis	catalysis	trifocals	owle-glass	pieceless
epiclesis	emphlysis	ladlefuls	wine-glass	voiceless
oogenesis	atmolysis	housefuls	opal-glass	priceless
parenesis	zymolysis	pouchfuls	bell-glass	juiceless
phrenesis	pyrolysis	mouthfuls	isinglass	fenceless
anamnesis	autolysis	basinfuls	lamp-glass	forceless
diaeresis	cytolysis	cherubims	pier-glass	truceless
apheresis	phlebitis	seraphims	hour-glass	shadeless

tradeless	fleshless	dowerless	gelidness	freshness
prideless	blushless	powerless	solidness	apishness
guideless	deathless	towerless	timidness	harshness
knifeless	wrathless	odourless	humidness	flushness
imageless	faithless	classless	tumidness	nobbiness
liegeless	toothless	blissless	rapidness	tubbiness
surgeless	frothless	doubtless	vapidness	spiciness
natheless	trothless	bractless	tepidness	priciness
netheless	depthless	shaftless	luridness	juiciness
slakeless	mirthless	craftless	fetidness	sauciness
brakeless	worthless	shiftless	fluidness	headiness
smokeless	mouthless	driftless	lividness	readiness
scaleless	truthless	lightless	vividness	shadiness
smileless	fanciless	nightless	childness	faddiness
guileless	merciless	rightless	blandness	giddiness
titleless	penniless	sightless	grandness	muddiness
styleless	weariless	limitless	blindness	ruddiness
shameless	wreakless	fruitless	roundness	heediness
blameless	plackless	guiltless	soundness	neediness
flameless	trackless	faultless	weirdness	reediness
crimeless	fleckless	plantless	proudness	seediness
plumeless	speckless	scentless	douceness	weediness
rhymeless	frockless	taintless	snideness	handiness
shineless	stockless	jointless	crudeness	sandiness
spineless	Greekless	pointless	threeness	windiness
stoneless	stalkless	printless	largeness	goodiness
scapeless	thankless	stintless	litheness	moodiness
chapeless	clankless	frontless	staleness	woodiness
shapeless	sparkless	dauntless	nobleness	hardiness
grapeless	clerkless	countless	wholeness	tardiness
spareless	idealless	pilotless	ampleness	wordiness
fibreless	rivalless	heartless	primeness	curdiness
spireless	vowelless	chartless	aloneness	gaudiness
shoreless	shell-less	shirtless	proneness	bawdiness
ceaseless	smell-less	skirtless	spareness	dowdiness
phaseless	skill-less	sportless	awareness	rowdiness
noiseless	shawlless	boastless	thereness	leafiness
pulseless	dreamless	crestless	whereness	miffiness
menseless	realmless	frostless	obeseness	huffiness
senseless	qualmless	crustless	falseness	puffiness
horseless	bloomless	trustless	denseness	goofiness
causeless	charmless	spoutless	tenseness	turfiness
pauseless	stormless	troutless	closeness	staginess
houseless	queenless	strawless	looseness	podginess
stateless	chainless	sinewless	terseness	pudginess
tasteless	brainless	indexless	worseness	legginess
valueless	stainless	hobbyless	whiteness	bogginess
issueless	thornless	honeyless	triteness	dogginess
graveless	crownless	moneyless	wasteness	fogginess
valveless	strapless	sultaness	acuteness	sogginess
nerveless	sleepless	broadness	bruteness	bulginess
brazeless	scalpless	fadedness	vagueness	manginess
chiefless	graspless	nakedness	graveness	ranginess
briefless	sugarless	tiredness	stiffness	dinginess
griefless	udderless	satedness	bluffness	minginess
chaffless	riderless	notedness	gruffness	itchiness
proofless	orderless	vexedness	aloofness	washiness
beingless	cheerless	fixedness	beingness	fishiness
stingless	angerless	mixedness	thingness	bushiness
reachless	ownerless	staidness	dyingness	mushiness
teachless	waterless	rabidness	wrongness	rushiness
matchless	utterless	lucidness	youngness	pithiness
touchless	riverless	rigidness	roughness	leakiness
abashless	loverless	validness	toughness	shakiness

flakiness	funniness	jettiness	sharpness	foundress
snakiness	sunniness	pettiness	crispness	overdress
quakiness	phoniness	wittiness	clearness	coat-dress
tackiness	stoniness	dottiness	unharness	sorceress
wackiness	horniness	nuttiness	soberness	panderess
cockiness	tawniness	goutiness	queerness	murderess
rockiness	downiness	heaviness	eagerness	archeress
luckiness	soapiness	nerviness	otherness	Quakeress
muckiness	pulpiness	viewiness	taperness	jaileress
spikiness	bumpiness	spewiness	utterness	ostleress
milkiness	dumpiness	showiness	Inverness	farmeress
silkiness	jumpiness	snowiness	governess	pauperess
bulkiness	lumpiness	craziness	sweirness	writeress
sulkiness	happiness	wooziness	crassness	porteress
lankiness	nappiness	gauziness	crossness	coheiress
pinkiness	sappiness	jazziness	grossness	anchoress
funkiness	soppiness	dizziness	greatness	authoress
punkiness	gaspiness	fuzziness	squatness	tailoress
smokiness	weariness	muzziness	exactness	rectoress
larkiness	chariness	bleakness	erectness	victoress
jerkiness	hoariness	blackness	fleetness	doctoress
perkiness	beeriness	slackness	sweetness	hand-press
corkiness	fieriness	thickness	quietness	wine-press
forkiness	angriness	slickness	swiftness	drop-press
murkiness	hairiness	quickness	lightness	stop-press
riskiness	tarriness	sleekness	rightness	overpress
boskiness	merriness	blankness	tightness	creatress
duskiness	sorriness	crankness	oughtness	exactress
huskiness	noisiness	frankness	tacitness	electress
muskiness	prosiness	starkness	unfitness	traitress
gawkiness	tipsiness	briskness	scantness	arbitress
pawkiness	horsiness	vocalness	faintness	auditress
scaliness	massiness	shoalness	jointness	janitress
mealiness	messiness	ruralness	gauntness	monitress
godliness	bossiness	equalness	bluntness	heritress
soiliness	mossiness	usualness	inaptness	visitress
hilliness	fussiness	cruelness	unaptness	psaltress
silliness	mussiness	frailness	ineptness	chantress
dolliness	gutsiness	smallness	smartness	paintress
jolliness	lousiness	chillness	apartness	jointress
manliness	newsiness	stillness	swartness	temptress
earliness	meatiness	drollness	alertness	procuress
burliness	slatiness	wofulness	inertness	repossess
curliness	niftiness	awfulness	apertness	prelatess
surliness	loftiness	solemness	shortness	varletess
lowliness	saltiness	buxomness	ghastness	hermitess
beaminess	cantiness	cleanness	moistness	priestess
seaminess	tintiness	humanness	curstness	Hebrewess
loaminess	sootiness	tyranness	stoutness	edelweiss
sliminess	emptiness	greenness	glueyness	Judas-kiss
griminess	dirtiness	oftenness	bishopess	hit-or-miss
balminess	hastiness	givenness	dock-cress	scale-moss
filminess	nastiness	plainness	rockcress	rose-cross
jemminess	pastiness	sternness	wall-cress	ring-cross
dumminess	testiness	brownness	wart-cress	backcross
gumminess	mistiness	deaconess	gala-dress	motocross
rumminess	dustiness	dragoness	head-dress	autocross
roominess	fustiness	pythoness	readdress	albatross
barminess	gustiness	patroness	mini-dress	megagauss
raininess	lustiness	Britoness	minidress	scrog-buss
whininess	rustiness	sextoness	maxi-dress	repercuss
spininess	fattiness	cheapness	ball-dress	Anschluss
canniness	nattiness	steepness	full-dress	long-coats
bonniness	tattiness	plumpness	laundress	bile-ducts

pantalets	type-genus	bounteous	imperious	exogamous
entremets	Elaeagnus	courteous	unserious	unanimous
castanets	Trachinus	beauteous	delirious	isodomous
bath-salts	Delphinus	unduteous	laborious	bonhomous
corybants	cincinnus	analogous	notorious	isonomous
crowfoots	Coregonus	isologous	incurious	abnormous
inter-arts	cothurnus	astichous	uncurious	anonymous
carap-nuts	succubous	amorphous	injurious	eponymous
harquebus	exsuccous	scirrhous	penurious	manganous
Psittacus	dithecous	acanthous	luxurious	villanous
umbilicus	synoicous	ananthous	vexatious	larcenous
lumbricus	paroicous	indubious	fractious	burdenous
Leviticus	lubricous	bibacious	facetious	biogenous
Leuciscus	posticous	dicacious	ambitious	zoogenous
uraniscus	verrucous	audacious	seditious	erogenous
Autolycus	palladous	sagacious	bumptious	isogenous
ceratodus	molybdous	fugacious	gumptious	exogenous
esophagus	hybridous	salacious	adoptious	oxygenous
Areopagus	nefandous	solacious	unobvious	lichenous
asparagus	pudendous	tenacious	oblivious	neotenous
Crataegus	isopodous	minacious	lixivious	glutenous
pemphigus	hazardous	capacious	unenvious	leavenous
Spatangus	epigaeous	rapacious	unanxious	sphagnous
mundungus	plumbeous	feracious	obnoxious	uredinous
ray-fungus	fabaceous	veracious	innoxious	tendinous
demiurgus	sebaceous	voracious	scybalous	uliginous
Ophiuchus	micaceous	furacious	unjealous	diclinous
clianthus	theaceous	vivacious	unzealous	criminous
amianthus	oleaceous	triecious	cephalous	fulminous
ailanthus	tufaceous	monecious	anomalous	verminous
Ceanothus	fagaceous	dioecious	asepalous	torminous
bathybius	filaceous	parecious	apetalous	aluminous
perradius	limaceous	judicious	troublous	fibrinous
stapedius	ulmaceous	officious	urodelous	platinous
dupondius	pomaceous	malicious	nickelous	cretinous
Marasmius	vinaceous	delicious	cautelous	chitinous
Asclepius	ceraceous	cilicious	libellous	glutinous
retiarius	moraceous	silicious	orgillous	tyrannous
sartorius	rosaceous	ferocious	papillous	trigonous
Mauritius	musaceous	atrocious	aphyllous	zoogonous
trapezius	cetaceous	prescious	subdolous	unisonous
Amygdalus	setaceous	conscious	luteolous	poisonous
sphacelus	rutaceous	astucious	variolous	prisonous
strobilus	siliceous	insidious	frivolous	consonous
trochilus	pumiceous	invidious	globulous	syntonous
Olenellus	sericeous	melodious	oraculous	cavernous
pulvillus	lapideous	ambagious	calculous	alburnous
peribolus	volageous	egregious	musculous	epigynous
nucleolus	spongeous	religious	credulous	trigynous
malleolus	hypogeous	litigious	acidulous	eutropous
gladiolus	ceruleous	spongious	pendulous	barbarous
superplus	untimeous	ingenious	tremulous	cellarous
flocculus	cutaneous	selenious	granulous	deiparous
Pediculus	rubineous	arsenious	spinulous	uniparous
funiculus	vimineous	felonious	crapulous	oviparous
utriculus	erroneous	simonious	querulous	nonparous
novodamus	eburneous	pecunious	garrulous	nectarous
gaudeamus	ethereous	self-pious	fistulous	tenebrous
ignoramus	venereous	vicarious	pustulous	slumbrous
nystagmus	cinereous	nefarious	trigamous	ludicrous
mumpsimus	glaireous	bifarious	syngamous	chancrous
sumpsimus	arboreous	vagarious	zoogamous	meandrous
prodromus	righteous	malarious	apogamous	diandrous
ginglymus	plenteous	hilarious	isogamous	anandrous

thundrous	ambiguous	heart-beat	milk-float	Blackfeet
anhydrous	irriguous	bloodheat	cut-throat	freesheet
enhydrous	ingenuous	superheat	butter-pat	time-sheet
cancerous	strenuous	fever-heat	ochlocrat	mane-sheet
sorcerous	congruous	buckwheat	millocrat	packsheet
panderous	fructuous	mincemeat	cosmocrat	mainsheet
ponderous	impetuous	forcemeat	hierocrat	tear-sheet
wonderous	theftuous	horsemeat	plutocrat	news-sheet
murderous	sumptuous	flesh-meat	slavocrat	dust-sheet
oviferous	longevous	spoonmeat	boodie-rat	draw-sheet
ovigerous	acclivous	sheepmeat	dandiprat	parrakeet
dangerous	declivous	duck's-meat	dandyprat	court-leet
gingerous	festivous	sweetmeat	beaver-rat	off-street
lecherous	cantharus	roast-meat	Reichsrat	mum-budget
cankerous	Juniperus	overgreat	camass-rat	trebuchet
trimerous	rotavirus	manor-seat	heliostat	pea-jacket
isomerous	myxovirus	mercy-seat	coelostat	bed-jacket
lyomerous	Corchorus	muck-sweat	haemostat	air-jacket
jasperous	zoophorus	butter-fat	chemostat	pay-packet
craterous	Polyporus	marrowfat	klinostat	mid-wicket
dipterous	dioestrus	stonechat	hydrostat	hip-pocket
pesterous	thesaurus	entrechat	hygrostat	hop-pocket
tetterous	Centaurus	cockle-hat	cheese-vat	air-pocket
dexterous	Cynosurus	slouch-hat	panchayat	sea-rocket
pulverous	consensus	shovel-hat	small-debt	sky-rocket
podagrous	prolapsus	bowler-hat	self-doubt	ice-bucket
rancorous	discursus	sailor-hat	overreact	ash-bucket
inodorous	Parnassus	river-flat	ventifact	gutbucket
meteorous	Cupressus	dichromat	recompact	newmarket
fulgorous	narcissus	tanka-boat	substract	eel-basket
clamorous	semilatus	speed-boat	over-exact	princelet
glamorous	peripatus	sauce-boat	disaffect	tiercelet
stuporous	apparatus	whale-boat	disinfect	tonguelet
flavorous	quadratus	seine-boat	imperfect	camouflet
apivorous	saleratus	shore-boat	unperfect	springlet
fervorous	literatus	house-boat	unsubject	branchlet
monstrous	comitatus	swingboat	retroject	surmullet
goustrous	decubitus	track-boat	introject	streamlet
mercurous	introitus	canal-boat	interject	flageolet
verdurous	subsultus	dreamboat	preselect	cabriolet
furfurous	Amarantus	steamboat	genuflect	dog-violet
fulgurous	redivivus	wager-boat	predilect	epistolet
perjurous	complexus	peter-boat	intellect	multiplet
tellurous	amphioxus	river-boat	recollect	septuplet
murmurous	kickshaws	powerboat	reconnect	sextuplet
macrurous	Ember-days	motor-boat	reinspect	landaulet
vulturous	chair-days	pilot-boat	unsuspect	cassoulet
venturous	canal-rays	waistboat	misdirect	sun-helmet
rapturous	backstays	jollyboat	incorrect	gas-helmet
torturous	jack-stays	ferry-boat	resurrect	diamagnet
edematous	broadways	gravy-boat	wax-insect	bar-magnet
gummatous	spoonways	wylie-coat	intersect	towing-net
spiritous	slantways	house-coat	architect	dolphinet
fatuitous	frontways	petticoat	unpredict	stockinet
momentous	leastways	frock-coat	interdict	estaminet
tomentous	hendiadys	undercoat	constrict	funnel-net
dicrotous	Didelphys	dress-coat	unextinct	tunnel-net
asbestous	T	greatcoat	periproct	bobbin-net
schistous	tittlebat	short-coat	ventiduct	sun-bonnet
innocuous	holderbat	waistcoat	by-product	cushionet
deciduous	supplicat	scapegoat	substruct	clarionet
residuous	weasel-cat	billy-goat	construct	shrimp-net
assiduous	concordat	nanny-goat	videlicet	insect-net
dividuous	storm-beat	firefloat	sugar-beet	safety-net

mythopoet	rushlight	whodunnit	redundant	culminant
water-poet	tail-light	maladroit	regardant	fulminant
red-carpet	moonlight	plague-pit	retardant	germinant
swimmeret	lamplight	rock-pipit	accordant	unisonant
spinneret	loop-light	gravel-pit	well-meant	consonant
interpret	rear-light	potato-pit	procreant	dissonant
sulphuret	starlight	bitter-pit	miscreant	amazon-ant
bed-closet	footlight	cherry-pit	termagant	alternant
summerset	spotlight	assumpsit	turmagant	declarant
dinner-set	good-night	canefruit	inelegant	celebrant
toilet-set	forenight	bush-fruit	intrigant	terebrant
sobriquet	weeknight	jack-fruit	trenchant	exuberant
parroquet	overnight	wall-fruit	sycophant	itinerant
palm-civet	fortnight	space-suit	officiant	cooperant
Glenlivet	eyebright	dress-suit	négociant	co-operant
love-shaft	sun-bright	affidavit	irradiant	jesserant
rock-shaft	folk-right	mother-wit	allegiant	reiterant
butt-shaft	downright	latter-wit	humiliant	cauterant
road-craft	copyright	white-salt	brilliant	integrant
handcraft	hindsight	supersalt	defoliant	immigrant
woodcraft	foresight	sword-belt	compliant	deodorant
bard-craft	backsight	storm-belt	suppliant	perforant
redecraft	peep-sight	waistbelt	bivariant	commorant
homecraft	oversight	underfelt	invariant	cormorant
rune-craft	wind-tight	well-built	covariant	susurrant
kingcraft	raintight	slop-built	inebriant	penetrant
songcraft	skin-tight	down-quilt	deliriant	re-entrant
bushcraft	onslaught	panic-bolt	luxuriant	obscurant
folk-craft	indraught	wring-bolt	predikant	fulgurant
overdraft	up-draught	chain-bolt	tremblant	colourant
homograft	ore-raught	drift-bolt	assailant	nurturant
xenograft	unfraught	screw-bolt	ungallant	soi-disant
autograft	mistaught	archivolt	libellant	cognisant
whip-graft	bethought	find-fault	repellant	corposant
makeshift	methought	step-fault	appellant	incessant
half-shift	inbrought	footfault	expellant	uncessant
gear-shift	upbrought	withhault	vacillant	croissant
chairlift	inwrought	pole-vault	thrillant	combatant
spindrift	unwrought	wine-vault	pétillant	humectant
star-drift	upwrought	snake-cult	tremolant	expectant
snowdrift	far-sought	difficult	seed-plant	reductant
wind-swift	whitebait	hydropult	rock-plant	reluctant
mould-loft	spoon-bait	impeccant	musk-plant	crepitant
home-croft	reinhabit	desiccant	coal-plant	palpitant
candytuft	centre-bit	exsiccant	loco-plant	annuitant
Wehrmacht	racing-bit	predicant	moss-plant	resultant
Gaeltacht	devil's-bit	mendicant	snow-plant	insultant
land-yacht	sheep's-bit	applicant	coagulant	repentant
sand-yacht	discredit	formicant	tremulant	remontant
benedight	miscredit	fabricant	stimulant	acceptant
overdight	discomfit	lubricant	gratulant	exceptant
flyweight	disprofit	nigricant	postulant	important
cockfight	identikit	provocant	pustulant	resistant
bullfight	bethankit	coruscant	affirmant	assistant
headlight	forjaskit	confidant	informant	executant
sidelight	disjaskit	trepidant	subtenant	pollutant
undelight	forjeskit	demandant	indignant	computant
limelight	full-split	ascendant	malignant	disputant
pipe-light	wagons-lit	defendant	benignant	attenuant
firelight	time-limit	dependant	repugnant	clinquant
lovelight	pretermit	appendant	oppugnant	fluctuant
half-light	close-knit	intendant	declinant	gallivant
top-flight	interknit	attendant	examinant	observant
highlight	tight-knit	extendant	eliminant	chatoyant

decumbent	expedient	inurement	arrayment	forepoint
recumbent	resilient	abasement	enjoyment	reef-point
incumbent	emollient	erasement	herryment	seal-point
absorbent	ebullient	avisement	foreanent	ball-point
adsorbent	recipient	passement	permanent	autopoint
resorbent	incipient	amusement	prominent	reappoint
subjacent	excipient	rousement	continent	pourpoint
conticent	desipient	abatement	pertinent	viewpoint
demulcent	insipient	statement	abstinent	blueprint
adnascent	disorient	amazement	sustinent	hoofprint
renascent	transient	feoffment	component	rain-print
tabescent	impatient	parchment	proponent	overprint
albescent	in-patient	catchment	secernent	newsprint
pubescent	volitient	hatchment	well-spent	footprint
rubescent	Jack-a-Lent	abashment	overspent	flesh-tint
rufescent	maltalent	fleshment	godparent	mezzotint
quiescent	prevalent	condiment	bioparent	undertint
tumescent	univalent	hardiment	different	stegodont
canescent	trivalent	jolliment	white-rent	lophodont
senescent	tervalent	herriment	deterrent	halobiont
ignescent	sexvalent	merriment	abhorrent	aerobiont
virescent	pestilent	worriment	occurrent	forefront
latescent	excellent	detriment	decurrent	wavefront
lutescent	repellent	nutriment	recurrent	full-front
dehiscent	impellent	sentiment	incurrent	shop-front
fatiscent	expellent	vestiment	uncurrent	chorizont
precedent	divellent	recalment	up-current	grand-aunt
procident	attollent	ravelment	excurrent	puissaunt
diffident	condolent	bevelment	penny-rent	great-aunt
confident	somnolent	devilment	represent	paravaunt
president	turbulent	enrolment	co-present	mouse-hunt
dissident	succulent	extolment	competent	slave-hunt
provident	truculent	annulment	prepotent	still-hunt
ascendent	crapulent	alignment	advertent	no-account
splendent	corpulent	eloinment	resistent	overcount
dependent	flatulent	adornment	insistent	paramount
impendent	fundament	equipment	remittent	catamount
obtundent	lineament	debarment	diffluent	overmount
implodent	firmament	deferment	confluent	self-begot
corrodent	sacrament	determent	profluent	hot-and-hot
occludent	passament	interment	obsequent	bloodshot
imprudent	testament	amassment	congruent	rifle-shot
road-agent	embedment	rabatment	obstruent	stoneshot
land-agent	amendment	treatment	connivent	grapeshot
bank-agent	placement	enactment	resolvent	grief-shot
newsagent	educement	exactment	insolvent	sling-shot
negligent	abodement	ejectment	obvolvent	slung-shot
corrigent	agreement	besetment	vol-au-vent	chain-shot
indulgent	lodgement	revetment	complaint	undershot
refulgent	judgement	refitment	lead-paint	water-shot
effulgent	vengement	remitment	overpaint	wrist-shot
cotangent	inclement	allotment	restraint	arrow-shot
impingent	addlement	apartment	distraint	Phanariot
stringent	exilement	blastment	skinflint	copatriot
detergent	implement	agistment	flay-flint	heptaglot
divergent	événement	emolument	air-splint	land-pilot
resurgent	alinement	engoûment	horsemint	helipilot
insurgent	atonement	strewment	spearmint	autopilot
assurgent	scapement	endowment	knee-joint	underplot
attrahent	elopement	annexment	juke-joint	grass-plot
deficient	decrement	embayment	fish-joint	guillemot
efficient	recrement	allayment	clip-joint	thumb-knot
prescient	increment	repayment	disanoint	sword-knot
conscient	excrement	inpayment	dead-point	witch-knot

9 -OOT

ankle-boot	windswept	sallyport	kink-hoast	paysagist
theftboot	pole-clipt	gas-retort	overroast	falangist
welly-boot	subscript	woundwort	antispast	dialogist
baldi-coot	prescript	stonewort	paederast	analogist
bandicoot	conscript	mitre-wort	shouldest	ecologist
board-foot	proscript	lousewort	disinfest	geologist
spade-foot	transumpt	marshwort	predigest	neologist
three-foot	interrupt	toothwort	decongest	ufologist
goosefoot	incorrupt	birthwort	strongest	biologist
horse-foot	uncorrupt	moudiwort	wind-chest	zoologist
wrong-foot	taxed-cart	mowdiwort	hope-chest	apologist
Blackfoot	apple-cart	coral-wort	steadiest	orologist
underfoot	water-cart	navelwort	goodliest	urologist
stairfoot	night-cart	quillwort	seemliest	otologist
bird's-foot	dandy-cart	pearl-wort	trustiest	myologist
hare's-foot	honey-cart	strapwort	high-blest	synergist
dove's-foot	lion-heart	spearwort	dishonest	theurgist
calf's-foot	wind-chart	adderwort	bird's-nest	liturgist
wolf's-foot	supermart	laserwort	mare's-nest	monachist
cocksfoot	three-part	liverwort	crow's-nest	catechist
duck's-foot	cameo-part	glasswort	goldcrest	fetichist
bear's-foot	apple-tart	crosswort	firecrest	masochist
coltsfoot	push-start	sweetwort	unredrest	anarchist
crow's-foot	kick-start	moneywort	slide-rest	exarchist
fleet-foot	bump-start	pennywort	knife-rest	fetishist
swift-foot	jump-start	gypsywort	ratherest	aquariist
eight-foot	medaewart	well-faurt	disforest	swarajist
light-foot	moudiwart	forecourt	night-rest	autarkist
poult-foot	mowdiwart	basecourt	overwrest	cabbalist
first-foot	Camembert	moot-court	means-test	tribalist
splay-foot	misdesert	clay-court	disinvest	cembalist
pussyfoot	intersert	bandobast	undervest	cymbalist
dusty-foot	extravert	broadcast	transvest	herbalist
cockshoot	reconvert	stone-cast	north-west	verbalist
overshoot	discovert	roughcast	south-west	feudalist
shire-moot	retrovert	simulcast	Mithraist	cerealist
haanepoot	introvert	undercast	theorbist	frugalist
chinaroot	extrovert	love-feast	mosaicist	nephalist
breadroot	unpervert	beanfeast	mythicist	racialist
bloodroot	overexert	north-east	biblicist	socialist
snakeroot	overshirt	south-east	publicist	aerialist
coral-root	hair-shirt	redbreast	anglicist	serialist
tulip-root	tube-skirt	steadfast	metricist	curialist
brier-root	foreskirt	shamefast	physicist	animalist
orris-root	midi-skirt	soothfast	eroticist	formalist
arrowroot	mini-skirt	earthfast	vorticist	carnalist
hooped-pot	miniskirt	breakfast	Haggadist	amoralist
coffee-pot	maxi-skirt	stern-fast	Poujadist	pluralist
pottle-pot	overskirt	Hesychast	balladist	mentalist
Chassepot	gillflirt	scholiast	lampadist	visualist
fining-pot	jillflirt	encomiast	orchidist	actualist
pepper-pot	sea-squirt	ecdysiast	legendist	ritualist
flowerpot	Roquefort	sand-blast	Girondist	sexualist
on-the-spot	recomfort	fire-blast	methodist	bicyclist
nightspot	cold-short	full-blast	prosodist	price-list
monkey-pot	misreport	endoblast	Talmudist	crewelist
potato-rot	chase-port	idioblast	zeitgeist	prize-list
sea-parrot	vertiport	hypoblast	Weltgeist	profilist
owl-parrot	steam-port	mesoblast	tritheist	subtilist
Hottentot	davenport	ectoblast	pantheist	tactilist
hottentot	devonport	entoblast	misoneist	blacklist
procaryot	sternport	periplast	pinchfist	checklist
prokaryot	hoverport	beech-mast	massagist	stock-list
intercept	transport	snort-mast	massagist	medallist

metallist	saloonist	posturist	bloodlust	wapinshaw
panellist	Platonist	spagyrist	self-trust	heronshaw
Sibyllist	centonist	fantasist	anti-trust	wapper-jaw
symbolist	Teutonist	geodesist	overtrust	parrot-jaw
short-list	Plutonist	solipsist	cholecyst	phossy-jaw
dactylist	modernist	defeatist	lithocyst	wolf's-claw
trigamist	internist	prelatist	sporocyst	sons-in-law
Ockhamist	saturnist	dramatist	statocyst	heir-at-law
Gothamist	communist	dogmatist	xenocryst	score-draw
academist	Neptunist	thanatist	Hallstatt	rough-draw
alchemist	frescoist	emanatist	microwatt	sneck-draw
extremist	voodooist	exegetist	polyglott	underdraw
rhythmist	tattooist	magnetist	water-butt	deid-thraw
pessimist	Averroist	sonnetist	Fomalhaut	jack-straw
economist	Shintoist	phonetist	cosmonaut	Johnny-raw
zoonomist	hylozoist	cornetist	hydronaut	coping-saw
anatomist	therapist	decretist	astronaut	scroll-saw
epitomist	red-tapist	spiritist	scrape-gut	interview
zootomist	Pindarist	occultist	physic-nut	Bartlemew
reformist	welfarist	scientist	ground-nut	prize-crew
Targumist	Eucharist	Adventist	candle-nut	cabin-crew
volcanist	Catharist	narcotist	sleeve-nut	grub-screw
vulcanist	citharist	orthotist	souari-nut	hand-screw
Orleanist	topiarist	hypnotist	poison-nut	sand-screw
mechanist	cellarist	se-baptist	mocker-nut	wood-screw
Fabianist	pillarist	motettist	butternut	cork-screw
Indianist	summarist	fagottist	hereabout	twin-screw
shamanist	scenarist	computist	walkabout	turn-screw
Germanist	Caesarist	Utraquist	roll-about	tree-shrew
campanist	guitarist	archivist	thenabout	musk-shrew
timpanist	Dekabrist	passivist	turnabout	overstrew
tympanist	tenebrist	reservist	stirabout	saddle-bow
sopranist	ex-librist	Spinozist	west-about	fiddle-bow
Montanist	Octobrist	Pentecost	washed-out	violin-bow
galvanist	hetaerist	northmost	booked-out	eye-shadow
larcenist	careerist	southmost	played-out	jut-window
Origenist	spagerist	sternmost	out-and-out	bow-window
lichenist	Lutherist	undermost	strikeout	row-dow-dow
euthenist	Hitlerist	innermost	raccahout	raree-show
hygienist	mesmerist	uppermost	dish-clout	peach-blow
ripienist	Wagnerist	aftermost	odd-man-out	death-blow
Hellenist	mannerist	uttermost	sand-spout	underflow
Jansenist	zooperist	outermost	sour-crout	water-flow
cocainist	preterist	lowermost	setter-out	interflow
rabbinist	neoterist	sound-post	putter-out	afterglow
imaginist	dipterist	guide-post	revel-rout	dishallow
machinist	hetairist	hovel-post	bull-trout	oddfellow
violinist	spagirist	woman-post	goings-out	bedfellow
Paulinist	memoirist	queen-post	mangetout	pew-fellow
terminist	herborist	stern-post	proof-text	vow-fellow
routinist	meteorist	crown-post	U	snail-slow
Calvinist	Gongorist	penny-post	chalumeau	mud-minnow
columnist	meliorist	star-crost	gaspereau	scald-crow
Sorbonist	apriorist	landdrost	Cointreau ®	scarecrow
aniconist	tutiorist	hoar-frost	trousseau	galli-crow
jargonist	terrorist	renfierst	double-you	night-crow
visionist	cultorist	bratwurst	impromptu	gally-crow
fusionist	Camorrist	blutwurst	V	intergrow
actionist	questrist	holocaust	Baltoslav	down-throw
motionist	petaurist	hypocaust	leitmotiv	overthrow
notionist	labourist	bundobust	W	fire-arrow
mnemonist	colourist	blood-dust	scrimshaw	love-arrow
mammonist	culturist	brick-dust	oakenshaw	sea-sorrow
harmonist	rapturist	Dryasdust	wapenshaw	misbestow

kabeljouw	underclay	theomancy	appetency	preachify
X	roundelay	belomancy	penitency	speechify
earthflax	swordplay	oenomancy	renitency	Frenchify
prothorax	stage-play	aeromancy	impotency	unqualify
hearth-tax	horseplay	ceromancy	frequency	exemplify
window-tax	match-play	gyromancy	captaincy	indignify
myrtle-wax	underplay	pyromancy	surgeoncy	undignify
thorow-wax	interplay	co-tenancy	God-a-mercy	indemnify
card-index	shield-may	stagnancy	baronetcy	solemnify
dorsiflex	strike-pay	pregnancy	make-ready	personify
retroflex	slate-gray	poignancy	oven-ready	chondrify
prepollex	steel-gray	dominancy	white-lady	corporify
multiplex	pearl-gray	squinancy	saleslady	historify
decomplex	hair-spray	flippancy	fore-caddy	electrify
unperplex	crumb-tray	occupancy	grandaddy	denitrify
antihelix	storm-stay	flagrancy	orthopedy	devitrify
spondulix	thereaway	fragrancy	triploidy	demulsify
piscatrix	breakaway	aberrancy	sound-body	intensify
mediatrix	throw-away	inerrancy	disembody	diversify
Bellatrix	cruiseway	dilatancy	woman-body	objectify
dictatrix	churchway	dubitancy	everybody	pelletify
testatrix	milken-way	oscitancy	staminody	refortify
directrix	streetway	excitancy	tetrapody	cockneyfy
executrix	xenophoby	militancy	pentapody	mycophagy
pounce-box	autophoby	irritancy	heptapody	endophagy
dredge-box	stander-by	hesitancy	chiropody	theophagy
paddle-box	passers-by	latitancy	half-hardy	monophagy
goggle-box	reprobacy	exultancy	foolhardy	xerophagy
sneeze-box	intricacy	constancy	whipcordy	autophagy
spring-box	pervicacy	adjutancy	case-study	polyphagy
strong-box	candidacy	relevancy	self-study	sortilegy
signal-box	immediacy	arrivancy	overstudy	dune-buggy
balaam-box	supremacy	adjuvancy	ice-hockey	cardialgy
pillar-box	diplomacy	adjacency	tuning-key	nephralgy
tinder-box	contumacy	indecency	okey-dokey	odontalgy
powder-box	obstinacy	reticency	cipher-key	mystagogy
pepper-box	mobocracy	innocency	master-key	genealogy
letter-box	theocracy	acescency	culver-key	mammalogy
butter-box	dulocracy	decadency	pot-barley	tetralogy
ballot-box	democracy	stridency	gorblimey	festilogy
window-box	timocracy	residency	wild-honey	palillogy
sentry-box	nomocracy	subagency	wood-honey	diabology
vanity-box	monocracy	indigency	hive-honey	tribology
heterodox	Eurocracy	plangency	palm-honey	symbology
silver-fox	autocracy	emergency	baldmoney	sarcology
draught-ox	itineracy	pruriency	gate-money	muscology
flambeaux	procuracy	esuriency	ring-money	phycology
Esquimaux	intestacy	sentiency	risk-money	paedology
Chartreux	haruspicy	bivalency	call-money	atheology
superflux	marshalcy	covalency	poll-money	teleology
prehallux	colonelcy	redolency	ship-money	museology
pompholyx	titubancy	indolency	beer-money	osteology
Y	abundancy	feculency	salt-money	archology
dapple-bay	sergeancy	temulency	slate-grey	euchology
alack-a-day	serjeancy	virulency	steel-grey	nephology
second-day	fainéancy	purulency	pearl-grey	pathology
degree-day	recreancy	vehemency	ashen-grey	lithology
school-day	arrogancy	remanency	two-storey	anthology
yesterday	wanchancy	immanency	trot-cosey	mythology
latter-day	mischancy	imminency	dispurvey	sociology
Wednesday	sibilancy	opponency	niff-naffy	radiology
ticket-day	jubilancy	apparency	syllabify	audiology
market-day	undulancy	inherency	decalcify	hagiology
brick-clay	petulancy	coherency	demi-deify	ophiology

caliology	sciamachy	untunably	refinedly	unshapely
heliology	skiamachy	incapably	learnedly	eutrapely
semiology	theomachy	reparably	usurpedly	sincerely
koniology	logomachy	separably	retiredly	austerely
Mariology	monomachy	execrably	assuredly	obscurely
agriology	seannachy	tolerably	unbasedly	leisurely
dosiology	entelechy	numerably	advisedly	featurely
aetiology	ulotrichy	venerably	reposedly	precisely
sitiology	oligarchy	superbly	sparsedly	concisely
philology	hagiarchy	miserably	blessedly	immensely
haplology	phylarchy	admirably	limitedly	intensely
hoplology	ethnarchy	desirably	stiltedly	verbosely
anemology	hierarchy	memorably	pointedly	purposely
gemmology	tetrarchy	inerrably	stintedly	operosely
cosmology	pentarchy	incurably	devotedly	obversely
etymology	heptarchy	endurably	avertedly	adversely
uranology	polyarchy	advisably	reputedly	reversely
phenology	archduchy	excusably	subduedly	diversely
poenology	epigraphy	palatably	unmovedly	inversely
irenology	geography	vegetably	allowedly	diffusely
ichnology	biography	habitably	unmixedly	profusely
ethnology	zoography	dubitably	flaccidly	reclusely
rhinology	orography	heritably	squalidly	plicately
urinology	urography	veritably	invalidly	radiately
limnology	myography	irritably	unsolidly	mediately
hymnology	zootrophy	equitably	insipidly	seriately
iconology	dystrophy	refutably	languidly	philately
phonology	theosophy	immutably	impavidly	prolately
hypnology	sciosophy	reputably	cuckoldly	palmately
bumpology	zoomorphy	imputably	unworldly	pinnately
tropology	camera-shy	derivably	husbandly	ternately
hippology	flourishy	revivably	unsoundly	sinuately
acarology	opsimathy	removably	haggardly	privately
macrology	polymathy	immovably	niggardly	obovately
necrology	telepathy	unmovably	bastardly	eruditely
micrology	antipathy	allowably	dastardly	obliquely
andrology	theopathy	enjoyably	seawardly	antiquely
hydrology	idiopathy	evincibly	awkwardly	brusquely
therology	allopathy	coercibly	frowardly	concavely
hierology	unhealthy	irascibly	forwardly	ungravely
hygrology	seaworthy	inaudibly	outwardly	suasively
chirology	airworthy	illegibly	waywardly	evasively
onirology	nick-nacky	indelibly	comradely	pensively
chorology	pockmanky	divisibly	strangely	cursively
coprology	thelytoky	invisibly	fragilely	massively
patrology	rye-whisky	plausibly	subtilely	passively
petrology	tim-whisky	dissembly	fertilely	abusively
astrology	marrowsky	insolubly	hostilely	elusively
neurology	revocably	politicly	servilely	unitively
scatology	peaceably	crabbedly	supremely	furtively
skatology	traceably	trancedly	extremely	festively
hyetology	agreeably	decidedly	sublimely	restively
cartology	vengeably	dividedly	awesomely	costively
festology	permeably	guardedly	noisomely	pomace-fly
pestology	proveably	allegedly	irksomely	warble-fly
histology	ineffably	parchedly	fulsomely	dragonfly
nostology	laughably	studiedly	winsomely	salmon-fly
battology	unpliably	impliedly	contumely	cuckoo-fly
dittology	semblably	hurriedly	mundanely	turnip-fly
tautology	availably	crookedly	profanely	robber-fly
plutology	untamably	ashamedly	germanely	butterfly
phytology	estimably	alarmedly	obscenely	caddis-fly
Maryology	assumably	assumedly	terrenely	forest-fly
argy-bargy	definably	feignedly	genuinely	sobbingly

mincingly	glaringly	mawkishly	statelily	diurnally
maddingly	roaringly	hellishly	torch-lily	sugar-ally
abidingly	soaringly	bullishly	tiger-lily	liberally
glidingly	sparingly	foolishly	waterlily	numerally
slidingly	staringly	girlishly	subfamily	generally
bendingly	jeeringly	stylishly	uncannily	laterally
windingly	leeringly	swinishly	scrimpily	literally
puffingly	veeringly	tonnishly	unhappily	severally
laggingly	adoringly	dronishly	scrappily	preorally
beggingly	jarringly	rompishly	primarily	immorally
tuggingly	purringly	dumpishly	summarily	aurorally
ringingly	louringly	lumpishly	plenarily	centrally
singingly	teasingly	mumpishly	cursorily	ventrally
longingly	hissingly	foppishly	savourily	neutrally
sighingly	missingly	waspishly	throatily	dextrally
dashingly	pausingly	whorishly	ricketily	naturally
gushingly	amusingly	boorishly	thriftily	suturally
pushingly	rousingly	currishly	weightily	edictally
soakingly	gratingly	sourishly	flightily	capitally
quakingly	pratingly	saltishly	haughtily	maritally
mockingly	weetingly	doltishly	naughtily	book-tally
balkingly	siftingly	pettishly	doughtily	pivotally
winkingly	waitingly	sottishly	thirstily	gradually
healingly	haltingly	loutishly	unwittily	lingually
feelingly	meltingly	brutishly	tri-weekly	unequally
reelingly	peltingly	roguishly	berserkly	coequally
railingly	joltingly	slavishly	cubically	sensually
wailingly	pantingly	knavishly	radically	unusually
smilingly	rantingly	peevishly	medically	tactually
gallingly	hintingly	wolvishly	magically	virtually
tellingly	dartingly	twelfthly	logically	textually
willingly	lastingly	youngthly	ethically	asexually
lollingly	jestingly	seventhly	helically	unroyally
beamingly	fittingly	bimonthly	comically	swag-belly
flamingly	wittingly	unearthly	manically	thin-belly
foamingly	juttingly	uncouthly	finically	genteelly
seemingly	poutingly	unreadily	conically	rakehelly
meaningly	flowingly	unheedily	cynically	star-jelly
shiningly	glowingly	unhandily	stoically	flannelly
whiningly	knowingly	scraggily	topically	mongrelly
foiningly	coaxingly	springily	typically	hill-billy
twiningly	prayingly	stringily	lyrically	narghilly
winningly	undyingly	preachily	basically	Chantilly
cunningly	denyingly	starchily	musically	uncivilly
runningly	pityingly	snatchily	optically	knee-holly
droningly	amazingly	sketchily	civically	cockyolly
atoningly	buzzingly	grouchily	lexically	heedfully
warningly	staunchly	notaphily	toxically	needfully
fawningly	throughly	halophily	illegally	mindfully
yawningly	unfleshly	oenophily	specially	wakefully
weepingly	rubbishly	Sinophily	cordially	balefully
gripingly	prudishly	xerophily	spatially	dolefully
limpingly	raffishly	toxophily	initially	banefully
rompingly	huffishly	splashily	martially	tunefully
slopingly	selfishly	squashily	partially	hopefully
gropingly	wolfishly	breathily	trivially	carefully
nippingly	haggishly	lengthily	coaxially	direfully
rippingly	waggishly	healthily	decimally	musefully
toppingly	piggishly	wealthily	maximally	fatefully
carpingly	doggishly	streakily	thermally	hatefully
gaspingly	hoggishly	squeakily	abysmally	songfully
raspingly	sickishly	unluckily	seminally	bashfully
lispingly	duskishly	ungodlily	nominally	wishfully
flaringly	hawkishly	stone-lily	eternally	pushfully

ruthfully	godlessly	mordantly	dichotomy	inharmony
pitifully	uselessly	elegantly	lithotomy	synchrony
dutifully	aimlessly	radiantly	necrotomy	monopsony
skilfully	sinlessly	defiantly	microtomy	brimstony
soulfully	haplessly	valiantly	uterotomy	philogyny
harmfully	witlessly	gallantly	neurotomy	androgyny
moanfully	artlessly	rampantly	cystotomy	protogyny
gainfully	lawlessly	blatantly	phytotomy	errand-boy
painfully	joylessly	distantly	colostomy	office-boy
fearfully	expressly	instantly	taxidermy	stable-boy
tearfully	submissly	piquantly	diathermy	ploughboy
tactfully	gibbously	lambently	panspermy	schoolboy
fretfully	raucously	evidently	teknonymy	corner-boy
hurtfully	hideously	pendently	polyonymy	street-boy
restfully	hugeously	prudently	theophany	yellow-boy
zestfully	timeously	fulgently	accompany	barrow-boy
wistfully	piteously	pungently	pericrany	zircalloy
lustfully	duteously	turgently	momentany	permalloy
playfully	dubiously	anciently	osteogeny	pre-employ
uniformly	viciously	saliently	pathogeny	disemploy
uncleanly	tediously	leniently	phylogeny	misemploy
ruffianly	biliously	sapiently	cosmogeny	macrocopy
workmanly	copiously	patiently	hypnogeny	microcopy
unwomanly	variously	violently	sporogeny	photocopy
inhumanly	seriously	opulently	iatrogeny	skiascopy
showmanly	curiously	clemently	photogeny	telescopy
spartanly	furiously	eminently	histogeny	endoscopy
unqueenly	obviously	currently	phytogeny	horoscopy
drunkenly	deviously	presently	zootechny	poroscopy
condignly	enviously	fervently	latrociny	ouroscopy
certainly	anxiously	unsaintly	paraffiny	autoscopy
cullionly	noxiously	corruptly	moonshiny	cryoscopy
forlornly	jealously	uncourtly	matriliny	allotropy
amphiboly	zealously	confestly	hootnanny	presbyopy
allicholy	callously	earnestly	arle-penny	bomb-happy
oligopoly	emulously	unghostly	Rome-penny	fool-happy
radial-ply	heinously	patchouly	ninepenny	slap-happy
empanoply	ominously	shallowly	truepenny	overhappy
unclearly	ruinously	complexly	fivepenny	allocarpy
similarly	pompously	pantagamy	halfpenny	preoccupy
scholarly	onerously	hercogamy	lickpenny	chemitypy
tabularly	odorously	dichogamy	luck-penny	stenotypy
secularly	amorously	herkogamy	twalpenny	phonotypy
jocularly	riotously	hypergamy	turn-penny	phototypy
regularly	routously	music-demy	fourpenny	syllabary
tegularly	vacuously	blasphemy	goldfinny	columbary
popularly	nocuously	arch-enemy	goldsinny	pothecary
insularly	arduously	eurhythmy	calcedony	formicary
titularly	tenuously	thingummy	cosmogony	lampadary
allenarly	sinuously	froth-fomy	telephony	dromedary
slenderly	nervously	teleonomy	antiphony	subahdary
unorderly	compactly	chironomy	cacophony	legendary
butcherly	inexactly	astronomy	colophony	zemindary
weatherly	perfectly	plutonomy	homophony	secondary
brotherly	correctly	loxodromy	monophony	tracheary
northerly	adjunctly	lobectomy	acrophony	Dundreary
southerly	inquietly	tubectomy	autophony	camsteary
soldierly	unquietly	lipectomy	polyphony	life-weary
painterly	sprightly	topectomy	eudaemony	bone-weary
quarterly	uprightly	vasectomy	querimony	overweary
clouterly	unsightly	leucotomy	matrimony	judiciary
deliverly	illicitly	iridotomy	patrimony	fiduciary
traitorly	peccantly	cordotomy	parsimony	nobiliary
endlessly	verdantly	osteotomy	testimony	auxiliary

pecuniary	termitary	mesentery	dogmatory	snow-berry
vitellary	dignitary	dysentery	emanatory	crow-berry
bacillary	pituitary	splintery	signatory	bob-cherry
ancillary	sedentary	dicastery	damnatory	cutchery
sigillary	momentary	monastery	phonatory	overmerry
mamillary	voluntary	slaistery	culpatory	paediatry
armillary	sagittary	magistery	raspatory	hippiatry
capillary	tributary	huckstery	libratory	epeolatry
papillary	residuary	spluttery	vibratory	monolatry
pupillary	reliquary	engravery	migratory	pyrolatry
artillary	antiquary	discovery	narratory	autolatry
maxillary	electuary	salmon-fry	pulsatory	trinketry
vexillary	sanctuary	Englishry	dictatory	telemetry
corollary	fructuary	garnishry	saltatory	perimetry
medullary	sumptuary	airy-fairy	hortatory	dosimetry
exemplary	cassowary	Puck-hairy	gestatory	asymmetry
calculary	coxcombry	camstairy	gustatory	hodometry
nummulary	battle-cry	triumviry	elevatory	bolometry
formulary	parrot-cry	gimmickry	salvatory	barometry
granulary	hemihedry	warlockry	olfactory	aerometry
scapulary	surquedry	co-rivalry	refectory	horometry
stipulary	freeze-dry	wassailry	dejectory	pyrometry
capsulary	cuckoldry	sokemanry	directory	gasometry
cartulary	husbandry	heathenry	emunctory	optometry
lacrimary	brigandry	citizenry	depletory	marquetry
customary	garlandry	captainry	expletory	parquetry
infirmary	protandry	penguinry	decretory	circuitry
nightmary	polyandry	mansionry	secretory	pageantry
custumary	surrendry	cautionry	excretory	gallantry
lacrymary	Lollardry	hunky-dory	placitory	peasantry
sea-canary	stewardry	amphigory	proditory	servantry
parcenary	shrubbery	seigniory	pellitory	studentry
mercenary	embracery	vainglory	dormitory	ancientry
duodenary	do-goodery	provisory	territory	serpentry
millenary	midwifery	impulsory	desultory	out-sentry
centenary	villagery	incensory	inventory	post-entry
septenary	malingery	ostensory	deceptory	up-country
imaginary	bleachery	aspersory	scriptory	stewartry
caulinary	treachery	accessory	offertory	poetastry
decennary	sprechery	remissory	repertory	fantastry
antennary	branchery	dimissory	assertory	cambistry
legionary	stitchery	reclusory	love-story	sophistry
regionary	periphery	exclusory	executory	chemistry
visionary	scouthery	prelusory	elocutory	palmistry
pulmonary	squeakery	prolusory	statutory	chymistry
sublunary	fallalery	extrusory	overcarry	floristry
polyzoary	chandlery	probatory	glengarry	dentistry
itinerary	whifflery	placatory	brinjarry	baptistry
vulnerary	missilery	precatory	shadberry	casuistry
sisserary	jewellery	evocatory	hindberry	provostry
temporary	scrollery	piscatory	blaeberry	Aylesbury
arbitrary	schoolery	educatory	pokeberry	strangury
adversary	gossamery	predatory	baneberry	party-jury
accessary	pentamery	mandatory	wine-berry	unsavoury
necessary	homeomery	laudatory	Juneberry	speak-easy
janissary	pleiomery	feudatory	naseberry	xerochasy
mandatary	perfumery	prefatory	blueberry	esemplasy
insectary	chicanery	purgatory	hackberry	homoplasy
budgetary	machinery	radiatory	cranberry	euthanasy
societary	millinery	mediatory	soapberry	theocrasy
proletary	baboonery	expiatory	raspberry	ups-a-daisy
planetary	cocoonery	deviatory	bear-berry	upsy-daisy
sonnetary	tycoonery	adulatory	deerberry	hypocrisy
secretary	leprosery	crematory	neesberry	catalepsy

arsy-versy	putridity	sterility	sincerity	congruity
outdoorsy	vastidity	puerility	procerity	concavity
chuprassy	liquidity	neurility	posterity	air-cavity
itsy-bitsy	gravidity	pensility	austerity	depravity
fratchety	fervidity	tensility	dexterity	longevity
crotchety	facundity	fissility	integrity	acclivity
inebriety	fecundity	subtility	jequirity	declivity
notoriety	jocundity	tactility	authority	passivity
propriety	rotundity	sectility	meliority	captivity
insatiety	commodity	ductility	seniority	festivity
subtilety	absurdity	gentility	juniority	incurvity
outcrafty	haecceity	fertility	apriority	convexity
unthrifty	femineity	tortility	obscurity	prolixity
improbity	verbality	hostility	insulsity	specialty
superbity	rascality	inutility	immensity	severalty
procacity	feudality	servility	intensity	Admiralty
predacity	lineality	isopolity	extensity	squiralty
mendacity	unreality	frivolity	gibbosity	ephoralty
mordacity	irreality	credulity	globosity	mayoralty
pugnacity	frugality	garrulity	verbosity	serjeanty
sequacity	lethality	fogramity	hircosity	certainty
loquacity	sociality	supremity	viscosity	viscounty
mendicity	radiality	extremity	hideosity	freebooty
publicity	geniality	sublimity	fungosity	wine-party
cyclicity	veniality	unanimity	dubiosity	stag-party
duplicity	aeriality	proximity	viciosity	lawn-party
atomicity	seriality	infirmity	tediosity	champerty
ethnicity	joviality	deformity	ebriosity	overhasty
atonicity	animality	abnormity	curiosity	anaplasty
febricity	primality	anonymity	furiosity	zooplasty
clericity	formality	mundanity	vitiosity	polymasty
tacticity	normality	profanity	callosity	hyponasty
pepticity	dismality	gigmanity	villosity	immodesty
septicity	atonality	obscenity	animosity	overlusty
verticity	carnality	indignity	gummosity	witchetty
rusticity	vernality	malignity	spinosity	house-duty
precocity	spirality	benignity	carnosity	staff-duty
intercity	plurality	virginity	adiposity	death-duty
morbidity	causality	asininity	pomposity	stamp-duty
turbidity	mentality	indemnity	operosity	point-duty
placidity	mortality	solemnity	amorosity	timenoguy
rancidity	brutality	perennity	leprosity	soliloquy
viscidity	visuality	modernity	ventosity	ground-ivy
frigidity	actuality	maternity	sinuosity	poison-ivy
turgidity	mutuality	paternity	adversity	cataplexy
callidity	sexuality	community	diversity	orthodoxy
pallidity	liability	barbarity	necessity	schmaltzy
stolidity	viability	linearity	nonentity	Z
limpidity	inability	vulgarity	innocuity	rose-topaz
torpidity	stability	uncharity	assiduity	rheumatiz
hispidity	suability	oviparity	ambiguity	slivovitz
stupidity	edibility	disparity	ingenuity	slivowitz
hybridity	gracility	celebrity	strenuity	megahertz
floridity	fragility	tenebrity	obliquity	gigahertz
torridity	febrility	salubrity	antiquity	kilohertz

A	aerophobia	ophthalmia	Heptandria	fenestella
asarabacca	nosophobia	xerostomia	Polyandria	granadilla
Phytolacca	mysophobia	xerodermia	Cortaderia	grenadilla
rhinotheca	sitophobia	leishmania	Pontederia	serradilla
hydrotheca	perithecia	methomania	Metatheria	seguidilla
Tardigrada	embryulcia	anthomania	diphtheria	aspergilla
autostrada	mixed-media	mythomania	gaultheria	chinchilla
Monaxonida	multimedia	anglomania	eubacteria	candelilla
Sauropsida	Pinnipedia	gallomania	groceteria	manzanilla
assafetida	cypripedia	hydromania	ministeria	cascarilla
asafoetida	Cirripedia	metromania	pararthria	banderilla
Lithistida	orthopedia	dipsomania	allochiria	Pulsatilla
propaganda	cyclopedia	Celtomania	scriptoria	Potentilla
corrigenda	sphaeridia	Keltomania	Dinosauria	premaxilla
floribunda	antheridia	erotomania	glucosuria	sarcocolla
barramunda	clostridia	nostomania	glycosuria	osteocolla
Scaphopoda	latifundia	sarracenia	haematuria	nulla-nulla
Cirrhopoda	Cassiopeia	parascenia	monochasia	Collembola
Phyllopoda	peripeteia	myasthenia	paraphasia	sdrucciola
Heteropoda	polyphagia	Rhodymenia	metaplasia	Gorgonzola
Arthropoda	florilegia	leucopenia	phlegmasia	incunabula
Gastropoda	paraplegia	algolagnia	euthanasia	retinacula
Chaetopoda	hemiplegia	scotodinia	tillandsia	Pinguicula
Schizopoda	monoplegia	Polyhymnia	hypalgesia	animalcula
Pelecypoda	cardialgia	quadrennia	Syngenesia	Fratercula
baking-soda	nephralgia	haemoconia	paramnesia	Anguillula
hemichorda	arthralgia	archegonia	framboesia	music-drama
Ahuramazda	gastralgia	paraphonia	aphrodisia	Bridgerama
palaeogaea	proctalgia	escallonia	afrormosia	epiphonema
Hyracoidea	odontalgia	eudaemonia	Lychnapsia	Sexagesima
Echinoidea	gametangia	salicornia	polydipsia	grandmamma
Asteroidea	monomachia	Cavicornia	teichopsia	neurilemma
Lemuroidea	Dibranchia	onirodynia	xanthopsia	sarcolemma
Nematoidea	Saurischia	Tetragynia	flindersia	neurolemma
Blastoidea	paronychia	Pentagynia	rickettsia	meningioma
turnip-flea	dysgraphia	Heptagynia	montbretia	staphyloma
Nemertinea	Diadelphia	cornucopia	marchantia	plasmosoma
seborrhoea	dystrophia	nyctalopia	Ruminantia	Etheostoma
logorrhoea	apomorphia	hemianopia	Constantia	Amblystoma
menorrhoea	Lupercalia	tritanopia	polymastia	terra-firma
gonorrhoea	rhinolalia	protanopia	poinsettia	mycoplasma
orthopnoea	coprolalia	emmetropia	Marcgravia	parenchyma
tachypnoea	Vulcanalia	presbyopia	echopraxia	aerenchyma
Marshalsea	marginalia	formicaria	Cecidomyia	rhinophyma
Sarcophaga	Terminalia	persicaria	strelitzia	victoriana
Mallophaga	Quirinalia	Trachearia	dharmshala	Arthuriana
wonga-wonga	personalia	Cochlearia	drosophila	Christiana
satyagraha	Saturnalia	Zoantharia	gypsophila	pozzuolana
synaloepha	penetralia	crotalaria	clarabella	Quadrumana
jinrikisha	Ambarvalia	Sigillaria	vorticella	tramontana
jinricksha	phocomelia	Radiolaria	serradella	Lippizzana
tatpurusha	eutrapelia	Avicularia	Lingulella	phagedaena
pyracantha	Crocodilia	Plumularia	fustanella	philopoena
anacolutha	paraphilia	Sertularia	Pimpinella	interregna
toxiphobia	canophilia	bipinnaria	Fraxinella	chinachina
theophobia	Lacertilia	Pulmonaria	salmonella	plastilina
algophobia	prothallia	Alcyonaria	petronella	philippina
ergophobia	hyperdulia	adversaria	citronella	scarlatina
canophobia	leuchaemia	planetaria	mozzarella	Skupshtina
panophobia	melanaemia	Sagittaria	Gibberella	concertina
xenophobia	tularaemia	Enneandria	Cinderella	quinaquina
monophobia	hyperaemia	Tetrandria	toccatella	belladonna
cynophobia	hypoxaemia	Icosandria	Turritella	piscifauna
acrophobia	arrhythmia	Pentandria	tarantella	anguifauna

tsesarevna	teratomata	apotropaic	oligarchic	cosmoramic
Pelmatozoa	odontomata	paradisaic	hierarchic	tularaemic
candelabra	Vertebrata	leaf-mosaic	heptarchic	hyperaemic
hiera-picra	desiderata	Ural-Altaic	diagraphic	hypoxaemic
icosahedra	Polychaeta	disyllabic	epigraphic	unacademic
pentahedra	tuftaffeta	galliambic	geographic	Polyphemic
ouvirandra	excrementa	choliambic	biographic	tetrasemic
Heterocera	Apterygota	choriambic	zoographic	arrhythmic
Indigofera	macrobiota	monophobic	orographic	eurhythmic
viscachera	microbiota	aerophobic	urographic	cherubimic
cordillera	barracoota	gonococcic	myographic	isocheimic
hog-cholera	Zend-Avesta	orthopedic	dysgraphic	arch-chimic
telecamera	Camorrista	cyclopedic	zootrophic	pantomimic
cine-camera	parramatta	caryatidic	dystrophic	ophthalmic
scorzonera	comedietta	pentapodic	theosophic	trigrammic
Dermaptera	canzonetta	heptapodic	anamorphic	tragi-comic
Rhipiptera	malaguetta	Arctogaeic	trimorphic	heroi-comic
Plecoptera	terracotta	stenpoaeic	biomorphic	seriocomic
Psocoptera	barracouta	gonorrheic	zoomorphic	uneconomic
Coleoptera	Protophyta	ricinoleic	isomorphic	teleonomic
orthoptera	Chautauqua	diarrhoeic	anaglyphic	chironomic
Dermoptera	portmantua	pyorrhoeic	triglyphic	metronomic
Chiroptera	pillow-lava	mythopoeic	polymathic	astronomic
Neuroptera	amritattva	air-traffic	prognathic	antidromic
phylloxera	wag-at-the-wa'	way-traffic	telepathic	loxodromic
cephalagra	chionodoxa	unspecific	antipathic	trichromic
chaulmugra	pileorhiza	unprolific	idiopathic	leptosomic
mangabeira	coleorhiza	tenebrific	allopathic	pentatomic
Leptospira	mycorrhiza	frigorific	felspathic	polyatomic
mandragora	morbidezza	scientific	megalithic	lithotomic
epanaphora	B	xiphopagic	monolithic	microtomic
Commiphora	mitten-crab	paraplegic	Mesolithic	taxidermic
Discophora	robber-crab	hemiplegic	epicanthic	endodermic
ciliophora	spider-crab	arthralgic	helminthic	hypodermic
Ctenophora	velvet-crab	gastralgic	Visigothic	xerodermic
Rhizophora	hermit-crab	odontalgic	acolouthic	ectodermic
passiflora	luffing-jib	paedagogic	didascalic	diathermic
onychopora	pseudobulb	sialagogic	encephalic	geothermic
tirra-lirra	candle-bomb	cholagogic	naphthalic	exothermic
kookaburra	marker-bomb	hypnagogic	hemicyclic	panspermic
epiplastra	letter-bomb	mystagogic	pericyclic	isochasmic
hyoplastra	pocket-comb	hypnogogic	homocyclic	phantasmic
aspidistra	bread-crumb	genealogic	monocyclic	strabismic
pietra-dura	thingumbob	teleologic	polycyclic	isoseismic
endopleura	heart-throb	nephologic	sapropelic	erethismic
Amphineura	willow-herb	pathologic	philatelic	embolismic
Euthyneura	loll-shraub	lithologic	notaphilic	Hieronymic
caricatura	rub-a-dub-dub	mythologic	coumarilic	matronymic
scordatura	underscrub	sociologic	post-exilic	patronymic
coloratura	undershrub	radiologic	pyrogallic	metronymic
Hitopadesa	mashing-tub	hagiologic	prothallic	polyonymic
paraglossa	C	ophiologic	bimetallic	suboceanic
terra-rossa	genethliac	philologic	ametabolic	disorganic
babiroussa	sacroiliac	tropologic	amphibolic	unmechanic
lithophysa	dysthymiac	necrologic	hyperbolic	theophanic
imbroccata	theomaniac	micrologic	hypergolic	Magellanic
Flagellata	melomaniac	hydrologic	workaholic	pozzolanic
Articulata	monomaniac	hierologic	peelgarlic	aldermanic
parabemata	pyromaniac	astrologic	phenogamic	talismanic
epithemata	opsomaniac	histologic	panislamic	thiocyanic
diastemata	phrenesiac	nostologic	geodynamic	phagedenic
syntagmata	paradisiac	tautologic	biodynamic	glycogenic
sterigmata	megaparsec	tribrachic	isodynamic	osteogenic
melanomata	dispondaic	tristichic	cycloramic	pathogenic

orthogenic	heptatonic	hupaithric	astigmatic	arithmetic
pythogenic	planktonic	orthoboric	kerygmatic	baphometic
radiogenic	orthotonic	metaphoric	dilemmatic	paraenetic
cariogenic	supertonic	theophoric	coelomatic	diagenetic
visiogenic	hypertonic	pyrophoric	diplomatic	epigenetic
mammogenic	polyaxonic	phosphoric	iconomatic	pangenetic
hypnogenic	misocapnic	perchloric	pleromatic	congenetic
androgenic	under-tunic	sophomoric	achromatic	syngenetic
saprogenic	anti-heroic	madreporic	endermatic	neogenetic
iatrogenic	mock-heroic	unhistoric	telesmatic	biogenetic
neurogenic	pleochroic	paediatric	schismatic	orogenetic
lactogenic	monochroic	chemiatric	melismatic	isogenetic
photogenic	polychroic	hippiatric	numismatic	exogenetic
erotogenic	Palaeozoic	dielectric	porismatic	cybernetic
histogenic	megascopic	parametric	morganatic	hysteretic
phytogenic	telescopic	hexametric	mobocratic	anchoretic
rhizogenic	periscopic	telemetric	theocratic	Massoretic
allergenic	endoscopic	perimetric	democratic	ischuretic
tumorgenic	horoscopic	asymmetric	timocratic	trilobitic
myasthenic	poroscopic	iodometric	monocratic	coenobitic
urosthenic	gyroscopic	bolometric	Eurocratic	exopoditic
unhygienic	autoscopic	manometric	autocratic	laryngitic
splanchnic	cryoscopic	barometric	metastatic	bronchitic
paraffinic	nyctalopic	aerometric	antistatic	Israelitic
monoclinic	tritanopic	pyrometric	hypostatic	Ismailitic
polyclinic	protanopic	gasometric	aerostatic	syphilitic
endocrinic	emmetropic	cryometric	gyrostatic	poikilitic
haematinic	hemitropic	volumetric	pyrostatic	tonsilitic
Ugro-Finnic	isentropic	concentric	subaquatic	satellitic
Napoleonic	laeotropic	geocentric	ecphractic	laccolitic
cosmogonic	rheotropic	egocentric	emphractic	Glagolitic
paraphonic	azeotropic	epigastric	paratactic	batholitic
cataphonic	allotropic	palaestric	asyntactic	tremolitic
telephonic	gamotropic	orchestric	hypotactic	phonolitic
antiphonic	aerotropic	glucosuric	aerotactic	miarolitic
cacophonic	presbyopic	glycosuric	synthectic	microlitic
allophonic	monocarpic	barbituric	catalectic	coprolitic
xylophonic	polycarpic	tetrabasic	idiolectic	nummulitic
homophonic	heliotypic	ultrabasic	apoplectic	granulitic
monophonic	phenotypic	paraphasic	peritectic	bathylitic
acrophonic	phonotypic	monophasic	epideictic	tympanitic
trithionic	phototypic	polyphasic	apodeictic	austenitic
ganglionic	cinnabaric	hypalgesic	diazeuctic	encrinitic
thermionic	hyperbaric	cellulosic	anaptyctic	monzonitic
scorpionic	hexaplaric	neoclassic	alphabetic	gabbroitic
histrionic	solfataric	Panglossic	pyro-acetic	dichroitic
cinnamonic	polyhedric	dance-music	diapedetic	margaritic
eudaemonic	monohydric	table-music	epexegetic	Himyaritic
Pandemonic	polyhydric	swing-music	apologetic	endocritic
phlegmonic	peripheric	water-music	synergetic	hypocritic
anharmonic	exospheric	metaphysic	catechetic	chondritic
enharmonic	diphtheric	hyperbatic	empathetic	enhydritic
inharmonic	alphameric	pancreatic	unpathetic	urethritic
euharmonic	homeomeric	unemphatic	metathetic	erythritic
diachronic	tautomeric	phosphatic	antithetic	Sanskritic
anachronic	subgeneric	acroamatic	epenthetic	meteoritic
synchronic	congeneric	undramatic	nomothetic	anchoritic
electronic	penteteric	mathematic	hypothetic	hippuritic
infrasonic	mesenteric	emblematic	prosthetic	gneissitic
ultrasonic	dysenteric	phonematic	ditheletic	pegmatitic
supersonic	amphoteric	episematic	epimeletic	Muscovitic
hypersonic	holosteric	aposematic	diphyletic	quartzitic
trans-sonic	Finno-Ugric	systematic	isogametic	diastaltic
pentatonic	pronephric	phlegmatic	alphametic	catapultic

corybantic	annalistic	histolytic	umbrellaed	all-dreaded
theomantic	moralistic	tachylytic	rock-ribbed	unthreaded
unromantic	fatalistic	Yugoslavic	unshrubbed	bastinaded
pyromantic	vitalistic	radiotoxic	trundle-bed	colonnaded
crescentic	novelistic	phytotoxic	truckle-bed	value-added
Acherontic	pugilistic	caoutchouc	wedding-bed	hand-weeded
thrombotic	nihilistic	D	subscribed	state-aided
diorthotic	familistic	prayer-bead	rose-combed	three-sided
parabiotic	sciolistic	bridgehead	multilobed	crank-sided
antibiotic	simplistic	fiddlehead	feather-bed	improvided
halobiotic	dynamistic	muddlehead	round-faced	unprovided
aerobiotic	optimistic	bufflehead	shamefaced	unheralded
variolotic	urbanistic	beetlehead	false-faced	unshielded
endosmotic	melanistic	rattle-head	horse-faced	many-folded
ecchymotic	Romanistic	bottle-head	white-faced	hard-handed
escharotic	humanistic	puzzle-head	doughfaced	free-handed
polycrotic	feministic	square-head	multifaced	forehanded
homoerotic	hedonistic	figurehead	blackfaced	high-handed
autoerotic	canonistic	springhead	smock-faced	weak-handed
eccoprotic	jingoistic	goodlihead	cream-faced	backhanded
asymptotic	aphoristic	livelihead	wizen-faced	cack-handed
ichthyotic	humoristic	lovelihead	sheep-faced	kack-handed
eucaryotic	naturistic	seemlihead	poker-faced	full-handed
eukaryotic	futuristic	drearihead	paper-faced	open-handed
cataleptic	donatistic	shovel-head	glass-faced	even-handed
metaleptic	Docetistic	maidenhead	Janus-faced	iron-handed
protreptic	quietistic	wooden-head	light-faced	overhanded
antiseptic	nepotistic	jerkinhead	pasty-faced	four-handed
apopemptic	inartistic	dragonhead	putty-faced	neat-handed
anaglyptic	unartistic	mutton-head	high-placed	left-handed
procryptic	linguistic	dunderhead	well-placed	fast-handed
stochastic	euphuistic	nigger-head	overplaced	unexpanded
chiliastic	altruistic	loggerhead	interlaced	unascended
epiblastic	nativistic	hammerhead	tight-laced	undefended
myoblastic	Jehovistic	copperhead	snail-paced	unoffended
anaclastic	essayistic	jolterhead	giddy-paced	unfriended
synclastic	Puseyistic	letterhead	well-graced	unintended
scholastic	diagnostic	flower-head	prejudiced	unattended
anaplastic	geognostic	snake's-head	unrejoiced	inextended
neoplastic	prognostic	death's-head	loud-voiced	unextended
zooplastic	diacaustic	sheep's-head	full-voiced	free-minded
totemastic	apolaustic	billet-head	precipiced	like-minded
docimastic	diacoustic	bullet-head	high-priced	base-minded
polymastic	anacrustic	lappet-head	unbalanced	high-minded
pleonastic	copesettic	goodlyhead	pronounced	weak-minded
epispastic	epiglottic	sleepy-head	undivorced	evil-minded
phantastic	isoglottic	pencil-lead	unproduced	well-minded
anapaestic	argonautic	interplead	club-headed	open-minded
undomestic	aeronautic	horse-bread	bald-headed	even-minded
anamnestic	digoneutic	crispbread	hard-headed	fair-minded
archaistic	leucocytic	laverbread	idle-headed	long-winded
Hebraistic	phagocytic	sweetbread	bareheaded	unseconded
Shivaistic	endophytic	shortbread	sore-headed	ill-founded
solecistic	halophytic	gold-thread	stag-headed	confounded
parodistic	holophytic	pack-thread	long-headed	ungrounded
ditheistic	xerophytic	widespread	weak-headed	red-blooded
phlogistic	mesophytic	wing-spread	nail-headed	hot-blooded
eulogistic	ectophytic	overspread	bull-headed	unregarded
Buddhistic	entophytic	winter-clad	cool-headed	unretarded
erethistic	unanalytic	armour-clad	hoar-headed	unrewarded
cabalistic	anxiolytic	frantic-mad	fair-headed	unhazarded
modalistic	haemolytic	hopping-mad	soft-headed	unrecorded
idealistic	hydrolytic	bridle-road	grey-headed	iron-worded
legalistic	photolytic	microfarad	many-headed	unexcluded

bottle-feed	moustached	sanctified	two-wheeled	bedevilled
breast-feed	unattached	stultified	paralleled	self-willed
knock-kneed	unbreeched	identified	unhouseled	controlled
crook-kneed	unenriched	Scottified	bedraggled	numskulled
interbreed	unbranched	revivified	newfangled	unschooled
crossbreed	unstanched	lethargied	rectangled	crêpe-soled
cottonseed	unblenched	big-bellied	unshingled	unconsoled
fricasseed	untrenched	tunbellied	commingled	principled
millet-seed	unquenched	gor-bellied	full-sailed	untrampled
canary-seed	four-inched	pot-bellied	unassailed	unexampled
guaranteed	unsearched	multiplied	ring-tailed	unscrupled
night-steed	unstarched	unsupplied	cocktailed	icy-pearled
tumble-weed	unsmirched	unoccupied	fork-tailed	unentitled
sneezeweed	unscorched	woewearied	unentailed	ivy-mantled
maidenweed	unthatched	war-wearied	whip-tailed	high-souled
ribbon-weed	far-fetched	day-wearied	unbewailed	self-styled
jimson-weed	low-pitched	unsalaried	coomceiled	unhouzzled
cotton-weed	unploughed	undescried	hard-boiled	unstreamed
silverweed	unrelished	smoke-dried	rear-boiled	uninflamed
yellow-weed	unpolished	spray-dried	soft-boiled	above-named
willow-weed	unfinished	new-married	shop-soiled	undernamed
furrow-weed	diminished	unquarried	three-piled	unredeemed
four-leafed	astonished	tapestried	unbeguiled	unsublimed
vouchsafed	unpunished	prophesied	self-exiled	wrong-timed
kerchiefed	unperished	courtesied	unshackled	undertimed
stubble-fed	flourished	tongue-tied	unwrinkled	programmed
middle-aged	languished	propertied	unrecalled	unbedimmed
disengaged	unravished	dough-baked	scandalled	horn-rimmed
treillaged	well-wished	hawk-beaked	marshalled	full-summed
unassuaged	hard-pushed	parbreaked	initialled	unwelcomed
new-fledged	unsheathed	stark-naked	unappalled	unfathomed
sharp-edged	unbreathed	start-naked	enthralled	unransomed
unabridged	unsmoothed	barebacked	unmetalled	accustomed
well-judged	gag-toothed	humpbacked	unequalled	uncustomed
privileged	gap-toothed	shellacked	victualled	unbottomed
sandbagged	saw-toothed	bivouacked	unrivalled	cross-armed
fool-begged	big-mouthed	ring-necked	thin-walled	light-armed
barelegged	hot-mouthed	high-necked	unlabelled	heavy-armed
gate-legged	wry-mouthed	bull-necked	spancelled	unreformed
long-legged	shanghaied	crew-necked	unexcelled	well-formed
duck-legged	unpolicied	trafficked	satchelled	uninformed
near-legged	unremedied	half-cocked	trammelled	unperfumed
four-legged	able-bodied	full-cocked	empanelled	unconsumed
gaff-rigged	full-bodied	land-locked	unpanelled	impostumed
full-rigged	unembodied	grimlooked	channelled	monorhymed
ship-rigged	soft-bodied	unprovoked	flannelled	unprofaned
jury-rigged	unbloodied	unremarked	unrepelled	Venetianed
periwigged	Yankeefied	pockmarked	misspelled	bartisaned
head-lugged	unpacified	well-marked	apparelled	unhardened
undivulged	silicified	handworked	quarrelled	unburdened
unarranged	principled	asterisked	handselled	unscreened
unrevenged	solidified	unannealed	counselled	shagreened
weak-hinged	lapidified	unrepealed	unravelled	unweakened
stockinged	unmodified	unrevealed	shrivelled	unawakened
unstringed	whiskified	untroubled	embowelled	self-opened
full-winged	stellified	unmanacled	vitrailled	threatened
spur-winged	simplified	spectacled	hard-billed	unsoftened
beeswinged	saponified	fernticled	duck-billed	frightened
slow-winged	unverified	carbuncled	hawk-billed	straitened
loud-lunged	unpurified	high-heeled	soft-billed	unfastened
surcharged	classified	lark-heeled	stencilled	unlistened
verandahed	unossified	cork-heeled	self-killed	unleavened
unbleached	unratified	well-heeled	tendrilled	non-aligned
unbreached	stratified	spur-heeled	imperilled	undesigned

unassigned	unendeared	hot-livered	unpromised	unexpiated
unordained	unindeared	unshowered	customised	fimbriated
mad-brained	round-eared	unanswered	unsurmised	asteriated
fat-brained	cloth-eared	wire-haired	volcanised	unstriated
hot-brained	prick-eared	shag-haired	cretinised	unsatiated
restrained	tulip-eared	long-haired	self-poised	unvitiated
unstrained	high-reared	fair-haired	stylopised	uninflated
unobtained	undeclared	grey-haired	unapprised	umbellated
maintained	unpillared	unrepaired	sensitised	lamellated
mountained	unprepared	unimpaired	epidotised	mamillated
unattained	incompared	uninspired	unbaptised	papillated
ill-defined	school-bred	woman-tired	unmortised	pixillated
uncoffined	heaven-bred	unrequired	ill-advised	decollated
unconfined	forest-bred	unanchored	misadvised	cucullated
unimagined	miswandred	undeplored	uncleansed	petiolated
crinolined	untimbered	unimplored	unlicensed	inviolated
right-lined	uncumbered	unexplored	unenclosed	unviolated
unexamined	unnumbered	uncensored	uninclosed	vacuolated
fore-damned	unbarbered	undoctored	anchylosed	sacculated
caravanned	bewildered	unrestored	ecchymosed	calculated
unbedinned	shouldered	unliquored	round-nosed	cellulated
soft-finned	squandered	undebarred	sharp-nosed	nummulated
beribboned	unrendered	spot-barred	incomposed	crenulated
unpardoned	untendered	ill-starred	unproposed	pinnulated
trunnioned	unhindered	undeterred	superposed	scapulated
positioned	ythundered	race-hatred	unpurposed	serrulated
unreckoned	disordered	self-hatred	indisposed	sublimated
unsummoned	unpowdered	concentred	undisposed	inanimated
unweaponed	untochered	unsceptred	uneclipsed	unanimated
squadroned	unfathered	unobscured	unreversed	hyphenated
unreasoned	ungathered	red-figured	outclassed	turbinated
unseasoned	untethered	unperjured	compressed	marginated
empoisoned	unwithered	unlaboured	suppressed	acuminated
unpoisoned	unpuckered	uncoloured	distressed	pectinated
unprisoned	untuckered	unarmoured	unstressed	pulvinated
unlessoned	streamered	unhonoured	unfocussed	columnated
undertoned	unsummered	immeasured	nonplussed	mucronated
unbuttoned	unmannered	unmeasured	unconfused	personated
hard-earned	ungarnered	unleisured	unanalysed	grey-coated
well-earned	unhampered	uncensured	trilobated	addle-pated
ungoverned	unpampered	unfeatured	eradicated	forcipated
unreturned	untempered	twi-natured	affricated	dissipated
well-turned	attempered	ill-natured	tossicated	syncopated
unfortuned	unpeppered	disnatured	corticated	celebrated
unrenowned	beweltered	twy-natured	tosticated	reiterated
irrenowned	unfiltered	impictured	bifurcated	perforated
mistrayned	man-entered	strictured	obfuscated	frustrated
square-toed	ungartered	structured	uneducated	pandurated
pigeon-toed	pilastered	uncultured	cuspidated	decussated
stilettoed	unmastered	debentured	short-dated	bidentated
bell-shaped	enfestered	enraptured	undefeated	orientated
star-shaped	registered	sculptured	tracheated	attenuated
maxilliped	cloistered	untortured	anucleated	antiquated
pin-striped	unsistered	unnurtured	cochleated	infatuated
pinnatiped	unfostered	unpastured	unrepeated	unactuated
escalloped	balustered	broad-based	miscreated	incurvated
snow-capped	unbattered	displeased	deep-seated	contracted
unstrapped	unbettered	unappeased	variegated	protracted
bird-hipped	unfettered	high-raised	conjugated	abstracted
worshipped	unlettered	moon-raised	corrugated	distracted
hare-lipped	embittered	unoxidised	brecciated	unaffected
rose-lipped	unbuttered	unrealised	gangliated	uneffected
unstripped	unbeavered	unutilised	laciniated	uninfected
end-stopped	dissevered	pulvilised	ammoniated	complected

unexpected	rosy-footed	undeprived	grant-in-aid	double-gild
undirected	deep-rooted	unabsolved	ungainsaid	grandchild
undetected	fore-quoted	unresolved	pseudo-acid	nurse-child
restricted	maladapted	uninvolved	translucid	woman-child
unbudgeted	unscripted	unreproved	scarabaeid	brainchild
ricocheted	sad-hearted	unimproved	palmatifid	underbuild
crotcheted	hen-hearted	unapproved	pinnatifid	craft-guild
lust-dieted	five-parted	unobserved	fringillid	myriadfold
unfilleted	unimparted	undeserved	sipunculid	centrefold
gauntleted	four-parted	unreserved	chironomid	twelvefold
unhelmeted	unreverted	underjawed	pycnogonid	twentyfold
unbonneted	undiverted	foreshewed	anthracoid	thirtyfold
uncarpeted	unescorted	well-thewed	lumbricoid	stream-gold
unuplifted	unreported	home-brewed	obeliscoid	placer-gold
twilighted	forecasted	unshadowed	molluscoid	ground-hold
unknighted	high-tasted	disendowed	zoogloeoid	stronghold
affrighted	indigested	foreshowed	diallagoid	button-hold
unfrighted	undigested	overflowed	pemphigoid	fingerhold
far-sighted	unhallowed	unhallowed	spatangoid	anchor-hold
slow-gaited	unmolested	unfellowed	struthioid	two-year-old
accredited	interested	unmellowed	bacterioid	unforetold
unprofited	unforested	unpillowed	amygdaloid	dream-world
unqualited	unattested	unwinnowed	epicycloid	underworld
sex-limited	undivested	dull-browed	strobiloid	otherworld
unrespited	uninvested	deep-browed	aryballoid	afterworld
dispirited	hard-fisted	unborrowed	paraboloid	backspauld
unspirited	sick-listed	unfurrowed	tetraploid	contraband
unrequited	unresisted	unbestowed	pentaploid	string-band
high-kilted	unassisted	undersexed	nystagmoid	sweathband
sky-planted	unadjusted	dorsifixed	ginglimoid	German-band
untenanted	mistrysted	undismayed	epidermoid	throat-band
covenanted	parquetted	unbetrayed	Africanoid	shield-hand
unaccented	unadmitted	causewayed	arytaenoid	behind-hand
crescented	unremitted	double-dyed	carotenoid	second-hand
accidented	manumitted	almond-eyed	hirudinoid	charge-hand
untalented	pockpitted	double-eyed	delphinoid	bridle-hand
unlamented	bird-witted	goggle-eyed	albuminoid	beforehand
casemented	beef-witted	single-eyed	gelatinoid	minute-hand
fragmented	half-witted	beetle-eyed	carotinoid	sleeve-hand
pedimented	dull-witted	falcon-eyed	anthropoid	hand-in-hand
vestmented	lean-witted	saucer-eyed	saccharoid	four-in-hand
unrepented	iron-witted	wapper-eyed	cylindroid	master-hand
unparented	unallotted	gimlet-eyed	chaudfroid	woolly-hand
unresented	complotted	squint-eyed	suspensoid	Angaraland
acquainted	top-knotted	unpurveyed	dispersoid	scent-gland
lap-jointed	eye-spotted	unsurveyed	rheumatoid	ploughland
disjointed	unexecuted	yellow-eyed	graphitoid	distilland
bow-fronted	unpolluted	hollow-eyed	parasitoid	bottom-land
surmounted	convoluted	bloody-eyed	trachytoid	hinderland
wainscoted	uncommuted	bleary-eyed	zoophytoid	wonderland
undernoted	undisputed	starry-eyed	confervoid	borderland
club-footed	colleagued	unemployed	ultra-rapid	fatherland
lobe-footed	purple-hued	self-glazed	monohybrid	mother-land
free-footed	arabesqued	care-crazed	polyhybrid	hinterland
barefooted	four-leaved	pince-nezed	eurypterid	Reichsland
surefooted	ill-behaved	blood-sized	cattle-grid	no-man's-land
wing-footed	misbehaved	undersized	notodontid	confirmand
horn-footed	unenslaved	hearing-aid	superfluid	stink-brand
four-footed	undepraved	hawser-laid	semi-liquid	glitterand
flat-footed	unbelieved	shield-maid	unwithheld	ance-errand
left-footed	unrelieved	kennel-maid	brickfield	once-errand
soft-footed	undeceived	schoolmaid	wheat-field	Krugerrand
polt-footed	unreceived	bridesmaid	paddy-field	magistrand
slow-footed	short-lived	pantrymaid	windshield	music-stand

grandstand	scrape-good	fishing-rod	churchyard	Aviculidae
coach-stand	tocher-good	tension-rod	timber-yard	Serranidae
still-stand	novicehood	unscabbard	lumber-yard	Lycaenidae
understand	princehood	postal-card	sand-lizard	Zygaenidae
cruet-stand	beadlehood	ration-card	rock-lizard	Sciaenidae
ampussy-and	gentlehood	master-card	wall-lizard	Muraenidae
condescend	squirehood	letter-card	abbey-laird	Cyprinidae
subtrahend	riding-hood	spade-beard	tropic-bird	Tyrannidae
comprehend	likelihood	white-beard	mallee-bird	Vireonidae
back-friend	livelihood	hawksbeard	wattle-bird	Trogonidae
girlfriend	kinglihood	goat's-beard	whidah-bird	Salmonidae
discommend	drearihood	peg-tankard	whydah-bird	Scombridae
underspend	bountihood	Montagnard	missel-bird	Colubridae
unreverend	orphanhood	bread-board	parson-bird	Tanagridae
finger's-end	maidenhood	mould-board	mutton-bird	Viverridae
convertend	hoydenhood	sound-board	bishop-bird	Dasyuridae
wunderkind	virginhood	knife-board	Quaker-bird	Haliotidae
stone-blind	cousinhood	barge-board	rafter-bird	Locustidae
mastermind	deaconhood	verge-board	butter-bird	Scolytidae
rough-grind	nationhood	smoke-board	weaver-bird	Salicaceae
nanosecond	matronhood	scale-board	tailor-bird	Punicaceae
hammer-pond	fatherhood	fibreboard	whore's-bird	Caricaceae
correspond	motherhood	score-board	tyrant-bird	Myricaceae
cummerbund	waiterhood	skateboard	regent-bird	Urticaceae
overabound	masterhood	pasteboard	yellow-bird	Naiadaceae
hinge-bound	sisterhood	above-board	gooney-bird	Resedaceae
housebound	knighthood	matchboard	whirlybird	Xyridaceae
earthbound	parenthood	patchboard	canary-bird	proteaceae
north-bound	priesthood	notch-board	laggen-gird	Araliaceae
south-bound	Christhood	weigh-board	needlecord	Rhyniaceae
shellbound	heart-blood	flash-board	tape-record	Clusiaceae
spellbound	photoflood	earth-board	misericord	Pyrolaceae
stormbound	water-flood	blackboard	russel-cord	Betulaceae
water-bound	understood	chalkboard	rutherford	Alismaceae
frostbound	orange-wood	pedal-board	tetrachord	Solanaceae
money-bound	spongewood	sternboard	pentachord	Rhamnaceae
bloodhound	paddle-wood	astarboard	heptachord	Tuberaceae
nursehound	fiddlewood	underboard	clarichord	Piperaceae
rough-hound	candle-wood	paperboard	clavichord	Cyperaceae
otter-hound	greasewood	otter-board	weasel-word	Onagraceae
shell-mound	sneezewood	floorboard	broadsword	Lythraceae
three-pound	springwood	chessboard	small-sword	Mimosaceae
decompound	sandalwood	float-board	short-sword	Isoetaceae
walk-around	brazil-wood	strawboard	court-sword	Sapotaceae
turnaround	sappan-wood	emery-board	towel-gourd	Filicineae
wraparound	cotton-wood	sea-leopard	storm-cloud	Mucorineae
dead-ground	button-wood	camelopard	night-cloud	proseuchae
foreground	calico-wood	dynamitard	purse-proud	Sympetalae
calf-ground	letter-wood	sword-guard	house-proud	trabeculae
background	bitterwood	watch-guard	collar-stud	valleculae
overground	beaver-wood	blackguard	parcel-bawd	corbiculae
fair-ground	splintwood	water-guard	rent-a-crowd	maxillulae
showground	walnutwood	after-guard	E	pennatulae
clay-ground	yellow-wood	dressguard	endamoebae	Phenogamae
playground	canary-wood	coastguard	entamoebae	Mustelinae
ultrasound	ornithopod	churchward	Seleucidae	Viverrinae
supersound	brachiopod	easselward	Bombycidae	primiparae
flesh-wound	cephalopod	uphillward	Limnaeidae	chelicerae
death-wound	steganopod	schoolward	Sphingidae	Cruciferae
interwound	gasteropod	heavenward	Cotingidae	Guttiferae
eisteddfod	stomatopod	netherward	Zoanthidae	Conjugatae
thunder-god	smørrebrød	hitherward	Crotalidae	Compositae
serpent-god	picture-rod	greensward	Scopelidae	redescribe
smooth-shod	gauging-rod	street-ward	Mustelidae	transcribe

paedotribe	accomplice	sunderance	refulgence	profluence
Turcophobe	cream-slice	sufferance	effulgence	congruence
anglophobe	undervoice	temperance	detergence	connivence
gallophobe	chest-voice	reiterance	divergence	snaphaunce
hippophobe	dentifrice	penetrance	resurgence	sand-launce
ombrophobe	cockatrice	re-entrance	insurgence	sovenaunce
negrophobe	cantatrice	monstrance	upsurgence	puissaunce
hygrophobe	apprentice	perdurance	somewhence	habitaunce
Russophobe	fore-notice	defeasance	deficience	disavaunce
photophobe	interstice	suffisance	efficience	incandesce
Slavophobe	red-lattice	cognisance	prescience	recrudesce
riding-robe	sea-service	chevisance	conscience	convalesce
mother-to-be	tea-service	pulsatance	bioscience	effloresce
klangfarbe	eye-service	expectance	expedience	deliquesce
vacuum-tube	lip-service	inductance	munifience	effervesce
pollen-tube	disservice	reluctance	resilience	caper-sauce
Morris-tube	reprobance	repentance	ebullience	circumduce
square-face	sword-dance	acceptance	recipience	sea-lettuce
faying-face	snake-dance	importance	incipience	Rolls-Royce ®
brazen-face	torch-dance	desistance	desipience	nightshade
face-to-face	ascendance	resistance	insipience	sword-blade
subsurface	attendance	assistance	experience	spuleblade
tallow-face	redundance	admittance	transience	razor-blade
blonde-lace	accordance	remittance	impatience	custom-made
bobbin-lace	belly-dance	disadvance	prevalence	tailor-made
birthplace	allegeance	connivance	univalence	mazarinade
everyplace	miscreance	survivance	trivalence	pasquinade
strait-lace	inelegance	approvance	pestilence	carbonnade
pillow-lace	suffigance	observance	excellence	dragonnade
tawdry-lace	irradiance	conveyance	repellence	flanconade
gas-furnace	allegiance	purveyance	condolence	masquerade
sinke-a-pace	brilliance	surveyance	somnolence	tardigrade
cinque-pace	compliance	chatoyance	turbulence	spinigrade
hydrospace	suppliance	upbuoyance	succulence	cirrigrade
hyperspace	invariance	decumbence	truculence	dorsigrade
interspace	covariance	recumbence	crapulence	saltigrade
hurdle-race	luxuriance	off-licence	corpulence	centigrade
scapegrace	outbalance	renascence	flatulence	retrograde
welter-race	fer-de-lance	tabescence	recommence	intergrade
grand-niece	lead-glance	albescence	permanence	slave-trade
great-niece	side-glance	pubescence	prominence	balustrade
thumbpiece	iron-glance	quiescence	continence	tally-trade
broadpiece	overglance	calescence	pertinence	velocipede
fieldpiece	repellance	tumescence	abstinence	cirrhipede
three-piece	imparlance	canescence	threepence	taeniacide
ridge-piece	affirmance	senescence	sevenpence	aphidicide
siege-piece	sustenance	virescence	thruppence	stillicide
mouse-piece	convenance	latescence	eightpence	spermicide
touch-piece	provenance	dehiscence	fifty-pence	sororicide
mouthpiece	indignance	fatiscence	preference	fratricide
crown-piece	malignance	precedence	difference	aborticide
altarpiece	repugnance	procidence	conference	ophicleide
afterpiece	ordonnance	diffidence	abhorrence	bisulphide
crosspiece	unisonance	confidence	occurrence	disulphide
nightpiece	consonance	subsidence	recurrence	oxy-bromide
assay-piece	dissonance	dissidence	incurrence	isocyanide
abbey-piece	alternance	providence	co-presence	antimonide
lucky-piece	governance	ascendence	competence	saccharide
pennypiece	come-upance	dependence	resentence	pyromeride
warrandice	comeupance	impendence	prepotence	polymeride
fire-office	appearance	imprudence	advertence	purse-pride
loan-office	exuberance	snake-fence	desistence	overstride
overoffice	hinderance	negligence	insistence	seven-a-side
post-office	ponderance	indulgence	confluence	hitherside

silverside	cornel-tree	surplusage	apostrophe	rascal-like
prompt-side	missel-tree	escheatage	philosophe	seamanlike
Shrovetide	manteltree	baronetage	dissheathe	maidenlike
springtide	dragon-tree	freightage	outbreathe	slovenlike
school-tide	cotton-tree	fraughtage	power-lathe	dragonlike
nucleotide	Tyburn-tree	exploitage	wanchancie	matron-like
mercaptide	calico-tree	percentage	cote-hardie	Amazon-like
summertide	timber-tree	anecdotage	seannachie	spider-like
winter-tide	summer-tree	culvertage	maconochie	tinder-like
Eastertide	butter-tree	colportage	seecatchie	summerlike
Lammas-tide	beaver-tree	multi-stage	kirn-dollie	sister-like
court-guide	silver-tree	apron-stage	corn-dollie	sailor-like
honey-guide	bullet-tree	uredo-stage	hootnannie	priest-like
disprovide	forest-tree	gillravage	custard-pie	Christlike
isoniazide	locust-tree	deckle-edge	sweetie-pie	unladylike
olde-worlde	tallow-tree	quick-hedge	pudding-pie	guilty-like
zinc-blende	covenantee	thorn-hedge	dinanderie	morris-pike
hornblende	distinguée	wheat-midge	minauderie	bush-shrike
radiosonde	chimpanzee	road-bridge	camsteerie	crow-shrike
photodiode	chasse-café	land-bridge	stoutherie	bird-strike
pistillode	pousse-café	wire-bridge	bizarrerie	moonstrike
discommode	table-knife	leaf-bridge	leproserie	overstrike
avant-garde	flick-knife	deck-bridge	rôtisserie	earth-smoke
interclude	clasp-knife	tollbridge	bijouterie	chain-smoke
inquietude	paper-knife	overbridge	brusquerie	water-smoke
mansuetude	fruit-knife	raft-bridge	knobkerrie	frost-smoke
consuetude	putty-knife	footbridge	seigneurie	stone-broke
solicitude	orange-wife	drawbridge	ride-and-tie	stony-broke
similitude	oyster-wife	skew-bridge	parmacitie	dead-stroke
definitude	butter-wife	hodgepodge	pockmantie	side-stroke
infinitude	safety-cage	touch-judge	water-nixie	push-stroke
crassitude	husbandage	blancmange	butter-bake	backstroke
spissitude	brigandage	rifle-range	sponge-cake	downstroke
colatitude	garlandage	mock-orange	cheesecake	hair-stroke
exactitude	impoundage	prearrange	simnel-cake	four-stroke
sanctitude	way-baggage	disarrange	pepper-cake	heatstroke
plentitude	remortgage	misarrange	bride's-cake	spot-stroke
inaptitude	macrophage	short-range	Johnny-cake	schipperke
ineptitude	remarriage	strap-hinge	madder-lake	craigfluke
pinguitude	assemblage	stamp-hinge	coral-snake	liver-fluke
husking-bee	persiflage	constringe	tiger-snake	Provençale
raising-bee	camouflage	perstringe	water-snake	worldscale
tweedledee	maquillage	maskalonge	glass-snake	scent-scale
nourice-fee	pit-village	maskanonge	grass-snake	Clydesdale
kitchen-fee	after-image	maskinonge	shieldrake	yaffingale
gallows-lee	pilgrimage	overcharge	shelldrake	martingale
distrainee	villainage	rent-charge	green-drake	hartie-hale
snick-a-snee	villeinage	lithomarge	put-and-take	scrag-whale
barley-bree	cartonnage	inselberge	double-take	ca'ing-whale
transferee	plunderage	dramaturge	sweepstake	sperm-whale
poll-degree	telpherage	broad-gauge	earthquake	pilot-whale
corroboree	lighterage	steam-gauge	waterquake	muslin-kale
pagoda-tree	quarterage	paper-gauge	heart-quake	aquamanale
almond-tree	seignorage	water-gauge	patchcocke	Whitsun-ale
coffee-tree	proctorage	centrifuge	princelike	jumble-sale
orange-tree	effleurage	subterfuge	unlifelike	succursale
doubletree	harbourage	sabretache	unwifelike	tattle-tale
saddle-tree	discourage	ultrafiche	riddle-like	unbribable
candle-tree	overdosage	microfiche	unhomelike	ascribable
randle-tree	sea-passage	synecdoche	sphere-like	improbable
singletree	expressage	mesoscaphe	squire-like	absorbable
nettle-tree	vernissage	limitrophe	hearse-like	uncurbable
bottle-tree	petrissage	anastrophe	unkinglike	unclubable
plough-tree	repoussage	epistrophe	springlike	implacable

impeccable	sketchable	stimulable	vulnerable	narratable
deprecable	avouchable	unblamable	temperable	rejectable
eradicable	ploughable	inflamable	inoperable	delectable
predicable	relishable	redeemable	filterable	aspectable
vindicable	polishable	sublimable	pulverable	detectable
applicable	punishable	fathomable	answerable	indictable
explicable	perishable	ransomable	integrable	round-table
despicable	enunciable	customable	repairable	targetable
extricable	insociable	affirmable	respirable	marketable
masticable	unsociable	deformable	inspirable	plane-table
chain-cable	associable	reformable	acquirable	earth-table
provocable	amerciable	presumable	requirable	creditable
ineducable	remediable	consumable	perforable	profitable
uneducable	repudiable	unamenable	deplorable	inimitable
manducable	rarefiable	listenable	evaporable	hospitable
unreadable	pacifiable	convenable	factorable	charitable
degradable	modifiable	designable	restorable	requitable
formidable	salifiable	assignable	inexorable	unsuitable
providable	verifiable	impugnable	deferrable	inevitable
demandable	notifiable	expugnable	inferrable	insultable
ascendable	clergiable	ordainable	incurrable	tenantable
defendable	unreliable	regainable	demurrable	lamentable
dependable	affiliable	obtainable	penetrable	patentable
expendable	compliable	retainable	arbitrable	heriotable
extendable	undeniable	attainable	procurable	unquotable
regardable	inexpiable	calcinable	perdurable	acceptable
rewardable	invariable	confinable	colourable	insertable
hazardable	unvariable	imaginable	honourable	assertable
accordable	quarriable	declinable	favourable	water-table
recordable	insatiable	reclinable	measurable	reportable
unfordable	unsatiable	inclinable	leisurable	importable
illaudable	negotiable	examinable	censurable	exportable
effaceable	unenviable	eliminable	mensurable	metastable
enticeable	unshakable	abominable	culturable	arrestable
noticeable	mistakable	germinable	pasturable	detestable
pierceable	attackable	terminable	releasable	attestable
unrideable	unpickable	pardonable	appeasable	accostable
decreeable	dislikable	actionable	inerasable	adjustable
damageable	shrinkable	commonable	unerasable	admittable
manageable	unsinkable	summonable	oxidisable	rebuttable
voyageable	provokable	reasonable	realisable	executable
pledgeable	remarkable	seasonable	utilisable	confutable
changeable	unworkable	poisonable	surmisable	commutable
chargeable	unscalable	personable	cognisable	permutable
unlikeable	unhealable	unatonable	despisable	computable
unsaleable	repealable	governable	cleansable	disputable
unnameable	appealable	returnable	licensable	statutable
untameable	revealable	unturnable	proposable	fatiguable
irremeable	recyclable	self-unable	supposable	unarguable
delineable	unbailable	dissipable	disposable	invaluable
untuneable	unmailable	impalpable	endorsable	unvaluable
debateable	assailable	inculpable	impassable	reissuable
unliveable	ventilable	exculpable	unpassable	achievable
unloveable	recallable	extirpable	assessable	believable
immoveable	untellable	unbearable	unamusable	relievable
unmoveable	unfillable	untearable	dialysable	deceivable
unsizeable	untillable	unwearable	analysable	receivable
unruffable	disyllable	declarable	combatable	forgivable
propagable	inviolable	comparable	unbeatable	deprivable
segregable	consolable	renderable	come-at-able	cultivable
detachable	calculable	ponderable	repeatable	resolvable
attachable	inoculable	unpeerable	inflatable	insolvable
quenchable	circulable	preferable	collatable	unsolvable
searchable	coagulable	sufferable	proratable	improvable

unprovable	defectible	boondoggle	demoiselle	hemp-nettle
approvable	effectible	mishguggle	brocatelle	case-bottle
observable	rejectible	quadrangle	immortelle	bluebottle
reservable	detectible	maxi-single	trouvaille	wash-bottle
reviewable	decoctible	chevesaile	déshabillé	junk-bottle
unknowable	deductible	locomobile	dishabille	tear-bottle
unplayable	inventible	automobile	escadrille	beer-bottle
prepayable	deceptible	snowmobile	espadrille	knat-bottle
defrayable	receptible	low-profile	vaudeville	somnambule
unswayable	impartible	muster-file	claircolle	ventricule
conveyable	revertible	letter-file	barcarolle	animalcule
clergyable	divertible	honey-chile	window-bole	crepuscule
employable	digestible	Turcophile	pratincole	corpuscule
squeezable	ingestible	discophile	pigeonhole	reschedule
unseizable	comestible	paedophile	button-hole	enschedule
unprizable	divestible	audiophile	spider-hole	plastidule
capsizable	resistible	gallophile	fingerhole	spinnerule
bescribble	reflexible	hippophile	pocket-hole	work-to-rule
soap-bubble	inflexible	ombrophile	eyelet-hole	egg-capsule
invincible	unscramble	necrophile	rabbit-hole	bel-accoyle
unforcible	reassemble	negrophile	heart-whole	enneastyle
immiscible	disennoble	Russophile	bronchiole	tetrastyle
conducible	onyx-marble	arctophile	strophiole	pentastyle
producible	dissoluble	cartophile	undecimole	araeostyle
incredible	semi-double	Slavophile	carmagnole	cyclostyle
uncredible	distrouble	wait-a-while	bibliopole	pycnostyle
ascendible	tabernacle	worthwhile	sugar-maple	metrostyle
extendible	hibernacle	dreamwhile	long-staple	schemozzle
invendible	receptacle	otherwhile	wool-staple	shlemozzle
unvendible	skene-occle	aquamanile	participle	trou-madame
corrodible	vitellicle	thermopile	rock-temple	school-dame
includible	grand-uncle	velvet-pile	work-people	cannon-game
eye-legible	great-uncle	prehensile	overpeople	stern-frame
re-eligible	semicircle	distensile	scrog-apple	water-frame
ineligible	full-circle	subsessile	thorn-apple	Peter-see-me
negligible	hour-circle	protrusile	sugar-apple	quadrireme
corrigible	multicycle	fluviatile	suboctuple	phantasime
intangible	motor-cycle	retractile	oversubtle	beforetime
untangible	fairy-cycle	projectile	flea-beetle	springtime
infallible	punch-ladle	productile	gold-beetle	school-time
unfallible	toddy-ladle	mercantile	pine-beetle	underntime
referrible	cat's-cradle	percentile	rose-beetle	summertime
inferrible	cock-paddle	biquintile	rove-beetle	dinner-time
defeasible	bestraddle	chrysotile	stag-beetle	suppertime
infeasible	side-saddle	subfertile	dung-beetle	Eastertime
unfeasible	pack-saddle	bissextile	bark-beetle	decagramme
inerasible	paradiddle	hamshackle	musk-beetle	decigramme
expansible	taradiddle	ramshackle	disentitle	kilogramme
defensible	nun's-fiddle	ranshackle	portmantle	aerogramme
insensible	bass-fiddle	stay-tackle	disgruntle	unovercome
unsensible	pine-needle	kenspeckle	half-kirtle	brachydome
ostensible	cock-paidle	outspeckle	Jew's-myrtle	foster-home
extensible	rush-candle	ferntickle	sand-castle	stay-at-home
corrosible	foot-candle	corncockle	card-castle	gastronome
reversible	whip-handle	shoebuckle	mile-castle	palindrome
impassible	pump-handle	turnbuckle	forecastle	cosmodrome
accessible	flapdoodle	besprinkle	bur-thistle	hippodrome
admissible	limb-girdle	periwinkle	sow-thistle	xylochrome
remissible	varicocele	penoncele	sea-whistle	monochrome
impossible	bubonocele	chaud-mellé	cacomistle	lipochrome
unpossible	enterocele	villanelle	neat-cattle	cytochrome
diffusible	steatocele	fontanelle	fish-kettle	polychrome
compatible	protostele	jargonelle	self-mettle	frolicsome
olfactible	harpy-eagle	ritornelle	dead-nettle	unhandsome

blithesome	paraselene	capitoline	travertine	grapestone
meddlesome	anadyomene	discipline	predestine	gravestone
cuddlesome	Hippocrene	timber-line	philistine	clingstone
gigglesome	subterrene	spider-line	laurustine	slingstone
tanglesome	benzpyrene	borderline	subroutine	peach-stone
mettlesome	contravene	ledger-line	ensanguine	march-stone
plaguesome	azobenzene	picket-line	exsanguine	pitchstone
healthsome	orthocaine	staphyline	margravine	touchstone
drearisome	lignocaine	pyroxyline	aberdevine	slickstone
burdensome	benzocaine	carthamine	semi-divine	chockstone
chromosome	châtelaine	ethylamine	sops-in-wine	sleekstone
plasmosome	gas-turbine	bellarmine	disentwine	chalkstone
centrosome	psittacine	iridosmine	intertwine	clinkstone
cumbersome	fettuccine	reillumine	pyridoxine	stinkstone
lumbersome	colchicine	strychnine	piperazine	pearl-stone
bothersome	Plasticine	unfeminine	tartrazine	logan-stone
laboursome	putrescine	creatinine	trade-falne	greenstone
humoursome	isoleucine	Fescennine	comédienne	satin-stone
brightsome	smaragdine	coregonine	sicilienne	quernstone
frightsome	sylphidine	cinchonine	Tyrolienne	brownstone
tediousome	pyrimidine	cowdie-pine	Parisienne	altar-stone
teleostome	piperidine	cowrie-pine	spauld-bone	adderstone
cyclostome	alabandine	antilopine	stifle-bone	cross-stone
bragadisme	brigandine	philippine	huckle-bone	float-stone
imposthume	farrandine	saccharine	cuttle-bone	troutstone
preconsume	ferrandine	aquamarine	coffin-bone	honey-stone
cyclothyme	muscardine	quinacrine	collar-bone	penny-stone
holoenzyme	purse-seine	methedrine	raven's-bone	fairy-stone
rumple-bane	sweep-seine	Benzedrine	splint-bone	paroxytone
parischane	over-refine	pantherine	breastbone	shard-borne
rhodophane	disimagine	adulterine	marrow-bone	underborne
lithophane	asparagine	papaverine	quadricone	water-borne
hyalophane	fire-engine	sapphirine	cone-in-cone	auto-immune
cellophane ®	rose-engine	euchlorine	cinder-cone	ill-fortune
hydrophane	tank-engine	lacustrine	spermogone	misfortune
multiplane	beam-engine	palustrine	vibraphone	heterodyne
datum-plane	aeroengine	tambourine	sousaphone	chlorodyne
hydroplane	pulp-engine	avanturine	dictaphone	trichogyne
rhizoplane	beer-engine	aventurine	videophone	ergatogyne
water-plane	pony-engine	Alphonsine	radiophone	Euphrosyne
rotor-plane	ice-machine	dessiatine	anglophone	panton-shoe
bibliomane	didelphine	dessyatine	gramophone	tennis-shoe
quadrumane	catarrhine	tetractine	microphone	death-throe
frangipane	earth-shine	polyactine	hydrophone	fire-escape
elecampane	cloacaline	univoltine	photophone	riverscape
window-pane	corydaline	brigantine	interphone	trans-shape
steam-crane	tourmaline	adamantine	Entryphone ®	ticker-tape
water-crane	penny-a-line	diamantine	arpeggione	stone-snipe
high-octane	disincline	amarantine	zabaglione	cul-de-lampe
tramontane	microcline	quarantine	sauce-alone	triniscope
submontane	shroud-line	Tridentine	sea-anemone	nephoscope
cismontane	sourdeline	barkentine	chitarrone	radioscope
penny-stane	anopheline	clementine	minestrone	hagioscope
anthracene	mousseline	serpentine	prednisone	helioscope
ante-Nicene	strobiline	porpentine	twelve-tone	myrioscope
post-Nicene	rosaniline	turpentine	demi-ditone	teinoscope
Palaeocene	isabelline	florentine	fieldstone	rhinoscope
vinylidene	Ghibelline	cispontine	grindstone	iconoscope
damasceene	streamline	pyrrhotine	bloodstone	colposcope
Palaeogene	fathom-line	guillotine	snakestone	microscope
seltzogene	rupicoline	Gilbertine	drakestone	hydroscope
Antiochene	arvicoline	Colbertine	eagle-stone	hygroscope
clomiphene	saxicoline	Norbertine	rhinestone	statoscope
zygosphene	trampoline	vespertine	swinestone	lactoscope

pantoscope	escritoire	mismeasure	paper-chase	scandalise
Vertoscope ®	repertoire	outmeasure	repurchase	illegalise
cystoscope	sea-vampire	entreasure	multiphase	specialise
radarscope	barbed-wire	untreasure	interphase	cordialise
bathyscope	smooth-bore	overinsure	oligoclase	patrialise
ox-antelope	threescore	disclosure	orthoclase	initialise
redevelope	seven-score	impressure	saccharase	bestialise
tiller-rope	underscore	expressure	luciferase	trivialise
heliotrope	eightscore	commissure	polymerase	decimalise
phototrope	compradore	judicature	paraphrase	optimalise
monkey-rope	dumbledore	caricature	metaphrase	eternalise
cantaloupe	battledore	disfeature	periphrase	journalise
chromatype	heretofore	misfeature	holophrase	liberalise
palaeotype	hydrochore	nunciature	head-cheese	federalise
stereotype	anthophore	calliature	sage-cheese	generalise
chromotype	ctenophore	tubulature	blue-cheese	mineralise
phaenotype	phonophore	maculature	pick-cheese	literalise
stannotype	carpophore	good-nature	Singhalese	demoralise
fluorotype	androphore	usurpature	journalese	centralise
somatotype	spirophore	crispature	Vietnamese	neutralise
threadbare	sporophore	quadrature	Johnsonese	naturalise
spring-hare	photophore	literature	chersonese	palatalise
timber-mare	rhizophore	compacture	Portuguese	capitalise
headsquare	alongshore	refracture	postchaise	devitalise
word-square	peacock-ore	prefecture	mayonnaise	revitalise
five-square	whiggamore	conjecture	reappraise	chaptalise
foursquare	nethermore	projecture	overpraise	sensualise
rustic-ware	Monsignore	sun-picture	Islamicise	evangelise
pebble-ware	blastopore	encincture	fanaticise	caramelise
lustreware	tetraspore	extincture	politicise	mongrelise
crouch-ware	swarm-spore	forfeiture	scepticise	demobilise
jasperware	uredospore	nourriture	asepticise	immobilise
hollow-ware	aeciospore	subculture	elasticise	solubilise
nerve-fibre	pycnospore	apiculture	plasticise	lyophilise
stavesacre	macrospore	aviculture	Gnosticise	volatilise
pillow-bere	microspore	zooculture	Scotticise	decivilise
hemisphere	saddle-sore	garmenture	circumcise	gospellise
atmosphere	plague-sore	misventure	emparadise	Boswellise
ionosphere	chain-store	attainture	imparadise	parabolise
mesosphere	superstore	supporture	unparadise	metabolise
barysphere	pied-à-terre	contexture	hypnoidise	alcoholise
uintathere	centimetre	prefixture	chloridise	spaniolise
otherwhere	micrometre	commixture	fluoridise	vitriolise
everywhere	hectometre	paradoxure	peroxidise	monopolise
vivandière	centilitre	dextrogyre	cuckoldise	epistolise
lavallière	hectolitre	orthophyre	gormandise	macadamise
jardinière	metacentre	granophyre	aggrandise	pilgrimise
ferronière	head-centre	ground-base	psalmodise	legitimise
couturière	hypocentre	needle-case	rhapsodise	compromise
corsetière	rest-centre	pencil-case	niggardise	lobotomise
arthromere	lack-lustre	caddis-case	jeopardise	presurmise
blastomere	roquelaure	pillowcase	sherardise	Africanise
kerseymere	nature-cure	vanity-case	hansardise	reorganise
hectostere	rejoindure	peroxidase	bastardise	Italianise
self-severe	four-figure	predecease	paralogise	utopianise
soup-meagre	debouchure	little-ease	theologise	Persianise
soup-maigre	embouchure	prerelease	homologise	Russianise
capillaire	craquelure	day-release	monologise	fustianise
debonnaire	circummure	underlease	lethargise	dehumanise
nécessaire	fish-manure	reincrease	monarchise	unhumanise
secretaire	encoignure	palm-grease	goliathise	puritanise
reliquaire	bellamoure	heart's-ease	sympathise	mutagenise
praemunire	engendrure	strip-tease	radicalise	indigenise
Directoire	commeasure	stern-chase	devocalise	homogenise

röntgenise	schematise	ember-goose	snake-house	dijudicate
heathenise	pragmatise	brant-goose	smoke-house	pacificate
albumenise	enigmatise	brent-goose	frame-house	nidificate
greisenise	stigmatise	puir's-hoose	whorehouse	indelicate
rejuvenise	traumatise	precompose	storehouse	spiflicate
citizenise	rheumatise	discompose	state-house	umbilicate
Jacobinise	apostatise	circumpose	proof-house	triplicate
vitaminise	synthetise	presuppose	coach-house	complicate
effeminise	demonetise	all-purpose	watch-house	supplicate
albuminise	remonetise	predispose	weigh-house	divaricate
bituminise	syncretise	overexpose	rough-house	hereticate
chlorinise	graphitise	saccharose	flash-house	elasticate
gelatinise	dolomitise	pease-brose	earth-house	detoxicate
keratinise	mylonitise	water-brose	steakhouse	intoxicate
scrutinise	parasitise	gelder-rose	blockhouse	trisulcate
antagonise	warrantise	oedematose	wheel-house	obtruncate
cinchonise	serpentise	caespitose	jewel-house	detruncate
missionise	anabaptise	sarmentose	still-house	reallocate
sectionise	burnettise	apocalypse	greenhouse	equivocate
decolonise	hey-de-guise	transverse	sugar-house	trifurcate
recolonise	epiloguise	blood-horse	dower-house	confiscate
infamonise	prologuise	trace-horse	power-house	lemniscate
uncanonise	colloquise	stage-horse	manor-house	exheredate
enthronise	fore-advise	stonehorse	doll's-house	dilucidate
gluttonise	bolshevise	shire-horse	puir's-house	revalidate
fraternise	relativise	white-horse	poor's-house	invalidate
westernise	fesseewise	coach-horse	glasshouse	intimidate
episcopise	squarewise	wheel-horse	lighthouse	dilapidate
penelopise	ploughwise	towel-horse	night-house	mithridate
Philippise	lengthwise	thill-horse	plant-house	chloridate
plagiarise	parcelwise	troop-horse	pilot-house	fluoridate
burglarise	scrollwise	water-horse	charthouse	subcordate
depolarise	tandemwise	river-horse	court-house	transudate
tabularise	anthemwise	shaft-horse	guest-house	chlamydate
secularise	randomwise	draft-horse	trust-house	chalybeate
regularise	stolenwise	light-horse	bawdy-house	trilineate
popularise	cornerwise	hobby-horse	ferry-house	ebracteate
laminarise	dexterwise	dandy-horse	whale-louse	illaqueate
militarise	mirrorwise	redisburse	grape-louse	sluice-gate
slenderise	streetwise	racecourse	prick-louse	congregate
grangerise	thwartwise	forecourse	sheep-louse	corpse-gate
weatherise	recondense	golf-course	plant-louse	ploughgate
earlierise	superdense	main-course	fieldmouse	smifligate
bowdlerise	recompense	damp-course	creepmouse	profligate
euhemerise	no-nonsense	matellasse	water-mouse	vitiligate
polymerise	undersense	nathelesse	shrew-mouse	easselgate
adulterise	subglobose	seemelesse	honey-mouse	promulgate
allegorise	ventricose	gentilesse	disespouse	prolongate
categorise	disenclose	entremesse	sand-grouse	theologate
devalorise	disinclose	vicomtesse	wood-grouse	homologate
revalorise	fibrillose	tropopause	sage-grouse	wicket-gate
decolorise	radiculose	harquebuse	white-hawse	bisulphate
proctorise	siliculose	chauffeuse	lithophyse	disulphate
enterprise	vesiculose	Betelgeuse	proteolyse	unilabiate
idolatrise	squamulose	Chartreuse	plasmolyse	depreciate
symmetrise	anastomose	raconteuse	stereobate	appreciate
geometrise	lachrymose	tricoteuse	conglobate	patriciate
pasteurise	toffee-nose	circumfuse	exacerbate	denunciate
sulphurise	pumple-nose	hypotenuse	perturbate	annunciate
pressurise	bottle-nose	opera-house	masturbate	consociate
denaturise	lanuginose	music-house	coradicate	dissociate
moisturise	shovelnose	round-house	irradicate	excruciate
panegyrise	copper-nose	guard-house	rededicate	digladiate
synthesise	quink-goose	glebe-house	adjudicate	triradiate

tripudiate	water-plate	palatinate	land-pirate	menstruate
collegiate	screw-plate	gelatinate	arch-pirate	effectuate
arpeggiate	infibulate	septennate	deaspirate	perpetuate
fastigiate	immaculate	cincinnate	perspirate	tumultuate
branchiate	flocculate	cachinnate	duumvirate	accentuate
conciliate	pediculate	tripinnate	redecorate	margravate
trifoliate	paniculate	sulphonate	edulcorate	insalivate
perfoliate	geniculate	dithionate	stercorate	deactivate
vindemiate	funiculate	propionate	invigorate	reactivate
calumniate	auriculate	passionate	camphorate	inactivate
univariate	vesiculate	antimonate	ameliorate	coacervate
uniseriate	reticulate	incoronate	decolorate	polychaete
repatriate	articulate	embryonate	advisorate	odontocete
expatriate	operculate	quaternate	electorate	ascomycete
ingratiate	emasculate	triternate	perpetrate	zygomycete
propitiate	inosculate	semi-lunate	trinitrate	myxomycete
licentiate	stridulate	curled-pate	infiltrate	diothelete
potentiate	spathulate	rattle-pate	calyptrate	dyothelete
annuntiate	stellulate	anticipate	fenestrate	decathlete
abbreviate	accumulate	emancipate	magistrate	incomplete
khediviate	manipulate	principate	birostrate	indiscrete
asphyxiate	estipulate	constipate	illustrate	semiterete
cheapskate	depopulate	disculpate	inaccurate	asynartete
sphacelate	repopulate	episcopate	effigurate	Rebeccaite
trachelate	punctulate	dunderpate	inaugurate	Capernaite
marprelate	capitulate	tricuspate	sulphurate	coquimbite
insufflate	salicylate	saccharate	marquisate	anthracite
exsufflate	amalgamate	exhilarate	condensate	benedicite
assibilate	desquamate	vertebrate	compensate	erubescite
strobilate	stablemate	exprobrate	incrassate	plebiscite
obnubilate	disanimate	consecrate	inspissate	overexcite
invigilate	legitimate	second-rate	exorbitate	smaragdite
annihilate	school-mate	deliberate	capacitate	alabandite
assimilate	consummate	dilacerate	felicitate	heulandite
deoppilate	bichromate	exulcerate	expedilate	endopodite
flabellate	dichromate	eviscerate	excogitate	argyrodite
barbellate	steersmate	desiderate	egurgitate	Wycliffite
cancellate	Italianate	immoderate	habilitate	Areopagite
flagellate	complanate	vociferate	debilitate	urostegite
crenellate	halogenate	exaggerate	nobilitate	limburgite
stipellate	homogenate	morigerate	facilitate	redruthite
tessellate	rejuvenate	accelerate	delimitate	flake-white
rostellate	impregnate	decelerate	infinitate	pearl-white
scutellate	deracinate	intemerate	decapitate	riebeckite
fibrillate	vaticinate	innumerate	auscultate	laurvikite
cantillate	ecardinate	degenerate	predentate	samarskite
distillate	inordinate	regenerate	tridentate	laurdalite
pistillate	co-ordinate	ingenerate	segmentate	polyhalite
postillate	coordinate	intenerate	commentate	Thermalite ®
calceolate	invaginate	incinerate	sustentate	retinalite
lanceolate	emarginate	remunerate	archontate	australite
nucleolate	desalinate	exasperate	dissertate	Ishmaelite
capreolate	delaminate	recuperate	solid-state	diothelite
spaniolate	effeminate	vituperate	life-estate	dyothelite
vitriolate	ingeminate	inveterate	real-estate	carnallite
apostolate	inseminate	obliterate	unicostate	Parnellite
blood-plate	denominate	alliterate	tricostate	Russellite
whole-plate	innominate	illiterate	understate	whewellite
terneplate	albuminate	adulterate	super-state	metabolite
sieve-plate	illuminate	exenterate	interstate	phlebolite
touch-plate	bituminate	asseverate	subarcuate	lepidolite
earth-plate	resupinate	deflagrate	continuate	ripidolite
steel-plate	chlorinate	church-rate	inadequate	theodolite
stall-plate	fluorinate	fourth-rate	colliquate	actinolite

siderolite	pyrolusite	bouillotte	interleave	applausive
staurolite	Triphysite	contribute	interweave	preclusive
chrysolite	diophysite	distribute	spokeshave	conclusive
troctolite	dyophysite	superacute	aftershave	protrusive
odontolite	halloysite	hyperacute	disenslave	incubative
graptolite	stalactite	water-chute	Rhinegrave	dedicative
topazolite	tennantite	irresolute	architrave	medicative
lherzolite	kersantite	last-minute	wind-sleeve	indicative
kimberlite	peridotite	miscompute	oversleeve	judicative
novaculite	pyrrhotite	substitute	shire-reeve	permeative
spherulite	unipartite	constitute	disbelieve	recreative
sperrylite	tripartite	prostitute	misbelieve	entreative
chessylite	sexpartite	lymphocyte	Fastens-eve	nauseative
pre-Adamite	convertite	troglodyte	apperceive	indagative
Benthamite	ballistite	osteophyte	twenty-five	Rh-negative
Adullamite	Trotskyite	lithophyte	well-to-live	irrigative
wolframite	galleryite	heliophyte	chain-drive	mitigative
cheese-mite	yellow-yite	cormophyte	underdrive	abrogative
anti-Semite	confidante	tropophyte	whist-drive	derogative
stalagmite	intrigante	microphyte	gainstrive	palliative
pandermite	governante	hydrophyte	persuasive	spoliative
exurbanite	dilettante	hygrophyte	dissuasive	ampliative
stephanite	sordamente	sporophyte	incohesive	initiative
Buchmanite	lentamente	saprophyte	indecisive	babblative
teschenite	dolcemente	protophyte	undecisive	semblative
pyroxenite	homozygote	squeteague	compulsive	unrelative
vanadinite	table-d'hôte	fowl-plague	propulsive	co-relative
indefinite	macrobiote	blue-tongue	convulsive	irrelative
gadolinite	gnotobiote	wasp-tongue	prehensive	revelative
melaconite	twelve-note	dog's-tongue	prepensive	similative
cryoconite	packet-note	disembogue	propensive	oppilative
glauconite	prompt-note	paedagogue	suspensive	regulative
palagonite	tetraptote	sialagogue	protensive	simulative
paragonite	underquote	cholagogue	distensive	cumulative
arragonite	procaryote	hydragogue	responsive	copulative
Marcionite	prokaryote	mystagogue	dispersive	estimative
antimonite	verkrampte	sialogogue	abstersive	splenative
Jamesonite	pianoforte	travelogue	subversive	dominative
Camptonite	mezzo-forte	philologue	perversive	nominative
torbernite	toothpaste	truth-value	precursive	ruminative
sporozoite	aftertaste	eigenvalue	discursive	inchoative
phlogopite	aubergiste	undervalue	successive	occupative
cylindrite	planchette	transvalue	concessive	reparative
glauberite	fourchette	indigo-blue	redressive	separative
cordierite	corselette	spirit-blue	degressive	execrative
garnierite	crinolette	cobalt-blue	regressive	lacerative
sphalerite	cassolette	recontinue	aggressive	ulcerative
dopplerite	toilinette	semi-opaque	digressive	federative
sombrerite	poplinette	bank-cheque	ingressive	generative
marguerite	balconette	communique	depressive	imperative
televérité	marionette	catafalque	repressive	alterative
epidiorite	sermonette	semicirque	impressive	admirative
lithotrite	mignonette	antimasque	oppressive	decorative
saussurite	maisonette	Kafkaesque	expressive	pejorative
underwrite	canzonette	Romanesque	possessive	memorative
ghost-write	collarette	Japanesque	submissive	indurative
porphyrite	leaderette	Titanesque	promissive	figurative
thaumasite	ulsterette	picaresque	permissive	depurative
dyscrasite	genevrette	Tudoresque	dismissive	maturative
crocoisite	chemisette	humoresque	succussive	accusative
perquisite	silhouette	satyresque	concussive	cunctative
martensite	blanquette	blottesque	percussive	vegetative
inapposite	éprouvette	statuesque	discussive	dubitative
andalusite	winceyette	shore-leave	unplausive	recitative

incitative	expeditive	misobserve	plate-proof	arc-welding
excitative	tonalitive	launcegaye	crash-proof	upbuilding
meditative	definitive	weather-eye	shock-proof	commanding
cogitative	affinitive	Chamber-lye	shellproof	upstanding
limitative	infinitive	underglaze	stormproof	descending
comitative	admonitive	land-breeze	underproof	week-ending
irritative	exploitive	wage-freeze	waterproof	contending
hesitative	transitive	antifreeze	press-proof	egg-binding
visitative	depositive	deep-freeze	lightproof	desponding
denotative	Rh-positive	Louis-Seize	idiot-proof	redounding
adaptative	appositive	catalogize	G	resounding
co-optative	oppositive	partialize	pudding-bag	astounding
constative	expositive	underprize	growing-bag	foreboding
reputative	repetitive	booby-prize	wampumpeag	fair-boding
imputative	appetitive	rheumatize	marker-flag	date-coding
evacuative	quantitive	Judenhetze	Nachschlag	orcharding
evaluative	subsultive	Betelgeuze	Brobdignag	forwarding
adequative	consultive	F	Kentish-rag	miswording
derivative	pendentive	wheatsheaf	blitzkrieg	applauding
innovative	fermentive	silver-leaf	trouser-leg	concluding
enervative	presentive	cloverleaf	scissor-leg	foreseeing
relaxative	sustentive	velvet-leaf	clothes-peg	bordraging
refractive	preventive	spirit-leaf	ostrich-egg	outlodging
detractive	appointive	horse-thief	truffle-pig	ungrudging
retractive	affrontive	sneak-thief	sucking-pig	unflagging
attractive	locomotive	water-thief	thimble-rig	zigzagging
extractive	automotive	make-belief	scratch-wig	humbugging
perfective	inadaptive	poor-relief	poison-fang	unchanging
subjective	preceptive	heart-grief	slang-whang	scavenging
projective	conceptive	stouthrief	alang-alang	inbringing
deflective	perceptive	shandygaff	ilang-ilang	upbringing
reflective	susceptive	monkey-gaff	ylang-ylang	scrounging
inflective	subreptive	chiff-chaff	Kuomintang	converging
neglective	redemptive	wring-staff	swing-swang	beseeching
collective	pre-emptive	torch-staff	ski-bobbing	squelching
connective	resumptive	broomstaff	hobjobbing	flaunching
respective	assumptive	churn-staff	hobnobbing	scratching
inspective	absorptive	cross-staff	wall-facing	bewitching
corrective	resorptive	undercliff	drag-racing	unweighing
dissective	corruptive	bumbailiff	boat-racing	triumphing
protective	disruptive	hippogriff	foot-racing	upflashing
convective	supportive	ticking-off	unnoticing	refreshing
predictive	contortive	falling-off	bratticing	rubbishing
vindictive	distortive	telling-off	tap-dancing	sea-fishing
afflictive	suggestive	cooling-off	entrancing	cod-fishing
inflictive	congestive	damping-off	convincing	rodfishing
astrictive	tempestive	stroganoff	subheading	net-fishing
convictive	persistive	written-off	misleading	fly-fishing
extinctive	exhaustive	powder-puff	undreading	plenishing
defunctive	combustive	breadstuff	map-reading	garnishing
adjunctive	resolutive	rough-stuff	lip-reading	varnishing
injunctive	diminutive	greenstuff	misreading	burnishing
concoctive	slide-valve	sweetstuff	forbidding	nourishing
traductive	clack-valve	mutessarif	succeeding	unblushing
conductive	redissolve	centre-half	proceeding	sea-bathing
productive	disinvolve	swing-shelf	inbreeding	sunbathing
completive	intervolve	timber-wolf	upbraiding	Landsthing
suppletive	ground-dove	untalked-of	law-abiding	Odelsthing
concretive	turtle-dove	saddle-roof	invaliding	first-thing
discretive	light-o'-love	child-proof	hard-riding	everything
inhibitive	undergrove	soundproof	surf-riding	bird-skiing
cohibitive	disimprove	swordproof	rank-riding	unspeaking
exhibitive	misimprove	smokeproof	overriding	road-making
impeditive	disapprove	shame-proof	unyielding	shoemaking

rope-making	cudgelling	uncharming	unswearing	unaspiring
love-making	bushelling	confirming	rip-roaring	undesiring
sick-making	nickelling	performing	cup-and-ring	napkin-ring
bookmaking	enamelling	unassuming	slubbering	wood-boring
bootmaking	pummelling	costeaning	chambering	well-boring
muck-raking	kennelling	caravaning	slumbering	skikjöring
moonraking	tunnelling	shebeening	shuddering	handspring
skyjacking	compelling	stiffening	broidering	land-spring
barracking	propelling	toughening	meandering	well-spring
hopsacking	dispelling	slackening	brandering	mainspring
mafficking	teaselling	thickening	maundering	hairspring
rollicking	chiselling	quickening	thundering	salt-spring
frolicking	hanselling	sweetening	blundering	preferring
chemicking	tinselling	quietening	loundering	conferring
picnicking	houselling	lightening	scowdering	anchor-ring
nit-picking	hostelling	shortening	proffering	concurring
fossicking	gravelling	scrivening	staggering	curmurring
physicking	travelling	arraigning	swaggering	signet-ring
good-liking	snivelling	unfeigning	sniggering	band-string
well-liking	drivelling	sustaining	butchering	shoestring
jaywalking	shovelling	mainlining	feathering	lutestring
unthinking	grovelling	land-mining	leathering	slip-string
unblinking	marvelling	iron-mining	weathering	draw-string
by-drinking	indwelling	unrepining	blethering	accoutring
die-sinking	trowelling	contemning	blithering	unrecuring
non-smoking	pencilling	trepanning	smothering	enamouring
odd-looking	fulfilling	inspanning	southering	outpouring
ill-looking	ice-hilling	ski-running	soldiering	flavouring
skylarking	distilling	rum-running	cashiering	reassuring
bitter-king	instilling	gunrunning	smickering	unpleasing
priest-king	gambolling	ballooning	stammering	increasing
scribbling	log-rolling	gadrooning	shimmering	vitalising
scrambling	patrolling	dethroning	glimmering	minimising
resembling	petrolling	concerning	whimpering	surprising
encircling	pistolling	discerning	clappering	practising
tricycling	leg-pulling	mid-morning	whispering	appetising
shieldling	streamling	May-morning	trousering	disguising
rehandling	air-cooling	sojourning	unaltering	unreposing
unbundling	nidderling	fine-tuning	sheltering	unimposing
groundling	sanderling	land-owning	sweltering	rehearsing
princeling	tenderling	embrowning	re-entering	traversing
ill-feeling	niggerling	wrong-doing	sauntering	outgassing
fledgeling	fingerling	shore-going	quartering	compassing
changeling	dapperling	forthgoing	plastering	surpassing
cringeling	easterling	ocean-going	blistering	professing
squireling	fosterling	embargoing	glistering	undressing
starveling	bitterling	undergoing	bolstering	depressing
scraggling	silverling	beekeeping	blustering	ear-kissing
straggling	priestling	unsleeping	clustering	engrossing
struggling	unsettling	ski-jumping	scattering	ear-bussing
wassailing	belittling	sky-jumping	chattering	untrussing
unavailing	throttling	developing	flattering	toad-eating
prevailing	tarpauling	trolloping	smattering	worm-eating
tasseiling	batfowling	undrooping	chittering	uncreating
pot-boiling	unmuzzling	unstooping	glittering	entreating
subsoiling	undreaming	kidnapping	twittering	nauseating
top-soiling	misdeeming	enwrapping	shuttering	dirt-eating
sprinkling	misseeming	unslipping	sputtering	undulating
strinkling	declaiming	dry-cupping	stuttering	air-grating
signalling	unbecoming	swan-upping	lacquering	vegetating
installing	home-coming	copy-typing	conquering	enervating
corbelling	blossoming	overdaring	unwavering	undoubting
cancelling	lead-arming	forbearing	despairing	self-acting
parcelling	ley-farming	God-fearing	unadmiring	refracting

detracting	sunsetting	signifying	basmitsvah	band-clutch
unexacting	jet-setting	scarifying	batmitsvah	Pentateuch
play-acting	outsetting	clarifying	bathmizvah	Heptateuch
projecting	coquetting	glorifying	barmitzvah	scaramouch
reflecting	brevetting	terrifying	basmitzvah	brood-pouch
collecting	curvetting	horrifying	batmitzvah	cheek-pouch
respecting	bed-wetting	petrifying	gallabiyah	shillelagh
dissecting	outfitting	nitrifying	wolf's-peach	breast-high
protecting	submitting	falsifying	stagecoach	usquebaugh
afflicting	committing	versifying	motor-coach	horselaugh
tea-meeting	permitting	gratifying	glass-coach	overslaugh
crocheting	acquitting	rectifying	turnbroach	belly-laugh
cricketing	outwitting	Scotifying	amphibrach	underbough
blanketing	garrotting	certifying	horse-leech	disc-plough
trinketing	gem-cutting	fortifying	folk-speech	fire-plough
trumpeting	outjutting	mortifying	tetrastich	snow-plough
whippeting	off-putting	testifying	pentastich	dray-plough
banqueting	intriguing	justifying	vine-branch	sure-enough
unshifting	haranguing	mystifying	nudibranch	see-through
in-fighting	face-saving	brutifying	palm-branch	Yarborough
benighting	life-saving	satisfying	zygobranch	rajpramukh
Jew-baiting	time-saving	kite-flying	crossbench	bathyscaph
crib-biting	flag-waving	high-flying	front-bench	pentagraph
backbiting	hair-waving	sail-flying	slit-trench	planigraph
nail-biting	retrieving	underlying	pipe-wrench	zincograph
soliciting	free-diving	companying	zebra-finch	mimeograph
unexciting	skin-diving	destroying	greenfinch	tachograph
surfeiting	perceiving	unwearying	penny-pinch	nephograph
benefiting	life-giving	semi-drying	snaphaunch	lithograph
unmeriting	self-giving	pillorying	overlaunch	orthograph
sky-writing	gaingiving	unhurrying	honeybunch	radiograph
recruiting	ever-living	bulk-buying	quick-lunch	audiograph
uninviting	dissolving	star-gazing	squirearch	heliograph
consulting	self-loving	chittagong	heresiarch	cyclograph
enchanting	slow-moving	triphthong	manna-larch	stylograph
warranting	unswerving	thereamong	route-march	anemograph
tormenting	misdrawing	headstrong	frog's-march	stenograph
dissenting	bronze-wing	overstrong	cornstarch	phonograph
repainting	pigeon-wing	patter-song	safety-arch	vibrograph
untainting	outflowing	tumble-dung	paper-birch	micrograph
imprinting	shallowing	double-hung	Ubermensch	hydrograph
unstinting	perplexing	underslung	thumb-latch	hierograph
affronting	undelaying	Aufklärung	night-latch	hygrograph
cub-hunting	pipe-laying	quersprung	quick-match	chirograph
rat-hunting	non-playing	high-strung	cross-match	spirograph
pot-hunting	overlaying	overstrung	crosspatch	hectograph
fox-hunting	gainsaying	Anschauung	death-watch	vectograph
accounting	journeying	hunting-cog	lever-watch	Dictograph
excerpting	stupefying	Iceland-dog	night-watch	pictograph
supporting	torrefying	sausage-dog	wrist-watch	hyetograph
unsporting	putrefying	prairie-dog	outstretch	pantograph
die-casting	liquefying	truffle-dog	clove-hitch	photograph
tea-tasting	specifying	raccoon-dog	rope-stitch	tachygraph
contesting	crucifying	jiggety-jog	backstitch	jellygraph
untwisting	unedifying	Battenberg	lockstitch	water-nymph
flyposting	acidifying	harvest-bug	open-stitch	gastrosoph
upbursting	qualifying	safety-plug	whip-stitch	Tetramorph
disgusting	mollifying	Struldbrug	galravitch	homeomorph
pargetting	nullifying	H	tsarevitch	ophiomorph
forgetting	amplifying	halleluiah	czarevitch	rhizomorph
outjetting	mummifying	hallelujah	water-witch	ditriglyph
subletting	magnifying	Methuselah	time-switch	lithoglyph
regretting	dignifying	topi-wallah	pear-switch	hieroglyph
dew-retting	lignifying	barmitsvah	hotchpotch	petroglyph

photoglyph	vinegarish	lukewarmth	piccalilli	smoke-stack
hippogryph	pantherish	tragacanth	canaliculi	harman-beck
balderdash	flapperish	coelacanth	Teleostomi	saloon-deck
weeping-ash	tripperish	nineteenth	frangipani	flight-deck
clish-clash	all-overish	eighteenth	Hindustani	cross-check
stone-brash	empoverish	thirteenth	fantoccini	smart-Aleck
water-brash	impoverish	fourteenth	tortellini	bottle-neck
nettlerash	Anglo-Irish	trillionth	cannelloni	rubber-neck
window-sash	amateurish	honeymonth	hippocampi	limber-neck
colour-wash	sybaritish	crumb-cloth	devanagari	smart-Alick
yellow-wash	coquettish	broadcloth	certiorari	pilgarlick
prickly-ash	Watteauish	table-cloth	Stradivari	holing-pick
backsheesh	extinguish	horse-cloth	raiyatwari	spawn-brick
proud-flesh	relinquish	greencloth	septemviri	whitterick
goose-flesh	flunkeyish	altar-cloth	centumviri	quick-trick
horseflesh	cockneyish	paper-cloth	millefiori	under-trick
madonnaish	old-fogyish	floorcloth	Monsignori	saddle-sick
old-maidish	mackintosh	glass-cloth	chota-hazri	travel-sick
invalidish	hobble-bush	habit-cloth	perdendosi	bread-stick
Hollandish	button-bush	waistcloth	tibiotarsi	sword-stick
Laplandish	calico-bush	mummy-cloth	Pediculati	matchstick
outlandish	crumb-brush	emery-cloth	illuminati	quick-stick
awkwardish	flesh-brush	kitten-moth	spermaceti	broomstick
butter-dish	toothbrush	codlin-moth	dilettanti	night-stick
needle-fish	underbrush	veneer-moth	pentimenti	throw-stick
candle-fish	paint-brush	antler-moth	intermezzi	toddy-stick
nettle-fish	dandy-brush	burnet-moth	**K**	candlewick
bottle-fish	reed-thrush	carpet-moth	parrot-beak	spatchcock
cuttlefish	woodthrush	sphinx-moth	stone-break	spitchcock
sleeve-fish	song-thrush	sabre-moth	water-break	midden-cock
Tartuffish	sponge-bath	cheek-tooth	heartbreak	turkey-cock
sheath-fish	needle-bath	small-tooth	hairstreak	butterdock
werwolfish	silver-bath	flesh-broth	opera-cloak	sea-burdock
bottom-fish	shower-bath	Mishnayoth	yackety-yak	shellshock
ribbon-fish	vapour-bath	open-hearth	saddleback	bubbly-jock
dragon-fish	leaf-sheath	brick-earth	fiddle-back	brake-block
rudder-fish	wing-sheath	japan-earth	turtleback	heart-block
coffer-fish	root-sheath	underearth	centre-back	watch-clock
pufferfish	underneath	childbirth	ahorseback	alarm-clock
archer-fish	self-breath	still-birth	switchback	four-o-clock
hammer-fish	snow-wreath	afterbirth	splash-back	water-clock
butter-fish	lattermath	cross-birth	canvas-back	spring-lock
silver-fish	bridle-path	fourscorth	yellowback	Bramah-lock
doctor-fish	towing-path	henceforth	sticky-back	badderlock
rabbit-fish	kinesipath	pennyworth	paddy-whack	hammerlock
parrot-fish	homoeopath	altazimuth	crackajack	fetterlock
peacockish	psychopath	round-mouth	minute-jack	lady's-smock
genteelish	naturopath	flute-mouth	lumber-jack	Kilmarnock
tomfoolish	cinder-path	river-mouth	natter-jack	honey-crock
accomplish	Reichsrath	frog's-mouth	whisky-jack	smock-frock
phantomish	thousandth	overgrowth	smoke-black	schorl-rock
ruffianish	seventieth	nature-myth	pitch-black	garnet-rock
heathenish	methinketh	**I**	ivory-black	quartz-rock
displenish	shibboleth	micrococci	click-clack	bloodstock
dead-finish	knee-length	coati-mondi	knick-knack	swing-stock
griffinish	wavelength	jaguarondi	shrinkpack	alpenstock
bumpkinish	half-length	salmagundi	sound-track	understock
Babylonish	full-length	barramundi	multi-track	upper-stock
gluttonish	rhabdolith	burramundi	trick-track	joint-stock
disgarnish	palaeolith	coati-mundi	storm-track	pin-buttock
disfurnish	enterolith	jaguarundi	sheep-track	jabberwock
picayunish	verse-smith	sarcophagi	sugar-wrack	springbuck
hidalgoish	whitesmith	vermicelli	grasswrack	herald-duck
trollopish	blacksmith	ritornelli	hackmatack	raven's-duck

velvet-duck
spirit-duck
burrow-duck
zumbooruck
dumbstruck
moonstruck
overstruck
ingle-cheek
maiden-meek
pinakothek
kibbutznik
Ostpolitik
randle-balk
double-talk
honey-stalk
cradlewalk
gravel-walk
lapper-milk
butter-milk
thrown-silk
tusser-silk
gentlefolk
tradesfolk
Herrenvolk
barrel-bulk
mountebank
oyster-bank
Reichsbank
scrimshank
skrimshank
greenshank
sheepshank
point-blank
marking-ink
writing-ink
copying-ink
water-blink
sleeve-link
kiddiewink
tiddlywink
dunderfunk
blind-drunk
swine-drunk
punch-drunk
source-book
phrase-book
minute-book
cheque-book
sketch-book
school-book
ration-book
cellar-book
muster-book
letter-book
prayer-book
pocket-book
prompt-book
pastrycook
swivel-hook
button-hook
tenter-hook
sister-hook
Donnybrook
cassia-bark

wattlebark
whale-shark
tiger-shark
meadow-lark
second-mark
ripple-mark
fingermark
banker-mark
reichsmark
shadow-mark
double-park
oyster-park
check-clerk
under-clerk
sales-clerk
tuning-fork
tarsia-work
rustic-work
groundwork
rubble-work
needlework
wattle-work
tongue-work
branch-work
stitchwork
crewelwork
scrollwork
schoolwork
grotto-work
ashlar-work
collar-work
spider-work
wonder-work
wickerwork
copper-work
master-work
canvas-work
basketwork
breastwork
donkey-work
Dewar-flask
vizard-mask
litany-desk
huntiegowk

L

catacumbal
dochmiacal
demoniacal
simoniacal
ammoniacal
Genesiacal
gonococcal
monothecal
forinsecal
spondaical
syllabical
cherubical
romancical
sporadical
premedical
geomedical
biomedical
conoidical
falsidical

methodical
periodical
episodical
prosodical
Talmudical
specifical
prolifical
magnifical
beatifical
pontifical
salvifical
anagogical
apagogical
analogical
ecological
geological
neological
biological
zoological
orological
urological
myological
theurgical
liturgical
anarchical
seraphical
autarkical
unbiblical
encyclical
diabolical
symbolical
academical
epidemical
alchemical
rhythmical
coxcomical
economical
anatomical
epitomical
zootomical
endermical
mechanical
ecumenical
rabbinical
flaminical
Sorbonical
sardonical
euphonical
mnemonical
gnomonical
harmonical
sermonical
geoponical
parsonical
Platonical
unheroical
hylozoical
satrapical
haruspical
spagerical
unclerical
chimerical
mesmerical
neoterical

exoterical
hysterical
podagrical
spagirical
oratorical
pictorical
rhetorical
historical
theatrical
electrical
unmetrical
dioptrical
geodesical
phthisical
sabbatical
emphatical
prelatical
dramatical
noematical
ragmatical
climatical
primatical
umbratical
Socratical
didactical
diabetical
syndetical
geodetical
exegetical
pathetical
hermetical
cosmetical
planetical
frenetical
magnetical
phonetical
unpoetical
dietetical
mephitical
apolitical
Adamitical
eremitical
hermitical
uncritical
Jesuitical
pedantical
romantical
despotical
elliptical
panoptical
synoptical
autoptical
monastical
dynastical
majestical
domestical
theistical
logistical
monistical
papistical
poristical
juristical
puristical
artistical

acoustical
analytical
matrifocal
patrifocal
hyperfocal
uxorilocal
matrilocal
patrilocal
reciprocal
multivocal
homocercal
wrap-rascal
grand-ducal
hebdomadal
Barmecidal
herbicidal
fungicidal
prolicidal
germicidal
vermicidal
parricidal
matricidal
patricidal
foeticidal
septicidal
pesticidal
larvicidal
rhomboidal
pinacoidal
helicoidal
lambdoidal
conchoidal
trochoidal
pinakoidal
homaloidal
prismoidal
paranoidal
sphenoidal
solenoidal
dendroidal
spheroidal
asteroidal
thyrsoidal
sinusoidal
botryoidal
schizoidal
triapsidal
caryatidal
intertidal
internodal
urochordal
hymeneaeal
phalangeal
pharyngeal
gonorrheal
parapineal
peritoneal
diarrhoeal
pyorrhoeal
golden-seal
ribbon-seal
symphyseal
periosteal
commonweal

interregal	categorial	epithermal	fractional	epicentral
vermifugal	immemorial	geothermal	tractional	palaestral
febrifugal	incisorial	isothermal	functional	orchestral
unconjugal	scansorial	exothermal	additional	campestral
oligarchal	sponsorial	paranormal	volitional	procedural
hierarchal	gressorial	decinormal	positional	perineural
Petrarchal	infusorial	phantasmal	devotional	intramural
acronychal	senatorial	strabismal	eruptional	extra-mural
apocryphal	venatorial	isoseismal	solutional	subnatural
air-marshal	natatorial	embolismal	squadronal	connatural
bequeathal	equatorial	organismal	synchronal	non-natural
Simmenthal	lavatorial	aneurismal	isochronal	structural
proverbial	electorial	aneurysmal	impersonal	accultural
subglacial	tinctorial	paroxysmal	interzonal	sepultural
pre-glacial	proctorial	subdecanal	unmaternal	scriptural
carapacial	volitorial	stone-canal	substernal	sculptural
zoothecial	janitorial	epagomenal	episternal	brachyural
apothecial	monitorial	phenomenal	glance-coal	supervisal
injudicial	visitorial	suprarenal	candle-coal	interposal
maleficial	state-trial	time-signal	cannel-coal	transposal
beneficial	semestrial	home-signal	kennel-coal	metatarsal
unofficial	bimestrial	subordinal	splint-coal	duniwassal
artificial	industrial	testudinal	parrot-coal	isoglossal
rectricial	tree-burial	aboriginal	cherry-coal	hypabyssal
tectricial	trophesial	unoriginal	hemitropal	menopausal
provincial	paradisial	monorhinal	metacarpal	substratal
semi-uncial	carnassial	periclinal	archetypal	idiolectal
praecocial	symphysial	anticlinal	prototypal	notonectal
antisocial	natalitial	monoclinal	ambulacral	mischmetal
commercial	solstitial	trigeminal	involucral	scrap-metal
threnodial	instantial	subliminal	decahedral	sheet-metal
parapodial	credential	cognominal	octahedral	suborbital
monopodial	evidential	pronominal	hexahedral	cucurbital
myocardial	tendential	surnominal	hemihedral	congenital
precordial	prudential	endocrinal	holohedral	urogenital
concordial	tangential	triactinal	polyhedral	encrinital
primordial	sapiential	monactinal	confederal	sincipital
sporangial	eminential	hexactinal	peripheral	premarital
apterygial	torrential	intestinal	unicameral	meteorital
monarchial	presential	enneagonal	tetrameral	intervital
epithelial	sentential	tetragonal	outgeneral	assonantal
non-gremial	sequential	pentagonal	unilateral	quadrantal
nosocomial	sclerotial	heptagonal	trilateral	aplacental
agronomial	preceptial	orthogonal	collateral	accidental
polynomial	colloquial	antiphonal	uniliteral	occidental
prostomial	quadrivial	salicional	triliteral	incidental
subcranial	homotaxial	meridional	parenteral	nidamental
self-denial	nicrosilal	obsidional	hemipteral	ligamental
catamenial	interramal	occasional	peripteral	ornamental
millennial	duodecimal	revisional	monopteral	atramental
centennial	isocheimal	divisional	sepulchral	tenemental
septennial	pack-animal	sponsional	hypaethral	fragmental
perigonial	millesimal	delusional	disenthral	pedimental
hegemonial	centesimal	vocational	disinthral	rudimental
ceremonial	approximal	ideational	xenarthral	regimental
antimonial	microsomal	creational	decemviral	documental
principial	hydrosomal	oblational	triumviral	tegumental
urticarial	peristomal	relational	extemporal	monumental
seminarial	peridermal	irrational	incorporal	immanental
glossarial	taxidermal	durational	unpastoral	thiopental
managerial	endodermal	gyrational	parametral	unparental
immaterial	hypodermal	notational	triquetral	prefrontal
unmaterial	ectodermal	rotational	subcentral	horizontal
acroterial	diathermal	nutational	unicentral	balibuntal

sacerdotal	wind-tunnel	untranquil	powder-mill	scuttleful
holophotal	pine-kernel	thorn-devil	peppermill	diseaseful
transeptal	palm-kernel	boll-weevil	pewter-mill	promiseful
unimmortal	antechapel	corn-weevil	quartz-mill	purposeful
isoglottal	disapparel	cow-chervil	churn-drill	remorseful
entophytal	beer-barrel	masked-ball	power-drill	ingrateful
individual	wood-sorrel	cup-and-ball	quarter-ill	ungrateful
sublingual	rose-laurel	cannonball	shirt-frill	despiteful
prelingual	cold-chisel	button-ball	Yggdrasill	requiteful
unilingual	discounsel	tennis-ball	groundsill	untasteful
trilingual	miscounsel	object-ball	window-sill	meaningful
sign-manual	bomb-vessel	basketball	standstill	stomachful
semi-annual	seed-vessel	brandy-ball	stone-still	unwatchful
televisual	dickcissel	volley-ball	stockstill	refreshful
consensual	swan-mussel	dining-hall	goose-quill	unfaithful
contactual	overmantel	market-hall	Eatanswill	untruthful
unpunctual	pari-mutuel	once-for-all	cotton-boll	unmerciful
conventual	datum-level	free-for-all	muster-roll	unthankful
conceptual	water-level	Tattersall	toilet-roll	misdeemful
perceptual	split-level	thumb-stall	sdeignfull	disdainful
contextual	dumpy-level	line-squall	throat-full	worshipful
homosexual	fire-shovel	shieldwall	thick-skull	slumberful
gerundival	crown-jewel	parpen-wall	sporophyll	uncheerful
non-arrival	disembowel	wall-to-wall	hypsophyll	pitcherful
adjectival	fish-trowel	minute-bell	pyrogallol	tumblerful
decennoval	witch-hazel	diving-bell	cannabinol	despairful
withdrawal	schlimazel	sleigh-bell	resorcinol	successful
blood-royal	water-ouzel	school-bell	free-school	unblissful
rhyme-royal	coffin-nail	muffin-bell	life-school	undoubtful
super-royal	fingernail	vesper-bell	dame-school	neglectful
pennyroyal	dinner-pail	silver-bell	song-school	respectful
mycorhizal	centre-rail	flower-bell	playschool	suspectful
endorhizal	breastrail	market-bell	music-stool	delightful
influenzal	monkey-rail	curfew-bell	close-stool	unrightful
skew-corbel	square-sail	thread-cell	frithstool	sprightful
coromandel	mizzen-sail	nettle-cell	grith-stool	insightful
down-at-heel	daggle-tail	mother-cell	piano-stool	thoughtful
tread-wheel	springtail	music-shell	night-stool	conceitful
brake-wheel	plough-tail	mitre-shell	joint-stool	unfruitful
scape-wheel	cottontail	olive-shell	cutty-stool	uneventful
mitre-wheel	racket-tail	tooth-shell	fleece-wool	unboastful
swing-wheel	forkit-tail	chank-shell	cotton-wool	wanrestful
coach-wheel	monkey-tail	snail-shell	calciferol	disgustful
pitch-wheel	lead-pencil	pearl-shell	tocopherol	untrustful
brushwheel	blue-pencil	acorn-shell	ergosterol	object-soul
snail-wheel	hair-pencil	cameo-shell	eucalyptol	vice-consul
crown-wheel	francophil	auger-shell	ethambutol	otter-trawl
water-wheel	bibliophil	tower-shell	errand-girl	fingerbowl
count-wheel	psammophil	razor-shell	office-girl	shriche-owl
emery-wheel	thermophil	venus-shell	schoolgirl	guinea-fowl
daisy-wheel	eosinophil	death-knell	shrimp-girl	mallee-fowl
manchineel	verbena-oil	night-spell	flower-girl	screech-owl
orange-peel	linseed-oil	groundsell	chorus-girl	scritch-owl
vinegar-eel	mustard-oil	ne'er-do-well	ballet-girl	shritch-owl
shear-steel	spindle-oil	Camberwell	yellow-girl	chlorophyl
ne'er-do-weel	quatrefoil	sickle-bill	discordful	tetraethyl
Owlspiegel	hop-trefoil	sheath-bill	unpeaceful	zygodactyl
Ahithophel	cinque-foil	cranesbill	ungraceful	polydactyl
Achitophel	silver-foil	stork's-bill	rejoiceful	M
kriegsspiel	lumbang-oil	parrot-bill	courageful	schoolma'am
unparallel	disembroil	louping-ill	presageful	tarmacadam
ruby-spinel	coconut-oil	coffee-mill	revengeful	sealed-beam
dog's-fennel	whereuntil	cotton-mill	dislikeful	collar-beam
skip-kennel	Jugendstil	lumber-mill	thimbleful	hammer-beam

10 -EAM

head-stream	vestry-room	chloroform	nothingism	dichromism
mill-stream	disembosom	outperform	bantingism	pancosmism
mainstream	rum-blossom	salverform	pedagogism	Africanism
downstream	may-blossom	brainstorm	demagogism	Vaticanism
slipstream	reaccustom	guinea-worm	paralogism	Hobbianism
plough-team	rock-bottom	thread-worm	ostrichism	Grobianism
siphonogam	full-bottom	ribbon-worm	revanchism	lesbianism
phanerogam	sewage-farm	cotton-worm	monarchism	ruffianism
scintigram	oyster-farm	canker-worm	monorchism	Wolfianism
stereogram	school-marm	palmer-worm	pansophism	Italianism
psychogram	phelloderm	copper-worm	dimorphism	utopianism
lymphogram	echinoderm	galley-worm	Swadeshism	Messianism
cardiogram	scleroderm	enthusiasm	Englishism	Russianism
chromogram	blastoderm	iconoclasm	Britishism	Noetianism
thermogram	angiosperm	sarcoplasm	Lamarckism	Kantianism
seismogram	gymnosperm	hyaloplasm	radicalism	Marxianism
organogram	school-term	neuroplasm	bipedalism	Brahmanism
sphenogram	medium-term	protoplasm	unidealism	Rachmanism
chronogram	amoebiform	deutoplasm	surrealism	Buchmanism
dendrogram	limaciform	karyoplasm	stibialism	puritanism
cryptogram	radiciform	plasmodesm	specialism	Genevanism
barrow-tram	culiciform	Rebeccaism	patrialism	Saracenism
self-esteem	calyciform	Krishnaism	martialism	monogenism
protoxylem	monadiform	pharisaism	partialism	polygenism
post-mortem	glandiform	Pan-Arabism	bestialism	heathenism
root-system	calceiform	lambdacism	trivialism	oecumenism
apophthegm	malleiform	archaicism	decimalism	strychnism
polyrhythm	clypeiform	Hebraicism	minimalism	Jacobinism
cross-claim	proteiform	prosaicism	nominalism	caffeinism
alternatim	strigiform	pacificism	journalism	griffinism
Ashkenazim	spongiform	phallicism	liberalism	morphinism
weeping-elm	conchiform	organicism	federalism	maudlinism
crippledom	scyphiform	laconicism	literalism	Brahminism
sheriffdom	cyathiform	empiricism	chloralism	illuminism
subkingdom	phialiform	classicism	immoralism	femininism
enthraldom	gangliform	Asiaticism	humoralism	nicotinism
kitchendom	moniliform	fanaticism	centralism	chauvinism
heathendom	ypsiliform	asceticism	neutralism	Bourbonism
demirepdom	mytiliform	scepticism	naturalism	antagonism
fresherdom	thalliform	asepticism	capitalism	cinchonism
flunkeydom	stelliform	Gnosticism	gradualism	pyrrhonism
cockneydom	poculiform	Scotticism	sensualism	reunionism
cacodaemom	raduliform	Neofascism	virtualism	hegemonism
kaffir-boom	cumuliform	old-maidism	textualism	Bergsonism
peach-bloom	cotyliform	invalidism	revivalism	Johnsonism
water-bloom	squamiform	Chassidism	Froebelism	westernism
tappet-loom	cucumiform	gormandism	genteelism	hidalgoism
dyer's-broom	cribriform	Lollardism	evangelism	Averrhoism
coffee-room	cancriform	bastardism	diothelism	Lysenkoism
stable-room	quadriform	cicisbeism	dyothelism	trichroism
saddle-room	dendriform	Manicheism	mongrelism	diatropism
engine-room	tuberiform	antitheism	immobilism	geotropism
throne-room	viperiform	hylotheism	symphilism	isotropism
bridegroom	vaporiform	henotheism	zoophilism	solidarism
robing-room	cultriform	monotheism	Parnellism	blepharism
dining-room	elytriform	autotheism	Boswellism	plagiarism
tiring-room	securiform	polytheism	catabolism	secularism
living-room	incisiform	conacreism	katabolism	insularism
strong-room	medusiform	microseism	metabolism	luminarism
schoolroom	stratiform	bradyseism	alcoholism	viviparism
lumber-room	digitiform	Tartuffism	asystolism	monetarism
powder-room	cristiform	werwolfism	gargoylism	militarism
locker-room	linguiform	geophagism	Benthamism	gynandrism
street-room	overinform	suffragism	dysphemism	Chaucerism

Grangerism	stamp-album	honorarium	cockalorum	adamantean
Wertherism	ammoniacum	sanitarium	thalictrum	Philistean
Fourierism	tweedledum	seaquarium	triquetrum	teleostean
cottierism	memorandum	opprobrium	emplastrum	Zimbabwean
bowdlerism	referendum	synandrium	sense-datum	xylophagan
metamerism	stomodaeum	desiderium	surrogatum	Balbriggan
euhemerism	propylaeum	puerperium	petrolatum	shenanigan
mesomerism	Prometheum	osmeterium	postulatum	sense-organ
polymerism	peritoneum	psalterium	substratum	mouth-organ
spoonerism	periosteum	acroterium	Pennisetum	pedal-organ
Voltairism	fee-fi-fo-fum	sudatorium	nidamentum	piano-organ
hypocorism	chewing-gum	fumatorium	indumentum	chair-organ
traitorism	dendrobium	sanatorium	argumentum	choir-organ
pentaprism	euphorbium	moratorium	post-partum	light-organ
orthoprism	zoothecium	natatorium	individuum	scent-organ
macroprism	apothecium	praetorium	N	Petrarchan
sinecurism	paramecium	auditorium	arrière-ban	chrysophan
amateurism	androecium	digitorium	intra-urban	tryptophan
pasteurism	lawrencium	vomitorium	interurban	Cisleithan
speciesism	stichidium	haustorium	republican	Phoenician
narcissism	chromidium	dysprosium	Pentelican	technician
acrobatism	nephridium	perimysium	Copernican	practician
schematism	osmiridium	spermatium	un-American	politician
pragmatism	praesidium	pancratium	Pan-African	ekistician
stigmatism	ommatidium	technetium	Eurafrican	beautician
automatism	compendium	panaritium	Franciscan	Ordovician
traumatism	plasmodium	Dracontium	chimney-can	Cistercian
rheumatism	parapodium	sclerotium	Muhammadan	amphiscian
aplanatism	Lycopodium	sestertium	Mohammedan	Chalcidian
separatism	monopodium	consortium	Muhammedan	solifidian
moderatism	Polypodium	nasturtium	Mahommedan	cycloidian
prostatism	anacardium	colloquium	Seleucidan	Amerindian
convictism	myocardium	quadrivium	Heraclidan	hypolydian
prophetism	primordium	compluvium	arachnidan	mixolydian
obsoletism	praeludium	chrome-alum	shandrydan	Heracleian
concretism	sporangium	pentathlum	Maccabaean	Berkeleian
syncretism	horologium	cerebellum	Sadducaean	shereefian
Jacobitism	Horologium	ante-bellum	hymeneaean	Tartuffian
ebionitism	eponychium	post-bellum	Arctogaean	Glaswegian
sybaritism	promethium	capitellum	Manichaean	salpingian
Nazaritism	hypanthium	haustellum	Nabathaean	theologian
parasitism	Gnaphalium	tropaeolum	Ptolemaean	Zaporogian
fortuitism	epithelium	mussel-plum	coffee-bean	Wallachian
patriotism	subsellium	cherry-plum	string-bean	batrachian
tricrotism	prostomium	acetabulum	runner-bean	Eustachian
anabaptism	iridosmium	vestibulum	butter-bean	Antiochian
consortism	sparganium	vibraculum	locust-bean	Monarchian
concettism	proscenium	umbraculum	kidney-bean	Malpighian
absolutism	lenocinium	spiraculum	cherry-bean	epitaphian
deaf-mutism	tirocinium	tentaculum	crustacean	didelphian
epiphytism	peridinium	corniculum	theodicean	Karmathian
Pan-Slavism	delphinium	curriculum	crinoidean	Cerinthian
bolshevism	triclinium	tuberculum	cestoidean	Corinthian
anticivism	gadolinium	propagulum	antipodean	Purbeckian
recidivism	millennium	molybdenum	ditrochean	Lamarckian
negativism	septennium	presternum	promethean	Juvenalian
relativism	perigonium	episternum	nepenthean	Australian
positivism	stramonium	Illecebrum	Sophoclean	Froebelian
flunkeyism	polemonium	ambulacrum	filicinean	pre-exilian
cockneyism	principium	simulacrum	hirudinean	rampallian
Trotskyism	tepidarium	involucrum	Trollopean	Boswellian
Tammanyism	spermarium	kettledrum	Voltairean	capitolian
meerschaum	oceanarium	panjandrum	daguerrean	Verulamian
Lebensraum	cinerarium	eriophorum	paradisean	didynamian

antinomian	Chaucerian	tutworkman	horse-gowan	fair-spoken
Panamanian	Luciferian	councilman	heavy-laden	soft-spoken
Pomeranian	Wertherian	Abraham-man	muck-midden	wind-broken
Ruritanian	Spenserian	gombeen-man	room-ridden	frithsoken
Lusitanian	psalterian	javelin-man	bestridden	death-token
Lithuanian	Mousterian	Greco-Roman	handmaiden	windfallen
Tyrrhenian	Hanoverian	freedwoman	gleemaiden	sick-fallen
Madelenian	Voltairian	spacewoman	swan-maiden	downfallen
Bourignian	hypodorian	noblewoman	corn-maiden	chapfallen
peridinian	infusorian	apple-woman	unbeholden	chopfallen
viraginian	praetorian	tripewoman	withholden	root-fallen
Carolinian	stentorian	horse-woman	herb-garden	arch-flamen
Abyssinian	symmetrian	Dutchwoman	rose-garden	freedwomen
Eleusinian	pedestrian	Irishwoman	roof-garden	Dutchwomen
Riemannian	rupestrian	bowerwoman	back-garden	bowerwomen
Heliconian	equestrian	chairwoman	rock-garden	catechumen
Caledonian	palustrian	beadswoman	beer-garden	table-linen
Aberdonian	centaurian	bondswoman	case-harden	underlinen
Patagonian	Pasteurian	saleswoman	fire-warden	veldschoen
Trophonian	Manchurian	markswoman	overburden	drawing-pen
pyrrhonian	Athanasian	clanswoman	carragheen	dukkeripen
Erewhonian	Melanesian	townswoman	mavourneen	pine-barren
Scillonian	Indonesian	Scotswoman	hand-screen	willow-wren
Apollonian	Polynesian	tally-woman	windscreen	forechosen
Babylonian	paradisian	midshipman	rood-screen	well-chosen
Solomonian	circensian	triggerman	widescreen	lederhosen
Ciceronian	Waldensian	telpherman	telescreen	Munchausen
Cameronian	Dickensian	weatherman	fire-screen	outsweeten
Bergsonian	Circassian	brother-man	silk-screen	disquieten
Morisonian	thalassian	lighterman	meatscreen	straighten
Johnsonian	Parnassian	groundsman	rifle-green	affrighten
Selbornian	Malthusian	roberdsman	crown-green	unfoughten
decagynian	Carthusian	strokesman	grass-green	dishearten
hexagynian	Andalusian	estatesman	lovat-green	pine-marten
monogynian	homoousian	honours-man	gaudy-green	rechristen
polygynian	pancratian	expressman	bluey-green	unchristen
Aethiopian	peripetian	robertsman	soup-tureen	flea-bitten
Trollopian	Neo-Kantian	upright-man	well-beseen	hard-bitten
cacotopian	Vincentian	draughtman	unforeseen	hard-gotten
Philippian	Laurentian	servant-man	mangosteen	unbegotten
Arimaspian	Herbartian	harvestman	Nibelungen	well-gotten
lapidarian	Gilbertian	infrahuman	hogen-mogen	dirt-rotten
tubularian	Philistian	superhuman	carcinogen	overleaven
stigmarian	rumfustian	highwayman	fibrinogen	night-raven
grammarian	Gravettian	trolley-man	electrogen	yestereven
catenarian	Algonquian	hackneyman	dermatogen	unforgiven
laminarian	subclavian	journeyman	forfeuchen	self-driven
seminarian	Belgravian	laundry-man	prairie-hen	wanthriven
octonarian	Leibnizian	kempery-man	forfoughen	half-a-dozen
tractarian	hyalomelan	nurseryman	strengthen	interreign
vegetarian	groundplan	mystery-man	disburthen	whisky-john
solitarian	militiaman	cavalryman	wind-shaken	foreordain
limitarian	husbandman	countryman	unforsaken	rue-bargain
sanitarian	gold-end-man	liberty-man	undertaken	outbargain
fruitarian	orchard-man	mycetozoan	hamesucken	watch-chain
ubiquarian	surfaceman	warming-pan	padding-ken	block-chain
Cantuarian	serviceman	hemipteran	bousingken	disenchain
janizarian	garbageman	xiphosuran	mild-spoken	interchain
Trinacrian	machineman	bipartisan	kind-spoken	daisy-chain
decandrian	singing-man	Neapolitan	unbespoken	outvillain
triandrian	tithing-man	constantan	free-spoken	penny-plain
octandrian	serving-man	gargantuan	fine-spoken	crackbrain
hexandrian	Englishman	luggage-van	well-spoken	water-brain
Spencerian	Kentish-man	Villanovan	foul-spoken	catch-drain

underdrain	chloroquin	epilimnion	rescission	fumigation
Cassegrain	acriflavin	symphonion	discission	irrigation
paste-grain	riboflavin	phaelonion	submission	litigation
souterrain	bone-spavin	quaternion	commission	mitigation
red-murrain	picrotoxin	trade-union	permission	navigation
siege-train	neurotoxin	interunion	dismission	levigation
disentrain	phytotoxin	sticharion	succussion	elongation
wagon-train	precondemn	synaxarion	concussion	abrogation
hover-train	Ringelmann	acroterion	percussion	derogation
goods-train	landammann	zwitterion	discussion	arrogation
overstrain	baby-ribbon	pundigrion	preclusion	glaciation
chevrotain	archdeacon	omophorion	conclusion	emaciation
sea-captain	catholicon	persuasion	protrusion	speciation
bloodstain	diaconicon	dissuasion	delibation	fasciation
quatorzain	harmonicon	incohesion	dealbation	eradiation
state-cabin	panopticon	indecision	accubation	palliation
Portakabin ®	sore-falcon	misprision	incubation	spoliation
marsh-robin	Armageddon	television	titubation	ampliation
psilocybin	unsmiled-on	redivision	intubation	patriation
bacitracin	acotyledon	Eurovision	defecation	initiation
aureomycin	pteranodon	compulsion	radication	tritiation
gramicidin	Euroclydon	propulsion	abdication	exuviation
phalloidin	humdudgeon	convulsion	dedication	escalation
biliverdin	curmudgeon	descension	medication	inhalation
terreplein	wood-pigeon	prehension	indication	exhalation
bridle-rein	rock-pigeon	declension	judication	regelation
Zollverein	clay-pigeon	propension	lorication	anhelation
safety-rein	chirurgeon	suspension	aprication	co-relation
schalstein	sea-surgeon	out-pension	vesication	irrelation
ragamuffin	escutcheon	presension	urtication	revelation
humgruffin	chamaeleon	dissension	toxication	sufflation
double-chin	orpheoreon	pretension	truncation	conflation
buff-jerkin	hendecagon	protension	relocation	sibilation
slammerkin	flap-dragon	distension	bilocation	jubilation
copperskin	snapdragon	low-tension	allocation	depilation
silverskin	blood-wagon	displosion	advocation	oppilation
encephalin	stage-wagon	submersion	revocation	mutilation
enkephalin	chuck-wagon	dispersion	invocation	spallation
penicillin	water-wagon	abstersion	validation	ocellation
Ampicillin ®	honey-wagon	subversion	lapidation	areolation
gyre-carlin	mammy-wagon	conversion	emendation	etiolation
book-muslin	carrying-on	perversion	inundation	immolation
tuberculin	Demogorgon	discursion	foundation	desolation
provitamin	king-archon	còmpassion	denudation	insolation
agglutinin	soda-siphon	dispassion	trabeation	tabulation
tender-loin	apocryphon	outpassion	nucleation	ambulation
chinquapin	Antichthon	succession	malleation	lobulation
corking-pin	autochthon	precession	permeation	tubulation
rolling-pin	Cestracion	concession	alineation	jaculation
tirling-pin	pyramidion	procession	balneation	maculation
drawing-pin	gorgoneion	confession	recreation	peculation
clothes-pin	irreligion	profession	laureation	osculation
listener-in	Mabinogion	degression	indagation	nidulation
catch-basin	pincushion	regression	divagation	undulation
ocean-basin	air-cushion	aggression	delegation	modulation
river-basin	perihelion	digression	relegation	nodulation
pancreatin	triskelion	ingression	allegation	regulation
achromatin	rascallion	depression	abnegation	simulation
phenacetin	pennillion	repression	denegation	cumulation
precipitin	centillion	impression	renegation	annulation
sand-martin	septillion	oppression	obligation	papulation
freemartin	postillion	expression	deligation	vapulation
Chambertin	sextillion	possession	alligation	copulation
lambrequin	rumbullion	abscission	remigation	population

insulation	leviration	temptation	correction	wave-motion
ustulation	decoration	co-optation	porrection	self-motion
defamation	pejoration	quartation	subsection	link-motion
datamation	coloration	flirtation	trisection	locomotion
squamation	ignoration	substation	dissection	slow-motion
racemation	peroration	prestation	protection	love-potion
decimation	stupration	crustation	convection	usucaption
intimation	enarration	pay-station	provection	conception
estimation	aberration	way-station	prediction	perception
automation	filtration	refutation	non-fiction	subreption
inhumation	castration	salutation	affliction	correption
exhumation	lustration	volutation	infliction	conniption
immanation	obduration	deputation	astriction	ascription
impanation	induration	reputation	conviction	redemption
alienation	figuration	amputation	intinction	pre-emption
catenation	abjuration	imputation	extinction	diremption
stagnation	objuration	evacuation	defunction	resumption
ordination	adjuration	graduation	abjunction	assumption
pagination	depuration	evaluation	adjunction	readoption
sagination	maturation	inequation	injunction	excerption
lamination	saturation	excavation	expunction	absorption
gemination	obturation	tidivation	concoction	adsorption
semination	suturation	salivation	infarction	desorption
domination	nanisation	derivation	traduction	resorption
nomination	ionisation	activation	subduction	corruption
lumination	accusation	titivation	conduction	disruption
rumination	recusation	motivation	production	decryption
supination	dilatation	renovation	obsoletion	encryption
patination	floatation	innovation	completion	proportion
divination	cunctation	starvation	suppletion	contortion
umbonation	punctation	acervation	concretion	distortion
coronation	eructation	enervation	discretion	suggestion
detonation	hebetation	malaxation	imbibition	congestion
intonation	vegetation	relaxation	adhibition	exhaustion
eburnation	habitation	indexation	inhibition	combustion
inchoation	dubitation	annexation	cohibition	precaution
usurpation	recitation	denization	exhibition	allocution
crispation	incitation	abreaction	expedition	illocution
occupation	oscitation	arefaction	emollition	absolution
reparation	excitation	self-action	ebullition	resolution
separation	meditation	compaction	demolition	devolution
cribration	digitation	refraction	definition	revolution
execration	cogitation	infraction	admonition	involution
liberation	fugitation	detraction	ammunition	diminution
laceration	velitation	retraction	apparition	commixtion
maceration	volitation	attraction	contrition	complexion
ulceration	limitation	extraction	futurition	overreckon
federation	sanitation	confection	transition	encephalon
sideration	capitation	perfection	deposition	water-melon
moderation	irritation	trajection	reposition	paddymelon
toleration	hesitation	subjection	imposition	tetrathlon
cameration	visitation	projection	apposition	pentathlon
numeration	latitation	disjection	opposition	tourbillon
generation	equitation	re-election	exposition	Eriocaulon
veneration	cavitation	prelection	repetition	water-lemon
cineration	levitation	by-election	appetition	Podostemon
superation	invitation	deflection	contention	pentstemon
literation	exaltation	reflection	abstention	king-salmon
alteration	exultation	inflection	distention	rock-salmon
emigration	plantation	neglection	sustention	backgammon
deliration	denotation	collection	subvention	phenomenon
admiration	annotation	connection	prevention	champignon
aspiration	adaptation	inspection	convention	demi-cannon
expiration	coaptation	re-erection	hand-lotion	gander-moon

table-spoon	virgin-born	pseudimago	montero-cap	pursership
snuff-spoon	latter-born	touch-and-go	salmon-leap	writership
heart-spoon	forest-born	get-up-and-go	cellar-flap	mastership
trout-spoon	guinea-corn	wild-indigo	weather-map	authorship
quarteroon	sea-unicorn	intertrigo	gingersnap	censorship
musquetoon	peppercorn	camerlengo	brandy-snap	factorship
melocotoon	barleycorn	camerlingo	toilet-soap	hectorship
chief-baron	flugelhorn	supercargo	yellow-soap	lectorship
court-baron	powder-horn	you-know-who	police-trap	rectorship
decahedron	basset-horn	clock-radio	wentletrap	doctorship
octahedron	whitethorn	alarm-radio	rattle-trap	editorship
hexahedron	blackthorn	music-folio	stench-trap	pastorship
hemihedron	quickthorn	impresario	potato-trap	sun-worship
holohedron	goat's-thorn	cross-ratio	watch-strap	disworship
octohedron	yestermorn	cheechalko	shrinkwrap	misworship
polyhedron	near-begaun	estrangelo	pottle-deep	packet-ship
interferon	leprechaun	ritornello	breast-deep	turret-ship
night-heron	currant-bun	saltarello	firing-step	tenantship
Pentameron	machine-gun	peccadillo	heraldship	truantship
Heptameron	whaling-gun	piccadillo	friendship	regentship
hexaemeron	gatling-gun	octodecimo	cowardship	clientship
mesenteron	harpoon-gun	pianissimo	noviceship	thwartship
monopteron	scatter-gun	lentissimo	bailieship	priestship
hypaethron	chicken-run	fortissimo	beadleship	bashawship
waffle-iron	leprechawn	serrasalmo	aedileship	fellowship
toggle-iron	gambit-pawn	eighteenmo	battleship	jockeyship
plough-iron	right-drawn	mud-volcano	umpireship	suretyship
disenviron	upside-down	fortepiano	squireship	riding-whip
adiaphoron	sponge-down	cappuccino	legateship	pistol-whip
pome-citron	tumbledown	stracchino	curateship	spring-clip
quercitron	hand-me-down	maraschino	bedellship	letter-clip
trochotron	roping-down	peacherino	school-ship	pillowslip
chronotron	splashdown	concertino	consulship	cow-parsnip
emplastron	broken-down	tickety-boo	sachemship	aide-de-camp
stone-mason	powder-down	didgeridoo	seamanship	lumber-camp
comparison	dinner-gown	hullabaloo	penmanship	streetlamp
disherison	fresh-blown	view-halloo	airmanship	spirit-lamp
engarrison	snuff-brown	barley-broo	hetmanship	psychopomp
hyperbaton	whity-brown	comanchero	sultanship	butter-bump
checklaton	half-a-crown	estanciero	wardenship	donkey-pump
shecklaton	slave-grown	cancionero	ensignship	monkey-pump
feuilleton	thick-grown	ground-zero	coffin-ship	mutton-chop
Bedlington	woman-grown	capodastro	cousinship	archbishop
Kensington	undergrown	strepitoso	deaconship	schism-shop
antiproton	intergrown	affettuoso	archonship	barber-shop
rick-barton	liver-grown	martellato	matronship	repair-shop
Charleston	grass-grown	tree-tomato	prison-ship	policy-shop
phlogiston	market-town	illuminato	sextonship	hippety-hop
melicotton		seed-potato	dollarship	predevelop
silk-cotton	O	portamento	Caesarship	disenvelop
polycotton	angwantibo	pentimento	bursarship	hand-gallop
push-button	mumbo-jumbo	mezzotinto	membership	codswallop
meganewton	paramedico	fianchetto	leadership	nincompoop
periphyton	nero-antico	rondoletto	readership	nickumpoop
Anglo-Saxon	fantastico	allegretto	rangership	riding-crop
Amphitryon	aficionado	prosciutto	vergership	prison-crop
Amphictyon	adelantado	recitativo	fathership	minute-drop
shield-fern	ritardando	passamezzo	mother-ship	contraprop
knave-bairn	tremolando	intermezzo	viziership	razor-strop
town's-bairn	scherzando		dealership	humming-top
purple-born	stringendo	P	tellership	safety-stop
sphere-born	inquirendo	shuffle-cap	butlership	chimney-top
native-born	diminuendo	statute-cap	keepership	pseudocarp
heaven-born	how-do-you-do	wishing-cap	kaisership	pyrenocarp
	pichiciago	hunting-cap		

schizocarp	blue-collar	superaltar	first-aider	sidewinder
Australorp	rollcollar	almacantar	paraglider	wool-winder
digger-wasp	sand-dollar	almucantar	hang-glider	stemwinder
sapling-cup	half-dollar	life-mortar	backslider	up-and-under
parting-cup	day-scholar	sloop-of-war	bird-spider	thereunder
wassail-cup	south-polar	belshazzar	wolf-spider	whereunder
stirrup-cup	multipolar	wine-bibber	scrub-rider	dumfounder
cluster-cup	interpolar	land-jobber	horse-rider	compounder
buttoned-up	extra-solar	sea-blubber	rough-rider	ten-pounder
lighting-up	confabular	land-lubber	stock-rider	propounder
contrecoup	acetabular	root-rubber	besom-rider	all-rounder
candle-doup	mandibular	subscriber	night-rider	free-fooder
trou-de-loup	vestibular	prescriber	reconsider	wool-carder
manna-croup	unilobular	proscriber	subdivider	day-boarder
blood-group	vernacular	bedchamber	witch-alder	superorder
amido-group	spiracular	bond-timber	outfielder	money-order
amino-group	tentacular	knee-timber	water-elder	self-murder
nitro-group	trabecular	dive-bomber	backvelder	soft-sawder
turtle-soup	vallecular	wool-comber	spot-welder	face-powder
hydropolyp	fascicular	code-number	scaffolder	worm-powder
R	pellicular	back-number	manifolder	hair-powder
Ranzellaar	follicular	tight-lacer	stadholder	spruce-beer
bastard-bar	vermicular	amphimacer	landholder	commandeer
swingle-bar	curricular	air-officer	bond-holder	caravaneer
harbour-bar	matricular	law-officer	fund-holder	carabineer
draught-bar	versicular	sacrificer	card-holder	scrutineer
buttery-bar	lenticular	rope-dancer	freeholder	auctioneer
outside-car	particular	wire-dancer	type-holder	harpooneer
baggage-car	vorticular	taxi-dancer	rush-holder	wheresoe'er
touring-car	testicular	step-dancer	withholder	leafleteer
parlour-car	clavicular	freelancer	book-holder	banqueteer
freight-car	peduncular	insurancer	loan-holder	circuiteer
tramway-car	homuncular	reverencer	ship-holder	charioteer
trolley-car	caruncular	pronouncer	lampholder	understeer
hebdomadar	furuncular	sand-saucer	unitholder	hackbuteer
pillow-bear	unilocular	reproducer	copyholder	glendoveer
woolly-bear	trilocular	introducer	Africander	pine-chafer
switchgear	sexlocular	transducer	glad-hander	rose-chafer
uninuclear	tubercular	file-leader	backhander	cockchafer
pronuclear	minuscular	ringleader	left-hander	cross-refer
king's-spear	eglandular	bear-leader	Afrikander	umbellifer
womenswear	subangular	fair-leader	woodlander	retransfer
sportswear	triangular	loss-leader	Highlander	socdolager
wander-year	octangular	playleader	Thailander	sogdolager
yesteryear	campanular	news-reader	mainlander	scrimmager
bull-beggar	penannular	promenader	overlander	scrummager
paper-cigar	glomerular	Gasconader	calamander	disparager
budgerigar	peninsular	freeloader	salamander	encourager
khidmutgar	bivalvular	railroader	palisander	gilravager
khitmutgar	micropylar	kerb-trader	mind-bender	rock-badger
evangeliar	peristylar	curb-trader	hellbender	corn-dodger
unfamiliar	monostylar	free-trader	road-mender	sortileger
sweet-briar	polystylar	death-adder	quarrender	sandbagger
intercalar	beach-la-mar	air-bladder	goal-tender	bootlegger
cat-burglar	molendinar	rope-ladder	sand-binder	gold-digger
consimilar	reim-kennar	fish-ladder	self-binder	hill-digger
dissimilar	supralunar	trap-ladder	highbinder	head-hugger
cerebellar	plenilunar	step-ladder	bookbinder	stravaiger
wine-cellar	superlunar	overbidder	pathfinder	socdoliger
varicellar	interlunar	jury-rudder	viewfinder	sogdoliger
coal-cellar	translunar	interceder	baby-minder	self-danger
salt-cellar	cassumunar	self-feeder	subjoinder	voetganger
substellar	bitter-spar	self-seeder	non-joinder	bellhanger
tendrillar	Turko-Tatar	superseder	misjoinder	coat-hanger

bushranger	vanquisher	habit-maker	game-dealer	jackhammer
challenger	well-wisher	money-maker	junk-dealer	trip-hammer
stallenger	toolpusher	merrymaker	corn-dealer	drop-hammer
forefinger	jaw-crusher	thief-taker	newsdealer	tilt-hammer
five-finger	surf-bather	snuff-taker	mind-healer	claw-hammer
ring-finger	sea-feather	check-taker	man-stealer	windjammer
fish-finger	pen-feather	undertaker	wholesaler	programmer
wharfinger	pin-feather	painstaker	Emmentaler	head-bummer
stockinger	oak-leather	money-taker	pot-wabbler	bressummer
stallinger	good-father	highjacker	pot-wobbler	chironomer
mud-slinger	forefather	backpacker	dissembler	astronomer
ink-slinger	stepfather	wool-packer	chronicler	mushroomer
gunslinger	foregather	cat-cracker	panhandler	electromer
bell-ringer	altogether	wit-cracker	two-wheeler	fish-farmer
austringer	bell-wether	nutcracker	loudhailer	tank-farmer
outswinger	grey-wether	woodpecker	reconciler	baby-farmer
left-winger	come-hither	trafficker	Rottweiler	foot-warmer
love-monger	anywhither	arse-licker	soap-boiler	tobogganer
fishmonger	good-mother	bootlicker	free-soiler	musicianer
meal-monger	stepmother	foot-licker	baseballer	aquaplaner
fellmonger	shanghaier	wool-picker	footballer	Weimaraner
ironmonger	dog-fancier	pig-sticker	marshaller	Lippizaner
pearmonger	sea-soldier	self-cocker	victualler	Lipizzaner
starmonger	bombardier	comstocker	bierkeller	coparcener
newsmonger	halberdier	sand-sucker	trammeller	emboldener
peltmonger	humidifier	wind-sucker	quarreller	fourteener
land-hunger	simplifier	lumpsucker	bookseller	threatener
eard-hunger	calorifier	seersucker	slop-seller	intervener
yerd-hunger	emulsifier	goatsucker	bestseller	campaigner
yird-hunger	classifier	peat-reeker	tale-teller	complainer
socdologer	sanctifier	self-seeker	foreteller	pea-trainer
sogdologer	stultifier	hitch-hiker	man-queller	restrainer
mythologer	quantifier	race-walker	unraveller	distrainer
philologer	beautifier	rope-walker	out-dweller	maintainer
astrologer	chandelier	fire-walker	stenciller	cordwainer
surcharger	multiplier	wire-walker	self-filler	moonshiner
discharger	palfrenier	fell-walker	weedkiller	shale-miner
beefburger	carabinier	shop-walker	time-killer	underminer
sea-poacher	pontonnier	baby-walker	self-killer	determiner
encroacher	chiffonier	high-ranker	pain-killer	forty-niner
reproacher	sweet-brier	tea-drinker	lady-killer	submariner
cowpuncher	hen-harrier	well-sinker	corn-miller	caravanner
researcher	fox-terrier	deep-sinker	quadriller	leg-spinner
eye-catcher	prophesier	sand-bunker	bell-siller	road-runner
rat-catcher	plumassier	coal-bunker	well-willer	Rome-runner
cowcatcher	cuirassier	mossbunker	road-roller	forerunner
fly-catcher	perruquier	overlooker	high-roller	baserunner
dispatcher	sugar-baker	love-broker	controller	fell-runner
Hamburgher	ice-breaker	bill-broker	wire-puller	overrunner
epigrapher	tie-breaker	pawnbroker	wine-cooler	telephoner
geographer	jaw-breaker	ship-broker	pourparler	antiphoner
biographer	law-breaker	shin-barker	brow-antler	marathoner
zoographer	boneshaker	backmarker	trey-antler	religioner
theosopher	peacemaker	bookmarker	paper-ruler	occasioner
squabasher	frame-maker	tear-jerker	spin-bowler	petitioner
gold-washer	verse-maker	zinc-worker	wild-fowler	questioner
dish-washer	grave-maker	headworker	daydreamer	emblazoner
free-fisher	matchmaker	faceworker	horse-tamer	northerner
line-fisher	watchmaker	mine-worker	bêche-de-mer	southerner
kingfisher	brickmaker	wireworker	blasphemer	lime-burner
seal-fisher	clockmaker	case-worker	proclaimer	rick-burner
demolisher	trunk-maker	backworker	disclaimer	lamp-burner
skirmisher	paper-maker	evil-worker	longprimer	overturner
languisher	dressmaker	cornhusker	fore-hammer	importuner

slave-owner	treacherer	stone-eater	heliometer	life-renter
church-goer	decipherer	feed-heater	goniometer	rack-renter
horseshoer	cloisterer	flesh-eater	variometer	frequenter
music-paper	embitterer	opium-eater	opsiometer	ten-pointer
state-paper	splutterer	four-seater	cyclometer	calc-sinter
snuff-paper	discoverer	lotus-eater	coulometer	overwinter
watch-paper	deflowerer	honey-eater	anemometer	triaconter
touch-paper	quick-firer	woman-hater	trommeter	headhunter
flock-paper	stone-borer	psychiater	planometer	mine-hunter
satin-paper	adventurer	hagiolater	cyanometer	dung-hunter
stamp-paper	recapturer	ophiolater	pycnometer	moth-hunter
glass-paper	manoeuvrer	heliolater	clinometer	book-hunter
emery-paper	cockteaser	Mariolater	urinometer	lion-hunter
gut-scraper	fire-raiser	iconolater	pyknometer	tuft-hunter
skyscraper	dispraiser	necrolater	iconometer	pie-counter
night-taper	hair-raiser	Marylater	phonometer	rencounter
pike-keeper	mythiciser	granulater	vibrometer	discounter
gamekeeper	hybridiser	desecrater	ombrometer	map-mounter
time-keeper	liquidiser	dehydrater	micrometer	surmounter
gate-keeper	deoxidiser	floodwater	hydrometer	freebooter
cash-keeper	syllogiser	bilge-water	hygrometer	peashooter
lock-keeper	catechiser	table-water	spirometer	six-shooter
bookkeeper	franchiser	gripe-water	nitrometer	helicopter
parkkeeper	tantaliser	white-water	opisometer	gyrocopter
goal-keeper	visualiser	peach-water	pulsometer	non-starter
shopkeeper	stabiliser	ditch-water	drosometer	reredorter
door-keeper	steriliser	freshwater	hypsometer	rear-dorter
crowkeeper	fertiliser	breakwater	lactometer	ripsnorter
tub-thumper	symboliser	blackwater	hyetometer	coal-porter
buck-jumper	victimiser	slack-water	Tintometer ®	woolsorter
showjumper	randomiser	quick-water	photometer	telecaster
baby-jumper	economiser	shoal-water	piezometer	forecaster
horse-coper	epitomiser	angel-water	water-meter	medicaster
interloper	galvaniser	storm-water	pachymeter	newscaster
sandgroper	recogniser	shearwater	tachymeter	peat-caster
dive-dapper	solemniser	underwater	bathymeter	down-easter
fly-flapper	harmoniser	river-water	thereafter	clubmaster
wit-snapper	sermoniser	sweet-water	jack-rafter	headmaster
bird-pepper	patroniser	abstracter	rick-lifter	bandmaster
wall-pepper	moderniser	obstructer	shop-lifter	pond-master
worshipper	merceriser	tetrameter	gunfighter	yard-master
mud-skipper	tenderiser	voltameter	dumb-waiter	fire-master
tea-clipper	mesmeriser	pentameter	land-waiter	ring-master
day-tripper	pulveriser	heptameter	tide-waiter	bushmaster
sand-hopper	deodoriser	acidimeter	prohibiter	dock-master
clodhopper	temporiser	planimeter	sheep-biter	workmaster
leaf-hopper	terroriser	pulsimeter	telewriter	taskmaster
frog-hopper	dogmatiser	densimeter	typewriter	coalmaster
rock-hopper	magnetiser	passimeter	songwriter	iron-master
corn-popper	sensitiser	centimeter	sign-writer	ship-master
rere-supper	hypnotiser	gravimeter	news-writer	overmaster
super-duper	advertiser	pelvimeter	play-writer	mint-master
land-louper	improviser	pleximeter	copywriter	postmaster
stenotyper	boot-closer	tribometer	zootsuiter	ritt-master
calendarer	decomposer	viscometer	subchanter	quiz-master
mace-bearer	interposer	araeometer	trochanter	rib-roaster
tale-bearer	transposer	mileometer	mischanter	wine-taster
pall-bearer	free-verser	taseometer	dreikanter	Manchester
bull-roarer	discourser	diagometer	tea-planter	Winchester
rememberer	trespasser	tachometer	supplanter	arbalester
squanderer	bedpresser	bathometer	covenanter	tonguester
interferer	self-abuser	fathometer	residenter	reregister
endangerer	transfuser	radiometer	gradienter	enregister
malingerer	gold-beater	audiometer	ornamenter	corn-kister

arbalister	never-never	soothsayer	explicator	examinator
re-enlister	whomsoever	southsayer	fornicator	eliminator
beetmister	whensoever	cherimoyer	fabricator	abominator
administer	whatsoever	lake-lawyer	lubricator	terminator
encloister	pearl-diver	bumfreezer	rubricator	personator
uncloister	pile-driver	kieselguhr	masticator	gubernator
good-sister	taxi-driver	love-affair	rusticator	alternator
half-sister	wool-driver	wheel-chair	defalcator	syncopator
twin-sister	reap-silver	sedan-chair	inculcator	extirpator
stepsister	ruby-silver	king's-chair	provocator	declarator
linguister	table-cover	night-chair	depredator	preparator
jaw-twister	loose-cover	elbow-chair	elucidator	comparator
sea-monster	undercover	maidenhair	liquidator	celebrator
billposter	rediscover	pigeon-pair	delineator	calibrator
four-poster	spread-over	scale-stair	procreator	lucubrator
filibuster	warmed-over	fellow-heir	miscreator	desecrator
crop-duster	change-over	retrochoir	propagator	dehydrator
outbluster	switch-over	Drawcansir	variegator	enumerator
seed-oyster	ring-plover	quadrumvir	castigator	co-operator
wildcatter	rain-plover	jeistiecor	instigator	cooperator
anti-matter	wood-carver	ambassador	expurgator	integrator
overmatter	fish-carver	embassador	subjugator	denigrator
dead-letter	undeserver	drumbledor	corrugator	respirator
love-letter	time-server	corregidor	officiator	inspirator
ship-letter	bed-swerver	kerb-vendor	enunciator	elaborator
drop-letter	withdrawer	curb-vendor	repudiator	perforator
four-letter	rough-hewer	news-vendor	retaliator	meliorator
newsletter	televiewer	unhoped-for	humiliator	implorator
post-letter	crossbower	uncared-for	defoliator	evaporator
pace-setter	overshower	looking-for	elutriator	corporator
bonesetter	safe-blower	quint-major	expatiator	penetrator
typesetter	snow-blower	chancellor	negotiator	arbitrator
pirouetter	disc-flower	counsellor	alleviator	procurator
moss-litter	wind-flower	councillor	travelator	conjurator
baby-sitter	moth-flower	intervenor	compilator	triturator
bogtrotter	ball-flower	distrainor	ventilator	incantator
shea-butter	wallflower	quint-minor	oscillator	orientator
dika-butter	bell-flower	mainpernor	titillator	assentator
rock-butter	twinflower	closed-door	percolator	compotator
palm-butter	moon-flower	behind-door	variolator	devastator
salt-butter	cornflower	battledoor	travolator	commutator
wood-cutter	mist-flower	louvre-door	legislator	computator
file-cutter	crow-flower	prison-door	translator	attenuator
type-cutter	July-flower	door-to-door	turbulator	extenuator
leaf-cutter	hover-mower	louver-door	speculator	insinuator
cork-cutter	horsepower	street-door	calculator	punctuator
coal-cutter	steam-power	underfloor	inoculator	cultivator
corn-cutter	hydropower	first-floor	circulator	observator
fish-cutter	under-power	blackamoor	coagulator	calefactor
Herrnhuter	superpower	transferor	stimulator	malefactor
transmuter	water-power	tortfeasor	granulator	benefactor
instituter	wine-grower	supervisor	stipulator	corn-factor
ambidexter	silk-grower	antecessor	collimator	underactor
cataloguer	wool-grower	compressor	lacrimator	subtractor
coal-heaver	watch-tower	suppressor	lacrymator	contractor
note-shaver	water-tower	reprobator	oxygenator	protractor
semiquaver	stair-tower	desiccator	designator	abstractor
stage-fever	light-tower	exsiccator	vaccinator	transactor
swine-fever	bobbysoxer	deprecator	buccinator	prospector
marsh-fever	plate-layer	eradicator	fascinator	vivisector
dandy-fever	bricklayer	vindicator	originator	disjunctor
unbeliever	dice-player	syndicator	machinator	paradoctor
cantilever	underlayer	applicator	declinator	rain-doctor
howsomever	self-slayer	duplicator	pollinator	proproctor

obstructor	S	paedeutics	crossbones	Charollais
destructor	spring-haas	paideutics	crab-stones	Beaujolais
instructor	mustard-gas	halieutics	palisadoes	Dendrophis
propraetor	distringas	charabancs	innuendoes	fontinalis
proprietor	exhaust-gas	fairy-beads	Mandingoes	fleur-de-lis
prohibitor	galimatias	crossroads	flamingoes	portcullis
proveditor	erysipelas	niger-seeds	goloe-shoes	tetrapolis
progenitor	Michaelmas	chrysalids	patereroes	pentapolis
premonitor	Childermas	piece-goods	square-toes	cosmopolis
disheritor	contadinas	dress-goods	mosquitoes	necropolis
requisitor	ballerinas	foot-guards	timber-toes	metropolis
inquisitor	Orthoceras	fieldwards	jackanapes	endodermis
prepositor	Deinoceras	shorewards	small-pipes	hypodermis
ovipositor	Oireachtas	northwards	nyctalopes	epididymis
compositor	mulligrubs	southwards	small-wares	deck-tennis
dispositor	strategics	sternwards	pundonores	vichyssois
competitor	pedagogics	afterwards	Insessores	Osteolepis
absolvitor	hydraulics	rightwards	metastases	trichiasis
covenantor	graphemics	frontwards	metatheses	moniliasis
servo-motor	morphemics	coastwards	antitheses	ascariasis
water-motor	epistemics	appendices	hypotheses	filariasis
polyhistor	ergonomics	pontifices	hornfelses	scleriasis
thermistor	autonomics	anthelices	Albigenses	satyriasis
transistor	subatomics	haruspices	amanuenses	pityriasis
praepostor	toponymics	cicatrices	apotheoses	leontiasis
retributor	cacogenics	heritrices	sunglasses	metaplasis
prosecutor	cryogenics	Everglades	syllabuses	catastasis
persecutor	nucleonics	rhomboides	succubuses	metastasis
collocutor	eudemonics	Hesperides	nautiluses	hypostasis
prolocutor	environics	sobersides	calculuses	diapedesis
restitutor	ambisonics	caryatides	mandamuses	syneidesis
institutor	transonics	hydrazides	platypuses	periegesis
iron-liquor	subtropics	board-wages	excursuses	epexegesis
night-churr	geriatrics	interreges	paraphyses	catechesis
plesiosaur	biometrics	phorminges	othergates	parathesis
megalosaur	isometrics	Polianthes	disparates	metathesis
ankylosaur	obstetrics	bedclothes	Notoryctes	antithesis
brontosaur	catoptrics	subspecies	nomothetes	epenthesis
onocentaur	geophysics	ecospecies	actualités	hypothesis
pasticheur	biophysics	somebodies	satellites	prosthesis
accoucheur	aquabatics	macaronies	tympanites	biopoiesis
persifleur	acrobatics	vespiaries	draconites	uropoiesis
dérailleur	aerobatics	Stannaries	corybantes	paraenesis
tirailleur	kinematics	categories	quadrantes	diagenesis
répétiteur	axiomatics	toiletries	Stratiotes	epigenesis
colporteur	chromatics	vitalities	parkleaves	pangenesis
rapporteur	pneumatics	facilities	bull-beeves	syngenesis
free-labour	geostatics	cornflakes	themselves	neogenesis
overlabour	dialectics	Rhoeadales	yourselves	biogenesis
troubadour	energetics	Euglenales	appendixes	noogenesis
twenty-four	aesthetics	Uredinales	cicatrixes	orogenesis
dinner-hour	homiletics	Ginkgoales	heritrixes	pyogenesis
rose-colour	semeiotics	spectacles	squint-eyes	ecphonesis
dove-colour	thermotics	hot-cockles	hey-de-guyes	aphaeresis
self-colour	epizootics	oftentimes	strelitzes	synaeresis
plum-colour	orthoptics	hydrosomes	handicuffs	synderesis
overcolour	onomastics	gensdarmes	stridelegs	synteresis
bar-parlour	orchestics	hippomanes	belongings	hysteresis
sky-parlour	sophistics	testudines	polishings	proairesis
coat-armour	ballistics	serpigines	oughtlings	amanuensis
good-humour	stylistics	aborigines	screenings	thrombosis
love-favour	agonistics	lentigines	strippings	molybdosis
perfervour	floristics	vertigines	water-wings	pholidosis
imprimatur	patristics	rackabones	wafer-tongs	apotheosis

ornithosis	urethritis	catholicos	night-glass	thriveless
diorthosis	oophoritis	ambuscados	flint-glass	motiveless
parabiosis	fibrositis	desperados	groundmass	swerveless
antibiosis	stomatitis	acolouthos	white-brass	breezeless
aerobiosis	dermatitis	akolouthos	manna-grass	beliefless
ateleiosis	gingivitis	portfolios	melic-grass	reliefless
enantiosis	Dolichotis	chaparajos	panic-grass	springless
anchylosis	aquafortis	chaparejos	beard-grass	stringless
pterylosis	epiglottis	malapropos	sword-grass	speechless
endosmosis	proglottis	rhinoceros	spike-grass	breechless
ecchymosis	beef-brewis	monopteros	brome-grass	branchless
pollenosis	echopraxis	pronephros	plume-grass	stanchless
syntenosis	heliotaxis	Mosasauros	goose-grass	quenchless
paragnosis	chemotaxis	contraltos	shave-grass	searchless
telegnosis	hydrotaxis	Ramphastos	bunch-grass	churchless
carcinosis	phototaxis	pettichaps	couch-grass	thatchless
byssinosis	brachyaxis	pettychaps	quick-grass	sheathless
marmarosis	amphimixis	Homorelaps	sisal-grass	breathless
osmidrosis	'tween-decks	quadriceps	lemon-grass	wreathless
bagassosis	chopsticks	corn-thrips	spear-grass	scaithless
haematosis	back-blocks	paratroops	sugar-grass	skaithless
dermatosis	dreadlocks	beech-drops	supergrass	healthless
thanatosis	marshlocks	Chamaerops	aftergrass	remediless
asbestosis	goldilocks	rifle-corps	starr-grass	recoilless
synostosis	womenfolks	staff-corps	arrow-grass	streamless
ichthyosis	pilliwinks	camel-corps	ill-success	redeemless
zoothapsis	siege-works	prison-bars	sea-goddess	systemless
metalepsis	steelworks	wool-shears	war-goddess	rhythmless
antisepsis	sternworks	red-sanders	leopardess	fathomless
paralipsis	upperworks	alexanders	stewardess	ransomless
ecthlipsis	paintworks	sallenders	disprofess	bottomless
stereopsis	print-works	hip-huggers	comburgess	spleenless
ampelopsis	canonicals	leg-warmers	shieldless	fizzenless
meconopsis	bacchanals	mismanners	friendless	designless
Amblyopsis	altar-rails	hop-bitters	groundless	pardonless
procrypsis	lamb's-tails	backstairs	regardless	visionless
paraphysis	glassfulls	downstairs	rewardless	fusionless
hypophysis	barrelfuls	septemvirs	shroudless	nationless
uranalysis	shovelfuls	Monsignors	fleeceless	motionless
urinalysis	saucerfuls	out-of-doors	chanceless	weaponless
zincolysis	pocketfuls	flexihours	strifeless	patronless
radiolysis	bucketfuls	small-hours	bridgeless	reasonless
haemolysis	basketfuls	contrabass	changeless	seasonless
hydrolysis	biorhythms	double-bass	fringeless	foisonless
neurolysis	king-of-arms	third-class	chargeless	returnless
photolysis	coat-of-arms	underclass	scatheless	dollarless
histolysis	king-at-arms	upper-class	saddleless	cumberless
antiaditis	cocoa-beans	superclass	throneless	numberless
tracheitis	hinderlans	lower-class	escapeless	rudderless
meningitis	Mussulmans	first-class	stripeless	borderless
myringitis	cancrizans	opera-glass	sphereless	fingerless
syringitis	afterpains	wired-glass	desireless	tocherless
laryngitis	widershins	gauge-glass	lustreless	fatherless
bronchitis	thumbikins	Howleglass	recureless	motherless
cephalitis	'sbuddikins	fibreglass	futureless	hammerless
tonsilitis	spillikins	plate-glass	phraseless	dinnerless
papillitis	hinderlins	watch-glass	chaiseless	supperless
cellulitis	kettle-pins	plexiglass	praiseless	masterless
valvulitis	kittle-pins	storm-glass	opposeless	sisterless
tympanitis	operations	crown-glass	spouseless	matterless
duodenitis	pantaloons	dildo-glass	reputeless	fetterless
cerebritis	wafer-irons	galloglass	tongueless	letterless
ureteritis	automatons	water-glass	virtueless	showerless
hysteritis	beccaficos	sheet-glass	sleeveless	flowerless

10 -ESS

answerless	pettedness	severeness	bounciness	wambliness
prayerless	amazedness	meagreness	steadiness	deadliness
anchorless	morbidness	entireness	shoddiness	kindliness
authorless	turbidness	secureness	speediness	goodliness
sailorless	placidness	demureness	greediness	lordliness
tremorless	rancidness	impureness	untidiness	steeliness
terrorless	candidness	matureness	wieldiness	likeliness
colourless	sordidness	unwiseness	mouldiness	timeliness
armourless	frigidness	jocoseness	broodiness	comeliness
humourless	turgidness	moroseness	gourdiness	homeliness
honourless	pallidness	coarseness	sturdiness	loneliness
favourless	stolidness	hoarseness	cloudiness	liveliness
savourless	torpidness	sparseness	sniffiness	loveliness
stressless	stupidness	averseness	chuffiness	kingliness
effectless	floridness	obtuseness	fluffiness	gashliness
objectless	horridness	sedateness	snuffiness	weakliness
pocketless	torridness	oblateness	stuffiness	sickliness
thriftless	putridness	innateness	scurfiness	shelliness
weightless	liquidness	ornateness	stodginess	smelliness
flightless	fervidness	effeteness	smudginess	chilliness
knightless	unkindness	politeness	shagginess	woolliness
profitless	jocundness	finiteness	flagginess	seemliness
summitless	inwardness	remoteness	knagginess	unholiness
spiritless	towardness	chasteness	cragginess	pearliness
resultless	upwardness	arguteness	quagginess	measliness
tenantless	absurdness	diluteness	dregginess	grisliness
talentless	shrewdness	minuteness	clogginess	portliness
relentless	choiceness	astuteness	grogginess	costliness
parentless	scarceness	opaqueness	slanginess	unruliness
plaintless	fierceness	uniqueness	thinginess	creaminess
desertless	spruceness	untrueness	clinginess	dreaminess
effortless	unsafeness	nativeness	stinginess	steaminess
importless	savageness	activeness	sponginess	smalminess
Christless	blitheness	citizeness	poachiness	clamminess
resistless	unlikeness	takingness	bunchiness	gloominess
thirstless	femaleness	savingness	tetchiness	smarminess
shadowless	stableness	lovingness	bitchiness	storminess
windowless	feebleness	vexingness	pitchiness	braininess
marrowless	trebleness	stanchness	touchiness	skinniness
sorrowless	edibleness	Scotchness	doughiness	thorniness
superbness	nimbleness	modishness	dauphiness	brawniness
publicness	humbleness	rakishness	flashiness	sleepiness
heroicness	doubleness	mulishness	trashiness	steepiness
forcedness	singleness	owlishness	fleshiness	stripiness
handedness	facileness	tonishness	marshiness	clumpiness
mindedness	fickleness	impishness	wrathiness	grumpiness
jaggedness	tripleness	mopishness	filthiness	stumpiness
raggedness	simpleness	uppishness	frothiness	droopiness
doggedness	suppleness	garishness	earthiness	trappiness
ruggedness	subtleness	lavishness	worthiness	slippiness
pickedness	gentleness	Jewishness	sneakiness	floppiness
wickedness	littleness	boyishness	freakiness	sloppiness
hookedness	ugsomeness	coyishness	knackiness	chirpiness
forkedness	arcaneness	toyishness	trickiness	croupiness
maimedness	humaneness	smoothness	stickiness	bleariness
searedness	insaneness	villainess	stockiness	smeariness
sacredness	sereneness	scabbiness	pluckiness	dreariness
cursedness	supineness	shabbiness	chalkiness	sugariness
cussedness	divineness	flabbiness	crankiness	unwariness
elatedness	jejuneness	slabbiness	spookiness	tawdriness
giftedness	unripeness	drabbiness	quirkiness	cheeriness
unitedness	squareness	knobbiness	friskiness	wateriness
wontedness	unwareness	chubbiness	wabbliness	starriness
rootedness	sombreness	stubbiness	wobbliness	paltriness

sultriness	manfulness	augustness	otherguess	Lithodomus
wintriness	sinfulness	unjustness	hit-and-miss	Anthonomus
uneasiness	fitfulness	devoutness	school-miss	Chironomus
greasiness	artfulness	fallowness	candy-floss	strabismus
queasiness	lawfulness	sallowness	cyclo-cross	psellismus
cheesiness	joyfulness	mellowness	intercross	vaginismus
cocksiness	seldomness	yellowness	criss-cross	synthronus
folksiness	lissomness	hollowness	harquebuss	zoophobous
whimsiness	infirmness	narrowness	short-coats	veridicous
flimsiness	leadenness	convexness	dead-lights	veneficous
clumsiness	hiddenness	prolixness	deck-quoits	ventricous
glassiness	soddenness	phoneyness	wine-vaults	monotocous
brassiness	suddenness	thale-cress	underpants	polytocous
grassiness	woodenness	watercress	emblements	subfuscous
glossiness	brokenness	pennycress	fieldboots	molluscous
drossiness	sullenness	maladdress	grass-roots	solipedous
drowsiness	barrenness	offendress	hoots-toots	tremendous
sweatiness	rottenness	underdress	three-parts	stupendous
sleetiness	cravenness	nightdress	cashew-nuts	horrendous
craftiness	unevenness	court-dress	hereabouts	decapodous
shiftiness	brazenness	manageress	thenabouts	octopodous
mightiness	solemnness	avengeress	whatabouts	jeopardous
stiltiness	commonness	pantheress	houts-touts	hypogaeous
guiltiness	wantonness	divineress	trolley-bus	herbaceous
faultiness	modernness	fruiteress	gonococcus	ericaceous
scantiness	scrimpness	adulteress	Diplodocus	juncaceous
daintiness	wilderness	conqueress	hocus-pocus	predaceous
paintiness	tenderness	retrogress	flea-circus	iridaceous
flintiness	sickerness	transgress	trochiscus	lardaceous
jauntiness	properness	warrioress	Spheniscus	paleaceous
heartiness	dapperness	electoress	Scarabaeus	tuffaceous
sportiness	betterness	drill-press	coryphaeus	tophaceous
reastiness	bitterness	decompress	pronucleus	typhaceous
yeastiness	cleverness	recompress	oesophagus	rubiaceous
frostiness	unfairness	cider-press	xiphopagus	meliaceous
crustiness	remissness	power-press	antitragus	liliaceous
trustiness	odiousness	screw-press	rust-fungus	tiliaceous
scattiness	famousness	mediatress	smut-fungus	alliaceous
prettiness	porousness	idolatress	mystagogus	foliaceous
grittiness	joyousness	emulatress	epicanthus	coriaceous
clottiness	intactness	dictatress	Helianthus	violaceous
knottiness	abjectness	directress	Haemanthus	amylaceous
snottiness	selectness	seductress	agapanthus	palmaceous
spottiness	directness	servitress	Amaranthus	gemmaceous
smuttiness	strictness	inventress	polyanthus	glumaceous
cliquiness	unmeetness	chauntress	octonarius	acanaceous
scurviness	secretness	sculptress	Charadrius	arenaceous
sleaziness	slightness	ancestress	astragalus	avenaceous
wheeziness	brightness	songstress	Bucephalus	acinaceous
breeziness	straitness	ministress	Crocodilus	spinaceous
quizziness	adroitness	cloistress	prothallus	pennaceous
socialness	eye-witness	huckstress	discobolus	anonaceous
genialness	ear-witness	seamstress	holus-bolus	drupaceous
jovialness	occultness	spinstress	fasciculus	aceraceous
dismalness	pliantness	sempstress	cauliculus	oleraceous
casualness	recentness	overstress	panniculus	ochraceous
subtilness	silentness	mulattress	fonticulus	porraceous
unwellness	intentness	executress	monticulus	ostraceous
shrillness	fluentness	jointuress	Didunculus	lauraceous
woefulness	quaintness	prepossess	homunculus	byssaceous
irefulness	promptness	dispossess	ranunculus	cactaceous
usefulness	abruptness	prophetess	glomerulus	cretaceous
ruefulness	expertness	baroness	Hyoscyamus	pultaceous
wilfulness	robustness	air-hostess	Polyphemus	myrtaceous

testaceous	precocious	morbillous	gangrenous	slanderous
olivaceous	palladious	fibrillous	villainous	thunderous
malvaceous	perfidious	tubicolous	mucedinous	plunderous
curvaceous	fastidious	nidicolous	libidinous	founderous
spadiceous	commodious	fimicolous	cupidinous	sebiferous
triticeous	preludious	limicolous	paludinous	nubiferous
orchideous	contagious	rupicolous	hirudinous	vociferous
jaspideous	prodigious	viticolous	proteinous	luciferous
florideous	struthious	saxicolous	oleaginous	muciferous
rampageous	reptilious	miraculous	viraginous	nuciferous
umbrageous	rebellious	pediculous	voraginous	oleiferous
outrageous	abstemious	ridiculous	rubiginous	saliferous
courageous	ruthenious	periculous	caliginous	piliferous
petroleous	insomnious	meticulous	fuliginous	pomiferous
extraneous	calumnious	monoculous	lanuginous	laniferous
coetaneous	euphonious	flosculous	aeruginous	omniferous
coccineous	harmonious	stridulous	trichinous	coniferous
gramineous	precarious	glandulous	foraminous	poriferous
stamineous	trifarious	scrofulous	moliminous	auriferous
fulmineous	gregarious	irregulous	abdominous	ossiferous
ultroneous	uproarious	unpopulous	albuminous	vitiferous
calcareous	tenebrious	scrupulous	cacuminous	rotiferous
nectareous	lugubrious	puberulous	leguminous	armigerous
tartareous	salubrious	edentulous	voluminous	lanigerous
despiteous	mysterious	spondylous	ceruminous	pupigerous
dispiteous	suspirious	symphylous	bituminous	morigerous
subaqueous	inglorious	monoxylous	subspinous	decamerous
geophagous	censorious	endogamous	gelatinous	octamerous
omophagous	amatorious	allogamous	keratinous	hexamerous
zoophagous	victorious	homogamous	serotinous	ephemerous
exophagous	perjurious	monogamous	velutinous	innumerous
pemphigous	quotatious	autogamous	scrutinous	polymerous
antilogous	infectious	polygamous	concinnous	ungenerous
homologous	flagitious	didynamous	treasonous	streperous
lucifugous	mollitious	equanimous	homotonous	prosperous
nidifugous	propitious	pompelmous	monotonous	adulterous
homozygous	nutritious	theonomous	gluttonous	tripterous
stomachous	factitious	autonomous	decagynous	isopterous
distichous	fictitious	anadromous	hexagynous	boisterous
didelphous	licentious	hylotomous	perigynous	roisterous
dimorphous	deceptious	xylotomous	monogynous	blusterous
catarrhous	exceptious	dispermous	hypogynous	roysterous
synanthous	goloptious	posthumous	misogynous	cadaverous
amphibious	goluptious	homonymous	octogynous	papaverous
procacious	robustious	synonymous	polygynous	pellagrous
predacious	incautious	paronymous	anatropous	anarthrous
mendacious	obsequious	acronymous	apotropous	undesirous
mordacious	lascivious	diaphanous	isotropous	chivalrous
fallacious	multivious	membranous	syncarpous	indecorous
pugnacious	impervious	nubigenous	apocarpous	malodorous
rampacious	prolixious	indigenous	omniparous	clangorous
ungracious	scandalous	omnigenous	pupiparous	zoochorous
sequacious	acephalous	lysigenous	viviparous	uniflorous
loquacious	disepalous	endogenous	penumbrous	facinorous
curvacious	bipetalous	halogenous	decandrous	ring-porous
trioecious	dipetalous	xylogenous	triandrous	zoosporous
monoecious	procoelous	homogenous	monandrous	aposporous
synoecious	symphilous	xenogenous	gynandrous	isosporous
pernicious	geophilous	monogenous	synandrous	exosporous
auspicious	zoophilous	acrogenous	octandrous	traitorous
suspicious	unperilous	pyrogenous	hexandrous	stertorous
avaricious	scurrilous	ectogenous	slumberous	languorous
lubricious	cancellous	autogenous	monocerous	nucivorous
capricious	marvellous	polygenous	glanderous	ranivorous

omnivorous	uredosorus	stratocrat	vest-pocket	river-craft
ossivorous	pro-oestrus	meritocrat	life-rocket	hovercraft
non-ferrous	Allosaurus	aristocrat	mini-rocket	courtcraft
idolatrous	dolichurus	bureaucrat	wall-rocket	scoutcraft
zoolatrous	Trichiurus	malabar-rat	step-rocket	rough-draft
barratrous	metatarsus	humidistat	whip-socket	crown-graft
disastrous	foederatus	thermostat	fire-bucket	three-cleft
sinistrous	perforatus	siderostat	kerb-market	sound-shift
colostrous	conspectus	autodidact	curb-market	night-shift
sulphurous	prospectus	counteract	down-market	spoondrift
porphyrous	Benedictus	Pontefract	Euromarket	river-drift
oedematous	tersanctus	cataphract	meat-market	undercroft
eczematous	unigenitus	subprefect	test-market	steam-yacht
stemmatous	Pterygotus	side-effect	hand-basket	lanzknecht
gliomatous	eucalyptus	pluperfect	fire-basket	way-freight
lipomatous	mumble-news	free-select	flag-basket	dead-weight
stromatous	All-Hallows	disconnect	buck-basket	make-weight
astomatous	law-burrows	disrespect	work-basket	live-weight
myxomatous	leastaways	retrospect	chip-basket	overweight
miasmatous	strideways	introspect	eyas-musket	glove-fight
felicitous	lengthways	miscorrect	rock-violet	prize-fight
solicitous	colour-ways	quadrisect	quadruplet	fire-blight
calamitous	thwartways	leaf-insect	quintuplet	floodlight
strepitous	fleur-de-lys	contradict	lansquenet	overflight
ancipitous	T	drug-addict	landing-net	test-flight
inebritous	vampire-bat	sacrosanct	fowling-net	torchlight
immeritous	spectre-bat	indistinct	casting-net	watch-light
circuitous	leopard-cat	spermaduct	trammel-net	flashlight
ubiquitous	hunting-cat	spermiduct	herb-bennet	earth-light
iniquitous	Magnificat	circumduct	poke-bonnet	microlight
gratuitous	requiescat	misconduct	blue-bonnet	after-light
fortuitous	peel-and-eat	end-product	torpedo-net	crosslight
sarmentous	whole-wheat	analphabet	clew-garnet	night-light
portentous	mummy-wheat	trench-feet	draught-net	watch-night
tricrotous	jerked-meat	tenderfeet	ear-trumpet	birthnight
contiguous	ready-to-eat	broadsheet	pine-carpet	guest-night
continuous	misentreat	title-sheet	cork-carpet	first-night
menstruous	window-seat	score-sheet	phosphoret	fly-by-night
insensuous	fallow-chat	proof-sheet	disc-floret	gaudy-night
spirituous	steeple-hat	stern-sheet	bell-turret	merry-night
tumultuous	picture-hat	plate-fleet	phosphuret	star-bright
voluptuous	Homburg-hat	watersmeet	sack-posset	birthright
unvirtuous	scarlet-hat	indiscreet	tourniquet	forthright
incestuous	double-flat	honey-sweet	soubriquet	millwright
implexuous	anastigmat	tweet-tweet	mutton-suet	wainwright
saxicavous	Laundromat	minibuffet	mock-privet	shipwright
longaevous	trichromat	mini-budget	fore-and-aft	cartwright
rendezvous	apochromat	fuss-budget	crankshaft	playwright
pedipalpus	advice-boat	life-jacket	spear-shaft	mouse-sight
Pliohippus	paddle-boat	bluejacket	aftershaft	night-sight
Aristippus	rowing-boat	cork-jacket	swordcraft	smoketight
metacarpus	butter-boat	dust-jacket	spacecraft	hug-me-tight
Podocarpus	packet-boat	nick-nacket	stagecraft	chock-tight
Pilocarpus	narrow-boat	wage-packet	siegecraft	steamtight
artocarpus	monkey-boat	age-bracket	housecraft	watertight
Mindererus	riding-coat	gas-bracket	statecraft	light-tight
Polypterus	trench-coat	fan-cricket	leechcraft	overcaught
Eurypterus	shellycoat	fen-cricket	witchcraft	overraught
parvovirus	Serbo-Croat	zone-ticket	smithcraft	bestraught
semichorus	shove-groat	meal-ticket	handicraft	distraught
canephorus	bluethroat	pawnticket	small-craft	foretaught
pyrophorus	ruby-throat	soup-ticket	queencraft	self-taught
cryophorus	physiocrat	pick-pocket	under-craft	dearbought
phosphorus	technocrat	slit-pocket	water-craft	overbought

hard-fought	blood-guilt	compearant	munificent	prosilient
misthought	somersault	exhilarant	subnascent	dissilient
fearnought	wagon-vault	vociferant	connascent	prevenient
ore-wrought	antepenult	accelerant	erubescent	convenient
outwrought	heath-poult	intolerant	marcescent	usucapient
unbesought	perturbant	adulterant	iridescent	concipient
groundbait	disturbant	infragrant	candescent	percipient
ledger-bait	complicant	conspirant	turgescent	suscipient
straw-plait	supplicant	edulcorant	coalescent	innutrient
sage-rabbit	detoxicant	invigorant	opalescent	scaturient
jack-rabbit	intoxicant	decolorant	pallescent	abiturient
rock-rabbit	commandant	redcurrant	adolescent	parturient
buck-rabbit	descendant	subintrant	caulescent	out-patient
snaffle-bit	pretendant	registrant	fremescent	insentient
reaming-bit	concordant	ministrant	spumescent	co-sentient
disinhibit	discordant	restaurant	evanescent	assentient
inexplicit	solivagant	denaturant	spinescent	balbutient
cash-credit	congregant	malfeasant	torpescent	percutient
self-deceit	Flamingant	unpleasant	accrescent	discutient
preconceit	disenchant	degreasant	decrescent	ambivalent
misconceit	plain-chant	practisant	increscent	equivalent
Gesundheit	triumphant	convulsant	excrescent	sexivalent
Fahrenheit	hierophant	dispersant	nigrescent	monovalent
speed-limit	deforciant	conversant	florescent	zero-valent
retransmit	insouciant	depressant	vitrescent	polyvalent
primogenit	submediant	impuissant	putrescent	propellent
strong-knit	supergiant	percussant	lactescent	prepollent
forcing-pit	pot-valiant	surfactant	liquescent	graveolent
costean-pit	univariant	attractant	flavescent	suaveolent
cuckoo-spit	euphoriant	extractant	fervescent	non-violent
disinherit	asphyxiant	respectant	semilucent	malevolent
wood-spirit	nonchalant	inhabitant	antecedent	benevolent
time-spirit	resemblant	cohabitant	soricident	flocculent
team-spirit	pasquilant	exorbitant	coincident	inesculent
reinspirit	top-gallant	solicitant	descendent	fraudulent
corn-spirit	installant	incogitant	propendent	puberulent
sea-biscuit	flagellant	infinitant	pretendent	medicament
dog-biscuit	propellant	strepitant	contendent	paludament
trekschuit	shade-plant	revisitant	despondent	palliament
breadfruit	stove-plant	consultant	respondent	parliament
stone-fruit	rosin-plant	marcantant	protrudent	loculament
grapefruit	sheep-plant	accountant	house-agent	rearmament
sling-fruit	water-plant	accomptant	crown-agent	tournament
first-fruit	interplant	contestant	underagent	additament
lounge-suit	power-plant	protestant	press-agent	enjambment
riding-suit	transplant	inconstant	viceregent	entombment
diving-suit	pilot-plant	unconstant	tassel-gent	benumbment
romper-suit	yeast-plant	coadjutant	prefulgent	enfoldment
sailor-suit	stridulant	intriguant	profulgent	intendment
monkey-suit	capitulant	continuant	subtangent	attendment
devastivit	polysemant	colliquant	refringent	refundment
spring-halt	declaimant	irrelevant	astringent	retardment
stringhalt	reclaimant	pursuivant	contingent	defacement
superexalt	life-tenant	eye-servant	abstergent	effacement
wampum-belt	lieutenant	man-servant	convergent	enfacement
safety-belt	impregnant	conservant	contrahent	enlacement
parcel-gilt	unpregnant	flamboyant	sufficient	solacement
silver-gilt	illuminant	foudroyant	proficient	enticement
basket-hilt	altisonant	procumbent	perficient	evincement
cloud-built	altitonant	coadjacent	omniscient	scarcement
coach-built	discrepant	complacent	inobedient	amercement
woman-built	anticipant	maledicent	unobedient	deducement
yacht-built	episcopant	maleficent	ingredient	seducement
jerry-built	forbearant	beneficent	consilient	inducement

engagement	attachment	disbarment	miscontent	coquelicot
management	fleechment	endearment	armipotent	pistol-shot
enragement	enrichment	cumberment	ignipotent	cannon-shot
obligement	avouchment	wilderment	omnipotent	musket-shot
avengement	encashment	ponderment	totipotent	compatriot
revokement	polishment	wonderment	equipotent	groundplot
regalement	famishment	sunderment	idempotent	touch-me-not
impalement	banishment	affeerment	subsistent	lover's-knot
babblement	vanishment	preferment	consistent	breast-knot
gabblement	punishment	conferment	persistent	wellie-boot
rabblement	lavishment	sapperment	inexistent	riding-boot
mumblement	ravishment	pesterment	co-existent	weasel-coot
tanglement	ambushment	betterment	infrequent	bumble-foot
minglement	assythment	impairment	unfrequent	tanglefoot
defilement	impediment	devourment	subsequent	single-foot
revilement	embodiment	harassment	consequent	tenderfoot
cajolement	enregiment	assessment	delinquent	hounds-foot
graplement	habiliment	embossment	ineloquent	calves'-foot
dimplement	compliment	indebtment	dissolvent	sheep's-foot
complement	unruliment	indictment	circumvent	undershoot
supplement	dreariment	infeftment	constraint	water-shoot
couplement	experiment	commitment	reacquaint	orange-root
jostlement	embankment	acquitment	Septuagint	square-root
battlement	embarkment	insultment	peppermint	dragon-root
settlement	revealment	relentment	latter-mint	pillar-root
epaulement	instalment	resentment	hinge-joint	cancer-root
éboulement	propelment	department	mitre-joint	bitter-root
dazzlement	derailment	impartment	scarf-joint	costus-root
puzzlement	assailment	deportment	match-joint	yellow-root
definement	retailment	assortment	dowel-joint	melting-pot
refinement	entailment	arrestment	water-joint	chamberpot
repinement	fulfilment	divestment	standpoint	lobster-pot
attunement	assoilment	investment	fesse-point	plague-spot
escapement	entoilment	enlistment	flash-point	mother-spot
retirement	instilment	adjustment	pedal-point	yellow-spot
attirement	recallment	encystment	organ-point	beauty-spot
securement	embalmment	integument	embonpoint	chimney-pot
allurement	malignment	instrument	preappoint	poll-parrot
immurement	eloignment	bestowment	disappoint	turkey-trot
debasement	designment	prepayment	spear-point	nympholept
embasement	resignment	non-payment	power-point	tapescript
encasement	assignment	defrayment	cuckoo-pint	typescript
incasement	impugnment	supplyment	thumbprint	transcript
advisement	ordainment	deployment	voice-print	postscript
accusement	regainment	employment	lithoprint	manuscript
rebatement	obtainment	thereanent	microprint	stiff-rumpt
incitement	detainment	pre-eminent	ferroprint	spell-stopt
excitement	retainment	sea-serpent	heterocont	tumble-cart
inditement	attainment	unapparent	zeuglodont	chaise-cart
invitement	enjoinment	step-parent	selenodont	spring-cart
denotement	prisonment	ground-rent	dicynodont	egg-and-dart
tapotement	cantonment	incoherent	heterodont	white-heart
subduement	secernment	unreverent	pleurodont	blackheart
engouement	internment	irreverent	glyptodont	greenheart
dénouement	government	concurrent	diphyodont	sweetheart
imbruement	attornment	non-current	heterokont	faint-heart
enlevement	disownment	percurrent	tête-de-pont	flint-heart
revivement	entrapment	heaven-sent	break-front	bairn's-part
evolvement	enwrapment	disconsent	waterfront	moudiewart
engulfment	reshipment	inappetent	river-front	mowdiewart
abridgment	decampment	impenitent	shirt-front	overthwart
adjudgment	encampment	malcontent	heresy-hunt	herb-robert
preachment	escarpment	non-content	tantamount	preconcert
detachment	recoupment	discontent	rock-turbot	pop-concert

disconcert	steam-chest	algologist	virtualist	misogynist
animadvert	arch-priest	ethologist	textualist	torpedoist
controvert	jack-priest	axiologist	revivalist	Averrhoist
Blackshirt	mass-priest	gemologist	tricyclist	orthoepist
Brownshirt	thriftiest	nomologist	evangelist	emancipist
undershirt	rinderpest	pomologist	zoophilist	varitypist
dress-shirt	undercrest	atmologist	enamellist	calotypist
sweat-shirt	polychrest	zymologist	parabolist	copy-typist
nightshirt	reafforest	oenologist	monopolist	solidarist
underskirt	rain-forest	penologist	epistolist	lapidarist
discomfort	deer-forest	Sinologist	vocabulist	plagiarist
ultrashort	musket-rest	vinologist	monogamist	secularist
table-sport	palimpsest	monologist	misogamist	seminarist
spoil-sport	breath-test	topologist	polygamist	luminarist
moudiewort	reconquest	typologist	Wykehamist	glossarist
mowdiewort	galley-west	aerologist	geochemist	monetarist
nipplewort	Ptolemaist	serologist	biochemist	militarist
sneezewort	algebraist	agrologist	problemist	sanitarist
springwort	shirtwaist	virologist	legitimist	obituarist
stitchwort	panty-waist	horologist	ergonomist	Decembrist
spleen-wort	diatribist	misologist	aeronomist	Sanhedrist
barrenwort	pharmacist	nosologist	agronomist	misandrist
spider-wort	Spartacist	batologist	autonomist	ephemerist
motherwort	pacificist	ontologist	taxonomist	euhemerist
pepperwort	pyrrhicist	optologist	conformist	Antichrist
masterwort	Islamicist	cytologist	synonymist	allegorist
setterwort	dynamicist	sexologist	Africanist	categorist
butterwort	ceramicist	Mayologist	Vaticanist	folklorist
adder's-wort	polemicist	bryologist	Italianist	podiatrist
throatwort	organicist	revanchist	Paulianist	geriatrist
yellow-wort	technicist	monarchist	Messianist	belletrist
quinsy-wort	empiricist	autarchist	Russianist	geometrist
prize-court	classicist	mica-schist	fustianist	sinecurist
shadowcast	geneticist	talc-schist	abiogenist	pedicurist
narrowcast	demoticist	epitaphist	monogenist	manicurist
smell-feast	kenoticist	pansophist	polygenist	panegyrist
bluebreast	Neofascist	Volapükist	libidinist	consubsist
saddle-fast	pyramidist	arcubalist	illuminist	synthesist
colour-fast	Bollandist	surrealist	chauvinist	discursist
gymnasiast	psalmodist	glacialist	Sorbonnist	narcissist
ecclesiast	spasmodist	specialist	trombonist	schematist
enthusiast	threnodist	martialist	Bourbonist	chrematist
whirl-blast	rhapsodist	partialist	antagonist	pragmatist
cnidoblast	orchardist	fluvialist	theogonist	enigmatist
osteoblast	antitheist	decimalist	symphonist	stigmatist
planoblast	hylotheist	minimalist	pyrrhonist	grammatist
fibroblast	henotheist	maximalist	Marcionist	automatist
neuroblast	monotheist	nominalist	fashionist	spermatist
histoblast	autotheist	eternalist	pillionist	separatist
osteoclast	polytheist	diurnalist	bullionist	pancratist
lithoclast	mutton-fist	journalist	opinionist	pandectist
idoloclast	geophagist	liberalist	reunionist	synthetist
iconoclast	suffragist	federalist	versionist	concretist
leucoplast	strategist	generalist	Passionist	syncretist
protoplast	phalangist	mineralist	factionist	fortuitist
mizzen-mast	decalogist	literalist	fictionist	trecentist
jigger-mast	oncologist	immoralist	portionist	anecdotist
paraphrast	mycologist	humoralist	fluxionist	anabaptist
metaphrast	pedologist	centralist	hegemonist	orthoptist
diaskeuast	podologist	neutralist	balloonist	concettist
second-best	ideologist	naturalist	lampoonist	vignettist
mock-modest	rheologist	capitalist	bassoonist	librettist
wildebeest	theologist	gradualist	cartoonist	operettist
hartebeest	oreologist	sensualist	lanternist	absolutist

bilinguist	litter-lout	disc-harrow	kinchin-lay	stimulancy
colloquist	horned-pout	bush-harrow	stroke-play	postulancy
conclavist	water-spout	rest-harrow	strokeplay	spodomancy
Pan-Slavist	chucker-out	good-morrow	cudgel-play	lithomancy
bolshevist	striker-out	cony-burrow	screenplay	axinomancy
recidivist	through-put	**X**	puppet-play	capnomancy
relativist	church-text	anticlimax	closet-play	necromancy
positivist	**U**	metathorax	shadow-play	hydromancy
water-twist	fricandeau	mesothorax	cathode-ray	hieromancy
intertwist	couscousou	sealing-wax	passageway	cleromancy
paradoxist	**W**	thumb-index	right-of-way	nigromancy
Trotskyist	weather-gaw	circumflex	throughway	chiromancy
middlemost	wapenschaw	contraplex	telpherway	oniromancy
hiddenmost	wapinschaw	googolplex	expressway	cartomancy
hindermost	tattie-shaw	quadruplex	moucharaby	athermancy
highermost	wappenshaw	separatrix	subshrubby	subtenancy
nethermost	weapon-shaw	quadratrix	namby-pamby	prevenancy
hithermost	whillywhaw	moderatrix	standers-by	malignancy
eastermost	tattie-claw	generatrix	inefficacy	benignancy
lattermost	statute-law	spectatrix	indelicacy	repugnancy
bettermost	pease-straw	trisectrix	complicacy	oppugnancy
pigeon-post	turning-saw	protectrix	profligacy	consonancy
fingerpost	ripping-saw	inheritrix	immaculacy	dissonancy
permafrost	compass-saw	precentrix	legitimacy	exuberancy
cloudburst	vine-mildew	coadjutrix	inordinacy	ponderancy
knackwurst	Bartholmew	crio-sphinx	effeminacy	itinerancy
liverwurst	thumbscrew	prattlebox	episcopacy	penetrancy
theopneust	otter-shrew	squeeze-box	snobocracy	re-entrancy
wanderlust	ready-to-sew	bathing-box	hagiocracy	expectancy
upper-crust	knuckle-bow	packing-box	ochlocracy	reluctancy
time-thrust	weather-bow	hunting-box	millocracy	acceptancy
home-thrust	torrent-bow	nesting-box	doulocracy	importancy
overthrust	foreshadow	driving-box	pornocracy	executancy
nematocyst	rain-shadow	journal-box	hierocracy	connivancy
blastocyst	overshadow	thunder-box	plutocracy	observancy
phenocryst	grass-widow	weather-box	slavocracy	decumbency
crack-tryst	rose-window	chatterbox	immoderacy	recumbency
juggernaut	sash-window	witness-box	innumeracy	incumbency
sauerkraut	shop-window	pouncet-box	degeneracy	absorbency
emerald-cut	shot-window	country-box	regeneracy	quiescency
scissor-cut	flower-show	unorthodox	inveteracy	precedency
bathing-hut	puppet-show	chickenpox	illiteracy	confidency
locking-nut	blow-by-blow	groundprox	conspiracy	subsidency
marking-nut	tree-mallow	Scombresox	magistracy	presidency
saouari-nut	rose-mallow	chalumeaux	inaccuracy	ascendency
burr-walnut	musk-mallow	trousseaux	inadequacy	dependency
buffalo-nut	Jew's-mallow	Clarenceux	fire-policy	impendency
bladder-nut	goat-sallow	billet-doux	impeccancy	indulgency
roundabout	sea-swallow	nectocalyx	mendicancy	refulgency
thereabout	good-fellow	**Y**	ascendancy	stringency
whereabout	yoke-fellow	pressed-day	intendancy	detergency
rouseabout	work-fellow	wedding-day	attendancy	divergency
knockabout	hail-fellow	washing-day	redundancy	insurgency
whirl-about	room-fellow	working-day	accordancy	assurgency
right-about	playfellow	sealing-day	miscreancy	deficiency
roustabout	lace-pillow	mumping-day	termagancy	efficiency
track-scout	goat-willow	Sabbath-day	inelegancy	expediency
scooped-out	yellow-snow	twelfth-day	trenchancy	resiliency
clapped-out	middlebrow	seventh-day	sycophancy	ebulliency
down-and-out	hoodie-crow	unbirthday	irradiancy	recipiency
topping-out	stone-throw	Whit-Monday	brilliancy	incipiency
barring-out	hand-barrow	Whitsunday	compliancy	transiency
fitting-out	hurl-barrow	quarter-day	luxuriancy	cecutiency
throughout	broad-arrow	present-day	repellancy	prevalency

trivalency	idle-pulley	psephology	brachylogy	noteworthy
excellency	dog-parsley	trophology	metallurgy	loveworthy
repellency	cow-parsley	carphology	dramaturgy	newsworthy
somnolency	blood-money	morphology	iconomachy	hystericky
turbulency	knife-money	exobiology	tauromachy	phthisicky
succulency	table-money	glaciology	leiotrichy	cockyleeky
truculency	rogue-money	cardiology	cymotrichy	talky-talky
corpulency	glove-money	semeiology	parastichy	walky-talky
flatulency	prize-money	bibliology	Whiggarchy	hanky-panky
inclemency	drink-money	craniology	chiliarchy	corn-whisky
permanency	shell-money	storiology	matriarchy	acromegaly
prominency	token-money	gnosiology	patriarchy	improbably
continency	petromoney	physiology	trierarchy	implacably
pertinency	press-money	deltiology	squirarchy	impeccably
abstinency	smart-money	histiology	telegraphy	applicably
componency	ready-money	angelology	serigraphy	despicably
difference	fairy-money	typhlology	pasigraphy	formidably
abhorrency	strathspey	potamology	lexigraphy	dependably
decurrency	dapple-grey	docimology	cacography	illaudably
recurrency	hodden-grey	entomology	ideography	noticeably
competency	lovey-dovey	thermology	oleography	manageably
prepotency	niffy-naffy	seismology	areography	changeably
advertency	dehumidify	enzymology	oreography	chargeably
insistency	pre-qualify	urbanology	logography	untameably
congruency	disqualify	oceanology	holography	irremeably
connivency	presignify	satanology	xylography	unmoveably
insolvency	consignify	phaenology	demography	perishably
revolvency	saccharify	selenology	mimography	unsociably
chaplaincy	disglorify	emmenology	nomography	remediably
paramouncy	declassify	phrenology	tomography	undeniably
sergeantcy	reclassify	technology	monography	inexpiably
serjeantcy	decrassify	demonology	lipography	invariably
viscountcy	subjectify	chronology	topography	insatiably
bankruptcy	unsanctify	immunology	typography	unenviably
ragged-lady	dissatisfy	palynology	aerography	unshakably
granddaddy	sarcophagy	escapology	cerography	remarkably
sugar-daddy	hippophagy	timbrology	xerography	inviolably
hoddy-doddy	coprophagy	dendrology	horography	calculably
fuddy-duddy	scatophagy	numerology	pyrography	unblamably
orthopaedy	pantophagy	ponerology	nosography	presumably
overgreedy	onychopagy	heterology	autography	imaginably
octaploidy	bibliopegy	nephrology	doxography	abominably
octoploidy	mineralogy	cheirology	polygraphy	terminably
polyploidy	malacology	oneirology	cacotrophy	pardonably
sugar-candy	synecology	gastrology	philosophy	reasonably
jack-a-dandy	bioecology	futurology	gymnosophy	seasonably
handy-dandy	autecology	papyrology	endomorphy	impalpably
corn-brandy	codicology	glossology	pleomorphy	inculpably
quick-sandy	musicology	nematology	zygomorphy	unbearably
cock-a-bondy	lexicology	somatology	mesomorphy	comparably
salmagundi	toxicology	hepatology	ectomorphy	preferably
goody-goody	monadology	teratology	wishy-washy	sufferably
self-parody	pseudology	oryctology	coconut-shy	inoperably
hirdy-girdy	archeology	mycetology	philomathy	answerably
hurdy-gurdy	balneology	cometology	unsympathy	deplorably
child-study	choreology	pyretology	homeopathy	inexorably
understudy	gnoseology	odontology	osteopathy	penetrably
rowdy-dowdy	spongology	deontology	sociopathy	perdurably
disc-jockey	trichology	Egyptology	hydropathy	colourably
hokey-pokey	stichology	cryptology	neuropathy	honourably
tim-whiskey	conchology	heortology	nostopathy	favourably
blind-alley	psychology	aristology	roadworthy	measurably
tea-trolley	edaphology	glottology	nameworthy	leisurably
half-volley	graphology	embryology	hateworthy	censurably

inerasably	measuredly	overwisely	cabbage-fly	hobblingly
cognisably	agonisedly	prepensely	dolphin-fly	ramblingly
supposably	composedly	propensely	vinegar-fly	wamblingly
impassably	supposedly	conversely	smother-fly	fumblingly
delectably	disposedly	perversely	blister-fly	humblingly
creditably	reversedly	retrorsely	harvest-fly	jumblingly
profitably	harassedly	introrsely	stabbingly	mumblingly
inimitably	diffusedly	abstrusely	snubbingly	rumblingly
hospitably	confusedly	delicately	defacingly	warblingly
charitably	repeatedly	truncately	menacingly	riddlingly
unsuitably	animatedly	derogately	enticingly	dawdlingly
inevitably	agitatedly	stellately	glancingly	bafflingly
lamentably	affectedly	desolately	prancingly	triflingly
acceptably	dejectedly	undulately	piercingly	stiflingly
detestably	expectedly	ultimately	seducingly	jugglingly
disputably	spiritedly	intimately	pleadingly	tanglingly
statutably	dementedly	ordinately	unfadingly	minglingly
invaluably	unwontedly	nominately	ploddingly	bunglingly
deceivably	thwartedly	inchoately	incedingly	availingly
insolvably	invertedly	separately	deridingly	revilingly
improvably	reportedly	moderately	yieldingly	tinklingly
observably	digestedly	accurately	unendingly	spellingly
invincibly	admittedly	obdurately	soundingly	swellingly
incredibly	besottedly	digitately	broodingly	ripplingly
ineligibly	pollutedly	adequately	chaffingly	rustlingly
negligibly	depravedly	obsoletely	sniffingly	tattlingly
intangibly	resolvedly	completely	scoffingly	drawlingly
infallibly	deservedly	concretely	engagingly	scowlingly
inerasibly	reservedly	discretely	drudgingly	growlingly
expansibly	unavowedly	impolitely	grudgingly	prowlingly
defensibly	convexedly	unpolitely	braggingly	dazzlingly
insensibly	pellucidly	definitely	obligingly	puzzlingly
unsensibly	uncandidly	infinitely	slangingly	dreamingly
ostensibly	splendidly	contritely	twangingly	skimmingly
impassibly	intrepidly	appositely	cringingly	trimmingly
accessibly	overboldly	oppositely	stingingly	swimmingly
compatibly	manifoldly	unchastely	swingingly	becomingly
resistibly	unfriendly	absolutely	loungingly	charmingly
inflexibly	purblindly	resolutely	filchingly	alarmingly
reassembly	overfondly	coercively	pinchingly	assumingly
absorbedly	profoundly	adhesively	witchingly	repiningly
enforcedly	backwardly	cohesively	touchingly	stunningly
unforcedly	downwardly	decisively	laughingly	swooningly
unheededly	untowardly	incisively	gnashingly	intoningly
one-sidedly	leftwardly	derisively	blushingly	yearningly
intendedly	westwardly	effusively	crushingly	mourningly
extendedly	blizzardly	delusively	scathingly	frowningly
groundedly	overnicely	allusively	loathingly	creepingly
secludedly	unprincely	illusively	writhingly	sweepingly
enlargedly	overfreely	creatively	soothingly	skimpingly
detachedly	overtimely	negatively	sneakingly	droopingly
starchedly	gladsomely	relatively	speakingly	stoopingly
wretchedly	handsomely	illatively	shockingly	snappingly
troubledly	dolesomely	optatively	strikingly	skippingly
deformedly	lonesomely	reactively	skulkingly	trippingly
consumedly	tiresomely	inactively	spankingly	usurpingly
designedly	toilsomely	electively	prankingly	graspingly
resignedly	fearsomely	additively	thinkingly	fleeringly
strainedly	inurbanely	fugitively	stinkingly	sneeringly
declaredly	femininely	genitively	friskingly	taperingly
preparedly	sanguinely	positively	rebukingly	waveringly
cankeredly	insecurely	adaptively	stealingly	hoveringly
temperedly	creaturely	abortively	dabblingly	coweringly
all-firedly	immaturely	sportively	nibblingly	loweringly

admiringly	sparkishly	ironically	infernally	truthfully
aspiringly	devilishly	heroically	supernally	fancifully
retiringly	ticklishly	tropically	maternally	mercifully
untiringly	churlishly	rubrically	paternally	wearifully
unerringly	ghoulishly	hydrically	internally	thankfully
stirringly	qualmishly	metrically	externally	stormfully
enduringly	womanishly	physically	communally	unmanfully
alluringly	clannishly	statically	integrally	womanfully
debasingly	clownishly	tactically	temporally	scornfully
pleasingly	sheepishly	hectically	corporally	mournfully
praisingly	scampishly	thetically	pectorally	cheerfully
imposingly	snappishly	emetically	pastorally	powerfully
pressingly	pokerishly	poetically	spectrally	blissfully
guessingly	feverishly	critically	binaurally	doubtfully
debatingly	tightishly	tritically	culturally	rightfully
floatingly	skittishly	septically	gutturally	fruitfully
gloatingly	sluttishly	vertically	texturally	unartfully
doubtingly	thievishly	vortically	societally	sportfully
fleetingly	shrewishly	rustically	varietally	ghastfully
covetingly	eleventhly	mystically	orientally	boastfully
incitingly	trimonthly	nautically	parentally	trustfully
invitingly	unsteadily	univocally	teetotally	unlawfully
exultingly	unwieldily	suicidally	immortally	lukewarmly
slantingly	scratchily	dilly-dally	sagittally	musicianly
stintingly	anemophily	ethereally	punctually	aldermanly
hauntingly	acarophily	tilly-fally	habitually	unmaidenly
tauntingly	necrophily	prodigally	eventually	unshakenly
vauntingly	hydrophily	conjugally	medievally	forsakenly
gruntingly	photophily	homothally	tilly-vally	mistakenly
temptingly	cartophily	especially	disloyally	unbrokenly
startingly	stealthily	judicially	underbelly	unbenignly
flirtingly	unworthily	officially	parallelly	uncommonly
snortingly	friendlily	unsocially	rockabilly	southernly
sportingly	orange-lily	fiducially	silly-billy	slatternly
questingly	ordinarily	remedially	piccadilly	stubbornly
trustingly	literarily	unfilially	daffodilly	taciturnly
twittingly	contrarily	biennially	willy-nilly	melancholy
plottingly	militarily	colonially	tranquilly	bibliopoly
shoutingly	solitarily	notarially	allycholly	oversupply
floutingly	sanitarily	imperially	black-bully	half-yearly
pursuingly	salutarily	materially	dreadfully	familiarly
grievingly	slipperily	sororially	speedfully	peculiarly
thrivingly	dilatorily	tutorially	fraudfully	globularly
strivingly	semi-weekly	uniaxially	peacefully	oracularly
revivingly	cannibally	proximally	gracefully	circularly
unlovingly	heliacally	informally	forcefully	vascularly
delayingly	maniacally	abnormally	pridefully	muscularly
edifyingly	Judaically	cardinally	vengefully	singularly
rallyingly	mosaically	originally	guilefully	granularly
annoyingly	iambically	marginally	shamefully	Decemberly
queryingly	farcically	virginally	blamefully	untenderly
worryingly	tragically	criminally	pausefully	disorderly
hurryingly	surgically	terminally	unusefully	unfatherly
whizzingly	sophically	autumnally	gratefully	unmotherly
thoroughly	mythically	diagonally	spitefully	cavalierly
overrashly	biblically	regionally	tastefully	courtierly
snobbishly	cyclically	visionally	wastefully	chandlerly
childishly	chemically	nationally	wrongfully	unmannerly
dwarfishly	inimically	rationally	watchfully	improperly
Whiggishly	cosmically	notionally	wrathfully	unproperly
priggishly	scenically	optionally	faithfully	daughterly
sluggishly	irenically	seasonally	slothfully	sinisterly
sneakishly	ethnically	unisonally	mirthfully	unsisterly
freakishly	clinically	personally	youthfully	spinsterly

debonairly	fabulously	flagrantly	thymectomy	sanctimony
inferiorly	nebulously	fragrantly	adenectomy	disharmony
superiorly	sedulously	ignorantly	lumpectomy	cockernony
ulteriorly	populously	pleasantly	uterectomy	asynchrony
anteriorly	infamously	puissantly	neurectomy	oligophrony
interiorly	bigamously	oscitantly	mastectomy	message-boy
exteriorly	venomously	militantly	strabotomy	reading-boy
hurly-burly	enormously	exultantly	phlebotomy	clapperboy
half-hourly	ravenously	constantly	varicotomy	quarter-boy
princessly	luminously	pursuantly	stereotomy	charity-boy
heedlessly	resinously	relevantly	trichotomy	ferro-alloy
needlessly	mutinously	adjacently	craniotomy	superalloy
mindlessly	cumbrously	indecently	herniotomy	zootherapy
fadelessly	wondrously	innocently	ovariotomy	opotherapy
lifelessly	ulcerously	decadently	pogonotomy	carbon-copy
namelessly	temerously	stridently	laparotomy	radioscopy
timelessly	numerously	impudently	sclerotomy	rhinoscopy
tonelessly	generously	indigently	enterotomy	urinoscopy
hopelessly	viperously	diligently	nephrotomy	colposcopy
carelessly	desirously	plangently	gastrotomy	necroscopy
tirelessly	decorously	emergently	pleurotomy	microscopy
movelessly	rigorously	obediently	embryotomy	hieroscopy
ruthlessly	vigorously	pruriently	rent-an-army	oniroscopy
pitilessly	valorously	redolently	homoplasmy	cystoscopy
fecklessly	dolorously	indolently	miscellany	prompt-copy
recklessly	timorously	insolently	teeny-weeny	overcanopy
lucklessly	humorously	luculently	morphogeny	zoanthropy
soullessly	canorously	temulently	dynamogeny	orthotropy
harmlessly	sonorously	virulently	organogeny	heliotropy
formlessly	vaporously	purulently	heterogeny	aeolotropy
painlessly	lustrously	vehemently	epeirogeny	anisotropy
helplessly	dextrously	imminently	teratogeny	phototropy
fearlessly	covetously	apparently	odontogeny	thixotropy
peerlessly	sensuously	inherently	embryogeny	slipsloppy
tactlessly	unctuously	coherently	phillumeny	counter-spy
bootlessly	virtuously	reverently	theotechny	stereotypy
spotlessly	tortuously	penitently	pyrotechny	apothecary
hurtlessly	grievously	affluently	matricliny	prebendary
restlessly	abstractly	frequently	patricliny	world-weary
listlessly	indirectly	eloquently	matrocliny	justiciary
viewlessly	succinctly	conjointly	patrocliny	subsidiary
mistressly	distinctly	stalwartly	postliminy	presidiary
gorgeously	conjunctly	malapertly	turpentiny	incendiary
nauseously	discreetly	immodestly	predestiny	tripudiary
feateously	disquietly	manifestly	hootananny	conciliary
wrongously	unthriftly	unpriestly	hootenanny	silentiary
edaciously	straightly	syndactyly	threepenny	potentiary
spaciously	unknightly	chasmogamy	pinchpenny	revestiary
graciously	implicitly	plasmogamy	catchpenny	carpellary
speciously	explicitly	heterogamy	sevenpenny	fibrillary
preciously	abundantly	cryptogamy	thruppenny	fritillary
lusciously	recreantly	plastogamy	arles-penny	pistillary
studiously	arrogantly	clistogamy	eightpenny	epistolary
gloriously	jubilantly	pathognomy	piccaninny	vocabulary
uxoriously	vigilantly	chirognomy	pickaninny	patibulary
spuriously	petulantly	diseconomy	chalcedony	reticulary
usuriously	stagnantly	heteronomy	death-agony	capitulary
factiously	pregnantly	cheironomy	psychogony	chartulary
captiously	poignantly	gastronomy	heterogony	lachrymary
cautiously	dominantly	orthodromy	schizogony	sexagenary
previously	ruminantly	homochromy	radiophony	octogenary
perviously	resonantly	monochromy	gramophony	unordinary
frabjously	flippantly	polychromy	photophony	veterinary
perilously	tolerantly	iridectomy	tautophony	sanguinary

10 -ARY

millionary	festoonery	sibilatory	breadberry	pleasantry
pensionary	copartnery	depilatory	scald-berry	low-country
passionary	Japanesery	stillatory	cloudberry	puff-pastry
cessionary	condensery	desolatory	crake-berry	phantastry
missionary	phylactery	tabulatory	chokeberry	linguistry
stationary	charactery	ambulatory	Rhineberry	canterbury
factionary	slaughtery	jaculatory	gooseberry	Bloomsbury
lectionary	drysaltery	osculatory	youngberry	hygrochasy
dictionary	effrontery	undulatory	blackberry	paronomasy
auctionary	poetastery	regulatory	salal-berry	Christmasy
tuitionary	baptistery	simulatory	coral-berry	lackadaisy
cautionary	upholstery	copulatory	loganberry	night-palsy
fluxionary	forgettery	defamatory	rowan-berry	palsy-walsy
quaternary	presbytery	divinatory	Rheinberry	minstrelsy
unliterary	redelivery	usurpatory	elderberry	acatalepsy
stercorary	higry-pigry	reparatory	wheat-berry	parablepsy
registrary	eard-hungry	separatory	strawberry	narcolepsy
dispensary	yerd-hungry	execratory	wild-cherry	wind-dropsy
commissary	yird-hungry	liberatory	sand-cherry	popsy-wopsy
consectary	aldermanry	emigratory	bird-cherry	halfe-horsy
hereditary	microhenry	aspiratory	motor-lorry	governessy
unmilitary	chaplainry	expiratory	psychiatry	hitty-missy
insanitary	emblazonry	laboratory	bardolatry	tuftaffety
unsanitary	plerophory	adjuratory	lordolatry	non-society
infinitary	cauliflory	depuratory	litholatry	subvariety
depositary	word-memory	advisatory	hagiolatry	insobriety
ubiquitary	folk-memory	excusatory	ophiolatry	pernickety
elementary	persuasory	cunctatory	heliolatry	perjinkety
segmentary	dissuasory	excitatory	Mariolatry	arty-crafty
pigmentary	compulsory	hesitatory	cosmolatry	fifty-fifty
alimentary	propulsory	invitatory	iconolatry	efficacity
commentary	prehensory	salutatory	necrolatry	incapacity
unguentary	suspensory	innovatory	hierolatry	inveracity
insalutary	responsory	refractory	astrolatry	unveracity
tumultuary	precursory	detractory	plutolatry	ergodicity
promptuary	percursory	trajectory	Maryolatry	impudicity
voluptuary	discursory	correctory	acidimetry	infelicity
quaestuary	possessory	protectory	planimetry	triplicity
sculduddry	rescissory	completory	densimetry	simplicity
cobwebbery	promissory	suppletory	gravimetry	complicity
embroidery	dismissory	inhibitory	pelvimetry	endemicity
commandery	conclusory	exhibitory	pleximetry	seismicity
goliardery	incubatory	plauditory	unsymmetry	canonicity
zigzaggery	dedicatory	ambagitory	viscometry	chronicity
humbuggery	indicatory	admonitory	araeometry	sphericity
scavengery	judicatory	transitory	tachometry	centricity
chirurgery	vesicatory	depository	sociometry	stypticity
bewitchery	advocatory	repository	goniometry	elasticity
debauchery	revocatory	expository	coulometry	plasticity
spreaghery	invocatory	consultory	anemometry	spasticity
triumphery	amendatory	promontory	uranometry	causticity
cod-fishery	emendatory	locomotory	clinometry	mother-city
net-fishery	indagatory	preceptory	iconometry	subacidity
henpeckery	obligatory	redemptory	micrometry	flaccidity
peacockery	fumigatory	peremptory	hydrometry	squalidity
crewellery	mitigatory	clerestory	hygrometry	invalidity
distillery	derogatory	faldistory	spirometry	insolidity
tomfoolery	gladiatory	prehistory	hypsometry	unsolidity
homoeomery	palliatory	consistory	photometry	insipidity
subdeanery	spoliatory	multistory	tachymetry	scabridity
penguinery	initiatory	clear-story	bathymetry	pinguidity
stationery	escalatory	ghost-story	serjeantry	iracundity
buffoonery	revelatory	absolutory	merchantry	profundity
lampoonery	habilatory	intermarry	pheasantry	orotundity

extraneity	pliability	difformity	protensity	commonalty
corporeity	amiability	uniformity	varicosity	personalty
perjinkity	friability	conformity	vitreosity	temporalty
radicality	salability	homonymity	graciosity	shrievalty
logicality	tamability	synonymity	speciosity	disloyalty
comicality	tenability	inurbanity	preciosity	difficulty
finicality	non-ability	inhumanity	spuriosity	parchmenty
topicality	capability	betweenity	fabulosity	suzerainty
typicality	dupability	alkalinity	nebulosity	self-bounty
musicality	curability	femininity	squamosity	vice-county
illegality	durability	sanguinity	luminosity	third-party
speciality	disability	Patavinity	tuberosity	peace-party
cordiality	ratability	concinnity	numerosity	house-party
spatiality	actability	fraternity	generosity	homoblasty
nuptiality	notability	quaternity	literosity	autoplasty
partiality	mutability	co-eternity	vaporosity	nyctinasty
bestiality	equability	eviternity	unctuosity	chemonasty
feminality	movability	diuturnity	virtuosity	photonasty
seminality	taxability	capernoity	tortuosity	paederasty
bitonality	docibility	hoity-toity	university	dishonesty
liberality	audibility	solidarity	perversity	pine-beauty
generality	legibility	similarity	klendusity	picket-duty
laterality	risibility	bipolarity	unchastity	mixty-maxty
literality	visibility	tubularity	contiguity	dulciloquy
squirality	fusibility	secularity	continuity	somniloquy
immorality	immobility	jocularity	perpetuity	multiloquy
unmorality	ignobility	regularity	pulp-cavity	superheavy
centrality	solubility	angularity	proclivity	topsyturvy
neutrality	volubility	annularity	emissivity	steam-navvy
dextrality	imbecility	popularity	creativity	metagalaxy
graduality	indocility	insularity	negativity	anaphylaxy
inequality	juvenility	titularity	relativity	orthopraxy
coequality	feminility	omniparity	reactivity	phyllotaxy
sensuality	scurrility	viviparity	inactivity	heterotaxy
factuality	volatility	muliebrity	coactivity	nephropexy
tactuality	tractility	mediocrity	electivity	heterodoxy
virtuality	erectility	prosperity	positivity	tuzzi-muzzy
asexuality	non-utility	lithotrity	protervity	rose-quartz
infidelity	disutility	insecurity	complexity	Z
ridability	incivility	immaturity	perplexity	Hakenkreuz
sueability	gratillity	propensity	officialty	razzmatazz
affability	equanimity			

A	olla-podrida	counterplea	Chilognatha
Sanguisorba	Eurypterida	miscellanea	wood-naphtha
maceranduba	assafoetida	collectanea	Della-Robbia
Thyrostraca	Ornithopoda	spade-guinea	agoraphobia
saltimbocca	Brachiopoda	leucorrhoea	astraphobia
spermatheca	Cephalopoda	sialorrhoea	taphephobia
pinacotheca	Gasteropoda	amenorrhoea	taphophobia
bibliotheca	Stomatopoda	rhinorrhoea	bathophobia
glyptotheca	washing-soda	staging-area	pathophobia
Atharvaveda	Ornithogaea	mountain-tea	sitiophobia
Gregarinida	Panathenaea	gutta-percha	anglophobia
Pycnogonida	Proboscidea	ipecacuanha	ochlophobia
Scorpionida	Ophiuroidea	Hagiographa	gallophobia
Pedipalpida	Phasmatodea	Theromorpha	dromophobia

phonophobia	tulipomania	terebratula	sinfonietta
scopophobia	timbromania	psychodrama	Spermaphyta
necrophobia	etheromania	closet-drama	Thallophyta
hydrophobia	kleptomania	epicheirema	Spermophyta
negrophobia	acronymania	epithelioma	Schizophyta
hypsophobia	sideropenia	tuberculoma	interlingua
Russophobia	hebephrenia	enchondroma	conjunctiva
nyctophobia	saprolegnia	Trypanosoma	contrayerva
pantophobia	Caesalpinia	Schistosoma	Bodhisattva
photophobia	quadriennia	scyphistoma	coleorrhiza
bone-breccia	quinquennia	rhabdomyoma	B
cyclopaedia	somatotonia	Echinoderma	spectre-crab
hypnopaedia	Clavicornia	scleroderma	calling-crab
Cirrhipedia	oneirodynia	hypocorisma	soldier-crab
pseudopodia	pleurodynia	collenchyma	paschal-lamb
bradycardia	glossodynia	coenenchyma	cluster-bomb
tachycardia	Dodecagynia	prosenchyma	redding-comb
prosopopeia	hemeralopia	Johnsoniana	deaf-and-dumb
hyperphagia	heterotopia	amphisbaena	rule-of-thumb
menorrhagia	Convallaria	prolegomena	hop-o'-my-thumb
tetraplegia	Turbellaria	Cochin-China	fuller's-herb
cephalalgia	Procellaria	globigerina	mallee-scrub
steatopygia	calceolaria	orchestrina	lignum-scrub
Escherichia	Utricularia	burnt-sienna	C
Zonotrichia	Spergularia	spermatozoa	toxiphobiac
welwitschia	dolphinaria	taratantara	pericardiac
paragraphia	Sanguinaria	abracadabra	endocardiac
typographia	Dodecandria	rhombohedra	zygocardiac
Monadelphia	Prototheria	pyritohedra	coprolaliac
Monodelphia	sansevieria	Scolopendra	paraphiliac
anacoluthia	Cryptomeria	Rhopalocera	anthomaniac
Marsupialia	Vallisneria	Aphaniptera	mythomaniac
glossolalia	Anthesteria	Lepidoptera	anglomaniac
bacchanalia	allocheiria	Trichoptera	dipsomaniac
Placentalia	plerophoria	Hymenoptera	erotomaniac
psychedelia	Pterosauria	Heteroptera	Pandemoniac
paranthelia	albuminuria	Cheiroptera	aphrodisiac
passacaglia	hyperplasia	Plectoptera	poison-sumac
memorabilia	paronomasia	chaulmoogra	clog-almanac
paedophilia	antonomasia	Rhabdophora	Panathenaic
anglophilia	anaesthesia	Cotylophora	trisyllabic
haemophilia	telesthesia	retinispora	dithyrambic
scopophilia	cenesthesia	retinospora	agoraphobic
necrophilia	paragenesia	Insectivora	heliophobic
coprophilia	hemianopsia	Interglossa	anglophobic
melancholia	idioglossia	hydromedusa	hydrophobic
Saintpaulia	xenoglossia	Subungulata	photophobic
Cryptogamia	mycodomatia	exanthemata	pseudocubic
epithalamia	Corrodentia	treponemata	prothoracic
prothalamia	differentia	Monotremata	metasilicic
septicaemia	orthodontia	condylomata	Mohorovicic
thalassemia	periodontia	carcinomata	Asclepiadic
pachydermia	paraphraxia	hydrosomata	orthopaedic
hypothermia	stereotaxia	phantasmata	cyclopaedic
cyclothymia	gentianella	empyreumata	cantharidic
Christiania	selaginella	Mahabharata	ribonucleic
toxicomania	trichinella	understrata	seborrhoeic
francomania	subumbrella	Oligochaeta	gonorrhoeic
nymphomania	air-umbrella	Spirochaeta	subspecific
bibliomania	fothergilla	tufftaffeta	conspecific
megalomania	chrysocolla	tufttaffeta	non-specific
petalomania	hibernacula	ejectamenta	coprophagic
phyllomania	receptacula	impedimenta	phytophagic
demonomania	cicatricula	hälleflinta	bibliopegic

cephalalgic	hylomorphic	psychonomic	nonharmonic
diphthongic	homomorphic	cheironomic	disharmonic
ptyalagogic	xenomorphic	gastronomic	dysharmonic
emmenagogic	monomorphic	hydrobromic	decameronic
synecologic	xeromorphic	palindromic	freemasonic
autecologic	mesomorphic	orthodromic	stereosonic
psychologic	ectomorphic	hippodromic	Neoplatonic
graphologic	automorphic	polychromic	geotectonic
morphologic	polymorphic	osteodermic	somatotonic
physiologic	philomathic	pachydermic	Pan-Slavonic
seismologic	osteopathic	adiathermic	proterozoic
phrenologic	sociopathic	endothermic	hypnopompic
demonologic	hydropathic	homothermic	orthoscopic
chronologic	neuropathic	ectothermic	hagioscopic
somatologic	protopathic	eurythermic	helioscopic
teratologic	feldspathic	perispermic	rhinoscopic
odontologic	laccolithic	endospermic	macroscopic
embryologic	Aeneolithic	cataclasmic	necroscopic
metallurgic	batholithic	endoplasmic	microscopic
dramaturgic	granolithic	ectoplasmic	hygroscopic
synecdochic	microlithic	hetaerismic	pantoscopic
parapsychic	bathylithic	hetairismic	zoanthropic
metapsychic	labyrinthic	macrocosmic	nyctitropic
paragraphic	Ostrogothic	microcosmic	orthotropic
telegraphic	Moeso-gothic	cataclysmic	pleiotropic
serigraphic	acromegalic	cyclothymic	dexiotropic
pasigraphic	procephalic	permanganic	aeolotropic
lexigraphic	tetracyclic	air-mechanic	chemotropic
cacographic	pentacyclic	transuranic	hydrotropic
ideographic	carbocyclic	charlatanic	neurotropic
oreographic	psychedelic	hydrocyanic	anisotropic
logographic	psychodelic	phagedaenic	phototropic
idiographic	archangelic	tumorigenic	haptotropic
holographic	paedophilic	psychogenic	thixotropic
xylographic	anglophilic	thermogenic	heterotropic
demographic	scopophilic	epeirogenic	rhizocarpic
tomographic	necrophilic	oestrogenic	palaeotypic
kymographic	hydrophilic	somatogenic	stereotypic
monographic	photophilic	teratogenic	heterotypic
topographic	cartophilic	odontogenic	centrobaric
typographic	ithyphallic	blastogenic	helispheric
cerographic	homothallic	schizogenic	hemispheric
nosographic	non-metallic	pantothenic	atmospheric
autographic	intervallic	calisthenic	ionospheric
polygraphic	gibberellic	Demosthenic	homoeomeric
monodelphic	melancholic	panhellenic	elastomeric
mycotrophic	Neo-Catholic	hebephrenic	phylacteric
endotrophic	bibliopolic	theotechnic	climacteric
autotrophic	unapostolic	zymotechnic	sphincteric
mixotrophic	isapostolic	pyrotechnic	cholesteric
diastrophic	somnambulic	polytechnic	paranephric
geostrophic	nostradamic	matriclinic	perinephric
apostrophic	chasmogamic	patriclinic	hydrochoric
philosophic	phaenogamic	matroclinic	sporophoric
paramorphic	cryptogamic	patroclinic	tetrasporic
metamorphic	epithalamic	cinchoninic	prehistoric
hemimorphic	aerodynamic	serpentinic	psychiatric
perimorphic	thalassemic	chalcedonic	kinesiatric
endomorphic	borborygmic	chameleonic	all-electric
theomorphic	logarithmic	radiophonic	non-electric
pleomorphic	algorithmic	anglophonic	isoelectric
lagomorphic	isorhythmic	gramophonic	myoelectric
zygomorphic	telegrammic	microphonic	planimetric
idiomorphic	subeconomic	photophonic	densimetric

gravimetric	haemostatic	anti-Semitic	ectoplastic
pleximetric	hydrostatic	stalagmitic	autoplastic
viscometric	hypallactic	glauconitic	nyctinastic
araeometric	parallactic	peritonitic	photonastic
sociometric	catallactic	onirocritic	antispastic
radiometric	chemotactic	hypercritic	Hudibrastic
audiometric	hydrotactic	lithotritic	paederastic
heliometric	phototactic	saussuritic	transvestic
goniometric	acatalectic	porphyritic	Haggadistic
coulometric	paraplectic	martensitic	methodistic
anemometric	cataplectic	stalactitic	Talmudistic
trommetric	amphimictic	periostitic	tritheistic
clinometric	Palaearctic	peristaltic	pantheistic
econometric	amino-acetic	sycophantic	zootheistic
axonometric	strategetic	Cisatlantic	misoneistic
micrometric	unprophetic	spodomantic	sphragistic
hydrometric	sympathetic	necromantic	dialogistic
hygrometric	dyspathetic	hydromantic	epilogistic
spirometric	synanthetic	chiromantic	syllogistic
hypsometric	parenthetic	unauthentic	neologistic
photometric	cosmothetic	paedodontic	dyslogistic
tautometric	anaesthetic	orthodontic	synergistic
bathymetric	telesthetic	mastodontic	catechistic
metacentric	diotheletic	Anacreontic	fetichistic
pericentric	dyotheletic	Phaethontic	masochistic
homocentric	hyperemetic	halobiontic	anarchistic
Eurocentric	epithymetic	monozygotic	fetishistic
barycentric	paragenetic	macrobiotic	cabbalistic
perigastric	metagenetic	saprobiotic	tribalistic
cacogastric	lysigenetic	gnotobiotic	unrealistic
hypogastric	abiogenetic	unpatriotic	socialistic
thermoduric	homogenetic	anastomotic	curialistic
disulphuric	xenogenetic	syndesmotic	anomalistic
orthophyric	monogenetic	biocoenotic	pluralistic
granophyric	merogenetic	trichinotic	ritualistic
stereobatic	pyrogenetic	hyperinotic	symbolistic
Mithradatic	ectogenetic	anaplerotic	euphemistic
Mithridatic	ontogenetic	aponeurotic	pessimistic
parabematic	polygenetic	procaryotic	Targumistic
erythematic	diamagnetic	acataleptic	mediumistic
problematic	geomagnetic	parableptic	mechanistic
theorematic	zoomagnetic	neuroleptic	shamanistic
diastematic	isomagnetic	bradypeptic	Germanistic
engrammatic	telekinetic	hemianoptic	Montanistic
ungrammatic	autokinetic	apocalyptic	Origenistic
unidiomatic	mythopoetic	scholiastic	Hellenistic
dichromatic	arch-heretic	encomiastic	Paulinistic
metasomatic	diaphoretic	idioblastic	Calvinistic
phantomatic	antipyretic	holoblastic	mammonistic
symptomatic	peripatetic	homoblastic	modernistic
charismatic	asynartetic	hypoblastic	communistic
synonymatic	Capernaitic	meroblastic	voodooistic
perihepatic	anthracitic	mesoblastic	hylozoistic
Pherecratic	Areopagitic	ectoblastic	eucharistic
ochlocratic	salpingitic	cataclastic	citharistic
cosmocratic	pharyngitic	pyroclastic	manneristic
Hippocratic	diothelitic	aeroelastic	Gongoristic
hierocratic	dyothelitic	metaplastic	terroristic
plutocratic	tonsillitic	esemplastic	voyeuristic
biquadratic	body-politic	endoplastic	solipsistic
cathedratic	staurolitic	alloplastic	spiritistic
magistratic	graptolitic	homoplastic	scientistic
homeostatic	spherulitic	xenoplastic	hypnotistic
orthostatic	pre-adamitic	ceroplastic	synoptistic

Spinozistic
pyrognostic
paracrostic
catacaustic
holocaustic
sporocystic
polyglottic
empiricutic
hermeneutic
therapeutic
emphyteutic
troglodytic
osteophytic
lithophytic
cormophytic
tropophytic
microphytic
hydrophytic
hygrophytic
sporophytic
saprophytic
protophytic
proteolytic
thermolytic
plasmolytic
Baltoslavic
stereotaxic
thermotaxic
D
chuckle-head
knuckle-head
feather-head
leather-head
dragon's-head
crappit-head
simnel-bread
wastel-bread
gingerbread
monkey-bread
screw-thread
girdlestead
middenstead
pseudomonad
trichomonad
quarter-road
walking-toad
blotting-pad
thick-ribbed
marriage-bed
standing-bed
spawning-bed
undescribed
uninscribed
loose-limbed
clean-limbed
honeycombed
well-thumbed
unperturbed
undisturbed
double-faced
mottle-faced
smooth-faced
weasel-faced
brazen-faced

bauson-faced
copper-faced
tallow-faced
bloody-faced
chitty-faced
strait-laced
smooth-paced
unjaundiced
unbeneficed
underpriced
short-priced
defeasanced
unevidenced
experienced
unsentenced
unconvinced
unannounced
self-induced
hydra-headed
round-headed
addle-headed
white-headed
wrong-headed
blackheaded
thick-headed
shock-headed
sleek-headed
steel-headed
level-headed
swell-headed
clear-headed
light-headed
arrow-headed
giddy-headed
muddy-headed
curly-headed
puppy-headed
empty-headed
heavy-headed
unpersuaded
false-bedded
interbedded
proxy-wedded
star-studded
unsucceeded
non-provided
uncuckolded
close-banded
crossbanded
unhusbanded
three-handed
large-handed
close-handed
white-handed
slack-handed
underhanded
light-handed
right-handed
short-handed
horny-handed
empty-handed
heavy-handed
undescended
uncommended

unsuspended
unrescinded
self-blinded
broad-minded
proud-minded
large-minded
noble-minded
wrong-minded
tough-minded
small-minded
sober-minded
light-minded
right-minded
short-winded
well-founded
well-rounded
cold-blooded
pure-blooded
blue-blooded
half-blooded
high-blooded
full-blooded
warm-blooded
chicken-feed
groundspeed
unpedigreed
jimpson-weed
three-leafed
close-reefed
overstuffed
solid-hoofed
whole-hoofed
trencher-fed
unmortgaged
hard-visaged
pale-visaged
long-visaged
marble-edged
double-edged
deckle-edged
full-fledged
three-legged
rough-legged
cross-legged
light-legged
bandy-legged
dandy-rigged
waterlogged
hamstringed
bowstringed
round-winged
eagle-winged
goose-winged
white-winged
swift-winged
light-winged
full-charged
unsubmerged
unimpeached
overreached
unstaunched
round-arched
unscratched
high-pitched

overpitched
undebauched
unretouched
forevouched
unrefreshed
potting-shed
established
unpublished
un-Englished
unabolished
unblemished
replenished
ungarnished
untarnished
unvarnished
unburnished
unfurnished
unnourished
freight-shed
missheathed
hard-mouthed
loud-mouthed
full-mouthed
foul-mouthed
open-mouthed
flap-mouthed
deep-mouthed
close-bodied
loose-bodied
disembodied
unliquefied
unspecified
unqualified
exemplified
undignified
indemnified
personified
unterrified
electrified
unvitrified
countrified
intensified
diversified
ungratified
unrectified
uncertified
unfortified
unmortified
unjustified
unsatisfied
whiskeyfied
countryfied
interallied
shad-bellied
swag-bellied
fish-bellied
uncompanied
ready-monied
preoccupied
shrubberied
territoried
unqualitied
necessitied
mother-naked

ring-straked	ill-informed	bastinadoed	unsuccoured
earthquaked	unperformed	mustachioed	sad-coloured
round-backed	transformed	sword-shaped	off-coloured
sling-backed	imposthumed	wedge-shaped	unicoloured
finch-backed	self-assumed	brickshaped	tricoloured
bunch-backed	unburthened	strap-shaped	tan-coloured
hunchbacked	unthickened	heart-shaped	discoloured
crookbacked	unquickened	white-rumped	sky-coloured
camel-backed	unsharpened	stiff-rumped	ill-humoured
well-stacked	unsweetened	undeveloped	ill-favoured
half-checked	unlightened	handicapped	unflavoured
crane-necked	unchastened	wide-chapped	self-assured
stiff-necked	unmoistened	close-lipped	misfeatured
rose-cheeked	undersigned	thick-lipped	good-natured
rosy-cheeked	unexplained	tight-lipped	literatured
index-linked	bird-brained	cloud-topped	untinctured
three-nooked	hare-brained	table-topped	ungenitured
thumb-marked	beef-brained	stereotyped	predeceased
death-marked	dull-brained	quarter-bred	unpurchased
unconcealed	hair-brained	beblubbered	unexercised
unsyllabled	clay-brained	dismembered	unvocalised
tabernacled	hard-grained	unofficered	unmoralised
semicircled	self-trained	enfouldered	uncivilised
overhandled	constrained	forwandered	inorganised
wedge-heeled	uncurtained	well-ordered	unorganised
light-heeled	tear-stained	web-fingered	unromanised
four-wheeled	unsustained	unfeathered	trichinised
unhandseled	well-defined	unweathered	uncanonised
right-angled	disinclined	ill-mannered	unpolarised
wedge-tailed	streamlined	ill-tempered	unsurprised
sharp-tailed	double-mined	distempered	unpractised
uncurtailed	unillumined	mistempered	unquantised
undespoiled	ensanguined	hot-tempered	unchastised
ferntickled	exsanguined	wide-watered	undisguised
unsprinkled	uncontemned	unsheltered	black-a-vised
unsandalled	undermanned	concentered	well-advised
pedestalled	thin-skinned	well-entered	undispensed
blind-felled	unguerdoned	unchartered	undisclosed
soft-shelled	truncheoned	unplastered	toffee-nosed
uncompelled	unparagoned	sequestered	saddle-nosed
untravelled	stanchioned	unflustered	bottle-nosed
dishevelled	unfashioned	uncluttered	undiagnosed
disbowelled	companioned	unconquered	trichinosed
white-billed	dimensioned	undelivered	snotty-nosed
unfulfilled	unpensioned	milk-livered	self-imposed
semi-skilled	impassioned	lily-livered	ill-disposed
undistilled	unpassioned	unrecovered	unrehearsed
protocolled	gradationed	self-covered	untraversed
water-cooled	carnationed	high-powered	unsurpassed
footstooled	affectioned	time-expired	embarrassed
single-soled	conditioned	well-desired	unprocessed
well-coupled	intentioned	Pompeian-red	unconfessed
disgruntled	unemotioned	smooth-bored	unprofessed
high-battled	unportioned	rubber-cored	unharnessed
high-mettled	pantalooned	unscissored	unwitnessed
close-hauled	caparisoned	close-barred	unaddressed
unscheduled	encrimsoned	crossbarred	unredressed
whole-souled	book-learned	evil-starred	well-dressed
unreclaimed	unconcerned	unpreferred	hard-pressed
itchy-palmed	undiscerned	transferred	undepressed
overbrimmed	unpatterned	self-centred	unimpressed
well-groomed	full-acorned	soft-centred	unexpressed
rosy-bosomed	prong-horned	self-figured	pre-stressed
unconfirmed	misfortuned	unharboured	unpossessed

star-crossed	unseparated	self-planted	unharvested
storm-tossed	vertebrated	unwarranted	long-waisted
undiscussed	obliterated	precedented	wasp-waisted
circumfused	unaspirated	unsegmented	close-fisted
self-misused	fenestrated	unaugmented	tight-fisted
overdrowsed	illustrated	ungarmented	white-listed
alembicated	unsaturated	unfermented	inexhausted
complicated	incrassated	untormented	unexhausted
elasticated	unmeditated	unprevented	maladjusted
trifurcated	sedigitated	hand-painted	superfatted
treble-dated	unannotated	unattainted	ricochetted
dilapidated	understated	unappointed	pantaletted
medium-dated	unexcavated	bullfronted	carburetted
self-created	unmotivated	unaccounted	telluretted
undelegated	uncompacted	unrecounted	uncommitted
congregated	unrefracted	whole-footed	intromitted
unmitigated	ill-affected	white-footed	transmitted
unnavigated	disaffected	rough-footed	hand-knitted
unabrogated	unsubjected	tiger-footed	thick-witted
consociated	unprojected	swift-footed	quick-witted
fastigiated	self-elected	light-footed	sharp-witted
intagliated	unreflected	splay-footed	blunt-witted
columniated	uninflected	true-devoted	ready-witted
historiated	predilected	self-devoted	hasty-witted
uninitiated	intellected	unreceipted	wainscotted
asphyxiated	recollected	self-tempted	toad-spotted
sphacelated	uncollected	unattempted	substituted
unmutilated	unconnected	interrupted	self-subdued
cancellated	unrespected	uncorrupted	free-tongued
flagellated	unsuspected	cold-hearted	long-tongued
crenellated	uncorrected	kind-hearted	wasp-tongued
tessellated	unprotected	hard-hearted	many-tongued
castellated	constricted	free-hearted	round-leaved
fibrillated	unconvicted	pale-hearted	three-leaved
lanceolated	unconcocted	wise-hearted	alder-leaved
nucleolated	uncompleted	true-hearted	cross-leaved
mentholated	undelighted	half-hearted	well-behaved
steel-plated	unbenighted	high-hearted	architraved
pediculated	foresighted	weak-hearted	unreprieved
paniculated	long-sighted	full-hearted	unconceived
geniculated	high-sighted	warm-hearted	unperceived
auriculated	weak-sighted	open-hearted	double-lived
vesiculated	dull-sighted	lion-hearted	well-derived
reticulated	near-sighted	iron-hearted	uncontrived
articulated	slow-sighted	down-hearted	undissolved
operculated	tardy-gaited	soft-hearted	self-evolved
unmodulated	uninhabited	peace-parted	well-beloved
unregulated	uninhibited	three-parted	half-starved
flammulated	fore-recited	unconcerted	wapper-jawed
unpopulated	unsolicited	unconverted	bow-windowed
punctulated	self-excited	unperverted	bay-windowed
foraminated	unforfeited	uncomforted	mishallowed
opinionated	unbenefited	unsupported	unswallowed
incoronated	discomfited	transported	black-browed
embryonated	self-limited	ill-assorted	retroflexed
rough-coated	capernoited	undistorted	unperplexed
parti-coated	hot-spirited	broadcasted	highly-sexed
petticoated	low-spirited	unballasted	storm-stayed
black-coated	stalactited	three-masted	unpathwayed
sugar-coated	three-suited	undermasted	sessile-eyed
party-coated	civil-suited	rear-roasted	unhackneyed
rattle-pated	sober-suited	uncontested	two-storeyed
constipated	self-invited	unprotested	disemployed
saccharated	unenchanted	woman-vested	undestroyed

middle-sized
pocket-sized
tripe-visag'd
waiting-maid
between-maid
kitchen-maid
chambermaid
parlour-maid
servant-maid
laundry-maid
nurserymaid
crappit-heid
tyroglyphid
white-eyelid
gonococcoid
scarabaeoid
epitrochoid
paratyphoid
haemorrhoid
felspathoid
helminthoid
sclerotioid
encephaloid
hypocycloid
prothalloid
crystalloid
varicelloid
hyperboloid
sipunculoid
strongyloid
characinoid
paraffinoid
pycnogonoid
phlegmonoid
diphtheroid
eurypteroid
parathyroid
hypothyroid
goniatitoid
elephantoid
paramastoid
antherozoid
multicuspid
ichthyopsid
battlefield
bleach-field
oyster-field
glove-shield
dress-shield
school-child
foster-child
hundredfold
unblindfold
severalfold
millionfold
bur-marigold
middle-world
spirit-world
double-form'd
driving-band
swingle-hand
running-hand
station-hand
charter-hand

seconds-hand
husbandland
pasture-land
morning-land
poison-gland
monkey-gland
slumberland
coral-island
blarney-land
self-command
countermand
surtarbrand
surturbrand
yince-errand
weather-fend
mouth-friend
superintend
distribuend
kaisar-i-Hind
double-blind
gravel-blind
colour-blind
window-blind
burn-the-wind
quarter-wind
counter-bond
microsecond
split-second
quaternion'd
rose-diamond
ducking-pond
curling-pond
herring-pond
sinking-fund
superabound
unhidebound
strike-bound
muscle-bound
fardel-bound
honour-bound
sleuth-hound
basset-hound
azocompound
oxy-compound
stoneground
above-ground
sharp-ground
underground
bergschrund
honest-to-God
photoperiod
scattergood
old-maidhood
invalidhood
brotherhood
flapperhood
widowerhood
traitorhood
jealoushood
prophethood
gutter-blood
heart's-blood
unwithstood
amboina-wood

amboyna-wood
palmyra-wood
leopard-wood
shawnee-wood
rhodium-wood
sanderswood
trumpet-wood
branchiopod
sounding-rod
divining-rod
picture-card
mailing-card
scoring-card
playing-card
compass-card
Barclaycard
substandard
cool-tankard
fascia-board
notice-board
bridgeboard
wobble-board
paddle-board
baffle-board
centre-board
louvre-board
cheese-board
sleeve-board
scrive-board
springboard
string-board
diving-board
thatch-board
switchboard
splash-board
shovel-board
school-board
mortar-board
luffer-board
fingerboard
teeter-board
letter-board
louver-board
follow-board
monkey-board
cameleopard
snow-leopard
wall-mustard
castle-guard
fingerguard
picket-guard
land-steward
shop-steward
thitherward
whitherward
lock-forward
propforward
prop-forward
overforward
fence-lizard
moor-buzzard
bonnet-laird
singing-bird
mocking-bird

mockingbird
humming-bird
dragoon-bird
buffalo-bird
butcher-bird
gallows-bird
smörgasbőrd
picture-cord
harpsichord
trouble-word
bottle-gourd
disenshroud

E

Lumbricidae
Tortricidae
Dasipodidae
Hydrophidae
Hesperiidae
Nymphalidae
Trochilidae
Loliginidae
Trachinidae
Delphinidae
Atherinidae
Procyonidae
Ephemeridae
Geometridae
Phasmatidae
Buprestidae
Bombacaceae
Styracaceae
Dipsacaceae
Orchidaceae
Oxalidaceae
Sapindaceae
Osmundaceae
Cyatheaceae
Moringaceae
Acanthaceae
Pedaliaceae
Lobeliaceae
Loganiaceae
Geraniaceae
Begoniaceae
Fumariaceae
Ribesiaceae
Santalaceae
Canellaceae
Bacillaceae
Primulaceae
Pandanaceae
Platanaceae
Verbenaceae
Sphagnaceae
Apocynaceae
Droseraceae
Burseraceae
Marantaceae
Psilotaceae
Myxophyceae
Scitamineae
leishmaniae
rickettsiae
salmonellae

premaxillae	misguidance	erubescence	impenitence
Monocotylae	dinner-dance	iridescence	omnipotence
Phaenogamae	concordance	candescence	subsistence
paraselenae	discordance	turgescence	consistence
Lycopodinae	morris-dance	coalescence	persistence
Equisetinae	ballet-dance	opalescence	re-existence
Cupuliferae	insouciance	pallescence	inexistence
Glumiflorae	mésalliance	adolescence	co-existence
windlestrae	misalliance	fremescence	infrequence
Leguminosae	equibalance	spumescence	subsequence
paraglossae	overbalance	evanescence	consequence
lithophysae	nonchalance	spinescence	ineloquence
Incompletae	resemblance	torpescence	preannounce
lignum-vitae	assemblance	accrescence	transpierce
Therapeutae	performance	excrescence	police-force
superscribe	maintenance	nigrescence	point-source
interscribe	countenance	florescence	rejuvenesce
sternotribe	mountenance	vitrescence	precognosce
francophobe	co-ordinance	putrescence	superinduce
ailurophobe	coordinance	lactescence	overproduce
buffalo-robe	chrominance	liquescence	mass-produce
pickelhaube	illuminance	antecedence	reintroduce
torpedo-tube	discrepance	coincidence	unbarricade
working-face	comeuppance	abscondence	fire-brigade
seaming-lace	come-uppance	despondence	double-shade
hiding-place	forbearance	respondence	switchblade
burial-place	compearance	home-defence	scutch-blade
commonplace	remembrance	self-defence	phylloclade
market-place	encumbrance	self-offence	bottom-glade
wind-furnace	vociferance	picket-fence	machine-made
counter-pace	furtherance	contingence	hand-grenade
double-space	intolerance	submergence	fanfaronade
hammer-brace	deliverance	re-emergence	unguligrade
herb-of-grace	disentrance	convergence	laterigrade
walking-race	reinsurance	everywhence	digitigrade
scant-o'-grace	co-insurance	sufficience	plantigrade
battle-piece	reassurance	proficience	arquebusade
centre-piece	malfeasance	omniscience	crescentade
string-piece	non-feasance	inobedience	rodomontade
doting-piece	misfeasance	regredience	mispersuade
mantelpiece	conversance	preaudience	maxillipede
museum-piece	renaissance	consilience	bacillicide
masterpiece	impuissance	dissilience	tyrannicide
pocket-piece	reflectance	prevenience	bactericide
bonnet-piece	conductance	convenience	insecticide
gambit-piece	inhabitance	provenience	infanticide
coach-office	exorbitance	percipience	giganticide
stamp-office	capacitance	insentience	rodenticide
paper-office	inheritance	ambivalence	liberticide
market-price	susceptance	equivalence	parasuicide
malpractice	supportance	monovalence	race-suicide
net-practice	outdistance	prepollence	trypanocide
walnut-juice	permittance	non-violence	nikethamide
point-device	acquittance	malevolence	tolbutamide
bond-service	continuance	benevolence	thalidomide
time-service	perpetuance	flocculence	oxy-chloride
self-service	irrelevance	fraudulence	oxy-fluoride
sick-service	contrivance	pre-eminence	giant-stride
perturbance	flamboyance	postponence	therebeside
disturbance	complacence	co-inherence	spindle-side
contra-dance	maleficence	incoherence	slickenside
forbiddance	beneficence	irreverence	weather-side
square-dance	munificence	concurrence	countryside
figure-dance	connascence	inappetence	morning-tide

hunting-tide	miscarriage	hypostrophe	irrevocable
Twelfth-tide	mismarriage	underclothe	leader-cable
Passion-tide	victuallage	appleringie	confiscable
Whitsuntide	post-village	argie-bargie	persuadable
polypeptide	mirror-image	cockaleekie	undecidable
nectar-guide	stage-manage	kiddywinkie	unavoidable
countrywide	concubinage	baron-bailie	bestridable
sesquioxide	libertinage	water-bailie	individable
pitchblende	cloisonnage	water-purpie	undividable
anticathode	chaperonage	camaraderie	descendable
pneumathode	squarsonage	supercherie	unamendable
misericorde	tea-equipage	espièglerie	commendable
disquietude	life-peerage	gendarmerie	impoundable
decrepitude	hucksterage	chinoiserie	unsoundable
pulchritude	seigniorage	marqueterie	unwoundable
vicissitude	re-encourage	charcuterie	protrudable
ingratitude	deck-passage	bourgeoisie	unpeaceable
promptitude	telemessage	capernoitie	replaceable
incertitude	retroussage	gaberlunzie	retraceable
metalhedyde	décolletage	linseed-cake	untraceable
paraldehyde	high-voltage	wedding-cake	serviceable
spelling-bee	beaumontage	Twelfth-cake	imperceable
quilting-bee	working-edge	saffron-cake	enforceable
fiddle-de-dee	frank-pledge	pomfret-cake	divorceable
skilligalee	about-sledge	currant-cake	unagreeable
semi-jubilee	window-ledge	shimmy-shake	foreseeable
skilligolee	acknowledge	rattlesnake	unwedgeable
cypress-knee	feather-edge	garter-snake	negligeable
snickersnee	swing-bridge	carpet-snake	unshakeable
surrenderee	weigh-bridge	vacuum-brake	dislikeable
riddle-me-ree	chain-bridge	barley-brake	unmalleable
gallows-free	underbridge	stubble-rake	unblameable
mustard-tree	paint-bridge	unchildlike	impermeable
service-tree	pivot-bridge	husbandlike	illaqueable
cabbage-tree	police-judge	purpose-like	humbuggable
sausage-tree	overindulge	ostrich-like	immitigable
spindle-tree	quick-change	peacock-like	unmitigable
whiffletree	interchange	spaniel-like	innavigable
swingletree	shortchange	ruffian-like	unnavigable
whippletree	ion-exchange	workmanlike	prolongable
rigging-tree	navel-orange	unqueenlike	impeachable
wishing-tree	rocket-range	scholar-like	unreachable
weeping-tree	rechallenge	thunder-like	unteachable
varnish-tree	maskallonge	brotherlike	unmatchable
mammoth-tree	muskellunge	soldierlike	untouchable
quicken-tree	proof-charge	unloverlike	publishable
lacquer-tree	depth-charge	serpentlike	abolishable
gallows-tree	undercharge	marlinspike	tarnishable
trumpet-tree	supercharge	heart-strike	nourishable
interviewee	hypercharge	death-stroke	uncrushable
pedder-coffe	call-at-large	loup-the-dyke	appreciable
sheath-knife	caper-spurge	Chippendale	justiciable
oyster-knife	thaumaturge	Wensleydale	dissociable
butter-knife	narrow-gauge	halfendeale	putrefiable
pocket-knife	insectifuge	farthingale	liquefiable
loose-strife	bonnet-rouge	nightingale	specifiable
rouping-wife	stomach-ache	caaing-whale	acidifiable
palm-cabbage	papier-mâché	point-of-sale	qualifiable
scaffoldage	Callitriche	unclubbable	magnifiable
vagabondage	schottische	describable	signifiable
Marivaudage	bonne-bouche	inscribable	vitrifiable
weather-gage	bathyscaphe	perturbable	falsifiable
ostreophage	catastrophe	immedicable	rectifiable
haemorrhage	antistrophe	practicable	certifiable

fortifiable	intolerable	extractable	contrivable
justifiable	denumerable	neglectable	dissolvable
satisfiable	innumerable	collectable	unremovable
conciliable	regenerable	connectable	irremovable
companiable	unvenerable	respectable	disprovable
unweariable	remunerable	suspectable	preservable
unmarriable	recuperable	correctable	conservable
propitiable	insuperable	predictable	unallowable
repleviable	vituperable	ineluctable	destroyable
imperviable	inalterable	coffee-table	convincible
unspeakable	unalterable	completable	incoercible
unbreakable	inutterable	inking-table	marcescible
uncheckable	unutterable	gaming-table	vitrescible
unshockable	conquerable	dining-table	putrescible
unthinkable	inseverable	inhabitable	cognoscible
undrinkable	deliverable	unhabitable	unreducible
concealable	recoverable	indubitable	irreducible
congealable	perspirable	inexcitable	descendible
unavailable	undesirable	unexcitable	refrangible
assimilable	unmemorable	hereditable	infrangible
compellable	inenarrable	forfeitable	submergible
distillable	preferrable	incogitable	discernible
trisyllable	conferrable	illimitable	persuasible
articulable	perpetrable	indomitable	indivisible
manipulable	unfiltrable	exploitable	convulsible
reclaimable	registrable	inheritable	prehensible
inestimable	unendurable	unmeritable	suspensible
inflammable	succourable	unvisitable	subsensible
confirmable	pleasurable	inequitable	distensible
conformable	increasable	unequitable	responsible
performable	purchasable	corbel-table	collapsible
inalienable	appraisable	warrantable	submersible
unalienable	exercisable	augmentable	concessible
impregnable	civilisable	fermentable	depressible
consignable	organisable	presentable	repressible
explainable	vaporisable	preventable	impressible
undrainable	comprisable	unpaintable	expressible
containable	chastisable	unprintable	submissible
unstainable	inadvisable	accountable	permissible
sustainable	unadvisable	uncountable	dismissible
medicinable	condensable	demountable	compossible
indefinable	dispensable	inadaptable	discussible
undefinable	collapsable	unadaptable	implausible
denominable	traversable	attemptable	unplausible
innominable	conversable	accomptable	protrusible
illuminable	compassable	dinner-table	extractible
condemnable	surpassable	unavertable	perfectible
unshunnable	discussable	comfortable	collectible
fashionable	unaccusable	supportable	connectible
pensionable	irrecusable	contestable	correctible
fissionable	inexcusable	forgettable	dissectible
mentionable	escheatable	toilet-table	conductible
emotionable	entreatable	regrettable	preventible
treasonable	untreatable	irrefutable	usucaptible
inescapable	unpalatable	inscrutable	perceptible
unescapable	uncomatable	unsubduable	susceptible
worshipable	ungetatable	continuable	redemptible
developable	redoubtable	colliquable	pre-emptible
unflappable	undoubtable	construable	corruptible
unstoppable	refractable	non-issuable	convertible
irreparable	retractable	perpetuable	pervertible
inseparable	intractable	retrievable	suggestible
unseparable	untractable	conceivable	congestible
inexecrable	attractable	perceivable	exhaustible

combustible	swallow-hole	maisterdome	chaff-engine
disassemble	sporangiole	home-and-home	steam-engine
salmon-coble	cornice-pole	harvest-home	water-engine
irresoluble	clothes-pole	oligochrome	goods-engine
conceptacle	profiterole	heliochrome	time-machine
conventicle	eucalyptole	stenochrome	tape-machine
dress-circle	short-staple	phytochrome	rope-machine
push-bicycle	rood-steeple	troublesome	slot-machine
doggy-paddle	condisciple	wheedlesome	trisulphine
stock-saddle	submultiple	wranglesome	diamorphine
intermeddle	self-example	unwholesome	apomorphine
tarradiddle	townspeople	venturesome	tichorrhine
mollycoddle	toffee-apple	quarrelsome	leptorrhine
microneedle	queene-apple	X-chromosome	platyrrhine
mould-candle	eating-apple	Y-chromosome	cookie-shine
fetch-candle	potato-apple	trypanosome	monkey-shine
sperm-candle	winter-apple	schistosome	amaranthine
swing-handle	bitter-apple	slumbersome	hyacinthine
cock-a-doodle	pipe-stapple	shuddersome	encephaline
meningocele	pipe-stopple	furthersome	enkephaline
haematocele	barge-couple	flavoursome	geanticline
saloon-rifle	supersubtle	delightsome	geosyncline
spread-eagle	shard-beetle	unlightsome	thermocline
double-eagle	black-beetle	plagiostome	service-line
hornswoggle	click-beetle	sarcenchyme	down-the-line
disentangle	tiger-beetle	riding-rhyme	washing-line
intertangle	water-beetle	Malacca-cane	nitraniline
intermingle	lady's-mantle	walking-cane	crystalline
christingle	cloud-castle	swagger-cane	fringilline
tattie-bogle	overwrestle	transpadane	gyre-carline
potato-bogle	milk-thistle	antemundane	telpher-line
argle-bargle	musk-thistle	tryptophane	clothes-line
francophile	star-thistle	hyalomelane	unmasculine
bibliophile	wolf-whistle	psilomelane	scopolamine
psammophile	store-cattle	leesome-lane	methylamine
thermophile	sabre-rattle	battleplane	propylamine
spermophile	death-rattle	rocket-plane	nitrosamine
scripophile	lickspittle	thrust-plane	amphetamine
ailurophile	three-bottle	sea-purslane	hyoscyamine
minute-while	white-bottle	balletomane	theobromine
self-sterile	greenbottle	quarrel-pane	redetermine
contractile	water-bottle	counterpane	countermine
protractile	scent-bottle	vicar-forane	gelseminine
self-fertile	coal-scuttle	sclate-stane	anti-heroine
areosystile	microtubule	weather-vane	transalpine
fernitickle	disseminule	cyclohexane	pilocarpine
fernytickle	sliding-rule	Pleistocene	cluster-pine
spang-cockle	dodecastyle	mise-en-scène	cinnabarine
honeysuckle	troll-my-dame	hypersthene	ultramarine
pennywinkle	redding-kame	naphthalene	transmarine
pinnywinkle	window-frame	philhellene	alexandrine
pennoncelle	rhyme-scheme	chloroprene	cycloserine
ritournelle	quinquereme	polystyrene	epinephrine
chantarelle	pudding-time	aminobutene	helleborine
chanterelle	milking-time	rhododaphne	accipitrine
pipistrelle	leaping-time	alycompaine	brankursine
pastourelle	pairing-time	internecine	Benedictine
tagliatelle	closing-time	geomedicine	elephantine
barbastelle	whiting-time	biomedicine	Diophantine
spirituelle	betweentime	pentazocine	Ignorantine
ratatouille	counter-time	incarnadine	barquentine
Baskerville	calligramme	benzylidine	clandestine
placket-hole	centigramme	deserpidine	Trappistine
grummet-hole	hectogramme	transandine	vincristine

langoustine	exhaust-pipe	savoir-faire	manufacture
amethystine	sinking-ripe	Vendémiaire	contracture
consanguine	weeping-ripe	doctrinaire	word-picture
chloroquine	gallows-ripe	legionnaire	overpicture
acriflavine	candy-stripe	billionaire	distincture
waldgravine	epidiascope	millionaire	conjuncture
landgravine	CinemaScope ®	sepiostaire	disjuncture
palsgravine	polariscope	barrage-fire	acupuncture
balloon-vine	stroboscope	Kentish-fire	restructure
currant-wine	opeidoscope	curtain-fire	portraiture
tragedienne	pseudoscope	broach-spire	decumbiture
cracovienne	stereoscope	cushion-tire	expenditure
varsovienne	stethoscope	night-attire	unigeniture
shackle-bone	benthoscope	apple-squire	progeniture
knuckle-bone	chromoscope	service-wire	divestiture
wishing-bone	thermoscope	picture-wire	investiture
herring-bone	seismoscope	priming-wire	aquaculture
stirrup-bone	lychnoscope	chicken-wire	self-culture
twitter-bone	chronoscope	theretofore	pomiculture
heckelphone	laparoscope	Terpsichore	viniculture
francophone	dichroscope	melanophore	mariculture
chordophone	fluoroscope	nematophore	sericulture
anticyclone	gastroscope	ommatophore	agriculture
wood-anemone	proctoscope	common-shore	viticulture
malakatoone	kinetoscope	anthochlore	aquiculture
tautochrone	vectorscope	clinochlore	monoculture
disenthrone	forlorn-hope	farthermore	king-vulture
thiopentone	deuteranope	furthermore	disaventure
quarter-tone	lycanthrope	forevermore	insculpture
pumice-stone	misanthrope	urediospore	self-torture
scythe-stone	thaumatrope	aplanospore	hill-pasture
pebble-stone	platinotype	arthrospore	purpresture
cobblestone	electrotype	insectivore	pyrogravure
rubble-stone	throughfare	amour-propre	rotogravure
copple-stone	jumping-hare	news-theatre	autogravure
turtle-stone	ploughshare	reconnoitre	savoir-vivre
coping-stone	three-square	nerve-centre	lamprophyre
upping-stone	eight-square	Skillcentre	keratophyre
pavingstone	graniteware	storm-centre	cushion-tyre
hearth-stone	earthenware	orthocentre	staging-base
pencil-stone	supersedere	supersedure	counterbase
loggan-stone	planisphere	transfigure	attaché-case
spleen-stone	lithosphere	countermure	thimble-case
parpen-stone	cosmosphere	displeasure	packing-case
sarsen-stone	ozonosphere	land-measure	writing-case
rottenstone	troposphere	wine-measure	tweezer-case
amazon-stone	hydrosphere	tape-measure	scissor-case
corner-stone	photosphere	half-measure	elbow-grease
magnesstone	rhizosphere	long-measure	vine-disease
cement-stone	bathysphere	overmeasure	single-phase
kidney-stone	carabiniere	foreclosure	plagioclase
cherry-stone	bonbonnière	compressure	histaminase
trumpet-tone	ferronnière	acupressure	glutaminase
estramazone	mentonnière	low-pressure	·catch-phrase
window-barne	boutonnière	duplicature	chrysoprase
inopportune	bouquetière	candidature	archdiocese
steepe-downe	condottiere	entablature	cream-cheese
tick-tack-toe	crémaillère	legislature	rheumateese
guttersnipe	genouillère	vasculature	officialese
weasand-pipe	milliampere	musculature	Camaldolese
service-pipe	microampere	declinature	Indo-Chinese
pudding-pipe	Wanderjahre	supernature	diplomatese
tobacco-pipe	ensepulchre	temperature	underpraise
clyster-pipe	nickel-ochre	incurvature	superpraise

over-precise	hand-promise	hypothetise	barrel-house
catholicise	dichotomise	demagnetise	bastel-house
phonemicise	taxidermise	propylitise	schoolhouse
hispanicise	suburbanise	desensitise	custom-house
Slavonicise	Americanise	fainéantise	schism-house
hibernicise	europeanise	half-baptise	garden-house
historicise	neopaganise	readvertise	pigeon-house
theatricise	disorganise	proselytise	prison-house
cosmeticise	unmechanise	cataloguise	summer-house
phoneticise	plebeianise	monologuise	frater-house
pedanticise	Socinianise	soliloquise	porter-house
romanticise	Prussianise	stone-bruise	porterhouse
domesticise	nitrogenise	point-devise	market-house
spheroidise	deoxygenise	objectivise	hurley-house
merchandise	phenomenise	madonnawise	biting-louse
gourmandise	masculinise	shuttlewise	cat-and-mouse
vagabondise	defibrinise	breadthwise	church-mouse
standardise	decarbonise	weather-wise	pampelmouse
sluggardise	religionise	saltierwise	pompelmouse
galliardise	emulsionise	chequerwise	blackgrouse
genealogise	fractionise	scissorwise	breathalyse
anthologise	synchronise	worldly-wise	electrolyse
mythologise	isochronise	proper-false	multilobate
etymologise	skeletonise	commonsense	hypothecate
tautologise	northernise	deoxyribose	premedicate
affranchise	southernise	radicellose	revendicate
enfranchise	vichyssoise	folliculose	subindicate
Petrarchise	unvulgarise	tuberculose	revindicate
theosophise	familiarise	eglandulose	prejudicate
telepathise	peculiarise	anthracnose	specificate
cannibalise	circularise	lentiginose	significate
defeudalise	vascularise	pampelmoose	pontificate
unfeudalise	singularise	pompelmoose	certificate
etherealise	formularise	superimpose	testificate
prodigalise	sanctuarise	dual-purpose	spifflicate
naphthalise	decerebrise	cabbage-rose	divellicate
deracialise	schillerise	guelder-rose	reduplicate
imperialise	depauperise	gelders-rose	induplicate
materialise	aspheterise	phagocytose	octuplicate
arterialise	canisterise	semi-ellipse	communicate
memorialise	computerise	intersperse	haruspicate
marginalise	desilverise	saddle-horse	prevaricate
criminalise	phosphorise	riding-horse	decorticate
regionalise	exteriorise	sinistrorse	excorticate
nationalise	extemporise	charge-nurse	domesticate
rationalise	hexametrise	foster-nurse	averruncate
personalise	decarburise	rhumb-course	translocate
encarnalise	decolourise	watercourse	reciprocate
internalise	miniaturise	intercourse	inturbidate
externalise	re-emphasise	snatch-purse	consolidate
communalise	metastasise	heathenesse	bicuspidate
gutturalise	hypostasise	stratopause	accommodate
hospitalise	hypothesise	accoucheuse	urochordate
orientalise	apotheosise	hypothenuse	nudicaudate
immortalise	mathematise	orchid-house	discalceate
eventualise	emblematise	coffee-house	uninucleate
desexualise	systematise	bridge-house	confarreate
parallelise	acclimatise	change-house	extravagate
destabilise	diplomatise	charge-house	desegregate
crystallise	achromatise	senate-house	suffumigate
hyperbolise	schismatise	gaming-house	investigate
protocolise	democratise	tiring-house	interrogate
tuberculise	hypostatise	spring-house	assubjugate
astronomise	alphabetise	eating-house	multijugate

dendrachate	testiculate	decarbonate	perlustrate
tetrarchate	unguiculate	bicarbonate	prefigurate
persulphate	recalculate	trithionate	configurate
beneficiate	pedunculate	stellionate	barbiturate
stipendiate	carunculate	decurionate	acculturate
abranchiate	tuberculate	fractionate	extravasate
domiciliate	recirculate	functionate	improvisate
antimoniate	triangulate	impersonate	marquessate
contorniate	strangulate	reincarnate	hydrolysate
impropriate	subungulate	consternate	superfetate
appropriate	papillulate	unfortunate	resuscitate
expropriate	dissimulate	importunate	premeditate
instantiate	reformulate	participate	regurgitate
renegotiate	campanulate	feather-pate	ingurgitate
margraviate	exstipulate	shatter-pate	periclitate
roller-skate	glomerulate	preoccupate	decrepitate
intercalate	peninsulate	decerebrate	precipitate
cardinalate	encapsulate	equilibrate	necessitate
arch-prelate	incapsulate	involucrate	reorientate
dissimilate	serratulate	reverberate	latiseptate
horripilate	expostulate	protuberate	transeptate
pedicellate	carbonylate	incarcerate	ground-state
constellate	meprobamate	confederate	police-state
haustellate	dephlegmate	considerate	trust-estate
penicillate	penultimate	proliferate	buffer-state
refocillate	misestimate	verbigerate	indeciduate
scintillate	guesstimate	refrigerate	individuate
machicolate	approximate	agglomerate	objectivate
bracteolate	semipalmate	connumerate	oligochaete
bifoliolate	inkhorn-mate	oppignerate	spirochaete
extrapolate	midshipmate	obtemperate	analphabete
interpolate	impostumate	intemperate	discomycete
baffle-plate	pomegranate	depauperate	phycomycete
contemplate	thiocyanate	commiserate	thesmothete
fingerplate	miscegenate	perseverate	monothelete
copperplate	hydrogenate	conflagrate	pentathlete
butter-plate	deoxygenate	reintegrate	planogamete
silver-plate	concatenate	decemvirate	macrogamete
armour-plate	indesignate	triumvirate	microgamete
breastplate	revaccinate	inelaborate	epistilbite
retranslate	ratiocinate	unelaborate	ophicalcite
confabulate	hallucinate	collaborate	pentlandite
mandibulate	incardinate	orthoborate	annabergite
preambulate	subordinate	corroborate	acolouthite
funambulate	disordinate	imperforate	Plymouthite
perambulate	compaginate	phosphorate	Hepplewhite
umbraculate	unoriginate	deteriorate	silver-white
spiraculate	immarginate	perchlorate	greenockite
tentaculate	contaminate	unicolorate	carbonalite
trabeculate	disseminate	concolorate	heteroclite
valleculate	incriminate	commemorate	monothelite
corbiculate	predominate	impignorate	sapropelite
fasciculate	prenominate	oppignorate	crocodilite
forficulate	cognominate	bicorporate	toxophilite
cauliculate	determinate	incorporate	crystallite
vermiculate	interminate	expectorate	Campbellite
corniculate	exterminate	directorate	apophyllite
turriculate	mandarinate	constuprate	amphibolite
matriculate	defibrinate	impenetrate	crocidolite
bursiculate	peregrinate	concentrate	Camaldolite
denticulate	assassinate	orchestrate	cosmopolite
monticulate	deglutinate	sequestrate	meteorolite
particulate	agglutinate	demonstrate	chiastolite
gesticulate	paripinnate	remonstrate	ichthyolite

tentaculite	spinnerette	subdivisive	appellative
vermiculite	vinaigrette	inoffensive	oscillative
hellgramite	marquisette	unoffensive	superlative
harvest-mite	sansculotte	inexpensive	legislative
itacolumite	knee-tribute	unexpensive	ejaculative
Hieronymite	electrocute	hypotensive	speculative
suburbanite	fipple-flute	co-extensive	calculative
luxulianite	octave-flute	discoursive	inoculative
vesuvianite	supervolute	progressive	circulative
sillimanite	thrombocyte	compressive	coagulative
luxulyanite	poikilocyte	suppressive	stimulative
molybdenite	granulocyte	irremissive	granulative
nephelinite	erythrocyte	antitussive	exclamative
franklinite	spermaphyte	transfusive	affirmative
napoleonite	thallophyte	unexclusive	reformative
smithsonite	psammophyte	disillusive	informative
trophozoite	spermophyte	inobtrusive	explanative
octahedrite	gametophyte	unobtrusive	designative
alexandrite	schizophyte	reprobative	combinative
yttro-cerite	electrolyte	improbative	imaginative
cassiterite	beach-rescue	approbative	originative
melanterite	seven-league	rebarbative	eliminative
peristerite	hart's-tongue	desiccative	criminative
labradorite	woody-tongue	exsiccative	comminative
phosphorite	psychagogue	deprecative	carminative
madreporite	ptyalagogue	eradicative	germinative
water-sprite	emmenagogue	predicative	terminative
cerargyrite	grammalogue	vindicative	personative
pyrargyrite	market-value	implicative	alternative
unrequisite	washing-blue	applicative	coadunative
decomposite	peacock-blue	duplicative	dissipative
incomposite	discontinue	explicative	extirpative
phillipsite	discothèque	fabricative	nuncupative
monophysite	téléférique	lubricative	declarative
spessartite	verd-antique	affricative	preparative
hatchettite	appropinque	inculcative	comparative
monchiquite	Carlylesque	suffocative	enumerative
baddeleyite	Ossianesque	provocative	exonerative
McCarthyite	Titianesque	altercative	temperative
gouvernante	Germanesque	elucidative	inoperative
pococurante	Runyonesque	retardative	unoperative
concertante	barbaresque	delineative	co-operative
intriguante	Wagneresque	procreative	cooperative
flamboyante	Turneresque	miscreative	reiterative
cognoscente	plateresque	propagative	integrative
aguardiente	Pinteresque	segregative	inspirative
passing-note	picturesque	aggregative	elaborative
quarter-note	soldatesque	colligative	perforative
casting-vote	gigantesque	instigative	meliorative
counter-vote	misconstrue	prerogative	explorative
Sachertorte	basket-weave	objurgative	evaporative
cotton-waste	galley-slave	conjugative	corporative
suffragette	superoctave	enunciative	restorative
historiette	thought-wave	bisociative	penetrative
flannelette	trunksleeve	associative	impetrative
aiguillette	undersleeve	irradiative	substrative
landaulette	shirt-sleeve	repudiative	suppurative
caravanette	.overachieve	retaliative	mensurative
kitchenette	make-believe	humiliative	defensative
stockinette	internecive	exfoliative	intensative
maisonnette	swallow-dive	expatiative	adversative
chansonette	preconceive	alleviative	expectative
launderette	misconceive	correlative	qualitative
leatherette	bridge-drive	ventilative	crepitative

gravitative	dispositive	mansard-roof	backsliding
facultative	competitive	grease-proof	horse-riding
resultative	investitive	virtue-proof	cold-welding
voluntative	deglutitive	splashproof	butt-welding
connotative	substantive	shrink-proof	wash-gilding
dehortative	unretentive	cudgel-proof	outbuilding
cohortative	irretentive	cannon-proof	scaffolding
exhortative	inattentive	shower-proof	roadholding
assortative	unattentive	musket-proof	landholding
devastative	uninventive	bullet-proof	half-landing
attestative	terremotive	galley-proof	undemanding
confutative	maladaptive	unthought-of	outstanding
commutative	unreceptive	Kulturkampf	mind-bending
computative	irreceptive	sang-de-boeuf	nerve-ending
disputative	descriptive	oeil-de-boeuf	unoffending
extenuative	inscriptive	G	road-mending
insinuative	subsumptive	sleeping-bag	undepending
punctuative	presumptive	shoulder-bag	never-ending
deprivative	consumptive	Brobdingnag	goal-tending
observative	discerptive	mulberry-fig	unattending
calefactive	unassertive	thingumajig	half-binding
rarefactive	contrastive	walking-twig	bookbinding
radioactive	indigestive	travail-pang	fact-finding
retroactive	locorestive	gammerstang	self-winding
photoactive	retributive	orang-outang	ring-winding
hyperactive	attributive	wine-bibbing	pair-bonding
interactive	consecutive	land-jobbing	lip-rounding
diffractive	persecutive	subscribing	surrounding
subtractive	dissolutive	dive-bombing	black-boding
contractive	restitutive	wool-combing	wool-carding
protractive	institutive	mould-facing	unregarding
abstractive	weapon-salve	interfacing	unrewarding
distractive	poppet-valve	tight-lacing	sightseeing
ineffective	puppet-valve	unrejoicing	vouchsafing
non-elective	safety-valve	unit-pricing	windsurfing
prospective	circumvolve	wire-dancing	encouraging
perspective	nubbing-cove	step-dancing	well-judging
vivisective	kinchin-cove	pronouncing	flag-wagging
maledictive	riding-glove	ear-piercing	bootlegging
benedictive	boxing-glove	mispleading	tent-pegging
conflictive	counter-move	mind-reading	gold-digging
restrictive	microgroove	forereading	periwigging
distinctive	Lochaber-axe	bespreading	disobliging
instinctive	quick-freeze	mistreading	back-ganging
subjunctive	Louis-Treize	never-fading	wide-ranging
conjunctive	Louis-Quinze	bastinading	challenging
disjunctive	needle-furze	freeloading	mud-slinging
obstructive	F	self-loading	bell-ringing
destructive	lattice-leaf	wing-loading	part-singing
instructive	walking-leaf	overtrading	cold-forging
disquietive	currant-loaf	overbidding	drop-forging
prohibitive	barrier-reef	rice-pudding	unpreaching
recognitive	neckerchief	Jack-pudding	far-reaching
premonitive	infangthief	pock-pudding	unblenching
preteritive	snatch-thief	milk-pudding	unflinching
acquisitive	photo-relief	plum-pudding	eye-catching
inquisitive	plough-staff	hand-feeding	rat-catching
insensitive	Jacob's-staff	self-feeding	spud-bashing
unsensitive	bull-mastiff	high-feeding	bond-washing
intensitive	counter-buff	ill-breeding	buck-washing
diapositive	hatti-sherif	outbreeding	line-fishing
prepositive	half-and-half	paragliding	haaf-fishing
compositive	mantelshelf	hang-gliding	seal-fishing
suppositive	prairie-wolf	metalliding	punt-fishing

skirmishing	dissembling	aquaplaning	time-sharing
unfinishing	self-feeling	damascening	none-sparing
diminishing	paralleling	overweening	cornice-ring
astonishing	parasailing	reawakening	considering
unperishing	dovetailing	unawakening	bewildering
flourishing	nun's-veiling	threatening	shouldering
brattishing	soap-boiling	unsoftening	smouldering
languishing	stockpiling	frightening	squandering
well-wishing	name-calling	unlistening	unwandering
surf-bathing	unrecalling	christening	calendering
unbreathing	tear-falling	good-evening	all-cheering
know-nothing	marshalling	undesigning	engineering
shanghaiing	initialling	complaining	domineering
water-skiing	enthralling	unremaining	sin-offering
handshaking	victualling	restraining	ingathering
peacemaking	snorkelling	undeclining	unwithering
verse-making	trammelling	interlining	scouthering
epoch-making	empanelling	undermining	chandlering
matchmaking	channelling	drift-mining	untempering
watch-making	colonelling	cross-tining	unfaltering
brickmaking	misspelling	caravanning	ministering
paper-making	apparelling	unbeginning	embittering
dressmaking	quarrelling	hand-running	spluttering
money-making	handselling	fell-running	persevering
merrymaking	bookselling	overrunning	wedding-ring
purse-taking	counselling	unpardoning	quick-firing
leave-taking	unravelling	petitioning	sky-aspiring
snuff-taking	shrivelling	questioning	uninspiring
stocktaking	pit-dwelling	unreasoning	unenquiring
undertaking	embowelling	wage-earning	uninquiring
painstaking	stencilling	forewarning	watch-spring
night-waking	landfilling	good-morning	water-spring
shellacking	time-killing	unreturning	neck-herring
fish-packing	soul-killing	root-pruning	concentring
cat-cracking	bedevilling	importuning	latch-string
bivouacking	high-rolling	slave-owning	rough-string
trafficking	controlling	church-going	check-string
arse-licking	wire-pulling	schoolgoing	navel-string
bootlicking	scatterling	steady-going	apron-string
politicking	chitterling	stilettoing	heart-string
pig-sticking	keelhauling	townscaping	unmurmuring
self-cocking	antifouling	safe-keeping	unlabouring
self-locking	spin-bowling	home-keeping	off-scouring
self-seeking	wild-fowling	bookkeeping	sculpturing
race-walking	gas-guzzling	shopkeeping	cheese-wring
fire-walking	instreaming	tub-thumping	displeasing
fell-walking	unbeseeming	show-jumping	heart-easing
high-ranking	true-seeming	knee-capping	fund-raising
unshrinking	fair-seeming	worshipping	fire-raising
well-sinking	programming	clodhopping	hair-raising
good-looking	up-and-coming	swan-hopping	catechising
well-looking	misbecoming	boot-topping	tantalising
unprovoking	forthcoming	audiotyping	unpromising
tear-jerking	thick-coming	load-bearing	sloganising
hard-working	shortcoming	tale-bearing	patronising
wireworking	fish-farming	rush-bearing	cauterising
fell-lurking	tank-farming	wool-bearing	temporising
cornhusking	self-harming	overbearing	advertising
fair-dealing	rock-forming	soul-fearing	self-closing
mind-healing	uninforming	worm-gearing	transposing
self-healing	platforming	spur-gearing	sick-nursing
self-sealing	unpresuming	hard-wearing	buck-passing
unrevealing	well-meaning	spacefaring	tap-dressing
untrembling	tobogganing	night-faring	top-dressing

fly-dressing
distressing
outcrossing
nonplussing
warehousing
suffocating
gold-beating
conjugating
rival-hating
humiliating
unsatiating
undeviating
vacillating
oscillating
calculating
circulating
stimulating
lancinating
fascinating
fulminating
personating
alternating
overcoating
knock-rating
penetrating
devastating
extenuating
insinuating
fluctuating
aggravating
captivating
distracting
unaffecting
prospecting
conflicting
race-meeting
town-meeting
go-to-meeting
camp-meeting
mass-meeting
ricocheting
disquieting
zoografting
face-lifting
shop-lifting
bull-baiting
bear-baiting
sheep-biting
unprofiting
dispiriting
inspiriting
handwriting
typewriting
sign-writing
part-writing
rib-vaulting
unrelenting
unrepenting
unresenting
oil-painting
wax-painting
reed-bunting
snow-bunting
headhunting

tuft-hunting
surmounting
wainscoting
freebooting
undiverting
ripsnorting
cold-casting
overcasting
newscasting
peat-casting
handfasting
everlasting
rib-roasting
wine-tasting
bird-nesting
interesting
ill-wresting
unresisting
unassisting
crop-dusting
bird-batting
wire-netting
type-setting
filmsetting
down-setting
unbefitting
hard-hitting
unremitting
manumitting
down-sitting
baby-sitting
complotting
bogtrotting
wood-cutting
side-cutting
rate-cutting
leaf-cutting
fish-gutting
sea-scouting
colleaguing
unbelieving
power-diving
unforgiving
clean-living
unconniving
unreproving
unapproving
wood-carving
chip-carving
unobserving
undeserving
time-serving
self-serving
reed-drawing
wire-drawing
self-drawing
wash-drawing
deep-drawing
bias-drawing
wing-and-wing
bastard-wing
mind-blowing
safe-blowing
overflowing

foreknowing
self-knowing
cock-crowing
wine-growing
wool-growing
price-fixing
track-laying
bricklaying
role-playing
long-playing
tithe-paying
soothsaying
tender-dying
solidifying
lapidifying
stellifying
simplifying
saponifying
classifying
stratifying
sanctifying
stultifying
identifying
Scottifying
revivifying
night-flying
multiplying
uncomplying
self-denying
non-marrying
prophesying
courtesying
glass-gazing
zero-grazing
overgrazing
monophthong
scuppernong
hunting-song
wither-wrung
sea-hedgehog
fishing-frog
Enghalskrug
H
meshuggenah
bathmitsvah
bathmitzvah
clairschach
copper-beech
stump-speech
bear's-breech
schrecklich
tsesarevich
tectibranch
lophobranch
pulmobranch
church-bench
widow's-bench
horse-drench
Anglo-French
screw-wrench
oyster-wench
weaver-finch
fallow-finch
steam-launch

motor-launch
ticket-punch
rabbit-punch
ramgunshoch
gymnasiarch
ecclesiarch
symposiarch
randle-perch
stave-church
tallow-catch
safety-catch
throat-latch
tennis-match
safety-match
backscratch
minute-watch
home-stretch
overstretch
kidney-vetch
sonofabitch
timber-hitch
cable-stitch
whole-stitch
queen-stitch
chain-stitch
satin-stitch
cross-stitch
gillravitch
cesarevitch
cesarewitch
knife-switch
double-dutch
rabbit-hutch
Kommersbuch
such-and-such
meshuggeneh
swing-plough
wheel-plough
drill-plough
steam-plough
pull-through
peep-through
headborough
tharborough
leach-trough
coronagraph
Stevengraph
helicograph
pseudograph
stereograph
choreograph
psychograph
glyphograph
cardiograph
torsiograph
dynamograph
thermograph
seismograph
selenograph
chronograph
coronograph
kinetograph
odontograph
cryptograph

shadowgraph
heterotroph
pseudomorph
homoeomorph
theriomorph
allelomorph
ergatomorph
dendroglyph
spatterdash
water-splash
mountain-ash
synchromesh
horseradish
chafing-dish
vagabondish
whistle-fish
stand-offish
sucking-fish
walking-fish
peacock-fish
werewolfish
pelican-fish
dolphin-fish
surgeon-fish
bellows-fish
trumpet-fish
sea-crawfish
sea-crayfish
road-hoggish
re-establish
lukewarmish
old-womanish
satin-finish
photo-finish
preadmonish
nail-varnish
nightmarish
Decemberish
Micawberish
cavalierish
spinsterish
Scotch-Irish
straightish
Israelitish
novelettish
distinguish
pedagoguish
wishtonwish
bramble-bush
steeple-bush
bottle-brush
hearth-brush
water-thrush
underbreath
bribery-oath
hand-breadth
acre-breadth
hair-breadth
footbreadth
corner-teeth
cable-length
whole-length
dress-length
peristalith

coppersmith
silversmith
livable-with
seventeenth
decillionth
nonillionth
octillionth
twelvemonth
gander-month
sponge-cloth
saddle-cloth
nettle-cloth
cheesecloth
hearse-cloth
hammercloth
butter-cloth
toilet-cloth
ground-sloth
cabbage-moth
tussock-moth
unicorn-moth
clothes-moth
luckenbooth
chisel-tooth
wisdom-tooth
hound's-tooth
barley-broth
middle-earth
rivet-hearth
down-to-earth
bitter-earth
yellow-earth
saddle-girth
thenceforth
whenceforth
setter-forth
twopenn'orth
east-by-north
west-by-north
littleworth
groatsworth
money's-worth
plaice-mouth
word-of-mouth
cottonmouth
hand-to-mouth
east-by-south
west-by-south
undergrowth
aftergrowth
intergrowth

I
schwärmerei
Chondrostei
cuir-bouilli
douroucouli
lapis-lazuli
hippopotami
Plagiostomi
Xanthochroi
Melanochroi
bersaglieri
condottieri
svarabhakti

cognoscenti
rifacimenti
tutti-frutti

K
make-or-break
riding-cloak
biofeedback
prickle-back
stickleback
scratch-back
balloon-back
leather-back
quarter-back
steeplejack
jumping-jack
crackerjack
quarter-jack
cinder-track
sherris-sack
yackety-yack
quarter-deck
double-check
leather-neck
killikinick
kinnikinick
pick-and-pick
monkey-trick
thought-sick
orange-stick
fiddlestick
candle-stick
singlestick
poking-stick
poting-stick
silver-stick
shinty-stick
harvest-tick
double-quick
kiss-me-quick
shuttlecock
brissel-cock
weathercock
graving-dock
spatter-dock
chock-a-block
office-block
upping-block
snatch-block
swivel-block
pillow-block
monkey-block
cuckoo-clock
master-clock
flower-clock
turret-clock
mortice-lock
mortise-lock
olivine-rock
weeping-rock
country-rock
upping-stock
gazing-stock
netherstock
anchor-stock

muscovy-duck
panic-struck
stage-struck
heart-struck
shrew-struck
hide-and-seek
Passion-week
Whitsun-week
night-shriek
apparatchik
realpolitik
chimney-nuik
Muschelkalk
flower-stalk
Bristol-milk
coconut-milk
country-folk
double-think
crambo-clink
skating-rink
kitchen-sink
countersink
service-book
fortune-book
picture-book
statute-book
reading-book
writing-book
account-book
cookery-book
cornice-hook
weeding-hook
pruning-hook
reaping-nook
chimney-nook
winter's-bark
stringy-bark
Deutschmark
section-mark
countermark
mother's-mark
vestry-clerk
weeding-fork
worsted-work
lattice-work
trestle-work
machine-work
scratch-work
plumber-work
sampler-work
counter-work
plaster-work
spatter-work
chequer-work
trellis-work
journey-work
scuttle-cask
harness-cask
vacuum-flask
powder-flask
reading-desk
writing-desk
bashi-bazouk
screech-hawk

sparrow-hawk	epistolical	prismatical	rumbustical
hunt-the-gowk	apostolical	rheumatical	scorbutical
glimmer-gowk	pre-adamical	pneumatical	epiphytical
L	geochemical	quadratical	zoophytical
intertribal	biochemical	leviratical	catalytical
parheliacal	zoochemical	apostatical	paradoxical
egomaniacal	synonimical	stalactical	unequivocal
micrococcal	antinomical	climactical	anisocercal
protococcal	autonomical	impractical	leptocercal
intrathecal	taxonomical	unpractical	diphycercal
algebraical	toponymical	syntactical	sesquipedal
pharisaical	metonymical	geotactical	quadrupedal
coxcombical	Brahmanical	cachectical	loculicidal
paramedical	puritanical	dialectical	spermicidal
pyramidical	oecumenical	syntectical	fratricidal
spasmodical	untechnical	apodictical	coralloidal
rhapsodical	Jacobinical	apomictical	metalloidal
honorifical	subclinical	energetical	arachnoidal
strategical	Brahminical	prophetical	hysteroidal
pedagogical	Sorbonnical	apathetical	ellipsoidal
demagogical	theogonical	synthetical	planetoidal
synagogical	gnathonical	aesthetical	ichthyoidal
bibliogical	hegemonical	homiletical	trapezoidal
mycological	uncanonical	splenetical	cantharidal
pedological	thrasonical	phrenetical	arthropodal
ideological	orthoepical	threnetical	schizopodal
theological	anthropical	baronetical	octachordal
oreological	subtropical	theoretical	notochordal
algological	Neotropical	toploftical	proctodaeal
ethological	antitypical	Jacobitical	peritonaeal
axiological	cylindrical	impolitical	oesophageal
gemological	chiragrical	unpolitical	linseed-meal
homological	unsatirical	sodomitical	matrilineal
nomological	allegorical	sybaritical	patrilineal
pomological	categorical	diacritical	rectilineal
zymological	anaphorical	subcritical	multilineal
oenological	plethorical	dendritical	curvilineal
penological	ahistorical	nephritical	gonorrhoeal
Sinological	diametrical	pleuritical	thunder-peal
monological	trimetrical	parasitical	incorporeal
topological	symmetrical	authentical	counterseal
typological	geometrical	anecdotical	quarter-seal
aerological	isometrical	thermotical	interosseal
serological	obstetrical	epileptical	sarcophagal
agrological	eccentrical	sylleptical	septifragal
virological	panegyrical	proleptical	medico-legal
horological	nonsensical	dyspeptical	diphthongal
nosological	intrinsical	cathartical	centrifugal
posological	extrinsical	subvertical	hexastichal
batological	unclassical	subcortical	hemistichal
ontological	geophysical	sarcastical	matriarchal
cytological	schematical	gymnastical	patriarchal
bryological	kinematical	fantastical	trierarchal
lethargical	pragmatical	Hobbistical	squirarchal
demiurgical	enigmatical	atheistical	hexateuchal
chemurgical	stigmatical	sophistical	microcephal
hierurgical	asthmatical	Thomistical	vice-marshal
chirurgical	grammatical	agonistical	fire-marshal
stomachical	idiomatical	dioristical	isolecithal
monarchical	axiomatical	patristical	therewithal
autarchical	automatical	statistical	wherewithal
pansophical	spermatical	pietistical	labyrinthal
evangelical	plasmatical	egotistical	neanderthal
parabolical	spasmatical	casuistical	interfacial

post-glacial	inventorial	subdiaconal	rear-admiral
multiracial	scriptorial	subregional	port-admiral
interracial	reportorial	previsional	multispiral
perithecial	quaestorial	provisional	vicar-choral
prejudicial	ancestorial	expansional	extra-floral
carnificial	executorial	ascensional	protectoral
sacrificial	endometrial	dimensional	sublittoral
superficial	trimestrial	extensional	pericentral
quincuncial	terrestrial	reversional	epiplastral
interradial	seigneurial	recessional	hyoplastral
intermedial	monochasial	secessional	conirostral
clostridial	hysteresial	obsessional	latirostral
internodial	rickettsial	probational	zygopleural
chiropodial	equinoctial	educational	interneural
pericardial	gentilitial	gradational	behavioural
endocardial	tribunitial	variational	intercrural
praecordial	substantial	summational	commissural
interludial	residential	emanational	caricatural
lymphangial	obediential	librational	prefectural
moustachial	desinential	vibrational	conjectural
paronychial	exponential	operational	subcultural
prothallial	deferential	sensational	hydrargyral
sinupallial	referential	gestational	vomeronasal
multinomial	inferential	valuational	reappraisal
peristomial	reverential	situational	intercensal
pericranial	inessential	affectional	intertarsal
primigenial	unessential	directional	sex-reversal
uncongenial	co-essential	inductional	transversal
archegonial	penitential	secretional	duniewassal
matrimonial	existential	traditional	paraglossal
patrimonial	influential	conditional	hypoglossal
testimonial	antenuptial	coalitional	exoskeletal
participial	post-nuptial	abolitional	cannon-metal
under-espial	pugilistial	cognitional	yellow-metal
polyzoarial	diaphragmal	attritional	centripetal
secretarial	wheel-animal	nutritional	anteorbital
pluriserial	nonagesimal	intuitional	stalactital
rectiserial	sexagesimal	attuitional	consonantal
multiserial	chromosomal	intentional	implacental
mesenterial	osteodermal	unemotional	labiodental
monasterial	pachydermal	commotional	interdental
magisterial	homothermal	exceptional	fundamental
ministerial	hypothermal	insertional	firmamental
spinsterial	eurythermal	evolutional	sacramental
seigniorial	perispermal	deflexional	testamental
accessorial	supernormal	inflexional	implemental
insessorial	catechismal	unipersonal	recremental
assessorial	ruridecanal	tripersonal	incremental
piscatorial	storm-signal	contubernal	excremental
prefatorial	latitudinal	sempiternal	detrimental
purgatorial	altitudinal	semi-diurnal	nutrimental
mediatorial	attitudinal	procerebral	sentimental
crematorial	submarginal	enneahedral	vestimental
dictatorial	gymnorhinal	tetrahedral	apartmental
saltatorial	disciplinal	icosahedral	emolumental
raptatorial	subterminal	pentahedral	continental
gestatorial	conterminal	anti-federal	componental
redactorial	air-terminal	cook-general	periodontal
selectorial	interspinal	ipsilateral	full-frontal
directorial	tetractinal	equilateral	nasofrontal
escritorial	pentactinal	sphincteral	interseptal
territorial	polyactinal	coleopteral	intersertal
institorial	vespertinal	presbyteral	transportal
servitorial	mediastinal	vice-admiral	infracostal

supracostal
Pentecostal
sacrocostal
intercostal
holocaustal
rock-crystal
monocrystal
polycrystal
recommittal
transmittal
polyglottal
surrebuttal
monolingual
audio-visual
contractual
ineffectual
instinctual
prepunctual
unspiritual
intersexual
transsexual
nominatival
accusatival
infinitival
pop-festival
disapproval
misbestowal
mycorrhizal
bog-asphodel
paddle-wheel
Pelton-wheel
spider-wheel
master-wheel
prayer-wheel
bucket-wheel
breast-wheel
monkey-wheel
sliding-keel
chrome-steel
damask-steel
nickel-steel
land-spaniel
kinderspiel
kriegsspiel
cupro-nickel
ferronickel
paper-enamel
water-tunnel
rhynchocoel
Whitechapel
sea-dotterel
water-barrel
storm-petrel
blood-vessel
steam-vessel
pearl-mussel
river-mussel
space-travel
summit-level
spirit-level
steam-shovel
roller-towel
surface-mail
buttock-mail

cornice-rail
picture-rail
quarter-rail
gaff-topsail
maintopsail
crag-and-tail
trendle-tail
trindle-tail
trundle-tail
draggle-tail
bristle-tail
flickertail
scissor-tail
swallow-tail
countervail
slate-pencil
town-council
Germanophil
gerontophil
choking-coil
rosewood-oil
counterfoil
paraffin-oil
macassar-oil
quarter-evil
claw-and-ball
skittle-ball
what-d'ye-call
trumpet-call
weather-gall
booking-hall
concert-hall
disenthrall
incorporall
coffee-stall
fingerstall
passing-bell
bubble-shell
cockleshell
turtle-shell
trough-shell
mussel-shell
oyster-shell
helmet-shell
fortune-tell
wishing-well
hedging-bill
pruning-bill
scissor-bill
sparrow-bill
tucking-mill
rolling-mill
woollen-mill
linen-scroll
rock-and-roll
sausage-roll
weather-roll
counter-roll
cock-and-bull
herring-gull
xanthophyll
sclerophyll
chlorophyll
wood-alcohol

axerophthol
paracetamol
board-school
hedge-school
piano-school
under-school
night-school
machine-tool
rocking-tool
fender-stool
litany-stool
cholesterol
coprosterol
phytosterol
telecontrol
fire-control
self-control
dual-control
gain-control
stilbestrol
water-pistol
message-girl
dancing-girl
sweater-girl
servant-girl
charity-girl
amplexicaul
disgraceful
resourceful
overcareful
pleasureful
increaseful
suspenseful
unreposeful
distasteful
reproachful
researchful
dispatchful
strengthful
unhealthful
unbeautiful
teaspoonful
all-powerful
distressful
misdoubtful
disquietful
affrightful
unresentful
distrustful
mistrustful
begging-bowl
wassail-bowl
chrysoberyl
tetradactyl
pentadactyl
artiodactyl
macrodactyl
pterodactyl
leptodactyl
hyperdactyl
pachydactyl
M

queez-maddam
landing-beam

walking-beam
working-beam
bloodstream
third-stream
spill-stream
ocean-stream
trout-stream
stirrup-dram
marconigram
phraseogram
oscillogram
dactylogram
sphygmogram
steganogram
harmonogram
meteorogram
spectrogram
caprolactam
staff-system
block-system
tally-system
tetradrachm
cabbage-palm
feather-palm
coconut-palm
weather-helm
overfreedom
archdukedom
officialdom
Christendom
spinsterdom
bachelordom
penny-wisdom
attorneydom
Dogberrydom
torpedo-boom
nickel-bloom
winter-bloom
hall-bedroom
service-room
reading-room
morning-room
keeping-room
waiting-room
sitting-room
drawing-room
harness-room
grog-blossom
plum-blossom
disaccustom
riverbottom
ostrich-farm
straight-arm
ostracoderm
isogeotherm
pullet-sperm
dress-reform
acinaciform
scoleciform
verruciform
naupliiform
coralliform
lamelliform
patelliform

bacilliform
mamilliform
lapilliform
papilliform
corolliform
vasculiform
planuliform
granuliform
campaniform
tympaniform
antenniform
calcariform
scalariform
dolabriform
cerebriform
colubriform
crateriform
scalpriform
panduriform
insectiform
zeolitiform
granitiform
asbestiform
sagittiform
cabbage-worm
bristle-worm
sea-longworm
bladder-worm
trophoplasm
somatoplasm
disyllabism
demoniacism
supremacism
heteroecism
Mithraicism
catholicism
academicism
hispanicism
ecumenicism
Platonicism
Teutonicism
Hibernicism
esotericism
exotericism
historicism
theatricism
dramaticism
didacticism
eclecticism
athleticism
cosmeticism
phoneticism
apoliticism
pedanticism
Atlanticism
romanticism
neuroticism
monasticism
agnosticism
Mohammedism
gourmandism
vagabondism
landlordism
Manichaeism

Sadduceeism
phariseeism
absenteeism
tetratheism
physitheism
cosmotheism
werewolfism
teleologism
sociologism
tautologism
hierarchism
Petrarchism
panpsychism
theosophism
trimorphism
zoomorphism
isomorphism
prognathism
hylopathism
Plymouthism
comstockism
cannibalism
syndicalism
clericalism
physicalism
officialism
unsocialism
colonialism
imperialism
materialism
abnormalism
regionalism
nationalism
rationalism
personalism
paternalism
externalism
communalism
cerebralism
pastoralism
neovitalism
Orientalism
teetotalism
medievalism
monothelism
parallelism
probabilism
possibilism
notaphilism
Sinophilism
infantilism
bimetallism
pointillism
ametabolism
hyperbolism
panislamism
panspermism
suburbanism
Anglicanism
Gallicanism
Americanism
Europeanism
neopaganism
hooliganism

Arcadianism
plebeianism
Pelagianism
Hegelianism
Stahlianism
Bohemianism
Socinianism
Arminianism
Baconianism
demonianism
agrarianism
Rotarianism
Prussianism
creatianism
Novatianism
adoptianism
Erastianism
Moravianism
Lutheranism
Wesleyanism
Burschenism
phenomenism
larrikinism
inquilinism
determinism
Michurinism
Byzantinism
libertinism
Weismannism
Napoleonism
religionism
histrionism
revisionism
divisionism
illusionism
creationism
relationism
Adoptionism
eudaemonism
diachronism
anachronism
synchronism
prochronism
isochronism
northernism
southernism
opportunism
pleochroism
polychroism
malapropism
rheotropism
allotropism
gamotropism
aerotropism
singularism
mercenarism
millenarism
Carbonarism
fissiparism
voluntarism
hemihedrism
holohedrism
Micawberism
cavalierism

courtierism
tetramerism
pentamerism
tautomerism
consumerism
aspheterism
catheterism
gangsterism
Pythagorism
adiaphorism
phosphorism
deteriorism
bachelorism
brachyprism
adventurism
scripturism
progressism
immediatism
suprematism
systematism
astigmatism
achromatism
corporatism
ditheletism
martinetism
Rechabitism
coenobitism
dithelitism
shunamitism
favouritism
diphysitism
corybantism
vigilantism
irredentism
immanentism
polycrotism
homoerotism
autoerotism
parabaptism
braggartism
Bonapartism
polymastism
phagocytism
holophytism
proselytism
pedagoguism
demagoguism
Gargantuism
exclusivism
objectivism
primitivism
intuitivism
highbrowism
attorneyism
McCarthyism
whiteboyism
literaryism
Dogberryism
corrigendum
Carborundum ®
proctodaeum
peritonaeum
succedaneum
Polytrichum

Polystichum
cork-cambium
paramaecium
perithecium
paramoecium
Laserpicium
intermedium
cypripedium
zoogonidium
sphaeridium
antheridium
hesperidium
clostridium
antependium
latifundium
staminodium
stylopodium
Chenopodium
pericardium
endocardium
diascordium
cassiopeium
florilegium
gametangium
xenodochium
promycelium
prothallium
Penicillium
taurobolium
gynostemium
zoospermium
peridesmium
pericranium
parascenium
postscenium
latrocinium
einsteinium
tridominium
condominium
quadrennium
archegonium
carpogonium
sporogonium
pelargonium
phosphonium
pandemonium
californium
Telescopium
syllabarium
columbarium
formicarium
frigidarium
ophidiarium
polyzoarium
leprosarium
insectarium
planetarium
termitarium
equilibrium
zoodendrium
Megatherium
Sivatherium
Dinotherium
Nototherium

eubacterium
magisterium
ministerium
apodyterium
subdelirium
aspersorium
muscatorium
crematorium
maggotorium
scriptorium
endometrium
epigastrium
perineurium
monochasium
capillitium
Laserpitium
mendelevium
intervallum
aspergillum
Podophyllum
Zygophyllum
incunabulum
retinaculum
Xanthoxylum
Zanthoxylum
xeranthemum
menispermum
interregnum
antirrhinum
mediastinum
sempiternum
harum-scarum
panjandarum
candelabrum
procerebrum
hippeastrum
hydrargyrum
helichrysum
polygonatum
desideratum
excrementum
sempervivum

N

watering-can
Pan-Anglican
all-American
Pan-American
Heracleidan
sauropsidan
panomphaean
jumping-bean
tonquin-bean
Calabar-bean
scarlet-bean
Archimedean
caryatidean
callipygean
Nietzschean
spring-clean
vacuum-clean
hyperborean
Pythagorean
Theocritean
Bonapartean

Procrustean
coprophagan
cinema-organ
barrel-organ
Elizabethan
Fontarabian
Aurignacian
academician
mechanician
rhetorician
electrician
cosmetician
magnetician
phonetician
logistician
acoustician
heteroscian
Rosicrucian
nullifidian
scincoidian
Gallovidian
Portlandian
Anglo-Indian
pericardian
monocardian
Perigordian
hyperlydian
peripeteian
Falstaffian
humgruffian
Kimeridgian
Gallowegian
Carolingian
Merovingian
mythologian
philologian
Petrarchian
saurischian
Pickwickian
madrigalian
Westphalian
antithalian
saturnalian
penetralian
Argathelian
crocodilian
lacertilian
post-exilian
hypoaeolian
Polyphemian
syndyasmian
Hieronymian
Sandemanian
Magdalenian
Valentinian
Palestinian
Augustinian
Poseidonian
myrmidonian
Torridonian
Marathonian
Pandemonian
Smithsonian
Hamiltonian

Gladstonian
tetragynian
pentagynian
Aesculapian
cornucopian
abecedarian
trachearian
Rastafarian
zoantharian
fustilarian
sigillarian
radiolarian
hexaplarian
plumularian
sertularian
infirmarian
millenarian
centenarian
alcyonarian
necessarian
Sabbatarian
unsectarian
societarian
proletarian
egalitarian
utilitarian
Trinitarian
libertarian
antiquarian
monomyarian
Pre-Cambrian
enneandrian
tetrandrian
icosandrian
pentandrian
Alexandrian
Mulciberian
eleutherian
Shaksperian
spinsterian
Finno-Ugrian
fustilarian
hyperdorian
purgatorian
refectorian
Lancastrian
Zoroastrian
campestrian
silvestrian
sylvestrian
holothurian
Micronesian
Rabelaisian
Aphrodisian
Paracelsian
Albigensian
Tironensian
Tyronensian
Maglemosian
Panglossian
Belorussian
homoiousian
heterousian
gentilitian

tribunitian	angst-ridden	time-bargain	stone-falcon
Taliacotian	well-trodden	closed-chain	dicotyledon
unchristian	downtrodden	kibble-chain	fauxbourdon
lilliputian	bridemaiden	tiller-chain	nickelodeon
Yugoslavian	disemburden	arch-villain	stool-pigeon
Leibnitzian	smokescreen	chamberlain	tree-surgeon
Highlandman	small-screen	legerdemain	river-dragon
turnpike-man	organ-screen	travail-pain	patrol-wagon
medicine-man	choir-screen	tickle-brain	dinner-wagon
hardwareman	sight-screen	beetlebrain	honey-waggon
sandwich-man	split-screen	rattle-brain	octastichon
Scottishman	jungle-green	starch-grain	harmoniphon
Graeco-Roman	bottle-green	pollen-grain	anacoluthon
policewoman	Kendal-green	silver-grain	eccaleobion
needlewoman	wintergreen	mine-captain	unsuspicion
gentlewoman	Fastern's-e'en	flag-captain	enchiridion
tiring-woman	oxy-hydrogen	ship-captain	euchologion
churchwoman	calyptrogen	post-captain	leaf-cushion
Scotchwoman	progestogen	drop-curtain	rapscallion
bushel-woman	manna-lichen	prothrombin	perduellion
patrolwoman	soup-kitchen	antijacobin	tourbillion
Mussulwoman	overburthen	anti-Jacobin	quadrillion
washerwoman	Brotstudien	haemoglobin	quintillion
oyster-woman	god-forsaken	chrysarobin	self-opinion
butter-woman	game-chicken	ragged-robin	hypolimnion
tribeswoman	awe-stricken	ground-robin	excommunion
tradeswoman	stalling-ken	phycophaein	rose-campion
spokeswoman	rough-spoken	fluorescein	sea-scorpion
stateswoman	plain-spoken	gegenschein	septentrion
yachtswoman	short-spoken	snaffle-rein	orchestrion
sportswoman	house-broken	lipoprotein	imprecision
market-woman	trade-fallen	listening-in	subincision
clergy-woman	crestfallen	heart-urchin	subdivision
trencher-man	gentlewomen	therewithin	supervision
Anglo-Norman	merchantmen	table-napkin	re-expansion
subtacksman	undershapen	gibberellin	reascension
businessman	fountain-pen	podophyllin	high-tension
congressman	men-children	paper-muslin	hypotension
draughtsman	Lepidosiren	anti-vitamin	inextension
aircraftman	Munchhausen	phycocyanin	co-extension
merchantman	storm-beaten	anthocyanin	anteversion
foremastman	catch-the-ten	haemocyanin	ambiversion
subterhuman	forfoughten	carrageenin	progression
preterhuman	stone-marten	canting-coin	compression
crossbowman	beech-marten	crisping-pin	suppression
assemblyman	foreshorten	heliotropin	kirk-session
delivery-man	underbitten	thyrotropin	prescission
infantryman	frostbitten	cholesterin	readmission
property-man	handwritten	listeners-in	irremission
carrageenan	typewritten	vasopressin	manumission
Cypro-Minoan	misbegotten	cater-cousin	superfusion
dripping-pan	unforgotten	cross-cousin	interfusion
tetrapteran	nook-shotten	high-falutin	transfusion
orthopteran	clean-shaven	king-penguin	disillusion
chiropteran	steam-driven	lactoflavin	prelibation
discophoran	chain-driven	blood-spavin	reprobation
ctenophoran	under-driven	enterotoxin	improbation
non-partisan	power-driven	radiocarbon	approbation
black-and-tan	motor-driven	hydrocarbon	conurbation
Chautauquan	blood-frozen	radio-beacon	desiccation
delivery-van	quick-frozen	synonymicon	exsiccation
luckengowan	weather-sign	apollonicon	deprecation
unforbidden	countersign	panegyricon	imprecation
witch-ridden	plea-bargain	onomasticon	eradication

predication	variegation	decollation	lancination
vindication	segregation	percolation	fascination
syndication	aggregation	hariolation	imagination
edification	colligation	variolation	evagination
deification	castigation	consolation	origination
reification	instigation	vacuolation	machination
unification	fustigation	legislation	declination
publication	divulgation	translation	reclination
vellication	subrogation	tribulation	inclination
villication	prorogation	ejaculation	pollination
replication	surrogation	sacculation	examination
implication	aspergation	speculation	elimination
application	objurgation	calculation	crimination
duplication	expurgation	inoculation	culmination
explication	subjugation	circulation	fulmination
formication	conjugation	musculation	commination
fornication	corrugation	coagulation	abomination
fabrication	enunciation	pullulation	germination
imbrication	bisociation	stimulation	termination
lubrication	association	gemmulation	vermination
rubrication	reradiation	nummulation	acumination
affrication	irradiation	formulation	pectination
metrication	remediation	granulation	destination
extrication	dimidiation	stipulation	festination
mastication	repudiation	sporulation	inquination
tostication	brachiation	serrulation	perennation
rustication	retaliation	gratulation	carbonation
defalcation	defiliation	postulation	condonation
inculcation	affiliation	pustulation	personation
suffocation	humiliation	methylation	incarnation
collocation	defoliation	acclamation	hibernation
dislocation	exfoliation	declamation	gubernation
embrocation	laciniation	reclamation	alternation
convocation	inebriation	exclamation	subornation
provocation	fimbriation	incremation	coadunation
debarcation	excoriation	sublimation	mancipation
embarcation	elutriation	acclimation	forcipation
demarcation	luxuriation	collimation	dissipation
altercation	expatiation	reanimation	obstipation
bifurcation	negotiation	inanimation	inculpation
expiscation	alleviation	exanimation	exculpation
obfuscation	lixiviation	proximation	syncopation
coruscation	debarkation	affirmation	apocopation
re-education	embarkation	deformation	extirpation
coeducation	demarkation	reformation	nuncupation
manducation	imparkation	information	declaration
degradation	congelation	deplumation	preparation
aggradation	correlation	despumation	celebration
upgradation	misrelation	profanation	cerebration
depredation	stagflation	explanation	terebration
elucidation	reinflation	subpanation	calibration
trepidation	bombilation	trepanation	obumbration
liquidation	compilation	oxygenation	adumbration
deoxidation	ventilation	hyphenation	lucubration
fecundation	appellation	indignation	obsecration
retardation	cupellation	obsignation	desecration
recordation	vacillation	designation	dehydration
infeudation	oscillation	resignation	rehydration
enucleation	sigillation	assignation	verberation
delineation	mamillation	expugnation	canceration
allineation	fusillation	bombination	ponderation
procreation	titillation	combination	botheration
miscreation	cavillation	vaccination	glomeration
propagation	vexillation	calcination	enumeration

vulneration	pectisation	disputation	malfunction
exoneration	unitisation	devaluation	dysfunction
cooperation	peptisation	revaluation	conjunction
co-operation	nitrosation	upvaluation	disjunction
desperation	decussation	attenuation	box-junction
reiteration	ablactation	extenuation	compunction
mutteration	affectation	insinuation	irreduction
deuteration	delectation	obliquation	obstruction
pulveration	humectation	illiquation	destruction
integration	expectation	antiquation	instruction
demigration	coarctation	infatuation	carburetion
remigration	reluctation	punctuation	prohibition
immigration	elicitation	fluctuation	extradition
denigration	suscitation	fructuation	suraddition
respiration	venditation	habituation	recondition
inspiration	flagitation	aggravation	subaudition
suspiration	gurgitation	depravation	pre-ignition
enquiration	crepitation	re-elevation	recognition
inquiration	palpitation	deprivation	premonition
elaboration	mussitation	cultivation	preterition
perforation	inusitation	aestivation	innutrition
melioration	jactitation	tittivation	micturition
defloration	nictitation	innervation	parturition
deploration	gravitation	observation	acquisition
imploration	occultation	reservation	requisition
exploration	decantation	incurvation	inquisition
pignoration	recantation	subluxation	preposition
evaporation	incantation	labefaction	oviposition
corporation	indentation	tabefaction	malposition
restoration	orientation	rubefaction	composition
subarration	lamentation	madefaction	proposition
saburration	cementation	calefaction	supposition
susurration	fomentation	malefaction	disposition
penetration	assentation	tumefaction	competition
impetration	ostentation	benefaction	repartition
arbitration	connotation	rarefaction	bipartition
denitration	compotation	check-action	deglutition
eventration	acceptation	pedal-action	irretention
prostration	impartation	retroaction	inattention
flustration	dehortation	underaction	misdevotion
frustration	exhortation	interaction	contraption
carburation	deportation	diffraction	adscription
procuration	importation	subtraction	description
obscuration	asportation	contraction	inscription
perduration	exportation	protraction	rumgumption
fulguration	impastation	abstraction	subsumption
conjuration	devastation	distraction	presumption
murmuration	head-station	transaction	consumption
colouration	infestation	pre-election	discerption
suppuration	molestation	non-election	reinsertion
mensuration	forestation	reselection	reassertion
trituration	arrestation	prospection	reapportion
nervuration	obtestation	indirection	demi-bastion
Judaisation	detestation	venesection	indigestion
arabisation	attestation	vivisection	moxibustion
laicisation	reinstation	malediction	retribution
iridisation	aerostation	valediction	attribution
dockisation	degustation	benediction	consecution
realisation	encystation	dereliction	prosecution
utilisation	confutation	confliction	persecution
stylisation	commutation	abstriction	inexecution
solmisation	permutation	obstriction	prolocution
atomisation	dismutation	restriction	perlocution
ozonisation	computation	distinction	dissolution

convolution	self-concern	alto-relievo	creatorship
comminution	ultra-modern	alto-rilievo	senatorship
destitution	bristle-fern	cavo-rilievo	curatorship
restitution	dark-lantern	P	electorship
institution	morgenstern	watering-cap	proctorship
irreflexion	natural-born	trencher-cap	praetorship
genuflexion	lamellicorn	rubbish-heap	traitorship
crucifixion	shoeing-horn	compost-heap	auditorship
transfixion	morsing-horn	thunder-clap	janitorship
solifluxion	hunting-horn	shaving-soap	monitorship
Callistemon	sallow-thorn	Windsor-soap	tree-worship
phaenomenon	weather-worn	throat-strap	fire-worship
water-cannon	counter-turn	beauty-sleep	self-worship
fire-balloon	through-gaun	curtail-step	will-worship
kite-balloon	bourtree-gun	kindredship	hero-worship
hunter's-moon	magazine-gun	stewardship	amateurship
ungazed-upon	choice-drawn	justiceship	goddess-ship
diatessaron	watered-down	comradeship	hostess-ship
enneahedron	thistle-down	vaivodeship	prefectship
tetrahedron	reach-me-down	waivodeship	subjectship
icosahedron	backing-down	voivodeship	prophetship
pentahedron	damping-down	grandeeship	servantship
Eriodendron	talk-you-down	traineeship	studentship
archenteron	morning-gown	trusteeship	provostship
orthopteron	unforeknown	baillieship	viceroyship
katabothron	Cappah-brown	apostleship	mystery-ship
katavothron	meadow-brown	tribuneship	factory-ship
turfing-iron	copple-crown	lectureship	hunting-whip
jagging-iron	trouble-town	prelateship	trouser-clip
pinking-iron	burrowstown	primateship	mussel-scalp
burling-iron	O	sheriffship	aides-de-camp
priming-iron	frigorifico	landing-ship	reading-lamp
searing-iron	verde-antico	sailing-ship	rubber-stamp
stirrup-iron	saltimbanco	Messiahship	letter-stamp
wrought-iron	amontillado	marshalship	lignum-swamp
synchrotron	fish-torpedo	generalship	brine-shrimp
epiplastron	whiskerando	admiralship	turbine-pump
hyoplastron	accelerando	co-rivalship	forcing-pump
antineutron	rallentando	colonelship	stomach-pump
night-season	rinforzando	bondmanship	stirrup-pump
master-mason	decrescendo	lifemanship	machine-shop
arrow-poison	archipelago	bushmanship	fitting-shop
state-prison	internuncio	workmanship	leaving-shop
disimprison	braggadocio	oarsmanship	pattern-shop
disgarrison	comprimario	batsmanship	overdevelop
hedge-parson	estranghelo	showmanship	hunting-crop
chairperson	violoncello	denizenship	clothes-prop
salesperson	Punchinello	citizenship	hedge-hyssop
schecklaton	sextodecimo	captainship	whipping-top
potamogeton	vivacissimo	milk-kinship	mountain-top
exoskeleton	legatissimo	surgeonship	whistle-stop
skimmington	prestissimo	patroonship	achaenocarp
quarrington	thirty-twomo	scholarship	dipterocarp
zooplankton	player-piano	managership	double-sharp
nitrocotton	tickettyboo	teachership	mussel-scaup
pearl-button	rat-kangaroo	benchership	standing-cup
press-button	sancho-pedro	weather-ship	tantalus-cup
shirt-button	guerrillero	soldiership	trous-de-loup
belly-button	chiaroscuro	premiership	R
tummy-button	capriccioso	speakership	retrobulbar
leg-of-mutton	contrabasso	partnership	Liquidambar
Psilophyton	sweet-potato	advisership	dorsolumbar
hydrophyton	cinquecento	emperorship	luncheon-bar
sauce-crayon	rifacimento	sponsorship	splinter-bar

armoured-car	serpent-star	slave-holder	whole-hogger
sleeping-car	land-grabber	stock-holder	footslogger
jaunting-car	stock-jobber	smallholder	sockdoliger
pencil-cedar	abbey-lubber	cigar-holder	Grenzgänger
landing-gear	india-rubber	stadtholder	autochanger
chafing-gear	brass-rubber	hog-shoulder	crapehanger
running-gear	sheet-rubber	right-hander	crepehanger
driving-gear	transcriber	marshlander	cliffhanger
mononuclear	fume-chamber	southlander	strap-hanger
matrilinear	antechamber	gerrymander	paper-hanger
patrilinear	sick-chamber	jerrymander	lady's-finger
rectilinear	bill-chamber	withstander	index-finger
multilinear	rain-chamber	double-ender	opera-singer
curvilinear	disremember	reprehender	minnesinger
interlinear	misremember	money-lender	torch-singer
salmon-spear	lobby-member	recommender	sight-singer
prickly-pear	leaf-climber	nurse-tender	right-winger
anchovy-pear	rock-climber	sea-lavender	relic-monger
wash-and-wear	hook-climber	spellbinder	panic-monger
ready-to-wear	root-climber	rangefinder	peace-monger
wood-vinegar	belly-timber	witch-finder	place-monger
gally-beggar	beachcomber	water-finder	scaremonger
barley-sugar	disencumber	comet-finder	whoremonger
curtal-friar	sea-cucumber	fault-finder	verse-monger
verisimilar	strait-lacer	childminder	state-monger
night-cellar	hurdle-racer	transponder	flesh-monger
earth-pillar	flag-officer	dumbfounder	maxim-monger
caterpillar	park-officer	type-founder	yeard-hunger
horse-collar	opera-dancer	bell-founder	earth-hunger
white-collar	belly-dancer	iron-founder	sockdologer
sword-dollar	necromancer	half-pounder	chronologer
circumpolar	conveyancer	four-pounder	gastrologer
circumsolar	baby-bouncer	echo-sounder	Steinberger
incunabular	greengrocer	blackbirder	backbencher
somnambular	stickleader	clam-chowder	bird-catcher
subglobular	cheer-leader	plate-powder	molecatcher
semi-tubular	class-leader	tooth-powder	mail-catcher
retinacular	proof-reader	pearl-powder	gull-catcher
spectacular	stall-reader	giant-powder	gnatcatcher
canalicular	sight-reader	yeast-powder	want-catcher
adminicular	homesteader	emery-powder	boot-catcher
ventricular	pasquinader	curry-powder	cony-catcher
animalcular	masquerader	putty-powder	bird-watcher
carbuncular	slave-trader	jumping-deer	fire-watcher
octonocular	gall-bladder	chanticleer	doomwatcher
interocular	swim-bladder	mountaineer	pork-butcher
crepuscular	underbidder	culverineer	Antiburgher
corpuscular	stock-feeder	electioneer	paragrapher
equiangular	paper-feeder	munitioneer	telegrapher
rectangular	velocipeder	crotcheteer	serigrapher
multangular	water-spider	pamphleteer	cacographer
pentangular	money-spider	glue-sniffer	logographer
unicellular	circle-rider	foraminifer	xylographer
semi-annular	ground-elder	sockdolager	demographer
subscapular	reef-builder	pilgrimager	mimographer
proconsular	shipbuilder	bank-manager	nomographer
univalvular	boat-builder	honey-badger	monographer
trivalvular	body-builder	devil-dodger	topographer
circumlunar	paper-folder	draft-dodger	typographer
testamentar	music-holder	gally-bagger	horographer
brittle-star	title-holder	grave-digger	nosographer
evening-star	shareholder	steam-digger	doxographer
morning-star	leaseholder	hair-trigger	philosopher
feather-star	householder	pettifogger	queer-basher

haberdasher
gatecrasher
whitewasher
sweep-washer
whale-fisher
black-fisher
pearl-fisher
establisher
republisher
embellisher
replenisher
four-flusher
share-pusher
tail-feather
bell-heather
shoe-leather
buff-leather
half-leather
wash-leather
rock-leather
overleather
spur-leather
whitleather
overweather
fair-weather
grandfather
housefather
get-together
somewhither
elsewhither
grandmother
housemother
queen-mother
good-brother
half-brother
twin-brother
stepbrother
bird-fancier
foot-soldier
lammergeier
Biedermeier
speechifier
personifier
demulsifier
intensifier
montgolfier
Amelanchier
pigeon-flier
turcopolier
electrolier
accompanier
chansonnier
gonfalonier
photocopier
speech-crier
tumble-drier
ring-carrier
bulk-carrier
mail-carrier
bull-terrier
arquebusier
catapultier
loudspeaker
code-breaker

safe-breaker
backbreaker
rock-breaker
ship-breaker
shopbreaker
poodle-faker
mantua-maker
threadmaker
phrasemaker
speech-maker
system-maker
sailor-maker
basket-maker
bushwhacker
safe-cracker
fire-cracker
corn-cracker
three-decker
city-slicker
tooth-picker
billsticker
beta-blocker
back-blocker
door-knocker
bloodsucker
honey-sucker
voortrekker
deerstalker
track-walker
sleep-walker
floorwalker
night-walker
stilt-walker
puppy-walker
front-ranker
supertanker
free-thinker
forethinker
dram-drinker
opium-smoker
chain-smoker
underlooker
stockbroker
money-broker
fieldworker
metal-worker
steelworker
underworker
glassworker
shift-worker
nightworker
cat's-whisker
horse-dealer
plain-dealer
interdealer
faith-healer
Emmenthaler
reed-warbler
wood-warbler
wax-chandler
four-wheeler
blackmailer
steam-boiler
hospitaller

teetotaller
forestaller
stonewaller
music-seller
underseller
print-seller
truth-teller
story-teller
lake-dweller
cave-dweller
town-dweller
giant-killer
dusty-miller
steam-roller
comptroller
ob-and-soller
disannuller
proof-puller
water-cooler
preschooler
wool-stapler
crown-antler
pipe-dreamer
tin-streamer
Rüdesheimer
penthemimer
Stahlhelmer
stone-hammer
helve-hammer
steam-hammer
water-hammer
ninny-hammer
yellow-ammer
coal-trimmer
chance-comer
cheironomer
gastronomer
store-farmer
stock-farmer
truck-farmer
sheep-farmer
plate-warmer
misinformer
transformer
barnstormer
physician
collegianer
Lippizzaner
refreshener
zip-fastener
pop-fastener
overgrainer
entertainer
purse-seiner
Niersteiner
penny-a-liner
man-milliner
discipliner
after-dinner
breadwinner
prize-winner
front-runner
truncheoner
scrimshoner

parishioner
reversioner
probationer
refectioner
traditioner
conditioner
coalitioner
partitioner
extortioner
executioner
pot-walloner
honeymooner
catercorner
afterburner
theatre-goer
picture-goer
concert-goer
thread-paper
marble-paper
needle-paper
tissue-paper
starch-paper
filter-paper
butter-paper
silver-paper
toilet-paper
garnet-paper
velvet-paper
ballot-paper
road-scraper
linen-draper
moss-cheeper
pound-keeper
peace-keeper
lodge-keeper
storekeeper
housekeeper
hotel-keeper
green-keeper
under-keeper
lightkeeper
soul-sleeper
tree-creeper
mine-sweeper
screen-wiper
claim-jumper
pot-walloper
paratrooper
moss-trooper
handicapper
betel-pepper
water-pepper
high-stepper
doorstepper
snuff-dipper
transhipper
coal-whipper
sand-skipper
teeny-bopper
sheet-copper
froth-hopper
grasshopper
name-dropper
snow-dropper

ring-stopper
show-stopper
aftersupper
card-sharper
pig's-whisper
horse-couper
stereotyper
sword-bearer
purse-bearer
torch-bearer
train-bearer
underbearer
water-bearer
crossbearer
embroiderer
philanderer
surrenderer
tax-gatherer
slaughterer
upholsterer
redeliverer
transferrer
forespurrer
day-labourer
dishonourer
disfavourer
map-measurer
time-pleaser
brain-teaser
stern-chaser
paraphraser
reappraiser
plasticiser
circumciser
gormandiser
theologiser
sympathiser
specialiser
mineraliser
literaliser
neutraliser
monopoliser
utopianiser
homogeniser
gelatiniser
scrutiniser
fraterniser
populariser
bowdleriser
allegoriser
enterpriser
pasteuriser
moisturiser
synthesiser
pragmatiser
vine-dresser
hairdresser
flax-dresser
world-beater
windcheater
space-heater
superheater
bibliolater
physiolater

demonolater
shell-crater
second-rater
ground-water
spring-water
potash-water
laurel-water
mother-water
potass-water
cement-water
barley-water
quarry-water
Azotobacter
constructer
permeameter
torque-meter
alkalimeter
polarimeter
solarimeter
calorimeter
chlorimeter
colorimeter
vaporimeter
fluorimeter
zymosimeter
plessimeter
strabometer
speedometer
tacheometer
stereometer
swingometer
trochometer
psychometer
gradiometer
craniometer
pluviometer
dynamometer
thermometer
seismometer
volumometer
auxanometer
salinometer
actinometer
chronometer
dendrometer
spherometer
sclerometer
chlorometer
fluorometer
stactometer
quantometer
Comptometer ®
interpreter
hereinafter
home-crofter
fire-fighter
bullfighter
pipe-lighter
firelighter
moonlighter
lamplighter
goddaughter
coast-waiter
simpliciter

hedge-writer
prose-writer
slate-writer
underwriter
ghost-writer
mossbluiter
crack-halter
sesquialter
pole-vaulter
representer
word-painter
sign-painter
teleprinter
line-printer
penteconter
place-hunter
still-hunter
night-hunter
gully-hunter
span-counter
hunt-counter
first-footer
pussyfooter
line-shooter
snapshooter
intercepter
ornithopter
interrupter
self-starter
prêt-à-porter
transporter
night-porter
frankfurter
broadcaster
criticaster
north-easter
south-easter
cotoneaster
shin-plaster
music-master
grandmaster
pound-master
three-master
barge-master
whoremaster
housemaster
beach-master
wreck-master
flock-master
stall-master
drill-master
burgomaster
sheep-master
choir-master
stentmaster
toastmaster
scout-master
assay-master
north-wester
south-wester
tea-canister
bar-sinister
Westminster
paternoster

blockbuster
trust-buster
pearl-oyster
backscatter
lick-platter
stand-patter
bloodletter
rhyme-letter
chain-letter
underletter
wood-fretter
vine-fretter
carburetter
trend-setter
disembitter
pinch-hitter
horse-litter
intromitter
transmitter
cocoa-butter
surrebutter
fairy-butter
stone-cutter
chaff-cutter
wheel-cutter
paper-cutter
glass-cutter
grass-cutter
straw-cutter
daisy-cutter
distributer
out-and-outer
undervaluer
howsomdever
trench-fever
disbeliever
misbeliever
whatsomever
wheresoever
whosesoever
whichsoever
transceiver
thanksgiver
whisky-liver
stage-driver
slave-driver
quill-driver
owner-driver
river-driver
screw-driver
quacksalver
quicksilver
sheep-silver
toilet-cover
working-over
stone-plover
stilt-plover
sallee-rover
tooth-drawer
sneck-drawer
underviewer
interviewer
froth-blower
glass-blower

blood-flower	vinificator	illustrator	water-colour
globe-flower	purificator	instaurator	liver-colour
stage-flower	equivocator	inaugurator	straw-colour
goose-flower	confiscator	sulphurator	out-paramour
cauliflower	dilapidator	totalisator	scale-armour
snail-flower	commendator	compensator	plate-armour
elder-flower	promulgator	dispensator	chain-armour
tiger-flower	compurgator	inspissator	bed-of-honour
night-flower	depreciator	habilitator	mouth-honour
gillyflower	appreciator	facilitator	treachetour
candle-power	denunciator	auscultator	mystery-tour
sand-thrower	annunciator	commentator	non-sequitur
mine-thrower	digladiator	sustentator	protomartyr
silk-thrower	conciliator	disceptator	S
overthrower	calumniator	dissertator	supersedeas
multiplexer	centuriator	sternutator	laughing-gas
swordplayer	propitiator	continuator	pseudomonas
stage-player	abbreviator	perpetuator	Trichomonas
piano-player	asphyxiator	conservator	candelabras
sight-player	nomenclator	house-factor	chapeau-bras
whist-player	insufflator	substractor	galliambics
lammergeyer	vasodilator	disinfector	orthopedics
pigeon-flyer	invigilator	preselector	telearchics
crown-lawyer	annihilator	resurrector	geodynamics
under-sawyer	flagellator	constrictor	biodynamics
trail-blazer	postillator	horse-doctor	eurhythmics
steeple-fair	articulator	witch-doctor	loxodromics
sledge-chair	emasculator	water-doctor	orthogenics
swivel-chair	stridulator	transductor	zootechnics
basket-chair	accumulator	constructor	cataphonics
self-despair	manipulator	arch-traitor	thermionics
umbrella-fir	depopulator	co-inheritor	histrionics
rouge-et-noir	consummator	lithotritor	eudaemonics
air-corridor	confirmator	perquisitor	hydroponics
hydrometeor	lachrymator	compulsitor	electronics
unsighed-for	rejuvenator	interventor	ultrasonics
unwished-for	vaticinator	psychomotor	hypersonics
unlooked-for	desalinator	cardiomotor	transsonics
uncalled-for	inseminator	rocket-motor	paediatrics
bower-anchor	denominator	interceptor	hippiatrics
sheet-anchor	illuminator	interruptor	cliometrics
drift-anchor	anticipator	carburettor	pataphysics
waist-anchor	emancipator	contributor	metaphysics
kwashiorkor	consecrator	distributor	cryophysics
paper-sailor	Pantocrator	prostitutor	mathematics
earth-tremor	deliberator	ornithosaur	systematics
misdemeanor	vociferator	tyrannosaur	informatics
contra-tenor	exaggerator	ichthyosaur	numismatics
Heldentenor	accelerator	arbitrageur	aerostatics
misgovernor	decelerator	mitrailleur	gyrostatics
folding-door	regenerator	Monseigneur	apologetics
whicket-door	incinerator	carilloneur	catechetics
without-door	remunerator	franc-tireur	prosthetics
second-floor	exasperator	connoisseur	epigenetics
surrenderor	recuperator	provocateur	cybernetics
predecessor	vituperator	littérateur	geopolitics
intercessor	adulterator	slave-labour	meteoritics
vasopressor	deflagrator	three-colour	stereoptics
expromissor	conspirator	stone-colour	linguistics
perturbator	edulcorator	mouse-colour	diagnostics
masturbator	invigorator	snuff-colour	diacoustics
adjudicator	stump-orator	flesh-colour	aquanautics
trafficator	perpetrator	multicolour	aeronautics
pacificator	infiltrator	monticolour	chars-à-bancs

hinderlands	chain-plates	aposiopesis	prostatitis
petropounds	ascomycetes	catachresis	sclerotitis
churchwards	Zygomycetes	synchoresis	periostitis
schoolwards	Myxomycetes	diaphoresis	stephanotis
heavenwards	pantalettes	ecblastesis	sarcocystis
netherwards	troglodytes	anagnorisis	anaphylaxis
hitherwards	harbour-dues	peristalsis	prophylaxis
streetwards	interleaves	canariensis	paraphraxis
prothoraces	wring-staves	anthracosis	orthopraxis
farm-offices	torch-staves	psittacosis	stereotaxis
antihelices	executrixes	syssarcosis	trophotaxis
mediatrices	spindle-legs	sarcoidosis	phyllotaxis
directrices	furnishings	homozygosis	thermotaxis
executrices	hinderlings	necrobiosis	heterotaxis
Actinomyces	netherlings	gnotobiosis	spondulicks
proboscides	May-meetings	synoeciosis	tarry-breeks
chrysalides	gas-fittings	coccidiosis	pilniewinks
lanthanides	oyster-tongs	bacteriosis	copper-works
cantharides	necropoleis	brucellosis	pontificals
ephemerides	Kulturkreis	spirillosis	theatricals
Paradoxides	lumbricalis	anadiplosis	grease-heels
port-charges	fleurs-de-lis	pediculosis	bevel-wheels
dead-clothes	torticollis	anastomosis	Tattersall's
long-clothes	megalopolis	syndesmosis	choir-stalls
type-species	table-tennis	biocoenosis	patent-rolls
superficies	Ichthyornis	trichinosis	nautch-girls
butterflies	tous-les-mois	hyperinosis	John-a-dreams
halfpennies	avoirdupois	hypotyposis	compendiums
twalpennies	Cephalaspis	bromidrosis	moratoriums
hostilities	Hydrocharis	anaplerosis	colloquiums
death-duties	orbicularis	metachrosis	smithereens
sweepstakes	Pedicularis	diarthrosis	curly-greens
Equisetales	Apollinaris	enarthrosis	widdershins
immoveables	doch-an-doris	aponeurosis	withershins
lady-trifles	candidiasis	gliomatosis	od's-bodikins
snow-goggles	phthiriasis	lipomatosis	od's-pitikins
otherwhiles	osteoclasis	myxomatosis	autochthons
fiançailles	metaphrasis	parasitosis	responsions
long-purples	periphrasis	epanalepsis	octahedrons
animalcules	antiphrasis	parablepsis	wellingtons
seldom-times	haemostasis	monoblepsis	peccadillos
plainstanes	iconostasis	paraleipsis	paranephros
subimagines	synanthesis	xerotripsis	Rhamphastos
impetigines	parenthesis	thanatopsis	corbie-steps
bloody-bones	anaesthesis	eremacausis	potato-chips
Struthiones	cenesthesis	hyperacusis	thwartships
barge-stones	hyperemesis	emphyteusis	contretemps
plainstones	paragenesis	diapophysis	shock-troops
ambuscadoes	metagenesis	proteolysis	storm-troops
reformadoes	perigenesis	thermolysis	triceratops
desperadoes	abiogenesis	plasmolysis	eurodollars
orbiculares	hylogenesis	haemoptysis	fivefingers
carpospores	gamogenesis	thyroiditis	Coulommiers
Grallatores	homogenesis	mastoiditis	frighteners
periphrases	xenogenesis	parotiditis	nose-nippers
parentheses	monogenesis	myocarditis	lotus-eaters
proboscises	merogenesis	salpingitis	outquarters
chrysalises	ectogenesis	pharyngitis	self-affairs
anastomoses	ontogenesis	tonsillitis	belowstairs
gladioluses	autogenesis	spondylitis	millefleurs
ignoramuses	cytogenesis	staphylitis	second-class
narcissuses	polygenesis	pneumonitis	middle-class
apparatuses	telekinesis	peritonitis	master-class
diapophyses	autokinesis	blepharitis	bottle-glass

minute-glass	meaningless	belatedness	profaneness
tiring-glass	stomachless	relatedness	germaneness
cheval-glass	scratchless	limitedness	obsceneness
garden-glass	stretchless	exaltedness	genuineness
finger-glass	Sabbathless	stiltedness	unawareness
object-glass	victualless	pointedness	sincereness
pocket-glass	fushionless	stintedness	austereness
toilet-glass	passionless	stuntedness	obscureness
window-glass	emotionless	devotedness	preciseness
gallowglass	portionless	spottedness	conciseness
brandy-glass	worshipless	subduedness	immenseness
leaguer-lass	slumberless	removedness	intenseness
servant-lass	thunderless	renewedness	verboseness
hunting-mass	shelterless	unfixedness	operoseness
gyrocompass	harbourless	unstaidness	adverseness
guinea-grass	succourless	flaccidness	diffuseness
tussac-grass	flavourless	squalidness	profuseness
orange-grass	successless	invalidness	recluseness
sesame-grass	respectless	insipidness	mediateness
rescue-grass	suspectless	languidness	prolateness
quitch-grass	delightless	twofoldness	cognateness
twitch-grass	sprightless	unsoundness	privateness
bottom-grass	thoughtless	dastardness	repleteness
ribbon-grass	conceitless	awkwardness	hirsuteness
cotton-grass	servantless	frowardness	obliqueness
finger-grass	garmentless	forwardness	antiqueness
pepper-grass	contentless	outwardness	brusqueness
clover-grass	comfortless	waywardness	forgiveness
pampas-grass	supportless	strangeness	suasiveness
millet-grass	purportless	warlikeness	evasiveness
meadow-grass	exhaustless	pliableness	pensiveness
monkey-grass	eyebrowless	amiableness	massiveness
canary-grass	victoryless	friableness	passiveness
scurvy-grass	prosaicness	salableness	abusiveness
jury-process	graphicness	tenableness	amusiveness
demigoddess	franticness	tunableness	amativeness
moon-goddess	elasticness	capableness	furtiveness
shepherdess	moon-madness	curableness	restiveness
archduchess	horn-madness	durableness	costiveness
trafficless	scabbedness	notableness	nothingness
husbandless	crabbedness	mutableness	smilingness
garlandless	roundedness	equableness	willingness
serviceless	guardedness	savableness	seemingness
defenceless	shaggedness	movableness	shiningness
offenceless	craggedness	docibleness	winningness
vantageless	parchedness	audibleness	cunningness
revengeless	loathedness	legibleness	fawningness
nonetheless	studiedness	visibleness	glaringness
perfumeless	hurriedness	ignobleness	sparingness
confineless	crookedness	volubleness	meltingness
fortuneless	settledness	fragileness	lastingness
sceptreless	ashamedness	pensileness	flowingness
verdureless	untamedness	subtileness	knowingness
measureless	feignedness	ductileness	undyingness
featureless	refinedness	brittleness	staunchness
cultureless	learnedness	supremeness	caddishness
raptureless	kindredness	sublimeness	faddishness
pastureless	retiredness	welcomeness	reddishness
textureless	assuredness	awesomeness	wordishness
promiseless	debasedness	noisomeness	prudishness
purposeless	advisedness	irksomeness	raffishness
reverseless	reposedness	fulsomeness	toffishness
remorseless	exposedness	winsomeness	huffishness
requiteless	blessedness	lissomeness	selfishness

waggishness	grouchiness	squattiness	foreignness
piggishness	squashiness	shadowiness	forlornness
doggishness	breathiness	seasickness	unknownness
hoggishness	lengthiness	cubicalness	marchioness
snakishness	healthiness	radicalness	championess
peckishness	wealthiness	logicalness	unclearness
sickishness	swarthiness	comicalness	slenderness
pinkishness	drouthiness	finicalness	endlessness
bookishness	streakiness	cynicalness	godlessness
duskishness	squeakiness	stoicalness	uselessness
luskishness	unluckiness	typicalness	awelessness
mawkishness	treacliness	musicalness	leglessness
hellishness	worldliness	cordialness	aimlessness
dollishness	ungodliness	trivialness	sinlessness
bullishness	shapeliness	literalness	sunlessness
foolishness	stateliness	naturalness	haplessness
girlishness	thingliness	sensualness	saplessness
stylishness	fleshliness	unusualness	toplessness
swinishness	deathliness	factualness	hatlessness
mannishness	loathliness	genteelness	witlessness
tonnishness	earthliness	gladfulness	artlessness
nunnishness	prickliness	heedfulness	lawlessness
dronishness	cleanliness	needfulness	sexlessness
dampishness	unmanliness	mindfulness	joylessness
rompishness	womanliness	wakefulness	expressness
dumpishness	queenliness	balefulness	submissness
lumpishness	elderliness	dolefulness	gibbousness
mumpishness	orderliness	banefulness	viscousness
foppishness	miserliness	tunefulness	raucousness
waspishness	sightliness	hopefulness	hideousness
bearishness	saintliness	carefulness	hugeousness
whorishness	courtliness	direfulness	gaseousness
boorishness	beastliness	fatefulness	piteousness
currishness	ghastliness	hatefulness	duteousness
missishness	bristliness	songfulness	dubiousness
goatishness	ghostliness	bashfulness	viciousness
whitishness	streaminess	wishfulness	tediousness
saltishness	uncanniness	pushfulness	biliousness
doltishness	scrimpiness	pitifulness	copiousness
pettishness	unhappiness	dutifulness	variousness
sottishness	scrappiness	skilfulness	seriousness
loutishness	primariness	soulfulness	curiousness
brutishness	summariness	brimfulness	furiousness
roguishness	pepperiness	harmfulness	obviousness
slavishness	silveriness	branfulness	deviousness
knavishness	showeriness	gainfulness	enviousness
peevishness	floweriness	painfulness	anxiousness
wheyishness	cursoriness	helpfulness	noxiousness
uncouthness	elusoriness	fearfulness	jealousness
shrubbiness	savouriness	tearfulness	zealousness
threadiness	tricksiness	overfulness	callousness
unreadiness	leg-business	fretfulness	emulousness
unhandiness	throatiness	hurtfulness	heinousness
scruffiness	fidgetiness	restfulness	ominousness
scragginess	ricketiness	zestfulness	ruinousness
springiness	velvetiness	wistfulness	pompousness
stringiness	thriftiness	lustfulness	onerousness
preachiness	weightiness	playfulness	odorousness
Frenchiness	flightiness	uniformness	amorousness
raunchiness	haughtiness	uncleanness	riotousness
crunchiness	naughtiness	betweenness	vacuousness
starchiness	doughtiness	druckenness	nocuousness
sketchiness	thirstiness	drunkenness	arduousness
blotchiness	frowstiness	condignness	tenuousness

sinuousness	undershorts	tuberaceous	inconscious
fatuousness	towing-bitts	piperaceous	unconscious
nervousness	palmyra-nuts	cyperaceous	coconscious
gallowsness	whereabouts	onagraceous	overtedious
compactness	micrococcus	arboraceous	uninvidious
inexactness	Protococcus	papyraceous	compendious
perfectness	cysticercus	butyraceous	stupendious
correctness	Machaerodus	mimosaceous	unmelodious
unquietness	Machairodus	amentaceous	unreligious
uprightness	Lepidosteus	sapotaceous	irreligious
illicitness	sarcophagus	chartaceous	prestigious
glaikitness	cardophagus	crustaceous	atrabilious
defiantness	cunnilingus	chlamydeous	antibilious
gallantness	slime-fungus	demiurgeous	punctilious
distantness	physiologus	membraneous	ignominious
buoyantness	oxyrhynchus	subitaneous	symphonious
ancientness	Tragelaphus	spontaneous	ceremonious
currentness	apostrophus	homogeneous	acrimonious
presentness	Tyroglyphus	albugineous	antimonious
corruptness	scrub-typhus	stramineous	impecunious
earnestness	calycanthus	sanguineous	urticarious
shallowness	Schizanthus	subvitreous	omnifarious
complexness	interradius	sulphureous	burglarious
farawayness	septenarius	unrighteous	temerarious
winter-cress	Sagittarius	uncourteous	contrarious
bitter-cress	Straduarius	terraqueous	opprobrious
swine's-cress	ithyphallus	meliphagous	facinerious
battledress	Craterellus	toxiphagous	jocoserious
diving-dress	aspergillus	endophagous	deleterious
life-peeress	canaliculus	theophagous	unlaborious
hucksteress	ventriculus	creophagous	gressorious
superioress	dracunculus	hylophagous	meritorious
cheese-press	Convolvulus	xylophagous	industrious
bramah-press	Nostradamus	monophagous	illustrious
cotton-press	borborygmus	autophagous	unluxurious
letterpress	laryngismus	polyphagous	cunctatious
racket-press	parabolanus	xiphopagous	temptatious
spectatress	Pentacrinus	noctivagous	flirtatious
detractress	laurustinus	tautologous	unambitious
play-actress	monothecous	calcifugous	expeditious
inspectress	noctilucous	multijugous	cineritious
protectress	splendidous	callipygous	lateritious
conductress	multifidous	ulotrichous	icteritious
inhabitress	tetrapodous	tristichous	ablatitious
inheritress	amphipodous	diadelphous	repetitious
expositress	sauropodous	anamorphous	ascititious
enchantress	unhazardous	trimorphous	addititious
precentress	blizzardous	isomorphous	tendentious
preceptress	salicaceous	syngnathous	dissentious
supportress	punicaceous	prognathous	pretentious
upholstress	urticaceous	rhizanthous	sententious
coadjutress	cycadaceous	helminthous	contentious
adventuress	xyridaceous	triphibious	carnaptious
viscountess	ostreaceous	scribacious	curnaptious
second-guess	proteaceous	efficacious	conceptious
double-cross	spathaceous	incapacious	scrumptious
market-cross	araliaceous	unveracious	combustious
herring-buss	scoriaceous	disgracious	rumbustious
blunderbuss	ferulaceous	injudicious	precautious
manna-groats	alismaceous	veneficious	over-anxious
sternsheets	solanaceous	inofficious	unobnoxious
first-fruits	farinaceous	unofficious	thelytokous
smartypants	rhamnaceous	unmalicious	dicephalous
men-servants	saponaceous	tendencious	encephalous

episepalous
epipetalous
tripetalous
sympetalous
halophilous
xylophilous
ammophilous
xerophilous
umbratilous
cerebellous
varicellous
quarrellous
tendrillous
epiphyllous
triphyllous
ametabolous
amphibolous
calcicolous
piscicolous
caulicolous
arenicolous
terricolous
nudicaulous
folliculous
vermiculous
somniculous
monticulous
carunculous
furunculous
tuberculous
incredulous
untremulous
cavernulous
scaberulous
perichylous
endochylous
didactylous
hippodamous
hercogamous
dichogamous
phenogamous
hypergamous
blasphemous
longanimous
magnanimous
multanimous
lithodomous
catadromous
katadromous
dichotomous
lithotomous
diathermous
teknonymous
tautonymous
polyonymous
cymophanous
autophanous
athermanous
cauligenous
terrigenous
osteogenous
pathogenous
lithogenous
hypnogenous

hydrogenous
sporogenous
saprogenous
nitrogenous
erotogenous
rhizogenous
intravenous
mountainous
torpedinous
lumbaginous
farraginous
serpiginous
porriginous
pruriginous
lentiginous
tentiginous
vertiginous
vortiginous
ferruginous
salsuginous
monoclinous
inquilinous
tetragonous
cacophonous
homophonous
phlegmonous
diachronous
anachronous
trichronous
synchronous
isochronous
horrisonous
tetragynous
pentagynous
heptagynous
philogynous
androgynous
protogynous
hemitropous
allotropous
xylocarpous
monocarpous
polycarpous
nulliparous
primiparous
gemmiparous
uniparous
fissiparous
multiparous
larviparous
unslumbrous
enneandrous
tetrandrous
icosandrous
pentandrous
protandrous
heptandrous
polyandrous
imponderous
bulbiferous
morbiferous
bacciferous
calciferous
zinciferous

furciferous
cruciferous
frugiferous
lethiferous
zinkiferous
cheliferous
celliferous
melliferous
proliferous
ovuliferous
styliferous
culmiferous
mammiferous
gemmiferous
gummiferous
glumiferous
guaniferous
spiniferous
uriniferous
somniferous
manniferous
ozoniferous
corniferous
umbriferous
odoriferous
floriferous
cupriferous
ferriferous
yttriferous
thuriferous
dorsiferous
lactiferous
septiferous
mortiferous
pestiferous
guttiferous
calcigerous
crucigerous
plumigerous
spinigerous
crinigerous
cornigerous
scapigerous
dentigerous
clavigerous
treacherous
tetramerous
pentamerous
heptamerous
homeomerous
oligomerous
pleiomerous
anisomerous
congenerous
hemipterous
homopterous
sepulchrous
splendorous
adiaphorous
Eriophorous
pyrophorous
phosphorous
pot-valorous
tubiflorous

unicolorous
concolorous
homosporous
herbivorous
baccivorous
piscivorous
frugivorous
mellivorous
vermivorous
granivorous
lignivorous
carnivorous
monolatrous
triquetrous
thysanurous
adventurous
brachyurous
sarcomatous
adenomatous
scotomatous
rhizomatous
disquietous
duplicitous
precipitous
necessitous
obliquitous
acclivitous
declivitous
ligamentous
filamentous
atramentous
pedetentous
entophytous
conspicuous
perspicuous
promiscuous
indeciduous
unambiguous
dulcifluous
mellifluous
lactifluous
superfluous
interfluous
incongruous
anfractuous
infructuous
unfructuous
torrentuous
tempestuous
mischievous
hippocampus
Uranoscopus
Eoanthropus
Hydnocarpus
papovavirus
enterovirus
Istiophorus
Teleosaurus
Ceteosaurus
Stegosaurus
Apatosaurus
tibiotarsus
illuminatus
hircocervus

urchin-shows	straight-jet	overfreight	custom-built
breadthways	hurly-hacket	pound-weight	shackle-bolt
Pterichthys	shell-jacket	underweight	through-bolt
fleurs-de-lys	steam-jacket	paper-weight	thunderbolt
T	water-jacket	lightweight	strike-fault
mountain-cat	pilot-jacket	pennyweight	double-fault
spring-wheat	steam-packet	heavyweight	trough-fault
prickly-heat	mole-cricket	muffin-fight	umbrella-ant
sausage-meat	balm-cricket	pillow-fight	prejudicant
witches'-meat	smart-ticket	apple-blight	significant
hunting-seat	out-of-pocket	self-delight	communicant
pillion-seat	patch-pocket	candle-light	reciprocant
ejector-seat	watch-pocket	riding-light	extravagant
country-seat	retro-rocket	searchlight	noctivagant
bloody-sweat	dyer's-rocket	troth-plight	interrogant
you-know-what	overblanket	streetlight	intrenchant
proletariat	flesh-market	yesternight	law-merchant
secretariat	black-market	stage-fright	sea-elephant
service-flat	stock-market	mother-right	pad-elephant
monochromat	supermarket	patent-right	tire-valiant
passage-boat	hypermarket	wheelwright	incompliant
incense-boat	money-market	wagon-wright	uncompliant
vedette-boat	bread-basket	second-sight	unluxuriant
sailing-boat	siege-basket	fire-flaught	horripilant
berthon-boat	plate-basket	dreadnaught	surveillant
torpedo-boat	waste-basket	back-draught	scintillant
liberty-boat	trout-basket	down-draught	switch-plant
hacking-coat	pearl-millet	overdraught	contemplant
scratch-coat	fractionlet	full-fraught	cotton-plant
swagger-coat	ultraviolet	overfraught	oyster-plant
leather-coat	water-violet	blood-bought	proclaimant
whitethroat	dame's-violet	free-thought	transhumant
pantisocrat	smoke-helmet	forethought	undertenant
pedantocrat	crash-helmet	dreadnought	appurtenant
kangaroo-rat	white-bonnet	handwrought	joint-tenant
subcontract	cross-garnet	highwrought	unbenignant
precontract	field-cornet	overwrought	unrepugnant
malt-extract	stair-carpet	riding-habit	complainant
stage-effect	reinterpret	paper-credit	recombinant
after-effect	stair-turret	motor-bandit	contaminant
word-perfect	disulphuret	self-conceit	subdominant
circumflect	earth-closet	counterfeit	predominant
self-neglect	water-closet	sick-benefit	determinant
circumspect	wringing-wet	double-digit	agglutinant
overcorrect	paddle-shaft	tightly-knit	horrisonant
palmatisect	upcast-shaft	haematocrit	multisonant
pinnatisect	needlecraft	proof-spirit	inconsonant
scale-insect	speechcraft	water-spirit	participant
stick-insect	stitchcraft	party-spirit	preoccupant
subdistrict	schoolcraft	safe-deposit	reverberant
safe-conduct	screencraft	open-circuit	protuberant
agriproduct	mothercraft	rice-biscuit	refrigerant
misinstruct	authorcraft	wine-biscuit	intemperant
reconstruct	priestcraft	ship-biscuit	perseverant
superstruct	heterograft	belle-de-nuit	conflagrant
spinach-beet	nothing-gift	bathing-suit	corroborant
groundsheet	morning-gift	trouser-suit	pig-ignorant
charge-sheet	festschrift	supplicavit	expectorant
winter-sweet	spendthrift	plume-pluckt	auld-farrant
bittersweet	rigging-loft	pissasphalt	dock-warrant
meadow-sweet	landsknecht	plough-stilt	sequestrant
water-bouget	Fehmgericht	square-built	remonstrant
shoe-latchet	Vehmgericht	carvel-built	displeasant
turbo-ram-jet	dead-freight	system-built	complaisant

incognisant	restringent	divergement	nourishment
suppressant	rubefacient	engorgement	betrothment
supernatant	calefacient	provokement	intendiment
interactant	tumefacient	disablement	dissepiment
inexpectant	inefficient	entablement	concealment
unexpectant	coefficient	brabblement	congealment
unreluctant	inconscient	tremblement	enthralment
concubitant	disobedient	ennoblement	empanelment
resuscitant	inexpedient	dwindlement	apparelment
regurgitant	transilient	compilement	unravelment
concomitant	unexperient	beguilement	embowelment
precipitant	omnipatient	tracklement	engrailment
unrepentant	presentient	condolement	curtailment
unimportant	consentient	consolement	prevailment
equidistant	dissentient	entitlement	despoilment
inobservant	subservient	prattlement	embroilment
unobservant	transcalent	contenement	imperilment
maid-servant	tetravalent	confinement	bedevilment
bondservant	pentavalent	estrepement	installment
body-servant	multivalent	acquirement	controlment
clairvoyant	equipollent	requirement	chastenment
superjacent	overviolent	arbitrement	enlivenment
interjacent	somnivolent	procurement	bedizenment
magnificent	pulverulent	obscurement	arraignment
glaucescent	predicament	conjurement	realignment
lapidescent	amerciament	measurement	consignment
viridescent	disarmament	subbasement	enchainment
frondescent	temperament	surbasement	detrainment
acquiescent	arbitrament	releasement	entrainment
recalescent	disbandment	appeasement	containment
incalescent	commandment	incensement	sustainment
alkalescent	reamendment	endorsement	abandonment
virilescent	impoundment	restatement	environment
obsolescent	astoundment	instatement	concernment
acaulescent	bombardment	emboîtement	discernment
intumescent	discardment	requitement	adjournment
juvenescent	defraudment	rabattement	sojournment
luminescent	enjambement	confutement	development
concrescent	replacement	bereavement	envelopment
arborescent	emplacement	enslavement	overgarment
fluorescent	embracement	depravement	cashierment
delitescent	empiecement	achievement	reinterment
obmutescent	rejoicement	deprivement	flusterment
languescent	enhancement	devolvement	embowerment
revivescent	advancement	involvement	self-torment
indehiscent	water-cement	premovement	impressment
reminiscent	deforcement	improvement	engrossment
resipiscent	afforcement	enfeoffment	escheatment
reviviscent	enforcement	dislodgment	entreatment
noctilucent	divorcement	prejudgment	re-enactment
translucent	traducement	misjudgment	projectment
retrocedent	conducement	impeachment	engraftment
intercedent	producement	appeachment	benightment
non-resident	presagement	bewitchment	recruitment
self-evident	assuagement	debauchment	enchantment
improvident	abridgement	debouchment	presentment
unprovident	adjudgement	refreshment	contentment
resplendent	besiegement	abolishment	attainment
independent	derangement	blemishment	appointment
prescindent	arrangement	evanishment	recountment
double-agent	revengement	garnishment	reallotment
queen-regent	unhingement	burnishment	compartment
intelligent	impingement	furnishment	comportment
tassell-gent	enlargement	cherishment	supportment

disportment	running-knot	phonemicist	logomachist
dismastment	gallows-foot	historicist	Petrarchist
encrustment	sulphur-root	phoneticist	heptarchist
entrustment	biscuit-root	Atlanticist	panpsychist
re-endowment	watering-pot	semanticist	epigraphist
forepayment	shell-parrot	romanticist	zoographist
cash-payment	self-concept	orthopedist	myographist
overpayment	nondescript	chiropodist	theosophist
part-payment	superscript	scarabaeist	telepathist
impermanent	thunder-dart	poltergeist	antipathist
incontinent	lonely-heart	mythopoeist	allopathist
impertinent	bottle-chart	mycophagist	hylopathist
appertinent	walking-part	sacrilegist	Plymouthist
grandparent	counterpart	genealogist	syndicalist
houseparent	foot-lambert	mammalogist	clericalist
transparent	café-concert	tribologist	physicalist
indifferent	parsley-pert	garbologist	madrigalist
belligerent	undercovert	phycologist	colonialist
bloodsprent	riding-skirt	paedologist	imperialist
omnipresent	counter-fort	teleologist	materialist
incompetent	kinchin-mort	museologist	memorialist
self-content	whaling-port	osteologist	diluvialist
plenipotent	self-support	nephologist	criminalist
multipotent	sea-colewort	pathologist	regionalist
inadvertent	rupturewort	lithologist	nationalist
pre-existent	sea-milkwort	anthologist	rationalist
non-existent	bladderwort	mythologist	notionalist
unremittent	slipperwort	sociologist	personalist
mellifluent	sulphurwort	radiologist	externalist
interfluent	swallow-wort	audiologist	communalist
incongruent	whitlow-wort	hagiologist	cerebralist
deobstruent	police-court	ophiologist	pastoralist
substituent	church-court	Mariologist	neovitalist
constituent	tennis-court	philologist	Orientalist
finger-paint	racket-court	hoplologist	punctualist
unrestraint	rebroadcast	gemmologist	medievalist
pillar-saint	counter-cast	cosmologist	parallelist
preacquaint	rother-beast	etymologist	philatelist
stifle-joint	unsteadfast	phenologist	waiting-list
toggle-joint	hard-and-fast	poenologist	probabilist
master-joint	flabbergast	ethnologist	possibilist
rabbet-joint	phantasiast	rhinologist	notaphilist
needle-point	pancratiast	limnologist	canophilist
fusing-point	trophoblast	hymnologist	oenophilist
strongpoint	megaloblast	iconologist	facsimilist
school-point	gonimoblast	phonologist	footballist
silver-point	odontoblast	hippologist	bimetallist
honour-point	chromoplast	acarologist	aquarellist
fingerprint	chloroplast	necrologist	vitraillist
butter-print	Elastoplast ®	micrologist	pointillist
electrotint	mooring-mast	hydrologist	protocolist
rhynchodont	gynaecomast	hierologist	funambulist
diprotodont	foretopmast	chirologist	hairstylist
anaerobiont	maintopmast	chorologist	hippodamist
cash-account	rascalliest	metrologist	panislamist
book-account	hedge-priest	petrologist	love-in-a-mist
cost-account	underhonest	neurologist	pantomimist
scattershot	overearnest	pestologist	Soroptimist
tessaraglot	disinterest	histologist	ophthalmist
branch-pilot	disafforest	tautologist	plutonomist
counter-plot	house-arrest	plutologist	dichotomist
witenagemot	pre-conquest	phytologist	lithotomist
forget-me-not	theophobist	Maryologist	microtomist
Jacqueminot	supremacist	theomachist	phytotomist

taxidermist
panspermist
Americanist
Europeanist
tobogganist
Priscianist
Novatianist
adoptianist
accompanist
miscegenist
phenomenist
clavecinist
masculinist
determinist
Byzantinist
tobacconist
Napoleonist
tritagonist
protagonist
cosmogonist
telephonist
xylophonist
saxophonist
polyphonist
coercionist
religionist
non-unionist
disunionist
revisionist
delusionist
illusionist
vacationist
creationist
negationist
relationist
mutationist
reactionist
petitionist
devotionist
adoptionist
abortionist
questionist
solutionist
carillonist
eudaemonist
monopsonist
opportunist
philogynist
galley-foist
landscapist
telescopist
horoscopist
touch-typist
audio-typist
stenotypist
phonotypist
calendarist
singularist
Mekhitarist
voluntarist
equilibrist
verslibrist
Septembrist
artillerist

consumerist
plein-airist
adiaphorist
metaphorist
paed?atrist
hippiatrist
hexametrist
optometrist
bellettrist
miniaturist
adventurist
scripturist
epigenesist
photo-resist
progressist
speculatist
emblematist
suprematist
systematist
diplomatist
numismatist
democratist
corporatist
prosthetist
portraitist
Sanskritist
Esperantist
irredentist
ornamentist
immanentist
Bonapartist
aquafortist
novelettist
parachutist
institutist
monologuist
Gargantuist
exclusivist
objectivist
detectivist
primitivist
ideopraxist
unbeknownst
easternmost
westernmost
weathermost
farthermost
northermost
furthermost
southermost
rubbing-post
staging-post
winning-post
pendant-post
tempest-tost
underthirst
groundburst
honey-locust
diamond-dust
Nothofagust
underthrust
brains-trust
scuttle-butt
straight-cut

silkworm-gut
open-and-shut
sapucaia-nut
clearing-nut
quandong-nut
wassail-bout
rinthereout
stopping-out
counting-out
cold-without
whiting-pout
salmon-trout
straight-out
double-stout
U
Politbureau
portmanteau
W
wappenschaw
weapon-schaw
jinrickshaw
clapperclaw
father-in-law
mother-in-law
sister-in-law
counterdraw
windlestraw
cheese-straw
wheat-mildew
mountain-dew
grandnephew
great-nephew
counter-view
stone-curlew
Bartholomew
merry-andrew
water-meadow
sound-shadow
gable-window
wheel-window
oriel-window
storm-window
Judas-window
dak-bungalow
counter-blow
sea-furbelow
counter-glow
marshmallow
wood-swallow
blackfellow
class-fellow
lemon-yellow
king's-yellow
sweet-willow
pussywillow
carrion-crow
stone's-throw
wheelbarrow
drill-barrow
hoverbarrow
drill-harrow
chain-harrow
reed-sparrow
song-sparrow

cock-sparrow
rock-sparrow
X
sceuophylax
hydrothorax
thoroughwax
paraffin-wax
plano-convex
negotiatrix
consolatrix
speculatrix
arbitratrix
proprietrix
progenitrix
life-rentrix
prosecutrix
prolocutrix
Eurypharynx
stuffing-box
dredging-box
sembling-box
tumbling-box
coupling-box
shooting-box
dispatch-box
fricandeaux
Clarencieux
billets-doux
chalcedonyx
Y
loblolly-bay
settling-day
visiting-day
trysting-day
half-holiday
bank-holiday
contango-day
transfer-day
judgment-day
boulder-clay
picture-play
Passion-play
mystery-play
clanjamfray
home-and-away
carriageway
steerage-way
out-of-the-way
cash-railway
rack-railway
ship-railway
straightway
prolificacy
diathermacy
determinacy
importunacy
ptochocracy
physiocracy
technocracy
demonocracy
chrysocracy
ergatocracy
stratocracy
meritocracy

plantocracy	infrequency	volcanology	scenography
aristocracy	delinquency	vulcanology	stenography
bureaucracy	chieftaincy	campanology	ichnography
confederacy	heterocercy	lichenology	ethnography
cosmopolicy	paramountcy	sphagnology	hymnography
discordancy	walking-lady	arachnology	iconography
physiciancy	leaguer-lady	carcinology	phonography
rhabdomancy	chick-a-biddy	criminology	pornography
onychomancy	tragi-comedy	terminology	micrography
crithomancy	tetraploidy	eccrinology	hydrography
bibliomancy	pentaploidy	sindonology	hierography
botanomancy	scrimshandy	gnomonology	chirography
tephromancy	peach-brandy	meteorology	chorography
cheiromancy	daring-hardy	electrology	reprography
oneiromancy	nature-study	spectrology	ferrography
gastromancy	water-monkey	martyrology	petrography
lieutenancy	scrub-turkey	perissology	hypsography
concernancy	brush-turkey	eschatology	pictography
discrepancy	pearl-barley	haematology	hyetography
conversancy	lamp-chimney	dogmatology	pantography
inhabitancy	hearth-money	climatology	photography
exorbitancy	ration-money	primatology	cartography
incogitancy	pocket-money	stomatology	dittography
consultancy	blind-storey	dermatology	phytography
accountancy	multistorey	thanatology	tachygraphy
inconstancy	disyllabify	olfactology	paedotrophy
irrelevancy	foresignify	insectology	hypertrophy
conservancy	presanctify	cosmetology	gastrosophy
flamboyancy	ostreophagy	planetology	stasimorphy
coadjacency	entomophagy	herpetology	homeomorphy
complacency	pyroballogy	gigantology	photoglyphy
connascency	amphibology	Scientology	kinesipathy
erubescency	gynaecology	gerontology	homoeopathy
turgescency	myrmecology	Christology	psychopathy
excrescency	synoecology	agrostology	naturopathy
liquescency	Etruscology	reflexology	unseaworthy
coincidency	orchidology	ichthyology	shameworthy
despondency	pteridology	Titanomachy	blameworthy
respondency	methodology	orthostichy	quoteworthy
refringency	archaeology	squirearchy	laughworthy
astringency	spelaeology	water-souchy	faithworthy
contingency	pantheology	choregraphy	thankworthy
convergency	venereology	calligraphy	sightworthy
sufficiency	phraseology	snobography	trustworthy
proficiency	laryngology	zincography	knick-knacky
prosiliency	ornithology	discography	pilgarlicky
conveniency	cine-biology	osteography	rheumaticky
concipiency	aerobiology	pathography	jabberwocky
percipiency	agrobiology	lithography	arrhenotoky
insentiency	cryobiology	orthography	mackerel-sky
ambivalency	endemiology	mythography	logodaedaly
equivalency	malariology	radiography	anencephaly
monovalency	soteriology	hagiography	mesocephaly
prepollency	Assyriology	angiography	autocephaly
fraudulency	semasiology	heliography	rectipetaly
vicegerency	kinesiology	sialography	practicably
incoherency	heresiology	pyelography	irrevocably
concurrency	syphilology	haplography	unavoidably
inappetency	vexillology	stylography	commendably
impenitency	diabolology	filmography	serviceably
omnipotency	symbolology	mammography	unshakeably
idempotency	dactylology	dermography	unblameably
consistency	sphygmology	cosmography	impermeably
persistency	victimology	uranography	immitigably

unmitigably	susceptibly	importunely	tentatively
innavigably	corruptibly	opportunely	privatively
appreciably	convertibly	insincerely	defectively
dissociably	disassembly	unleisurely	affectively
certifiably	irresolubly	prematurely	effectively
justifiably	impoliticly	bellicosely	objectively
unweariably	perturbedly	grandiosely	adjectively
unspeakably	barefacedly	lacrimosely	selectively
unavailably	pigheadedly	lacrymosely	invectively
reclaimably	unimpededly	intricately	deductively
inestimably	undecidedly	aggregately	reductively
inflammably	misguidedly	immediately	seductively
conformably	undividedly	insatiately	inductively
inalienably	offhandedly	umbellately	secretively
unalienably	pretendedly	inviolately	primitively
impregnably	unboundedly	proximately	cognitively
indefinably	unfoundedly	pectinately	nutritively
fashionably	unguardedly	obstinately	sensitively
treasonably	debauchedly	festinately	partitively
unstoppably	qualifiedly	alternately	intuitively
irreparably	unweariedly	fortunately	attuitively
inseparably	unhurriedly	disparately	retentively
intolerably	unsettledly	temperately	attentively
denumerably	unashamedly	desperately	inventively
innumerably	unfeignedly	elaborately	plaintively
insuperably	sustainedly	corporately	deceptively
unalterably	abandonedly	insensately	irruptively
unutterably	unlearnedly	decussately	assertively
undesirably	concernedly	exquisitely	digestively
unendurably	scatteredly	dissolutely	resistively
pleasurably	surprisedly	grotesquely	executively
unadvisably	disguisedly	pervasively	reflexively
dispensably	unadvisedly	repulsively	scorpion-fly
conversably	dispersedly	impulsively	throbbingly
unaccusably	unbiassedly	expansively	absorbingly
irrecusably	confessedly	defensively	embracingly
inexcusably	professedly	offensively	rejoicingly
unpalatably	undoubtedly	expensively	traducingly
intractably	compactedly	intensively	spreadingly
respectably	collectedly	ostensively	exceedingly
indubitably	connectedly	extensively	unheedingly
illimitably	suspectedly	explosively	confidingly
indomitably	delightedly	corrosively	unbendingly
inequitably	conceitedly	extorsively	dependingly
warrantably	unlimitedly	decursively	accordingly
presentably	unmeritedly	excursively	swingeingly
accountably	tormentedly	impassively	besiegingly
comfortably	contentedly	recessively	revengingly
supportably	untaintedly	excessively	divergingly
regrettably	undauntedly	diffusively	flinchingly
irrefutably	purportedly	inclusively	searchingly
inscrutably	disgustedly	exclusively	scorchingly
retrievably	continuedly	prelusively	snatchingly
conceivably	perplexedly	collusively	vanishingly
perceivably	northwardly	obtrusively	perishingly
irremovably	southwardly	intrusively	ravishingly
irreducibly	sweet-cicely	purgatively	squeakingly
discernibly	housewifely	talkatively	shriekingly
indivisibly	versatilely	lucratively	shrinkingly
responsibly	unwelcomely	operatively	unwinkingly
repressibly	wholesomely	iteratively	provokingly
permissibly	loathsomely	narratively	appealingly
unplausibly	wearisomely	causatively	quibblingly
perceptibly	masculinely	imitatively	scamblingly

tremblingly	unamusingly	prelusorily	chaotically
grumblingly	carousingly	predatorily	idiotically
stumblingly	inflatingly	prefatorily	osmotically
unfeelingly	animatingly	desultorily	zymotically
shufflingly	affectingly	statutorily	sceptically
twanglingly	expectingly	unsavourily	cryptically
unfailingly	unweetingly	overhastily	elastically
unsmilingly	upliftingly	brainsickly	spastically
beguilingly	blightingly	archaically	drastically
sparklingly	slightingly	Hebraically	deistically
appallingly	revoltingly	prosaically	gnostically
repellingly	insultingly	aerobically	caustically
thrillingly	lamentingly	nomadically	quizzically
unwillingly	repentingly	veridically	equivocally
startlingly	resentingly	juridically	pyramidally
whistlingly	assentingly	fatidically	sigmoidally
scrawlingly	squintingly	synodically	corporeally
screamingly	flauntingly	malefically	adverbially
streamingly	thwartingly	pacifically	connubially
beseemingly	divertingly	mirifically	financially
thrummingly	reportingly	illogically	sympodially
affirmingly	unrestingly	psychically	parochially
presumingly	resistingly	graphically	congenially
unmeaningly	befittingly	angelically	triennially
maddeningly	unfittingly	dynamically	perennially
sickeningly	unwittingly	endemically	octennially
endearingly	struttingly	polemically	sexennially
unsparingly	fatiguingly	thermically	actuarially
jabberingly	depravingly	organically	subaerially
wanderingly	believingly	satanically	uniserially
ponderingly	reprovingly	botanically	amatorially
wonderingly	improvingly	eugenically	pictorially
pilferingly	approvingly	technically	editorially
lingeringly	observingly	laconically	sartorially
witheringly	deservingly	canonically	mercurially
simperingly	unknowingly	chronically	ambrosially
loiteringly	harrowingly	Byronically	essentially
falteringly	unpityingly	spherically	potentially
banteringly	unselfishly	numerically	impartially
pesteringly	fallalishly	generically	celestially
yatteringly	squeamishly	empirically	convivially
potteringly	lickerishly	satirically	baptismally
totteringly	semi-monthly	centrically	medicinally
mutteringly	bibliophily	whimsically	abdominally
slaveringly	entomophily	classically	doctrinally
quaveringly	scripophily	unmusically	abactinally
shiveringly	timbrophily	somatically	octagonally
quiveringly	unhealthily	fanatically	hexagonally
inspiringly	Madonna-lily	venatically	polygonally
inquiringly	superfamily	agnatically	sessionally
deploringly	secondarily	piratically	sectionally
imploringly	pecuniarily	erratically	emotionally
murmuringly	exemplarily	practically	fraternally
vapouringly	customarily	deictically	co-eternally
devouringly	mercenarily	ascetically	eviternally
venturingly	temporarily	eidetically	nocturnally
torturingly	arbitrarily	mimetically	municipally
unceasingly	necessarily	genetically	principally
appeasingly	sedentarily	tonetically	episcopally
promisingly	momentarily	heretically	vertebrally
agonisingly	voluntarily	politically	illiberally
disposingly	tributarily	levitically	puerperally
harassingly	provisorily	frantically	bilaterally
caressingly	accessorily	identically	diametrally

sinistrally	orbicularly	sagaciously	slumbrously
unnaturally	auricularly	salaciously	ludicrously
commensally	reticularly	tenaciously	ponderously
universally	binocularly	capaciously	murderously
dialectally	irregularly	rapaciously	dangerously
acropetally	unpopularly	veraciously	lecherously
occipitally	capitularly	voraciously	dexterously
elementally	unbrotherly	vivaciously	rancorously
segmentally	unsoldierly	judiciously	inodorously
anecdotally	posteriorly	officiously	clamorously
continually	neighbourly	maliciously	glamorously
effectually	dreadlessly	deliciously	monstrously
perpetually	soundlessly	ferociously	murmurously
spiritually	cloudlessly	atrociously	venturously
accentually	gracelessly	consciously	rapturously
unisexually	tracelessly	astuciously	momentously
mediaevally	pricelessly	insidiously	innocuously
genitivally	smokelessly	invidiously	assiduously
peelie-wally	guilelessly	melodiously	ambiguously
yellow-belly	shamelessly	egregiously	ingenuously
ungenteelly	blamelessly	religiously	strenuously
scoundrelly	spinelessly	litigiously	congruously
cuir-bouilly	ceaselessly	ingeniously	impetuously
unheedfully	noiselessly	feloniously	theftuously
unneedfully	senselessly	vicariously	sumptuously
unmindfully	causelessly	nefariously	imperfectly
regardfully	pauselessly	hilariously	unperfectly
changefully	tastelessly	imperiously	incorrectly
rebukefully	matchlessly	deliriously	fortnightly
untunefully	blushlessly	laboriously	maladroitly
unhopefully	faithlessly	notoriously	difficultly
reposefully	mirthlessly	incuriously	redundantly
healthfully	worthlessly	injuriously	accordantly
unpitifully	mercilessly	penuriously	termagantly
plentifully	tracklessly	luxuriously	inelegantly
bountifully	thanklessly	vexatiously	trenchantly
beautifully	sparklessly	fractiously	brilliantly
undutifully	dreamlessly	facetiously	compliantly
unskilfully	charmlessly	ambitiously	suppliantly
unharmfully	stainlessly	seditiously	luxuriantly
sdeignfully	sleeplessly	bumptiously	ungallantly
unfearfully	powerlessly	obliviously	repellantly
wonderfully	doubtlessly	obnoxiously	indignantly
masterfully	shiftlessly	innoxiously	malignantly
wasterfully	sightlessly	troublously	benignantly
prayerfully	limitlessly	libellously	consonantly
forgetfully	fruitlessly	frivolously	dissonantly
regretfully	guiltlessly	oraculously	exuberantly
frightfully	faultlessly	credulously	itinerantly
deceitfully	taintlessly	pendulously	incessantly
resentfully	pointlessly	tremulously	expectantly
unhurtfully	frontlessly	querulously	reluctantly
sorrowfully	dauntlessly	garrulously	repentantly
dismayfully	heartlessly	apogamously	importantly
patricianly	hazardously	unanimously	observantly
Christianly	untimeously	anonymously	decumbently
gentlemanly	erroneously	villanously	recumbently
statesmanly	righteously	larcenously	incumbently
forbiddenly	plenteously	glutinously	quiescently
sovereignly	bounteously	tyrannously	precedently
uncertainly	courteously	poisonously	diffidently
water-supply	beauteously	cavernously	confidently
unscholarly	analogously	barbarously	providently
molecularly	audaciously	oviparously	imprudently

negligently	gastrectomy	coparcenary	chancellery
indulgently	glossectomy	unmercenary	coparcenery
effulgently	hepatectomy	octingenary	cordwainery
stringently	tracheotomy	bimillenary	poltroonery
divergently	myringotomy	bicentenary	Podsnappery
deficiently	syringotomy	concubinary	freebootery
efficiently	laryngotomy	molendinary	self-mastery
presciently	arteriotomy	subordinary	phalanstery
expediently	cephalotomy	testudinary	pedagoguery
incipiently	tonsilotomy	preliminary	demagoguery
insipiently	hysterotomy	antiphonary	grotesquery
transiently	enterostomy	obsidionary	non-delivery
impatiently	gastrostomy	religionary	rediscovery
prevalently	angelophany	revisionary	gallimaufry
pestilently	satanophany	divisionary	yeard-hungry
excellently	metallogeny	oblationary	goldsmithry
repellently	hysterogeny	reactionary	dare-devilry
somnolently	scrape-penny	fractionary	charlatanry
turbulently	twelve-penny	functionary	chieftainry
succulently	hearth-penny	seditionary	hobgoblinry
truculently	dodecaphony	volitionary	subdeaconry
corpulently	quadraphony	petitionary	freemasonry
flatulently	stereophony	questionary	subcategory
inclemently	quadrophony	locutionary	chancellory
permanently	autochthony	ablutionary	heterospory
prominently	Amphictyony	dilutionary	supervisory
continently	peppercorny	superlunary	reprobatory
pertinently	orange-tawny	interlunary	improbatory
abstinently	proterogyny	translunary	approbatory
differently	whipping-boy	dishonorary	deprecatory
abhorrently	loblolly-boy	extemporary	imprecatory
decurrently	hobbledehoy	subcontrary	predicatory
recurrently	pelotherapy	caravansary	vindicatory
competently	serotherapy	anniversary	edificatory
advertently	cryotherapy	unnecessary	applicatory
insistently	stereoscopy	proprietary	explicatory
remittently	stethoscopy	ligamentary	masticatory
confluently	cranioscopy	filamentary	inculcatory
paramountly	retinoscopy	tenementary	provocatory
incorruptly	metoposcopy	fragmentary	expiscatory
steadfastly	laparoscopy	sedimentary	manducatory
soothfastly	oneiroscopy	rudimentary	depredatory
dishonestly	fluoroscopy	documentary	elucidatory
sclerocauly	hepatoscopy	tegumentary	trepidatory
polydactyly	proctoscopy	involuntary	retardatory
heterostyly	lycanthropy	protonotary	castigatory
siphonogamy	theanthropy	rallying-cry	intergatory
geitonogamy	misanthropy	proterandry	objurgatory
deuterogamy	bumble-puppy	type-foundry	expurgatory
cleistogamy	electrotypy	bell-foundry	enunciatory
chalazogamy	hypothecary	iron-foundry	retaliatory
craniognomy	hebdomadary	sculduddery	humiliatory
physiognomy	referendary	skulduddery	expatiatory
cheirognomy	beneficiary	whigmaleery	alleviatory
Deuteronomy	stipendiary	housewifery	compilatory
lithochromy	evangeliary	sculduggery	vacillatory
heliochromy	domiciliary	skulduggery	oscillatory
stenochromy	evidentiary	ironmongery	condolatory
photochromy	intercalary	tree-surgery	consolatory
orchiectomy	codicillary	cryosurgery	translatory
craniectomy	subaxillary	nick-nackery	ejaculatory
splenectomy	preambulary	gimcrackery	speculatory
enterectomy	sea-rosemary	comstockery	inoculatory
nephrectomy	accustomary	seal-rookery	circulatory

coagulatory	premonitory	lithotripsy	internality
stipulatory	requisitory	controversy	externality
gratulatory	suppository	Christmassy	cleverality
postulatory	deglutitory	seamstressy	integrality
acclamatory	life-history	Dukhobortsy	balmorality
declamatory	polyhistory	tufftaffety	temporality
exclamatory	retributory	tufttaffety	corporality
lacrimatory	persecutory	loan-society	spectrality
affirmatory	collocutory	contrariety	hospitality
reformatory	restitutory	impropriety	orientality
informatory	drap-de-berry	over-anxiety	immortality
chrismatory	coffee-berry	pervicacity	punctuality
lacrymatory	candle-berry	contumacity	eventuality
profanatory	huckleberry	pertinacity	probability
explanatory	hurtleberry	syllabicity	placability
obsignatory	sallal-berry	periodicity	peccability
designatory	goldenberry	specificity	amicability
co-signatory	boysenberry	prolificity	educability
combinatory	pigeon-berry	catholicity	readability
vaccinatory	salmon-berry	rhythmicity	weldability
buccinatory	winter-berry	volcanicity	saleability
declinatory	hounds-berry	vulcanicity	tameability
inclinatory	curlew-berry	isotonicity	rateability
eliminatory	quinsy-berry	historicity	moveability
criminatory	chokecherry	electricity	hangability
fulminatory	Tom-and-Jerry	hermeticity	sociability
comminatory	muffin-worry	eupepticity	reliability
terminatory	hurry-scurry	ellipticity	variability
mancipatory	hurry-skurry	domesticity	satiability
inculpatory	bibliolatry	rumti-iddity	inviability
exculpatory	theriolatry	pellucidity	workability
extirpatory	physiolatry	intrepidity	isolability
nuncupatory	angelolatry	illiquidity	amenability
declaratory	demonolatry	pudibundity	damnability
preparatory	dendrolatry	moribundity	palpability
respiratory	alkalimetry	infecundity	culpability
inspiratory	polarimetry	rubicundity	wearability
elaboratory	calorimetry	incommodity	exorability
imploratory	chlorimetry	diaphaneity	versability
exploratory	colorimetry	spontaneity	imitability
impetratory	plessimetry	homogeneity	suitability
procuratory	dissymmetry	farcicality	quotability
incantatory	tacheometry	cyclicality	portability
cementatory	stereometry	inimicality	instability
compotatory	stichometry	physicality	salvability
dehortatory	psychometry	criticality	solvability
exhortatory	craniometry	verticality	vincibility
degustatory	tensiometry	ethereality	forcibility
extenuatory	dynamometry	prodigality	miscibility
insinuatory	thermometry	conjugality	inedibility
observatory	seismometry	officiality	credibility
reservatory	chronometry	unsociality	vendibility
calefactory	chlorometry	imperiality	eligibility
malefactory	sycophantry	materiality	tangibility
benefactory	double-entry	informality	fallibility
manufactory	single-entry	abnormality	gullibility
ex-directory	calf-country	originality	terribility
maledictory	back-country	criminality	feasibility
valedictory	dog's-mercury	nationality	sensibility
benedictory	subtreasury	rationality	tensibility
succinctory	free-and-easy	commonality	torsibility
perfunctory	palingenesy	seasonality	passibility
prohibitory	discourtesy	personality	possibility
recognitory	nympholepsy	infernality	partibility

flexibility	piacularity	crapulosity	sheriffalty
consimility	oracularity	tenebrosity	spiritualty
vibratility	circularity	ponderosity	viceroyalty
versatility	vascularity	monstrosity	blood-guilty
inductility	muscularity	schistosity	sovereignty
ungentility	singularity	strenuosity	superdainty
infertility	granularity	impetuosity	uncertainty
incredulity	columnarity	sumptuosity	bottle-party
longanimity	nulliparity	conspicuity	search-party
magnanimity	primiparity	perspicuity	muster-party
parvanimity	fissiparity	promiscuity	leze-liberty
omniformity	multiparity	superfluity	disproperty
suburbanity	equilibrity	life-annuity	osteoplasty
aldermanity	insalubrity	longinquity	uranoplasty
convicinity	insincerity	propinquity	rhinoplasty
inquilinity	sinisterity	incongruity	thermonasty
masculinity	indexterity	incendivity	seismonasty
peregrinity	inferiority	impulsivity	mock-modesty
herb-trinity	superiority	expansivity	lese-majesty
taciturnity	deteriority	impassivity	leze-majesty
importunity	anteriority	diffusivity	theopneusty
opportunity	interiority	affectivity	oyster-patty
cappernoity	exteriority	objectivity	Nancy-pretty
serendipity	non-priority	selectivity	nitty-gritty
self-charity	top-priority	directivity	fatigue-duty
familiarity	prematurity	inductivity	transit-duty
peculiarity	bellicosity	cognitivity	ventriloquy
capillarity	grandiosity	sensitivity	stultiloquy
pupillarity	religiosity	retentivity	litholapaxy
unipolarity	incuriosity	acceptivity	unorthodoxy
exemplarity	ampullosity	receptivity	Z
globularity	pendulosity	resistivity	razzamatazz

A	ailurophobia	hypoglycemia	hypochondria
massaranduba	osteomalacia	exophthalmia	mitochondria
masseranduba	encyclopedia	sclerodermia	alstroemeria
Malacostraca	dextrocardia	hyperthermia	Thesmophoria
Entomostraca	rhythmopoeia	schizothymia	amphigastria
rhamphotheca	prosopopoeia	orchidomania	Ankylosauria
pearl-tapioca	onomatopoeia	pteridomania	phosphaturia
ichthyopsida	rhinorrhagia	potichomania	heteroplasia
coloquintida	metrorrhagia	hysteromania	enhypostasia
primigravida	quadraplegia	theatromania	hyperalgesia
Branchiopoda	quadriplegia	balletomania	telaesthesia
Sipunculacea	Aristolochia	phonasthenia	panaesthesia
Scorpionidea	Zantedeschia	neurasthenia	kinaesthesia
Molluscoidea	Ornithischia	hypersthenia	synaesthesia
Spatangoidea	Polyadelphia	washingtonia	paraesthesia
dysmenorrhea	stichomythia	Wellingtonia	dysaesthesia
blennorrhoea	anencephalia	Darlingtonia	radiesthesia
Myrmecophaga	ephebophilia	cerebrotonia	coenesthesia
Theriomorpha	ailurophilia	viscerotonia	palingenesia
Enteromorpha	scoptophilia	xanthochroia	cryptomnesia
Nematomorpha	bougainvilia	deuteranopia	pre-eclampsia
toxicophobia	Phanerogamia	pedicellaria	chromatopsia
bibliophobia	tetradynamia	scrophularia	acaridomatia
satanophobia	thalassaemia	Campanularia	acarodomatia

Bertholletia
tradescantia
respondentia
Theriodontia
Zeuglodontia
sesquitertia
hyperpyrexia
Rhizocephala
Rhynchonella
sarsaparilla
intermaxilla
ichthyocolla
tintinnabula
Artiodactyla
Quadragesima
Septuagesima
hypersarcoma
mesothelioma
sclerenchyma
Shaksperiana
antilegomena
epiphenomena
paralipomena
homologumena
Euglenoidina
vitro-di-trina
herpetofauna
Foraminifera
sesquialtera
Siphonaptera
Strepsiptera
Rhipidoptera
Thysanoptera
Mastigophora
Rhynchophora
Siphonophora
Panchatantra
streptoneura
acciaccatura
appoggiatura
Hemichordata
Dibranchiata
taramasalata
Heterosomata
Cyclostomata
Pachydermata
mycoplasmata
Invertebrata
Coelenterata
parasyntheta
mammee-sapota
Pteridophyta
extravaganza
      B
smash-and-grab
Zeitvertreib
miller's-thumb
seasoning-tub
powdering-tub
      C
Anglophabiac
intracardiac
paedophiliac
haemophiliac

scopophiliac
necrophiliac
melancholiac
nymphomaniac
bibliomaniac
megalomaniac
timbromaniac
etheromaniac
kleptomaniac
hebephreniac
Volga-Baltaic
photovoltaic
decasyllabic
parisyllabic
monosyllabic
octosyllabic
polysyllabic
orthorhombic
orthoboracic
metathoracic
mesothoracic
orthosilicic
Netherlandic
Hildebrandic
antiperiodic
onomatopoeic
slave-traffic
intertraffic
unscientific
haemorrhagic
archipelagic
bathypelagic
quadraplegic
quadriplegic
phlegmagogic
myrmecologic
phraseologic
meteorologic
eschatologic
herpetologic
thaumaturgic
amphibrachic
tetrastichic
zincographic
lithographic
orthographic
radiographic
hagiographic
heliographic
stylographic
anemographic
cosmographic
scenographic
stenographic
ichnographic
ethnographic
phonographic
pornographic
micrographic
hydrographic
hierographic
hygrographic
chorographic
reprographic

petrographic
hectographic
pictographic
hyetographic
pantographic
photographic
cartographic
phytographic
tachygraphic
peristrephic
oligotrophic
hypertrophic
catastrophic
octastrophic
antistrophic
monostrophic
tetramorphic
isodimorphic
paedomorphic
homeomorphic
ophiomorphic
protomorphic
ditriglyphic
hieroglyphic
petroglyphic
photoglyphic
orthognathic
kinesipathic
homoeopathic
psychopathic
naturopathic
chalcolithic
palaeolithic
pseudo-Gothic
stichomythic
intervocalic
logodaedalic
anencephalic
epencephalic
mesocephalic
heterocyclic
thermophilic
monometallic
non-alcoholic
anticatholic
subapostolic
hexadactylic
zygodactylic
phanerogamic
cleistogamic
chalazogamic
monothalamic
hypothalamic
hydrodynamic
hippopotamic
thalassaemic
idiorhythmic
polyrhythmic
exophthalmic
physiognomic
Deuteronomic
heliochromic
photochromic
alexipharmic

sclerodermic
homeothermic
sarcoplasmic
protoplasmic
deutoplasmic
microseismic
schizothymic
interoceanic
transoceanic
superorganic
chrysophanic
Aristophanic
councilmanic
Indo-Germanic
amphisbaenic
carcinogenic
hysterogenic
electrogenic
neurasthenic
callisthenic
hypersthenic
philhellenic
mnemotechnic
dodecaphonic
quadraphonic
chordophonic
stereophonic
quadrophonic
anticyclonic
antimnemonic
philharmonic
peristeronic
opisthotonic
cerebrotonic
viscerotonic
electrotonic
amphictyonic
xanthochroic
melanochroic
spermatozoic
stroboscopic
stethoscopic
thermoscopic
seismoscopic
metoposcopic
dichroscopic
deuteranopic
lycanthropic
theanthropic
misanthropic
gonadotropic
diageotropic
apogeotropic
stereotropic
psychotropic
trophotropic
morphotropic
plagiotropic
thigmotropic
thermotropic
schizocarpic
electrotypic
mixobarbaric
pyrotartaric

planispheric	technocratic	compatriotic	pharmaceutic
lithospheric	stratocratic	post-hypnotic	propaedeutic
tropospheric	meritocratic	rhinocerotic	probouleutic
photospheric	aristocratic	nympholeptic	granulocytic
electromeric	bureaucratic	organoleptic	spermaphytic
alphanumeric	homoeostatic	lithotriptic	psammophytic
trochanteric	thermostatic	phonocamptic	spermophytic
hydrochloric	enhypostatic	anacathartic	schizophytic
polyhistoric	autodidactic	hygrochastic	electrolytic
hydrofluoric	metagalactic	ecclesiastic	scanning-disc
pyro-electric	anaphylactic	enthusiastic	D
isodiametric	prophylactic	iconoclastic	fountain-head
polarimetric	cataphractic	viscoelastic	cylinder-head
chlorimetric	chiropractic	hydroelastic	sounding-lead
fluorimetric	stereotactic	photoelastic	counterplead
plessimetric	trophotactic	osteoplastic	currant-bread
dissymmetric	phyllotactic	cosmoplastic	quinquenniad
stereometric	thermotactic	rhinoplastic	turnpike-road
stichometric	heterotactic	protoplastic	launching-pad
psychometric	subantarctic	superplastic	unsubscribed
pluviometric	analphabetic	hyperplastic	unprescribed
dynamometric	antipathetic	paronomastic	self-absorbed
thermometric	theopathetic	seismonastic	pudding-faced
seismometric	biosynthetic	paraphrastic	hatchet-faced
chronometric	telaesthetic	metaphrastic	unprejudiced
chlorometric	kinaesthetic	periphrastic	gravel-voiced
fluorometric	synaesthetic	antiphrastic	shrill-voiced
heliocentric	dysaesthetic	holophrastic	silver-voiced
ethnocentric	monotheletic	catachrestic	self-balanced
catadioptric	etepimeletic	antitheistic	weal-balanced
Zarathustric	schindyletic	henotheistic	well-balanced
persulphuric	monophyletic	monotheistic	uninfluenced
lamprophyric	polyphyletic	polytheistic	unpronounced
hyperalgesic	spectrometic	monarchistic	home-produced
cryptomnesic	paedogenetic	unidealistic	self-produced
passion-music	osteogenetic	surrealistic	mass-produced
melodramatic	pathogenetic	specialistic	unintroduced
monodramatic	orthogenetic	nominalistic	double-headed
epirrhematic	phylogenetic	journalistic	muddleheaded
exanthematic	hypnogenetic	liberalistic	triple-headed
meristematic	petrogenetic	naturalistic	beetle-headed
unsystematic	histogenetic	capitalistic	rattle-headed
apothegmatic	phytogenetic	sensualistic	puzzle-headed
paradigmatic	rhizogenetic	revivalistic	spring-headed
anastigmatic	paramagnetic	evangelistic	wooden-headed
antasthmatic	gyromagnetic	monopolistic	mutton-headed
diagrammatic	acrophonetic	dysphemistic	dunderheaded
anagrammatic	hyperpyretic	monogenistic	loggerheaded
epigrammatic	antirachitic	chauvinistic	hammer-headed
trigrammatic	encephalitic	antagonistic	bullet-headed
programmatic	heteroclitic	reunionistic	yellow-headed
undiplomatic	toxophilitic	secularistic	oughly-headed
trichromatic	cosmopolitic	militaristic	woolly-headed
panchromatic	ichthyolitic	Fourieristic	glassy-headed
apochromatic	oneirocritic	euhemeristic	dough-kneaded
isochromatic	diphtheritic	hypocoristic	spring-bladed
leptosomatic	antarthritic	belletristic	spring-loaded
peristomatic	antipruritic	narcissistic	slickensided
xerodermatic	monophysitic	chrematistic	double-handed
panspermatic	hierophantic	syncretistic	single-handed
zoospermatic	cheiromantic	anabaptistic	understanded
empyreumatic	anthelmintic	relativistic	unbefriended
physiocratic	trophobiotic	positivistic	feeble-minded
undemocratic	anaerobiotic	sansculottic	single-minded

simple-minded
strong-minded
carnal-minded
absent-minded
narrow-minded
bloody-minded
motley-minded
broken-winded
uncompounded
well-grounded
sober-blooded
white-bearded
landing-speed
orchilla-weed
strangle-weed
pickerel-weed
understaffed
cloven-hoofed
black-visaged
sharp-visaged
fully-fledged
unprivileged
stridelegged
spider-legged
badger-legged
yellow-legged
square-rigged
unchallenged
unstockinged
rushy-fringed
wire-stringed
yellow-ringed
sheath-winged
turbocharged
undischarged
shrill-gorged
bare-breached
unreproached
unapproached
semi-detached
semi-attached
undispatched
wire-stitched
overscutched
accomplished
undiminished
unadmonished
unvanquished
long-breathed
well-breathed
lust-breathed
underclothed
sharp-toothed
sweet-toothed
round-mouthed
close-mouthed
splay-mouthed
honey-mouthed
mealy-mouthed
disprivacied
pottle-bodied
unclassified
unstratified
unsanctified

unquantified
unidentified
unscottified
dissatisfied
white-bellied
great-bellied
overcanopied
self-occupied
world-wearied
vocabularied
unseminaried
unpropertied
ring-streaked
saddlebacked
huckle-backed
broken-backed
yellow-backed
vacuum-packed
tongue-tacked
double-decked
turtle-necked
halter-necked
yellow-necked
hydraulicked
shellshocked
double-locked
self-disliked
double-banked
ripple-marked
counter-paled
undissembled
bespectacled
unspectacled
unchronicled
spring-heeled
unparalleled
obtuse-angled
star-spangled
culvertailed
racket-tailed
unreconciled
irreconciled
travel-soiled
unenthralled
revictualled
sickle-celled
untrammelled
jet-propelled
unapparelled
uncounselled
yellow-billed
uncontrolled
thick-skulled
self-schooled
unprincipled
underpeopled
undismantled
muddy-mettled
non-scheduled
heterostyled
unproclaimed
unaccustomed
cane-bottomed
rush-bottomed

bell-bottomed
full-bottomed
well-informed
self-consumed
unthreatened
affrightened
unfrightened
disheartened
unchristened
self-ordained
addle-brained
crackbrained
barmy-brained
close-grained
rough-grained
cross-grained
house-trained
unrestrained
overstrained
unmaintained
bloodstained
indetermined
undetermined
double-manned
whole-skinned
thick-skinned
pro-and-conned
twitterboned
escutcheoned
old-fashioned
new-fashioned
unpavilioned
possessioned
commissioned
unsanctioned
unmunitioned
proportioned
unquestioned
complexioned
unchaperoned
high-seasoned
unimprisoned
unforewarned
yellow-horned
triple-turned
unimportuned
white-crowned
shield-shaped
saddle-shaped
sickle-shaped
salver-shaped
yellow-rumped
lizard-hipped
unworshipped
intercropped
self-endeared
self-indeared
thoroughbred
unremembered
half-timbered
well-timbered
unencumbered
unincumbered
unconsidered

undisordered
unendangered
rosy-fingered
pen-feathered
pin-feathered
well-mannered
good-tempered
evil-tempered
well-tempered
tax-sheltered
unregistered
uncloistered
unembittered
white-livered
undiscovered
solar-powered
underpowered
unsepulchred
woolly-haired
three-centred
wine-coloured
rose-coloured
self-coloured
high-coloured
varicoloured
Cain-coloured
rust-coloured
ruby-coloured
many-coloured
rosy-coloured
good-humoured
time-honoured
hard-favoured
evil-favoured
well-favoured
hard-featured
sky-tinctured
unstructured
unsculptured
unsubsidised
unmethodised
unfranchised
unsocialised
unformalised
internalised
unsterilised
unfossilised
unfertilised
unmechanised
unrecognised
unpatronised
unmodernised
unauthorised
mathematised
unsensitised
unsupervised
tuberculosed
superimposed
undecomposed
well-disposed
underdressed
obcompressed
unsuppressed
prepossessed

dispossessed	uninstructed	slouch-hatted	cigarette-end
journey-bated	multifaceted	interfretted	misapprehend
certificated	tender-hefted	sulphuretted	school-friend
domesticated	heaven-gifted	pretermitted	hoodman-blind
self-educated	overweighted	nimble-witted	festoon-blind
well-educated	floodlighted	sodden-witted	swimming-pond
consolidated	well-plighted	unpersecuted	outward-bound
unliquidated	cross-lighted	untransmuted	weather-bound
non-nucleated	eagle-sighted	close-tongued	quarter-bound
earth-created	thick-sighted	sharp-tongued	para-compound
hundred-gated	quick-sighted	honey-tongued	ring-compound
unvariegated	sharp-sighted	uncatalogued	mono-compound
unsegregated	clear-sighted	intertissued	parade-ground
unexpurgated	short-sighted	smooth-leaved	battleground
unassociated	low-thoughted	burnet-leaved	teeing-ground
absinthiated	unprohibited	self-depraved	burial-ground
unventilated	unaccredited	self-deceived	cumber-ground
machicolated	base-spirited	prerogatived	winter-ground
silver-plated	high-spirited	self-involved	racket-ground
armour-plated	weak-spirited	lantern-jawed	hollow-ground
untranslated	mean-spirited	beetle-browed	merry-go-round
mandibulated	poor-spirited	smooth-browed	counter-round
trabeculated	uncovenanted	ready-moneyed	quarter-round
fasciculated	quick-scented	self-employed	unlikelihood
folliculated	sweet-scented	double-glazed	spinsterhood
vermiculated	unornamented	scullery-maid	bachelorhood
turriculated	battlemented	carriage-paid	quarter-blood
denticulated	unregimented	semipellucid	pigeon's-blood
testiculated	experimented	hypotrochoid	dragon's-blood
unguiculated	undocumented	feldspathoid	mountain-wood
uncalculated	instrumented	parasphenoid	southernwood
pedunculated	malcontented	subarachnoid	levelling-rod
tuberculated	discontented	pentacrinoid	lightning-rod
strangulated	miscontented	bioflavonoid	measuring-rod
unstimulated	unfrequented	antherozooid	visiting-card
unformulated	unacquainted	salamandroid	lamp-standard
unsublimated	self-anointed	hemispheroid	shuffle-board
unhyphenated	disappointed	orthopteroid	surfing-board
unvaccinated	sharp-pointed	xanthochroid	washing-board
unoriginated	microprinted	spermatozoid	running-board
disseminated	white-fronted	leucoplastid	ironing-board
unterminated	nimble-footed	diamond-field	scoring-board
smooth-coated	cloven-footed	stubble-field	drawing-board
full-throated	silver-footed	landing-field	flannelboard
ruby-throated	yellow-footed	hunting-field	council-board
periwig-pated	proud-hearted	playing-field	Bristol-board
uncelebrated	large-hearted	chesterfield	fume-cupboard
agglomerated	whole-hearted	harvest-field	weather-board
unintegrated	false-hearted	nipple-shield	checker-board
unelaborated	stiff-hearted	heater-shield	scraper-board
imperforated	black-hearted	thousandfold	clapperboard
unperforated	cruel-hearted	corn-marigold	plasterboard
unextenuated	plain-hearted	stranglehold	draughtboard
unpunctuated	great-hearted	subthreshold	chimney-board
unhabituated	light-hearted	trouble-world	hedge-mustard
uncultivated	faint-hearted	mourning-band	counter-guard
undistracted	flint-hearted	house-husband	quarter-guard
self-affected	stout-hearted	multiplicand	house-steward
retroflected	stony-hearted	Gondwanaland	henceforward
disconnected	heavy-hearted	Newfoundland	flash-forward
self-directed	timely-parted	farthingland	lounge-lizard
well-directed	time-bewasted	gangsterland	honey-buzzard
unrestricted	white-crested	concert-grand	umbrella-bird
unobstructed	uninterested	counter-stand	cardinal-bird

rifleman-bird	Umbelliferae	precipitance	self-violence
harmonichord	Calyciflorae	unrepentance	insomnolence
hunting-sword	Tubuliflorae	acquaintance	pulverulence
thunder-cloud	Liguliflorae	unacceptance	impermanence
E	Discomedusae	unimportance	incontinence
Scolopacidae	Hydromedusae	long-distance	impertinence
Scarabaeidae	Heterocontae	demi-distance	inabstinence
Paradiseidae	circumscribe	equidistance	mill-sixpence
Syngnathidae	Germanophobe	irresistance	transparence
Charadriidae	ailourophobe	circumstance	subreference
Lymantriidae	drainage-tube	happenstance	indifference
Cicindelidae	speaking-tube	readmittance	interference
Fringillidae	delivery-tube	inobservance	transference
Chironomidae	landing-place	unobservance	belligerence
Scorpaenidae	parking-place	disallowance	sir-reverence
Characinidae	lurking-place	reconveyance	omnipresence
Torpedinidae	nesting-place	clairvoyance	pearl-essence
Papilionidae	resting-place	magnificence	quintessence
Trichiuridae	burying-place	glaucescence	incompetence
Notonectidae	blast-furnace	lapidescence	plenipotence
Notodontidae	counter-brace	viridescence	inadvertence
Didelphyidae	river-terrace	frondescence	pre-existence
Simarubaceae	birding-piece	acquiescence	non-existence
Tamaricaceae	fowling-piece	decalescence	mellifluence
Hypericaceae	doating-piece	recalescence	interfluence
Epacridaceae	frontispiece	incalescence	mountenaunce
Juglandaceae	chimney-piece	alkalescence	cherry-bounce
Nymphaeaceae	police-office	virilescence	mispronounce
Schizaeaceae	Jack-in-office	emollescence	counter-force
Marsileaceae	ticket-office	obsolescence	phosphoresce
Nepenthaceae	flower-delice	detumescence	under-produce
Bromeliaceae	selling-price	intumescence	subintroduce
Magnoliaceae	chief-justice	juvenescence	flower-deluce
Vacciniaceae	bed-of-justice	luminescence	lamb's-lettuce
Salviniaceae	space-lattice	concrescence	spurtle-blade
Bignoniaceae	interservice	arborescence	scissor-blade
Krameriaceae	heart-service	calorescence	rifle-grenade
Gesneriaceae	significance	fluorescence	harlequinade
Marattiaceae	country-dance	delitescence	church-parade
Velloziaceae	extravagance	obmutescence	stock-in-trade
Polygalaceae	come-by-chance	revivescence	transit-trade
Crassulaceae	incompliance	indehiscence	rhodomontade
Gentianaceae	microbalance	reminiscence	overpersuade
Boraginaceae	dissemblance	resipiscence	molluscicide
Polygonaceae	copper-glance	obliviscence	parasiticide
Papaveraceae	silver-glance	revivescence	radionuclide
Combretaceae	surveillance	noctilucence	nicotinamide
Equisetaceae	air-ambulance	translucence	sulphonamide
Cordaitaceae	transhumance	supersedence	ferricyanide
Amarantaceae	appurtenance	non-residence	ferrocyanide
Rhodophyceae	preordinance	self-evidence	disaccharide
Phaeophyceae	predominance	improvidence	triglyceride
Cyanophyceae	inconsonance	resplendence	giant's-stride
Vaccinoideae	reappearance	independence	electrosonde
Lycopodineae	protuberance	intelligence	inexactitude
Ustilagineae	intemperance	multiscience	correctitude
Saurognathae	perseverance	inter-science	formaldehyde
differentiae	disseverance	disobedience	acetaldehyde
choripetalae	remonstrance	inexpedience	benzaldehyde
trichinellae	preassurance	inexperience	carpenter-bee
terebratulae	complaisance	consentience	talkee-talkee
Phanerogamae	recognisance	subservience	Hindoostanee
Angiospermae	incognisance	multivalence	brandy-pawnee
globigerinae	concomitance	equipollence	carriage-free

angelica-tree	grotesquerie	irremediable	ungovernable
umbrella-tree	clamjamphrie	solidifiable	unreturnable
trysting-tree	temperalitie	unmodifiable	participable
snowball-tree	mixtie-maxtie	saponifiable	inextirpable
benjamin-tree	capercailzie	unverifiable	incomparable
snowdrop-tree	aldermanlike	classifiable	rememberable
cucumber-tree	courtierlike	quantifiable	considerable
loblolly-tree	stickler-like	identifiable	imponderable
interrogatee	unsailorlike	multipliable	insufferable
subcommittee	business-like	expropriable	unsufferable
palette-knife	merchantlike	renegotiable	transferable
pruning-knife	unartistlike	undertakable	decipherable
hunting-knife	boarding-pike	unmistakable	invulnerable
carving-knife	marlinespike	unshrinkable	unvulnerable
drawing-knife	drongo-shrike	unremarkable	commiserable
leather-knife	second-strike	unrepealable	unfilterable
skunk-cabbage	hunger-strike	irrepealable	unbetterable
squirrel-cage	masterstroke	unappealable	discoverable
patrilineage	breaststroke	unrevealable	unanswerable
forecarriage	unicorn-whale	unassailable	unrepairable
mail-carriage	subscribable	reconcilable	irrepairable
slip-carriage	equiprobable	unrecallable	irrespirable
pony-carriage	ineradicable	inappellable	transpirable
reassemblage	inapplicable	counsellable	corroborable
bertillonage	unapplicable	controllable	imperforable
disadvantage	inexplicable	decasyllable	commemorable
photomontage	communicable	monosyllable	impenetrable
landing-stage	inextricable	octosyllable	demonstrable
resting-stage	domesticable	polysyllable	unprocurable
paralanguage	informidable	interpolable	unfavourable
metalanguage	unformidable	inconsolable	immeasurable
misknowledge	unascendable	contemplable	unmeasurable
straight-edge	undependable	incalculable	immensurable
milk-porridge	accommodable	incoagulable	manoeuvrable
plum-porridge	ineffaceable	unredeemable	inappeasable
hunting-lodge	displaceable	irredeemable	unappeasable
disprivilege	unnoticeable	non-flammable	criticisable
staff-college	impierceable	programmable	hybridisable
corn-exchange	disagreeable	unfathomable	irrealisable
part-exchange	carriageable	unreformable	vulcanisable
cooking-range	marriageable	irreformable	recognisable
kitchen-range	unmanageable	inconsumable	incognisable
mischallenge	unvoyageable	unassignable	pulverisable
cough-lozenge	unchangeable	unimpugnable	authorisable
double-charge	exchangeable	inexpugnable	dramatisable
gas-discharge	unriddleable	unexpugnable	magnetisable
weather-gauge	irrefragable	restrainable	hypnotisable
counter-gauge	unassuagable	distrainable	replevisable
sick-headache	investigable	unobtainable	unrepulsable
carte-blanche	interrogable	maintainable	decomposable
interwreathe	unbreachable	unattainable	uncomposable
turning-lathe	reproachable	unconfinable	unsupposable
cradle-scythe	approachable	unimaginable	superposable
boogie-woogie	unstanchable	indeclinable	transposable
kickie-wickie	unquenchable	contaminable	unanalysable
cockieleekie	unsearchable	determinable	uncomeatable
walkie-talkie	unpolishable	interminable	unrepeatable
kiddiewinkie	diminishable	exterminable	correlatable
capercaillie	unpunishable	agglutinable	translatable
tirlie-wirlie	imperishable	unpardonable	cultivatable
curliewurlie	unperishable	conscionable	contractable
whigmaleerie	vanquishable	questionable	undelectable
tapsieteerie	unbreathable	unreasonable	indetectable
tapsalteerie	bequeathable	unseasonable	unmarketable

console-table	indefensible	fairnitickle	polyurethane
trestle-table	inextensible	fairnytickle	lepidomelane
writing-table	incorrosible	pinniewinkle	compass-plane
drawing-table	irreversible	mademoiselle	cyclopropane
resuscitable	inaccessible	antimetabole	ultramontane
extraditable	compressible	watering-hole	transmontane
uncreditable	suppressible	starting-hole	chuckie-stane
unprofitable	inadmissible	eighteen-hole	through-stane
precipitable	irremissible	stocking-sole	channel-stane
inhospitable	transfusible	spire-steeple	polysiloxane
unhospitable	incompatible	equimultiple	trimethylene
uncharitable	contractible	churchpeople	polyethylene
merchantable	protractible	tribespeople	oxy-acetylene
untenantable	distractible	tradespeople	schizophrene
discountable	indefectible	custard-apple	polyisoprene
surmountable	indetectible	cooking-apple	nitrotoluene
unacceptable	destructible	thermo-couple	nitrobenzene
unreportable	instructible	ground-beetle	demi-mondaine
manifestable	contemptible	spring-beetle	steam-turbine
afforestable	discerptible	sexton-beetle	water-turbine
hog-constable	indivertible	bastard-title	folk-medicine
thermostable	manifestible	tercel-gentle	cantharidine
livery-stable	indigestible	tassel-gentle	donkey-engine
irrebuttable	unresistible	falcon-gentle	monkey-engine
attributable	irresistible	globe-thistle	fruit-machine
prosecutable	stone-bramble	torch-thistle	blanc-de-Chine
inexecutable	rumble-tumble	spear-thistle	crêpe-de-chine
incommutable	indissoluble	lady's-thistle	tragelaphine
transmutable	antiparticle	steam-whistle	terebinthine
disreputable	vibratiuncle	penny-whistle	labyrinthine
incomputable	root-tubercle	yellow-rattle	tetracycline
indisputable	motor-bicycle	tittle-tattle	sounding-line
unstatutable	fiddle-faddle	giant's-kettle	spilling-line
trolley-table	chick-a-diddle	Woulfe-bottle	nitroaniline
unachievable	niddle-noddle	brandy-bottle	intercolline
unbelievable	corpse-candle	gram-molecule	theophylline
unrelievable	tallow-candle	jointing-rule	vaginicoline
undeceivable	yankee-doodle	microcapsule	indiscipline
uncultivable	breast-girdle	pentadactyle	undiscipline
unresolvable	spermatocele	pterodactyle	calendar-line
irresolvable	siphonostele	araeosystyle	multicauline
unreprovable	higgle-haggle	razzle-dazzle	pyrithiamine
irreprovable	raggle-taggle	monkey-puzzle	diethylamine
inobservable	wiggle-waggle	cuisse-madame	cross-examine
unobservable	wallydraigle	what's-her-name	etheostomine
unshadowable	dingle-dangle	what's-his-name	picrocarmine
disallowable	jingle-jangle	what's-its-name	predetermine
unemployable	mingle-mangle	picture-frame	sea-porcupine
uncapsizable	disembrangle	drawing-frame	salamandrine
bibble-babble	crambo-jingle	shriving-time	intra-uterine
gibble-gabble	thermolabile	sprechstimme	extra-uterine
ribble-rabble	semi-imbecile	middle-income	vulvo-uterine
hubble-bubble	myrmecophile	stereochrome	paradoxurine
reproducible	Germanophile	chondriosome	multivoltine
introducible	ailourophile	pointillisme	brilliantine
unascendible	gerontophile	nursery-rhyme	Observantine
incorrodible	cross-and-pile	leopard's-bane	transpontine
intelligible	circumfusile	supramundane	trypaflavine
incorrigible	supersubtile	ultramundane	Rhinegravine
diffrangible	soughing-tile	intramundane	school-divine
inexpungible	interfertile	extra-mundane	pulp-magazine
indefeasible	saddle-hackle	supermundane	equestrienne
subdivisible	salmon-tackle	intermundane	circassienne
inexpansible	ledger-tackle	nitromethane	marriage-bone

shoulder-bone	chromosphere	recomforture	demilitarise
splinter-bone	thermosphere	intertexture	co-polymerise
dropped-scone	centrosphere	cough-mixture	containerise
Picturephone ®	stratosphere	intermixture	dispauperise
harmoniphone	blastosphere	heliogravure	characterise
kaleidophone	laisser-faire	photogravure	disauthorise
metallophone	laissez-faire	outmanoeuvre	contemporise
sphygmophone	mousquetaire	dressing-case	desulphurise
theatrophone	air-commodore	ribonuclease	depressurise
sarrusophone	hereinbefore	steeplechase	parenthesise
detectophone	conidiophore	hire-purchase	anathematise
speakerphone	siphonophore	asparaginase	symptomatise
stentorphone	neverthemore	telegraphese	Hippocratise
phytonadione	resting-spore	Marseillaise	anaesthetise
hydroquinone	aecidiospore	grammaticise	lithotritise
second-to-none	conidiospore	aestheticise	sycophantise
progesterone	basidiospore	depoliticise	parchmentise
androsterone	teleutospore	propagandise	somniloquise
testosterone	carton-pierre	diphthongise	subjectivise
chuckie-stone	amphitheatre	mineralogise	collectivise
staddle-stone	circumcentre	entomologise	contrariwise
rubbing-stone	clare-obscure	phrenologise	parallelwise
pudding-stone	clear-obscure	disfranchise	sinisterwise
logging-stone	clair-obscure	apostrophise	business-wise
wishing-stone	somatopleure	philosophise	colossus-wise
rocking-stone	double-figure	corporealise	frankincense
curling-stone	single-figure	adverbialise	counter-sense
putting-stone	father-figure	dissocialise	suffruticose
through-stone	mother-figure	parochialise	metamorphose
peacock-stone	shadow-figure	editorialise	stubble-goose
channel-stone	heart-failure	mercurialise	harvest-goose
thunder-stone	police-manure	fictionalise	fast-and-loose
plasterstone	board-measure	municipalise	multipurpose
serpent-stone	passemeasure	illiberalise	cross-purpose
winter-bourne	water-measure	decentralise	semicomatose
intercommune	passy-measure	denaturalise	rocking-horse
finger-and-toe	discomposure	unnaturalise	sumpter-horse
seaside-grape	time-exposure	universalise	quarter-horse
throttle-pipe	overexposure	decapitalise	clothes-horse
delivery-pipe	high-pressure	recapitalise	draught-horse
kaleidoscope	overpressure	unsensualise	string-course
myringoscope	root-pressure	spiritualise	mizzen-course
laryngoscope	subminiature	insolubilise	ballanwrasse
bronchoscope	abbreviature	underutilise	parrot-wrasse
ebullioscope	nomenclature	tranquillise	self-applause
aethrioscope	ring-armature	Hispaniolise	mitrailleuse
oscilloscope	magistrature	break-promise	orchard-house
sphygmoscope	vitrifacture	phlebotomise	trouble-house
galvanoscope	architecture	trichotomise	steeple-house
praxinoscope	venepuncture	sectarianise	spittle-house
dichrooscope	venipuncture	christianise	picture-house
electroscope	substructure	porcellanise	front-of-house
spectroscope	constructure	decitizenise	forcing-house
goat-antelope	discomfiture	porcelainise	lodging-house
skipping-rope	pisciculture	attitudinise	washing-house
philanthrope	floriculture	serpentinise	working-house
radio-isotope	horticulture	Philistinise	rooming-house
woodburytype	silviculture	haussmannise	corning-house
devil-may-care	sylviculture	excursionise	burning-house
thoroughfare	water-culture	disharmonise	leaping-house
mountain-hare	peradventure	embourgeoise	meeting-house
market-square	disadventure	counterpoise	charnel-house
porte-cochère	misadventure	chassé-croisé	council-house
rhabdosphere	discoverture	missionarise	mansion-house

session-house	pudding-plate	unadulterate	porcellanite
station-house	futtock-plate	coelenterate	Macmillanite
house-to-house	stencil-plate	presbyterate	microgranite
weather-house	fashion-plate	redintegrate	arfvedsonite
chapter-house	electroplate	disintegrate	babingtonite
Charterhouse	quarter-plate	transmigrate	wollastonite
draught-house	mistranslate	septemvirate	grossularite
country-house	somnambulate	centumvirate	tetrahedrite
harvest-louse	conglobulate	reinvigorate	aerosiderite
jumping-mouse	scrobiculate	tricorporate	granodiorite
flitter-mouse	canaliculate	concorporate	hypochlorite
cole-titmouse	adminiculate	discorporate	chalcopyrite
coal-titmouse	dearticulate	professorate	hemiparasite
harvest-mouse	inarticulate	collectorate	semiparasite
willow-grouse	unarticulate	inspectorate	endoparasite
autocatalyse	miscalculate	protectorate	ectoparasite
exsufflicate	inoperculate	recalcitrate	root-parasite
metasilicate	multungulate	pyrotartrate	prerequisite
multiplicate	overpopulate	administrate	syntagmatite
subduplicate	proconsulate	latirostrate	multipartite
conduplicate	congratulate	desulphurate	transvestite
centuplicate	absquatulate	commensurate	stakhanovite
prefabricate	recapitulate	contriturate	heterozygote
disintricate	microclimate	circumgyrate	reciting-note
intrinsicate	illegitimate	dextrogyrate	shoulder-note
authenticate	overestimate	tergiversate	pointilliste
fantasticate	monochromate	paraglossate	stockingette
sophisticate	imposthumate	interpretate	espagnolette
multisulcate	permanganate	incapacitate	munitionette
promuscidate	predesignate	rehabilitate	micropipette
longicaudate	incoordinate	multidentate	vinegarrette
curvicaudate	decaffeinate	disorientate	redistribute
subinfeudate	discriminate	multiseptate	circumlocute
supererogate	conterminate	trouble-state	reconstitute
billingsgate	indoctrinate	fissicostate	spermatocyte
matriarchate	predestinate	multicostate	pteridophyte
patriarchate	conglutinate	curvicostate	phanerophyte
hyposulphate	exsanguinate	circumnutate	phreatophyte
disassociate	longipennate	post-graduate	dermatophyte
intermediate	brevipennate	superannuate	cattle-plague
dibranchiate	subdiaconate	mispunctuate	beaumontague
disaffiliate	companionate	schizomycete	chaise-longue
sinupalliate	impassionate	aplanogamete	egg-and-tongue
multifoliate	unpassionate	Fehmgerichte	wooden-tongue
curvifoliate	affectionate	Vehmgerichte	mother-tongue
interfoliate	conditionate	hydrozincite	hound's-tongue
archegoniate	extortionate	skutterudite	adder's-tongue
proletariate	dispersonate	Theopaschite	phlegmagogue
secretariate	subalternate	synadelphite	galactagogue
multivariate	concelebrate	hyposulphite	exhaust-value
pluriseriate	invertebrate	hemimorphite	black-and-blue
multiseriate	deconsecrate	pyromorphite	mountain-blue
dispropriate	reconsecrate	marbled-white	cinematheque
substantiate	unconsecrate	cabbage-white	Alhambresque
landgraviate	paraquadrate	blatherskite	macaberesque
bletherskate	carbohydrate	cristobalite	Thurberesque
lenticellate	undeliberate	hydrophilite	Grolieresque
interpellate	preponderate	monticellite	plano-concave
verticillate	seraskierate	biosatellite	kitchen-knave
oblanceolate	conglomerate	pyrophyllite	borough-reeve
ebracteolate	unregenerate	agalmatolite	underachieve
strophiolate	obstreperate	hellgrammite	dead-and-alive
unifoliolate	subtemperate	luxullianite	thunder-drive
disconsolate	distemperate	strontianite	unpersuasive

self-adhesive	recuperative	apperceptive	penny-wedding
retropulsive	vituperative	interceptive	blood-pudding
reprehensive	obliterative	insusceptive	hodge-pudding
apprehensive	alliterative	subscriptive	pease-pudding
hypertensive	edulcorative	prescriptive	white-pudding
unresponsive	ameliorative	proscriptive	blackpudding
irresponsive	ministrative	transumptive	force-feeding
introversive	illustrative	interruptive	nose-bleeding
unsuccessive	compulsative	incorruptive	good-breeding
retrocessive	dispensative	introvertive	bate-breeding
unimpressive	incrassative	transportive	cloud-seeding
unoppressive	quidditative	decongestive	circle-riding
inexpressive	incogitative	intempestive	common-riding
unexpressive	excogitative	inexhaustive	water-gilding
unsubmissive	debilitative	contributive	word-building
intromissive	facilitative	distributive	shipbuilding
intermissive	delimitative	substitutive	body-building
transmissive	exploitative	constitutive	shareholding
repercussive	quantitative	mourning-dove	slave-holding
unapplausive	consultative	cupboard-love	smallholding
inconclusive	augmentative	pheasant's-eye	cold-moulding
unconclusive	alimentative	F	hood-moulding
perturbative	fermentative	quartern-loaf	neck-moulding
disturbative	presentative	handkerchief	blow-moulding
modificative	sustentative	outfangthief	crossbanding
purificative	preventative	walking-staff	crash-landing
complicative	dissertative	quarter-staff	belly-landing
gram-negative	sternutative	bound-bailiff	free-standing
depreciative	continuative	water-bailiff	long-standing
appreciative	colliquative	under-sheriff	parascending
renunciative	preservative	kitchen-stuff	money-lending
annunciative	conservative	do-it-yourself	fence-mending
dissociative	stupefactive	sunshine-roof	heart-rending
conciliative	putrefactive	pavilion-roof	unpretending
propitiative	petrifactive	weather-proof	nurse-tending
nomenclative	psychoactive	counterproof	fault-finding
annihilative	unattractive	shatter-proof	underfunding
assimilative	non-effective	soixante-neuf	type-founding
deoppilative	imperfective	oeils-de-boeuf	high-sounding
compellative	non-objective	G	echo-sounding
accumulative	self-elective	sprechgesang	backwounding
manipulative	unreflective	ourang-outang	unforeboding
amalgamative	irreflective	land-grabbing	surf-boarding
desquamative	intellective	stock-jobbing	sailboarding
consummative	recollective	brass-rubbing	safeguarding
confirmative	unrespective	rock-climbing	blackbirding
preformative	irrespective	beachcombing	undiscording
performative	resurrective	undisturbing	unforeseeing
co-ordinative	interdictive	self-effacing	fricasseeing
coordinative	jurisdictive	strait-lacing	guaranteeing
denominative	constrictive	hurdle-racing	horseshoeing
illuminative	reproductive	still-piecing	glue-sniffing
opinionative	unproductive	skirt-dancing	fireproofing
anticipative	introductive	conveyancing	discouraging
exhilarative	constructive	unconvincing	draft-dodging
exprobrative	interpretive	scare-heading	level-pegging
deliberative	precognitive	proof-reading	price-rigging
desiderative	disquisitive	outspreading	pettifogging
exaggerative	intransitive	sight-reading	footslogging
accelerative	gram-positive	homesteading	brick-nogging
degenerative	postpositive	horse-trading	leap-frogging
regenerative	disincentive	interbedding	wind-changing
remunerative	imperceptive	cross-bedding	cliffhanging
exasperative	unperceptive	camp-shedding	sound-ranging

sight-singing	free-wheeling	peace-keeping	predisposing
high-reaching	mind-boggling	swine-keeping	well-dressing
bird-catching	never-failing	housekeeping	hairdressing
bird-watching	coat-trailing	queue-jumping	unpossessing
fire-watching	rhumb-sailing	pot-walloping	cloud-kissing
doomwatching	unprevailing	moss-trooping	self-focusing
photo-etching	stone-boiling	wife-swapping	supplicating
queer-bashing	blackballing	high-stepping	intoxicating
brainwashing	forestalling	snuff-dipping	carbon-dating
paper-washing	stonewalling	transhipping	world-beating
unrefreshing	sun-expelling	lorry-hopping	space-heating
whale-fishing	quick-selling	name-dropping	excruciating
seine-fishing	truth-telling	ring-dropping	ingratiating
black-fishing	story-telling	tissue-typing	speed-boating
pearl-fishing	dishevelling	stereotyping	waistcoating
disrelishing	lake-dwelling	childbearing	exhilarating
unnourishing	pile-dwelling	underbearing	degenerating
slop-clothing	disbowelling	chain-gearing	exasperating
all-or-nothing	mouth-filling	cheese-paring	asseverating
span-farthing	rope-drilling	unslumbering	unhesitating
evil-speaking	protocolling	buccaneering	double-acting
code-breaking	disannulling	still-peering	single-acting
safe-breaking	water-cooling	privateering	self-electing
oath-breaking	daughterling	racketeering	unreflecting
backbreaking	caterwauling	sonneteering	unsuspecting
shopbreaking	kerb-crawling	profiteering	camp-sheeting
speech-making	curb-crawling	orienteering	whip-grafting
basket-making	tin-streaming	wood-offering	home-crofting
street-raking	ill-beseeming	wave-offering	land-yachting
breathtaking	overwhelming	meat-offering	sand-yachting
action-taking	free-swimming	marriage-ring	fire-fighting
mickey-taking	well-becoming	scavengering	cockfighting
earthquaking	house-warming	warmongering	bullfighting
bushwhacking	heart-warming	self-catering	self-lighting
safe-cracking	unconforming	concentering	moonlighting
wisecracking	unperforming	poetastering	double-biting
nerve-racking	transforming	trickstering	self-exciting
back-tracking	habit-forming	unflattering	discomfiting
bluestocking	self-cleaning	wallcovering	Speedwriting ®
corn-shucking	foretokening	overpowering	slate-writing
bloodsucking	benightening	mourning-ring	underwriting
north-seeking	aye-remaining	undespairing	unconsenting
south-seeking	appertaining	awe-inspiring	word-painting
pony-trekking	entertaining	sheep-scoring	vase-painting
deerstalking	unsustaining	saddle-spring	nose-painting
sleep-walking	serpentining	transferring	wall-painting
free-thinking	intertwining	white-herring	still-hunting
self-thinking	town-planning	soul-stirring	otter-hunting
index-linking	underpinning	fiddle-string	wing-shooting
sharp-looking	spear-running	violin-string	snapshooting
knee-crooking	underrunning	raconteuring	trap-shooting
stockbroking	conditioning	neighbouring	water-parting
kilfud-yoking	off-reckoning	misfeaturing	backstarting
epoch-marking	misreckoning	eternity-ring	transporting
metal-working	book-learning	self-pleasing	broadcasting
shift-working	storm-warning	well-pleasing	sand-blasting
unconcealing	unconcerning	stock-raising	star-blasting
death-dealing	undiscerning	overpraising	shot-blasting
plain-dealing	afterburning	gormandising	bird's-nesting
faith-healing	heartburning	demoralising	unprotesting
undersealing	half-mourning	unmoralising	blacklisting
motor-cycling	table-turning	scrutinising	non-resisting
shepherdling	bastinadoing	enterprising	blockbusting
sack-doudling	through-going	unappetising	ricochetting

bloodletting
underletting
trend-setting
photosetting
close-fitting
retrofitting
ear-splitting
unsubmitting
intromitting
transmitting
wainscotting
price-cutting
stone-cutting
glass-cutting
press-cutting
crosscutting
forth-putting
high-faluting
gem-engraving
labour-saving
misbelieving
thanksgiving
quill-driving
quacksalving
undissolving
route-proving
tooth-drawing
sneck-drawing
underdrawing
standard-wing
sapphire-wing
glass-blowing
water-flowing
childcrowing
cock-throwing
shadow-boxing
sight-playing
exemplifying
indemnifying
personifying
unterrifying
electrifying
intensifying
diversifying
unsatisfying
pigeon-flying
non-complying
microcopying
photocopying
freeze-drying
card-carrying
trail-blazing
highly-strung
bull-of-the-bog
lightning-bug
sparking-plug

H

hip-hip-hurrah
poison-sumach
doch-an-dorach
elasmobranch
Norman-French
monkey-wrench
kitchen-wench

bramble-finch
wedding-march
countermarch
eleutherarch
weeping-birch
mother-church
Stellenbosch
Platt-Deutsch
buttery-hatch
lucifer-match
bandersnatch
morning-watch
pencil-sketch
diamond-hitch
spider-stitch
garter-stitch
basket-stitch
tsesarevitch
toggle-switch
master-switch
butterscotch
bolting-hutch
scattermouch
tobacco-pouch
counter-weigh
mountain-high
shoulder-high
hooping-cough
trench-plough
breastplough
therethrough
wherethrough
breakthrough
thirdborough
marconigraph
flannelgraph
cathodograph
phraseograph
opisthograph
oscillograph
sphygmograph
steganograph
harmonograph
keraunograph
meteorograph
evaporograph
electrograph
spectrograph
ellipsograph
magnetograph
Telautograph ®
ornithomorph
enantiomorph
pythonomorph
synchroflash
weaning-brash
marrow-squash
scabbard-fish
paradise-fish
saucepan-fish
scorpion-fish
sergeant-fish
pre-establish
disestablish

disembellish
pound-foolish
French-polish
fore-admonish
Septemberish
buccaneerish
gazetteerish
dissenterish
overflourish
Rembrandtish
Ishmaelitish
sycophantish
dilettantish
uncoquettish
schoolboyish
devil-in-a-bush
shaving-brush
scratch-brush
clothes-brush
scouring-rush
missel-thrush
swimming-bath
life-and-death
hand's-breadth
acre's-breadth
hair's-breadth
straw-breadth
canvas-length
cable's-length
shoeing-smith
commonwealth
wood-hyacinth
centillionth
chrisom-cloth
leather-cloth
weather-cloth
polling-booth
scissor-tooth
Cologne-earth
trouble-mirth
three-ha'porth
foot-and-mouth
mouth-to-mouth
blabbermouth

I

caravansarai
caravanserai
streptococci
Plectognathi
gastrocnemii
chiquichiqui

K

make-and-break
Czechoslovak
straddle-back
roasting-jack
bladder-wrack
dressing-sack
chimney-stack
countercheck
Bristol-brick
message-stick
swizzle-stick
walking-stick

shaving-stick
swagger-stick
get-rich-quick
throstle-cock
patience-dock
electroshock
plumber-block
clinker-block
plummer-block
process-block
buzzard-clock
water-hemlock
pease-bannock
rolling-stock
jesting-stock
mouse-buttock
cross-buttock
wonder-struck
horror-struck
planet-struck
putting-cleek
Machtpolitik
chimney-stalk
lappered-milk
clearing-bank
whistle-drunk
custom-shrunk
exercise-book
spelling-book
visiting-book
transfer-book
birthday-book
Domesday-book
Doomsday-book
pressure-cook
gobbledegook
gobbledygook
shilling-mark
question-mark
shoulder-mark
low-watermark
sheriff-clerk
booking-clerk
session-clerk
mountain-cork
knife-and-fork
toasting-fork
clincher-work
stocking-mask

L

genethliacal
monomaniacal
pyromaniacal
paradisiacal
spermathecal
paradisaical
orthopedical
immethodical
unmethodical
scientifical
mystagogical
genealogical
mammalogical
phycological

paedological	strabismical	antithetical	prosopopeial
atheological	unmechanical	nomothetical	intracranial
teleological	talismanical	hypothetical	duodecennial
osteological	plano-conical	dithetelical	quadriennial
nephological	cosmogonical	arithmetical	bicentennial
pathological	antiphonical	paraenetical	quinquennial
lithological	cacophonical	anchoretical	antimalarial
mythological	histrionical	coenobitical	cancellarial
sociological	enharmonical	geopolitical	commissarial
radiological	inharmonical	Balaamitical	sphincterial
audiological	synchronical	self-critical	barristerial
hagiological	mock-heroical	hypocritical	presbyterial
ophiological	telescopical	anchoritical	prehensorial
aetiological	semitropical	unromantical	suspensorial
philological	archetypical	asymptotical	responsorial
gemmological	phenotypical	metaleptical	professorial
cosmological	phonotypical	protreptical	dedicatorial
etymological	prototypical	scholastical	gladiatorial
phenological	rhinocerical	pleonastical	grallatorial
poenological	peripherical	anapaestical	divinatorial
ethnological	exospherical	solecistical	imperatorial
rhinological	anticlerical	ditheistical	accusatorial
limnological	alphamerical	cabalistical	spectatorial
phonological	congenerical	donatistical	visitatorial
tropological	metaphorical	inartistical	prefectorial
necrological	unhistorical	linguistical	inspectorial
micrological	parametrical	Puseyistical	prosectorial
hydrological	asymmetrical	geognostical	protectorial
chorological	rheometrical	aeronautical	subeditorial
petrological	manometrical	phagocytical	preceptorial
astrological	barometrical	unanalytical	consistorial
neurological	horometrical	irreciprocal	diapophysial
scatological	pyrometrical	heterocercal	interspatial
cartological	gasometrical	tyrannicidal	perichaetial
pestological	volumetrical	bactericidal	interstitial
histological	concentrical	infanticidal	precedential
nostological	geocentrical	trypanocidal	confidential
battological	palaestrical	amygdaloidal	presidential
tautological	preclassical	epicycloidal	providential
phytological	neoclassical	paraboloidal	expediential
oligarchical	cataphysical	anthropoidal	experiential
hierarchical	metaphysical	saccharoidal	pestilential
tetrarchical	unprelatical	tetrachordal	componential
geographical	acroamatical	mountain-meal	preferential
biographical	mathematical	rhinorrhoeal	differential
zoographical	emblematical	cylinder-seal	conferential
orographical	systematical	Solomon's-seal	non-essential
myographical	diplomatical	triphthongal	court-martial
theosophical	telesmatical	tetrastichal	subcelestial
hyperbolical	schismatical	squirearchal	antediluvial
geodynamical	porismatical	pentateuchal	post-diluvial
agrochemical	theocratical	brachycephal	planetesimal
pyrochemical	democratical	interglacial	echinodermal
unrhythmical	timocratical	extra-special	homeothermal
pantomimical	hypostatical	unbeneficial	hydrothermal
tragi-comical	paratactical	semi-official	hyperthermal
heroi-comical	apoplectical	inartificial	angiospermal
seriocomical	epideictical	unartificial	protoplasmal
uneconomical	apodeictical	internuncial	rheumatismal
astronomical	alphabetical	psychosocial	nasolacrymal
loxodromical	epexegetical	uncommercial	isocheimenal
lithotomical	apologetical	anteprandial	superordinal
microtomical	catechetical	post-prandial	longitudinal
phantasmical	metathetical	enarthrodial	quarter-final

geanticlinal

geosynclinal

centroclinal

subabdominal

hendecagonal

televisional

convulsional

descensional

declensional

successional

precessional

processional

confessional

professional

digressional

expressional

percussional

dedicational

recreational

irrigational

navigational

revelational

anti-national

occupational

emigrational

maturational

volitational

visitational

salutational

derivational

motivational

projectional

deflectional

inflectional

inspectional

correctional

convectional

non-fictional

productional

discretional

apparitional

transitional

appositional

oppositional

repetitional

conventional

perceptional

proportional

contortional

precautional

revolutional

involutional

complexional

spermatozoal

subprincipal

subvertebral

dodecahedral

rhombohedral

pyritohedral

procathedral

rhopaloceral

nychthemeral

superhumeral

vicar-general

major-general

agent-general

isobilateral

multilateral

septilateral

cross-lateral

pluriliteral

odontophoral

tubulifloral

ligulifloral

interfemoral

post-doctoral

multicentral

dorsiventral

entoplastral

fissirostral

rectirostral

dentirostral

tenuirostral

curvirostral

unprocedural

interpleural

supernatural

manufactural

vocicultural

vinicultural

agricultural

unscriptural

bomb-disposal

interspersal

quaquaversal

sinistrorsal

dunniewassal

protonematal

endoskeletal

infraorbital

supra-orbital

interorbital

interdigital

extra-limital

primogenital

urinogenital

share-capital

party-capital

suboccipital

paroccipital

multicipital

lock-hospital

extra-marital

coincidental

medicamental

unornamental

complemental

supplemental

impedimental

complimental

experimental

governmental

departmental

instrumental

Septuagintal

superfrontal

interfrontal

contrapuntal

watch-crystal

non-committal

fissilingual

multilingual

dentilingual

interlingual

premenstrual

ultrasensual

supersensual

hypersensual

intellectual

psychosexual

heterosexual

perspectival

conjunctival

substantival

self-approval

self-betrayal

working-model

apfelstrudel

diamond-wheel

balance-wheel

canting-wheel

driving-wheel

pattern-wheel

counter-wheel

ratchet-wheel

trolley-wheel

blister-steel

field-spaniel

water-spaniel

glockenspiel

pumpernickel

copper-nickel

antiparallel

chrome-spinel

ring-dotterel

stormy-petrel

spurge-laurel

cherry-laurel

mangel-wurzel

studding-sail

water-wagtail

squirrel-tail

grapeseed-oil

water-milfoil

falcon-gentil

billiard-ball

medicine-ball

watering-call

judgment-hall

wag-at-the-wall

wag-by-the-wall

swimming-bell

gambling-hell

spindle-shell

unicorn-shell

scallop-shell

trumpet-shell

dropping-well

shealing-hill

sheeling-hill

shieling-hill

run-of-the-mill

spinning-mill

stamping-mill

sleeping-pill

diamond-drill

whip-poor-will

tenant-at-will

sneeshin-mull

public-school

riding-school

swimming-pool

snarling-tool

cucking-stool

ducking-stool

milking-stool

paddock-stool

servo-control

stilboestrol

saloon-pistol

pocket-pistol

bachelor-girl

spindle-whorl

disregardful

mischanceful

unrevengeful

unremorseful

unworshipful

wine-glassful

unsuccessful

undelightful

foresightful

unthoughtful

standing-bowl

burrowing-owl

heterodactyl

brachydactyl

M

thank-you-ma'am

weather-gleam

barrier-cream

exhaust-steam

sweet-william

battering-ram

röntgenogram

chromatogram

counter-claim

underkingdom

scoundreldom

newspaperdom

swinging-boom

Jacquard-loom

witches'-broom

standing-room

checking-room

dressing-room

counting-room

property-room

apple-blossom

pease-blossom

peach-blossom

heir-by-custom

double-bottom

copper-bottom

counter-charm

pteridosperm

lumbriciform
hydatidiform
campodeiform
strobiliform
flabelliform
flagelliform
morbilliform
anguilliform
pulvilliform
cylindriform
stalactiform
equisetiform
placentiform
serpentiform
underperform
thunder-storm
deuteroplasm
laryngospasm
gynodioecism
evangelicism
apostolicism
oecumenicism
grammaticism
chromaticism
dialecticism
syntheticism
aestheticism
psychoticism
fantasticism
patristicism
eunuchoidism
propagandism
avant-gardism
do-nothingism
prosyllogism
psychologism
synecdochism
patriarchism
Low-Churchism
parapsychism
diastrophism
philosophism
paramorphism
metamorphism
hemimorphism
theomorphism
pleomorphism
zygomorphism
hylomorphism
homomorphism
automorphism
polymorphism
paragnathism
hypognathism
practicalism
corporealism
superrealism
collegialism
parochialism
trinomialism
mercurialism
essentialism
factionalism
sectionalism

emotionalism
municipalism
episcopalism
bilateralism
commensalism
universalism
elementalism
bilingualism
perpetualism
spiritualism
pansexualism
mediaevalism
scoundrelism
Aristotelism
automobilism
Turcophilism
iconophilism
necrophilism
negrophilism
Russophilism
mercantilism
homothallism
aeroembolism
somnambulism
noctambulism
syndactylism
transformism
Laodiceanism
Manicheanism
Epicureanism
Traducianism
Confucianism
palladianism
Edwardianism
Zwinglianism
Sabellianism
neonomianism
Rosminianism
Febronianism
Hibernianism
gregarianism
semi-Arianism
sectarianism
unitarianism
Wagnerianism
Victorianism
Nestorianism
Hobbesianism
Keynesianism
Cartesianism
precisianism
Christianism
Pan-Germanism
stercoranism
charlatanism
Samaritanism
Panhellenism
Neohellenism
hobgoblinism
strychninism
philistinism
Neo-Darwinism
expansionism
immersionism

secessionism
diffusionism
exclusionism
deviationism
inflationism
isolationism
sensationism
causationism
salvationism
reductionism
coalitionism
abolitionism
intuitionism
evolutionism
parachronism
metachronism
asynchronism
Parkinsonism
Neoplatonism
nyctitropism
orthotropism
pleiotropism
heliotropism
chemotropism
hydrotropism
phototropism
haptotropism
incendiarism
newspaperism
characterism
dissenterism
shamateurism
behaviourism
hydrargyrism
mithridatism
dichromatism
metasomatism
Hippocratism
conservatism
Rembrandtism
dyotheletism
diamagnetism
geomagnetism
zoomagnetism
anti-Semitism
Marcionitism
obscurantism
dilettantism
paedobaptism
transvestism
stand-pattism
troglodytism
saprophytism
somniloquism
subjectivism
collectivism
Stakhanovism
voluntaryism
periostracum
etymologicum
stomatodaeum
cork-linoleum
pseudopodium
perionychium

epithalamium
praseodymium
transuranium
panhellenium
duraluminium
protactinium
quadriennium
bimillennium
quinquennium
spermogonium
pandaemonium
cuprammonium
dolphinarium
unguentarium
Uintatherium
Deinotherium
perinephrium
radio-thorium
synclinorium
suspensorium
inhalatorium
hypogastrium
pleiochasium
progymnasium
mycodomatium
perichaetium
kurchatovium
ornithogalum
sporangiolum
hibernaculum
supernaculum
receptaculum
diverticulum
suboperculum
orphan-asylum
xylobalsamum
Helianthemum
Lithospermum
xiphisternum
wide-spectrum
Ophioglossum
water-opossum
understratum
superstratum
paludamentum
calceamentum
crassamentum
N
anti-Gallican
Afro-American
Euro-American
Della-Cruscan
Panathenaean
Asclepiadean
velocipedean
proboscidean
non-Euclidean
Aristotelean
subterranean
Indo-European
baccalaurean
winnowing-fan
transleithan
geriatrician

geometrician	Schneiderian	hydromedusan	noradrenalin
biometrician	prototherian	tetrapolitan	butter-muslin
obstetrician	Lancasterian	pentapolitan	haematoxylin
dialectician	Presbyterian	cosmopolitan	phenylalanin
aesthetician	fustillirian	metropolitan	phaeomelanin
theoretician	Thermidorian	heterokontan	carragheenin
statistician	Montessorian	whooping-swan	gonadotropin
velocipedian	gladiatorian	cliché-ridden	xanthopterin
proboscidian	salutatorian	priest-ridden	demi-culverin
diprionidian	mid-Victorian	shield-maiden	fibrinolysin
cantharidian	prehistorian	unwithholden	griseofulvin
ephemeridian	consistorian	winter-garden	fluorocarbon
antemeridian	teleosaurian	flower-garden	marker-beacon
post-meridian	stegosaurian	market-garden	genethliacon
Pre-Dravidian	pterosaurian	church-warden	panpharmacon
paradoxidian	Australasian	window-screen	etymologicon
Little-endian	Austronesian	bowling-green	pantechnicon
Pecksniffian	Tardenoisian	putting-green	stereopticon
Semi-Pelagian	Patripassian	Lincoln-green	unbreathed-on
Kimmeridgian	Byelorussian	aesthesiogen	ground-pigeon
Cantabrigian	heteroousian	paracyanogen	bronze-pigeon
Carlovingian	Tagliacotian	hallucinogen	house-surgeon
hypophrygian	prechristian	agglutinogen	staff-surgeon
Archilochian	non-Christian	moonstricken	microsurgeon
monodelphian	Neo-Christian	smooth-spoken	neurosurgeon
labyrinthian	Southcottian	pretty-spoken	inescutcheon
bacchanalian	Scandinavian	heaven-fallen	station-wagon
episcopalian	antediluvian	footplatemen	antistrophon
Liverpudlian	post-diluvian	rabbit-warren	encheiridion
Aristotelian	Pestalozzian	spiegeleisen	king's-cushion
Torricellian	East-Indiaman	delicatessen	lady's-cushion
vaudevillian	backswordman	winter-beaten	pericynthion
cryptogamian	ex-serviceman	kindergarten	paranthelion
transuranian	longshoreman	hunger-bitten	mountain-lion
Neo-Darwinian	saltpetreman	sallow-kitten	epithalamion
Grandisonian	warehouseman	self-begotten	prothalamion
Jeffersonian	under-hangman	god-forgotten	pot-companion
Muggletonian	Low-Churchman	frankalmoign	panhellenion
dodecagynian	underworkman	feather-brain	non-communion
hippocrepian	servicewoman	scatter-brain	rock-scorpion
nothingarian	waiting-woman	shatter-brain	book-scorpion
turbellarian	Englishwoman	counter-drain	whip-scorpion
cancellarian	laundry-woman	baggage-train	circumcision
procellarian	countrywoman	through-train	long-division
epistolarian	remainder-man	freight-train	cell-division
vocabularian	cousin-german	soda-fountain	retropulsion
nonagenarian	Franco-German	catamountain	reprehension
sexagenarian	newspaperman	mill-mountain	apprehension
octogenarian	slaughterman	group-captain	hypertension
catilinarian	vice-chairman	weather-stain	extraversion
Apollinarian	swell-mobsman	antithrombin	reconversion
veterinarian	backwoodsman	erythromycin	introversion
doctrinarian	fish-salesman	streptomycin	extroversion
sublibrarian	meat-salesman	turacoverdin	transversion
Sublapsarian	man-of-war's-man	glucoprotein	underpassion
celibatarian	frontiersman	glycoprotein	retrocession
totalitarian	aircraftsman	lactoprotein	intercession
equalitarian	water-boatman	Frankenstein	supersession
futilitarian	artillery-man	thyrotrophin	repossession
humanitarian	spermatozoan	thick-and-thin	photo-fission
ubiquitarian	hymenopteran	strophanthin	non-admission
Gibraltarian	cheiropteran	phycoxanthin	recommission
Northumbrian	odontophoran	anthoxanthin	expromission
salamandrian	discomedusan	tercel-jerkin	intromission

intermission	self-creation	vesiculation	vertebration
transmission	illaqueation	reticulation	exprobration
repercussion	congregation	articulation	elucubration
circumfusion	disgregation	emasculation	consecration
inconclusion	promulgation	inosculation	deliberation
interclusion	prolongation	stridulation	dilaceration
self-delusion	homologation	flammulation	exulceration
non-intrusion	compurgation	accumulation	evisceration
conglobation	subarrhation	manipulation	desideration
exacerbation	depreciation	depopulation	immoderation
perturbation	appreciation	gastrulation	vociferation
masturbation	denunciation	punctulation	exaggeration
claudication	renunciation	capitulation	morigeration
adjudication	annunciation	blastulation	bletheration
dijudication	consociation	amalgamation	acceleration
pacification	dissociation	conclamation	deceleration
nidification	deforciation	proclamation	intoleration
codification	excruciation	disclamation	degeneration
modification	digladiation	desquamation	regeneration
palification	tripudiation	concremation	inteneration
salification	arpeggiation	legitimation	incineration
uglification	conciliation	inflammation	remuneration
vilification	prefoliation	consummation	disoperation
ramification	perfoliation	missummation	exasperation
humification	despoliation	confirmation	recuperation
panification	calumniation	preformation	vituperation
minification	columniation	malformation	obliteration
vinification	repatriation	conformation	alliteration
typification	expatriation	misformation	re-alteration
verification	centuriation	lachrymation	adulteration
purification	propitiation	complanation	exenteration
gasification	abbreviation	incatenation	asseveration
ossification	asphyxiation	rejuvenation	deflagration
ratification	antihalation	impregnation	deaspiration
notification	sphacelation	consignation	conspiration
vivification	insufflation	contignation	perspiration
spiflication	exsufflation	propugnation	edulcoration
triplication	disinflation	deracination	invigoration
complication	slumpflation	vaticination	amelioration
supplication	assibilation	reordination	prefloration
divarication	strobilation	inordination	decoloration
detoxication	obnubilation	co-ordination	tractoration
intoxication	invigilation	coordination	perpetration
detruncation	annihilation	invagination	infiltration
reallocation	assimilation	emargination	fenestration
equivocation	deoppilation	desalination	registration
trifurcation	installation	delamination	ministration
confiscation	flabellation	ingemination	colostration
miseducation	cancellation	insemination	claustration
disgradation	flagellation	denomination	illustration
exheredation	crenellation	illumination	instauration
dilucidation	compellation	resupination	effiguration
invalidation	tessellation	chlorination	inauguration
intimidation	scutellation	fluorination	sulphuration
dilapidation	fibrillation	gelatination	puncturation
fluoridation	cantillation	condemnation	nomadisation
peroxidation	distillation	cachinnation	faradisation
commendation	instillation	incoronation	fluidisation
refoundation	postillation	anticipation	localisation
defraudation	vitriolation	emancipation	vocalisation
subfeudation	infibulation	constipation	idealisation
transudation	flocculation	reoccupation	legalisation
sublineation	pediculation	inoccupation	canalisation
diffareation	geniculation	exhilaration	penalisation

moralisation	expeditation	stupefaction	proscription
ruralisation	excogitation	torrefaction	transumption
nasalisation	habilitation	putrefaction	reassumption
vitalisation	debilitation	liquefaction	reabsorption
totalisation	nobilitation	assuefaction	interruption
equalisation	facilitation	petrifaction	incorruption
novelisation	delimitation	vitrifaction	self-exertion
mobilisation	illimitation	satisfaction	overexertion
civilisation	insanitation	substraction	predigestion
nebulisation	exploitation	disaffection	decongestion
Islamisation	decapitation	disinfection	contribution
racemisation	strepitation	imperfection	distribution
minimisation	revisitation	unperfection	irresolution
optimisation	deposition	insubjection	substitution
urbanisation	auscultation	retrojection	constitution
organisation	consultation	introjection	prostitution
Romanisation	replantation	interjection	dorsiflexion
humanisation	implantation	self-election	retroflexion
tetanisation	explantation	preselection	disconnexion
splenisation	placentation	irreflection	diencephalon
cutinisation	segmentation	genuflection	epencephalon
unionisation	pigmentation	predilection	haematoxylon
colonisation	augmentation	intellection	prolegomenon
Polonisation	alimentation	recollection	perispomenon
canonisation	commentation	reinspection	pilot-balloon
immunisation	fermentation	misdirection	dessertspoon
velarisation	frumentation	resurrection	spermatozoon
polarisation	presentation	insurrection	dodecahedron
solarisation	sustentation	intersection	chiliahedron
suberisation	labanotation	cross-section	rhombohedron
maderisation	misquotation	interdiction	pyritohedron
etherisation	readaptation	jurisdiction	rhododendron
dimerisation	inadaptation	antifriction	liriodendron
laterisation	disceptation	prestriction	philodendron
arborisation	dissertation	constriction	nychthemeron
valorisation	subhastation	reproduction	branding-iron
memorisation	space-station	introduction	caulking-iron
vaporisation	contestation	transduction	snarling-iron
motorisation	protestation	solifluction	crimping-iron
hepatisation	power-station	substruction	crisping-iron
monetisation	rotor-station	construction	shooting-iron
Semitisation	pregustation	incompletion	toasting-iron
sanitisation	decrustation	indiscretion	entoplastron
quantisation	encrustation	precondition	march-treason
amortisation	incrustation	air-condition	Hobson-Jobson
condensation	effecutation	precognition	disinherison
compensation	sternutation	malnutrition	spokesperson
dispensation	subarcuation	vomiturition	object-lesson
malversation	continuation	perquisition	polysyndeton
conversation	colliquation	disquisition	endoskeleton
incrassation	menstruation	reimposition	nanoplankton
inspissation	perpetuation	postposition	aeroplankton
succussation	tumultuation	tripartition	sleeve-button
constatation	invultuation	superstition	trichophyton
perfectation	accentuation	non-attention	pay-as-you-earn
pernoctation	insalivation	supervention	staghorn-fern
colluctation	deactivation	intervention	Jack-a-lantern
engraftation	reactivation	tappet-motion	storm-lantern
inhabitation	inactivation	self-devotion	Jack-o'-lantern
cohabitation	coacervation	apperception	north-eastern
capacitation	preservation	interception	south-eastern
felicitation	conservation	subscription	north-western
solicitation	re-annexation	prescription	south-western
exercitation	overreaction	conscription	shawl-pattern

stock-and-horn
drinking-horn
sea-buckthorn
Christ's-thorn
dressing-down
freezing-down
dressing-gown
Cappagh-brown
steeple-crown
unoverthrown
man-about-town

O

incomunicado
clavicembalo
water-buffalo
marcatissimo
altaltissimo
twenty-four-mo
mezzo-soprano
antineutrino
tu-whit-tu-whoo
ground-cuckoo
drongo-cuckoo
tree-kangaroo
banderillero
Lillibullero
Lilliburlero
kidney-potato
unlistened-to
quattrocento
risorgimento
divertimento
contrapposto
basso-relievo
basso-rilievo
mezzo-rilievo

P

mountain-soap
kicking-strap
stirrup-strap
chimney-sweep
unfriendship
overlordship
prenticeship
discipleship
creatureship
laureateship
training-ship
cardinalship
corporalship
hospital-ship
musicianship
guardianship
horsemanship
freshmanship
brinkmanship
one-upmanship
aldermanship
watermanship
chairmanship
salesmanship
gamesmanship
huntsmanship
craftmanship

partisanship
chaplainship
championship
relationship
virtuosoship
recordership
preachership
wranglership
retainership
spinstership
seigniorship
superiorship
bachelorship
governorship
assessorship
mediatorship
dictatorship
directorship
servitorship
quaestorship
executorship
survivorship
image-worship
devil-worship
surveyorship
mistress-ship
sergeantship
serjeantship
residentship
viscountship
attorneyship
shoulder-slip
water-parsnip
pleasure-trip
landing-strip
weather-strip
tantalum-lamp
writer's-cramp
postage-stamp
cypress-swamp
thunder-plump
knocking-shop
prince-bishop
underdevelop
counterscarp
will-o'-the-wisp
moustache-cup
nitroso-group

R

dormitory-car
cinnamon-bear
steering-gear
crystal-clear
extranuclear
multinuclear
elephant's-ear
thousand-year
buckle-beggar
subumbrellar
quasi-stellar
interstellar
saddle-pillar
electropolar
infundibular

semiglobular
multilobular
interlobular
microtubular
tabernacular
supernacular
receptacular
appendicular
diverticular
plurilocular
multilocular
subopercular
semicircular
extra-regular
quadrangular
interlaminar
nail-head-spar
dogtooth-spar
schiller-spar
antimacassar
trench-mortar
shooting-star
bonny-clabber
sponge-rubber
money-grubber
cloud-chamber
bride-chamber
steam-chamber
guest-chamber
fellow-member
peace-officer
staff-officer
watch-officer
baron-officer
morris-dancer
ballet-dancer
oneiromancer
countenancer
remembrancer
encumbrancer
interpleader
muzzle-loader
breech-loader
rodomontader
salmon-ladder
Jacob's-ladder
cannon-fodder
ground-feeder
mouth-breeder
stock-breeder
bottle-slider
pillion-rider
circuit-rider
water-strider
brickfielder
mound-builder
coachbuilder
organ-builder
underbuilder
jerry-builder
office-holder
candle-holder
kettleholder
bottle-holder

ticket-holder
policy-holder
cold-shoulder
scrimshander
Netherlander
understander
object-finder
type-cylinder
semicylinder
seal-cylinder
surrejoinder
knife-grinder
organ-grinder
stage-thunder
brass-bounder
brassfounder
three-pounder
Bible-pounder
skateboarder
tape-recorder
pebble-powder
baking-powder
insect-powder
specktioneer
waistcoateer
pro-marketeer
slockdolager
stage-manager
queen-dowager
carpetbagger
double-dagger
square-rigger
plough-jogger
hugger-mugger
doppel-ganger
interchanger
shortchanger
money-changer
slang-whanger
way-passenger
sponge-finger
potato-finger
klipspringer
mastersinger
balladmonger
phrasemonger
cheese-monger
system-monger
gossip-monger
barber-monger
wonder-monger
costermonger
prayer-monger
carpetmonger
turbocharger
supercharger
cheeseburger
camp-preacher
music-teacher
crossbencher
front-bencher
lick-trencher
thief-catcher
baby-snatcher

body-snatcher	sword-breaker	hephthemimer	armour-bearer
clock-watcher	peace-breaker	sledge-hammer	sheep-shearer
slink-butcher	truce-breaker	tuning-hammer	self-murderer
check-weigher	image-breaker	yellow-hammer	bunko-steerer
calligrapher	frame-breaker	monkey-hammer	toll-gatherer
iambographer	stone-breaker	katzenjammer	filibusterer
snobographer	horse-breaker	snow-in-summer	baby-batterer
zincographer	house-breaker	breastsummer	rediscoverer
discographer	heartbreaker	stereoisomer	hair-restorer
lithographer	hallan-shaker	snake-charmer	reconnoitrer
orthographer	cuckold-maker	chloroformer	dock-labourer
mythographer	troublemaker	strengthener	farm-labourer
radiographer	posture-maker	bottle-opener	subtreasurer
hagiographer	leasing-maker	straightener	manufacturer
heliographer	pattern-maker	clip-fastener	instep-raiser
cosmographer	harness-maker	horse-trainer	standardiser
stenographer	gallows-maker	paper-stainer	mythologiser
ethnographer	cabinetmaker	sugar-refiner	Prussianiser
hymnographer	holidaymaker	freight-liner	synchroniser
phonographer	horse-knacker	water-diviner	Septembriser
pornographer	double-decker	money-spinner	systematiser
necrographer	single-decker	Jenny-spinner	demagnetiser
micrographer	three-pricker	Marcobrunner	proselytiser
hydrographer	alpha-blocker	out-pensioner	gas-condenser
hierographer	mother-fucker	processioner	horse-courser
chirographer	rabbit-sucker	commissioner	filter-passer
reprographer	office-seeker	foundationer	kirschwasser
petrographer	street-walker	law-stationer	stone-dresser
pantographer	skrimshanker	confectioner	court-dresser
photographer	stratotanker	correctioner	Besserwisser
cartographer	underskinker	exhibitioner	rabble-rouser
phytographer	water-drinker	practitioner	breathalyser
tachygrapher	headshrinker	conventioner	silver-beater
pocket-gopher	wonder-worker	redemptioner	single-seater
gastrosopher	double-dealer	resolutioner	serpent-eater
father-lasher	sheep-stealer	revolutioner	roller-skater
sage-thrasher	Simmenthaler	gander-mooner	milk-and-water
bottle-washer	paper-marbler	tracing-paper	surface-water
sponge-fisher	hedge-warbler	packing-paper	trocheameter
salmon-fisher	sedge-warbler	writing-paper	semi-diameter
accomplisher	conventicler	drawing-paper	coulombmeter
extinguisher	intermeddler	spring-keeper	isoperimeter
quill-feather	corn-chandler	saloon-keeper	evaporimeter
plate-leather	ship-chandler	street-keeper	extensimeter
sprat-weather	stern-wheeler	wicket-keeper	viscosimeter
foster-father	quarter-miler	hedge-creeper	effusiometer
everywhither	swashbuckler	Bible-thumper	nephelometer
through-other	laisser-aller	storm-trooper	sphygmometer
foster-mother	laissez-aller	flint-knapper	arithmometer
guild-brother	pearl-sheller	spirit-rapper	rhythmometer
blood-brother	forset-seller	cherry-pepper	endosmometer
craft-brother	fosset-seller	bread-chipper	galvanometer
water-soldier	woman-queller	transshipper	declinometer
boulevardier	spine-chiller	lady's-slipper	inclinometer
dehumidifier	vermin-killer	bodice-ripper	trigonometer
disqualifier	Pralltriller	cement-copper	harmonometer
butty-collier	inking-roller	cheese-hopper	psychrometer
tumbler-drier	butter-cooler	share-cropper	electrometer
crush-barrier	sabre-rattler	eavesdropper	tellurometer
troop-carrier	machine-ruler	stage-whisper	extensometer
water-carrier	night-brawler	electrotyper	galactometer
marsh-harrier	night-crawler	hebdomadarer	cathetometer
vaunt-courier	bobby-dazzler	shield-bearer	magnetometer
pedal-clavier	screw-steamer	office-bearer	densitometer

sensitometer	engine-fitter	domesticator	interoceptor
fore-and-after	lath-splitter	averruncator	exteroceptor
thereinafter	rail-splitter	reciprocator	lithotriptor
scene-shifter	hair-splitter	consolidator	pepper-castor
cattle-lifter	train-spotter	accommodator	interlocutor
weight-lifter	globe-trotter	investigator	mother-liquor
prize-fighter	teeter-totter	interrogator	charter-mayor
first-nighter	marble-cutter	prestigiator	road-surveyor
stepdaughter	cheese-cutter	impropriator	land-surveyor
manslaughter	storm-shutter	appropriator	hippocentaur
Gastarbeiter	down-and-outer	scintillator	entrepreneur
turbidimiter	mixter-maxter	extrapolator	carillonneur
screen-writer	school-leaver	interpolator	restaurateur
gossip-writer	wood-engraver	contemplator	spectre-lemur
letter-writer	line-engraver	confabulator	eleventh-hour
mirror-writer	whencesoever	funambulator	kilowatt-hour
ticket-writer	self-deceiver	perambulator	misbehaviour
script-writer	engine-driver	matriculator	technicolour
disenchanter	nickel-silver	gesticulator	salmon-colour
transplanter	crossing-over	dissimulator	Quaker-colour
supplementer	winter-clover	expostulator	splint-armour
complimenter	half-seas-over	dephlegmator	misdemeanour
experimenter	virgin's-bower	miscegenator	sweet-and-sour
scene-painter	wedding-dower	disseminator	pseudomartyr
office-hunter	grass-widower	recriminator	S
legacy-hunter	orange-flower	exterminator	semiwater-gas
heresy-hunter	pasque-flower	peregrinator	orthopaedics
snack-counter	fennel-flower	assassinator	metapsychics
abbey-counter	calico-flower	fractionator	aerodynamics
velvet-scoter	cuckoo-flower	impersonator	biorhythmics
motor-scooter	monkey-flower	participator	psychonomics
sharpshooter	camp-follower	equilibrator	orthodromics
interchapter	staying-power	reverberator	biomechanics
teleprompter	flame-thrower	refrigerator	calisthenics
three-quarter	spear-thrower	commiserator	zymotechnics
black-quarter	conning-tower	perseverator	pyrotechnics
animadverter	tennis-player	collaborator	radiophonics
ticket-porter	Penang-lawyer	corroborator	geotectonics
figure-caster	bottom-sawyer	commemorator	atmospherics
politicaster	crystal-gazer	incorporator	econometrics
pepper-caster	rocking-chair	concentrator	microphysics
theologaster	nursing-chair	orchestrator	astrophysics
court-plaster	Windsor-chair	sequestrator	problematics
riding-master	surface-to-air	demonstrator	hydrostatics
taxing-master	winding-stair	remonstrator	catallactics
chapelmaster	conquistador	stabilisator	phonotactics
schoolmaster	stream-anchor	improvisator	cytogenetics
muster-master	lord-superior	resuscitator	paedodontics
craftsmaster	brigade-major	precipitator	orthodontics
ballet-master	trumpet-major	water-reactor	periodontics
garret-master	counter-tenor	chiropractor	macrobiotics
quarrymaster	vice-governor	motor-tractor	gnotobiotics
cheese-taster	transgressor	free-selector	ceroplastics
candle-waster	decompressor	tax-collector	Hudibrastics
shirtwaister	dispossessor	subinspector	sphragistics
cash-register	hypothecator	self-director	catacoustics
water-blister	qualificator	zenith-sector	cosmonautics
bend-sinister	significator	mine-detector	astronautics
foster-sister	scarificator	contradictor	hermeneutics
bronco-buster	versificator	school-doctor	therapeutics
loss-adjuster	testificator	tithe-proctor	burnt-almonds
supercluster	justificator	non-conductor	wedding-cards
stone-chatter	communicator	primogenitor	velvet-guards
pitter-patter	prevaricator	electromotor	thitherwards

whitherwards	palingenesis	polyneuritis	moistureless
generatrices	paedogenesis	pancreatitis	disguiseless
nectocalyces	osteogenesis	trophallaxis	responseless
epididymides	pathogenesis	morphallaxis	farthingless
proglottides	orthogenesis	between-decks	stockingless
Steganopodes	mythogenesis	fiddlesticks	shillingless
knee-breeches	diplogenesis	draught-hooks	reproachless
grave-clothes	phylogenesis	substantials	strengthless
small-clothes	agamogenesis	wild-williams	fountainless
plain-clothes	hypnogenesis	master-at-arms	religionless
underclothes	sporogenesis	growing-pains	vacationless
night-clothes	petrogenesis	galligaskins	relationless
short-clothes	histogenesis	orthocousins	frictionless
heeby-jeebies	phytogenesis	combinations	functionless
namby-pambies	photokinesis	pinchcommons	ambitionless
pleasantries	karyokinesis	curling-irons	volitionless
incivilities	orthotonesis	phytobenthos	questionless
welter-stakes	cataphoresis	antigropelos	mistressless
Ulotrichales	ionophoresis	exophthalmos	distrustless
Lycopodiales	paracentesis	opisthodomos	mistrustless
collywobbles	heterauxesis	opisthotonos	prolificness
goose-pimples	pseudocyesis	misanthropos	majesticness
cashew-apples	anamorphosis	petrodollars	benumbedness
troll-my-dames	epanorthosis	lady's-fingers	one-sidedness
betweentimes	trophobiosis	pedal-pushers	two-sidedness
Strigiformes	anaerobiosis	live-feathers	scraggedness
Valenciennes	bilharziosis	camiknickers	enlargedness
antichthones	furunculosis	side-whiskers	detachedness
autochthones	tuberculosis	headquarters	starchedness
supercargoes	strongylosis	hindquarters	wretchedness
peccadilloes	paraphimosis	water-flowers	speckledness
necropolises	hallucinosis	night-terrors	deformedness
metropolises	avitaminosis	nail-scissors	resignedness
rhinoceroses	self-hypnosis	messeigneurs	preparedness
opera-glasses	autohypnosis	thorough-bass	witheredness
bow-compasses	bromhidrosis	working-class	cankeredness
polyanthuses	hyperidrosis	keeking-glass	pamperedness
ranunculuses	otosclerosis	looking-glass	favouredness
prospectuses	synarthrosis	larking-glass	diseasedness
eucalyptuses	osteoporosis	burning-glass	unbiasedness
zygapophyses	aeroneurosis	cupping-glass	despisedness
parapophyses	sarcomatosis	weather-glass	composedness
roller-skates	enteroptosis	liqueur-glass	diffusedness
Pleuronectes	nephroptosis	radio-compass	confusedness
Discomycetes	leucocytosis	orchard-grass	indebtedness
Phycomycetes	phagocytosis	quaking-grass	affectedness
Ecclesiastes	anacatharsis	tussock-grass	dejectedness
thousand-legs	zygapophysis	buffalo-grass	addictedness
ball-bearings	parapophysis	feather-grass	spiritedness
purse-strings	self-analysis	whitlow-grass	dementedness
apron-strings	electrolysis	sparrow-grass	unwontedness
weeding-tongs	haematolysis	timothy-grass	assortedness
curling-tongs	appendicitis	disembarrass	unfittedness
Hemerocallis	pericarditis	photo-process	besottedness
deuch-an-doris	endocarditis	philosophess	pollutedness
urolithiasis	lymphangitis	scabbardless	depravedness
trichiniasis	encephalitis	shepherdless	resolvedness
toxocariasis	crystallitis	distanceless	reservedness
dracontiasis	ophthalmitis	pretenceless	dismayedness
bilharziasis	diphtheritis	resourceless	pellucidness
biosynthesis	hamarthritis	languageless	uncandidness
kinaesthesis	panarthritis	nevertheless	splendidness
schindylesis	endometritis	backboneless	manifoldness
haematemesis	perineuritis	pleasureless	fourfoldness

overkindness
purblindness
day-blindness
overfondness
profoundness
all-roundness
backwardness
downwardness
untowardness
overniceness
placableness
amicableness
readableness
laudableness
saleableness
moveableness
singableness
sociableness
reliableness
variableness
pitiableness
enviableness
workableness
blamableness
amenableness
damnableness
palpableness
culpableness
bearableness
adorableness
passableness
suitableness
quotableness
unstableness
valuableness
knowableness
avowableness
forcibleness
credibleness
vendibleness
tangibleness
terribleness
horribleness
feasibleness
sensibleness
passibleness
flexibleness
juvenileness
volatileness
ungentleness
gladsomeness
handsomeness
gamesomeness
lonesomeness
tiresomeness
gruesomeness
toilsomeness
overfineness
feminineness
sanguineness
foregoneness
overripeness
immatureness
propenseness

perverseness
abstruseness
delicateness
desolateness
separateness
moderateness
accurateness
obdurateness
adequateness
obsoleteness
completeness
concreteness
discreteness
impoliteness
unpoliteness
definiteness
infiniteness
contriteness
appositeness
oppositeness
unchasteness
absoluteness
resoluteness
coerciveness
adhesiveness
cohesiveness
decisiveness
incisiveness
derisiveness
divisiveness
effusiveness
delusiveness
allusiveness
illusiveness
creativeness
negativeness
relativeness
vitativeness
laxativeness
reactiveness
covetiveness
fugitiveness
positiveness
adaptiveness
eruptiveness
abortiveness
sportiveness
piercingness
unfadingness
yieldingness
unendingness
engagingness
obligingness
touchingness
shockingness
strikingness
triflingness
drawlingness
swimmingness
becomingness
sweepingness
graspingness
waveringness
aspiringness

retiringness
unerringness
pleasingness
imposingness
invitingness
temptingness
thrivingness
unlovingness
thoroughness
overrashness
snobbishness
cloddishness
childishness
fiendishness
dwarfishness
Whiggishness
priggishness
sluggishness
sumphishness
sneakishness
freakishness
brackishness
trickishness
stockishness
ticklishness
churlishness
ghoulishness
qualmishness
womanishness
greenishness
swainishness
clannishness
clownishness
sheepishness
scampishness
snappishness
cheerishness
waterishness
feverishness
sweetishness
faintishness
skittishness
Scottishness
sluttishness
cliquishness
thievishness
shrewishness
chieftainess
unsteadiness
unwieldiness
scratchiness
stealthiness
unworthiness
friendliness
unkindliness
cowardliness
towardliness
princeliness
unlikeliness
untimeliness
uncomeliness
unliveliness
unloveliness
unseemliness

maidenliness
heavenliness
slovenliness
ungainliness
beggarliness
fatherliness
motherliness
mannerliness
masterliness
sisterliness
knightliness
priestliness
Christliness
literariness
contrariness
solitariness
salutariness
featheriness
smotheriness
slipperiness
plasteriness
nugatoriness
dilatoriness
agribusiness
agrobusiness
show-business
snippetiness
toploftiness
draughtiness
droughtiness
untrustiness
unprettiness
homesickness
gall-sickness
tragicalness
inimicalness
heroicalness
criticalness
triticalness
verticalness
mysticalness
materialness
brimfulness
overfullness
dreadfulness
peacefulness
gracefulness
voicefulness
pridefulness
vengefulness
guilefulness
shamefulness
blamefulness
unusefulness
gratefulness
spitefulness
tastefulness
wastefulness
wrongfulness
watchfulness
loathfulness
wrathfulness
faithfulness
slothfulness

mirthfulness	listlessness	explicitness	ombrophobous
youthfulness	gorgeousness	decrepitness	hydrophobous
truthfulness	vitreousness	flippantness	ochroleucous
fancifulness	nauseousness	fragrantness	untremendous
mercifulness	edaciousness	pleasantness	gastropodous
thankfulness	spaciousness	apparentness	schizopodous
stormfulness	graciousness	affluentness	ligniperdous
scornfulness	speciousness	frequentness	bombacaceous
mournfulness	preciousness	stalwartness	orchidaceous
cheerfulness	lusciousness	malapertness	sapindaceous
powerfulness	studiousness	inexpertness	acanthaceous
blissfulness	fashiousness	manifestness	santalaceous
doubtfulness	gloriousness	everydayness	cedrelaceous
rightfulness	uxoriousness	ambassadress	corallaceous
fruitfulness	spuriousness	fatigue-dress	argillaceous
sportfulness	usuriousness	wedding-dress	capillaceous
boastfulness	factiousness	bathing-dress	corollaceous
trustfulness	captiousness	evening-dress	salsolaceous
unlawfulness	cautiousness	morning-dress	schorlaceous
lukewarmness	greviousness	confessoress	primulaceous
forsakenness	previousness	professoress	plumulaceous
mistakenness	perviousness	packing-press	stipulaceous
unbrokenness	perilousness	copying-press	diatomaceous
uncommonness	fabulousness	clothes-press	pandanaceous
stubbornness	nebulousness	vindicatress	platanaceous
lovelornness	sedulousness	fornicatress	verbenaceous
forswornness	populousness	negotiatress	gallinaceous
oracularness	venomousness	legislatress	graminaceous
togetherness	enormousness	benefactress	pectinaceous
debonairness	ravenousness	instructress	carbonaceous
needlessness	luminousness	proprietress	apocynaceous
mindlessness	numinousness	progenitress	scolopaceous
woodlessness	mutinousness	inquisitress	droseraceous
lifelessness	scabrousness	headmistress	burseraceous
namelessness	cumbrousness	workmistress	cichoraceous
tamelessness	wondrousness	taskmistress	furfuraceous
timelessness	ulcerousness	postmistress	lomentaceous
homelessness	numerousness	interpretess	orichalceous
tonelessness	generousness	presidentess	calycoideous
hopelessness	desirousness	anotherguess	achlamydeous
carelessness	decorousness	weeping-cross	advantageous
tirelessness	rigorousness	pitch-and-toss	succedaneous
baselessness	vigorousness	portmanteaus	temporaneous
hatelessness	dolorousness	cumulo-nimbus	simultaneous
movelessness	timorousness	pneumococcus	momentaneous
selflessness	humorousness	echinococcus	assentaneous
ruthlessness	canorousness	Sivapithecus	subcutaneous
pitilessness	sonorousness	Oreopithecus	percutaneous
fecklessness	vaporousness	Neoceratodus	pergameneous
recklessness	dextrousness	thaumaturgus	pyroligneous
lucklessness	covetousness	oncorhynchus	testudineous
soullessness	exiguousness	philadelphus	ferrugineous
harmlessness	sensuousness	strophanthus	scitamineous
formlessness	unctuousness	antibacchius	interosseous
gainlessness	virtuousness	Stradivarius	discourteous
painlessness	tortuousness	logodaedalus	sarcophagous
helplessness	abstractness	Cynocephalus	lithophagous
fearlessness	indirectness	xiphophyllus	ophiophagous
peerlessness	succinctness	cirro-cumulus	mallophagous
tactlessness	distinctness	hypothalamus	hippophagous
bootlessness	discreetness	hippopotamus	carpophagous
spotlessness	disquietness	exophthalmus	necrophagous
hurtlessness	straightness	antoninianus	saprophagous
restlessness	implicitness	electrotonus	coprophagous

scatophagous
pantophagous
phytophagous
rhizophagous
dendrologous
heterologous
pompholygous
steatopygous
heterozygous
leiotrichous
cymotrichous
octastichous
monostichous
octostichous
triadelphous
monadelphous
monodelphous
perimorphous
pleomorphous
lagomorphous
zygomorphous
homomorphous
monomorphous
xeromorphous
mesomorphous
polymorphous
paragnathous
metagnathous
hypognathous
pervicacious
pachydacious
contumacious
turbinacious
pertinacious
self-gracious
heteroecious
semi-precious
inauspicious
unauspicious
unsuspicious
meretricious
tralaticious
subconscious
splendidious
unfastidious
incommodious
sacrilegious
contumelious
supercilious
cacophonious
querimonious
parsimonious
inharmonious
unharmonious
multifarious
multivarious
insalubrious
subdelirious
self-glorious
vainglorious
uncensorious
saltatorious
proditorious
syngenesious

ostentatious
disputatious
rambunctious
compunctious
inimicitious
gentilitious
unpropitious
innutritious
supposititious
tralatitious
adscititious
cementitious
adventitious
obreptitious
tricephalous
antisepalous
gamosepalous
monosepalous
octosepalous
polysepalous
antipetalous
gamopetalous
monopetalous
octopetalous
polypetalous
lithophilous
anthophilous
heliophilous
anemophilous
limnophilous
tropophilous
ombrophilous
necrophilous
hydrophilous
hygrophilous
coprophilous
photophilous
rhizophilous
verisimilous
endophyllous
gamophyllous
polyphyllous
dasyphyllous
radicicolous
silicicolous
lapidicolous
paludicolous
spongicolous
vaginicolous
unmiraculous
crepusculous
subacidulous
iracundulous
unscrupulous
tridactylous
syndactylous
phaenogamous
cryptogamous
heteronomous
homochromous
trichotomous
amphistomous
teleostomous
angiostomous

cyclostomous
osteodermous
pachydermous
idiothermous
homothermous
eurythermous
pseudonymous
cryptonymous
hydrophanous
porcellanous
quadrumanous
keratogenous
schizogenous
porcelainous
unlibidinous
hebetudinous
solitudinous
latitudinous
altitudinous
plumbaginous
mucilaginous
ustilaginous
impetiginous
matriclinous
patriclinous
matroclinous
patroclinous
postliminous
conterminous
exalbuminous
self-luminous
interspinous
serpentinous
exsanguinous
inconcinnous
cotyledonous
heterogonous
schizogonous
isostemonous
asynchronous
dodecagynous
amphitropous
orthotropous
stegocarpous
anthocarpous
angiocarpous
rhizocarpous
pachycarpous
sudoriparous
dodecandrous
precancerous
plumbiferous
siliciferous
laticiferous
glandiferous
frondiferous
conchiferous
moschiferous
petaliferous
stelliferous
soboliferous
papuliferous
cupuliferous
flammiferous

titaniferous
seminiferous
luminiferous
resiniferous
stanniferous
tuberiferous
sudoriferous
doloriferous
soporiferous
fructiferous
pyritiferous
amentiferous
salutiferous
sanguiferous
elytrigerous
synantherous
cantankerous
homoeomerous
homoiomerous
heteromerous
obstreperous
unprosperous
slaughterous
tetrapterous
plecopterous
coleopterous
orthopterous
macropterous
micropterous
chiropterous
neuropterous
preposterous
unchivalrous
discophorous
necrophorous
sporophorous
multiflorous
tetrasporous
radicivorous
fructivorous
sanguivorous
litholatrous
ophiolatrous
heliolatrous
Mariolatrous
Maryolatrous
disaventrous
ambidextrous
misventurous
erythematous
glaucomatous
xanthomatous
atheromatous
steatomatous
teratomatous
odontomatous
zygomycetous
infelicitous
unsolicitous
polyglottous
hydrophytous
transpicuous
incontiguous
circumfluous

disingenuous	lower-bracket	foreign-built	efflorescent
multiloquous	tennis-racket	clinker-built	deliquescent
untumultuous	Tyburn-ticket	electron-volt	ingravescent
contemptuous	single-wicket	jurisconsult	effervescent
presumptuous	underblanket	disaccordant	concupiscent
Sinanthropus	feeing-market	undiscordant	transcendent
habeas-corpus	Balaam-basket	supererogant	co-respondent
antibarbarus	pollen-basket	kerb-merchant	jurisprudent
Sciuropterus	mutton-cutlet	curb-merchant	counter-agent
Trachypterus	sun-and-planet	wine-merchant	intransigent
Histiophorus	cheese-rennet	coal-merchant	retromingent
cumulo-cirrus	sword-bayonet	corn-merchant	birefringent
Plesiosaurus	Tyburn-tippet	fent-merchant	constringent
megalosaurus	misinterpret	stoop-gallant	sorbefacient
Ankylosaurus	receiving-set	interpellant	stupefacient
Titanosaurus	powder-closet	grapple-plant	putrefacient
brontosaurus	breakfast-set	cushion-plant	liquefacient
egg-apparatus	Gesellschaft	tobacco-plant	febrifacient
nimbostratus	Gemeinschaft	vinegar-plant	non-efficient
cirro-stratus	driving-shaft	pitcher-plant	insufficient
Echinocactus	countershaft	compass-plant	unsufficient
Trismegistus	chimney-shaft	somnambulant	clairaudient
scapegallows	surface-craft	congratulant	inconvenient
water-bellows	landing-craft	misinformant	supervenient
peach-yellows	anti-aircraft	misdemeanant	intervenient
slantingways	right-and-left	queen-regnant	appercipient
straightways	scalping-tuft	disciplinant	intercipient
T	middleweight	discriminant	quadrivalent
nubbing-cheat	bantam-weight	conterminant	quantivalent
heather-bleat	summer-weight	conglutinant	sanguinolent
luncheon-meat	welter-weight	subalternant	mucopurulent
judgment-seat	winter-weight	concelebrant	monofilament
mutessarifat	letter-weight	preponderant	hereditament
commissariat	seventy-eight	carpenter-ant	withholdment
hierogrammat	potato-blight	transmigrant	displacement
collision-mat	shadow-flight	peace-warrant	misplacement
pleasure-boat	counterlight	fugie-warrant	entrancement
sculling-boat	harbour-light	bench-warrant	commencement
dispatch-boat	twelfth-night	death-warrant	convincement
coccidiostat	carpet-knight	knight-errant	denouncement
bacteriostat	ploughwright	blackcurrant	renouncement
judgment-debt	school-taught	recalcitrant	announcement
matter-of-fact	williewaught	administrant	forebodement
rough-perfect	aforethought	Premonstrant	disagreement
interconnect	afterthought	reed-pheasant	re-engagement
proof-correct	merry-thought	inconversant	endamagement
party-verdict	rough-wrought	unconversant	envisagement
herd-instinct	underwrought	non-combatant	dislodgement
self-destruct	interwrought	contranatant	prejudgement
preconstruct	trolling-bait	disinfectant	misjudgement
misconstruct	self-portrait	café-chantant	estrangement
balance-sheet	lickety-split	representant	infringement
swindle-sheet	potato-spirit	all-important	submergement
winding-sheet	microcircuit	decongestant	disgorgement
packing-sheet	short-circuit	non-resistant	accouchement
thunder-sheet	water-biscuit	circumjacent	enswathement
carriwitchet	passion-fruit	subterjacent	scribblement
pyjama-jacket	pressure-suit	privat-docent	enfeeblement
lumber-jacket	birthday-suit	contabescent	redoublement
dinner-jacket	speiss-cobalt	incandescent	encirclement
strait-jacket	Rochelle-salt	recrudescent	radio-element
monkey-jacket	shoulder-belt	convalescent	inveiglement
knick-knacket	conveyor-belt	somnolescent	stranglement
upper-bracket	purpose-built	spinulescent	entanglement

embattlement	confrontment	queen-consort	futurologist
resettlement	misallotment	service-court	papyrologist
unsettlement	reinvestment	sheriff-court	glossologist
belittlement	re-enlistment	harvest-feast	nematologist
bedazzlement	readjustment	erythroblast	hepatologist
embezzlement	withdrawment	haematoblast	teratologist
postponement	disendowment	counter-blast	odontologist
dethronement	underpayment	water-ballast	deontologist
enthronement	redeployment	alder-liefest	Egyptologist
accoutrement	unemployment	charter-chest	cryptologist
appraisement	supereminent	life-interest	embryologist
appetisement	subcontinent	self-interest	metallurgist
chastisement	semideponent	dithyrambist	dramaturgist
disguisement	heir-apparent	Russophobist	iconomachist
disbursement	foster-parent	geophysicist	quartz-schist
misstatement	price-current	aestheticist	paragraphist
embarquement	undercurrent	orthopaedist	telegraphist
retrievement	intercurrent	velocipedist	monographist
contrivement	cross-current	propagandist	typographist
forejudgment	misrepresent	avant-gardist	cerographist
self-judgment	multipresent	hippophagist	philosophist
encroachment	ventripotent	coprophagist	gymnosophist
reattachment	inconsistent	pantophagist	metamorphist
embranchment	impersistent	bibliopegist	homeopathist
retrenchment	self-existent	mineralogist	osteopathist
entrenchment	intromittent	malacologist	hydropathist
intrenchment	intermittent	musicologist	neuropathist
mismatchment	circumfluent	lexicologist	practicalist
blandishment	inconsequent	toxicologist	corporealist
stablishment	magniloquent	balneologist	superrealist
demolishment	multiloquent	choreologist	financialist
diminishment	reconstituent	spongologist	trinomialist
admonishment	privat-dozent	trichologist	mercurialist
astonishment	unconstraint	conchologist	essentialist
languishment	knuckle-joint	psychologist	convivialist
vanquishment	vantage-point	graphologist	semifinalist
bequeathment	talking-point	psephologist	factionalist
re-embodiment	boiling-point	morphologist	bicameralist
presentiment	burning-point	exobiologist	universalist
forestalment	turning-point	glaciologist	perpetualist
reinstalment	melting-point	cardiologist	spiritualist
dishevelment	growing-point	bibliologist	pansexualist
disannulment	point-to-point	craniologist	mediaevalist
non-alignment	counterpoint	storiologist	motor-cyclist
reassignment	zalambdodont	physiologist	automobilist
distrainment	machairodont	deltiologist	stegophilist
empoisonment	monophyodont	potamologist	ophiophilist
imprisonment	polyphyodont	entomologist	iconophilist
emblazonment	Berufsverbot	seismologist	negrophilist
undergarment	approach-shot	enzymologist	Russophilist
encumberment	canister-shot	urbanologist	Dantophilist
bewilderment	true-love-knot	oceanologist	cartophilist
endangerment	shoulder-knot	selenologist	mercantilist
decipherment	stocking-foot	phrenologist	vaudevillist
disinterment	pelican's-foot	technologist	bibliopolist
embitterment	buttress-root	demonologist	incunabulist
disseverment	pleurisy-root	chronologist	somnambulist
reassessment	intussuscept	immunologist	noctambulist
maltreatment	self-contempt	palynologist	animalculist
ill-treatment	tobacco-heart	escapologist	cryptogamist
mistreatment	heart-to-heart	timbrologist	iatrochemist
affrightment	weather-chart	dendrologist	Stahlhelmist
recommitment	parsley-piert	nephrologist	gastronomist
dispiritment	odd-come-short	cheirologist	palindromist

monochromist	redemptorist	**X**	impermanency
phlebotomist	psychiatrist	mountain-flax	locum-tenency
ovariotomist	econometrist	pneumothorax	incontinency
Cominformist	behaviourist	conservatrix	impertinency
transformist	caricaturist	resonance-box	transparency
harmoniumist	apiculturist	Jack-in-the-box	indifferency
Traducianist	theorematist	chocolate-box	belligerency
Confucianist	anaesthetist	portmanteaux	Eurocurrency
Zwinglianist	lithotritist	**Y**	incompetency
precisianist	relativitist	Ascension-day	plenipotency
miscellanist	obscurantist	snaffling-lay	inadvertency
stercoranist	bioscientist	morality-play	low-frequency
Panhellenist	orthodontist	straightaway	constituency
phillumenist	periodontist	superhighway	puzzle-monkey
pyrotechnist	chorizontist	cable-railway	grease-monkey
trampolinist	paedobaptist	cable-tramway	spider-monkey
Neo-Darwinist	clarinettist	companion-way	powder-monkey
vibraphonist	hermeneutist	minimotorway	bonnet-monkey
gramophonist	therapeutist	voiding-lobby	under-turnkey
accordionist	monolinguist	intermediacy	chance-medley
contagionist	somniloquist	inarticulacy	skittle-alley
precisionist	subjectivist	illegitimacy	bowling-alley
expansionist	collectivist	polypharmacy	tilley-valley
retensionist	accompanyist	gynaecocracy	hedge-parsley
extensionist	voluntaryist	cottonocracy	yellow-yowley
immersionist	Frauendienst	dollarocracy	passage-money
diversionist	thereagainst	pantisocracy	tribute-money
excursionist	whereagainst	pedantocracy	earnest-money
secessionist	hindforemost	gerontocracy	double-storey
obsessionist	northernmost	despotocracy	housey-housey
diffusionist	southernmost	kakistocracy	oversimplify
seclusionist	snubbing-post	squattocracy	transmogrify
exclusionist	swinging-post	unregeneracy	ichthyophagy
intrusionist	whipping-post	significancy	pharmacology
educationist	starting-post	extravagancy	hepaticology
variationist	sheriff's-post	scapulimancy	hydrogeology
deviationist	portrait-bust	lampadomancy	astrogeology
deflationist	enteropneust	ornithomancy	photogeology
inflationist	kissing-crust	omphalomancy	dysteleology
isolationist	cut-and-thrust	coscinomancy	pharyngology
cremationist	self-distrust	diathermancy	zoopathology
migrationist	cryptanalyst	undertenancy	sociobiology
sensationist	brilliant-cut	joint-tenancy	radiobiology
causationist	butterfly-nut	subordinancy	microbiology
salvationist	drinking-bout	predominancy	hydrobiology
defectionist	gang-there-out	preoccupancy	neurobiology
reductionist	long-drawn-out	inexpectancy	photobiology
traditionist	rainbow-trout	concubitancy	gnotobiology
coalitionist	passe-partout	concomitancy	liturgiology
abolitionist	**W**	precipitancy	stoechiology
nutritionist	brother-in-law	interjacency	stoichiology
partitionist	fathers-in-law	alkalescency	dactyliology
intuitionist	mothers-in-law	reviveancy	epidemiology
receptionist	walking-straw	resipiscency	paroemiology
extortionist	rabbeting-saw	reviviscency	bacteriology
elocutionist	butterfly-bow	translucency	historiology
evolutionist	louvre-window	resplendency	ecclesiology
neoplatonist	dormer-window	independency	hamartiology
microscopist	louver-window	inefficiency	epistemology
oniroscopist	schoolfellow	inexpediency	röntgenology
Mechitharist	chrome-yellow	transiliency	Kremlinology
coleopterist	Naples-yellow	subserviency	neurypnology
orthopterist	hedge-sparrow	multivalency	protozoology
neuropterist		equipollency	anthropology

traumatology	irrefragably	left-handedly	passionately
rheumatology	unquenchably	confoundedly	deliberately
pneumatology	unsearchably	ungroundedly	immoderately
dialectology	unpunishably	unrewardedly	intemerately
parasitology	imperishably	sanctifiedly	degenerately
protistology	irremediably	unprovokedly	inveterately
zoophytology	unmistakably	newfangledly	illiterately
paradoxology	irrepealably	undesignedly	inaccurately
gigantomachy	reconcilably	restrainedly	inadequately
stratigraphy	inconsolably	unconfinedly	incompletely
scintigraphy	incalculably	determinedly	indiscretely
lexicography	irredeemably	unpreparedly	indefinitely
chalcography	unfathomably	ill-naturedly	inappositely
pseudography	inconsumably	displeasedly	irresolutely
palaeography	inexpugnably	misadvisedly	statuesquely
biogeography	unattainably	suppressedly	persuasively
zoogeography	unimaginably	unconfusedly	dissuasively
stereography	indeclinably	dislocatedly	indecisively
choreography	determinably	dissipatedly	compulsively
psychography	interminably	reiteratedly	convulsively
lymphography	unpardonably	contractedly	suspensively
morphography	conscionably	protractedly	responsively
glyphography	questionably	abstractedly	discursively
cardiography	unreasonably	distractedly	successively
bibliography	unseasonably	unaffectedly	regressively
physiography	ungovernably	unexpectedly	aggressively
ampelography	incomparably	restrictedly	digressively
ceramography	rememberably	affrightedly	repressively
thermography	considerably	dispiritedly	impressively
seismography	insufferably	unrequitedly	oppressively
oceanography	invulnerably	disjointedly	expressively
organography	unanswerably	sure-footedly	possessively
selenography	impenetrably	interestedly	submissively
chronography	demonstrably	undivestedly	permissively
ectypography	unfavourably	unassistedly	percussively
polarography	immeasurably	unremittedly	applausively
cheirography	unmeasurably	undisputedly	preclusively
glossography	recognisably	unrelievedly	conclusively
cometography	unprofitably	unobservedly	protrusively
odontography	inhospitably	undeservedly	indicatively
glyptography	uncharitably	unreservedly	derogatively
cryptography	incommutably	otherworldly	irrelatively
chartography	transmutably	blackguardly	cumulatively
brachygraphy	disreputably	frolicsomely	nominatively
heterotrophy	indisputably	unhandsomely	ruminatively
homoeomorphy	unstatutably	blithesomely	execratively
heteromorphy	unbelievably	serpentinely	imperatively
chrestomathy	irresolvably	lachrymosely	decoratively
enantiopathy	irreprovably	transversely	pejoratively
praiseworthy	intelligibly	indelicately	figuratively
creditworthy	incorrigibly	profligately	vegetatively
happy-go-lucky	indefeasibly	uniseriately	dubitatively
whisky-frisky	indefensibly	lanceolately	meditatively
splenomegaly	irreversibly	immaculately	denotatively
macrocephaly	inaccessibly	paniculately	reputatively
microcephaly	inadmissibly	reticulately	imputatively
ineradicably	incompatibly	articulately	derivatively
inexplicably	contemptibly	legitimately	retractively
communicably	indigestibly	consummately	attractively
inextricably	irresistibly	inordinately	perfectively
ineffaceably	indissolubly	co-ordinately	subjectively
disagreeably	shamefacedly	coordinately	reflectively
unmanageably	pronouncedly	effeminately	collectively
unchangeably	unprovidedly	opinionately	connectively

respectively	blusteringly	compulsorily	platonically
protectively	scatteringly	promissorily	tectonically
vindictively	clatteringly	obligatorily	Hibernically
adjunctively	flatteringly	derogatorily	unheroically
injunctively	smatteringly	defamatorily	cholerically
productively	glitteringly	salutatorily	chimerically
discretively	twitteringly	refractorily	neoterically
definitively	sputteringly	transitorily	esoterically
infinitively	stutteringly	subsultorily	exoterically
transitively	conqueringly	peremptorily	hysterically
repetitively	unwaveringly	topsyturvily	meteorically
preventively	despairingly	demoniacally	oratorically
resumptively	unaspiringly	simoniacally	pictorically
disruptively	conspiringly	syllabically	rhetorically
suggestively	reassuringly	cherubically	historically
diminutively	unpleasingly	sporadically	theatrically
ichneumon-fly	decreasingly	heraldically	electrically
sea-butterfly	increasingly	methodically	emphatically
convincingly	surprisingly	periodically	prelatically
misleadingly	appetisingly	episodically	dramatically
forbiddingly	surpassingly	prosodically	thematically
unyieldingly	depressingly	specifically	noematically
commandingly	entreatingly	prolifically	dogmatically
pretendingly	undulatingly	magnifically	Socratically
despondingly	ruminatingly	terrifically	operatically
resoundingly	hesitatingly	horrifically	ecstatically
astoundingly	undoubtingly	beatifically	didactically
forebodingly	detractingly	pontifically	eclectically
applaudingly	attractingly	salvifically	syndetically
foreseeingly	reflectingly	anagogically	geodetically
ungrudgingly	neglectingly	apagogically	exegetically
unflaggingly	inspectingly	analogically	pathetically
unchangingly	protectingly	ecologically	athletically
beseechingly	enchantingly	geologically	balletically
scratchingly	tormentingly	neologically	hermetically
bewitchingly	consentingly	biologically	cosmetically
refreshingly	dissentingly	zoologically	frenetically
unblushingly	affrontingly	telergically	magnetically
unthinkingly	contestingly	liturgically	phonetically
unblinkingly	protestingly	anarchically	unpoetically
scribblingly	persistingly	seraphically	dietetically
scramblingly	disgustingly	metallically	enclitically
stragglingly	forgettingly	diabolically	apolitically
strugglingly	intriguingly	symbolically	uncritically
prevailingly	unswervingly	dactylically	Jesuitically
unbecomingly	perplexingly	academically	pedantically
unassumingly	horrifyingly	epidemically	gigantically
unrepiningly	gratifyingly	phonemically	semantically
forbearingly	satisfyingly	rhythmically	romantically
slubberingly	unwearyingly	economically	narcotically
slumberingly	outlandishly	anatomically	hypnotically
shudderingly	heathenishly	zootomically	despotically
thunderingly	amateurishly	volcanically	amitotically
blunderingly	coquettishly	mechanically	quixotically
staggeringly	nineteenthly	Germanically	elliptically
swaggeringly	eighteenthly	Hispanically	synoptically
sniggeringly	thirteenthly	hygienically	autoptically
smotheringly	fourteenthly	ecumenically	monastically
flickeringly	three-monthly	rabbinically	dynastically
stammeringly	myrmecophily	tyrannically	majestically
glimmeringly	ornithophily	sardonically	domestically
whimperingly	subsidiarily	gnomonically	egoistically
whisperingly	sanguinarily	harmonically	papistically
saunteringly	hereditarily	diatonically	juristically

artistically	parenterally	breathlessly	miraculously
autistically	connaturally	remedilessly	ridiculously
acoustically	structurally	prayerlessly	meticulously
analytically	scripturally	thriftlessly	scrupulously
reciprocally	sculpturally	profitlessly	polygamously
hebdomadally	congenitally	spiritlessly	equanimously
solenoidally	accidentally	relentlessly	posthumously
sinusoidally	occidentally	resistlessly	homonymously
acronychally	incidentally	tremendously	synonymously
shilly-shally	ornamentally	stupendously	diaphanously
heterothally	monumentally	horrendously	indigenously
proverbially	horizontally	jeopardously	villainously
injudicially	sacerdotally	umbrageously	libidinously
beneficially	counter-tally	outrageously	fuliginously
unofficially	individually	courageously	voluminously
artificially	semi-annually	extraneously	scrutinously
provincially	consensually	ultroneously	monotonously
antisocially	contextually	dispiteously	gluttonously
commercially	adjectivally	mendaciously	viviparously
monopodially	currant-jelly	mordaciously	slumberously
primordially	unpeacefully	fallaciously	slanderously
septennially	ungracefully	pugnaciously	thunderously
ceremonially	revengefully	ungraciously	vociferously
immaterially	purposefully	loquaciously	ungenerously
categorially	remorsefully	perniciously	whisperously
immemorially	ungratefully	auspiciously	prosperously
senatorially	despitefully	suspiciously	adulterously
equatorially	unwatchfully	avariciously	boisterously
proctorially	refreshfully	capriciously	anarthrously
monitorially	unfaithfully	precociously	chivalrously
industrially	untruthfully	perfidiously	indecorously
evidentially	unmercifully	fastidiously	clangorously
prudentially	unthankfully	commodiously	traitorously
tangentially	disdainfully	contagiously	stertorously
torrentially	worshipfully	prodigiously	idolatrously
presentially	uncheerfully	rebelliously	barratrously
sententially	successfully	abstemiously	disastrously
sequentially	neglectfully	calumniously	sinistrously
colloquially	respectfully	euphoniously	felicitously
millesimally	delightfully	harmoniously	solicitously
centesimally	unrightfully	precariously	calamitously
isothermally	sprightfully	gregariously	circuitously
phantasmally	thoughtfully	uproariously	ubiquitously
phenomenally	unfruitfully	lugubriously	iniquitously
aboriginally	uneventfully	salubriously	gratuitously
pronominally	disgustfully	mysteriously	fortuitously
pentagonally	sclerophylly	ingloriously	portentously
orthogonally	heterophylly	censoriously	contiguously
antiphonally	superhumanly	victoriously	continuously
meridionally	curmudgeonly	infectiously	tumultuously
occasionally	chirurgeonly	flagitiously	voluptuously
vocationally	overmultiply	propitiously	unvirtuously
ideationally	unfamiliarly	nutritiously	incestuously
relationally	dissimilarly	factitiously	indistinctly
irrationally	vernacularly	fictitiously	indiscreetly
fractionally	lenticularly	licentiously	softly-softly
functionally	particularly	robustiously	forthrightly
additionally	triangularly	incautiously	concordantly
volitionally	land-lubberly	obsequiously	discordantly
devotionally	stepmotherly	lasciviously	triumphantly
isochronally	groundlessly	imperviously	insouciantly
impersonally	regardlessly	scandalously	nonchalantly
unilaterally	speechlessly	scurrilously	stridulantly
collaterally	quenchlessly	marvellously	intolerantly

unpleasantly	anthropotomy	probationary	renunciatory
successantly	tracheostomy	deflationary	conciliatory
exorbitantly	sindonophany	reflationary	calumniatory
inconstantly	christophany	inflationary	propitiatory
irrelevantly	palaeobotany	traditionary	abbreviatory
flamboyantly	anthropogeny	abolitionary	vasodilatory
complacently	spermatogeny	extortionary	flagellatory
beneficently	thaumatogeny	quaestionary	cantillatory
munificently	niminy-piminy	elocutionary	distillatory
iridescently	earnest-penny	evolutionary	epistolatory
evanescently	singing-hinny	eleemosynary	deambulatory
antecedently	anthropogony	contemporary	articulatory
coincidently	laryngophony	plebiscitary	emasculatory
despondently	hemp-agrimony	paramilitary	stridulatory
astringently	heterochrony	sacramentary	manipulatory
contingently	polyembryony	testamentary	capitulatory
sufficiently	mulligatawny	vestimentary	proclamatory
proficiently	breeches-buoy	emolumentary	desquamatory
omnisciently	curietherapy	prothonotary	inflammatory
inobediently	serum-therapy	distributary	consummatory
conveniently	narcotherapy	usufructuary	confirmatory
equivalently	radiotherapy	gathering-cry	lachrymatory
malevolently	heliotherapy	stock-jobbery	consignatory
benevolently	chemotherapy	pettifoggery	condemnatory
fraudulently	hypnotherapy	microsurgery	cachinnatory
pre-eminently	hydrotherapy	neurosurgery	anticipatory
incoherently	phototherapy	fish-hatchery	exhilaratory
irreverently	tracheoscopy	haberdashery	exprobratory
concurrently	laryngoscopy	whale-fishery	consecratory
impenitently	bronchoscopy	pearl-fishery	exaggeratory
omnipotently	ornithoscopy	night-fishery	acceleratory
consistently	ebullioscopy	organ-gallery	regeneratory
persistently	dactyloscopy	press-gallery	remuneratory
infrequently	deuteroscopy	pantaloonery	recuperatory
unfrequently	spectroscopy	claptrappery	vituperatory
subsequently	philanthropy	phrontistery	perspiratory
consequently	psilanthropy	water-battery	stump-oratory
delinquently	enantiotropy	self-flattery	illustratory
high-priestly	trigger-happy	flesh-pottery	inauguratory
roundaboutly	intermediary	jail-delivery	compulsatory
trituberculy	supraciliary	gaol-delivery	compensatory
creepy-crawly	superciliary	quicksilvery	dispensatory
tetradactyly	residentiary	archdeaconry	auscultatory
pentadactyly	obedientiary	counter-flory	consultatory
macrodactyly	penitentiary	morning-glory	levorotatory
hyperdactyly	Post-Tertiary	extra-sensory	sternutatory
enantiostyly	dicarpellary	supersensory	preservatory
calycanthemy	submaxillary	intercessory	conservatory
lampadedromy	premaxillary	perturbatory	satisfactory
stereochromy	cataphyllary	pacificatory	interdictory
neuroanatomy	constabulary	modificatory	introductory
stapedectomy	somnambulary	verificatory	disquisitory
orchidectomy	septuagenary	purificatory	proto-history
rhytidectomy	tercentenary	supplicatory	contributory
appendectomy	sexcentenary	equivocatory	cash-and-carry
laryngectomy	valetudinary	confiscatory	service-berry
tonsilectomy	disciplinary	intimidatory	bramble-berry
duodenectomy	postliminary	commendatory	whortleberry
hysterectomy	cotyledonary	subfeudatory	roebuck-berry
oophorectomy	provisionary	transudatory	raccoon-berry
gingivectomy	revulsionary	compurgatory	buffalo-berry
pharyngotomy	expansionary	depreciatory	checker-berry
tetrachotomy	reversionary	appreciatory	whip-and-derry
tonsillotomy	diversionary	denunciatory	ground-cherry

winter-cherry	whimsicality	memorability	discommunity
symbololatry	classicality	filtrability	homopolarity
Christolatry	practicality	incurability	molecularity
ichthyolatry	quizzicality	figurability	irregularity
isoperimetry	corporeality	insurability	unpopularity
viscosimetry	connubiality	advisability	scissiparity
nephelometry	dissociality	opposability	posteriority
galvanometry	collegiality	palatability	prodigiosity
trigonometry	parochiality	dilatability	scrupulosity
psychrometry	congeniality	tractability	libidinosity
electrometry	perenniality	habitability	caliginosity
spectrometry	essentiality	excitability	fuliginosity
densitometry	potentiality	ignitability	voluminosity
lieutenantry	impartiality	heritability	vociferosity
unpleasantry	conviviality	irritability	spirituosity
north-country	subnormality	adaptability	voluptuosity
south-country	emotionality	temptability	multiversity
cross-country	polytonality	sportability	self-identity
geochemistry	municipality	immutability	disingenuity
biochemistry	principality	imputability	conspectuity
zoochemistry	illiberality	revivability	regressivity
agroindustry	ephemerality	removability	expressivity
monochromasy	sinistrality	immovability	self-activity
idiosyncrasy	commensality	irascibility	refractivity
kill-courtesy	universality	deducibility	subjectivity
kicksy-wicksy	effectuality	reducibility	projectivity
tootsy-wootsy	perpetuality	inaudibility	reflectivity
oversubtlety	spirituality	illegibility	collectivity
highty-tighty	accentuality	frangibility	conductivity
perspicacity	unisexuality	indelibility	productivity
treasure-city	high-fidelity	cohesibility	locomotivity
aperiodicity	revocability	divisibility	perceptivity
apostolicity	mixed-ability	invisibility	susceptivity
multiplicity	traceability	amissibility	absorptivity
genotypicity	agreeability	plausibility	permittivity
cylindricity	malleability	infusibility	fixed-penalty
eccentricity	permeability	ignitibility	seignioralty
chromaticity	navigability	insolubility	twenty-twenty
automaticity	teachability	verisimility	Humpty-dumpty
pneumaticity	unamiability	prehensility	fatigue-party
authenticity	unsalability	retractility	charterparty
inelasticity	availability	subfertility	one-and-thirty
cytotoxicity	pupilability	tranquillity	heteroblasty
high-velocity	flammability	multiformity	heteroplasty
rumpti-iddity	alienability	unconformity	keratoplasty
hyperacidity	untenability	pseudonymity	gynaecomasty
perfervidity	definability	churchianity	bloodthirsty
ororotundity	incapability	Christianity	none-so-pretty
discommodity	reparability	lese-humanity	pretty-pretty
simultaneity	separability	saccharinity	foolish-witty
incorporeity	tolerability	exsanguinity	spring-beauty
veridicality	numerability	inconcinnity	pectoriloquy
technicality	alterability	sempiternity	topside-turvy
sphericality	desirability	auto-immunity	heat-apoplexy

A			
spermatotheca	plagiostomata	macrodactylic	apophlegmatic
ethnographica	Echinodermata	psychodynamic	telegrammatic
physharmonica	Enteropneusta	thermodynamic	monogrammatic
terra-japonica	Spermatophyta	electrochemic	lipogrammatic
Cephalochorda	C	idiorrhythmic	monochromatic
Sipunculoidea	dextrocardiac	macroeconomic	polychromatic
Holothuroidea	orchidomaniac	microeconomic	psychosomatic
dysmenorrhoea	neurastheniac	enantiodromic	semi-automatic
galactorrhoea	hypochondriac	isogeothermic	idiosyncratic
syphilophobia	anaphrodisiac	homoeothermic	gynaecocratic
astrapophobia	pseudo-archaic	homoiothermic	pantisocratic
ailourophobia	tetrasyllabic	Rhaeto-Romanic	pedantocratic
thanatophobia	pentasyllabic	anthropogenic	gerontocratic
Syrophoenicia	heptasyllabic	spermatogenic	conglomeratic
encyclopaedia	polyphloisbic	schizophrenic	electrostatic
pharmacopoeia	meningococcic	pathognomonic	extra-galactic
megasporangia	streptococcic	heterochronic	intergalactic
Sauropterygia	encyclopaedic	isoelectronic	trophallactic
gigantomachia	photoperiodic	architectonic	anticlimactic
Tetrabranchia	antispasmodic	Baltoslavonic	schizomycetic
Stegocephalia	dysmenorrheic	polyembryonic	unsympathetic
paraphernalia	interspecific	kaleidoscopic	parasynthetic
syringomyelia	prescientific	laryngoscopic	polysynthetic
Germanophilia	bioscientific	bronchoscopic	psychogenetic
ailourophilia	stratigraphic	ebullioscopic	morphogenetic
gerontophilia	lexicographic	dichrooscopic	phellogenetic
suovetaurilia	palaeographic	deuteroscopic	thermogenetic
hypogylcaemia	zoogeographic	electroscopic	heterogenetic
polycythaemia	stereographic	spectroscopic	epeirogenetic
galactosaemia	choreographic	philanthropic	schizogenetic
hypercalcemia	psychographic	psilanthropic	hydromagnetic
hyperglycemia	glyphographic	hypermetropic	ferromagnetic
panophthalmia	bibliographic	apheliotropic	piezomagnetic
xerophthalmia	physiographic	enantiotropic	psychokinetic
enantiodromia	thermographic	stratospheric	onomatopoetic
xanthochromia	seismographic	gastroenteric	iontophoretic
scoleciformia	oceanographic	mastigophoric	theopaschitic
morphinomania	selenographic	proto-historic	microgrammitic
squandermania	glyptographic	archbishopric	antinephritic
psychasthenia	cryptographic	ferrosoferric	hemiparasitic
schizophrenia	gonadotrophic	volta-electric	semiparasitic
Lamellicornia	heterotrophic	turbo-electric	microfelsitic
hypermetropia	unphilosophic	hydroelectric	transatlantic
disequilibria	pseudomorphic	ferroelectric	scapulimantic
nitrobacteria	homoeomorphic	photoelectric	ornithomantic
lampadephoria	theriomorphic	piezoelectric	Phlegethontic
Dolichosauria	allelomorphic	viscosimetric	lithontriptic
Ichthyosauria	actinomorphic	monosymmetric	trophoblastic
achromatopsia	heteromorphic	nephelometric	heteroblastic
prosthodontia	ergatomorphic	endosmometric	phelloplastic
Diprotodontia	chrestomathic	trigonometric	thermoplastic
gynaecomastia	plectognathic	isobarometric	heteroplastic
eschscholtzia	anthelminthic	psychrometric	physitheistic
rebecca-eureka	mesencephalic	electrometric	sociologistic
Quinquagesima	macrocephalic	densitometric	panpsychistic
rhinoscleroma	microcephalic	Europocentric	cannibalistic
paraleipomena	hydrocephalic	pneumogastric	syndicalistic
homologoumena	leptocephalic	hyposulphuric	imperialistic
trisoctahedra	platycephalic	pyrosulphuric	materialistic
Ephemeroptera	psychrophilic	Austroasiatic	nationalistic
villeggiatura	heterothallic	categorematic	rationalistic
Protochordata	holometabolic	synaposematic	parallelistic
enchondromata	Anglo-Catholic	synallagmatic	probabilistic
	pentadactylic	diaphragmatic	antiballistic

oligopolistic
deterministic
diachronistic
anachronistic
synchronistic
monopsonistic
formularistic
voluntaristic
objectivistic
palaeocrystic
antiscorbutic
phreatophytic
autocatalytic
sympatholytic
bacteriolytic
pneumatolytic

D

woodcock's-head
scribbling-pad
mulberry-faced
thorough-paced
inexperienced
unexperienced
undifferenced
square-pierced
starch-reduced
swelled-headed
pudding-headed
waspish-headed
swollen-headed
weather-headed
unreprimanded
long-descended
unapprehended
unrecommended
Maginot-minded
worldly-minded
earthly-minded
wonder-wounded
coriander-seed
pineapple-weed
Jamestown-weed
butterfly-weed
shingle-roofed
undiscouraged
disadvantaged
spindle-legged
leather-winged
leather-lunged
thick-pleached
high-stomached
wide-stretched
unestablished
unembellished
unreplenished
distinguished
humble-mouthed
unexemplified
multiramified
unelectrified
undiversified
self-satisfied
hypertrophied
yellow-bellied

unaccompanied
unpreoccupied
owner-occupied
smooth-dittied
draggle-tailed
swallow-tailed
self-propelled
cock-thrappled
cock-throppled
estate-bottled
untransformed
unenlightened
cockle-brained
beetlebrained
rattle-brained
coarse-grained
school-trained
unconstrained
self-contained
unascertained
unentertained
travel-stained
self-sustained
undisciplined
self-condemned
smooth-chinned
unforeskinned
full-fashioned
uncompanioned
self-opinioned
unprovisioned
unimpassioned
disillusioned
unconditioned
dispositioned
forementioned
triple-crowned
copple-crowned
yellow-crowned
whiskerandoed
lozenge-shaped
spindle-shaped
trumpet-shaped
well-developed
wamble-cropped
underprepared
clean-timbered
ill-considered
unscavengered
light-fingered
tarry-fingered
sick-feathered
three-cornered
catercornered
quick-tempered
undistempered
sweet-tempered
short-tempered
blood-boltered
cross-gartered
headquartered
pigeon-livered
quicksilvered
yellow-covered

quick-answered
no-holds-barred
battle-scarred
unneighboured
sable-coloured
whole-coloured
flame-coloured
stone-coloured
mouse-coloured
slate-coloured
snuff-coloured
peach-coloured
versicoloured
multicoloured
parti-coloured
cream-coloured
lemon-coloured
liver-coloured
Judas-coloured
trout-coloured
straw-coloured
party-coloured
rusty-coloured
putty-coloured
undishonoured
white-favoured
sweet-savoured
double-natured
kindly-natured
unconjectured
misadventured
uncircumcised
unspecialised
fictionalised
unnaturalised
unmacadamised
unscrutinised
unsymmetrised
unpasteurised
unstigmatised
saussuritised
unrecompensed
unembarrassed
self-confessed
self-professed
self-addressed
tempest-tossed
uncomplicated
prefabricated
sophisticated
undepreciated
unappreciated
unabbreviated
unassimilated
verticillated
strophiolated
canaliculated
unarticulated
well-regulated
unconsummated
unimpregnated
unco-ordinated
uncoordinated
unilluminated

ensanguinated
unanticipated
unconsecrated
unexaggerated
unregenerated
unadulterated
unstercorated
unperpetrated
unillustrated
uninaugurated
uncompensated
superannuated
unaccentuated
unrecollected
self-collected
well-connected
well-respected
self-inflicted
self-convicted
well-conducted
silver-shafted
eagle-flighted
troth-plighted
sick-thoughted
self-conceited
undiscomfited
light-spirited
party-spirited
barrel-vaulted
well-warranted
unprecedented
unrepresented
travel-tainted
double-jointed
needle-pointed
self-appointed
well-appointed
rainbow-tinted
yellow-fronted
double-founted
silver-mounted
uninterrupted
marble-hearted
double-hearted
single-hearted
simple-hearted
gentle-hearted
broken-hearted
pigeon-hearted
tender-hearted
self-supported
white-breasted
barrel-chested
pigeon-chested
golden-crested
disinterested
gumple-foisted
power-assisted
phosphoretted
phosphuretted
unintermitted
untransmitted
subtile-witted
double-shotted

cinque-spotted
yellow-spotted
undistributed
urchin-snouted
double-tongued
smooth-tongued
shrill-tongued
maiden-tongued
silver-tongued
well-preserved
maiden-widowed
Gaidhealtachd
cook-housemaid
still-room-maid
hexactinellid
clinopinacoid
orthopinakoid
clinopinakoid
macropinakoid
histiophoroid
hydromedusoid
marsh-marigold
swaddling-band
sleight-of-hand
Chateaubriand
umbrella-stand
washhand-stand
misunderstand
miscomprehend
stretcher-bond
homeward-bound
thousand-pound
leuco-compound
ortho-compound
nitro-compound
vantage-ground
skittle-ground
landing-ground
hunting-ground
burying-ground
gentlemanhood
companionhood
neighbourhood
misunderstood
partridge-wood
porcupine-wood
caliature-wood
campeachy-wood
connecting-rod
cigarette-card
cribbage-board
drainage-board
building-board
moulding-board
sounding-board
chopping-board
shooting-board
skirting-board
court-cupboard
garlic-mustard
gauntlet-guard
thenceforward
centre-forward
north-eastward

south-eastward
north-westward
south-westward
chicken-hazard
serpent-lizard
turkey-buzzard
under-shepherd
boatswain-bird
coachwhip-bird
secretary-bird
cloak-and-sword
stick-in-the-mud
E
Aviculariidae
Tenebrionidae
Lasiocampidae
primigravidae
Portulacaceae
Myristicaceae
Lecythidaceae
Capparidaceae
Berberidaceae
Thymelaeaceae
Staphyleaceae
Dioscoreaceae
Saxifragaceae
Orobanchaceae
Cyclanthaceae
Amaranthaceae
Euphorbiaceae
Lycopodiaceae
Polypodiaceae
Anacardiaceae
Malpighiaceae
Aquifoliaceae
Sterculiaceae
Sparganiaceae
Frankeniaceae
Polemoniaceae
Rafflesiaceae
Tropaeolaceae
Eriocaulaceae
Ranunculaceae
Campanulaceae
Podostemaceae
Melastomaceae
Valerianaceae
nyctaginaceae
Commelinaceae
Balsaminaceae
Casuarinaceae
Papilionaceae
Caryocaraceae
Illecebraceae
Zingiberaceae
Cucurbitaceae
Chlorophyceae
Schizophyceae
Staphylindiae
Pedicellariae
Corolliflorae
Thalamiflorae
Scyphomedusae
Archegoniatae

oversubscribe
discharge-tube
lightning-tube
diffusion-tube
picture-palace
standing-place
sticking-place
skulking-place
dwelling-place
stopping-place
watering-place
trysting-place
thoroughbrace
changing-piece
mourning-piece
tenpenny-piece
booking-office
speaking-voice
starting-price
church-service
dinner-service
flower-service
toilet-service
knight-service
outrecuidance
non-attendance
overabundance
non-regardance
non-compliance
spring-balance
thermobalance
vraisemblance
somnambulance
Rhaeto-Romance
disaffirmance
appertainance
subappearance
non-appearance
disappearance
preponderance
redeliverance
recalcitrance
life-insurance
fire-insurance
self-insurance
overinsurance
life-assurance
self-assurance
co-inheritance
non-acceptance
transportance
non-resistance
non-observance
misobservance
dispurveyance
contabescence
incandescence
recrudescence
convalescence
consenescence
efflorescence
inflorescence
deliquescence
defervescence

effervescence
concupiscence
transcendence
jurisprudence
intransigence
birefringence
centrifugence
insufficience
clairaudience
inconvenience
supervenience
quadrivalence
quantivalence
supereminence
eighteen-pence
circumference
intercurrence
pluripresence
multipresence
misadvertence
inconsistence
self-existence
post-existence
intermittence
circumfluence
inconsequence
magniloquence
somniloquence
multiloquence
shoulder-blade
sex-intergrade
hydrosulphide
chlorobromide
trisaccharide
mourning-bride
tetrachloride
hydrochloride
Ascensiontide
Christmas-tide
All-hallowtide
mackerel-guide
semicarbazide
schadenfreude
consimilitude
dissimilitude
overmultitude
chinkerinchee
toothache-tree
wayfaring-tree
cornelian-tree
Christmas-tree
jack-crosstree
cranberry-tree
scalping-knife
chopping-knife
roller-bandage
bacteriophage
wheel-carriage
steam-carriage
undercarriage
water-carriage
hedge-marriage
intermarriage
woman-suffrage

13 -AGE

protolanguage
foreknowledge
self-knowledge
mackerel-midge
lattice-bridge
trestle-bridge
lifting-bridge
pontoon-bridge
pease-porridge
ball-cartridge
shooting-lodge
counterchange
shooting-range
countercharge
gas-centrifuge
drilling-lathe
Kletterschuhe
collieshangie
passementerie
tongue-doubtie
capercaillzie
shooting-brake
Christianlike
gentlemanlike
unworkmanlike
tradesmanlike
statesmanlike
sportsmanlike
chameleonlike
unscholarlike
unbrotherlike
unsoldierlike
thunder-strike
thunder-stroke
counterstroke
paraffin-scale
thresher-whale
indescribable
undescribable
imperturbable
multiplicable
impracticable
unpracticable
biodegradable
unpersuadable
indissuadable
undescendable
recommendable
uncommendable
unreplaceable
irreplaceable
unserviceable
pronounceable
unforeseeable
advantageable
knowledgeable
challengeable
semipermeable
unforgiveable
indefatigable
unimpeachable
unstaunchable
inappreciable
indissociable

exemplifiable
electrifiable
unvitrifiable
diversifiable
unjustifiable
unsatisfiable
unconcealable
unassimilable
tetrasyllable
congratulable
unreclaimable
irreclaimable
uninflammable
unconformable
transformable
unexplainable
constrainable
ascertainable
unsustainable
unmedicinable
disciplinable
unfashionable
companionable
objectionable
perditionable
unmentionable
exceptionable
non-returnable
unputdownable
unsmotherable
unconquerable
unrecoverable
irrecoverable
disintegrable
transferrable
administrable
dishonourable
unpleasurable
commeasurable
commensurable
conjecturable
unpurchasable
generalisable
volatilisable
non-cognisable
unpolarisable
unchastisable
undisguisable
incondensable
indispensable
untraversable
inconversable
unconversable
unsurpassable
undiscussable
manipulatable
unpredictable
constructable
billiard-table
interpretable
whirling-table
dressing-table
throwing-table
copyrightable

uninhabitable
overexcitable
discreditable
unwarrantable
representable
unpresentable
unpreventable
unaccountable
uncomfortable
insupportable
unsupportable
transportable
incontestable
uncontestable
unforgettable
transmittable
contributable
distributable
superannuable
unreprievable
irretrievable
inconceivable
unconceivable
unperceivable
indissolvable
ungainsayable
inconvincible
immarcescible
effervescible
incommiscible
concupiscible
incognoscible
undescendible
irrefrangible
indiscernible
undiscernible
transferrible
reprehensible
apprehensible
suprasensible
supersensible
irresponsible
introversible
immarcessible
irrepressible
unimpressible
inexpressible
unexpressible
impermissible
transmissible
incompossible
undiscussible
imperfectible
tax-deductible
constructible
imperceptible
insusceptible
unsusceptible
prescriptible
incorruptible
inconvertible
unconvertible
inexhaustible
incombustible

transit-circle
packing-needle
darning-needle
dipping-needle
netting-needle
snaffle-bridle
paschal-candle
encephalocele
splanchnocele
double-shuffle
magazine-rifle
passenger-mile
acrylonitrile
trysting-stile
fishing-tackle
water-sprinkle
dog-periwinkle
quatrefeuille
toad-in-the-hole
telegraph-pole
counter-parole
seeming-simple
kangaroo-apple
diamond-beetle
burying-beetle
blister-beetle
cotton-thistle
savanna-wattle
cuckoo-spittle
feeding-bottle
washing-bottle
sucking-bottle
pilgrim-bottle
macromolecule
sun-animalcule
climbing-frame
stocking-frame
quilting-frame
morphophoneme
breathing-time
Christmas-time
adventuresome
sex-chromosome
convertiplane
hydro-airplane
polypropylene
winding-engine
draught-engine
sewing-machine
mowing-machine
sowing-machine
rhadamanthine
noradrenaline
ship-of-the-line
twiddling-line
pyrimethamine
triethylamine
dimethylamine
naphthylamine
hydroxylamine
antihistamine
phenylalanine
oleomargarine
minisubmarine

scolopendrine	thrombokinase	pleasure-house	superordinate
xanthopterine	commercialese	treasure-house	interlaminate
contraterrine	self-dispraise	boarding-house	decontaminate
sulphadiazine	mathematicise	sponging-house	indeterminate
monotelephone	antisepticise	spunging-house	undeterminate
conversazione	demythologise	gambling-house	disilluminate
phylloquinone	theatricalise	dwelling-house	procrastinate
peacock-throne	proverbialise	tippling-house	imparipinnate
accident-prone	artificialise	spinning-house	polycarbonate
standing-stone	provincialise	clearing-house	compassionate
stepping-stone	commercialise	watering-house	dispassionate
cinnamon-stone	dematerialise	smelting-house	possessionate
clay-ironstone	immaterialise	vaulting-house	perfectionate
Saracen's-stone	industrialise	printing-house	proportionate
proparoxytone	phenomenalise	counting-house	contortionate
signature-tune	decriminalise	sessions-house	inconsiderate
measuring-tape	denationalise	prick-the-louse	equiponderate
dipleidoscope	irrationalise	psychoanalyse	multicamerate
sigmoidoscope	fractionalise	orthosilicate	transliterate
phonendoscope	depersonalise	subtriplicate	quadrumvirate
pharyngoscope	impersonalise	sesquiplicate	disinvigorate
tachistoscope	connaturalise	quadruplicate	supersaturate
daguerreotype	disnaturalise	quintuplicate	discapacitate
fair-and-square	occidentalise	excommunicate	multidigitate
robe-de-chambre	sacerdotalise	undomesticate	interdigitate
noli-me-tangere	individualise	phlogisticate	dishabilitate
asthenosphere	conceptualise	prognosticate	multicapitate
magnetosphere	contextualise	judge-advocate	semi-sagittate
questionnaire	recrystallise	reconsolidate	undergraduate
protospataire	metagrabolise	multinucleate	appropinquate
marsh-samphire	metagrobolise	baccalaureate	ferroconcrete
water-sapphire	Birminghamise	reinterrogate	hermaphrodite
conservatoire	republicanise	self-conjugate	hydrosulphite
telegraph-wire	un-Americanise	metaphosphate	hypophosphite
messenger-wire	Mohammedanise	pyrophosphate	black-and-white
thereinbefore	corinthianise	misappreciate	Pre-Raphaelite
chromatophore	pedestrianise	non-collegiate	chrysophilite
spermatophore	superhumanise	eusporangiate	anthophyllite
pneumatophore	platitudinise	quadrifoliate	sclerodermite
chlamydospore	dereligionise	cancellariate	hypersthenite
pycnidiospore	suggestionise	professoriate	ornithichnite
urediniospore	revolutionise	inappropriate	winter-aconite
square-measure	bone-turquoise	unappropriate	archimandrite
underexposure	vernacularise	differentiate	rensselaerite
time-signature	particularise	disassimilate	chlorargyrite
subprefecture	cheval-de-frise	circumvallate	launching-site
misconjecture	transistorise	involucellate	over-exquisite
motion-picture	apothegmatise	suspenciliate	carte-de-visite
primogeniture	reacclimatise	sublanceolate	rhodochrosite
sericiculture	anagrammatise	register-plate	quadripartite
ostreiculture	epigrammatise	infundibulate	Bloomsburyite
stirpiculture	empyreumatise	multilobulate	désobligeante
arboriculture	bureaucratise	interjaculate	avant-gardiste
vivisepulture	enhypostatise	appendiculate	up-to-the-minute
prisoners'-base	Protestantise	disarticulate	sheriff-depute
go-as-you-please	ventriloquise	diverticulate	spermatophyte
bowling-crease	substantivise	multiloculate	card-catalogue
popping-crease	anticlockwise	interosculate	sale-catalogue
coffee-disease	barnacle-goose	solidungulate	star-catalogue
grouse-disease	bernicle-goose	vice-consulate	turquoise-blue
salmon-disease	stalking-horse	underestimate	sculpturesque
potato-disease	vaulting-horse	hierogrammate	double-concave
parrot-disease	mermaid's-purse	catechumenate	ticket-of-leave
phosphorylase	bouillabaisse	insubordinate	pudding-sleeve

carriage-drive
comprehensive
corresponsive
high-explosive
unprogressive
retrogressive
transgressive
decompressive
insuppressive
subindicative
prejudicative
mundificative
qualificative
significative
justificative
reduplicative
communicative
reciprocative
unprovocative
consolidative
accommodative
investigative
interrogative
appropriative
intercalative
extrapolative
interpolative
contemplative
unspeculative
dissimulative
expostulative
approximative
uninformative
ratiocinative
hallucinative
subordinative
unimaginative
contaminative
disseminative
recriminative
determinative
exterminative
agglutinative
participative
reverberative
confederative
considerative
proliferative
refrigerative
agglomerative
uncooperative
unco-operative
post-operative
commiserative
collaborative
corroborative
deteriorative
commemorative
incorporative
expectorative
concentrative
demonstrative
remonstrative
prefigurative

resuscitative
premeditative
precipitative
authoritative
argumentative
frequentative
manifestative
transmutative
surface-active
counteractive
cost-effective
retrospective
introspective
contradictive
indistinctive
undistinctive
unconjunctive
non-productive
unobstructive
uninstructive
primogenitive
uninquisitive
transpositive
uncompetitive
circumventive
electromotive
magnetomotive
contraceptive
interoceptive
transcriptive
self-assertive
inconsecutive
plantie-cruive
throttle-valve
snifting-valve
mermaid's-glove
treasure-trove
autoschediaze
Louis-Quatorze
F
tenant-in-chief
roll-on-roll-off
blindman's-buff
mourning-stuff
thing-in-itself
splinter-proof
well-thought-of
G
carpet-bombing
self-sufficing
square-dancing
ballet-dancing
self-financing
still-piercing
muscle-reading
speech-reading
muzzle-loading
breechloading
carpet-bedding
breast-feeding
stock-breeding
interbreeding
crossbreeding
self-confiding

self-shielding
coachbuilding
jerry-building
unwithholding
cable-moulding
chain-moulding
understanding
water-standing
condescending
glass-grinding
corresponding
overabounding
brassfounding
sound-boarding
skateboarding
matchboarding
telerecording
tape-recording
soundproofing
waterproofing
unit-packaging
change-ringing
turbocharging
tent-preaching
stagecoaching
unreproaching
penny-pinching
soul-searching
cross-hatching
baby-snatching
clock-watching
square-bashing
tongue-lashing
sponge-fishing
salmon-fishing
camp-sheathing
underclothing
three-farthing
pitch-farthing
chuck-farthing
penny-farthing
plain-speaking
house-breaking
heartbreaking
leasing-making
cabinet-making
hydrocracking
nerve-wracking
hydraulicking
cotton-picking
pocket-picking
street-walking
mountebanking
right-thinking
mallemaroking
wonder-working
double-dealing
self-annealing
sheep-stealing
self-revealing
night-warbling
blood-curdling
fellow-feeling
ground-angling

hound-trailing
time-beguiling
swashbuckling
back-pedalling
road-metalling
revictualling
pearl-shelling
disgospelling
self-levelling
spine-chilling
cable-drilling
string-pulling
yellow-yorling
sabre-battling
otter-trawling
well-beseeming
summer-seeming
unforthcoming
nonconforming
time-consuming
self-consuming
case-hardening
strengthening
disheartening
yesterevening
uncomplaining
sugar-refining
chrome-tanning
pro-and-conning
processioning
proportioning
unquestioning
dead-reckoning
lead-poisoning
sleep-learning
index-learning
self-governing
yestermorning
engine-turning
thorough-going
flint-knapping
spirit-rapping
candle-dipping
transshipping
round-tripping
night-tripping
island-hopping
intercropping
eavesdropping
roller-bearing
sheep-shearing
profit-sharing
mortal-staring
sea-shouldring
unremembering
unconsidering
life-rendering
self-murdering
peace-offering
heave-offering
thank-offering
drink-offering
burnt-offering
long-suffering

wool-gathering
kiss-in-the-ring
mouthwatering
filibustering
baby-battering
time-bettering
weeping-spring
pickle-herring
heart-stirring
groin-centring
dead-colouring
land-measuring
manufacturing
merchandising
unrecognising
true-disposing
untrespassing
sempstressing
prepossessing
heaven-kissing
level-crossing
rabble-rousing
accommodating
carpet-beating
self-defeating
figure-skating
roller-skating
chrome-plating
nickel-plating
uncalculating
participating
self-operating
incorporating
undistracting
self-directing
non-conducting
satin-sheeting
prayer-meeting
tattie-lifting
cattle-lifting
weight-lifting
prize-fighting
floodlighting
badger-baiting
lady-in-waiting
non-forfeiting
mirror-writing
ticket-writing
cross-vaulting
transplanting
quick-scenting
parliamenting
discontenting
glass-painting
disappointing
plate-printing
microprinting
yellow-bunting
seine-shooting
sharpshooting
self-asserting
figure-casting
shadowcasting
narrowcasting

uninteresting
fire-resisting
thermosetting
word-splitting
side-splitting
vote-splitting
hair-splitting
pretermitting
train-spotting
globe-trotting
self-executing
school-leaving
figure-weaving
wood-engraving
line-engraving
seal-engraving
self-surviving
self-approving
wappenshawing
weaponshawing
unwithdrawing
badger-drawing
foreshadowing
land-surveying
counter-spying
crystal-gazing
double-glazing

H

promise-breach
Sabbath-breach
mourning-coach
root-and-branch
lamellibranch
perennibranch
opisthobranch
marsipobranch
Congreve-match
wristlet-watch
feather-stitch
blanket-stitch
railway-stitch
tumbler-switch
boulting-hutch
mountains-high
whooping-cough
button-through
follow-through
pocket-borough
Addressograph ®
cinematograph
kinematograph
chromatograph
phonautograph
anthropomorph
gynandromorph
otherworldish
Netherlandish
butterfly-fish
schoolgirlish
school-marmish
spirit-varnish
Romano-British
namby-pambyish
raspberry-bush

mocking-thrush
screech-thrush
finger-breadth
cupboard-faith
water-hyacinth
nemathelminth
quadrillionth
quintillionth
billiard-cloth
brattice-cloth
casement-cloth
honeycomb-moth
cloister-garth
sleeping-berth
straightforth
threepenn'orth
twopenceworth
twopennyworth

I

anthropophagi
actinobacilli
conversazioni

K

mourning-cloak
clickety-clack
counter-attack
hurricane-deck
mashie-niblick
clickety-click
porridge-stick
scouring-stick
shooting-stick
throwing-stick
constablewick
finnan-haddock
findon-haddock
building-block
swinging-block
chopping-block
mounting-block
cylinder-block
round-the-clock
cock-of-the-rock
sandy-laverock
laughing-stock
pointing-stock
floutingstock
quatch-buttock
thunder-struck
tongue-in-cheek
hide-and-go-seek
redding-straik
blankety-blank
whistled-drunk
grappling-hook
mackerel-shark
thresher-shark
reference-mark
quotation-mark
maid-of-all-work

L

pandemoniacal
meningococcal
streptococcal

trisyllabical
namby-pambical
orthopaedical
mineralogical
malacological
synecological
autecological
codicological
musicological
toxicological
untheological
trichological
conchological
psychological
graphological
psephological
morphological
glaciological
craniological
physiological
potamological
entomological
seismological
oceanological
phaenological
selenological
phrenological
technological
demonological
chronological
immunological
palynological
dendrological
nephrological
gastrological
futurological
glossological
somatological
teratological
odontological
deontological
Egyptological
cryptological
embryological
metallurgical
synecdochical
squirarchical
parapsychical
metapsychical
paragraphical
pasigraphical
lexigraphical
cacographical
ideographical
oreographical
logographical
xylographical
monographical
topographical
typographical
cerographical
philosophical
philomathical
hydropathical

neuropathical
labyrinthical
unevangelical
bibliopolical
unapostolical
aerodynamical
iatrochemical
petrochemical
photochemical
logarithmical
palindromical
microcosmical
charlatanical
zymotechnical
pyrotechnical
polytechnical
tautophonical
colposcopical
necroscopical
microscopical
hygroscopical
ultra-tropical
intratropical
extra-tropical
intertropical
helispherical
hemispherical
atmospherical
phylacterical
climacterical
prehistorical
psychiatrical
extra-metrical
planimetrical
gravimetrical
unsymmetrical
viscometrical
araeometrical
tachometrical
goniometrical
micrometrical
hydrometrical
hygrometrical
tautometrical
hypermetrical
tachymetrical
bathymetrical
lackadaisical
hobby-horsical
extra-physical
astrophysical
superphysical
hyperphysical
anathematical
problematical
theorematical
ungrammatical
symptomatical
ochlocratical
magistratical
hydrostatical
parallactical
quodlibetical
strategetical

unprophetical
sympathetical
parenthetical
cosmothetical
diotheletical
dyotheletical
homogenetical
peripatetical
diothelitical
dyothelitical
pre-adamitical
stalagmitical
onirocritical
supercritical
hypercritical
stalactitical
sycophantical
necromantical
chiromantical
apocalyptical
encomiastical
methodistical
tritheistical
pantheistical
dialogistical
syllogistical
neologistical
catechistical
cabbalistical
anomalistical
symbolistical
pessimistical
Hellenistical
Calvinistical
eucharistical
hermeneutical
troglodytical
molluscicidal
haemorrhoidal
hypocycloidal
dysmenorrheal
intersidereal
zygapophyseal
monophthongal
velt-mareschal
dolichocephal
knight-marshal
fluvioglacial
extra-judicial
tribuniticial
comprovincial
synarthrodial
prosopopoeial
premillennial
tercentennial
intercolonial
protonotarial
mitochondrial
crown-imperial
intra-arterial
unministerial
ambassadorial
expurgatorial
legislatorial

combinatorial
gubernatorial
procuratorial
subequatorial
propraetorial
proprietorial
progenitorial
exterritorial
inquisitorial
unterrestrial
controversial
zygapophysial
parapophysial
cardinalatial
cardinalitial
insubstantial
unsubstantial
beneficential
excrescential
irreverential
equipotential
subsistential
uninfluential
subsequential
consequential
courts-martial
ventriloquial
baggage-animal
draught-animal
quadragesimal
infinitesimal
isogeothermal
homoeothermal
homoiothermal
heterothermal
counter-signal
compass-signal
distant-signal
quadrigeminal
quadrinominal
cerebrospinal
archidiaconal
orthodiagonal
clinodiagonal
macrodiagonal
septentrional
subdivisional
congressional
progressional
compressional
convocational
coeducational
conjugational
appellational
translational
calculational
postulational
informational
supranational
inclinational
terminational
multinational
supernational
international

transnational
inspirational
unsensational
gravitational
computational
observational
contractional
abstractional
vivisectional
benedictional
dysfunctional
conjunctional
destructional
instructional
unconditional
inquisitional
prepositional
compositional
propositional
suppositional
dispositional
unintentional
unexceptional
inscriptional
institutional
interpersonal
intercommunal
gathering-coal
vice-principal
chorepiscopal
tetartohedral
foraminiferal
penthemimeral
states-general
quadrilateral
quadriliteral
spadicifloral
corollifloral
thalamifloral
supratemporal
lance-corporal
amphitheatral
xiphiplastral
nomenclatural
subternatural
preternatural
interjectural
architectural
substructural
piscicultural
crinicultural
floricultural
horticultural
waiting-vassal
intraparietal
interparietal
quadricipital
predicamental
temperamental
dissepimental
unsentimental
environmental
developmental
quartz-crystal

quadrilingual
semimenstrual
princess-royal
spinning-wheel
steering-wheel
sprocket-wheel
shabby-genteel
schutzstaffel
anti-personnel
cracker-barrel
weeding-chisel
surface-vessel
mangold-wurzel
drawing-pencil
copying-pencil
citronella-oil
hole-in-the-wall
partition-wall
tortoise-shell
thrashing-mill
threshing-mill
weather-symbol
writing-school
charity-school
dyed-in-the-wool
ground-control
mother-of-pearl
unreproachful
tablespoonful
disrespectful
self-forgetful
self-deceitful
discontentful
unmistrustful
perissodactyl
       M
straining-beam
whipping-cream
radiotelegram
encephalogram
parallelogram
what-d'ye-call-'em
semilogarithm
antilogarithm
Anglo-Saxondom
topsyturvydom
butcher's-broom
powdering-room
receiving-room
reception-room
breakfast-room
almond-blossom
orange-blossom
sulphur-bottom
scalpelliform
penicilliform
fringilliform
strombuliform
umbraculiform
telescopiform
cochleariform
alphabetiform
space-platform
measuring-worm

autoschediasm
monosyllabism
polysyllabism
androdioecism
gynomonoecism
histrionicism
metempiricism
geocentricism
neoclassicism
mathematicism
iconomaticism
self-criticism
homoeroticism
autoeroticism
antisepticism
scholasticism
neoplasticism
Neo-Plasticism
dunderheadism
contrabandism
Hildebrandism
blackguardism
dilettanteism
polysyllogism
thaumaturgism
sado-masochism
High-Churchism
catastrophism
isodimorphism
paedomorphism
homeomorphism
orthognathism
Neo-Lamarckism
mountebankism
academicalism
ecumenicalism
theatricalism
mesocephalism
proverbialism
provincialism
antisocialism
commercialism
primordialism
polynomialism
ceremonialism
immaterialism
industrialism
prudentialism
colloquialism
phenomenalism
aboriginalism
occasionalism
vocationalism
irrationalism
fractionalism
functionalism
unicameralism
unilateralism
triliteralism
structuralism
scripturalism
accidentalism
Occidentalism
sacerdotalism

individualism
conceptualism
Pre-Raphaelism
Pantagruelism
infallibilism
impossibilism
bibliophilism
monometallism
Machiavellism
zygodactylism
polydactylism
heterostylism
photochromism
republicanism
Pan-Africanism
Mohammedanism
Manichaeanism
Voltaireanism
micro-organism
solifidianism
Berkeleianism
antiochianism
monarchianism
Lamarckianism
Australianism
antinomianism
millennianism
Ciceronianism
Morisonianism
Johnsonianism
tractarianism
vegetarianism
sanitarianism
Spencerianism
Voltairianism
pedestrianism
equestrianism
Parnassianism
Malthusianism
Neo-Kantianism
Leibnizianism
philhellenism
catechumenism
indeterminism
autochthonism
trade-unionism
impressionism
expressionism
liberationism
generationism
perfectionism
protectionism
exhibitionism
contortionism
suggestionism
revolutionism
Saint-Simonism
tautochronism
feuilletonism
Eurocommunism
xanthochroism
caesaropapism
theanthropism
diageotropism

apogeotropism
stereotropism
trophotropism
plagiotropism
thigmotropism
thermotropism
semi-barbarism
millenniarism
vernacularism
particularism
reactionarism
electromerism
phalansterism
filibusterism
doctrinairism
ethnocentrism
Zarathustrism
anastigmatism
anagrammatism
trichromatism
panchromatism
apochromatism
panspermatism
aristocratism
panaesthetism
monotheletism
paramagnetism
gyromagnetism
monothelitism
cosmopolitism
monophysitism
flagellantism
pococurantism
Protestantism
compatriotism
self-hypnotism
Vansittartism
sansculottism
ventriloquism
progressivism
perspectivism
descriptivism
namby-pambyism
pycnoconidium
rutherfordium
zoosporangium
ferrochromium
radio-actinium
protoactinium
lectisternium
evangeliarium
vibracularium
armamentarium
Scolopendrium
perichondrium
hypochondrium
Palaeotherium
Titanotherium
Cheirotherium
anticlinorium
inclinatorium
vivisectorium
succinctorium
amphigastrium

acaridomatium
acarodomatium
Cyathophyllum
tintinnabulum
sustentaculum
chrysanthemum
broad-spectrum
odontoglossum
N
malacostracan
entomostracan
Latin-American
Anglo-American
ichthyopsidan
Pherecrataean
mediterranean
Shakespearean
terpsichorean
paediatrician
metaphysician
mathematician
systematician
informatician
arithmetician
geopolitician
tribunitician
linguistician
diagnostician
Brobdignagian
Swedenborgian
hyperphrygian
ornithischian
Philadelphian
Wordsworthian
Neo-Lamarckian
phantasmalian
tobaccanalian
Pantagruelian
Machiavellian
hippopotamian
transisthmian
platyrrhinian
Constantinian
Huntingdonian
Saint-Simonian
Hutchinsonian
Grumbletonian
semi-barbarian
suburbicarian
Shakespearian
anythingarian
neogrammarian
alphabetarian
communitarian
authoritarian
necessitarian
antiquitarian
phalansterian
valedictorian
propraetorian
polyhistorian
Zarathustrian
plesiosaurian
megalosaurian

Neo-Melanesian
Peloponnesian
Franco-Russian
Serbo-Croatian
antichristian
even-Christian
coastguardman
remittance-man
puss-gentleman
rag-and-bone-man
alongshoreman
light-horseman
lighthouseman
stagecoachman
High-Churchman
night-watchman
check-weighman
quartodeciman
Bildungsroman
Congresswoman
brother-german
line-fisherman
old-clothesman
privateersman
underclassman
parliament-man
skirl-in-the-pan
preserving-pan
mastigophoran
kitchen-midden
kitchen-garden
might-have-been
clothes-screen
draught-screen
sea-water-green
half-evergreen
quartz-halogen
ferricyanogen
ferrocyanogen
panic-stricken
grief-stricken
heart-stricken
representamen
women-children
weather-beaten
tempest-beaten
weather-bitten
first-begotten
weather-driven
fellow-citizen
half-sovereign
mountain-chain
semiporcelain
purple-in-grain
armoured-train
corridor-train
water-plantain
copper-captain
window-curtain
pressure-cabin
nucleo-protein
scleroprotein
custard-coffin
gonadotrophin

phthalocyanin
isoagglutinin
phycoerythrin
chlorocruorin
washhand-basin
drainage-basin
water-mocassin
bacteriolysin
Chloromycetin ®
screech-martin
diacatholicon
panharmonicon
boustrophedon
monocotyledon
carrier-pigeon
barber-surgeon
state-religion
parrot-fashion
epitrachelion
Pantagruelion
self-communion
post-communion
evangeliarion
mitochondrion
spheristerion
mispersuasion
cross-division
short-division
jet-propulsion
condescension
comprehension
interspersion
animadversion
master-passion
non-aggression
retrogression
introgression
transgression
decompression
recompression
prepossession
dispossession
self-admission
photo-emission
subcommission
discommission
pretermission
hypothecation
syllabication
premedication
revendication
subindication
revindication
prejudication
plebification
specification
calcification
dulcification
zincification
re-edificuation
acidification
mundification
zinkification
qualification

mellification
jollification
mollification
nullification
prolification
amplification
palmification
mummification
chymification
magnification
dignification
lignification
signification
damnification
cornification
reunification
scarification
clarification
scorification
glorification
caprification
metrification
petrification
nitrification
vitrification
thurification
falsification
versification
Russification
beatification
gratification
rectification
acetification
Scotification
certification
fortification
mortification
testification
justification
mystification
republication
spifflication
reapplication
reduplication
induplication
communication
haruspication
prevarication
decortication
excortication
domestication
averruncation
radiolocation
audio-location
interlocation
translocation
reciprocation
conspuration
consolidation
accommodation
backwardation
confarreation
noctivagation
desegregation

disobligation
suffumigation
subirrigation
investigation
interrogation
beneficiation
pronunciation
domiciliation
impropriation
appropriation
expropriation
instantiation
renegotiation
re-embarkation
intercalation
blood-relation
interrelation
dissimilation
horripilation
acceptilation
constellation
floccillation
refocillation
scintillation
machicolation
extrapolation
interpolation
contemplation
retranslation
confabulation
funambulation
perambulation
pandiculation
vermiculation
matriculation
graticulation
denticulation
gesticulation
tuberculation
triangulation
strangulation
dissimulation
subpopulation
encapsulation
expostulation
carbonylation
dephlegmation
disestimation
approximation
semipalmation
reaffirmation
back-formation
impostumation
miscegenation
hydrogenation
concatenation
recombination
revaccination
ratiocination
hallucination
subordination
preordination
compagination
contamination

re-examination
dissemination
recrimination
predomination
cognomination
determination
extermination
defibrination
peregrination
assassination
deglutination
agglutination
decarbonation
fractionation
impersonation
reincarnation
consternation
interlunation
participation
preoccupation
decerebration
equilibration
reverberation
protuberation
incarceration
confederation
consideration
proliferation
verbigeration
refrigeration
agglomeration
connumeration
commiseration
perseveration
disseveration
conflagration
reintegration
transpiration
collaboration
corroboration
imperforation
deterioration
discoloration
commemoration
impignoration
oppignoration
incorporation
expectoration
constupration
impenetration
concentration
orchestration
sequestration
demonstration
remonstration
perlustration
prefiguration
configuration
disfiguration
acculturation
intravasation
extravasation
italicisation
hybridisation

deoxidisation
periodisation
villagisation
syllogisation
globalisation
verbalisation
feudalisation
socialisation
radialisation
serialisation
animalisation
formalisation
normalisation
vernalisation
pluralisation
tantalisation
brutalisation
casualisation
visualisation
actualisation
ritualisation
mutualisation
dieselisation
cartelisation
stabilisation
syphilisation
sterilisation
fossilisation
subtilisation
fertilisation
metallisation
symbolisation
vacuolisation
systemisation
victimisation
randomisation
economisation
volcanisation
vulcanisation
mechanisation
Balkanisation
Germanisation
galvanisation
hyphenisation
cocainisation
luteinisation
hyalinisation
solemnisation
carbonisation
preconisation
jargonisation
harmonisation
peptonisation
Teutonisation
hibernisation
modernisation
barbarisation
vulgarisation
scenarisation
mercerisation
isomerisation
mesmerisation
pauperisation
cauterisation

pulverisation
herborisation
deodorisation
authorisation
glamorisation
temporisation
terrorisation
factorisation
cicatrisation
electrisation
carburisation
mediatisation
dramatisation
privatisation
palletisation
pelletisation
magnetisation
uralitisation
granitisation
sensitisation
epidotisation
hypnotisation
desertisation
improvisation
acclimatation
labefactation
superfetation
pollicitation
resuscitation
premeditation
accreditation
regurgitation
ingurgitation
sexploitation
decrepitation
precipitation
necessitation
tea-plantation
supplantation
displantation
reorientation
ornamentation
fragmentation
sedimentation
regimentation
documentation
argumentation
frequentation
confrontation
staff-notation
laevorotation
preadaptation
maladaptation
re-exportation
police-station
manifestation
deforestation
afforestation
contristation
transmutation
disreputation
perscrutation
individuation
overvaluation

objectivation
inobservation
counteraction
motor-traction
self-infection
self-injection
free-selection
retroflection
disconnection
retrospection
introspection
self-direction
miscorrection
quadrisection
mine-detection
contradiction
indistinction
interpunction
circumduction
self-induction
non-production
disinhibition
superaddition
irrecognition
predefinition
preadmonition
juxtaposition
decomposition
recomposition
superposition
interposition
indisposition
transposition
milk-dentition
contravention
circumvention
counter-motion
contraception
self-deception
preconception
misconception
transcription
rumlegumption
rumelgumption
disconcertion
self-assertion
disproportion
misproportion
autodigestion
cross-question
interlocution
electrocution
self-pollution
redissolution
circumflexion
parencephalon
mesencephalon
epiphenomenon
paralipomenon
trolling-spoon
contrabassoon
scalenohedron
leucitohedron
trapezohedron

Lepidodendron
meadow-saffron
grappling-iron
soldering-iron
photoelectron
xiphiplastron
great-grandson
counter-poison
Heath-Robinson
parasyntheton
phytoplankton
cornet-à-piston
trouser-button
homeoteleuton
turnip-lantern
Middle-Eastern
fiddle-pattern
kangaroo-thorn
submachine-gun
powdering-gown

O

incommunicado
generalissimo
fortississimo
staccatissimo
contrafagotto

P

percussion-cap
shoulder-strap
mountain-sheep
variable-sweep
housewifeskep
committeeship
housewifeship
constableship
candidateship
surrogateship
associateship
colleagueship
receiving-ship
seneschalship
principalship
proconsulship
suffraganship
physicianship
custodianship
librarianship
gentlemanship
swordsmanship
statesmanship
craftsmanship
draftsmanship
yachtsmanship
sportsmanship
chieftainship
subdeaconship
pendragonship
companionship
registrarship
commandership
pretendership
scrivenership
copartnership
land-ownership

treasurership
barristership
presbytership
successorship
confessorship
professorship
possessorship
gladiatorship
moderatorship
spectatorship
collectorship
inspectorship
prosectorship
protectorship
conductorship
solicitorship
subeditorship
precentorship
coadjutorship
nature-worship
animal-worship
presidentship
transport-ship
disfellowship
secretaryship
prairie-turnip
hurricane-lamp
bowstring-hemp
spectre-shrimp
whistling-shop
wills-o'-the-wisp

R

restaurant-car
thermonuclear
intrapetiolar
interpetiolar
tintinnabular
premandibular
unspectacular
sustentacular
perpendicular
subclavicular
quadrilocular
tritubercular
extra-vascular
fibrovascular
neurovascular
water-vascular
intramuscular
obtuse-angular
subtriangular
intracellular
extra-cellular
multicellular
intercellular
interscapular
intracapsular
supercolumnar
intercolumnar
circumscriber
bubble-chamber
single-chamber
widow's-chamber
founder-member

charter-member
canvas-climber
compass-timber
shock-absorber
ground-officer
police-officer
branch-officer
church-officer
intelligencer
thought-reader
scaling-ladder
pompier-ladder
dispatch-rider
boundary-rider
Schwenkfelder
bridge-builder
master-builder
heave-shoulder
wing-commander
wood-germander
first-offender
supercalender
sock-suspender
self-surrender
spike-lavender
gerund-grinder
letter-founder
non-compounder
lattice-girder
diamond-powder
washing-powder
priming-powder
whipping-cheer
audio-engineer
anti-marketeer
candle-snuffer
Flammenwerfer
thimble-rigger
deck-passenger
foot-passenger
wedding-finger
cross-springer
Meistersinger
costardmonger
miracle-monger
borough-monger
scandalmonger
species-monger
mystery-monger
school-teacher
hunger-marcher
clear-starcher
affenpinscher
oyster-catcher
purse-snatcher
backscratcher
weight-watcher
stratigrapher
lexicographer
chalcographer
palaeographer
biogeographer
zoogeographer
choreographer

morphographer
glyphographer
cardiographer
bibliographer
physiographer
seismographer
oceanographer
selenographer
chronographer
cheirographer
glossographer
cryptographer
distinguisher
beetle-crusher
saddle-feather
sickle-feather
flight-feather
chrome-leather
shammy-leather
mouth-breather
water-breather
nursing-father
foster-brother
seek-no-further
pigeon-fancier
owner-occupier
letter-carrier
Hammerklavier
strike-breaker
prison-breaker
mischief-maker
foot-land-raker
quarter-decker
knickerbocker
hunger-striker
wheeler-dealer
neanderthaler
sherry-cobbler
willow-warbler
fiddle-faddler
velvet-fiddler
swingebuckler
lawn-sprinkler
fortune-teller
tittle-tattler
paddle-steamer
kettledrummer
smoke-consumer
spring-cleaner
vacuum-cleaner
water-softener
paper-fastener
press-fastener
master-mariner
cotton-spinner
machine-gunner
quarter-gunner
scarlet-runner
heir-portioner
hole-and-corner
chimney-corner
incense-burner
kindergartner
manifold-paper

wrapping-paper
blotting-paper
plotting-paper
transfer-paper
woollen-draper
counsel-keeper
canary-creeper
street-sweeper
carpet-sweeper
wood-sandpiper
mutton-thumper
counter-jumper
understrapper
cayenne-pepper
sun-worshipper
carpet-slipper
asset-stripper
emerald-copper
peacock-copper
scandal-bearer
thunder-bearer
night-wanderer
electioneerer
tithe-gatherer
misadventurer
steeplechaser
rainbow-chaser
curtain-raiser
philosophiser
spiritualiser
tranquilliser
attitudiniser
desulphuriser
battle-cruiser
stratocruiser
laissez-passer
book-canvasser
double-crosser
plantain-eater
ecclesiolater
selling-plater
lavender-water
saccharimeter
semiperimeter
pyrheliometer
potentiometer
alcoholometer
stalagmometer
diaphanometer
volumenometer
saccharometer
weatherometer
accelerometer
decelerometer
sympiesometer
pneumatometer
refractometer
candle-lighter
granddaughter
self-slaughter
counterfeiter
helter-skelter
ship-carpenter
finger-pointer

calico-printer
fortune-hunter
bargain-hunter
thunder-darter
counter-caster
interpilaster
posture-master
dancing-master
fencing-master
singing-master
whaling-master
sailing-master
writing-master
drawing-master
station-master
thunder-master
quartermaster
harbour-master
concert-master
bottle-coaster
roller-coaster
salmon-leister
capellmeister
kapellmeister
chest-register
maladminister
baton-sinister
tongue-twister
Kidderminster
knuckleduster
feather-duster
silk-throwster
prairie-oyster
subject-matter
begging-letter
witches-butter
coconut-butter
revenue-cutter
section-cutter
microcomputer
ballast-heaver
clishmaclaver
underachiever
throttle-lever
whereinsoever
whithersoever
dress-improver
life-preserver
process-server
clapperclawer
thunder-shower
whistle-blower
peacock-flower
paschal-flower
flannel-flower
pelican-flower
carrion-flower
passion-flower
trumpet-flower
boundary-layer
bidding-prayer
morning-prayer
unprovided-for
weather-anchor

sergeant-major
steam-governor
burning-mirror
driving-mirror
air-compressor
simplificator
multiplicator
prefabricator
authenticator
sophisticator
intermediator
defibrillator
somnambulator
congratulator
monochromator
discriminator
indoctrinator
predestinator
conglutinator
multivibrator
aerogenerator
disintegrator
transmigrator
administrator
tergiversator
subcontractor
cine-projector
rent-collector
microdetector
semiconductor
tram-conductor
reconstructor
hedge-accentor
self-tormentor
chemoreceptor
photo-receptor
proprioceptor
lithontriptor
statute-labour
bonheur-du-jour
wedding-favour

S

materfamilias
paterfamilias
Chlamydomonas
photovoltaics
thaumaturgics
monostrophics
hydrodynamics
astrodynamics
photochromics
callisthenics
mnemotechnics
quadraphonics
quadrophonics
psychometrics
psychophysics
hydrokinetics
cosmopolitics
power-politics
party-politics
phonocamptics
magneto-optics
chrematistics

pharmaceutics	schizogenesis	quizzing-glass	peaceableness
hare-and-hounds	psychokinesis	prospect-glass	traceableness
clapperboards	synecphonesis	All-hallowmass	agreeableness
prosecutrices	onomatopoesis	pencil-compass	malleableness
Saccharomyces	iontophoresis	dog's-tail-grass	ineffableness
pseudomonades	photophoresis	scorpion-grass	fatigableness
circumambages	amniocentesis	kangaroo-grass	navigableness
ranz-des-vaches	mycotoxicosis	structureless	teachableness
trunk-breeches	hypersarcosis	unremorseless	touchableness
odontornithes	actinomycosis	beginningless	laughableness
riding-clothes	mononucleosis	suspicionless	unamiableness
heebie-jeebies	parapsychosis	companionless	breakableness
mutton-dummies	metamorphosis	dimensionless	drinkableness
preliminaries	homomorphosis	vibrationless	availableness
probabilities	leishmaniosis	inflexionless	untamableness
Protococcales	endometriosis	characterless	untenableness
Eubacteriales	salmonellosis	protectorless	untunableness
Rickettsiales	aspergillosis	foresightless	separableness
Ustilaginales	epanadiplosis	recomfortless	venerableness
Psilophytales	toxoplasmosis	barefacedness	miserableness
disagreeables	cytodiagnosis	pigheadedness	utterableness
irredeemables	narcohypnosis	many-sidedness	admirableness
imponderables	hyperhidrosis	undividedness	desirableness
betweenwhiles	synchondrosis	offhandedness	memorableness
millefeuilles	leptospirosis	unboundedness	incurableness
table-skittles	visceroptosis	unguardedness	endurableness
Passeriformes	haemodialysis	uncloudedness	advisableness
Testicardines	narco-analysis	estrangedness	excusableness
marriage-lines	hypno-analysis	debauchedness	uneatableness
ethanolamines	microanalysis	unbridledness	palatableness
Dicotyledones	cryptanalysis	unsettledness	tractableness
septentriones	autocatalysis	unfeignedness	habitableness
antigropeloes	bacteriolysis	unlearnedness	excitableness
belles-lettres	pneumatolysis	concernedness	irritableness
metamorphoses	labyrinthitis	disguisedness	equitableness
sarcophaguses	osteomyelitis	unadvisedness	temptableness
Hymenomycetes	poliomyelitis	dispersedness	immutableness
Pyrenomycetes	perityphlitis	unbiassedness	imputableness
Schizomycetes	perinephritis	unblessedness	cleavableness
arseno-pyrites	perigastritis	uncreatedness	immovableness
copper-pyrites	perihepatitis	compactedness	allowableness
prosecutrixes	cholecystitis	neglectedness	enjoyableness
daddy-long-legs	deoch-an-doruis	collectedness	deducibleness
Jenny-long-legs	spindle-shanks	suspectedness	reducibleness
level-peggings	tiddledywinks	delightedness	inaudibleness
paper-hangings	smelting-works	conceitedness	illegibleness
aqua-mirabilis	meals-on-wheels	unlimitedness	indelibleness
helminthiasis	cat-o'-nine-tails	contentedness	invisibleness
leishmaniasis	Winter-gardens	untaintedness	plausibleness
elephantiasis	Quaker-buttons	undauntedness	insolubleness
apocatastasis	Encephalartos	bespottedness	newfangleness
parasynthesis	will-o'-the-wisps	unspottedness	versatileness
polysynthesis	pinking-shears	continuedness	unwelcomeness
coenaesthesis	pruning-shears	complexedness	lithesomeness
psychogenesis	elephant's-ears	perplexedness	wholesomeness
morphogenesis	tickly-benders	perfervidness	loathsomeness
dynamogenesis	kittly-benders	threefoldness	toothsomeness
thermogenesis	walking-orders	word-blindness	wearisomeness
organogenesis	butter-fingers	snow-blindness	lightsomeness
heterogenesis	winkle-pickers	haphazardness	superfineness
epeirogenesis	walking-papers	underniceness	masculineness
gametogenesis	cross-quarters	wide-awakeness	ungenuineness
blastogenesis	conquistadors	revocableness	opportuneness
embryogenesis	probe-scissors	yieldableness	self-awareness

prematureness	unbendingness	satiricalness	worthlessness
intricateness	searchingness	centricalness	truthlessness
immediateness	scorchingness	whimsicalness	mercilessness
insatiateness	do-nothingness	classicalness	pennilessness
inviolateness	appealingness	ismaticalness	tracklessness
inanimateness	unfeelingness	practicalness	thanklessness
obstinateness	thrillingness	identicalness	dreamlessness
fortunateness	unwillingness	equivocalness	stainlessness
disparateness	beseemingness	essentialness	sleeplessness
temperateness	unmeaningness	impartialness	powerlessness
desperateness	endearingness	principalness	shiftlessness
elaborateness	unsparingness	unnaturalness	sightlessness
corporateness	unrestingness	effectualness	limitlessness
insensateness	unwittingness	spiritualness	fruitlessness
preteriteness	unknowingness	unmindfulness	guiltlessness
requisiteness	unselfishness	regardfulness	faultlessness
exquisiteness	squeamishness	changefulness	pointlessness
compositeness	lickerishness	scathefulness	dauntlessness
dissoluteness	vapourishness	untunefulness	heartlessness
grotesqueness	yellowishness	speechfulness	trustlessness
unforgiveness	left-handiness	healthfulness	hazardousness
pervasiveness	foolhardiness	unpitifulness	erroneousness
repulsiveness	unhealthiness	plentifulness	righteousness
impulsiveness	seaworthiness	bountifulness	plenteousness
expansiveness	airworthiness	undutifulness	bounteousness
offensiveness	unworldliness	unskilfulness	courteousness
expensiveness	niggardliness	wonderfulness	beauteousness
intensiveness	dastardliness	masterfulness	analogousness
extensiveness	unearthliness	wasterfulness	audaciousness
explosiveness	uncleanliness	prayerfulness	sagaciousness
purposiveness	unwomanliness	forgetfulness	fugaciousness
corrosiveness	scholarliness	frightfulness	salaciousness
excursiveness	brotherliness	deceitfulness	tenaciousness
impassiveness	northerliness	unhurtfulness	capaciousness
recessiveness	southerliness	unrestfulness	rapaciousness
excessiveness	soldierliness	sorrowfulness	voraciousness
diffusiveness	sprightliness	Christianness	furaciousness
exclusiveness	unsightliness	outspokenness	vivaciousness
obtrusiveness	unsaintliness	misshapenness	judiciousness
intrusiveness	uncourtliness	forgottenness	officiousness
combativeness	secondariness	uncertainness	maliciousness
evocativeness	exemplariness	dreadlessness	deliciousness
talkativeness	customariness	boundlessness	ferociousness
operativeness	visionariness	bloodlessness	atrociousness
imitativeness	temporariness	peacelessness	consciousness
defectiveness	arbitrariness	gracelessness	insidiousness
effectiveness	necessariness	voicelessness	invidiousness
infectiveness	sedentariness	pricelessness	melodiousness
objectiveness	momentariness	smokelessness	egregiousness
seductiveness	voluntariness	guilelessness	religiousness
secretiveness	tributariness	shamelessness	litigiousness
primitiveness	predatoriness	spinelessness	ingeniousness
sensitiveness	desultoriness	shapelessness	feloniousness
assentiveness	unsavouriness	noiselessness	vicariousness
retentiveness	unthriftiness	pulselessness	nefariousness
attentiveness	overhastiness	senselessness	imperiousness
inventiveness	horse-sickness	causelessness	deliriousness
plaintiveness	brainsickness	statelessness	laboriousness
deceptiveness	heart-sickness	tastelessness	notoriousness
receptiveness	prosaicalness	nervelessness	incuriousness
assertiveness	illogicalness	matchlessness	injuriousness
embracingness	satanicalness	deathlessness	penuriousness
sufficingness	technicalness	faithlessness	luxuriousness
confidingness	sphericalness	mirthlessness	vexatiousness

fractiousness	smelling-salts	isodimorphous	gymnospermous
facetiousness	three-per-cents	homeomorphous	diathermanous
ambitiousness	Lepidostrobus	ophiomorphous	coralligenous
seditiousness	meningococcus	tauromorphous	vitelligenous
bumptiousness	streptococcus	rhizomorphous	skeletogenous
obliviousness	Cercopithecus	orthognathous	prolegomenous
obnoxiousness	Galeopithecus	saurognathous	plenitudinous
innoxiousness	Semnopithecus	hysteranthous	platitudinous
troublousness	gastrocnemius	inefficacious	multitudinous
frivolousness	hydrocephalus	perspicacious	fortitudinous
oraculousness	leptocephalus	gynodioecious	cartilaginous
credulousness	lactobacillus	self-conscious	acotyledonous
pendulousness	strato-cumulus	semiconscious	autochthonous
tremulousness	Dendrocalamus	discommodious	tautochronous
querulousness	podophthalmus	melancholious	proterogynous
garrulousness	steganopodous	unceremonious	xanthochroous
criminousness	gasteropodous	sanctimonious	melanochroous
poisonousness	juglandaceous	disharmonious	plaigotropous
barbarousness	bromeliaceous	quadrifarious	heterocarpous
ludicrousness	magnoliaceous	stercorarious	schizocarpous
ponderousness	pucciniaceous	frumentarious	ovoviviparous
dangerousness	salviniaceous	disceptatious	semioviparous
lecherousness	bignoniaceous	stalactitious	proterandrous
dexterousness	amygdalaceous	profectitious	rhopalocerous
inodorousness	polygalaceous	fermentitious	splendiferous
clamorousness	strobilaceous	subreptitious	mammaliferous
monstrousness	gentianaceous	surreptitious	nickeliferous
venturousness	membranaceous	superstitious	fossiliferous
spiritousness	arundinaceous	conscientious	reptiliferous
momentousness	proteinaceous	unpretentious	coralliferous
innocuousness	boraginaceous	uncontentious	metalliferous
deciduousness	polygonaceous	megacephalous	umbelliferous
assiduousness	cinchonaceous	mesocephalous	papilliferous
ambiguousness	cylindraceous	autocephalous	petroliferous
ingenuousness	papaveraceous	dialypetalous	globuliferous
strenuousness	stercoraceous	malacophilous	celluliferous
congruousness	camphoraceous	psammophilous	granuliferous
impetuousness	equisetaceous	entomophilous	spinuliferous
sumptuousness	amarantaceous	thermophilous	balsamiferous
imperfectness	sarmentaceous	microphyllous	manganiferous
unperfectness	frumentaceous	anisophyllous	polliniferous
incorrectness	dichlamydeous	leptophyllous	staminiferous
downrightness	porcellaneous	sphagnicolous	aluminiferous
maladroitness	miscellaneous	sclerocaulous	platiniferous
brilliantness	subterraneous	overcredulous	antenniferous
stringentness	consectaneous	filipendulous	carboniferous
deficientness	instantaneous	solidungulous	stoloniferous
transientness	consentaneous	hexadactylous	nectariferous
incorruptness	inhomogeneous	zygodactylous	garnetiferous
steadfastness	heterogeneous	monodactylous	cobaltiferous
shamefastness	porcelaineous	polydactylous	argentiferous
soothfastness	ustilagineous	heterostylous	quartziferous
princess-dress	exsanguineous	geitonogamous	aphanipterous
millionairess	toxicophagous	phanerogamous	lepidopterous
printing-press	ostreophagous	cleistogamous	trichopterous
conspiratress	phyllophagous	monothalamous	hymenopterous
interpretress	entomophagous	polythalamous	heteropterous
music-mistress	lissotrichous	tetradynamous	cheiropterous
housemistress	tetrastichous	pusillanimous	plectopterous
toastmistress	pentastichous	plagiostomous	brachypterous
palpable-gross	orthostichous	sclerodermous	filibusterous
bridge-of-boats	pentadelphous	homeothermous	ambidexterous
traffic-lights	polyadelphous	angiospermous	odontophorous
double-or-quits	hypertrophous	cyclospermous	tubuliflorous

heterosporous
graminivorous
insectivorous
bibliolatrous
unadventurous
erysipelatous
exanthematous
monotrematous
emphysematous
papillomatous
granulomatous
condylomatous
carcinomatous
hydrosomatous
xerodermatous
ostodermatous
discomycetous
heteroclitous
serendipitous
inconspicuous
subcontiguous
unsuperfluous
subcontinuous
discontinuous
grandiloquous
ventriloquous
ultra-virtuous
Zinjanthropus
Dipterocarpus
electrophorus
Dolichosaurus
brachiosaurus
tyrannosaurus
Atlantosaurus
Ichthyosaurus
Balanoglossus
scambling-days
launching-ways
viol-de-gamboys
T
gathering-peat
protonotariat
future-perfect
preterperfect
letter-perfect
subject-object
spectre-insect
zebra-parakeet
shell-parakeet
reefing-jacket
hacking-jacket
leather-jacket
middle-bracket
walking-ticket
parking-ticket
through-ticket
trouser-pocket
saddle-blanket
clothes-basket
serving-mallet
cross-crosslet
electromagnet
feather-bonnet
foundation-net

keyhole-limpet
downcast-shaft
hundredweight
casting-weight
feather-weight
cruiser-weight
counter-weight
journey-weight
straight-pight
Gemütlichkeit
kissing-comfit
what-d'ye-call-it
millstone-grit
safety-deposit
butter-biscuit
pepper-and-salt
cartridge-belt
suspender-belt
clincher-built
soldering-bolt
insignificant
superabundant
lance-sergeant
staff-sergeant
drill-sergeant
scrap-merchant
rogue-elephant
extinguishant
tortoise-plant
creosote-plant
interosculant
anticoagulant
sublieutenant
decontaminant
superdominant
stop-consonant
equiponderant
imperseverant
search-warrant
knights-errant
uncomplaisant
self-important
fire-resistant
heat-resistant
rust-resistant
shop-assistant
fellow-servant
livery-servant
rejuvenescent
self-confident
over-confident
vice-president
self-dependent
correspondent
unintelligent
self-indulgent
overindulgent
circumambient
delirifacient
abortifacient
non-proficient
micronutrient
quinquevalent
electrovalent

multifilament
tooth-ornament
shell-ornament
interlacement
pronouncement
electrocement
re-enforcement
reinforcement
garnisheement
vouchsafement
pre-engagement
disengagement
mismanagement
disparagement
encouragement
forejudgement
disobligement
rearrangement
surchargement
rapprochement
embranglement
reconcilement
out-settlement
bamboozlement
frank-tenement
prefigurement
disfigurement
admeasurement
remeasurement
self-abasement
franchisement
advertisement
divertisement
reimbursement
reinstatement
overstatement
earth-movement
establishment
embellishment
replenishment
disembodiment
accompaniment
disembarkment
non-fulfilment
enlightenment
preordainment
ascertainment
appertainment
entertainment
refashionment
partitionment
apportionment
unconcernment
misgovernment
up-to-the-moment
redevelopment
dismemberment
beleaguerment
encompassment
embarrassment
self-treatment
affreightment
representment
reappointment

disinvestment
maladjustment
self-enjoyment
disemployment
misemployment
untransparent
equidifferent
co-belligerent
prices-current
letters-patent
omnicompetent
grandiloquent
stultiloquent
plumbisolvent
plumbosolvent
coursing-joint
shoulder-joint
breaking-point
sticking-point
starting-point
rallying-point
freezing-point
polyprotodont
elephant's-foot
gillie-wetfoot
bleeding-heart
bullock's-heart
state-of-the-art
princess-skirt
prince-consort
water-dropwort
squinancy-wort
east-north-east
east-south-east
chimney-breast
spermatoblast
phase-contrast
medicine-chest
treasure-chest
savanna-forest
metempiricist
neoclassicist
epigeneticist
cyberneticist
contrabandist
onychophagist
bibliophagist
gynaecologist
myrmecologist
Etruscologist
orchidologist
pteridologist
archaeologist
spelaeologist
pantheologist
venereologist
phraseologist
laryngologist
ornithologist
agrobiologist
cryobiologist
malariologist
Assyriologist
kinesiologist

heresiologist
syphilologist
vexillologist
victimologist
volcanologist
vulcanologist
campanologist
lichenologist
sphagnologist
arachnologist
carcinologist
criminologist
sindonologist
meteorologist
martyrologist
eschatologist
haematologist
climatologist
primatologist
dermatologist
olfactologist
insectologist
Sovietologist
planetologist
herpetologist
gerontologist
Christologist
agrostologist
ichthyologist
thaumaturgist
sado-masochist
calligraphist
orthographist
hagiographist
stenographist
phonographist
chirographist
photographist
tachygraphist
catastrophist
deipnosophist
hieroglyphist
kinesipathist
homoeopathist
psychopathist
periodicalist
proverbialist
non-specialist
antisocialist
commercialist
millennialist
immaterialist
industrialist
prudentialist
colloquialist
phenomenalist
occasionalist
irrationalist
fractionalist
functionalist
devotionalist
unicameralist
unilateralist
orchestralist

structuralist
scripturalist
Occidentalist
documentalist
sacerdotalist
individualist
conceptualist
homosexualist
Pantagruelist
infallibilist
impossibilist
bibliophilist
scripophilist
timbrophilist
monometallist
violoncellist
deuterogamist
thermochemist
physiognomist
Deuteronomist
nonconformist
chloroformist
philhellenist
mnemotechnist
indeterminist
dodecaphonist
co-religionist
quaternionist
trade-unionist
compulsionist
convulsionist
successionist
concessionist
impressionist
expressionist
percussionist
revelationist
undulationist
separationist
liberationist
tolerationist
emigrationist
recitationist
sanitationist
derivationist
innovationist
annexationist
perfectionist
projectionist
protectionist
exhibitionist
demolitionist
oppositionist
conventionist
conceptionist
redemptionist
assumptionist
corruptionist
contortionist
suggestionist
devolutionist
revolutionist
Saint-Simonist
feuilletonist

Eurocommunist
inopportunist
stereoscopist
stethoscopist
cranioscopist
retinoscopist
metoposcopist
oneiroscopist
lycanthropist
theanthropist
misanthropist
electrotypist
vernacularist
particularist
reactionarist
lepidopterist
trichopterist
phalansterist
bibliolatrist
psychometrist
viniculturist
sericulturist
agriculturist
viticulturist
palingenesist
papaprelatist
contemplatist
melodramatist
apothegmatist
anagrammatist
epigrammatist
pangrammatist
panspermatist
bureaucratist
rhabdomantist
pococurantist
experimentist
contrapuntist
Hemerobaptist
lithotriptist
controvertist
sansculottist
pharmaceutist
sociolinguist
ventriloquist
progressivist
destructivist
stern-foremost
listening-post
psychoanalyst
Messerschmitt
cigarette-butt
Queensland-nut
horse-chestnut
water-chestnut
well-worked-out
W
daughter-in-law
serjeant-at-law
squirrel-shrew
picture-window
compass-window
chamber-fellow
sulphur-yellow

weeping-willow
criss-cross-row
X
cephalothorax
concavo-convex
convexo-convex
improvisatrix
primogenitrix
interlocutrix
resistance-box
collecting-box
tic-douloureux
archaeopteryx
Y
varnishing-day
Passion-Sunday
porcelain-clay
street-railway
division-lobby
indeterminacy
thalassocracy
thalattocracy
dactyliomancy
preponderancy
circumjacency
recrudescency
convalescency
consenescency
defervescency
effervescency
transcendency
intransigency
retromingency
constringency
insufficiency
inconveniency
petrocurrency
inconsistency
intermittency
rough-and-ready
linsey-woolsey
topside-turvey
interstratify
anthropophagy
horse-and-buggy
genethlialogy
zoopsychology
geomorphology
aerolithology
helminthology
psychobiology
chronobiology
stoicheiology
ophthalmology
folk-etymology
phenomenology
biotechnology
endocrinology
synchronology
geochronology
palaeozoology
systematology
thremmatology
diplomatology

numismatology	irretrievably	transfusively	flourishingly
sedimentology	inconceivably	unexclusively	languishingly
palaeontology	unconceivably	inobtrusively	unshrinkingly
fifth-monarchy	unperceivably	unobtrusively	untremblingly
cathodography	irrefrangibly	predicatively	dissemblingly
opisthography	indiscernibly	implicatively	forefeelingly
autobiography	undiscernibly	provocatively	unbeseemingly
heresiography	reprehensibly	prerogatively	threateningly
metallography	supersensibly	correlatively	frighteningly
symbolography	irresponsibly	appellatively	complainingly
pterylography	irrepressibly	superlatively	questioningly
dactylography	inexpressibly	legislatively	unreasoningly
sphygmography	impermissibly	speculatively	unreturningly
steganography	imperceptibly	affirmatively	overbearingly
prosopography	insusceptibly	terminatively	consideringly
rhyparography	incorruptibly	alternatively	bewilderingly
electrography	inconvertibly	declaratively	squanderingly
spectrography	inexhaustibly	preparatively	interferingly
orchesography	incombustibly	comparatively	unfalteringly
climatography	undisturbedly	restoratively	splutteringly
dermatography	wrong-headedly	penetratively	perseveringly
thanatography	underhandedly	qualitatively	unmurmuringly
telautography	cold-bloodedly	facultatively	displeasingly
ichthyography	unqualifiedly	commutatively	dispraisingly
heterostrophy	constrainedly	disputatively	tantalisingly
anthroposophy	unconcernedly	retroactively	unpromisingly
enantiomorphy	undiscernedly	distractively	patronisingly
anthropopathy	ill-favouredly	ineffectively	temporisingly
untrustworthy	good-naturedly	prospectively	distressingly
mesaticephaly	undisguisedly	perspectively	deprecatingly
scaphocephaly	unmitigatedly	restrictively	suffocatingly
brachycephaly	disaffectedly	distinctively	instigatingly
indescribably	recollectedly	instinctively	undeviatingly
imperturbably	unsuspectedly	subjunctively	vacillatingly
impracticably	unwarrantedly	conjunctively	penetratingly
indissuadably	interruptedly	disjunctively	devastatingly
recommendably	hard-heartedly	obstructively	extenuatingly
uncommendably	half-heartedly	destructively	insinuatingly
irreplaceably	unsupportedly	instructively	aggravatingly
knowledgeably	transportedly	prohibitively	distractingly
indefatigably	unperceivedly	inquisitively	disquietingly
unjustifiably	troublesomely	insensitively	dispiritingly
unreclaimably	unwholesomely	dispositively	inspiritingly
irreclaimably	venturesomely	substantively	unrelentingly
unconformably	quarrelsomely	inattentively	unrepentingly
unfashionably	clandestinely	descriptively	everlastingly
companionably	inopportunely	inscriptively	interestingly
objectionably	appropriately	presumptively	unresistingly
exceptionably	triangulately	consumptively	mistrustingly
unconquerably	approximately	retributively	unremittingly
unrecoverably	subordinately	attributively	unbelievingly
irrecoverably	disordinately	consecutively	unapprovingly
dishonourably	determinately	institutively	undeservingly
unpleasurably	unfortunately	acquiescingly	overflowingly
commensurably	importunately	outstandingly	foreknowingly
indispensably	considerately	confoundingly	sanctifyingly
unsurpassably	intemperately	disparagingly	self-denyingly
discreditably	inelaborately	encouragingly	seventeenthly
unwarrantably	precipitately	disobligingly	thankworthily
unaccountably	picturesquely	challengingly	trustworthily
uncomfortably	inoffensively	encroachingly	preliminarily
insupportably	inexpensively	unflinchingly	extemporarily
incontestably	unexpensively	diminishingly	unnecessarily
unforgettably	progressively	astonishingly	fragmentarily

rudimentarily
involuntarily
vindicatorily
declamatorily
explanatorily
declaratorily
preparatorily
perfunctorily
premonitorily
algebraically
pharisaically
coxcombically
anaerobically
pyramidically
spasmodically
rhapsodically
honorifically
strategically
nostalgically
pedagogically
theologically
homologically
topologically
serologically
ontologically
lethargically
demiurgically
concyclically
evangelically
parabolically
apostolically
hydraulically
geochemically
graphemically
taxonomically
metonymically
inorganically
puritanically
antigenically
ontogenically
macaronically
thrasonically
geotropically
genotypically
cylindrically
allegorically
categorically
anaphorically
plethorically
diametrically
symmetrically
geometrically
isometrically
eccentrically
panegyrically
nonsensically
intrinsically
extrinsically
adiabatically
lymphatically
schematically
athematically
pragmatically
enigmatically

stigmatically
asthmatically
grammatically
idiomatically
axiomatically
chromatically
automatically
prismatically
traumatically
rheumatically
pneumatically
isostatically
climactically
unpractically
syntactically
geotactically
dialectically
apodictically
apomictically
energetically
prophetically
apathetically
synthetically
aesthetically
splenetically
phrenetically
theoretically
impolitically
sodomitically
parasitically
authentically
symbiotically
patriotically
sylleptically
proleptically
dyspeptically
bombastically
sarcastically
epinastically
gymnastically
peirastically
fantastically
Judaistically
atheistically
sophistically
realistically
dualistically
stylistically
atomistically
pianistically
agonistically
hubristically
dioristically
floristically
heuristically
statistically
egotistically
casuistically
catalytically
paradoxically
unequivocally
matrilineally
incorporeally
diphthongally

centrifugally
prejudicially
sacrificially
superficially
quincuncially
interradially
quadrennially
matrimonially
patrimonially
participially
magisterially
ministerially
prefatorially
mediatorially
dictatorially
territorially
inventorially
terrestrially
equinoctially
substantially
exponentially
deferentially
referentially
inferentially
reverentially
penitentially
influentially
sexagesimally
provisionally
extensionally
reversionally
educationally
sensationally
traditionally
conditionally
intentionally
unemotionally
exceptionally
conjecturally
transversally
interdentally
fundamentally
sacramentally
detrimentally
sentimentally
ineffectually
instinctually
unspiritually
nominativally
disgracefully
distastefully
reproachfully
unhealthfully
distressfully
distrustfully
mistrustfully
unchristianly
ungentlemanly
gentlewomanly
small-and-early
rectilinearly
verisimilarly
spectacularly
rectangularly

street-orderly
grandfatherly
grandmotherly
north-easterly
south-easterly
whoremasterly
north-westerly
south-westerly
unneighbourly
quarter-hourly
defencelessly
purposelessly
remorselessly
successlessly
thoughtlessly
spontaneously
sulphureously
unrighteously
uprighteously
efficaciously
injudiciously
inofficiously
unconsciously
compendiously
irreligiously
punctiliously
ignominiously
ceremoniously
acrimoniously
burglariously
temerariously
contrariously
opprobriously
deleteriously
meritoriously
industriously
illustriously
unambitiously
expeditiously
repetitiously
tendentiously
pretentiously
sententiously
contentiously
scrumptiously
over-anxiously
incredulously
blasphemously
magnanimously
dichotomously
vertiginously
anachronously
synchronously
isochronously
fissiparously
proliferously
odoriferously
pestiferously
treacherously
carnivorously
triquetrously
adventurously
precipitously
necessitously

conspicuously	balneotherapy	mountebankery	quadruplicity
perspicuously	psychotherapy	jiggery-pokery	exothermicity
promiscuously	physiotherapy	ship-chandlery	pathogenicity
unambiguously	organotherapy	sugar-refinery	iatrogenicity
mellifluously	actinotherapy	confectionery	tumorgenicity
superfluously	immunotherapy	good-King-Henry	synchronicity
incongruously	pyretotherapy	swine's-succory	concentricity
infructuously	pharyngoscopy	qualificatory	egocentricity
tempestuously	röntgenoscopy	significatory	phytotoxicity
mischievously	omoplatoscopy	certificatory	hypervelocity
circumspectly	diaphototropy	testificatory	irreciprocity
counterfeitly	parthenocarpy	justificatory	translucidity
significantly	daguerreotypy	communicatory	superfluidity
extravagantly	bibliothecary	disobligatory	instantaneity
predominantly	postliminiary	investigatory	consentaneity
inconsonantly	tricarpellary	interrogatory	inhomogeneity
participantly	interstellary	nick-nackatory	heterogeneity
protuberantly	supra-axillary	constellatory	pontificality
remonstrantly	extra-axillary	extrapolatory	theatricality
complaisantly	hypsophyllary	confabulatory	romanticality
concomitantly	quadringenary	preambulatory	matrifocality
precipitantly	prolegomenary	funambulatory	patrifocality
equidistantly	quincentenary	perambulatory	reciprocality
magnificently	octocentenary	matriculatory	artificiality
acquiescently	novocentenary	gesticulatory	provinciality
reminiscently	quingentenary	expostulatory	antisociality
translucently	extraordinary	ratiocinatory	commerciality
improvidently	superordinary	hallucinatory	primordiality
resplendently	multitudinary	recriminatory	immateriality
independently	genito-urinary	incriminatory	prudentiality
intelligently	televisionary	exterminatory	tangentiality
inefficiently	convulsionary	reverberatory	torrentiality
inconsciently	subversionary	refrigeratory	presentiality
disobediently	concessionary	transpiratory	sequentiality
inexpediently	processionary	corroboratory	phantasmality
subserviently	confessionary	commemoratory	phenomenality
incontinently	possessionary	demonstratory	aboriginality
impertinently	geostationary	remonstratory	unoriginality
transparently	confectionary	improvisatory	meridionality
indifferently	concretionary	laevorotatory	occasionality
belligerently	discretionary	contradictory	irrationality
incompetently	expeditionary	circumductory	impersonality
inadvertently	transitionary	disinhibitory	microtonality
unremittently	repetitionary	psychohistory	unilaterality
mellifluently	subventionary	interlocutory	connaturality
unsteadfastly	conventionary	sea-gooseberry	rectipetality
brachydactyly	precautionary	roe-blackberry	inhospitality
adenoidectomy	illocutionary	paper-mulberry	accidentality
salpingectomy	devolutionary	bladder-cherry	horizontality
sympathectomy	revolutionary	ecclesiolatry	individuality
tonsillectomy	supernumerary	anthropolatry	unpunctuality
pneumonectomy	extra-limitary	thaumatolatry	homosexuality
prostatectomy	primogenitary	saccharimetry	improbability
symphyseotomy	medicamentary	stoechiometry	absorbability
symphysiotomy	parliamentary	stoichiometry	implacability
encephalotomy	complementary	alcoholometry	impeccability
poikilothermy	supplementary	stalagmometry	predicability
electrothermy	complimentary	anthropometry	vindicability
livery-company	integumentary	light-infantry	applicability
spinning-jenny	evangelistary	mother-country	despicability
eighteen-penny	psychosurgery	counter-fleury	ineducability
traveller's-joy	salmon-fishery	rhombporphyry	formidability
kinesitherapy	oyster-fishery	pharmacognosy	expendability
musicotherapy	knick-knackery	spheroidicity	extendability

13 -ITY

manageability	perdurability	infeasibility	crystallinity
changeability	mensurability	expansibility	clandestinity
unsaleability	impassability	defensibility	consanguinity
sketchability	educatability	insensibility	confraternity
punishability	delectability	ostensibility	inopportunity
perishability	marketability	extensibility	unfamiliarity
insociability	profitability	corrosibility	consimilarity
unsociability	inimitability	reversibility	dissimilarity
associability	unsuitability	impassibility	vernacularity
verifiability	inevitability	accessibility	particularity
unreliability	acceptability	admissibility	triangularity
invariability	metastability	remissibility	peninsularity
insatiability	detestability	impossibility	ambidexterity
negotiability	commutability	diffusibility	impecuniosity
inviolability	permutability	compatibility	anfractuosity
inoculability	disputability	defectibility	sacrosanctity
coagulability	deceivability	deductibility	discontinuity
redeemability	receivability	deceptibility	appropinquity
deformability	resolvability	receptibility	associativity
reformability	insolvability	impartibility	correlativity
attainability	improvability	divertibility	radioactivity
terminability	squeezability	digestibility	retroactivity
impalpability	invincibility	resistibility	hyperactivity
comparability	immiscibility	reflexibility	instinctivity
ponderability	producibility	inflexibility	destructivity
preferability	incredibility	dissolubility	insensitivity
vulnerability	extendibility	self-sterility	substantivity
inoperability	invendibility	contractility	consumptivity
filterability	re-eligibility	self-fertility	vice-admiralty
answerability	ineligibility	overcredulity	prick-me-dainty
acquirability	negligibility	pusillanimity	storming-party
deplorability	corrigibility	nonconformity	galvanoplasty
factorability	intangibility	disconformity	stomatoplasty
inexorability	infallibility	superhumanity	traumatonasty
penetrability	defeasibility		

14 -IDA

A	trichobacteria	dodecasyllabic	ornithomorphic
Gnathobdellida	phantasmagoria	imparisyllabic	enantiomorphic
Hexactinellida	achondroplasia	quadrisyllabic	coelanaglyphic
bougainvillaea	pseudaesthesia	claustrophobic	anthropopathic
Neuropteroidea	hyperaesthesia	dysmenorrhoeic	mesaticephalic
spermatorrhoea	cryptaesthesia	through-traffic	rhinencephalic
pseudepigrapha	intelligentsia	stereospecific	prosencephalic
symmetrophobia	intelligentzia	antiodontalgic	scaphocephalic
claustrophobia	Acanthocephala	genethlialogic	brachycephalic
tetrasporangia	Perissodactyla	geomorphologic	Mephistophelic
macrosporangia	Shakespeariana	helminthologic	organometallic
microsporangia	interambulacra	opisthographic	vicar-apostolic
Ornithodelphia	Monoplacophora	metallographic	brachydactylic
imponderabilia	Polyplacophora	pterylographic	morphophonemic
hypercalcaemia	Prototracheata	sphygmographic	edriophthalmic
hyperglycaemia	Nudibranchiata	steganographic	poikilothermic
leucocythaemia	Zygobranchiata	rhyparographic	electrothermic
oligocythaemia	C	spectrographic	aesthesiogenic
hypernatraemia	archgenethliac	telautographic	hallucinogenic
leucocytopenia	morphinomaniac	ornithodelphic	stentorophonic
Appendicularia	antaphrodisiac	heterostrophic	optoelectronic

submicroscopic
tachistoscopic
palaeanthropic
therianthropic
diaheliotropic
diaphototropic
parthenocarpic
stereoisomeric
phantasmagoric
metaphosphoric
pyrophosphoric
diesel-electric
dynamo-electric
thermo-electric
stoechiometric
stoichiometric
pyrheliometric
potentiometric
anthropometric
stomatogastric
hydrosulphuric
hyperaesthesic
psychodramatic
pantopragmatic
apophthegmatic
hierogrammatic
lithochromatic
orthochromatic
protoplasmatic
proceleusmatic
hydropneumatic
telangiectatic
bacteriostatic
photosynthetic
hyperaesthetic
cryptaesthetic
galactopoietic
hermaphroditic
pyelonephritic
triconsonantic
pneumoconiotic
hydronephrotic
psychoneurotic
lithonthryptic
unenthusiastic
galvanoplastic
antiphlogistic
philosophistic
universalistic
spiritualistic
somnambulistic
transformistic
oligopsonistic
characteristic
filiopietistic
paralinguistic
metalinguistic
subjectivistic
spermatophytic
psychoanalytic
   D
neck-sweetbread
street-railroad
uncomprehended

heavenly-minded
dyer's-greenweed
unacknowledged
straddle-legged
schooner-rigged
counter-changed
proud-stomached
widow-bewitched
old-established
unaccomplished
undernourished
unextinguished
leather-mouthed
transmogrified
spindle-shanked
stiletto-heeled
self-controlled
high-principled
flowery-kirtled
self-proclaimed
promise-crammed
copper-bottomed
unstrengthened
copper-fastened
scatter-brained
shatter-brained
parallel-veined
self-determined
over-determined
disimpassioned
ill-conditioned
air-conditioned
aforementioned
above-mentioned
undermentioned
unproportioned
highly-seasoned
steeple-crowned
parallelepiped
parallelopiped
underdeveloped
night-foundered
nimble-fingered
butter-fingered
sticky-fingered
chicken-livered
double-flowered
nuclear-powered
orange-coloured
purple-coloured
salmon-coloured
unmanufactured
self-displeased
mathematicised
unmaterialised
uncrystallised
plane-polarised
unsystematised
death-practised
extra-condensed
unprepossessed
uncertificated
uncommunicated
undomesticated

unreciprocated
unconsolidated
unaccommodated
multinucleated
unappropriated
uncontemplated
unmatriculated
diverticulated
under-populated
uncontaminated
unconfederated
uncorroborated
unincorporated
unpremeditated
heaven-directed
uncontradicted
self-affrighted
public-spirited
outward-sainted
well-acquainted
intussuscepted
willing-hearted
chicken-hearted
uncontroverted
marble-breasted
double-breasted
single-breasted
pigeon-breasted
yellow-breasted
sparrow-blasted
self-interested
blood-bespotted
trumpet-tongued
galeopithecoid
brachypinakoid
neanderthaloid
lepidodendroid
corticosteroid
never-never-land
trencher-friend
stretching-bond
slug-foot-second
Bristol-diamond
ocean-greyhound
pleasure-ground
breeding-ground
standing-ground
spawning-ground
stamping-ground
stomping-ground
apprenticehood
high-priesthood
chittagong-wood
dragon-standard
across-the-board
solitaire-board
scrubbing-board
telegraph-board
hunting-leopard
treacle-mustard
skunk-blackbird
rhinoceros-bird
   E
Scombresocidae

Trachypteridae
osteoglossidae
Pleuronectidae
Chaetodontidae
Rhinocerotidae
Phytolaccaceae
Asclepiadaceae
Haloragidaceae
Hamamelidaceae
Amaryllidaceae
Calycanthaceae
Chenopodiaceae
Caprifoliaceae
Sarraceniaceae
Sigillariaceae
Pontederiaceae
Rickettsiaceae
Marchantiaceae
Marcgraviaceae
Zygophyllaceae
Convolvulaceae
Menispermaceae
Plumbaginaceae
Ustilaginaceae
Plantaginaceae
Rhizophoraceae
Passifloraceae
Hydropterideae
Monochlamydeae
breathing-space
straining-piece
murdering-piece
fivepenny-piece
printing-office
blood-sacrifice
multiple-choice
interlocutrice
dessert-service
insignificance
superabundance
torsion-balance
counterbalance
non-performance
discountenance
self-sustenance
non-compearance
disencumbrance
equiponderance
reconnaissance
self-inductance
disinheritance
reacquaintance
unacquaintance
self-importance
middle-distance
zenith-distance
discontinuance
exacerbescence
rejuvenescence
colliquescence
self-confidence
over-confidence
condescendence
self-dependence

correspondence	disqualifiable	striking-circle	sporangiospore
self-indulgence	unidentifiable	knitting-needle	gold-of-pleasure
overindulgence	unreconcilable	shoulder-girdle	counter-measure
circumambience	irreconcilable	breathing-while	fellow-creature
quinquevalence	incontrollable	circumscissile	microminiature
three-halfpence	uncontrollable	sulphathiazole	contemperature
cross-reference	dodecasyllable	snapping-turtle	distemperature
non-concurrence	quadrisyllable	prittle-prattle	infrastructure
omnicompetence	disconformable	medicine-bottle	ultrastructure
sonnet-sequence	unrestrainable	smelling-bottle	microstructure
grandiloquence	irrestrainable	bear-animalcule	superstructure
stultiloquence	indeterminable	third-programme	ultimogeniture
worcester-sauce	undeterminable	whispering-dome	disinfranchise
cabbage-lettuce	inconscionable	overburdensome	electroculture
wood-nightshade	unconscionable	ultramicrotome	heather-mixture
sesquisulphide	compassionable	bathing-costume	scale-staircase
sulphanilamide	impressionable	rabbeting-plane	ferro-manganese
monosaccharide	proportionable	aerohydroplane	hypercriticise
polysaccharide	unquestionable	hydro-aeroplane	bird-of-paradise
endoradiosonde	inconsiderable	pseudomembrane	monophthongise
verisimilitude	untransferable	louping-on-stane	disenfranchise
furfuraldehyde	indecipherable	dinitrobenzene	centrifugalise
chincherinchee	undecipherable	galeopithecine	overspecialise
turpentine-tree	unsplinterable	sulphapyridine	superficialise
cannonball-tree	indiscoverable	dividing-engine	testimonialise
maidenhair-tree	undiscoverable	traction-engine	territorialise
traveller's-tree	indemonstrable	folding-machine	substantialise
flamboyant-tree	undemonstrable	washing-machine	overcapitalise
strawberry-tree	unrecapturable	bathing-machine	sentimentalise
watch-committee	self-torturable	talking-machine	unspiritualise
spring-carriage	crystallisable	burling-machine	hysterectomise
saloon-carriage	unrecognisable	planing-machine	proletarianise
fibrocartilage	irrecognisable	reaping-machine	utilitarianise
Jack-by-the-hedge	indecomposable	pararosaniline	dechristianise
disacknowledge	undecomposable	hydrocoralline	unchristianise
blank-cartridge	untranslatable	self-discipline	disillusionise
water-privilege	disrespectable	trimethylamine	chevaux-de-frise
sansculotterie	contradictable	triphenylamine	subminiaturise
whittie-whattie	irresuscitable	phthalocyanine	radiosensitise
Pontefract-cake	unpremeditable	benzodiazepine	photosensitise
parliament-cake	unmerchantable	nitroglycerine	hypersensitise
swoopstake-like	transplantable	norepinephrine	hydrocellulose
salamander-like	insurmountable	Russo-Byzantine	nitrocellulose
unbusinesslike	unsurmountable	gooseberry-wine	general-purpose
approach-stroke	discomfortable	powder-magazine	provincial-rose
Internationale	under-constable	chlorpromazine	Wilhelmstrasse
telegraph-cable	breakfast-table	videotelephone	percussion-fuse
incommunicable	intransmutable	radiotelephone	preaching-house
uncommunicable	untransmutable	hydrocortisone	receiving-house
excommunicable	unforeknowable	phenobarbitone	slaughter-house
understandable	pribble-prabble	shell-limestone	succulent-house
discommendable	fermentescible	stumbling-stone	sacrament-house
decompoundable	unreproducible	cairngorm-stone	contraindicate
disserviceable	irreproducible	asparagus-stone	unsophisticate
unmarriageable	unintelligible	phenylbutazone	ultracrepidate
unpurchaseable	comprehensible	self-heterodyne	multicuspidate
unconceiveable	incompressible	spinthariscope	disaccommodate
irreproachable	insuppressible	scintilloscope	circumnavigate
inapproachable	indestructible	ophthalmoscope	orthophosphate
unapproachable	indiscerptible	chromatosphere	superphosphate
accomplishable	controvertible	Protospathaire	nudibranchiate
undiminishable	skimble-skamble	concessionaire	zygobranchiate
extinguishable	witches'-thimble	commissionaire	forisfamiliate
unvanquishable	rough-and-tumble	sporangiophore	quinquefoliate

angustifoliate
malappropriate
disappropriate
misappropriate
ferroprussiate
bletheranskate
dinoflagellate
multifoliolate
greywacke-slate
ottrelite-slate
polishing-slate
tintinnabulate
circumambulate
discombobulate
multarticulate
trituberculate
quadrigeminate
indiscriminate
predeterminate
rostrocarinate
polyembryonate
discomboberate
disincarcerate
disincorporate
interpenetrate
incommensurate
overcompensate
quinquecostate
interpunctuate
yttro-columbite
yttro-tantalite
Praeraphaelite
Anglo-Israelite
kinetheodolite
Porphyrogenite
micro-meteorite
micropegmatite
palmatipartite
pinnatipartite
polishing-paste
undergraduette
heliosciophyte
non-electrolyte
shelf-catalogue
Rembrandtesque
concavo-concave
convexo-concave
inapprehensive
unapprehensive
disapprobative
simplificative
multiplicative
supererogative
inappreciative
unappreciative
congratulative
recapitulative
transformative
discriminative
predestinative
conglutinative
unremunerative
retro-operative
disintegrative

transmigrative
administrative
interpretative
rehabilitative
representative
circumspective
self-protective
overprotective
non-restrictive
reconstructive
superstructive
radiosensitive
photosensitive
supersensitive
hypersensitive
contrapositive
chemoreceptive
proprioceptive
mackerel-breeze
phosphor-bronze

F

strawberry-leaf
examine-in-chief
colonel-in-chief
levelling-staff
palagonite-tuff
inflation-proof

G

country-dancing
subject-heading
thought-reading
counter-trading
current-bedding
silver-shedding
diamond-wedding
cabinet-pudding
electrogilding
castle-building
empire-building
ribbon-building
thimble-rigging
through-ganging
scandalmonging
fashionmonging
school-teaching
heart-searching
clear-starching
purse-snatching
backscratching
distinguishing
water-breathing
silversmithing
good-for-nothing
strike-breaking
prison-breaking
mischief-making
shrill-shriking
forward-looking
wheeler-dealing
fiddle-faddling
fortune-telling
self-fulfilling
sheep-whistling
tittle-tattling

soul-confirming
blood-consuming
spring-cleaning
counter-opening
foreshortening
plea-bargaining
self-explaining
speech-training
unentertaining
self-sustaining
self-condemning
electrowinning
malfunctioning
blood-poisoning
chain-lightning
sheet-lightning
promise-keeping
counsel-keeping
understrapping
leaden-stepping
asset-stripping
window-shopping
double-stopping
yellow-yoldring
night-wandering
mountaineering
bioengineering
electioneering
pamphleteering
scaremongering
verse-mongering
self-flattering
quicksilvering
night-flowering
spirit-stirring
engagement-ring
strand-scouring
steeplechasing
unsympathising
uncompromising
attitudinising
unenterprising
teleprocessing
window-dressing
unintoxicating
electroplating
discriminating
unilluminating
self-generating
contrarotating
self-neglecting
self-correcting
self-protecting
semiconducting
pillow-fighting
picture-writing
self-tormenting
dazzle-painting
finger-painting
finger-pointing
nature-printing
fingerprinting
cost-accounting
self-supporting

coconut-matting
unintermitting
steel-engraving
photo-engraving
daylight-saving
pleasure-giving
wappenschawing
weapon-schawing
working-drawing
whistle-blowing
pigeon-fancying
self-justifying
self-satisfying
self-destroying
soul-destroying
huckleberrying
bremsstrahlung
Sturmabteilung
Durchmusterung
interior-sprung

H

companion-hatch
stocking-stitch
double-declutch
kneading-trough
watering-trough
radiotelegraph
phototelegraph
autoradiograph
encephalograph
plethysmograph
telephotograph
pyrophotograph
radioautograph
borough-English
quicksilverish
hobbledehoyish
gooseberry-bush
scrubbing-brush
finger's-breadth
starch-hyacinth
swaddling-cloth
gooseberry-moth
star-of-the-earth
farthingsworth
shillingsworth
half-pennyworth

I

Malacopterygii
Crossopterygii
Elasmobranchii

K

devil-on-the-neck
davenport-trick
composing-stick
stumbling-block
percussion-lock
serpentine-rock
swingling-stock
scribbling-book
strawberry-mark
tabernacle-work

L

bibliomaniacal

staphylococcal	extracanonical	semi-centennial	circumlittoral
polysyllabical	stereoscopical	prothonotarial	lamellirostral
amphibological	stethoscopical	prince-imperial	serratirostral
gynaecological	metoposcopical	intercessorial	recurvirostral
myrmecological	misanthropical	compurgatorial	arboricultural
archaeological	alphanumerical	nomenclatorial	antiscriptural
spelaeological	unmetaphorical	conspiratorial	dress-rehearsal
phraseological	isodiametrical	commentatorial	opisthoglossal
laryngological	dissymmetrical	disceptatorial	triconsonantal
ornithological	tacheometrical	subterrestrial	transcendental
aerobiological	stereometrical	intramercurial	suprasegmental
agrobiological	stichometrical	excrementitial	presentimental
cryobiological	psychometrical	consubstantial	subcontinental
soteriological	pluviometrical	circumstantial	sphaerocrystal
volcanological	dynamometrical	reminiscential	unintellectual
vulcanological	thermometrical	intelligential	parliament-heel
campanological	seismometrical	interferential	Catherine-wheel
arachnological	chronometrical	superessential	blistered-steel
carcinological	catadioptrical	quintessential	wearing-apparel
terminological	commonsensical	plenipotential	tumbling-barrel
meteorological	unmetaphysical	supercelestial	ground-squirrel
spectrological	psychophysical	quinquagesimal	rabbit-squirrel
martyrological	unmathematical	poikilothermal	mountain-laurel
eschatological	enthymematical	electrothermal	chamber-counsel
climatological	unsystematical	intra-abdominal	resistance-coil
dermatological	apothegmatical	brachydiagonal	banqueting-hall
Sovietological	paradigmatical	semi-occasional	megasporophyll
herpetological	anagrammatical	tridimensional	trinitrophenol
gerontological	epigrammatical	two-dimensional	gooseberry-fool
Christological	empyreumatical	intercessional	boarding-school
agrostological	aristocratical	unprofessional	trinitrotoluol
reflexological	stereotactical	transmissional	forethoughtful
ichthyological	phyllotactical	perturbational	temperamentful
thaumaturgical	antipathetical	congregational	M
squirearchical	monotheletical	consociational	centimetre-gram
calligraphical	palingenetical	denominational	what-d'you-call-'em
zincographical	phytogenetical	non-operational	hobbledehoydom
lithographical	cosmopolitical	illustrational	consulting-room
orthographical	metropolitical	organisational	bed-sitting-room
hagiographical	oneirocritical	compensational	recitation-room
cosmographical	cheiromantical	dispensational	stalactitiform
stenographical	semi-elliptical	conversational	hypochondriasm
ichnographical	ecclesiastical	presentational	pseudo-archaism
hydrographical	enthusiastical	dissertational	andromonoecism
hierographical	paronomastical	conservational	peripateticism
hygrographical	paraphrastical	interjectional	onirocriticism
chorographical	periphrastical	unidirectional	hypercriticism
petrographical	antiphrastical	resurrectional	encyclopaedism
hyetographical	catachrestical	insurrectional	hypothyroidism
pantographical	monotheistical	intersectional	photoperiodism
photographical	polytheistical	cross-sectional	spread-eagleism
cartographical	misogynistical	jurisdictional	pococuranteism
tachygraphical	hypocoristical	constructional	know-nothingism
bathygraphical	belletristical	disquisitional	pseudomorphism
hypertrophical	pharmaceutical	postpositional	homoeomorphism
hieroglyphical	propaedeutical	unconventional	theriomorphism
contracyclical	hemispheroidal	conscriptional	allelomorphism
hydrodynamical	dysmenorrhoeal	distributional	heteromorphism
psychochemical	extracorporeal	substitutional	evangelicalism
thermochemical	air-vice-marshal	constitutional	oecumenicalism
physiognomical	provost-marshal	archiepiscopal	incorporealism
Deuteronomical	pharmacopoeial	hephthemimeral	matriarchalism
microseismical	extra-parochial	captain-general	patriarchalism
catechumenical	post-millennial	spatiotemporal	multiracialism

neocolonialism	polysynthetism	Supralapsarian	identification
territorialism	piezomagnetism	uniformitarian	prettification
substantialism	Theopaschitism	universitarian	Scottification
existentialism	transvestitism	sacramentarian	beautification
extensionalism	quattrocentism	early-Victorian	sanguification
sensationalism	indifferentism	ichthyosaurian	revivification
traditionalism	anthropophuism	ferromagnesian	detoxification
intuitionalism	constructivism	maintenance-man	quizzification
tripersonalism	hobbledehoyism	newspaper-woman	eutrophication
anti-federalism	sceuophylacium	aircraftswoman	multiplication
centripetalism	megasporangium	coastguardsman	disapplication
fundamentalism	Protevangelium	fellow-townsman	misapplication
sacramentalism	chondrocranium	handicraftsman	centuplication
sentimentalism	spermatogonium	Hierosolymitan	prefabrication
continentalism	organ-harmonium	common-or-garden	authentication
monolingualism	disciplinarium	Jack-in-the-green	sophistication
transsexualism	disequilibrium	turquoise-green	biodegradation
perfectibilism	Baluchitherium	prairie-chicken	retrogradation
heterothallism	clavicytherium	plague-stricken	intergradation
holometabolism	conservatorium	wonder-stricken	recommendation
trituberculism	radio-strontium	terror-stricken	subinfeudation
pentadactylism	crinkum-crankum	horror-stricken	interlineation
Pan-Americanism	trinkum-trankum	planet-stricken	self-abnegation
Nietzscheanism	Castanospermum	half-a-sovereign	vitilitigation
Pythagoreanism	omnium-gatherum	ivory-porcelain	supererogation
servo-mechanism	snip-snap-snorum	oxy-haemoglobin	centrifugation
Elizabethanism	N	phosphoprotein	inappreciation
Rosicrucianism	Middle-American	cyanocobalamin	disassociation
Petrarchianism	circumforanean	thromboplastin	intermediation
Valentinianism	contemporanean	andromedotoxin	reconciliation
Augustinianism	superterranean	cardinal-deacon	disaffiliation
millenarianism	Neopythagorean	potassium-argon	substantiation
centenarianism	Mohorovicician	piano-accordion	disembarkation
necessarianism	Syrophoenician	tatterdemalion	self-revelation
Sabbatarianism	audiometrician	intercommunion	hyperinflation
unsectarianism	econometrician	bladder-campion	interpellation
proletarianism	house-physician	uncircumcision	redistillation
egalitarianism	aeroelastician	self-propulsion	self-immolation
utilitarianism	French-Canadian	inapprehension	disconsolation
Trinitarianism	encyclopaedian	self-expression	mistranslation
libertarianism	monoprionidian	retransmission	somnambulation
antiquarianism	Schwenkfeldian	disapprobation	noctambulation
Zoroastrianism	hypomixolydian	imperturbation	conglobulation
Rabelaisianism	pharmacopoeian	silicification	inarticulation
Albigensianism	brobdingnagian	solidification	miscalculation
Leibnitzianism	sauropterygian	humidification	overpopulation
ultramontanism	sesquipedalian	lapidification	congratulation
anti-Jacobinism	stegocephalian	zinckification	recapitulation
predeterminism	opisthocoelian	simplification	superovulation
progressionism	perfectibilian	resinification	illegitimation
inspirationism	ultra-Neptunian	saponification	overestimation
restorationism	corpuscularian	eburnification	disaffirmation
interactionism	miscellanarian	etherification	pre-Reformation
prohibitionism	quadragenarian	esterification	disinformation
dissolutionism	septuagenarian	calorification	misinformation
restitutionism	premillenarian	gentrification	transformation
heterochronism	valetudinarian	emulsification	plant-formation
psilanthropism	solitudinarian	classification	imposthumation
apheliotropism	latitudinarian	Prussification	predesignation
penny-a-linerism	altitudinarian	stratification	foreordination
probabiliorism	attitudinarian	sanctification	incoordination
synaposematism	disciplinarian	fructification	disinclination
lipogrammatism	predestinarian	stultification	discrimination
monochromatism	infralapsarian	quantification	indoctrination

predestination	greisenisation	circumspection	postmastership
conglutination	trichinisation	stage-direction	ambassadorship
subalternation	bituminisation	overcorrection	chancellorship
concelebration	gelatinisation	microdetection	counsellorship
deconsecration	keratinisation	self-conviction	supervisorship
reconsecration	antagonisation	superinduction	legislatorship
conglomeration	cinchonisation	overproduction	procuratorship
contemperation	decolonisation	mass-production	proprietorship
non-cooperation	recolonisation	reintroduction	progenitorship
contesseration	enthronisation	misinstruction	prolocutorship
redintegration	fraternisation	reconstruction	serpent-worship
disintegration	westernisation	superstruction	sempstress-ship
intermigration	depolarisation	cabinet-edition	commandantship
transmigration	tabularisation	retrocognition	lieutenantship
self-admiration	secularisation	contraposition	accountantship
reinvigoration	regularisation	circumposition	good-fellowship
recalcitration	popularisation	presupposition	commissaryship
defenestration	militarisation	subterposition	skeleton-shrimp
administration	grangerisation	predisposition	cardinal-bishop
exclaustration	bowdlerisation	chemoreception	peppermint-drop
desulphuration	polymerisation	superscription	foundation-stop
discolouration	allegorisation	rumblegumption	R
commensuration	devalorisation	rummlegumption	preaching-friar
circumgyration	revalorisation	rummelgumption	palato-alveolar
politicisation	decolorisation	self-assumption	intramolecular
Finlandisation	symmetrisation	self-absorption	intermolecular
bastardisation	pasteurisation	self-suggestion	slantendicular
radicalisation	schematisation	auto-suggestion	slantindicular
scandalisation	stigmatisation	redistribution	extravehicular
specialisation	remonetisation	circumlocution	cardiovascular
patrialisation	sericitisation	pseudosolution	nebuchadnezzar
trivialisation	graphitisation	rubber-solution	council-chamber
decimalisation	dolomitisation	circumvolution	sheriff-officer
optimalisation	mylonitisation	reconstitution	warrant-officer
liberalisation	chloritisation	interconnexion	squadron-leader
federalisation	recondensation	alexipharmakon	follow-my-leader
generalisation	tergiversation	rhinencephalon	scorpion-spider
mineralisation	self-accusation	prosencephalon	transport-rider
demoralisation	vasodilatation	paraleipomenon	parlour-boarder
centralisation	castrametation	barrage-balloon	mourning-border
neutralisation	superfoetation	sausage-bassoon	flight-recorder
naturalisation	interpretation	trisoctahedron	receiving-order
capitalisation	incapacitation	stretching-iron	reception-order
devitalisation	rehabilitation	self-comparison	Rochelle-powder
chaptalisation	disorientation	person-to-person	black-marketeer
sensualisation	implementation	tetragrammaton	Kupferschiefer
evangelisation	representation	quilting-cotton	traffic-manager
caramelisation	vibroflotation	lavender-cotton	station-manager
demobilisation	dextrorotation	homoeoteleuton	cloak-and-dagger
immobilisation	misacceptation	alder-buckthorn	Johannisberger
strobilisation	transportation	O	glove-stretcher
solubilisation	disinfestation	cock-a-doodle-doo	Charley-pitcher
lyophilisation	uterogestation	pronunciamento	cathodographer
volatilisation	weather-station	vicesimo-quarto	autobiographer
alcoholisation	circumnutation	vigesimo-quarto	heresiographer
vitriolisation	miscomputation	P	metallographer
macadamisation	undervaluation	apprenticeship	steganographer
Africanisation	transvaluation	under-clerkship	rhyparographer
reorganisation	subinsinuation	vice-consulship	French-polisher
inorganisation	superannuation	catechumenship	ostrich-feather
Italianisation	mispunctuation	supercargoship	stirrup-leather
Russianisation	superelevation	controllership	horse-godmother
indigenisation	unsatisfaction	multi-ownership	fairy-godmother
homogenisation	cross-infection	tide-waitership	shilly-shallier

luggage-carrier	mustard-plaster	north-westwards	psychoanalysis
promise-breaker	blister-plaster	south-westwards	psephoanalysis
Sabbath-breaker	question-master	futtock-shrouds	leucocytolysis
circuit-breaker	property-master	sansculottides	diverticulitis
night-fossicker	clitter-clatter	riding-breeches	pyelonephritis
pleasure-seeker	bread-and-butter	Archaeornithes	osteo-arthritis
marriage-broker	heather-blutter	Trochelminthes	conjunctivitis
discount-broker	mountain-beaver	indescribables	hypercatalexis
billiard-marker	demi-semiquaver	unmentionables	traffic-signals
munition-worker	sea-gilliflower	inexpressibles	two-for-his-heels
tallow-chandler	cardinal-flower	snow-spectacles	petticoat-tails
swindge-buckler	moccasin-flower	Mephistopheles	sergeant-at-arms
screw-propeller	sea-gillyflower	mesdemoiselles	serjeant-at-arms
space-traveller	sword-swallower	conversaziones	hen-and-chickens
stocking-filler	orange-squeezer	semicarbazones	prostaglandins
food-controller	heavier-than-air	conquistadores	cornet-à-pistons
turbine-steamer	lighter-than-air	metempsychoses	traffic-returns
knapping-hammer	unaccounted-for	hippopotamuses	alloiostrophos
tariff-reformer	mushroom-anchor	pleurapophyses	Arctostaphylos
market-gardener	knight-bachelor	Basidiomycetes	weeding-forceps
kindergartener	vice-chancellor	Gasteromycetes	Crutched-friars
money-scrivener	town-councillor	handkerchieves	Crouched-friars
painter-stainer	thrashing-floor	rice-polishings	pyjama-trousers
blockade-runner	threshing-floor	three-farthings	porcupine-grass
fellow-commoner	withering-floor	leading-strings	dog's-tooth-grass
cartridge-paper	rear-view-mirror	kissing-strings	thought-process
saltpetre-paper	microprocessor	Camelopardalis	serpent-goddess
cigarette-paper	denitrificator	xiphihumeralis	experienceless
chimney-sweeper	prognosticator	Mephistophilis	successionless
whippersnapper	differentiator	onchocerciasis	expressionless
snipper-snapper	broncho-dilator	cholelithiasis	reflectionless
tree-worshipper	decontaminator	trichomoniasis	inflectionless
fire-worshipper	procrastinator	telangiectasis	proportionless
counter-skipper	turbo-generator	bronchiectasis	complexionless
hunt-the-slipper	transliterator	antiperistasis	shamefaceness
tobacco-stopper	hydroextractor	bacteriostasis	long-headedness
daguerreotyper	stamp-collector	antimetathesis	bull-headedness
standard-bearer	chest-protector	narcosynthesis	high-handedness
gyrostabiliser	boa-constrictor	chemosynthesis	open-handedness
self-advertiser	superconductor	photosynthesis	left-handedness
heather-bleater	circumferentor	erythropoiesis	unfriendedness
radiotelemeter	milking-parlour	onomatopoiesis	high-mindedness
absorptiometer	grace-and-favour	carcinogenesis	weak-mindedness
scintillometer	marriage-favour	chondrogenesis	book-mindedness
ophthalmometer	rhombenporphyr	electrogenesis	open-mindedness
geothermometer	S	haematogenesis	long-windedness
strabismometer	patresfamilias	plasmapheresis	ungroundedness
water-barometer	psychodynamics	enterocentesis	disengagedness
interferometer	thermodynamics	thyrotoxicosis	newfangledness
diffractometer	pneumodynamics	mucoviscidosis	accustomedness
misinterpreter	macroeconomics	metempsychosis	undesignedness
foster-daughter	microeconomics	paedomorphosis	restrainedness
manifold-writer	hydromechanics	pneumoconiosis	unpreparedness
teletypewriter	biomathematics	pneumokoniosis	ill-naturedness
heather-bluiter	biosystematics	diverticulosis	displeasedness
ship's-carpenter	psychosomatics	hydronephrosis	misadvisedness
over-the-counter	electrostatics	osteoarthrosis	indisposedness
bargain-counter	hydromagnetics	psychoneurosis	contractedness
bill-discounter	prosthodontics	trophoneurosis	abstractedness
troubleshooter	phelloplastics	carcinomatosis	distractedness
prick-the-garter	shifting-boards	spirochaetosis	unaffectedness
grammaticaster	sandwich-boards	trichophytosis	unexpectedness
philosophaster	north-eastwards	narcocatharsis	dispiritedness
verticillaster	south-eastwards	pleurapophysis	disjointedness

sure-footedness	deceivableness	meditativeness	despoticalness
flat-footedness	receivableness	attractiveness	majesticalness
interestedness	improvableness	subjectiveness	beneficialness
unresolvedness	observableness	reflectiveness	artificialness
undeservedness	unknowableness	protectiveness	connaturalness
unreservedness	invincibleness	vindictiveness	incidentalness
loving-kindness	incredibleness	productiveness	ungracefulness
night-blindness	intangibleness	inhabitiveness	revengefulness
implacableness	defeasibleness	definitiveness	purposefulness
despicableness	insensibleness	transitiveness	remorsefulness
unreadableness	impassibleness	repetitiveness	ungratefulness
formidableness	compatibleness	alimentiveness	despitefulness
rewardableness	inflexibleness	presentiveness	stomachfulness
manageableness	dissolubleness	preventiveness	unwatchfulness
changeableness	love-in-idleness	perceptiveness	unfaithfulness
chargeableness	frolicsomeness	absorptiveness	untruthfulness
untameableness	unhandsomeness	suggestiveness	unmercifulness
perishableness	blithesomeness	diminutiveness	unthankfulness
unsociableness	meddlesomeness	forbiddingness	disdainfulness
unreliableness	mettlesomeness	unyieldingness	worshipfulness
undeniableness	lumbersomeness	beseechingness	uncheerfulness
inexpiableness	humoursomeness	unthinkingness	successfulness
invariableness	threadbareness	unbecomingness	neglectfulness
insatiableness	immaculateness	unassumingness	respectfulness
remarkableness	articulateness	unaspiringness	delightfulness
inviolableness	legitimateness	surprisingness	unrightfulness
unblamableness	inordinateness	surpassingness	sprightfulness
attainableness	coordinateness	disgustingness	thoughtfulness
imaginableness	co-ordinateness	outlandishness	unfruitfulness
inclinableness	effeminateness	heathenishness	disgustfulness
abominableness	passionateness	all-overishness	free-spokenness
terminableness	deliberateness	amateurishness	particularness
pardonableness	immoderateness	coquettishness	friendlessness
reasonableness	degenerateness	namby-pambiness	groundlessness
seasonableness	inveterateness	road-worthiness	regardlessness
personableness	illiterateness	noteworthiness	motivelessness
unbearableness	inadequateness	newsworthiness	speechlessness
comparableness	incompleteness	unfriendliness	breathlessness
sufferableness	indiscreteness	untowardliness	healthlessness
vulnerableness	indefiniteness	slatternliness	remedilessness
inoperableness	inappositeness	disorderliness	fatherlessness
deplorableness	hyperacuteness	unmannerliness	prayerlessness
restorableness	irresoluteness	daughterliness	thriftlessness
inexorableness	statuesqueness	unsisterliness	weightlessness
penetrableness	persuasiveness	unknightliness	spiritlessness
honourableness	indecisiveness	sanguinariness	resultlessness
favourableness	convulsiveness	stationariness	relentlessness
measurableness	responsiveness	hereditariness	resistlessness
censurableness	discursiveness	insanitariness	tremendousness
impassableness	successiveness	obligatoriness	stupendousness
unpassableness	regressiveness	derogatoriness	rampageousness
delectableness	aggressiveness	refractoriness	umbrageousness
marketableness	impressiveness	transitoriness	outrageousness
creditableness	oppressiveness	peremptoriness	courageousness
profitableness	expressiveness	pernicketiness	extraneousness
inimitableness	possessiveness	heart-heaviness	ultroneousness
hospitableness	submissiveness	topsyturviness	nectareousness
charitableness	permissiveness	sleepy-sickness	dispiteousness
unsuitableness	conclusiveness	methodicalness	predaciousness
inevitableness	protrusiveness	symbolicalness	fallaciousness
acceptableness	irrelativeness	tyrannicalness	pugnaciousness
detestableness	decorativeness	theatricalness	ungraciousness
disputableness	figurativeness	emphaticalness	sequaciousness
fatiguableness	vegetativeness	unpoeticalness	loquaciousness

perniciousness
auspiciousness
suspiciousness
avariciousness
capriciousness
precociousness
perfidiousness
fastidiousness
commodiousness
contagiousness
prodigiousness
rebelliousness
abstemiousness
harmoniousness
precariousness
gregariousness
uproariousness
salubriousness
mysteriousness
ingloriousness
censoriousness
victoriousness
infectiousness
flagitiousness
propitiousness
nutritiousness
factitiousness
licentiousness
robustiousness
incautiousness
obsequiousness
lasciviousness
imperviousness
scandalousness
scurrilousness
marvellousness
miraculousness
ridiculousness
meticulousness
scrupulousness
synonymousness
diaphanousness
libidinousness
oleaginousness
voluminousness
monotonousness
viviparousness
slanderousness
vociferousness
prosperousness
boisterousness
cadaverousness
chivalrousness
indecorousness
malodorousness
facinorousness
traitorousness
stertorousness
solicitousness
calamitousness
circuitousness
iniquitousness
fortuitousness
portentousness

contiguousness
continuousness
spirituousness
tumultuousness
voluptuousness
incestuousness
indistinctness
indiscreetness
forthrightness
watertightness
unpleasantness
roundaboutness
princesse-dress
philosopheress
immunosuppress
disenchantress
schoolmistress
ballet-mistress
spring-mattress
interlocutress
preaching-cross
longs-and-shorts
swathing-clouts
circumbendibus
Staphylococcus
Ecclesiasticus
scaphocephalus
Mephostophilus
actinobacillus
proventriculus
periophthalmus
malacostracous
entomostracous
lecythidaceous
capparidaceous
berberidaceous
thymelaeaceous
dioscoreaceous
saxifragaceous
orobanchaceous
cyclanthaceous
amaranthaceous
euphorbiaceous
anacardiaceous
aquifoliaceous
polemoniaceous
fringillaceous
ranunculaceous
campanulaceous
pennatulaceous
melastomaceous
valerianaceous
nyctaginaceous
papilionaceous
zingiberaceous
zinziberaceous
cucurbitaceous
schizophyceous
extraforaneous
extemporaneous
consanguineous
myrmecophagous
ichthyophagous
pseudomorphous

homoeomorphous
theriomorphous
heteromorphous
plectognathous
schizognathous
androdioecious
gynomonoecious
hyperconscious
class-conscious
quinquefarious
unostentatious
contradictious
supposititious
non-contentious
stegocephalous
macrocephalous
microcephalous
androcephalous
hydrocephalous
platycephalous
opisthocoelous
myrmecophilous
ornithophilous
sclerophyllous
heterophyllous
tintinnabulous
overscrupulous
tetradactylous
pentadactylous
macrodactylous
anisodactylous
leptodactylous
enantiostylous
heterochromous
tetrachotomous
homoeothermous
homoiothermous
xanthomelanous
spermatogenous
quadrigeminous
dicotyledonous
haplostemonous
diplostemonous
geosynchronous
heterochronous
campylotropous
dipterocarpous
diamondiferous
flagelliferous
glanduliferous
foraminiferous
sacchariferous
stigmatiferous
diamantiferous
strepsipterous
thysanopterous
mastigophorous
rhynchophorous
galactophorous
corolliflorous
sanguinivorous
ichthyolatrous
hyposulphurous
disadventurous

misadventurous
heterosomatous
angiostomatous
pachydermatous
parenchymatous
aerenchymatous
pyrenomycetous
schizomycetous
subtersensuous
unpresumptuous
Palaeanthropus
                T
prothonotariat
claw-hammer-coat
shawl-waistcoat
counter-subject
finger-alphabet
gentleman-cadet
zebra-parrakeet
weather-prophet
dressing-jacket
shooting-jacket
transfer-ticket
luncheon-basket
dogtooth-violet
pressure-helmet
knight-banneret
running-banquet
Burschenschaft
propeller-shaft
shoulder-height
mosquito-weight
star-of-the-night
trencher-knight
counter-wrought
what-d'you-call-it
contraindicant
non-communicant
auto-intoxicant
colour-sergeant
gutter-merchant
telegraph-plant
artillery-plant
tintinnabulant
flag-lieutenant
antiperspirant
interpenetrant
anticonvulsant
counter-passant
antidepressant
turf-accountant
cost-accountant
child-resistant
water-resistant
marble-constant
superincumbent
self-complacent
hundred-per-cent
subarborescent
phosphorescent
interdependent
superintendent
absorbefacient
self-sufficient

counter-salient
inquisiturient
gram-equivalent
superexcellent
water-repellent
omnibenevolent
spring-ligament
wreath-filament
self-effacement
apprenticement
recommencement
self-management
discouragement
prearrangement
disarrangement
misarrangement
over-refinement
intertwinement
mismeasurement
reappraisement
aggrandisement
bouleversement
arrondissement
divertissement
understatement
disemboguement
non-involvement
pincer-movement
misimprovement
acknowledgment
self-enrichment
accomplishment
displenishment
disfurnishment
self-punishment
impoverishment
extinguishment
relinquishment
disenthralment
disembowelment
self-fulfilment
disentrainment
proportionment
self-government
predevelopment
wedding-garment
self-commitment
disenchantment
discontentment
miscontentment
disappointment
disconcertment
reed-instrument
wind-instrument
self-employment
supercontinent
microcomponent
counter-current
self-consistent
self-consequent
labyrinthodont
stoope-gallaunt
penny-in-the-slot
true-lover's-knot

deposit-receipt
smoking-concert
princesse-skirt
durchkomponirt
pennystone-cast
north-north-east
south-south-east
hypochondriast
cardinal-priest
riding-interest
north-north-west
south-south-west
aerodynamicist
astrophysicist
encyclopaedist
ichthyophagist
pharmacologist
hepaticologist
hydrogeologist
astrogeologist
dysteleologist
sociobiologist
microbiologist
hydrobiologist
photobiologist
liturgiologist
epidemiologist
bacteriologist
ecclesiologist
epistemologist
Kremlinologist
protozoologist
anthropologist
rheumatologist
pneumatologist
dialectologist
parasitologist
protistologist
zoophytologist
antimonarchist
chlorite-schist
stratigraphist
lexicographist
chalcographist
palaeographist
cheirographist
cryptographist
ministerialist
territorialist
substantialist
existentialist
educationalist
sensationalist
traditionalist
intuitionalist
tripersonalist
anti-federalist
fundamentalist
sacramentalist
sentimentalist
continentalist
Pentecostalist
perfectibilist
pteridophilist

pharmacopolist
electrochemist
neuroanatomist
Petrarchianist
ultramontanist
palaeobotanist
progressionist
transfusionist
convocationist
segregationist
repudiationist
retaliationist
reformationist
integrationist
inspirationist
restorationist
interactionist
abstractionist
vivisectionist
restrictionist
obstructionist
destructionist
prohibitionist
requisitionist
dissolutionist
restitutionist
laryngoscopist
spectroscopist
philanthropist
psilanthropist
probabiliorist
water-colourist
pisciculturist
floriculturist
horticulturist
paragrammatist
lipogrammatist
quattrocentist
indifferentist
prosthodontist
lithontriptist
psycholinguist
well-thought-out

U
holier-than-thou

W
daughters-in-law
butterfly-screw
casement-window
mountain-tallow
chimney-swallow
mountain-marrow
savanna-sparrow
Christ-cross-row

X
administratrix

Y
plutodemocracy
major-generalcy
insignificancy
crystallomancy
vice-presidency
correspondency
circumambiency

electrovalency
eigen-frequency
audio-frequency
squirrel-monkey
palaeopedology
otolaryngology
parapsychology
metapsychology
neuropathology
histopathology
phytopathology
electrobiology
neuroradiology
terotechnology
palaeethnology
neurohypnology
orthopterology
symptomatology
periodontology
pseudepigraphy
palaegeography
phytogeography
dactyliography
paroemiography
historiography
epistolography
röntgenography
anthropography
xylotypography
autotypography
xylopyrography
thalassography
cinematography
enigmatography
chromatography
thaumatography
gynandromorphy
myocardiopathy
cardiomyopathy
unpraiseworthy
dolichocephaly
incommunicably
irreproachably
inapproachably
unapproachably
unreconcilably
irreconcilably
incontrollably
uncontrollably
indeterminably
unconscionably
proportionably
unquestionably
inconsiderably
undiscoverably
unrecognisably
untranslatably
irresuscitably
insurmountably
unintelligibly
comprehensibly
insuppressibly
indestructibly
controvertibly

muddleheadedly
feeble-mindedly
absent-mindedly
uncontrolledly
unrestrainedly
good-humouredly
premeditatedly
undistractedly
disconnectedly
unrestrictedly
short-sightedly
malcontentedly
discontentedly
whole-heartedly
light-heartedly
faint-heartedly
stout-heartedly
preconcertedly
roundaboutedly
intermediately
disconsolately
inarticulately
illegitimately
discriminately
affectionately
extortionately
commensurately
reprehensively
apprehensively
unresponsively
irresponsively
inconclusively
appreciatively
denominatively
opinionatively
anticipatively
deliberatively
regeneratively
vituperatively
illustratively
dispensatively
quantitatively
unattractively
imperfectively
irrespectively
reproductively
unproductively
constructively
intransitively
postpositively
insusceptively
prescriptively
proscriptively
interruptively
distributively
substitutively
effervescingly
unpretendingly
discouragingly
embellishingly
overwhelmingly
entertainingly
serpentiningly
intertwiningly

unflatteringly
overpoweringly
undespairingly
scrutinisingly
enterprisingly
supplicatingly
excruciatingly
exhilaratingly
asseveratingly
unhesitatingly
unreflectingly
unsuspectingly
transportingly
intermittingly
disapprovingly
sycophantishly
praiseworthily
traditionarily
testamentarily
propitiatorily
anticipatorily
dispensatorily
satisfactorily
introductorily
genethliacally
immethodically
scientifically
genealogically
teleologically
pathologically
mythologically
philologically
etymologically
ethnologically
tropologically
micrologically
petrologically
astrologically
tautologically
hierarchically
geographically
biographically
theosophically
telepathically
idiopathically
hyperbolically
unrhythmically
pantomimically
tragi-comically
astronomically
hypodermically
histogenically
telephonically
antiphonically
histrionically
enharmonically
diachronically
anachronically
synchronically
electronically
mock-heroically
telescopically
alphamerically
subgenerically

semaphorically
metaphorically
asymmetrically
barometrically
volumetrically
concentrically
geocentrically
metaphysically
hyperbatically
mathematically
emblematically
phonematically
systematically
phlegmatically
astigmatically
diplomatically
achromatically
telesmatically
schismatically
morganatically
theocratically
democratically
autocratically
hypostatically
paratactically
apoplectically
apodeictically
alphabetically
epexegetically
apologetically
catechetically
antithetically
hypothetically
arithmetically
hypocritically
unromantically
aerobiotically
endosmotically
asymptotically
antiseptically
procryptically
pleonastically
anamnestically
hebraistically
solecistically
eulogistically
idealistically
legalistically
vitalistically
pugilistically
simplistically
optimistically
jingoistically
aphoristically
inartistically
linguistically
euphuistically
altruistically
geognostically
semi-officially
inartificially
unartificially
quadriennially
quinquennially

presbyterially
professorially
interspatially
confidentially
providentially
pestilentially
preferentially
differentially
antediluvially
longitudinally
successionally
professionally
discretionally
transitionally
conventionally
proportionally
supernaturally
unscripturally
quaquaversally
sinistrorsally
coincidentally
medicamentally
supplementally
experimentally
departmentally
instrumentally
interlingually
intellectually
substantivally
daffadowndilly
disregardfully
unremorsefully
unsuccessfully
unthoughtfully
old-gentlemanly
semicircularly
quadrangularly
schoolmasterly
advantageously
simultaneously
subcutaneously
percutaneously
discourteously
contumaciously
pertinaciously
inauspiciously
unsuspiciously
meretriciously
subconsciously
incommodiously
sacrilegiously
contumeliously
superciliously
querimoniously
parsimoniously
inharmoniously
multifariously
insalubriously
vaingloriously
ostentatiously
disputatiously
rambunctiously
compunctiously
unpropitiously

adventitiously
unscrupulously
trichotomously
pseudonymously
soporiferously
cantankerously
obstreperously
unprosperously
slaughterously
preposterously
incontiguously
disingenuously
contemptuously
presumptuously
preponderantly
transcendently
insufficiently
inconveniently
supereminently
inconsistently
intermittently
inconsequently
magniloquently
odd-come-shortly
radioastronomy
appendicectomy
ultramicrotomy
cholecystotomy
three-halfpenny
shove-halfpenny
radiotelephony
electrotherapy
ophthalmoscopy
monocarpellary
inframaxillary
intermaxillary
tintinnabulary
octingentenary
consuetudinary
progressionary
disillusionary
contractionary
prohibitionary
requisitionary
suppositionary
perlocutionary
institutionary
interplanetary
under-secretary
spade-husbandry
drill-husbandry
herring-fishery
hickery-pickery
bashi-bazoukery
joukery-pawkery
picture-gallery

singing-gallery
quarter-gallery
siege-artillery
woollen-drapery
counter-battery
disapprobatory
classificatory
recommendatory
subinfeudatory
supererogatory
intermediatory
reconciliatory
unconciliatory
congratulatory
recapitulatory
predesignatory
discriminatory
transmigratory
circumgyratory
self-accusatory
vasodilatatory
dextrorotatory
circumnutatory
unsatisfactory
circumlocutory
partridge-berry
worcesterberry
photogrammetry
pseudosymmetry
stoicheiometry
ophthalmometry
interferometry
knight-errantry
radiochemistry
microchemistry
iatrochemistry
photochemistry
histochemistry
piezochemistry
yellow-centaury
quartz-porphyry
subcontrariety
hippety-hoppety
tumorigenicity
hygroscopicity
bioelectricity
unauthenticity
muzzle-velocity
diathermaneity
extemporaneity
coxcombicality
nonsensicality
intrinsicality
extrinsicality
pragmaticality
impracticality

unpracticality
fantasticality
sesquipedality
incorporeality
superficiality
uncongeniality
territoriality
substantiality
co-essentiality
extensionality
traditionality
conditionality
intentionality
tripersonality
transversality
fundamentality
sentimentality
ineffectuality
intersexuality
practicability
irrevocability
unavoidability
serviceability
unmalleability
impermeability
dissociability
falsifiability
imperviability
unthinkability
inflammability
conformability
inalienability
impregnability
unflappability
irreparability
inseparability
intolerability
innumerability
insuperability
inalterability
deliverability
recoverability
deflagrability
undesirability
organisability
inadvisability
condensability
dispensability
collapsability
inexcusability
intractability
extractability
respectability
predictability
indubitability
hereditability

incogitability
fermentability
presentability
preventability
accountability
attemptability
irrefutability
inscrutability
construability
conceivability
dissolvability
irremovability
preservability
vitrescibility
irreducibility
refrangibility
infrangibility
submergibility
discerpibility
persuasibility
indivisibility
suspensibility
distensibility
responsibility
collapsibility
submersibility
impressibility
permissibility
compossibility
implausibility
perfectibility
conductibility
productibility
perceptibility
susceptibility
corruptibility
convertibility
suggestibility
combustibility
irresolubility
school-divinity
intercommunity
rectilinearity
curvilinearity
spectacularity
equiangularity
rectangularity
hebetudinosity
transmissivity
reproductivity
unproductivity
intempestivity
sweet-and-twenty

Z

sapphire-quartz

A
Rhynchobdellida
Tetractinellida
ophthalmoplegia
Ichthyopterygia
Opisthobranchia
Rhynchocephalia
pleuro-pneumonia
sulphur-bacteria
phenylketonuria
Polyprotodontia
icositetrahedra
Megacheiroptera
Microchiroptera
Tetrabranchiata
Tectibranchiata

B
strawberry-shrub

C
hendecasyllabic
perissosyllabic
anticholinergic
anthropopsychic
pseudepigraphic
phytogeographic
historiographic
xylotypographic
thalassographic
cinematographic
chromatographic
phonautographic
allotriomorphic
anthropomorphic
gynandromorphic
nemathelminthic
dysmenorrhealic
dolichocephalic
dieselhydraulic
perissodactylic
thanatognomonic
microelectronic
ophthalmoscopic
paraheliotropic
orthophosphoric
psychogeriatric
magneto-electric
photogrammetric
stoicheiometric
interferometric
anthropocentric
phenylketonuric
hypercatalectic
parasympathetic
sympathomimetic
psychosomimetic
psychotomimetic
parthenogenetic
spermatogenetic
schizophrenetic
electromagnetic
electrophoretic
micropegmatitic
antiperistaltic
autoschediastic

spermatoblastic
interscholastic
achondroplastic
sado-masochistic
phenomenalistic
irrationalistic
individualistic
conceptualistic
Pre-Raphaelistic
monarchianistic
impressionistic
expressionistic
exhibitionistic
particularistic
sociolinguistic
ventriloquistic
pharmacognostic

D
middle-of-the-road
micromicrofarad
uncircumscribed
dyer's-yellowweed
under-privileged
undistinguished
interstratified
peasecod-bellied
double-barrelled
non-commissioned
good-conditioned
well-conditioned
before-mentioned
well-intentioned
misproportioned
shoulder-slipped
round-shouldered
crook-shouldered
supercalendered
self-slaughtered
well-upholstered
counter-flowered
rainbow-coloured
unauthenticated
unsophisticated
unsubstantiated
self-opinionated
untransmigrated
polyunsaturated
vehicle-actuated
unreconstructed
softly-sprighted
self-constituted
great-grandchild
cloud-cuckoo-land
second-in-command
world-without-end
high-gravel-blind
gathering-ground
hobbledehoyhood
carriage-forward
straightforward
victualling-yard
all-changing-word
portmanteau-word

E
Callitrichaceae
Caesalpiniaceae
Selaginellaceae
Caryophyllaceae
Eriocaulonaceae
Ophioglossaceae
Archichlamydeae
Hydrocorallinae
smelting-furnace
consolation-race
receiving-office
Cinderella-dance
counterfeisance
self-capacitance
preacquaintance
superincumbence
self-complacence
marriage-licence
reconvalescence
bioluminescence
phosphorescence
counter-evidence
interdependence
superintendence
subintelligence
misintelligence
superexcellence
omnibenevolence
phase-difference
self-consequence
woody-nightshade
Bartholomew-tide
flamboyante-tree
riding-committee
landing-carriage
railway-carriage
hackney-carriage
meadow-saxifrage
nature-knowledge
training-college
parliament-hinge
ultracentrifuge
resurrection-pie
kilogram-calorie
micromicrocurie
unchristianlike
ungentlemanlike
unstatesmanlike
unsportsmanlike
circumscribable
machine-readable
countermandable
unrecommendable
unpronounceable
acknowledgeable
interchangeable
unchallengeable
circumnavigable
distinguishable
democratifiable
unreconciliable
countervailable
hendecasyllable

unconstrainable
unascertainable
indisciplinable
undisciplinable
predeterminable
uncompanionable
unobjectionable
unexceptionable
interpenetrable
incommensurable
uninterpretable
police-constable
indistributable
irreprehensible
inapprehensible
unapprehensible
intransmissible
untransmissible
biodestructible
imprescriptible
mountain-bramble
jerry-come-tumble
landscape-marble
wheel-animalcule
stretching-frame
shadow-pantomime
hexachlorophane
hexachlorophene
polychloroprene
trinitrotoluene
trinitrobenzene
sulphaguanidine
wringing-machine
weighing-machine
franking-machine
drilling-machine
stapling-machine
whirling-machine
stamping-machine
crimping-machine
printing-machine
knitting-machine
slotting-machine
dimethylaniline
hemicrystalline
holocrystalline
monocrystalline
polycrystalline
radiogramophone
brachistochrone
foundation-stone
gooseberry-stone
superheterodyne
boning-telescope
ultramicroscope
phenakistoscope
substratosphere
lob-lie-by-the-fire
micromillimetre
counter-pressure
semimanufacture
pillow-structure
self-portraiture
secundogeniture

paulo-post-future
freezing-mixture
deindustrialise
professionalise
conventionalise
supernaturalise
experimentalise
departmentalise
intellectualise
Presbyterianise
resurrectionise
apophthegmatise
unprotestantise
comprehensivise
spread-eaglewise
evening-primrose
banqueting-house
parliament-house
dephlogisticate
intercollegiate
tetrabranchiate
dorsibranchiate
tectibranchiate
lophobranchiate
pulmobranchiate
consubstantiate
circumstantiate
multinucleolate
multiarticulate
antepenultimate
metropolitanate
transilluminate
uncompassionate
disaffectionate
unproportionate
archiepiscopate
angustirostrate
extra-illustrate
anthropophagite
ichthyodorulite
ichthyodorylite
montmorillonite
stilpnosiderite
sphaerosiderite
incomprehensive
uncomprehensive
misapprehensive
manic-depressive
insignificative
co-significative
incommunicative
uncommunicative
prognosticative
testament-dative
electronegative
misappreciative
disassimilative
decontaminative
procrastinative
undemonstrative
unauthoritative
experimentative
nitro-derivative
intersubjective

photoconductive
superconductive
self-destructive
electropositive
intussusceptive
circumscriptive
heir-presumptive
F
conscience-proof
G
picture-moulding
notwithstanding
uncomprehending
feather-boarding
weather-boarding
question-begging
standing-rigging
middle-stitching
packet-switching
French-polishing
Sabbath-breaking
non-profit-making
pleasure-seeking
cloud-compelling
space-travelling
market-gardening
window-gardening
self-determining
air-conditioning
self-considering
wonder-mongering
schoolmastering
unprepossessing
railway-crossing
self-liquidating
unaccommodating
procrastinating
proof-correcting
photoconducting
superconducting
troubleshooting
crease-resisting
flutter-tonguing
quick-conceiving
transmogrifying
Götterdämmerung
Gleichschaltung
H
counter-approach
photozincograph
photolithograph
chromoxylograph
photomicrograph
hyetometrograph
microphotograph
electromyograph
ergatandromorph
schoolmasterish
Pre-Raphaelitish
whirling-dervish
new-Commonwealth
threepenceworth
threepennyworth

I
chondropterygii
Marsipobranchii

K
bubble-and-squeak
drawn-threadwork

L
hypochondriacal
tetrasyllabical
encyclopaedical
hepaticological
dysteleological
sociobiological
hydrobiological
gnotobiological
stoechiological
stoichiological
epidemiological
bacteriological
ecclesiological
epistemological
protozoological
anthropological
traumatological
rheumatological
pneumatological
zoophytological
antimonarchical
stratigraphical
lexicographical
palaeographical
biogeographical
zoogeographical
stereographical
psychographical
bibliographical
physiographical
seismographical
oceanographical
selenographical
glossographical
unphilosophical
chrestomathical
physicochemical
electrochemical
photomechanical
palaeobotanical
architectonical
bronchoscopical
ebullioscopical
spectroscopical
philanthropical
quasihistorical
amphitheatrical
isoperimetrical
viscosimetrical
monosymmetrical
trigonometrical
psychrometrical
electrometrical
idiosyncratical
polysynthetical
psychogenetical
theosophistical

materialistical
synchronistical
microanalytical
air-chief-marshal
extra-provincial
interprovincial
phantasmagorial
improvisatorial
entrepreneurial
uncontroversial
self-substantial
jurisprudential
circumferential
field-sequential
inconsequential
pseudohexagonal
non-professional
retrogressional
transgressional
configurational
confrontational
omnidirectional
juxtapositional
transpositional
transcriptional
disproportional
interambulacral
receiver-general
governor-general
director-general
adjutant-general
attorney-general
saddler-corporal
superstructural
counter-proposal
tarsometatarsal
harvest-festival
Christy-minstrel
marsh-cinquefoil
victualling-bill
microsporophyll
chloramphenicol
dessertspoonful
eleutherodactyl

M
star-of-Bethlehem
withdrawing-room
refreshment-room
infundibuliform
scolopendriform
polysyllabicism
oneirocriticism
hyperthyroidism
fifth-monarchism
enantiomorphism
anthropopathism
anticlericalism
experientialism
preferentialism
hyperadrenalism
confessionalism
professionalism
conventionalism
supernaturalism

experimentalism
departmentalism
instrumentalism
intellectualism
thrombo-embolism
anti-Gallicanism
Semi-Pelagianism
bacchanalianism
episcopalianism
Aristotelianism
nothingarianism
Apollinarianism
doctrinarianism
sublapsarianism
totalitarianism
equalitarianism
humanitarianism
Presbyterianism
Patripassianism
cosmopolitanism
annihilationism
preformationism
conversationism
presentationism
resurrectionism
insurrectionism
constructionism
interventionism
therianthropism
diaheliotropism
diaphototropism
parliamentarism
stereoisomerism
palaeomagnetism
hermaphroditism
Pre-Raphaelitism
intransigentism
tetrasporangium
macrosporangium
microsporangium
seconds-pendulum
ferro-molybdenum
interambulacrum

N
catch-as-catch-can
Mephistophelean
polyphloesboean
psychometrician
malacopterygian
crossopterygian
Christadelphian
ornithodelphian
Czechoslovakian
Mephistophelian
edriophthalmian
quinquagenarian
post-millenarian
platitudinarian
antitrinitarian
parliamentarian
Pan-Presbyterian
psychohistorian
crypto-Christian
blast-furnaceman

hackney-coachman
resurrection-man
Erziehungsroman
north-countryman
pantechnicon-van
poverty-stricken
shoulder-shotten
vice-chamberlain
casement-curtain
phenolphthalein
passenger-pigeon
evangelistarion
incomprehension
misapprehension
circumincession
circuminsession
self-approbation
self-vindication
syllabification
decalcification
speechification
Frenchification
exemplification
indemnification
personification
chondrification
corporification
electrification
denitrification
devitrification
demulsification
intensification
diversification
objectification
granitification
desertification
refortification
cockneyfication
quadruplication
quintuplication
self-explication
excommunication
prognostication
self-degradation
reconsolidation
discommendation
steam-navigation
astronavigation
reinterrogation
misappreciation
self-humiliation
differentiation
malassimilation
contravallation
circumvallation
disarticulation
interosculation
phosphorylation
underestimation
self-affirmation
malconformation
insubordination
superordination
self-pollination

interlamination
decontamination
self-examination
redetermination
indetermination
undetermination
procrastination
owner-occupation
reconsideration
inconsideration
transliteration
transfiguration
supersaturation
phonemicisation
romanticisation
spheroidisation
standardisation
etherealisation
materialisation
arterialisation
criminalisation
regionalisation
nationalisation
rationalisation
personalisation
externalisation
communalisation
hospitalisation
immortalisation
desexualisation
crystallisation
tuberculisation
suburbanisation
disorganisation
decarbonisation
fractionisation
synchronisation
vascularisation
singularisation
formularisation
schillerisation
canisterisation
computerisation
desilverisation
exteriorisation
extemporisation
decarburisation
decolourisation
miniaturisation
systematisation
acclimatisation
democratisation
demagnetisation
granulitisation
propylitisation
unpremeditation
interdigitation
dishabilitation
superexaltation
transplantation
supplementation
experimentation
instrumentation
malpresentation

weather-notation
reafforestation
clearing-station
dressing-station
roundaboutation
discontinuation
appropinquation
self-observation
dissatisfaction
subintellection
interconnection
proof-correction
antivivisection
microdissection
rent-restriction
under-production
self-destruction
preconstruction
misconstruction
superimposition
quadripartition
non-intervention
sense-perception
introsusception
intussusception
circumscription
marriage-portion
maldistribution
rhombencephalon
properispomenon
cloud-cuckoo-town

P

victualling-ship
chamberlainship
compotationship
probationership
interpretership
conservatorship
ancestor-worship
connoisseurship

R

intertentacular
interfascicular
slantingdicular
extra-curricular
interclavicular
cerebrovascular
presence-chamber
scripture-reader
companion-ladder
cigarette-holder
direction-finder
seventeen-hunder
blood-and-thunder
polishing-powder
saloon-passenger
sensation-monger
canvas-stretcher
phytogeographer
paroemiographer
historiographer
thalassographer
cinematographer
herb-Christopher

mountain-leather
seaplane-carrier
aircraft-carrier
slave-trafficker
sword-and-buckler
contrapropeller
fellow-traveller
sergeant-drummer
kitchen-gardener
pencil-sharpener
subcommissioner
malpractitioner
prairie-schooner
Middle-Easterner
sleeping-partner
scribbling-paper
crossing-sweeper
shoulder-clapper
devil-worshipper
medicine-dropper
stretcher-bearer
picture-restorer
ambulance-chaser
photosensitiser
armoured-cruiser
bomb-calorimeter
radiogoniometer
katathermometer
portrait-painter
under-the-counter
torque-converter
sticking-plaster
butterfly-flower
wall-gillyflower
Johnny-head-in-air
subject-superior
circumnavigator
prestidigitator
ticket-collector
police-inspector
school-inspector
vasoconstrictor
subintelligitur
S
dermatoglyphics
electrodynamics
morphophonemics
electrothermics
electrotechnics
mole-electronics
optoelectronics
metamathematics
pantopragmatics
lithochromatics
electrokinetics
paralinguistics
metalinguistics
bioastronautics
Jack-of-all-trades
Nemathelminthes
Platyhelminthes
swathing-clothes
extraordinaries
Jungermanniales

Spheniseiformes
Monocotyledones
chargé-d'affaires
chamber-hangings
butterfly-orchis
trypanosomiasis
schistosomiasis
ankylostomiasis
hypochondriasis
parthenogenesis
anthropogenesis
spermatogenesis
electrophoresis
theriomorphosis
atherosclerosis
onychocryptosis
electroanalysis
panophthalmitis
gastroenteritis
diaphragmatitis
circumstantials
gentleman-at-arms
messenger-at-arms
quarter-sessions
half-wellingtons
two-pair-of-stairs
laughing-jackass
citronella-grass
peasecod-cuirass
double-facedness
wrong-headedness
light-headedness
underhandedness
right-handedness
noble-mindedness
sober-mindedness
light-mindedness
right-mindedness
cold-bloodedness
foul-mouthedness
unqualifiedness
unsatisfiedness
stiff-neckedness
thin-skinnedness
unconcernedness
ill-favouredness
good-naturedness
unpractisedness
consecratedness
disaffectedness
recollectedness
unsuspectedness
unprotectedness
long-sightedness
near-sightedness
low-spiritedness
kind-heartedness
hard-heartedness
free-heartedness
true-heartedness
half-heartedness
warm-heartedness
open-heartedness
transportedness

quick-wittedness
overforwardness
practicableness
irrevocableness
unavoidableness
commendableness
unpeaceableness
serviceableness
unblameableness
impermeableness
unteachableness
dissociableness
justifiableness
imperviableness
congealableness
unavailableness
inflammableness
fashionableness
treasonableness
irreparableness
intolerableness
innumerableness
inseperableness
insuperableness
unalterableness
conquerableness
recoverableness
undesirableness
pleasurableness
inadvisableness
unadvisableness
dispensableness
inexcusableness
intractableness
untractableness
respectableness
predictableness
indubitableness
illimitableness
warrantableness
presentableness
accountableness
supportableness
irrefutableness
inscrutableness
retrievableness
conceivableness
dissolvableness
irremovableness
irreducibleness
refrangibleness
infrangibleness
indivisibleness
susceptibleness
corruptibleness
combustibleness
troublesomeness
unwholesomeness
venturesomeness
quarrelsomeness
clandestineness
inopportuneness
appropriateness
subordinateness

unfortunateness
importunateness
considerateness
intemperateness
picturesqueness
inoffensiveness
inexpensiveness
progressiveness
inobtrusiveness
unobtrusiveness
vindicativeness
provocativeness
procreativeness
correlativeness
superlativeness
speculativeness
imaginativeness
inoperativeness
penetrativeness
disputativeness
ineffectiveness
prospectiveness
distinctiveness
conjunctiveness
destructiveness
instructiveness
prohibitiveness
acquisitiveness
inquisitiveness
insensitiveness
competitiveness
substantiveness
irretentiveness
inattentiveness
descriptiveness
consumptiveness
consecutiveness
disobligingness
misbecomingness
overbearingness
displeasingness
unrelentingness
everlastingness
interestingness
unremittingness
unforgivingness
stand-offishness
pedagoguishness
unseaworthiness
faithworthiness
thankworthiness
trustworthiness
gentlemanliness
neighbourliness
extemporariness
unnecessariness
fragmentariness
rudimentariness
involuntariness
perfunctoriness
blood-guiltiness
morning-sickness
pharisaicalness
evangelicalness

uncanonicalness
categoricalness
symmetricalness
nonsensicalness
intrinsicalness
pragmaticalness
impracticalness
parasiticalness
fantasticalness
paradoxicalness
superficialness
magisterialness
substantialness
ineffectualness
disgracefulness
resourcefulness
distastefulness
reproachfulness
unhealthfulness
distressfulness
distrustfulness
mistrustfulness
defencelessness
purposelessness
remorselessness
successlessness
thoughtlessness
comfortlessness
spontaneousness
homogeneousness
sulphureousness
unrighteousness
scribaciousness
efficaciousness
incapaciousness
injudiciousness
inofficiousness
unconsciousness
coconsciousness
compendiousness
irreligiousness
punctiliousness
ceremoniousness
opprobriousness
deleteriousness
meritoriousness
illustriousness
expeditiousness
repetitiousness
tendentiousness
pretentiousness
sententiousness
contentiousness
incredulousness
vertiginousness
synchronousness
odoriferousness
mortiferousness
treacherousness
carnivorousness
adventurousness
precipitousness
necessitousness
conspicuousness

perspicuousness
superfluousness
incongruousness
tempestuousness
mischievousness
circumspectness
transparentness
unsteadfastness
hard-and-fastness
quartermistress
Rhamphorhynchus
ornithorhynchus
protospatharius
asclepiadaceous
amaryllidaceous
chenopodiaceous
caprifoliaceous
zygophyllaceous
menispermaceous
plumbaginaceous
plantaginaceous
pergamentaceous
homochlamydeous
monochlamydeous
disadvantageous
circumforaneous
contemporaneous
co-instantaneous
unconsentaneous
anthropophagous
ornithodelphous
enantiomorphous
opisthognathous
andromonoecious
unselfconscious
circumambagious
recrementitious
excrementitious
unconscientious
mesaticephalous
lissencephalous
scaphocephalous
brachycephalous
heterodactylous
brachydactylous
edriophthalmous
pulchritudinous
vicissitudinous
unfossiliferous
strombuliferous
tentaculiferous
margaritiferous
hypophosphorous
myristicivorous
epitheliomatous
plagiostomatous
odontostomatous
echinodermatous
sclerodermatous
sarcenchymatous
collenchymatous
prosenchymatous
basidiomycetous
seeming-virtuous

Pithecanthropus
carpometacarpus
cytomegalovirus
tarsometatarsus

T

strait-waistcoat
flibbertigibbet
speaking-trumpet
powdering-closet
sleeping-draught
well-accomplisht
Schrecklichkeit
Jack-in-the-pulpit
nepheline-basalt
saddler-sergeant
provost-sergeant
dividend-warrant
peacock-pheasant
counter-irritant
ultra-Protestant
crease-resistant
shrink-resistant
semi-independent
commission-agent
water-equivalent
disentrancement
self-advancement
porcelain-cement
superinducement
acknowledgement
interchangement
disentanglement
intertanglement
irreconcilement
transfigurement
bargain-basement
affranchisement
enfranchisement
readvertisement
éclaircissement
counter-movement
self-improvement
re-establishment
distinguishment
self-sustainment
self-abandonment
disillusionment
reapportionment
disimprisonment
party-government
overdevelopment
disafforestment
under-employment
semitransparent
gillie-whitefoot
durchkomponiert
bed-and-breakfast
hydrodynamicist
astrodynamicist
psychophysicist
geomorphologist
helminthologist
psychobiologist
ophthalmologist

phenomenologist
geochronologist
palaeozoologist
numismatologist
sedimentologist
palaeontologist
fifth-monarchist
steganographist
anthroposophist
experientialist
preferentialist
processionalist
confessionalist
conventionalist
supernaturalist
agriculturalist
experimentalist
instrumentalist
intellectualist
non-intrusionist
preformationist
emancipationist
degenerationist
conversationist
presentationist
preservationist
conservationist
resurrectionist
insurrectionist
interventionist
conscriptionist
constitutionist
crypto-communist
psychotherapist
physiotherapist
daguerreotypist
sericiculturist
ostreiculturist
arboriculturist
pharmacognosist
apophthegmatist
hierogrammatist
intransigentist
Second-adventist

Y

Annunciation-day
continuation-day
mountain-railway
archiepiscopacy
superintendency
self-sufficiency
self-consistency
sandwort-spurrey
ethnomusicology
psychopathology
anthropobiology
anaesthesiology
neurophysiology
microtechnology
palaeolimnology
lepidopterology
palaeophytology
hydrometallurgy
staphylorrhaphy

radiotelegraphy
phototelegraphy
palaeogeography
psychobiography
xeroradiography
autoradiography
cholangiography
encephalography
crystallography
photoxylography
ultrasonography
cinemicrography
palaeontography
telephotography
pyrophotography
acknowledgeably
interchangeably
unchallengeably
distinguishably
unobjectionably
unexceptionably
incommensurably
irreprehensibly
unconstrainedly
unprecedentedly
uninterruptedly
single-heartedly
tender-heartedly
disinterestedly
unintermittedly
north-eastwardly
south-eastwardly
north-westwardly
south-westwardly
inappropriately
insubordinately
indeterminately
compassionately
dispassionately
proportionately
inconsiderately
comprehensively
unprogressively
retrogressively
transgressively
significatively
communicatively
interrogatively
contemplatively
unimaginatively
consideratively
uncooperatively
unco-operatively
demonstratively
authoritatively
argumentatively
counteractively
retrospectively
contradictively
indistinctively
transcriptively
understandingly
condescendingly
correspondingly

dishearteningly	stalagmitically	discommodiously
uncomplainingly	hypercritically	unceremoniously
prepossessingly	stalactitically	sanctimoniously
remonstratingly	peristaltically	disharmoniously
uninterestingly	sycophantically	surreptitiously
intertwistingly	necromantically	superstitiously
untrustworthily	anacreontically	conscientiously
extraordinarily	gnotobiotically	pusillanimously
discretionarily	unpatriotically	multitudinously
parliamentarily	apocalyptically	inconspicuously
complementarily	encomiastically	discontinuously
supplementarily	meroblastically	insignificantly
contradictorily	methodistically	superabundantly
trisyllabically	syllogistically	uncomplaisantly
dithyrambically	dyslogistically	self-confidently
subspecifically	socialistically	correspondently
mineralogically	anomalistically	grandiloquently
synecologically	ritualistically	cholecystectomy
physiologically	euphemistically	cholecystostomy
entomologically	pessimistically	röntgenotherapy
phrenologically	mechanistically	ultramicroscopy
technologically	hellenistically	plenipotentiary
chronologically	manneristically	sesquicentenary
synecdochically	hermeneutically	quatercentenary
paragraphically	therapeutically	disinflationary
telegraphically	extra-judicially	slumpflationary
ideographically	synarthrodially	interjectionary
logographically	intercolonially	resurrectionary
topographically	proprietorially	insurrectionary
typographically	inquisitorially	disquisitionary
autographically	controversially	substitutionary
philosophically	insubstantially	unparliamentary
automorphically	consequentially	uncomplimentary
homeopathically	ventriloquially	semi-documentary
hydropathically	infinitesimally	shooting-gallery
unapostolically	septentrionally	portrait-gallery
logarithmically	postulationally	greenery-yallery
macrocosmically	internationally	excommunicatory
cataclysmically	inspirationally	knick-knackatory
pyrotechnically	gravitationally	interjaculatory
gramophonically	observationally	self-explanatory
colposcopically	conjunctionally	procrastinatory
macroscopically	unconditionally	dissatisfactory
microscopically	prepositionally	non-contributory
heliotropically	suppositionally	orthopsychiatry
atmospherically	unintentionally	chemopsychiatry
prehistorically	unexceptionally	neuropsychiatry
unsymmetrically	institutionally	biogeochemistry
goniometrically	interpersonally	stereochemistry
problematically	preternaturally	psychochemistry
theorematically	temperamentally	thermochemistry
ungrammatically	developmentally	immunochemistry
unidiomatically	compartmentally	rhombenporphyry
symptomatically	disrespectfully	Michaelmas-daisy
ochlocratically	self-forgetfully	pyro-electricity
hydrostatically	antichristianly	photoelasticity
catallactically	perpendicularly	superplasticity
sympathetically	miscellaneously	contemporaneity
parenthetically	subterraneously	co-instantaneity
anaesthetically	instantaneously	heterocercality
abiogenetically	consentaneously	confidentiality
ontogenetically	heterogeneously	conventionality
diamagnetically	inefficaciously	proportionality
Capernaitically	perspicaciously	cross-laterality

dorsiventrality
instrumentality
intellectuality
heterosexuality
equiprobability
inapplicability
inexplicability
communicability
disagreeability
unchangeability
exchangeability
irrefragability
approachability
imperishability
unverifiability
irrepealability
reconcilability
controllability
incalculability
irredeemability
programmability
determinability

questionability
incomparability
imponderability
decipherability
invulnerability
impenetrability
demonstrability
immensurability
manoeuvrability
hypnotisability
decomposability
contractability
precipitability
incommutability
transmutability
disreputability
irresolvability
intelligibility
incorrigibility
diffrangibility
indefeasibility
indefensibility

inextensibility
irreversibility
inaccessibility
compressibility
inadmissibility
irremissibility
incompatibility
contractibility
distractibility
irreductibility
destructibility
contemptibility
indigestibility
irresistibility
indissolubility
shabby-gentility
roundaboutility
Neo-Christianity
complementarity
counter-security
transferribilty
self-sovereignty